Brief Contents *with Listing of Writing Projects*

P9-DFA-896

PART ONE A Guide to College and College Writing 1

1 Inside Colleges and Universities 3
Composing a Literacy Narrative 14
Interviewing a Scholar 15

2 Reading and Writing Rhetorically 20
Analyzing the Rhetorical Features of a Text 34

3 Developing Arguments 37
Composing a Rhetorical Analysis of an Advertisement 57

4 Academic Research 59
Writing an Annotated Bibliography 77
Developing a Supported Argument on a Controversial Issue 79

PART TWO Inside Academic Writing 87

5 Reading and Writing in Academic Disciplines 89
Writing a Rhetorical Analysis of an Academic Article 100
Writing a Comparative Rhetorical Analysis 101
Comparing Scholarly and Popular Articles 102
Translating a Scholarly Article for a Public Audience 106

6 Reading and Writing in the Humanities 108
Interpreting a Text 142
Creating an Artistic Text 150

7 Reading and Writing in the Social Sciences 152
Writing a Literature Review 185
Writing a Theory Response 197

8 Reading and Writing in the Natural Sciences 209
Keeping an Observation Logbook 228
Developing a Research Proposal 241
Composing a Lab Report 249

9 Reading and Writing in the Applied Fields 261
Discovering Genres of Writing in an Applied Field 304

PART THREE Entering Academic Conversations: Readings and Case Studies 307

10 Love, Marriage, and Family 309
Contributing to a Scholarly Conversation 379
Writing a Comparative Analysis of Research Methodologies 380

11 Crime, Punishment, and Justice 381
Writing a Brief Annotated Bibliography 448
Composing an Evaluative Rhetorical Analysis 449

12 Food, Sustainability, and Class 451
Writing a Persuasive Narrative 543
Translating a Scholarly Work for a Popular Audience 543

13 Global Climate Change and Natural Catastrophes 545
Composing a Research Proposal 611
Writing a Comparative Rhetorical Analysis: Popular and Academic Sources 612

Appendix: Introduction to Documentation Styles 613
Index 633

An Insider's Guide to Academic Writing

A Rhetoric and Reader

Susan Miller-Cochran

University of Arizona

Roy Stamper

North Carolina State University

Stacey Cochran

University of Arizona

Bedford/St. Martin's

A Macmillan Education Imprint

Boston • New York

For Bedford/St. Martin's

Vice President, Editorial, Macmillan Higher Education Humanities: Edwin Hill
Editorial Director, English and Music: Karen S. Henry
Publisher for Composition, Business and Technical Writing, and Developmental Writing:
   Leasa Burton
Senior Executive Editor: Stephen A. Scipione
Executive Editor: Molly Parke
Developmental Editor: Sherry Mooney
Senior Production Editor: Ryan Sullivan
Assistant Production Supervisor: Victoria Anzalone
Marketing Manager: Emily Rowin
Copy Editor: Alice Vigliani
Indexer: Schroeder Indexing Services
Director of Rights and Permissions: Hilary Newman
Senior Art Director: Anna Palchik
Text Design: Claire Seng-Niemoeller
Cover Design: William Boardman
Cover Art: Andrea Tsurumi
Composition: Jouve
Printing and Binding: RR Donnelley and Sons

Manufactured in the United States of America.

0   9   8   7   6   5
f   e   d   c   b

For information, write: Bedford/St. Martin's, 75 Arlington Street, Boston, MA 02116 (617-399-4000)

ISBN   978-0-312-56676-0

Acknowledgments

Preface for Instructors

What is an "insider"? In all walks of life, insiders are the ones who know the territory, speak the language, have the skills, understand the codes, keep the secrets. With *An Insider's Guide to Academic Writing*, we want to help college students, new to the world of higher education, learn the territory, language, skills, codes, and secrets of academic writing in disciplinary contexts. While no single book, or course, or teacher could train all students in all the details of scholarly writing in all disciplines, *An Insider's Guide* offers a flexible, rhetoric-based pedagogy that has helped our students navigate the reading and writing expectations of academic discourse communities across the curriculum. We have found that because the pedagogy is grounded in rhetorical principles and concepts, writing instructors who might otherwise be wary of teaching outside their scholarly expertise feel confident about the approach. Moreover, students quickly grasp the transferable benefits of the approach to their future courses, so their level of enthusiasm and personal investment is high.

As a unique enhancement to its rhetoric-based pedagogy, *An Insider's Guide to Academic Writing* integrates, through video and print interviews, the writing advice of scholars and undergraduates from many disciplines; they speak from and about their own experiences as academic writers. (We conducted, filmed, and curated the interviews ourselves, and they are available as part of the LaunchPad Solo package with the book.) Whether professor or student, these credible and compelling experts humanize and demystify disciplinary discourse, sharing their insider knowledge with academic novices.

An Insider's Guide to Academic Writing derives from the research and teaching that went into transitioning the first-year writing program at North Carolina State University to a writing-in-the-disciplines (WID) approach. This approach is gaining wider currency nationwide as calls for instruction in transferable college writing skills increase. At that time, more than a decade ago, faculty in the program (including the authors of this book) immersed themselves in scholarship on WID and WID pedagogy. We also began to seek supporting instructional materials, but did not find any existing textbooks that met our needs. While several texts focused, to varying degrees, on introducing students to writing in the academic disciplines, few texts employed a rhetorical approach to explore these kinds of writing. Fewer still employed a rhetorical approach to understanding the conventions of writing that characterize those disciplinary texts while also providing support for students' own production of disciplinary genres.

The book that emerged from these years of teaching and research, *An Insider's Guide to Academic Writing*, is a composition rhetoric with readings that distills much of the writing-in-the-disciplines approach that we and our colleagues have used with success for many years. This approach begins by applying rhetorical principles to the understanding of texts, and then shows those principles at work in various domains of academic inquiry, including the humanities, the social sciences, the natural sciences, and the applied fields. It does so mainly by (1) introducing students to rhetorical lenses through which they can view the genres and conventions they will be expected to read and produce in other courses, (2) providing examples of those genres and conventions to analyze and discuss, and (3) including carefully scaffolded writing activities and projects designed to help students explore and guide their production of those genres.

We believe that composition programs pursuing a WID-oriented approach to academic writing will find that *An Insider's Guide* provides a foundation of instruction in disciplinary thinking and writing but is flexible enough to accommodate the diverse teaching interests of individual instructors. Some faculty, for instance, use this approach to support themed courses; they examine how a particular topic or issue is explored by scholars across a range of disciplines. Other faculty situate principles of argument at the center of their course designs and explore disciplinary perspectives and writing in light of those principles. Still others organize their courses as step-by-step journeys through academic domains while attending to the similarities and distinctions in writing practices (rhetorical conventions and genres) of various fields.

The goal of each of these approaches is to foster students' understanding of the various academic communities they participate in as part of the typical undergraduate experience. With the support of *An Insider's Guide to Academic Writing*, these approaches can also foster a deepening rhetorical sensitivity in our students while providing opportunities for them to analyze and practice the kinds of genres they often encounter in college. The book encourages students to exercise rhetorical skills that are transferable from one writing situation to another and supports a rhetorical approach to understanding writing that should be at the core of any first-year writing experience.

A Closer Look at the Rhetoric

The nine chapters of the rhetoric take students inside the worlds of higher education, academic writing and research, and disciplinary writing.

- Part One, "A Guide to College and College Writing," begins by introducing students to colleges and universities, as well as to the kinds of writing expectations they will likely face in college. It introduces students to core principles of rhetoric and explores a number of frameworks for rhetorical analysis. This part of the book also reviews basic principles of argument and strategies for conducting library research.

- Part Two, "Inside Academic Writing," is an exploration of the research practices, rhetorical conventions, and genres that characterize the major academic disciplinary domains—the humanities, the social sciences, the natural sciences, as well as a number of applied fields. The first chapter in Part Two (Chapter 5) explores the role of the core principles from Part One—rhetoric, argument, and research—in the various academic disciplines. Each of the remaining chapters in Part Two focuses on a different domain, but they all begin with an exploration of research practices specific to those academic communities. Each chapter also employs a practical, three-part framework (SLR, or "structure, language, and reference")* for identifying and analyzing the conventions that characterize writing in each discipline. In addition, these chapters provide scaffolded support for students' production of discipline-appropriate genres. In the social sciences, for example, we offer support for students' production of theory-response position papers as well as for the literature review.

"INSIDER" FEATURES OF THE RHETORIC

The rhetoric chapters provide a number of features that help facilitate instruction and student learning:

"Insider's View" Sidebars and Videos Linked to LaunchPad Solo Students hear directly from scholars in various academic fields who explore disciplinary writing expectations and reflect on their own writing practices. These unique features provide a form of personal access to the academic world that students sometimes find alien, uninviting, or intimidating. Each video is accompanied by a pair of activities within LaunchPad Solo, one to confirm students' understanding of the content and the second inviting them to make larger connections and provide thoughtful written responses.

Sidebars and video links

---

*For the concept of the SLR framework, we are indebted to Patricia Linton, Robert Madigan, and Susan Johnson ("Introducing Students to Disciplinary Genres: The Role of the General Composition Course," *Language and Learning across the Disciplines* 1.2 [October 1994]: 63–78).

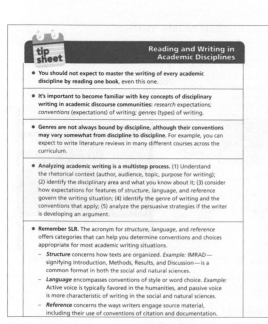

"Insider Example" Readings These readings appear throughout the chapters, providing models of writing by scholars and students. Most of the readings exemplify important genres of academic and disciplinary writing; many are annotated with marginal commentary that identifies writers' rhetorical moves and/or poses questions for students' further consideration. These annotations take students "inside" the production of various disciplinary texts and, by extension, inside the academy itself.

"Inside Work" and "Writing Project" Activities These activities appear strategically throughout the book's chapters. They are designed to provide opportunities for students to put their learning into action, to analyze and

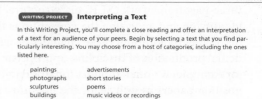

"Inside Work" and "Writing Project" activities

practice the skills and moves taught in the chapters. These activities function throughout the chapters to build a scaffold that supports students' mastery of skills needed to produce the various "Writing Projects" explored throughout the book, from rhetorical analyses and interpretations (in the humanities), theory-response papers and literature reviews (in the social sciences), research proposals and formal observation reports (in the natural sciences), to lesson plans and memoranda (in the applied fields).

Summary "Tip Sheets" Each chapter in the rhetoric concludes with a "Tip Sheet" that underscores critical concepts and insights for students as they move from novices to academic insiders.

"Tip Sheet"

A Closer Look at the Thematic Reader

Part Three, "Entering Academic Conversations: Readings and Case Studies," is a thematic anthology that takes students inside issues of cultural and academic interest. Along with many examples of writing from non-academic venues that you would expect to find in a composition reader, *An Insider's Guide* distinguishes itself from other texts by including many full-length examples of scholarly articles that highlight the research and communication practices explored through the rhetoric. Unlike so many other texts, which often provide only excerpted portions of scholarly works of interest, our reader provides full-on "academic case studies," as we explain below.

The reader is composed of four chapters: "Love, Marriage, and Family," "Crime, Punishment, and Justice," "Food, Sustainability, and Class," and "Global Climate Change and Natural Catastrophes." These are topics that claim students' attention all the time, popular issues that are real to them, newsworthy subjects that are staples of media coverage—and they are the kinds of topics that academic commentators are expected to weigh in on. Here are the specifics of how the chapters work:

- Each of the four thematic chapters begins with an introduction that offers a general overview of the chapter's contents, including identification of each chapter's case study focus. For example, the introduction to Chapter 10, "Love, Marriage, and Family," identifies a number of issues and perspectives offered by the popular readings, including an assessment of the current state of marriage in the United States, an exploration of the dynamics of control between parents and children, as well as an examination of various definitions of "family." Each chapter introduction further briefly describes the scholarly perspectives offered in the chapter's academic case study (see the next page for further description of the case studies).

- Each selection in the reader is framed by a brief introduction that provides insight into elements of the rhetorical context of each work, as well as by a series of questions that come at the end of each reading—some aimed at supporting reading comprehension ("Reading Questions"), some designed to foster consideration of the texts' rhetorical elements ("Rhetoric Questions"), and some designed to elicit and explore students' personal connections to ideas and to encourage further active knowledge-making and research ("Response and Research Questions").

- Each of the chapters includes a collection of engaging readings designed to highlight various aspects of the topic under consideration in the chapter. Writings are taken from such popular sources as print and online magazines (e.g., *Psychology Today*, *Marie Claire*, the *New Yorker*), as well as newspapers and sites for online news reporting (e.g., the *New York Times*, *Daily Beast*, *reason.com*), just to name a few. Collectively, these readings provide additional context for understanding the range of perspectives and approaches individuals assume in response to the topics.

- Each of the chapters in the reader also includes an academic case study that provides a scholarly perspective from the humanities, the social sciences, the natural sciences, and the applied fields on a more focused issue of inquiry related to the chapter's themes. For example, Chapter 11, "Crime, Punishment, and Justice," takes up capital punishment as its more focused case study topic and includes scholarly articles from the *Journal of American Folklore* (humanities), the *International Journal of Public Opinion Research* (social sciences), *PLoS Medicine* (natural sciences), and the *International Journal of Criminal Justice Sciences* (applied fields) to offer readers a range of academic perspectives on the topic. These readings highlight the research focus, forms of evidence, and communication practices that define these discourse communities. Students and instructors can use these readings to learn about the topics scholars explore and the ways they explore those topics, as well as about the literate practices of scholars across the academic domains.

- Each chapter in the reader concludes with two suggested writing projects. In each case, the first assignment asks students, in response to the chapter's readings, to produce a genre explored in the book's rhetoric. The second assignment asks students to consider further the rhetorical features of one or more of the texts in each chapter.

An instructor can draw on the readings selectively; we have included more options than can realistically be used in a semester. Some instructors may prefer to assign entire academic casebooks; others may choose to cherry-pick them to support a specific disciplinary emphasis at certain points during a semester or quarter; still others may elect to concentrate only on excerpts from scholarly articles, where certain structure, language, or reference features may be examined closely. We expect that some instructors will prefer to use exclusively the non-academic pieces, asking students to find their own academic examples from the literature of their majors or of other courses that interest them. In any case, we hope that instructors find our selections useful; the thematic chapters do not present a reading list to be marched through over the course of a semester, but a resource to be tapped to suit the particular needs of students as they explore the byways of academic reading and writing.

Finally, the appendix, "Introduction to Documentation Styles," discusses how specific citation styles reflect disciplinary concerns and emphases while concisely explaining and exemplifying the basics of MLA, APA, and CSE documentation.

In all walks of life, not all who are invited inside become insiders. Students taking your course in writing are there because they have accepted the invitation to higher education; they've crossed the first threshold. But to become insiders, they'll need the wisdom and counsel of other insiders. We have prepared this book, with its supporting videos and ancillary materials (detailed on p. xiii) to help them learn the territory, language, skills, codes, and secrets of academic writing. But a guidebook can only do so much. Students need insiders such as yourself and your colleagues to guide their understanding. We hope our *Insider's Guide* proves to be a resource you rely on as you start them on their journeys.

Acknowledgments

Writing this textbook has been a journey for all three of us as we have experimented with various pedagogical approaches, assignments, and content with students and faculty colleagues. We have had tremendous support from the team at Bedford, first and foremost from Steve Scipione, our editor, who has helped us see this project through to completion while providing insightful suggestions that have guided our approach. We are also indebted to composition publisher Leasa Burton, who understood our goals and championed this project from the beginning, and executive editor Molly Parke, whose creative thinking about the book's potential has been encouraging and invigorating. We have also received outstanding support and guidance from developmental editor Sherry Mooney, who has helped us successfully incorporate the voices of many scholars and students into this project, and Ryan Sullivan, who guided the book through the production process with great care and good humor. Claire Seng-Niemoeller created the superb design of the book, and Christine Voboril cleared the permissions. We thank Emily Rowin and Melissa Famiglietti for their marketing and market development efforts. We remain grateful to other contributors who helped in so many ways behind the scenes, including Edwin Hill, Karen Henry, Elise Kaiser, Anna Palchik, Kalina Ingham, Lindsey Jaroszewicz, Alyssa Demirjian, and Sophia Snyder, who made her mark during the earliest stages of the project.

We are also indebted to the students who were willing to try this approach and, in many cases, share their writing in this book. Their examples provide essential scaffolding for the book's approach, and their honest feedback helped us refine our explanation of various genres and disciplines.

We are also grateful to our colleagues in the First-Year Writing Program at North Carolina State University, who have shared their expertise and ideas about teaching writing in and about disciplines over the years. Without their support and their innovation, we would not have been able to complete this project. Specifically, we want to thank David Gruber, who helped us solicit responses from professionals in a range of fields early in the project. We also want to thank Brent Simoneaux, who provided outstanding feedback on early drafts of the chapters and helped us compile the selections and support for the reader. We are also indebted to Kate Lavia-Bagley, whose experience and success with teaching this approach is showcased in the outstanding Instructor's Manual she has written to accompany the book.

We also appreciate the outstanding comments and suggestions we received from reviewers throughout the development of this first edition: Steven Alvarez, Queens College of CUNY; Sonia Apgar Begert, Olympic College; JoAnn Buck, Guilford Technical Community College; Diana Kaye Campbell, Forsyth Technical Community College; Jennifer Cellio, Northern Kentucky University; Jill Channing, Mitchell Community College; Polina Chemishanova, University of North Carolina at Pembroke; Jason DePolo, North Carolina Agricultural and Technical State University; Brock Dethier, Utah State University; Anthony Edgington, University of Toledo; Stephanie Franco, Texas Tech; Sarah Hallenbeck, University of North Carolina at Chapel Hill; Michael Harker, Georgia State University; Kimberly Harrison, Florida International University; Jonathan Hartmann, University of New Haven; Elizabeth Finch Hedengren, Brigham Young University; Lisa Hirsch, Hostos Community College of CUNY; Karen Keaton Jackson, North Carolina Central University; Patricia Lynne, Framingham State University; Janel Mays, Durham Technical Community College; Jessie L. Moore, Elon University; Tracy Morse, East Carolina University; Alice J. Myatt, University of Mississippi; Carroll Ferguson Nardone, Sam Houston State University; Kristin Redfield, Forsyth Technical Community College; Georgia Rhoades, Appalachian State University; Kevin Roozen, Auburn University; Kathleen Ryan, University of Montana; Jessica Saxon, Craven Community College; Loreen Smith, Isothermal Community College; Donna Strickland, University of Missouri, Columbia; Elizabeth West, Central Piedmont Community College; Carl Whithaus, University of California, Davis; and Hui Wu, University of Texas at Tyler.

And finally, we are indebted to our friends and families, who provided a great deal of support as we worked on this project over several years. Without their patience and encouragement, we would not have been able to make this idea into a reality.

Susan Miller-Cochran
Roy Stamper
Stacey Cochran

Get the Most Out of Your Course with *An Insider's Guide to Academic Writing*

Bedford/St. Martin's offers resources and format choices that help you and your students get even more out of your book and course. To learn more about or to order any of the following products, contact your Bedford/St. Martin's sales representative, e-mail sales support (**sales_support@bfwpub.com**), or visit the website at **macmillanhighered.com/insidersguide/catalog**.

LaunchPad Solo for *An Insider's Guide to Academic Writing*: Where Students Learn LaunchPad Solo for *An Insider's Guide to Academic Writing* provides unique content and new ways to get the most out of your book. For students, "Insider's View" videos feature advice from scholars and students about thinking and writing in different academic fields, with accompanying questions and activities. A special set of "Insider Videos" for instructors gives tips and strategies for introducing students to a wide range of disciplines, including the social sciences and the sciences. You'll also find additional interactive exercises and tutorials for reading, writing, and research, as well as LearningCurve, adaptive, game-like practice that helps students focus on the topics where they need the most help.

To get the most out of your book, order LaunchPad Solo for *An Insider's Guide to Academic Writing* packaged with the print book. (LaunchPad Solo for *An Insider's Guide to Academic Writing* can also be purchased on its own.) An activation code is required. To order LaunchPad Solo for *An Insider's Guide to Academic Writing* with the print book, use ISBN 978-1-319-05354-3.

Alternative versions of *An Insider's Guide to Academic Writing* are available. *An Insider's Guide to Academic Writing: A Brief Rhetoric* (Chapters 1–9 of the rhetoric and reader, with the appendix on documentation) is available in both print and value-priced e-book versions. For details, visit **macmillanhighered .com/insidersguide/catalog**.

Bedford/St. Martin's offers a range of affordable formats, so students can choose what works best for them. For details, visit **macmillanhighered .com/insidersguide/catalog**.

Select value packages. Add value to your text by packaging one of the following resources with *An Insider's Guide to Academic Writing*. To learn more about package options for any of the following products, contact your Bedford/St. Martin's sales representative or visit **macmillanhighered.com/insidersguide /catalog**.

Writer's Help 2.0 is a powerful online writing resource that helps students find answers, whether they are searching for writing advice on their own or as part of an assignment.

- **Smart Search** Built on research with more than 1,600 student writers, the smart search in *Writer's Help 2.0* provides reliable results even when students use novice terms, such as *flow* and *unstuck*.

- **Trusted Content from Our Best-Selling Handbooks**   Choose *Writer's Help 2.0 for Hacker Handbooks* or *Writer's Help 2.0 for Lunsford Handbooks* and ensure that students have clear advice and examples for all of their writing questions.

- **Adaptive Exercises That Engage Students**   *Writer's Help 2.0* includes LearningCurve, game-like online quizzing that adapts to what students already know and helps them focus on what they need to learn.

Student access is packaged with *An Insider's Guide to Academic Writing* at a significant discount. Contact your Bedford/St. Martin's sales representative to ensure that your students have easy access to online writing support with *Writer's Help 2.0 for Hacker Handbooks* or *Writer's Help 2.0 for Lunsford Handbooks*. Students who rent a book or buy a used book can purchase access to *Writer's Help 2.0* at **macmillanhighered.com/writershelp2**.

Instructors may request free access by registering as an instructor at **macmillanhighered.com/writershelp2**. For technical support, visit **macmillanhighered.com/getsupport**.

Portfolio Keeping, **Third Edition, by Nedra Reynolds and Elizabeth Davis,** provides all the information students need to use the portfolio method successfully in a writing course. *Portfolio Teaching*, a companion guide for instructors, provides the practical information instructors and writing program administrators need to use the portfolio method successfully in a writing course. To order *Portfolio Keeping* packaged with this text, contact your sales representative for a package ISBN.

Instructor Resources

macmillanhighered.com/insidersguide/catalog

You have a lot to do in your course. Bedford/St. Martin's wants to make it easy for you to find the support you need—and to get it quickly.

Resources for Teaching An Insider's Guide to Academic Writing is available as a PDF that can be downloaded from the Bedford/St. Martin's online catalog at the URL above. In addition to chapter overviews and teaching tips, the instructor's manual includes sample syllabi, proposed answers or responses to the questions and activities throughout the text, and classroom activities.

Resources for Teaching North Carolina English 112 with An Insider's Guide to Academic Writing is available as a PDF that can be downloaded from the Bedford/St. Martin's online catalog at the URL above. This brief resource complements *Resources for Teaching An Insider's Guide to Academic Writing*, with teaching attention to specific course outcomes and transfer requirements articulated in the 2014 Comprehensive Articulation Agreement between the University of North Carolina and the North Carolina Community College System.

Teaching Central offers the entire list of Bedford/St. Martin's print and online professional resources. You'll find landmark reference works, sourcebooks on pedagogical issues, award-winning collections, and practical advice for the classroom—all free for instructors. Visit **macmillanhighered .com/teachingcentral**.

Join Our Community! The Macmillan English Community is now Bedford/St. Martin's home for professional resources, featuring *Bits*, our popular blog site offering new ideas for the composition classroom and composition teachers. Connect and converse with a growing team of Bedford authors and top scholars who blog on *Bits*: Andrea Lunsford, Nancy Sommers, Steve Bernhardt, Traci Gardner, Barclay Barrios, Jack Solomon, Susan Bernstein, Elizabeth Wardle, Doug Downs, Elizabeth Losh, Jonathan Alexander, and Donna Winchell.

In addition, you'll find an expanding collection of resources that support your teaching:

- Sign up for webinars.
- Download resources from our professional resource series.
- Start a discussion.
- Ask a question.
- Follow your favorite members.
- Review projects in the pipeline.

Visit **community.macmillan.com** to join the conversation with your fellow teachers.

How This Book Supports WPA Outcomes
for First-Year Composition

Note: This chart aligns with the latest WPA Outcomes Statement, ratified in July 2014.

WPA Outcomes	Relevant Features of *An Insider's Guide to Academic Writing*
Rhetorical Knowledge	
Learn and use key rhetorical concepts through analyzing and composing a variety of texts.	*An Insider's Guide to Academic Writing* is built on a foundation of rhetorical analysis and production that commences in Chapter 2, "Reading and Writing Rhetorically" (pp. 20–36), and is extended through the rest of the book. The book uses a variety of "rhetorical lenses" to help students become academic insiders who know what conventions to expect and adapt in disciplinary writing. And it brings in, via print and video, the insights of real academic professionals to help students become insiders.
Gain experience reading and composing in several genres to understand how genre conventions shape and are shaped by readers' and writers' practices and purposes.	Each of the nine chapters in Parts One and Two provide instruction in reading and composing a variety of key academic and disciplinary genres, from a rhetorical analysis (Chapter 2, "Reading and Writing Rhetorically," pp. 30–34) to a literature review (Chapter 7, "Reading and Writing in the Social Sciences," pp. 180–95) to a research proposal (Chapter 8, "Reading and Writing in the Natural Sciences," pp. 240–48).
Develop facility in responding to a variety of situations and contexts, calling for purposeful shifts in voice, tone, level of formality, design, medium, and/or structure.	*An Insider's Guide* is predicated on the practice of situational and contextual composition, where rhetorical context and attention to conventions of structure, language, and reference determine a writer's approach to material. For example, in Chapter 5, "Reading and Writing in Academic Disciplines" (pp. 94–99), an astronomer explains how he writes for different audiences, with examples of the same scientific research written up for two different audiences. The chapter introduces the "Structure/Language/Reference" heuristic.
Understand and use a variety of technologies to address a range of audiences.	The use of "Insider's View" videos, available in LaunchPad Solo for *An Insider's Guide to Academic Writing*, models and reinforces the principle of using different technologies to communicate to a range of audiences. The videos of academics explaining how and why they write represent a different channel of explanation, to students and instructors, than the pedagogy in the print book. See astronomer Mike Brotherton's interviews (Chapter 5, "Reading and Writing in Academic Disciplines," pp. 93, 96, 100) and "Insider's View" videos, for example.

WPA Outcomes	Relevant Features of *An Insider's Guide to Academic Writing*
Match the capacities of different environments (e.g., print and electronic) to varying rhetorical situations.	See the previous entry, and also the various discussions of genre and genre awareness throughout the book—for example, the opening pages of Chapter 2, "Reading and Writing Rhetorically" (pp. 20–24). See also the cluster of material in Chapter 6, "Reading and Writing in the Humanities," on interpreting images (pp. 109–12) and the Dale Jacobs essay on multimodality (pp. 114–23).
Critical Thinking, Reading, and Composing	
Use composing and reading for inquiry, learning, thinking, and communicating in various rhetorical contexts.	All of the discipline-specific chapters include detailed information about research and inquiry in their academic domains. See Chapter 6, "Reading and Writing in the Humanities" (pp. 111–29); Chapter 7, "Reading and Writing in the Social Sciences" (pp. 154–65); Chapter 8, "Reading and Writing in the Natural Sciences" (pp. 212–21); and Chapter 9, "Reading and Writing in the Applied Fields" (pp. 261–64).
Read a diverse range of texts, attending especially to relationships between assertion and evidence, to patterns of organization, to interplay between verbal and nonverbal elements, and how these features function for different audiences and situations.	Chapter 3, "Developing Arguments" (pp. 37–58), offers instruction in identifying claims and assertions and relating them to evidence. The genres sections of all the disciplinary chapters in Part Two, "Inside Academic Writing" (Chapters 5–9), help students pay attention to patterns of organization (e.g., the IMRAD format), with particular attention to the Structure, Language, and Reference systems in play. See, for example, "Genres of Writing in the Natural Sciences" (pp. 227–59).
Locate and evaluate primary and secondary research materials, including journal articles, essays, books, databases, and informal Internet sources.	See in particular Chapter 4, "Academic Research" (pp. 59–85), where information on locating and evaluating primary and secondary research materials—including journal articles, essays, books, databases, and informal Internet sources—can be found.
Use strategies—such as interpretation, synthesis, response, critique, and design/redesign—to compose texts that integrate the writer's ideas with those from appropriate sources.	Chapter 4, "Academic Research" (pp. 59–85), discusses working with sources. Furthermore, Chapter 6, "Reading and Writing in the Humanities" (pp. 108–51), explores textual interpretation, response, and critique; and Chapter 7, "Reading and Writing in the Social Sciences," pays particular attention to strategies of synthesis (pp. 183–95).
Processes	
Develop a writing project through multiple drafts.	*An Insider's Guide to Academic Writing* presents an overview of the writing process in Chapter 2 (the "Rhetorical Writing Processes" section, pp. 27–30), and many chapters include "Inside Work" activities that ask students to build on the previous activities to develop a paper. For example, Chapter 3, "Developing Arguments," includes a sequence of such activities on pp. 39, 42, 45, 46, and 48.

(continued)

WPA Outcomes	Relevant Features of *An Insider's Guide to Academic Writing*
Processes (continued)	
Develop flexible strategies for reading, drafting, reviewing, collaboration, revising, rewriting, rereading, and editing.	See the previous entry. Additionally, the "Writing Project" activities that generally close each chapter in the rhetoric are sequenced and scaffolded to support process writing. Throughout the book and in LaunchPad Solo interviews, academic insiders discuss the nature of collaborative writing and working with editors.
Use composing processes and tools as a means to discover and reconsider ideas.	All of the discipline-specific chapters include detailed information about research and inquiry in their academic domains, and pay attention to the notion of testing ideas with audiences. See in particular Chapter 8, "Reading and Writing in the Natural Sciences," which traces how the process of developing observation and research inevitably leads to a modification of ideas (contrast the two papers by student Kedric Lemon on pp. 230–39 and pp. 250–59).
Experience the collaborative and social aspects of writing processes.	Many of the "Inside Work" activities require collaborative work, and the ethos of collaboration comes through strongly in the chapters on social sciences (Chapter 7) and natural sciences (Chapter 8). The chapter on writing in the natural sciences explicitly discusses the importance of cooperation and collaboration in the conventions section (p. 226).
Learn to give and act on productive feedback to works in progress.	See the previous rubric. Many of the articles reprinted in the book were written by teams of researchers. In particular, check out the Academic Case Studies in Chapters 10–13.
Adapt composing processes for a variety of technologies and modalities.	*An Insider's Guide to Academic Writing*'s start-to-finish emphasis on rhetorically situated, genre-aware, and convention-informed writing makes this point.
Reflect on the development of composing practices and how those practices influence their work.	Many of the "Inside Work" activities throughout the book have students reflect on what they know, what they think they know, and what they learn. For example, see the "Inside Work" activities throughout Chapter 1, "Inside Colleges and Universities" (pp. 3–19).
Knowledge of Conventions	
Develop knowledge of linguistic structures, including grammar, punctuation, and spelling, through practice in composing and revising.	The distinctive SLR framework (Structure/Language/Reference) introduced in Part Two ("Inside Academic Writing," Chapters 5–9; see the introduction to SLR in Chapter 5, pp. 96–98) has a Language category that emphasizes the linguistic choices and conventions in disciplinary writing, and the Reference feature puts emphasis on formatting issues that include spelling and punctuation. Bedford/St. Martin's also offers a variety of writing handbooks that can be packaged inexpensively with *An Insider's Guide*. See the preface for information.

WPA Outcomes	Relevant Features of *An Insider's Guide to Academic Writing*
Understand why genre conventions for structure, paragraphing, tone, and mechanics vary.	Genre conventions across and within disciplines are emphasized throughout Part Two of the book. Beyond that, the Appendix on documentation styles (pp. 613–27) discusses disciplinary conventions in referencing, with implications for structure and mechanics.
Gain experience negotiating variations in genre conventions.	*An Insider's Guide* provides many opportunities for students to experiment and negotiate variations in disciplinary conventions. See, for example, the "Writing Projects" in Chapter 5, "Reading and Writing in Academic Disciplines," which include "Comparing Scholarly and Popular Articles" (p. 102) and "Translating a Scholarly Article for a Public Audience" (p. 106). In particular, some of the "Inside Work" activities in Chapter 9, "Reading and Writing in the Applied Fields" (pp. 272, 282, 294, 304), ask students to become professionals "for a day" and try writing important genres by extrapolating from models in the chapter.
Learn common formats and/or design features for different kinds of texts.	The design features of key genres, such as IMRAD, are highlighted (especially in Chapters 7 and 8, on the social sciences and natural sciences respectively). Chapter 4, "Academic Research," introduces different documentation formats (MLA, APA, CSE—pp. 76–77), which is expanded upon in the Appendix on documentation styles (pp. 613–27). Further, the range of multidisciplinary readings in Chapters 10–13 foregrounds a variety of formats used in the humanities, social sciences, and sciences.
Explore the concepts of intellectual property (such as fair use and copyright) that motivate documentation conventions.	The Appendix on documentation styles (MLA, APA, CSE formats) raises issues of different documentation conventions (pp. 613–27), and the discussion of plagiarism in Chapter 4, "Academic Research," raises concerns about intellectual property (pp. 75–76).
Practice applying citation conventions systematically in their own work.	The Appendix (pp. 613–27) enables students to apply citation conventions of MLA, APA, and CSE styles systematically in their own work.

Contents

LaunchPadSolo *Additional video material may be found online in LaunchPad Solo when the ▶ icon appears.*

Preface for Instructors v

PART ONE   A Guide to College and College Writing 1

1 Inside Colleges and Universities 3

What Is Higher Education? 3

How Do Colleges and Universities Differ from One Another? 4

- Inside Work: Choosing a College 5

What Is the Purpose of College? 5

- Inside Work: Writing about College 7

What Are Academic Disciplines? 7

How Many Different Academic Disciplines Are There? 8

- Inside Work: Understanding Disciplinarity 9

Why Do Academics Write? 10

- Inside Work: Thinking about What Academics Write 11
- ▶ Insider's View: Sam Stout, Gena Lambrecht, Alexandria Woods, Students 11

How Does Writing in College Compare with Writing in Other Contexts? 12

- ▶ Insider's View: Karen Keaton Jackson, Writing Studies 12
- Inside Work: Understanding the Goals of Your Writing Course 13

What Do You Already Know about Writing in Different Contexts? 14

- **WRITING PROJECT:** Composing a Literacy Narrative 14
- **WRITING PROJECT:** Interviewing a Scholar 15

Insider Example: Student Interview with a Faculty Member 16

Kaitie Gay, *Interview with Marvin Malecha* 16

Tip Sheet: Inside Colleges and Universities 19

2 Reading and Writing Rhetorically   20

Understanding Rhetorical Context   21
- ▶ Insider's View: Karen Keaton Jackson, Writing Studies   21
- ▪ Inside Work: Identifying Rhetorical Context   22

Understanding Genres   23
- ▶ Insider's View: Moriah McCracken, Writing Studies   23

Reading Rhetorically   24

Reading Visuals Rhetorically   25
- ▪ Inside Work: Reading Rhetorically   25

Writing Rhetorically   25
- ▪ Inside Work: Analyzing Rhetorical Context   27

Rhetorical Writing Processes   27
- ▶ Insider's View: Jonathan Morris and Jody Baumgartner, Political Science   28
- ▶ Insider's View: Patrick Bahls, Mathematics   29

Writing a Rhetorical Analysis   30

     George H. W. Bush, *Letter to Saddam Hussein*   31

   Insider Example: Student Rhetorical Analysis   32

     Sofia Lopez, *The Multiple Audiences of George H. W. Bush's Letter to Saddam Hussein*   33

- ▪ WRITING PROJECT: Analyzing the Rhetorical Features of a Text   34

Tip Sheet: Reading and Writing Rhetorically   35

3 Developing Arguments   37

Understanding Proofs and Appeals   38
- ▪ Inside Work: Writing about Arguments   39

Making Claims   39

     Thesis versus Hypothesis   40

Developing Reasons   41
- ▪ Inside Work: Constructing Thesis Statements   42

Supporting Reasons with Evidence   43
- ▶ Insider's View: Moriah McCracken, Writing Studies   44
- ▶ Insider's View: Michelle Richter, Criminal Justice   45
- ▪ Inside Work: Analyzing Audience Expectations   45

Understanding Assumptions   45
- ▪ Inside Work: Considering Assumptions and Audience   46

Anticipating Counterarguments 47

- ▶ **Insider's View:** Mike Brotherton, Astronomy   47
- ▪ **Inside Work:** Dealing with Counterarguments   48

Analyzing Arguments 48

Insider Example: Professional Analysis of an Advertisement 48

Jack Solomon, from *Masters of Desire: The Culture of American Advertising* 49

Insider Example: Student Analysis of an Advertisement 52

Timothy Holtzhauser, *Rhetoric of a 1943 War Bonds Ad* 52

- ▪ **WRITING PROJECT:** Composing a Rhetorical Analysis of an Advertisement 57

Tip Sheet: Developing Arguments 58

4 Academic Research 59

Conducting Research 59

Developing a Research Question 59

- ▪ **Inside Work:** Writing a Research Question 60

Choosing Primary and Secondary Sources 60

- ▶ **Insider's View:** Jody Baumgartner and Jonathan Morris, Political Science 60
- ▶ **Insider's View:** Moriah McCracken, Writing Studies 61
- ▪ **Inside Work:** Collecting Primary Evidence 61
- ▪ **Inside Work:** Using Primary and Secondary Sources 62

Searching for Sources 62

- ▪ **Inside Work:** Generating Search Terms 65

Evaluating Sources 69

- ▶ **Insider's View:** Jonathan Morris, Political Science 69
- ▪ **Inside Work:** Evaluating Sources 70

Summarizing, Paraphrasing, and Quoting from Sources 71

- ▪ **Inside Work:** Summarizing, Paraphrasing, and Quoting from Sources 74

Avoiding Plagiarism 75

- ▶ **Insider's View:** Karen Keaton Jackson, Writing Studies 75
- ▪ **Inside Work:** Understanding Plagiarism 75

Understanding Documentation Systems 76

- ▪ **WRITING PROJECT:** Writing an Annotated Bibliography 77
- ▪ **WRITING PROJECT:** Developing a Supported Argument on a Controversial Issue 79

Insider Example: Student Argument on a Controversial Issue 80

Ashlyn Sims, *Condom Distribution in High School* 80

Tip Sheet: Academic Research 84

PART TWO   Inside Academic Writing   87

5 Reading and Writing in Academic Disciplines   89

> ⊙ Insider's View: Karen Keaton Jackson, Writing Studies   90

Analyzing Genres and Conventions of Academic Writing   91

> ⊙ Insider's View: Moriah McCracken, Writing Studies   92

Adapting to Different Rhetorical Contexts: An Academic Writer at Work   92

> Insider's View: Mike Brotherton, Astronomy   93
> ▪ Inside Work: Reflecting on a Discipline   93

Using Rhetorical Context to Analyze Writing for a Non-Academic Audience   94

> **Mike Brotherton,** from *Hubble Space Telescope Spies Galaxy/Black Hole Evolution in Action*   94
> Insider's View: Mike Brotherton, Astronomy   96
> ▪ Inside Work: Reflecting on Rhetorical Context   96

Using Structure, Language, and Reference to Analyze Academic Writing   96

> ⊙ Insider's View: Mike Brotherton, Astronomy   97
> **M. S. Brotherton, Wil van Breugel, S. A. Stanford, R. J. Smith, B. J. Boyle, Lance Miller, T. Shanks, S. M. Croom, and Alexei V. Filippenko,** from *A Spectacular Poststarburst Quasar*   98
> ▪ Inside Work: Reflecting on Disciplinary Writing   99
> Insider's View: Mike Brotherton, Astronomy   100
> ▪ **WRITING PROJECT:** Writing a Rhetorical Analysis of an Academic Article   100
> ▪ **WRITING PROJECT:** Writing a Comparative Rhetorical Analysis   101
> ▪ **WRITING PROJECT:** Comparing Scholarly and Popular Articles   102

Translating Scholarly Writing for Different Rhetorical Contexts   102

> **Insider Example: Student Translation of a Scholarly Article**   102
> **Jonathan Nastasi,** *Life May Be Possible on Other Planets*   102
> ▪ **WRITING PROJECT:** Translating a Scholarly Article for a Public Audience   106

Tip Sheet: Reading and Writing in Academic Disciplines   107

6 Reading and Writing in the Humanities   108

Introduction to the Humanities   108

> Insider's View: John McCurdy, History   109

Texts and Meaning   109

> ▪ Inside Work: Thinking about Texts   110

Observation and Interpretation   110

> ▪ Inside Work: Observing and Asking Questions   110

Research in the Humanities 111

▷ **Insider's View:** Karen Keaton Jackson, Writing Studies   111

▪ **Inside Work:** Observing and Interpreting Images   112

The Role of Theory in the Humanities   113

Close Reading in the Humanities   113

Insider Example: Professional Close Reading   114

Dale Jacobs, *More Than Words: Comics as a Means of Teaching Multiple Literacies*   114

Strategies for Close Reading and Observation   123

Kate Chopin, from *The Story of an Hour*   124

▪ **Inside Work:** Annotating a Text   125

Kate Chopin, *The Story of an Hour*   126

▪ **Inside Work:** Preparing a Content/Form-Response Grid   128

Responding to the Interpretations of Others   128

▷ **Insider's View:** Moriah McCracken, Writing Studies   128

Conventions of Writing in the Humanities   129

Insider's View: Shelley Garrigan, Spanish Language and Literature   129

Structural Conventions   130

Developing Research Questions and Thesis Statements   130

▷ **Insider's View:** Karen Keaton Jackson, Writing Studies   130

▪ **Inside Work:** Developing *Why, What,* and *How* Questions   132

Developing Effective Thesis Statements   132

▪ **Inside Work:** Drafting Thesis Statements   133

Five-Paragraph Essays and Other Thesis-Driven Templates   134

▷ **Insider's View:** Karen Keaton Jackson, Writing Studies   134

Other Structural Conventions in the Humanities   135

Language Conventions in the Humanities   136

Reference Conventions in the Humanities   138

Documentation   139

▪ **Inside Work:** Analyzing Scholarly Writing in the Humanities   140

Genres of Writing in the Humanities   141

Insider's View: Shelley Garrigan, Spanish Language and Literature   141

Textual Interpretation   141

▪ **WRITING PROJECT:** Interpreting a Text   142

Insider Example: Student Interpretation of a Text   142

Sarah Ray, *Till Death Do Us Part: An Analysis of Kate Chopin's "The Story of an Hour"*   143

Artistic Texts   149

▪ **WRITING PROJECT:** Creating an Artistic Text   150

Tip Sheet: Reading and Writing in the Humanities   151

7 Reading and Writing in the Social Sciences 152

Introduction to the Social Sciences 152
> **Insider's View:** Kevin Rathunde, Social Sciences 153
> ■ Inside Work: Observing Behavior 153

Research in the Social Sciences 154
The Role of Theory 154

Insider Example: Exploring Social Science Theory 155
> **Kalervo Oberg,** from *Cultural Shock: Adjustments to New Cultural Environments* 155
> ■ Inside Work: Tracing a Theory's Development 158
Research Questions and Hypotheses 158
> ■ Inside Work: Developing Hypotheses 159
Methods 160
> **Insider's View:** Kevin Rathunde, Social Sciences 161
> ⊙ **Insider's View:** Jonathan Morris, Political Science 164
> ■ Inside Work: Considering Research Methods 164
The IRB Process and Use of Human Subjects 165

Conventions of Writing in the Social Sciences 165
> **Insider's View:** Aya Matsuda, Linguistics 166
Structural Conventions and IMRAD Format 166
Other Structural Conventions 174
> ■ Inside Work: Observing Structural Conventions 176
Language Conventions 176
> ■ Inside Work: Observing Language Features 178
Reference Conventions 178
> ■ Inside Work: Observing Reference Features 179

Genres of Writing in the Social Sciences 180
> **Insider's View:** Aya Matsuda, Linguistics 180
The Literature Review 180

Insider Example: An Embedded Literature Review 181
> **Mihaly Csikszentmihalyi and Jeremy Hunter,** from *Happiness in Everyday Life: The Uses of Experience Sampling* 181
Writing a Literature Review 182
> ■ **WRITING PROJECT:** Writing a Literature Review 185

Insider Example: Student Literature Review 186
> **William O'Brien,** *Effects of Sleep Deprivation: A Literature Review* 187
Theory Response Essay 196
> ■ **WRITING PROJECT:** Writing a Theory Response 197

Insider Example: Student Theory Response Paper 198

    Matt Kapadia, *Evaluation of the Attribution Theory* 199

Tip Sheet: Reading and Writing in the Social Sciences 208

8   Reading and Writing in the Natural Sciences   209

Introduction to the Natural Sciences 209

    Insider's View: Sian Proctor, Geology 210

Research in the Natural Sciences 212

    Insider's View: Paige Geiger, Molecular and Integrative Physiology 212

    ■ **Inside Work:** Considering a Natural Science Topic 213

  Observation and Description in the Natural Sciences 213

    ■ **Inside Work:** Thinking about Systematic Observation in the Sciences 214

  Moving from Description to Speculation 214

    ■ **Inside Work:** Practicing Description and Speculation 216

    ■ **Inside Work:** Developing Research Questions and a Hypothesis 217

  Designing a Research Study in the Natural Sciences 218

    Insider's View: Michelle LaRue, Conservation Biology 219

    ⊙ **Insider's View:** Patrick Bahls, Mathematics 219

    ■ **Inside Work:** Freewriting about an Experiment 220

Conventions of Writing in the Natural Sciences 221

    Insider's View: Michelle LaRue, Conservation Biology 222

  Objectivity 222

    ■ **Inside Work:** Looking for Conventions of Objectivity 223

  Replicability 224

  Recency 225

    ⊙ **Insider's View:** Patrick Bahls, Mathematics 225

    ■ **Inside Work:** Looking for Conventions of Replicability and Recency 225

  Cooperation and Collaboration 226

Genres of Writing in the Natural Sciences 227

  An Observation Logbook 227

    Insider's View: Paige Geiger, Molecular and Integrative Physiology 227

    ■ **WRITING PROJECT:** Keeping an Observation Logbook 228

  Insider Example: Student Observation Logbook 229

    Kedric Lemon, *Comparing the Efficiency of Various Batteries Being Used over Time* 230

  Research Proposal 240

    ■ **WRITING PROJECT:** Developing a Research Proposal 241

Insider Example: Research Proposal 241

    Gary Ritchison, *Hunting Behavior, Territory Quality, and Individual Quality of American Kestrels* (Falco sparverius) 242

Lab Report 248

    ■ **WRITING PROJECT:** Composing a Lab Report 249

Insider Example: Student Lab Report 249

    Kedric Lemon, *Which Type of Battery Is the Most Effective When Energy Is Drawn Rapidly?* 250

Tip Sheet: Reading and Writing in the Natural Sciences 260

9 Reading and Writing in the Applied Fields 261

Introduction to the Applied Fields 261

What Are Applied Fields? 261

    ■ Inside Work: Defining and Solving Problems 262

    ■ Inside Work: Considering Additional Applied Fields 263

Rhetoric and the Applied Fields 263

    ▶ **Insider's View:** Michelle Richter, Criminal Justice 263

Genres in Selected Applied Fields 264

Nursing 264

    Insider's View: Janna Dieckmann, Nursing 265

Insider Example: Professional Research Report in Nursing 266

    Margaret Shandor Miles, Diane Holditch-Davis, Suzanne Thoyre, and Linda Beeber, *Rural African-American Mothers Parenting Prematurely Born Infants: An Ecological Systems Perspective* 266

Insider Example: Discharge Instructions 269

    First Hospital, *Discharge Instructions for Heart Attack* 270

    ■ Inside Work: Nurse for a Day 272

Education 272

Insider Example: Student Lesson Plan 273

    Myra Moses, *Lesson Plan* 273

Insider Example: Student IEP 276

    Myra Moses, *IEP* 277

    ■ Inside Work: Teacher for a Day 282

Business 282

Insider Example: Student Memorandum 283

    James Blackwell, *Investigative Report on Hazen and Sawyer* 284

Insider Example: Student Business Plan   285

    Daniel Chase Mills, *The Electricity Monitor Company*   286

      ■ Inside Work: CFO for a Day   294

Law   294

Insider Example: Professional Legal Brief   296

    University of Texas at Austin, et al., *Brief for Respondents*   296

Insider Example: E-Mail Correspondence from Attorney   303

    Joseph E. Miller Jr., *Sample E-Mail*   303

      ■ Inside Work: Lawyer for a Day   304

      ■ **WRITING PROJECT:** Discovering Genres of Writing in an Applied Field   304

Tip Sheet: Reading and Writing in the Applied Fields   305

PART THREE   Entering Academic Conversations: Readings and Case Studies   307

10 Love, Marriage, and Family   309

Andrew Cherlin, *How American Family Life Is Different*   310

    "Both pictures, contradictory as they may be, are part of the way that Americans live their family lives. Together they spin the American merry-go-round of intimate partnerships."

Susan Krauss Whitbourne, *The Myth of the Helicopter Parent*   316

    "[T]he findings lead to a new understanding of parent-child support in the years of emerging adulthood."

Brian Powell, Catherine Bolzendahl, Claudia Geist, and Lala Carr Steelman, *Changing Counts, Counting Change: Toward a More Inclusive Definition of Family*   318

    "The United States includes a rich diversity of families whether or not they are officially recognized as such. In fact, 'the family,' although still invoked far too often in public and scholarly venues, is an increasingly untenable and obsolete concept."

Susan Saulny, *In Strangers' Glances at Family, Tensions Linger*   332

    "Many mixed-race youths say they feel wider acceptance than past generations, particularly on college campuses and in pop culture.... [W]hen they are alone, the family strives to be colorblind. But what they face outside their home is another story."

Academic Case Study: Perspectives on Love

Humanities

Warren E. Milteer Jr., *The Strategies of Forbidden Love: Family across Racial Boundaries in Nineteenth-Century North Carolina*   336

    Despite legal and social disapproval of the time, "free women of mixed ancestry and white men developed relationships that mimicked legally sanctioned marriages."

Social Sciences

Marissa A. Harrison and Jennifer C. Shortall, *Women and Men in Love: Who Really Feels It and Says It First?*   348

"[W]omen may not be the greater 'fools for love' that society assumes."

Natural Sciences

Donatella Marazziti and Domenico Canale, *Hormonal Changes When Falling in Love*   356

"[T]o fall in love provokes transient hormonal changes, some of which seem to be specific to each sex."

Applied Fields

Cara O. Peters, Jane B. Thomas, and Richard Morris, *Looking for Love on Craigslist: An Examination of Gender Differences in Self-Marketing Online*   363

"The results illustrate that language is an imprecise form in how people read and understand the written and spoken word."

- ■ **WRITING PROJECT:** Contributing to a Scholarly Conversation   379
- ■ **WRITING PROJECT:** Writing a Comparative Analysis of Research Methodologies   380

11 Crime, Punishment, and Justice   381

Barbara Bradley Hagerty, *Inside a Psychopath's Brain: The Sentencing Debate*   382

"'Neuroscience and neuroimaging is going to change the whole philosophy about how we punish and how we decide who to incapacitate and how we decide how to deal with people.'"

Sophia Kerby, *The Top 10 Most Startling Facts about People of Color and Criminal Justice in the United States: A Look at the Racial Disparities Inherent in Our Nation's Criminal-Justice System*   385

"[I]t is imperative that criminal-justice reform evolves as the civil rights issue of the 21st century."

Clark Merrefield, *Should Juvenile Criminals Be Sentenced Like Adults?*   388

"'While some teenagers can be astonishingly mature and others inconceivably childish, middle adolescence—roughly, ages 14 to 18—might be the worst time in a person's life for rational decision making.'"

Abigail Pesta (reporting), *I Survived Prison: What Really Happens behind Bars*   392

"I'm about to become a prisoner in a massive penitentiary, and I feel an overwhelming sense of dread. I'm surrounded by people who have been here before, who know the system, who know how to work the guards. But I know nothing."

Academic Case Study: Capital Punishment

Humanities

Michael Owen Jones, *Dining on Death Row: Last Meals and the Crutch of Ritual* 396

"'He ate a bite or two, and that was it.'" An examination of last-meal experiences of individuals facing capital punishment.

Social Sciences

Benedikt Till and Peter Vitouch, *Capital Punishment in Films: The Impact of Death Penalty Portrayals on Viewers' Mood and Attitude toward Capital Punishment* 416

"[T]hese films certainly deteriorate the viewer's mood, and have the potential to influence their social values and beliefs."

Natural Sciences

Teresa A. Zimmers, Jonathan Sheldon, David A. Lubarsky, Francisco López-Muñoz, Linda Waterman, Richard Weisman, and Leonidas G. Koniaris, *Lethal Injection for Execution: Chemical Asphyxiation?* 426

"We sought to determine whether the current drug regimen results in death in the manner intended."

Applied Fields

Cyndy Caravelis Hughes and Matthew Robinson, *Perceptions of Law Enforcement Officers on Capital Punishment in the United States* 438

According to the authors, their study is the first "to assess death penalty opinion among criminal justice practitioners."

- **WRITING PROJECT:** Writing a Brief Annotated Bibliography 448
- **WRITING PROJECT:** Composing an Evaluative Rhetorical Analysis 449

12 Food, Sustainability, and Class 451

Gustavo Arellano, *Taco USA: How Mexican Food Became More American Than Apple Pie* 452

"Food is a natural conduit of change, evolution, and innovation. Wishing for a foodstuff to remain static, uncorrupted by outside influence—especially in these United States—is as ludicrous an idea as barring new immigrants from entering the country."

Brent Cunningham, *Pastoral Romance* 457

"The reality of America's food past is far more complicated, and troubling, than is suggested by the romantic image at the heart of our foodie nostalgia."

Dana Goodyear, *Grub* 464

"Standing before a plate of brownies fortified with a mash of the sautéed mealworms, he said despondently, 'This is the future! You'll eat worms and like it. You gotta eat *something*.'"

Michael Pollan, *Why Cook?*   471

> "Cooking has the power to transform more than plants and animals: It transforms us, too, from mere consumers into producers."

Academic Case Study: Genetically Modified Food
Humanities

Daniel Gregorowius, Petra Lindemann-Matthies, and Markus Huppenbauer, *Ethical Discourse on the Use of Genetically Modified Crops: A Review of Academic Publications in the Fields of Ecology and Environmental Ethics*   478

> The study surveys more than three decades of "the moral reasoning on the use of GM crops expressed in academic publications."

Social Sciences

John C. Bernard, Katie Gifford, Kristin Santora, and Daria J. Bernard, *Willingness to Pay for Foods with Varying Production Traits and Levels of Genetically Modified Content*   501

> Are consumers willing to pay more for organic foods than for genetically modified foods? What about second-generation rather than first-generation GM foods?

Natural Sciences

Aziz Aris and Samuel Leblanc, *Maternal and Fetal Exposure to Pesticides Associated to Genetically Modified Foods in Eastern Townships of Quebec, Canada*   513

> The goal of this study is to help "develop procedures to avoid environmentally induced disease in susceptible populations such as pregnant women and their fetuses."

Applied Fields

Sherry Seethaler and Marcia Linn, *Genetically Modified Food in Perspective: An Inquiry-Based Curriculum to Help Middle School Students Make Sense of Tradeoffs*   525

> How do middle school students learn about the controversial scientific issue of genetically modified foods?

- ■ **WRITING PROJECT:** Writing a Persuasive Narrative   543
- ■ **WRITING PROJECT:** Translating a Scholarly Work for a Popular Audience   543

13 Global Climate Change and Natural Catastrophes   545

Sharon Begley, *Are You Ready for More?*   546

> "From these and other extreme-weather events, one lesson is sinking in with terrifying certainty. The stable climate of the last 12,000 years is gone."

Daniel Sarewitz and Roger A. Pielke Jr., *Rising Tide*   550

> "Global climate change is real, and developing alternative energy sources and reducing global carbon-dioxide emission is essential. But the claim that action to slow climate change is justified by the rising toll of natural disasters . . . is both scientifically and morally insupportable."

John Broome, *The Ethics of Climate Change*   555

"How should we—all of us living today—evaluate the well-being of future generations? . . . How should we respond to the small but real chance that climate change could lead to worldwide catastrophe?"

Ted Steinberg, *Disasters and Deregulation*   561

"From a statistical perspective, our nation's recent hurricane problem comes down to a case of bad luck. . . . But we can help load the dice in our favor by understanding what has gone wrong with the federal government's approach to natural hazards."

Academic Case Study: Hurricane Katrina
Humanities

Zenia Kish, *"My FEMA People": Hip-Hop as Disaster Recovery in the Katrina Diaspora*   565

This study examines musical responses to "the violence, racism, displacement, and vulnerability that came to represent the experiences of the Katrina diaspora."

Social Sciences

Barbara L. Allen, *Environmental Justice, Local Knowledge, and After-Disaster Planning in New Orleans*   580

The author explores social justice issues in the aftermath of Hurricane Katrina.

Natural Sciences

Tingzhi Su, Shi Shu, Honglan Shi, Jianmin Wang, Craig Adams, and Emitt C. Witt, *Distribution of Toxic Trace Elements*   588

Was there an increase of toxic trace elements in regional soil and sediments after the devastating landfall of Hurricane Katrina?

Applied Fields

Jacqueline Rhoads, Faye Mitchell, and Susan Rick, *Posttraumatic Stress Disorder after Hurricane Katrina*   601

The authors provide nurses with insight into the signs and symptoms of post-traumatic stress disorder (PTSD) in the aftermath of Hurricane Katrina in an effort "to prevent serious sequelae that can disrupt and even end a person's life."

- **WRITING PROJECT:** Composing a Research Proposal   611
- **WRITING PROJECT:** Writing a Comparative Rhetorical Analysis: Popular and Academic Sources   612

Appendix: Introduction to Documentation Styles   613
Index   633

A Guide to College and College Writing

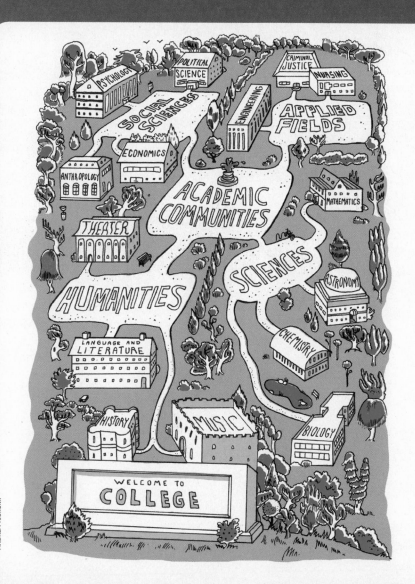

ANDREA TSURUMI

PART ONE

A Guide to College and College Writing

1

Inside Colleges and Universities 3

2

Reading and Writing Rhetorically 20

3

Developing Arguments 37

4

Academic Research 59

Inside Colleges and Universities

What Is Higher Education?

This book introduces the expectations about writing you'll likely encounter in college and gives you a set of tools to complete writing tasks successfully. To understand those expectations, you must first understand how colleges and universities are structured; how your other writing experiences in high school, college, and work might compare; and what expectations about writing you might encounter in your particular college or university classes. These expectations will likely differ according to the type of college or university you attend.

As you read through the chapters in this book, certain recurring features will help expand your knowledge of college writing:

- *Insider's View* boxes contain excerpts of comments by scholars and students discussing academic writing. Many of these are gleaned from video interviews that complement the instruction in this book. The videos, which are further referenced in the page margins, can be viewed for greater insight into the processes and productions of academic writers. Video content and other great resources are available on the LaunchPad Solo designed to accompany this text.

- *Inside Work* activities prompt you to reflect on what you have learned while trying out new insights and techniques.

- *Writing Projects* offer sequences of activities that will help you develop your own compositions.

- *Tip Sheets* summarize key lessons of the chapters.

Before we turn to college writing, however, we ask you to read about and reflect on some of the wider contexts of higher education—in particular, your place in it.

HOW DO COLLEGES AND UNIVERSITIES DIFFER FROM ONE ANOTHER?

As we discuss the expectations you might encounter related to writing in college, you should consider the specific context of the school you're attending. What kind of school is it? What types of students does it serve? What are the school's mission and focus? It's important to realize that different schools have differing missions and values that influence their faculty members' expectations for students.

How did you determine where to attend college? Some prospective students send out applications to multiple schools, while others know exactly where they want to start their college careers. Some students transfer from one school to another, and they do so for a variety of reasons. If you researched potential schools, and especially if you visited different campuses as part of your decision-making process, you likely realized that there are many different kinds of schools in the United States (not to mention the variety of institutions of higher education elsewhere in the world). If we just focus on the range of higher education options in the United States, we find:

- **Community Colleges:** schools that typically offer associate's degrees. Some community colleges prepare students to enter careers directly following graduation; others specialize in helping students transfer to bachelor's-granting institutions after completing most of their general education requirements or an associate's degree.

- **Liberal Arts Colleges/Universities:** schools that introduce students to a broad variety of disciplines as they pursue their bachelor's degrees. Liberal arts schools generally focus on undergraduate education, although some offer graduate degrees as well.

- **Doctoral-Granting/Research-Intensive Universities:** schools with an emphasis on research and a focus on both undergraduate and graduate education. Doctoral-granting universities, especially those that are research-intensive, can often be quite large, and they generally have higher expectations for faculty members' research activities than other types of institutions do. As a result, students may have more opportunities for collaborative research with faculty members, and graduate students might teach some undergraduate classes.

- **Master's-Granting Institutions:** schools that offer bachelor's degrees in addition to a selection of master's degrees. Such schools usually have a dual focus on undergraduate and graduate education, but they might not emphasize research expectations for their faculty as intensely as doctoral-granting institutions do.

- **Schools with a Specific Focus:** schools that serve specific populations or prepare students for particular careers. Such schools might be single-sex institutions, historically black colleges and universities, Hispanic-serving institutions, religious-affiliated schools, or agricultural, technical, and vocational schools.

- **For-Profit Institutions:** schools that operate on a business model and are privately held or publicly traded companies. Some are regionally accredited institutions; many focus on meeting the needs of students whose schedules or other commitments require a different approach from what a typical non-profit college or university provides.

What kind of school is the institution that you currently attend? Knowing how your particular college or university is structured, and how it fits into the larger context of higher education, can help you understand its institutional values and the emphasis it places on particular kinds of academic preparation. If you know these important factors, you'll be able to anticipate the expectations for your academic work and understand the reasoning behind the requirements for your degree.

INSIDE WORK) **Choosing a College**

Write brief responses to the following questions, and be prepared to discuss them with your classmates.

- What kind of institution do you attend? What characteristics of your school seem to match that category?

- What degree program or major are you most interested in? Why?

- Was your interest in a particular degree program or major a factor when you decided to go to college? Did it draw you to your particular college? Why or why not?

- What classes are you taking, and how did you choose them?

- What kinds of factors do you consider when choosing your classes? What guidance, requirements, or other influences help you make those choices? ▶

WHAT IS THE PURPOSE OF COLLEGE?

People's reasons for pursuing an undergraduate degree can differ, depending on the school and the individual student. Some schools and degree programs focus on preparing students for particular vocations that they can pursue directly after graduation. Others focus more broadly on developing well-rounded, informed graduates who will be active in their communities regardless of which careers they pursue. Still others emphasize different, and sometimes quite specific, outcomes for their graduates. If you have never done so, consider taking a look at the mission or values statements for your university, college, or department. What do the faculty members and administrators value? What are their expectations of you as a student?

For example, the mission statement of Texas A&M University begins by stating:

> Texas A&M University is dedicated to the discovery, development, communication, and application of knowledge in a wide range of academic and professional fields.

This statement shows a broad commitment to a range of academic interests and professions; therefore, students at Texas A&M can expect to find a wide range of majors represented at the university. The mission statement also emphasizes that knowledge discovery is important at Texas A&M, highlighting the school's role as a research-intensive university.

As another example, the mission statement of San Juan College in New Mexico reads:

> The mission of San Juan College is to improve the quality of life of the citizens it serves by meeting the educational and human needs of the entire community in concert with community agencies, businesses, industries, and other groups.

This statement illustrates San Juan College's emphasis on connection to the community and the agencies, businesses, and industries surrounding and connected to the college. San Juan's mission is connected intricately to the community it serves.

A third example is the mission statement of Endicott College in Massachusetts, which begins by stating:

> The mission of Endicott College is to instill in students an understanding of and an appreciation for professional and liberal studies. Deeply woven within this philosophy is the concept of applied learning, which has been the hallmark of Endicott. Linking classroom and off-campus work experience through required internships remains the most distinguishing feature of the College.

Endicott's mission mentions an emphasis on applied learning, which is evident through its requirement of internships to extend classroom learning. Students who enroll at Endicott College should expect to make practical, hands-on application of their learning throughout their coursework.

Of course, different students have different goals and reasons for pursuing undergraduate degrees. Sometimes those goals match the institution's mission fairly closely, but not always. What is your purpose in attending your college or university? How do your personal and professional goals fit within the school's goals and values? What will you need to do while in college to achieve your goals? What have you already accomplished, and what do you still need to know and do?

Read the following questions, and write a brief response to each.

• What goals do you hope to achieve by attending college?

• What steps should you take to maximize your opportunity to achieve your academic goals?

Next, find your college or university's mission statement (usually available on the school's website), and write a brief description that compares your goals for college to the mission statement. How does the mission of your school fit your goals? How might the strengths and mission of your college or university help you achieve your goals? ▶

What Are Academic Disciplines?

Another structural feature of colleges and universities is the way they are divided into academic disciplines. Depending on the school, this might take the form of departments, divisions, colleges, or other groupings. **Academic disciplines** are, broadly defined, areas of teaching, research, and inquiry that academics pursue. Sometimes these disciplines are listed in broad categories, such as psychology, English, biology, physics, and engineering.

At other times, disciplines are listed in more specialized categories that demonstrate the diversity of areas encompassed within higher education: for example, adolescent psychology, abnormal psychology, sociolinguistics, second language acquisition, molecular biology, physiology, astrophysics, quantum mechanics, civil engineering, mechanical engineering, computer science, Victorian poetry, and medieval literature.

While the specific divisions may differ according to the institution, most college and university faculties are grouped into departments. Larger schools are often further divided into colleges

ANDREA TSURUMI

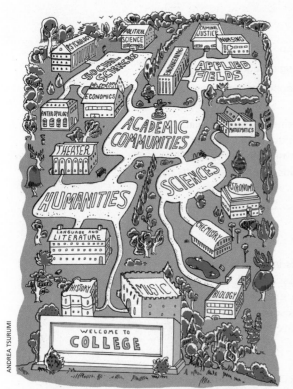

ANDREA TSURUMI

or divisions, which usually cluster departments together that are related in some way to one another. These divisions often, but not always, fall along common lines that divide departments into broader disciplinary areas of the humanities, social sciences, natural sciences, and applied fields. We describe these broad categories in more detail in the next section.

HOW MANY DIFFERENT ACADEMIC DISCIPLINES ARE THERE?

You might find that different faculty members give varying answers to the question, "How many different academic disciplines are there?" And those answers differ for good reason. Sometimes academic disciplines are seen as equivalent to departments. Faculty in the history department study history, right? But the subject of history can be divided into many different categories, too: antebellum U.S. history, Middle Eastern history, and African American history, for example. In addition, people in other departments might study and teach topics that are related to history, such as American religious history, medieval literature and culture, and ancient rhetoric. You can probably imagine how categorizing all these different areas of study and research would be difficult.

For the purposes of this text, we're going to explore writing in different disciplinary areas that are grouped together according to (1) the kinds of questions that scholars ask in those disciplines and (2) the research strategies, or methods of inquiry, that they use to answer those questions. As mentioned earlier, we've divided various academic disciplines into four broad disciplinary categories: humanities, social sciences, natural sciences, and applied fields. As we talk about these four areas of study and the disciplines associated with them, both here and in Part Two of the book, you'll notice some similarities and differences within the categories:

- Scholars in the **humanities** usually ask questions about the human condition. To answer these questions, they often employ methods of inquiry that are based on analysis, interpretation, and speculation. Examples of academic disciplines that are generally considered part of the humanities are history, literature, philosophy, foreign languages, religious studies, and the visual arts. For examples of the kinds of questions humanists ask, see Chapter 6.

- Scholars in the **social sciences** usually ask questions about human behavior and society. To answer these questions, they often employ methods of inquiry that are based on theory building or empirical research. Examples of academic disciplines that are generally considered part of the social sciences are communication, psychology, sociology, political science, economics, and anthropology. For examples of the kinds of questions social scientists ask, see Chapter 7.

- Scholars in the **natural sciences** usually ask questions about the natural world and the universe. To answer these questions, they often employ methods of inquiry that are based on experimentation and quantifiable data. Examples of academic disciplines that are generally considered part of the natural sciences are chemistry, biology, physics, astronomy, and mathematics. For examples of the kinds of questions natural scientists ask, see Chapter 8.

- Scholars in **applied fields** might have their foundation in any one (or more) of the disciplinary categories, but their work is generally focused on practical application. Some disciplines that could fall under the category of applied fields are criminal justice, medicine, nursing, education, business, agriculture, and engineering. Each of these fields has elements that are closely aligned with the humanities, social sciences, and/or natural sciences, but each also focuses on application of that knowledge in specific contexts. For examples of the kinds of questions scholars in applied fields ask, see Chapter 9.

These categories are not perfectly distinct, though; they sometimes overlap with one another. You'll see examples of overlap in the chapters in Part Two, in the student writing examples there, and when you undertake your own research in academic journals. However, the disciplinary categories of humanities, social sciences, natural sciences, and applied fields are useful for understanding some of the distinctions in the ways academics think and do research.

INSIDE WORK Understanding Disciplinarity

In your own words, write a brief description of the four academic disciplines mentioned in the previous section.

- humanities
- social sciences
- natural sciences
- applied fields

Next, list your current course schedule. How might you classify the classes you're taking in terms of these four categories? For each class, write for a few minutes about what characteristics of the class cause it to fit into the category you've chosen. Finally, compare your answers with a classmate's. ▶

WHY DO ACADEMICS WRITE?

As you think about the writing you will do in college, keep in mind that you are learning how to participate in the kinds of discussions that scholars and faculty members engage in about topics and issues of mutual interest. In other words, you're entering into academic conversations that have been going on for a while. As you are writing, you will need to think about who your audience is (other students? teachers? an audience outside of the academic setting?), who has already been participating in the conversations of interest to you (and perhaps who hasn't), and what expectations for your writing you'll need to follow in order to contribute to those conversations. (We'll have much more to say about the concept of audience in Chapter 2.)

As we explore the kinds of writing done in various disciplinary areas, you'll notice that different disciplines have different expectations for writing. In other words, faculty members in a particular discipline might expect a piece of writing to be structured in a particular way, or they might use specific kinds of language, or they might expect you to be familiar with certain research by others and refer to it in prescribed ways. Each of these expectations is an aspect of the writing *conventions* of a particular discipline. **Conventions** are the customs that scholars in a particular discipline follow in their writing. Sometimes those conventions take the form of repeated patterns in structure or certain choices in language use, just to name a few. As students learn these conventions, we sometimes say that they are developing *literacy* in the conventions of a discipline. **Literacy** generally refers to the ability to read and write, but it can also refer to the development of familiarity with the conventions and expectations of different situations. As a student, you will be developing academic literacy—or literacies, since you'll be navigating the expectations of several disciplinary contexts.

To prepare for writing in varied academic contexts, it might be helpful to think about why academics write. Most faculty members at institutions of higher education explain their responsibilities to the institution and their discipline in terms of three categories: their teaching, their research (which generates much of their writing), and their service (what they do outside of their research and teaching that contributes both to the school and to their discipline). Many academics' writing is related to communicating the results of their research, and it might be published or shared with academic audiences or more general audiences. In fact, a scholar might conduct a research project and then find that he or she needs to communicate the results of that project to a variety of audiences.

Imagine that a physiologist who studies diabetes has discovered a new therapy that could potentially benefit diabetic individuals. The researcher might want to publish the results of her study in an academic journal so that other scientists can read about the results, perhaps replicate the study (repeat it to confirm that the results are the same), and maybe expand on the research findings. She might also want to communicate the results of her research to doctors who work with diabetic patients but who don't necessarily read academic journals in physiology. They might read medical journals, though, so in this case the researcher would need to tailor her results to an audience that is primarily interested in the application of research results to patients. In addition, she might want to report the results of her research to the general public, in which case she might write a press release so that newspapers and magazines can develop news stories about her findings. Each of these writing situations involves reporting the same research results, but to different audiences and for different purposes. The physiologist would need to tailor her writing to meet the needs of each writing situation.

INSIDE WORK **Thinking about What Academics Write**

Look for a published piece that has been written by one of the professors that you have for another class. Try to find something that you can access in full, either online or through your school's library. Some colleges and universities have lists of recent publications by faculty on their websites. Additionally, some faculty members list their publications on personal websites. You might also seek help from librarians at your institution if you aren't familiar with the library's resources. Then write your responses to the following questions.

- What does the professor write about?

- Where was that work published?

- Who is the audience for your professor's work?

- What surprised you most about your professor's published work? ❱

Insider's View
Undergraduate students on academic writing
SAM STOUT, GENA LAMBRECHT, ALEXANDRIA WOODS, STUDENTS

Left to right: Sam, engineering; Gena, design; Alexandria, biology

QUESTION: How does the writing you did in high school compare to the writing you've done in college so far?

SAM: Well, in high school [teachers] mainly chose what we wrote about. And here in college they allow you to write about what you're going to be focusing on and choose something that's actually going to benefit you in the future instead of writing for an assignment grade.

GENA: Well, I thought I would be doing a lot more writing like in my AP English classes, which was analyzing literature and poems and plays and writing to a prompt that talked a lot about specific conventions for that type of literature.

ALEXANDRIA: I expected my college writing to be science-related—doing lab reports and research proposals—rather than what I did before college, in middle school and high school, which was just doing definition papers, analysis of books, and things like that.

 **LaunchPadSolo**

Hear more from students about college writing.

w

**g for students
own voices**

JACKSON, WRITING STUDIES

"eral, the sense that I get is that in high
writing is more focused on literature.
college level, we're more interested in
thinking. We're looking for students to
eir own voices in place. Really getting
nts to think stylistically about the choices
make, really thinking about purpose and
ence and the whole rhetorical context. I
k that's really key at the college level. By
ege we're looking at the purpose, and the
dience, and the style, and how all of this
determined based on the different writing
tuation you're in."

LaunchPadSolo

*Get expert advice
on transitioning to
college writing.*

How Does Writing in College Compare with Writing in Other Contexts?

Some students find that writing in college focuses less on personal experience and more on academic research than writing they've done in other contexts. Many of your expectations for writing in college might be based on prior experiences, such as the writing you did in high school or in a work setting. Some students are surprised to find that writing instruction in college is not always paired with discussion of literature, as it often is in high school. While some colleges and universities use literature as a starting point for teaching writing, many other schools offer writing instruction that is focused on principles of **rhetoric**—the study of how language is used to communicate—apart from the study of literature. (Rhetoric will be discussed in detail in subsequent chapters throughout this book.) If you are used to thinking about English courses, and the writing assigned in those courses, as being primarily about literature and literary analysis, you might find that the expectations in your college-level writing courses are somewhat different. Many writing courses at the college level will require you to write about different topics, in different forms, and for different audiences. Depending on your school, writing program, and instructor, the study of literature might be part of that approach, but you might also need to learn about the expectations of instructors in other disciplines.

When we compare the writing expectations in college with what you might have experienced in other contexts, we're making some general assumptions about your experience that may or may not be true. We're also making generalizations about colleges and universities that might differ from the school you're currently attending. One of the most important concepts we'll discuss in this book is the importance of context (see Chapter 2), so you'll need to balance the principles we talk about in this text with your firsthand experience of the context of your particular college or university. You might find that some of our assumptions are true to your particular experience and some are not. When possible, make note of the principles we discuss that are similar to your experience and the ones that are different. As you do so, you'll be learning about and applying these principles in a way that is much more useful than just memorizing information.

Although the approaches toward teaching writing at various colleges and universities differ, we can talk about some common expectations for college-level writing. The Council of Writing Program Administrators (CWPA), a professional organization of hundreds of writing program directors from across the country, published a list of common outcomes for first-year writing courses that has been adapted for use by many schools. The first list of common outcomes was published in 2000, and it has been revised twice since then, most recently in 2014. The purpose of the statement is to provide common expectations for what college students should be able to accomplish in terms of their writing after finishing a first-year course, but the details of those expectations are often revised to fit a specific institution's context. For example, the third outcome deals with "Processes" and states that:

> By the end of first-year composition, students should
> - Develop a writing project through multiple drafts
> - Develop flexible strategies for reading, drafting, reviewing, collaborating, revising, rewriting, rereading, and editing
> - Use composing processes and tools as a means to discover and reconsider ideas
> - Experience the collaborative and social aspects of writing processes
> - Learn to give and act on productive feedback to works in progress
> - Adapt composing processes for a variety of technologies and modalities
> - Reflect on the development of composing practices and how those practices influence their work
>
> http://wpacouncil.org/positions/outcomes.html

The statement doesn't specify which steps or strategies in a writing process students should practice, or what kinds of writing they should be doing. It is left up to individual schools to determine what will be most helpful for their students.

Some institutions follow the guidelines from the Council of Writing Program Administrators explicitly, while others do not. Even at institutions that use these outcomes as a foundation for the writing curriculum, however, it's often possible to find many different approaches to teaching writing that help students achieve academic literacy. How do your institution's outcomes for writing compare and contrast with your experience in high school English classes? How do the outcomes for writing compare and contrast with your writing experience outside of school (perhaps in work-related or personal settings)?

INSIDE WORK) **Understanding the Goals of Your Writing Course**

Take a look at the goals, objectives, or outcomes listed for the writing course you are currently taking. You might look for a course description on the school's website or in a course catalog, or you might find goals or learning objectives listed in the course syllabus.

- What surprised you about the goals or objectives for your writing course?

- What is similar to or different from the writing courses you have taken before?

- What is similar to or different from the expectations you had for this course?

- How do the outcomes for the course align with your goals for writing and for college?

- What does the list of goals for your course tell you about what is valued at your institution? ❯

WHAT DO YOU ALREADY KNOW ABOUT WRITING IN DIFFERENT CONTEXTS?

The culminating writing projects in this chapter ask you to explore your own writing and literacy experiences in more detail. Thinking about the experience and skills that you already bring to your college writing will help you to build on them and expand your abilities.

WRITING PROJECT **Composing a Literacy Narrative**

A *literacy narrative* is an essay that reflects on how someone has developed literacy over time. Literacy is sometimes defined as the ability to read and write, but in this context we'd like you to use a broader definition. Think of literacy not only as the ability to read and write, but also as the ability to successfully function in a specific context or contexts. Your instructor may give you more direction about how to define literacy for the purpose of this assignment, but you could focus on the following questions.

Academic Literacy

- What are your first memories of writing in school?

- How did you learn about the expectations for writing in school?

- Can you think of a time when you struggled to meet the requirements of a school writing assignment? What happened?

Technological Literacy

- What early memories do you have of using technology?

- How do you use technology now to communicate in your daily life? What technologies are most important to you for work, for school, and/or for personal commitments?

Workplace Literacy

- What writing and communication skills are expected in the occupation you aspire to when you graduate? How will you develop those skills?

- Can you think of a time when you encountered a task at work that you didn't know how to accomplish? What did you do? How did you address the challenge?

Social and/or Cultural Literacy

- Have you ever been in a social situation where you didn't know how to act? What did you do?

- What groups do you identify with, and what expectations and shared beliefs make that group cohesive?

A literacy narrative should do three things: (1) make a point about the author's literacy development, (2) read as a story and use narrative strategies to tell the story, and (3) provide specific details that support the point of the narrative.

In a narrative essay, explore the development of your own literacy. You might do this chronologically, at least as you start writing. Be specific in identifying how you define literacy and how you developed your abilities. In your narrative and analysis, provide examples from your experience, and show how they contribute to the development of that literacy. Ultimately, your narrative should be directed to a particular audience for a particular purpose, so think of a context in which you might tell this story. For example, a student who is studying to be a teacher might write about his early literacy experiences and how they led to an interest in teaching other children to read and write. Or an applicant for a job requiring specific technological ability might include a section in an application letter that discusses her development of expertise in technological areas relevant to the job. Be imaginative if you like, but make sure that your narrative provides specific examples and makes a point about your literacy development that you believe is important.

WRITING PROJECT   ## Interviewing a Scholar

Under the guidance of your instructor, find a professor at your college or university who teaches in a discipline that is of interest to you. You might choose a faculty member with whom you already have a connection, either through taking a class, having a mutual acquaintance, or enjoying a shared interest. Ask the scholar if you can interview him or her, either in person or through e-mail. Consider the descriptions of different disciplinary areas in this chapter, and write a profile of the faculty member that addresses questions about his or her writing, such as the following:

- What kinds of writing do scholars in your field do?

- What writing conventions are specific to and important to your field? How did you learn those conventions?

- What was your first experience of writing a scholarly article like? What did you learn through that experience?

- What kinds of writing do you do most often in your work?

- What expectations do you have for students who are learning to write in your field?

Be sure to follow up your questions by asking for specific examples if you need more information to understand the scholar's responses. In addition, you might ask to see an example of his or her academic writing to use as an illustration in your narrative. Above all, be sure to thank the faculty member for taking the time to respond to your questions.

A profile of a faculty member's writing should do two things: (1) make a point about the person being interviewed (in this case, your point should focus on the person's writing), and (2) include details about the person that help develop the point. You might write the questions and answers in an interview format, or you might incorporate the scholar's responses into an essay that uses the interview to make a specific point about his or her development and experience as a writer.

Insider Example
Student Interview with a Faculty Member

Kaitie Gay, a first-year student at North Carolina State University, conducted an interview via e-mail with Marvin Malecha, who is a professor of architecture and dean of the College of Design. Kaitie conducted her interview after reading a selection from one of Malecha's books, *Reconfiguration in the Study and Practice of Design Architecture* (2002). Her interview questions, and Malecha's responses, could lay the foundation for a writing profile.

COURTESY OF KAITIE GAY

KAITIE: In your article, you talk about the different ways that individuals learn about the field of architecture. Which do you find more beneficial to students studying architecture, learning by experience or learning in a classroom setting?

MALECHA: I believe both settings are important, as one complements the other. However, it is also true that certain individuals will have their epiphany on a construction site while others will gain insight from theoretical discourse. But in the end, both are important because each gives perspective to the other. For those interested in theory and classroom investigation, the construction site makes real what otherwise would be disconnected ideas. For the individual who is most likely to be inclined to build and ask questions later, the theoretical discussion forces them to be more reflective. It is for this reason that we maintain a close relationship with the architectural profession at NC State. We want students to work in offices as they progress through school. It is also the reason we offer design build experiences during the summer sessions. But the desire to balance a student's experience also justifies our desire to have students study abroad and to participate in scholarship and research. These experiences exercise the mind.

KAITIE: In the article you said, "Technology will reduce the need for a studio-based culture." Is it important that we balance technology and studio, or do you find it a good thing that the field is becoming more technology-driven?

MALECHA: It is easy to forget the rather primitive state of technology in the field of architecture when I wrote this article. The social media and the many tools at our discretion today really amplify my comments. I was speaking to a traditional studio-based culture where students sat at their desks almost solely dependent on the direction and handouts of their instructor. I believed that this sole relationship would be significantly changed by the ability to have incredible amounts of information at hand, including case studies, new materials, programming insights to push along scholarship, and plan development. I believed that it would be possible to check in with a studio instructor from anywhere in the world, blurring the difference between the virtual and the real. It was already true when I wrote this article that joint studios were conducted between schools on different continents utilizing the telephone and fax technology. Given this, I believed that new technologies would enhance such possibilities. I also believed that schools could conduct studios in professional offices, thereby making the bond between practice and education even stronger.

I have never been intimidated by new tools, only concerned that the tools might overwhelm our intentions. The new technologies have brought many wonderful possibilities to the conduct of the design professions. In architecture, ideas such as integrated project delivery would not be possible without the tools. We can build better with fewer errors using new technologies, we can communicate among a diverse set of users and clients using new technologies, and we can archive our work more effectively using new technologies.

It is important, however, that we teach students to control the technology, so as not to be overwhelmed by it.

KAITIE: Later in your piece you talk about the architecture field becoming more competitive, individual, and sometimes arrogant as opposed to cooperative. Throughout your career, have you found that the field is really more individual, or is there a sense of collaboration with other designers when working on a project?

MALECHA: I have found it to be both. There is a very strong culture of the individual within the architecture profession. At times, it will show itself in ugly ways. The prominent celebrity architects are referred to by some as the Black Cape Architects. This reveals the tension between those who take the lead in the concept phase of a project and those who see to the realization of a project through complex phases of design development, construction documents, and construction administration. It is true that great buildings have a personality that is derived most often from the personality of an individual or at least from an office working with a singular mind. It is equally true that the profession is wholly dependent on collaboration to realize even the smallest project.

When I wrote this particular section of the article, I was specifically addressing educators, because in the schools the teaching of collaborative practices was absent for the most part. The school experience had become focused on producing the next great cadre of superstar architects. Of course, this is a flawed strategy, since on a major project such as a hospital or skyscraper there may be a small team of designers led by a strong individual to bring about a design concept and then hundreds within the architectural office and related consultant offices to realize the project. It was my intention to advocate that educators face this dilemma and cause them to teach collaborative methods even as individual design skills were heightened. In addition, it is important to remember that there are many roles architects assume, complementing the obvious role of principal designer. There are those who manage the specification process, those who oversee construction document preparation, those who specialize in construction administration, and those who serve as the primary contact to the clients and users. Each of these roles serves an incredibly important purpose. Again, educators must make students aware of these many roles, give credence to their importance, and encourage students to seek their best place in an interesting and diverse professional culture.

Buildings need the bold ideas of individuals who are strong conceptually. Buildings also need individuals who can put a building together in the most effective way.

KAITIE: What audience were you trying to reach with this article, and what pushed you to write it?

MALECHA: At the time I was writing this article, I was primarily speaking to other educators. However, it is also true that the magazine had a broad audience, and therefore students and practicing architects were very much on my mind. I was trying to get the readers to think differently about the study and practice of architecture.

Discussion Questions

1. Read through Kaitie Gay's questions for Dr. Malecha. What was her purpose in interviewing Dr. Malecha? What did she want to understand?

2. Was there anything that surprised you in Dr. Malecha's responses? If so, what was it?

3. If you were going to add a question to Kaitie's interview, what would it be? Why would you add that question?

4. If Kaitie were to use this interview as the basis for a writing profile of Dr. Malecha, what other information would she need to find? What steps would she need to take?

tip sheet   Inside Colleges and Universities

- **Colleges and universities are not all the same.** Different kinds of colleges and universities have varying purposes, majors, and degrees, and they appeal to a variety of potential students.

- **The institution you attend has a specific focus.** You may find it helpful to identify this focus and understand how it fits with your academic and career goals.

- **Colleges and universities are divided into disciplinary areas.** You might see these areas at your school as departments, divisions, and/or colleges. In this book, we talk about four broad disciplinary areas: humanities, social sciences, natural sciences, and applied fields.

- **Academic writing follows unique conventions.** When academics write, they often follow conventions specific to their writing situations and to their disciplinary areas.

- **Writing in college is not always the same as writing in other contexts.** In college writing courses, we focus on principles of rhetoric, or how language is used to communicate.

2 Reading and Writing Rhetorically

You read and write in many different situations: at school, at home, with your friends, and maybe at work. Perhaps there are other situations in which you read and write, too, likely through a variety of different media. You might read and write in a journal, in a status update on Facebook, in a photo caption on Instagram, in a word processor as you prepare a paper for school, in a text message, or in a note to a friend. You could probably name many other situations in which you read and write on a daily basis.

Have you ever considered how different the processes of reading and writing are in these situations? You're performing the same act (reading or writing a text) in many ways, but several features might change from one situation to another:

- the way the text looks
- the medium or technology you use
- the tone you use
- the words you use (or avoid using)
- the grammar and mechanics that are appropriate

ANDREA TSURUMI

Even within the more specific category of "academic writing" that we address in this book, some of these features might shift depending on the context. In some disciplines, the structure, vocabulary, style, and documentation expectations are different from those in other disciplines. If you've ever written a lab report for a physics class and a literary analysis for a literature class, then you've likely experienced some of those differences. The differences arise because of the specific demands of each of the differing writing situations.

Understanding Rhetorical Context

As you read and write, we want you to consider closely the specific situation for which you are writing. In other words, you should always think about the **rhetorical context** in which your writing takes place. In this text, we'll define rhetorical context through four elements:

- who the author is, and what background and experience he or she brings to the text
- who the intended audience is for the text
- what issue or topic the author is addressing
- what the author's purpose is for writing

Each of these elements has an impact on the way a text is written and interpreted. Consider how you might write about your last job in a text message to a friend in comparison with how you might write about it in an application letter for a new job. Even though the author is the same (you) and the topic is the same (your last job), the audience and your purpose for writing are vastly different. These differences thus affect how you characterize your job and your choice in medium for writing the message.

Sometimes writing situations call for more than one audience as well. You might address a **primary audience**, the explicitly addressed audience for the text, but you might also have a **secondary audience**, an implied audience who also might read your text or be interested in it. Imagine you wrote a job application letter as an assignment for a business writing class. Your primary audience would likely be your instructor, but you might also write the letter as a template to use when actually sending out a job application letter in the future. So your future prospective employer might be a secondary audience.

In academic settings, also, these elements of rhetorical context shift depending on the disciplinary context within which you're writing. Consider another example: Imagine a student has decided to research the last presidential election for a school assignment. If the research assignment were given in a history class, then the student might research and write about other political elections that provide a precedent for the outcome of the recent election and the events surrounding it. The student would be approaching the topic from a historical perspective, which would be appropriate for the context of the discipline and audience (a history professor). If the student were writing for an economics class, he or she might focus on the economic impact of elections

and how campaign finance laws, voter identification laws, and voters' socioeconomic statuses affected the election. Even though the author, audience, topic, and purpose seem similar at first glance (they're all academic research assignments, right?), the student would focus on different questions and aspects of the topic when examining the election from different disciplinary perspectives and for different audiences. Other elements of the student's writing would likely shift, too, and we'll discuss those differences in Part Two of this book.

Why might it be important to consider the rhetorical context when reading or writing? As you read, noticing the rhetorical context of a text can help you understand choices that the author makes in writing that might at first seem confusing or inconsistent, even in academic writing. For example, writers might use the passive voice in an experimental study report ("the data were collected by . . .") but not in an essay on the poetry of John Donne. Or the same scholar might write in the first person in one kind of academic text (like this textbook) but not in another (perhaps a scholarly article). In all these writing situations, the author makes choices based on the rhetorical context. In this textbook, the first person ("I" or "We") helps to establish a personal tone that might not be appropriate for an academic journal article. We (first person) made this choice specifically because of our audience for the textbook—students who are learning to navigate academic writing. We wanted the text to have a friendlier and less academically distant tone. Such a conversational tone wouldn't always be appropriate in other rhetorical contexts, though. When you write, understanding the rhetorical context can help you be more effective in achieving your purpose and communicating with your audience because you make choices that are appropriate to the situation.

As you notice the kinds of choices a writer makes, you are analyzing the rhetorical context of the writing: that is, you are taking elements of the writing apart to understand how they work together. Analyzing rhetorical context is a key strategy we'll use throughout this book to understand how different forms of writing work and what the similarities and differences are in writing across various disciplines.

INSIDE WORK   Identifying Rhetorical Context

Think about a specific situation in the past that required you to write something. It could be any kind of text; it doesn't have to be something academic. Then create a map—by drawing a diagram, a chart, or some other visual image—of the rhetorical context of that piece of writing. Consider the following questions as you draw.

- What was your background and role as the author?

- Who was the audience?

- What was the topic?

- What was your purpose for writing? ▶

Understanding Genres

As you learn to analyze the rhetorical context of writing, keep in mind that much writing takes place within communities of people who are interested in similar subjects. They might use similar vocabulary, formats for writing, and grammatical and stylistic rules. In a sense, they speak the same "language." The common practices that they typically employ in their writing are called *conventions*, as we discussed in Chapter 1. As you read and analyze the writing of academic writers, we'll ask you to notice and comment on the conventions that different disciplines use in various rhetorical contexts. When you write, you'll want to keep those conventions in mind, paying attention to the ways you should shape your own writing to meet the expectations of the academic community you are participating in. We'll go into more detail about how to analyze the specific conventions of disciplinary writing in Part Two.

In addition to paying close attention to the conventions that writers employ, we'll ask you to consider the *genre* through which writers communicate their information. **Genres** are approaches to writing situations that share some common features, or conventions. You already write in many genres in your daily life: If you've sent or read e-mail messages, text messages, personal letters, and thank-you notes, then you've written and read examples of four different genres that are all associated with personal writing. If you like to cook, you've probably noticed that recipes in cookbooks follow similar patterns by presenting the ingredients first and then providing step-by-step directions for preparation. The ingredients usually appear in a list, and the instructions generally read as directives (e.g., "Add the eggs one at a time and mix well"), often in more of a prose style. Recipes are a genre. If you've looked for an office job before, you've probably encountered at least three different genres in the job application process: job advertisements, application letters, and résumés. How well you follow the expected conventions of the latter two genres often affects whether or not you get a job.

You've also likely had experience producing academic genres. If you've ever written a business letter, an abstract, a mathematical proof, a poem, a book review, a research proposal, or a lab report, then you might have noticed that these kinds of academic writing tasks have certain conventions that make them unique. Lab reports, for example, typically have specific expectations for the organization of information and for the kind of language used to communicate that information. Throughout Part Two of the book, we offer examples of a number of other academic genres — a literature review, an interpretation of an artistic text, as well as a theory response, just to name a few.

Because different writing situations, or rhetorical contexts, call for different approaches, we ask you to think about the genre, as well as associated conventions, that you might be reading or writing in any particular situation. Our goal is not to have you identify a formula to follow for every type of academic

See what writing studies instructor Moriah McCracken has to say about genres.

writing, but rather to understand the expectations of a writing situation — and how much flexibility you have in meeting those expectations — so that you can make choices appropriate to the genre.

Reading Rhetorically

Since we're talking about paying attention to rhetorical context, we want to explain the difference between the reading you do with an eye toward rhetorical context and the reading you might do in other circumstances. Whenever you read during a typical day, you probably do so for a variety of reasons. You might read:

- **To Communicate:** reading a text message, a letter from a friend, an e-mail, a birthday card, or a post on Instagram

- **To Learn:** reading instructions, a textbook, street signs while you drive, dosage instructions on a medication bottle, or the instructor's comments at the end of a paper that you turned in for a class

- **To Be Entertained:** reading novels, stories, comics, a joke forwarded in e-mail, or a favorite website

The details that you pay attention to, and the level at which you notice those details, vary according to your purpose in reading.

In this text, however, we will ask you to read in a way that is different from reading just to communicate, learn, or be entertained. We want you to *read rhetorically*, paying close attention to the rhetorical context of whatever you are reading. When you read rhetorically, you make note of the different elements of rhetorical context that help to shape the text. You'll notice who the **author** is (or, if there are multiple authors, who each one is) and what background, experience, knowledge, and potential biases the author brings to the text. In addition, you'll notice who the intended **audience** is for the text. Is the author writing to a group of peers? To other scholars in the field? How much prior knowledge does that audience have, and how does the intended audience shape the author's approach in the text? Are there multiple audiences (primary and secondary)? You'll also notice what the **topic** is and how it influences the text. Does the author use a specific approach related to the topic choice? Additionally, you'll notice the author's **purpose** for writing. Sometimes the purpose is stated explicitly, and sometimes it is implied. Why does the author choose to write about this topic at this point? What does the author hope to achieve? Finally, you'll want to notice how these four elements work together to shape the text. How is the choice of audience related to the author's background, topic, and purpose for writing?

Reading Visuals Rhetorically

We should stress that the strategies for understanding rhetorical context and for reading rhetorically are applicable to both verbal and visual texts. In fact, any rhetorical event, or any occasion that requires the production of a text, establishes a writing situation with a specific rhetorical context. Consider the places you might encounter visual advertisements, as one form of visual texts, over the course of a single day: in a magazine, on a website, in stores, on billboards, on television, and so on. Each encounter provides an opportunity to read the visual text rhetorically, or to consider how the four elements of author, audience, topic, and purpose work together to shape the text itself (in this case, an advertisement). This process is called **rhetorical analysis**.

In fact, noticing these elements when you read will help you become a careful and critical reader of all kinds of texts. When we use the term *critical*, we don't use it with any negative connotations. We use it in the way it works in the term *critical thinking*, meaning that you will begin to understand the relationships among author, audience, topic, and purpose by paying close attention to context.

INSIDE WORK   **Reading Rhetorically**

> With the direction of your instructor, choose a text (either verbal or visual) to read and analyze. As you read the text, consider the elements of rhetorical context. Write about who the author is, who the intended audience is, what the topic is, and what the author's purpose is for writing or for creating the text. Finally, consider how these elements work together to influence the way the text is written or designed. In future chapters, we'll ask you to engage in this kind of *rhetorical analysis* to understand the different kinds of texts produced by students and scholars in various academic contexts. ▶

Writing Rhetorically

Writing is about choices. Writing is not a firm set of rules to follow. There are multiple choices available to you anytime you take on a writing task, and the choices you make will help determine how effectively you communicate with your intended audience, about your topic, for your intended purpose. Some choices, of course, are more effective than others, based on the conventions expected for certain situations. And yet, sometimes you might break conventions in order to make a point or draw attention to what you are writing. In both cases, though, it's important to understand the expectations of the rhetorical context for which you are writing so that your choices will have the effect you intend.

When you write rhetorically, you'll analyze the four elements of rhetorical context, examining how those elements shape your text through the choices that you make as a writer. You'll think about the following elements:

- **What You, as the *Author,* Bring to the Writing Situation**   How do your background, experience, and relative position to the audience shape the way you write?

- **Who Your Intended *Audience* Is**   Is there a specific audience you should address? Has the audience already been determined for you (e.g., by your instructor)? What do you know about your audience? What does your audience value?

- **What Your *Topic* Is**   What are you writing about? Has the topic been determined for you, or do you have the freedom to focus your topic according to your interests? What is your relationship to the topic? What is your audience's relationship to it?

- **What Your *Purpose* Is for Writing**   Why are you writing about this topic, at this time? For example, are you writing to inform? To persuade? To entertain?

Outside of school contexts, we often write because we encounter a situation that calls for us to write. Imagine a parent who wants to write a note to thank her son's teacher for inviting her to assist in a class project. The audience is very specific, and the topic is determined by the occasion for writing. Depending on the relationship between the parent and the teacher, the note might be rather informal. But if the parent wants to commend the teacher and copy the school's principal, she might write a longer, more formal note that could be included in the teacher's personnel file. Understanding the rhetorical context would help the parent decide what choices to make in this writing situation.

For school assignments, thinking about the topic is typically the first step because students are often assigned to write about something specific. If your English professor asks you to write a literary interpretation of Toni Morrison's *Song of Solomon,* your topic choice is limited. Even in this situation, though, you have the freedom to determine what aspect of the text you'll focus on. Do you want to look at imagery in the novel? Would you like to examine Morrison's use of language? Would you like to analyze recurring themes, or perhaps interpret the text in the historical and cultural context in which it was written?

In this text, we would like you also to consider the other elements of rhetorical context—author, audience, and purpose—to see how they influence your topic. Considering your purpose in writing can often shape your audience and topic. Are you writing to communicate with a friend? If so, about what? Are you completing an assignment for a class? Are you writing to persuade someone to act on an issue that's important to you? If you are writing to argue for a change in a policy, to whom do you need to write in order to achieve your purpose? How will you reach that audience, and what would the audience's expectations be for your text? What information will you need to provide? Your understanding of the rhetorical context for writing will shape your writing and help you to communicate more effectively with your audience, about your topic, to meet your purpose.

INSIDE WORK   **Analyzing Rhetorical Context**

> Think back to the rhetorical situation you identified in the "Inside Work: Identifying Rhetorical Context" activity on page 22. Consider that situation more analytically now, using the questions from that activity and slightly revised here as a guide. Write your responses to the following questions.
>
> - As the *author*, how did your background, experience, and relative position to the audience shape the way you created your text?
>
> - Were you addressing a specific *audience*? Was the audience already determined for you? What did you know about your audience? What did your audience value or desire?
>
> - What was your text about? Was the *topic* determined for you, or did you have the freedom to focus your topic according to your interests? What was your relationship to the topic? What was your audience's relationship to it?
>
> - What was your *purpose* for creating a text about that topic, at that time? For example, were you writing to inform? To persuade? To entertain? ❱

Rhetorical Writing Processes

In addition to making choices related to the context of a writing situation, writers make choices about their own process of writing. Writers follow different processes, sometimes being influenced by their own writing preferences, their experience with writing, and the specific writing tasks they have to accomplish. Writing can be a messy process that involves lots of drafting, revising, researching, thinking, and sometimes even throwing things out, especially for longer writing tasks. With that said, though, there are several steps in the process that experienced writers often find useful, and each step can be adapted to the specific writing situation in which they find themselves.

You might already be familiar with some of the commonly discussed steps of the writing process from other classes you've taken. Often, writing teachers talk about some variation of the following elements of the writing process:

- **Prewriting/Invention**   The point at which you gather ideas for your writing. There are a number of useful brainstorming strategies that students find helpful to the processes of gathering their thoughts and arranging them for writing. A few of the most widely used strategies are *freewriting*, *listing*, and *idea mapping*.

  Freewriting   As the term implies, **freewriting** involves writing down your thoughts in a free-flow form, typically for a set amount of time. There's no judgment or evaluation of these ideas as they occur to you.

MORRIS: So often it's not about "I need to write this page." It's that "I have to spend hours and hours and hours doing the analysis. And even once I've done the analysis, taking the statistics and putting them in a way that the reader can understand and is relevant to the story will take days." Now, what I've adjusted to in this *writing process* is "Okay, I don't need to get a page a day. But I've got to have these sets of tasks for today." And it may be doing a series of statistics and then putting them into an Excel to make a nice, pretty chart that'll support the story.

BAUMGARTNER: Well, sure.

MORRIS: So it's about tasks.

Find additional advice on the writing process.

You simply write down whatever comes to mind as you consider a topic or idea. Later, of course, you revisit what you've written to see if it contains ideas or information worth examining further.

Listing   **Listing** is a way of quickly highlighting important information for yourself. The writer starts with a main idea and then just lists whatever comes to mind. These lists are typically done quickly the first time, but you can return to them and rework or refine them at any point in the writing process.

Idea Mapping   This brainstorming technique is a favorite among students because it allows you to represent your ideas in an easy-to-follow map. **Idea mapping** is sometimes referred to as cluster mapping because as you brainstorm, you use clusters of ideas and lines to keep track of the ideas and the relationships among them.

- **Research**   Sometimes research is considered a separate step in the writing process, and sometimes it is part of prewriting/invention. Of course, depending on the nature of your project, there might be a considerable amount of research or very little research involved. We explore some strategies for conducting research in more detail in Chapter 4.

- **Drafting**   At the drafting stage, you get ideas down on paper or screen. You might already realize that these stages don't happen in isolation in most cases; drafting might occur while you're doing prewriting/invention and research, and you might go back and forth between different stages as you work.

- **Peer Review**   Writers often benefit from seeking the feedback of others before considering a project complete. **Peer review** is the process of having other students, classmates, or audience members read your work and provide feedback. Later in this text, we'll use the term *peer review* to refer to the specific process that scholars go through when they submit academic writing for publication. It's similar: they submit work for publication, then peers in their discipline read and comment on it (they may or may not recommend it for publication), and then the scholars often revise it again prior to publication.

- **Revising** At the revision stage, a writer takes another look at his or her writing and makes content-level and organizational changes. This is different from the final step of editing/proofreading.

- **Editing/Proofreading** Finally, the writer focuses on correcting grammatical, mechanical, stylistic, and referential problems in the text.

Depending on the rhetorical context of a writing task, these processes might shift in importance and in the order in which you do them. Imagine you get a last-minute writing assignment at work. You would progress through these stages rather quickly, and you might not have time for more than a cursory peer review. If you're writing a term paper for a class, however, you might be able to do initial prewriting, research, and drafting well before the project's deadline. As we discuss different types of scholarly writing in this text, you might also consider how the writing process for each of these types of writing can vary. When conducting an experimental study, the research stage of the process will take a significant portion of the time allocated to the project.

You might be able to think of examples from your own experience when you wrote in different ways for different projects because the rhetorical context was not the same. We want to encourage you to plan your writing process deliberately and avoid the mistake that many inexperienced writers make—waiting until the last minute and quickly writing a first draft and then turning it in because there is no time left for anything else. The most effective writers carefully plan out their writing and take the time they need to work through different parts of the writing process.

As you consider the influence of rhetorical context on your writing process, also think about the specific preferences you have as a writer. In order to do your best writing, be aware of where and how you write best. Consider these questions: What physical space do you like to write in? Where are you most productive? At what time of day do you write best? If you have a pressing deadline, what environmental factors help you to meet the deadline? Do you need to work someplace quiet? Do you like to have noise in the background? What

Hear more about genres of writing.

kind of work space works best for you? Do you usually keep coffee or another favorite drink nearby? An awareness of preferences such as these will help you meet the challenges of different writing situations as you encounter them.

We'll ask you to practice different parts of your writing process throughout this book, both through the exercises you'll participate in and the larger writing assignments that you'll complete. As you work through the exercises, think about what part of the writing process you're addressing.

Writing a Rhetorical Analysis

When you read rhetorically, you analyze a text through a particular lens. Examining a text through the formal framework of author, audience, topic, and purpose can be a way of analyzing a text in a written assignment as well. Such an examination is called a *rhetorical analysis*, a genre of writing that explores elements of a text's rhetorical context. We'll provide several opportunities for you to conduct rhetorical analyses in this book, since it is one of the ways you will begin to discover the features of writing across different academic contexts.

In a rhetorical analysis, the writer uses a rhetorical framework to understand how the context of the text helps to create meaning. One framework you might use involves walking through the different elements of rhetorical context to examine the piece of writing in detail:

Rhetorical Context

Author	What does the author bring to the writing situation?
Audience	Who is the author addressing, and what do they know or think about this topic?
Topic	What is the author writing about, and why did he or she choose it?
Purpose	Why is the author writing about this topic, at this time?

These four components of the rhetorical context function together dynamically. You might analyze the author's background and experience and how he or she develops credibility in the text. Or you could make assertions about the author's primary and secondary audiences based on the author's choices regarding style and language. But in reality, all four of the rhetorical context components function together to shape how someone writes or speaks.

The following text is a letter that George H. W. Bush, the forty-first president of the United States (and father of the forty-third president, George W. Bush), sent to Iraqi president Saddam Hussein on January 9, 1991, shortly before the United States, in cooperation with over thirty other countries, launched an assault to expel Iraqi forces from Kuwait. This action came in response to Iraq's invasion and annexation of Kuwait in 1990, and it became a part of the history that is now referred to as the First Gulf War. While the events that precipitated this letter occurred a long time ago, it is a helpful arti-fact for understanding the complicated power dynamics at play in the United States' involvement in ongoing events in the Middle East. As you read the letter, pay close attention to the rhetorical moves that President Bush makes. Who are his primary and secondary audiences? Is his audience only Saddam Hussein? If not, then who else is his audience, and what in his letter suggests who the secondary audience is? What is the letter's purpose? Does Bush seem to think Saddam will leave Kuwait? How do you know?

Letter to Saddam Hussein

GEORGE H. W. BUSH

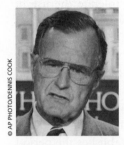

Mr. President,

We stand today at the brink of war between Iraq and the world. This is a war that began with your invasion of Kuwait; this is a war that can be ended only by Iraq's full and unconditional compliance with UN Security Council resolution 678.

I am writing to you now, directly, because what is at stake demands that no opportunity be lost to avoid what would be a certain calamity for the people of Iraq. I am writing, as well, because it is said by some that you do not understand just how isolated Iraq is and what Iraq faces as a result.

I am not in a position to judge whether this impression is correct; what I can do, though, is try in this letter to reinforce what Secretary of State James A. Baker told your foreign minister and eliminate any uncertainty or ambiguity that might exist in your mind about where we stand and what we are prepared to do.

The international community is united in its call for Iraq to leave all of Kuwait without condition and without further delay. This is not simply the pol-icy of the United States; it is the position of the world community as expressed in no less than twelve Security Council resolutions.

We prefer a peaceful outcome. However, anything less than full compliance with UN Security Council resolution 678 and its predecessors is unacceptable. There can be no reward for aggression.

Nor will there be any negotiation. Principles cannot be compromised. How-ever, by its full compliance, Iraq will gain the opportunity to rejoin the inter-national community. More immediately, the Iraqi military establishment will escape destruction. But unless you withdraw from Kuwait completely and without condition, you will lose more than Kuwait. What is at issue here is not the future of Kuwait—it will be free, its government restored—but rather the future of Iraq. This choice is yours to make.

The United States will not be separated from its coalition partners. Twelve Security Council resolutions, twenty-eight countries providing military units to enforce them, more than one hundred governments complying with sanctions—all highlight the fact that it is not Iraq against the United States, but Iraq against the world. That most Arab and Muslim countries are arrayed against you as well should reinforce what I am saying. Iraq cannot and will not be able to hold on to Kuwait or exact a price for leaving. You may be tempted to find solace in the diversity of opinion that is American democracy. You should resist any such temptation. Diversity ought not to be confused with division. Nor should you underestimate, as others have before you, America's will.

Iraq is already feeling the effects of the sanctions mandated by the United Nations. Should war come, it will be a far greater tragedy for you and your country. Let me state, too, that the United States will not tolerate the use of chemical or biological weapons or the destruction of Kuwait's oil fields and installations. Further, you will be held directly responsible for terrorist actions against any member of the coalition. The American people would demand the strongest possible response. You and your country will pay a terrible price if you order unconscionable acts of this sort.

I write this letter not to threaten, but to inform. I do so with no sense of satisfaction, for the people of the United States have no quarrel with the people of Iraq. Mr. President, UN Security Council resolution 678 establishes the period before January 15 of this year as a "pause of good will" so that this crisis may end without further violence. Whether this pause is used as intended, or merely becomes a prelude to further violence, is in your hands, and yours alone.

I hope you weigh your choice carefully and choose wisely, for much will depend upon it.

Discussion Questions

1. For what purpose(s) does President Bush write this letter?
2. How does Bush establish his credibility, honesty, and resolve in the letter?
3. Who is the primary audience? Who are the secondary audiences?
4. What conventional features for this form of writing (genre) does Bush's letter exhibit?

Insider Example
Student Rhetorical Analysis

The following is a student rhetorical analysis of the letter written from George H. W. Bush to Saddam Hussein. As you read this analysis, consider how the student, Sofia Lopez, uses audience, topic, and purpose to construct meaning from Bush's letter. Additionally, pay attention to how Sofia uses evidence from the letter to support her assertions. These moves will become more important when we discuss using evidence to support claims in Chapter 3 (see pp. 43–45).

Sofia Lopez
Mr. Harris
English 100
January 201-

The Multiple Audiences of George H. W. Bush's Letter
to Saddam Hussein

President George H. W. Bush's 1991 letter to Saddam Hussein, then the president of Iraq, is anything but a simple piece of political rhetoric. The topic of the letter is direct and confrontational. On the surface, Bush directly calls upon Hussein to withdraw from Kuwait, and he lays out the potential impact should Hussein choose not to withdraw. But when analyzed according to the rhetorical choices Bush makes in the letter, a complex rhetorical situation emerges. Bush writes to a dual audience in his letter and establishes credibility by developing a complex author position. By the conclusion of the letter, Bush accomplishes multiple purposes by creating a complex rhetorical situation.

While Bush's direct and primary audience is Saddam Hussein, Bush also calls upon a much larger secondary audience in the first sentence of the letter by identifying "the world" as the second party involved in the imminent war that the letter is written to prevent. Bush continues to write the letter directly to Hussein, using second person to address him and describe the choices before him. Bush also continues, however, to engage his secondary audience throughout the letter by referring to resolutions from the UN Security Council in five separate paragraphs (1, 4, 5, 7, and 9). The letter can even be interpreted to have tertiary audiences of the Iraqi and the American people because the letter serves to justify military action should Hussein not comply with the conditions of the letter.

Because Bush is addressing multiple audiences, he establishes a complex author position as well. He is the primary author of the letter, and he uses first person to refer to himself, arguably to emphasize the direct, personal confrontation in the letter. He constructs a more complex author position, however, by speaking for other groups in his letter and, in a sense, writing "for" them. In paragraph 4, he speaks for the international community when he writes, "The international community is united in its call for Iraq to leave all of Kuwait. . . ." He draws on the international community again in

The introduction outlines the writer's approach to analyzing Bush's letter. Based on the introduction, what do you see as the writer's overall purpose for this rhetorical analysis?

In this paragraph, the writer outlines potential audiences for Bush's letter in more detail. Who are those audiences?

In this paragraph, the writer explores the ways Bush is able to align himself with multiple audiences. What evidence does the writer use to demonstrate Bush's associations with his various audiences?

paragraph 6 and refers to his coalition partners in paragraph 7, aligning his position with the larger community. Additionally, in paragraph 7, he builds his credibility as an author by emphasizing that he is aligned with other Arab and Muslim countries in their opposition to Hussein's actions. Writing for and aligning himself with such a diverse group of political partners helps him address the multiple audiences of his letter to accomplish his purposes.

The writer frequently refers to Bush's "complex author position." What do you think the writer means by this?

While the primary and literal purpose of the letter is to call upon Iraq to withdraw from Kuwait and to outline the consequences of noncompliance, Bush accomplishes additional purposes directly related to his additional audiences and the complex author position he has established. The primary purpose of his letter, naturally, is addressed to his primary audience, Saddam Hussein. The construction of the letter, however, including the repeated mention of UN Security Council resolutions, the invocation of support from other Arab and Muslim countries, and the reference to other coalition partners and the international community, serves to call upon the world (and specifically the United Nations) to support military action should Hussein not comply with the conditions of the letter. The construction of a letter with a complex audience and author allows Bush to address multiple purposes that support future action.

·What other elements of the rhetorical situation might the writer explore to further analyze Bush's letter?

Discussion Questions

1. What does Sofia Lopez identify as Bush's purpose? How does she support that interpretation of Bush's purpose?

2. Whom does Sofia see as Bush's audience? How does she support that reading of the letter?

3. What might you add to the analysis, from a rhetorical perspective?

WRITING PROJECT   Analyzing the Rhetorical Features of a Text

In this paper, you will analyze the rhetorical situation of a text of your choosing. You might want to choose something publicly available (already published) that represents a piece of polished writing so that you know that the author(s) has finished making revisions and has had time to think through important rhetorical choices. Alternatively, you might choose something written for an academic, personal, work, or other context. Start by reading the text carefully and rhetorically. Use the elements of rhetorical context to analyze and understand the choices the writer has made in the text.

Rhetorical Context

- author
- audience

- topic
- purpose

In addition to describing the rhetorical features of the article, you will also explore why you believe the author made certain choices. For example, if you're analyzing a blog entry on a political website, you might discuss who the author is and review his or her background. Then you could speculate about the writing choices the author has made and how his or her background might have influenced those choices.

Consider what conclusion you can draw about the text, and highlight that as an assertion you can make in the introduction to your analysis. The body of your paper should be organized around the rhetorical features you are analyzing, demonstrating how you came to your conclusion about the text.

In your conclusion, reflect on what you have found. Are there other issues still to be addressed? What other rhetorical strategies could be explored to analyze the work further? Are there surprises in the choices the writer makes that you should mention?

Keep in mind that your essential aim is to analyze, not to evaluate.

tip sheet — Reading and Writing Rhetorically

- **It is important to consider rhetorical context as you read and write.** Think about how the following four elements have shaped or might shape a text:
  - who the *author* is, and what background and experience he or she brings to the text
  - who the intended *audience* is
  - what issue or *topic* the author is addressing
  - what the author's *purpose* is for writing

- **Genres are approaches to writing situations that share some common features, or conventional expectations.** As you read and write texts, consider the form of writing you're asked to read or produce: Is it a recognizable genre? What kinds of conventional expectations are associated with the genre? How should you shape your text in response to those expectations?

- **Reading rhetorically means reading with an eye toward how the four elements of author, audience, topic, and purpose work together** to influence the way an author shapes a text, verbal or visual or otherwise.

Continued

- **Writing rhetorically means crafting your own text based on an understanding of the four elements of your rhetorical context.** Specifically, you consider how your understanding of the rhetorical context should affect the choices you make as a writer, or how your understanding should ultimately shape your text.

- **A rhetorical writing process involves a set of steps that include prewriting, researching, drafting, revising, and editing/proofreading.** The order of the steps and their importance to any writer can be altered or repeated as needed.

- **A rhetorical analysis is a formal piece of writing that examines the different elements of the rhetorical context of a text.** It also often considers how these elements work together to explain the shape of a text targeted for analysis.

CHAPTER 3

Developing Arguments

M any writing situations, both academic and non-academic, require authors
to persuade audiences on a particular topic—in other words, to develop
an *argument*. When we refer to arguments, we don't mean heated, emotional
sparring matches that are often supported by little else than opinion. Rather,
we use **argument** to refer to the process of making a logical case for a particular position, interpretation, or conclusion. You experience and participate in
these kinds of arguments around you every day as you decide what to eat for a
meal, choose certain classes to take, determine what movie to see with a group
of friends, or read (or perhaps choose to ignore) online advertisements about
products to purchase.

In academic settings, arguments are frequently research-oriented because
the authors are presenting and arguing for a particular interpretation or conclusion from the results of their research. To make such an argument effectively, academics must develop clear, persuasive texts through which to present
their research. These arguments make **claims**—arguable assertions—that are
supported with evidence from research. The unifying element of any academic
argument is its primary or central claim, and although most
sustained arguments make a series of claims, there is usually
one central claim that makes an argument a coherent whole.
Our goal in this chapter is to introduce you to some of the basic
principles of argumentation and to help you write clear central
claims and develop successful arguments, especially in your academic writing.

If arguments are persuasive and effective, they are likely
well reasoned and well supported, and they draw on evidence
that is chosen for a specific rhetorical context. All writers must
pay attention to the audience and purpose of their argument.
Often, they do this by developing, either implicitly or explicitly,

ANDREA TSURUMI

proofs of their arguments and *appeals* that are appropriate to their audience. Proofs and appeals are elements specific to arguments that you'll need to pay attention to in addition to rhetorical context, which is relevant for all writing situations.

Understanding Proofs and Appeals

Aristotle, a rhetorician in ancient Greece, developed a method of analyzing arguments that can be useful to us in our own reading and writing today. He explained that arguments are based on a set of proofs that are used as evidence to support a claim. He identified two kinds of proofs: inartistic and artistic. **Inartistic proofs** are based on factual evidence, such as statistics, raw data, or contracts. **Artistic proofs**, by contrast, are created by the writer or speaker to support an argument. Many arguments contain a combination of inartistic and artistic proofs, depending on what facts are available for support. Aristotle divided the complex category of artistic proofs into three kinds of **rhetorical appeals** that speakers and writers can rely on to develop artistic proofs in support of an argument:

- Appeals to **ethos** are based on the author's or speaker's credibility or character. An example might be a brand of motor oil that is endorsed by a celebrity NASCAR driver. Another example could be a proposal for grant money to conduct a research study that discusses the grant writer's experience in successfully completing similar research studies in the past. In both examples, the speaker's or writer's experiences (as a NASCAR driver or as an established researcher) are persuasive elements in the argument. We might be more inclined to buy a certain brand of motor oil if our favorite driver says it's the best kind, and a grant-funding agency will likely feel more comfortable giving a large sum of money to a researcher who has demonstrated successful completion of research projects in the past.

- Appeals to **logos** are based on elements of logic and reason. An example might be an argument for change in an attendance policy that outlines the negative effects and potential repercussions of maintaining the current policy. The argument relies on logic and reason because it presents the negative effects and draws a connection to the policy, emphasizing how a change in the policy might reverse those effects.

- Appeals to **pathos** are based on the anticipated emotional response of the audience. Emotion can be a powerful motivator to convince an audience to hear an argument. An example might include telling the story of a particular community affected by current gun control regulation when arguing for a shift in policy. If a politician uses this strategy when arguing for passage of an important bill in Congress, for example, the emotional impact might influence other legislators to vote in favor of the bill.

These types of appeals are present in arguments in both academic and non-academic settings. Many arguments, and often the most effective ones, include elements of more than one kind of appeal, using several strategies to persuade an audience. In the example above of a politician arguing before Congress, the argument would be much stronger and likely more persuasive if other appeals were used in addition to an emotional appeal. The politician might develop an argument that includes raw data and statistics (an inartistic proof), the advice of experts in the field (ethos), a cause and effect relationship that points to a particular cause of the problem (logos), along with the story of a community affected by current gun control regulation (pathos). Understanding the structure of arguments, and knowing the potential ways you can develop your own arguments to persuade an audience, will help you to write more effectively and persuasively.

INSIDE WORK **Writing about Arguments**

Choose a text to read that makes either an explicit or an implicit claim. Consider something that interests you—perhaps an advertisement, or even your college's or university's website. Write about the kinds of rhetorical appeals you notice. Do you see evidence of ethos? Logos? Pathos? Is the argument drawing on statistics or raw data, an inartistic proof? Why do you think the author(s) or designer(s) structured the argument in this way? To answer this question, you'll also need to consider the rhetorical context. Who is the author, and who is the intended audience? What is the topic, and what is the purpose of the argument? In other words, what is the ultimate goal of the argument? ▶

Making Claims

As we mentioned earlier, the unifying element of any academic argument is its primary or central claim. In American academic settings, the central claim is often (but not always) presented near the beginning of a piece so that it can tie the elements of the argument together. A form of the central claim that you might be familiar with is the **thesis statement**. Thesis statements, whether revealed in an argument's introduction or delayed and presented later in an argument (perhaps even in the conclusion), are central claims of arguments that are typical of writing that is centrally focused on civic concerns, as well as writing in some academic fields such as those in the humanities (see Chapter 6).

Imagine for a moment that you've been asked to write an argument taking a position on a current social topic like cell phone usage, and you must decide whether or not to support legislation to limit cell phone use while driving. In this instance, the statement of your position is your claim. It might read something like this: "We should support legislation to limit the use of cell phones while driving," or "We should not support legislation to limit the use of cell phones while driving." There are many types of claims. The statement "We should pass legislation to limit the use of cell phones" is a claim of proposal or policy, indicating that the writer will propose some action or solution to a problem. We could also explore claims of definition ("Cheerleading is a sport") or claims of value ("Supporting a charity is a good thing to do"), just to name a few.

Literary analyses, a genre commonly taught in high school English classes, usually present a thesis statement as part of their introductions. You may be familiar with a thesis statement that reads something like this: "Nathaniel Hawthorne's 'The Birthmark' is a complex tale that cautions us against believing that science is capable of perfecting our natures." This thesis statement makes a claim in support of a specific interpretation of the story. Regardless of the specific type of claim offered, the argument that follows it provides evidence to demonstrate why an audience should find the claim persuasive.

THESIS VERSUS HYPOTHESIS

In an academic setting, thesis statements like those typical of arguments in the humanities are not the only kind of unifying claim you might encounter. In fact, arguments in the natural and social sciences are often organized around a statement of hypothesis, which is different from a thesis statement. Unlike a thesis statement, which serves to convey a final position or conclusion on a topic or issue that a researcher has arrived at based on study, a **hypothesis** is a proposed explanation or conclusion that is usually either confirmed or denied on the basis of rigorous examination or experimentation later in a paper. This means that hypothesis statements are, in a sense, still under consideration by a writer or researcher. A hypothesis is a proposed answer to a research question. Thesis statements, in contrast, represent a writer or researcher's conclusion(s) after much consideration of the issue or topic.

Consider the following examples of a hypothesis and a thesis about the same topic:

Hypothesis	Thesis
Decreased levels of sleep will lead to decreased levels of academic performance for college freshmen.	College freshmen should get at least seven hours of sleep per night because insufficient sleep has been linked to emotional instability and poor academic performance.

The hypothesis example above includes several elements that distinguish it from the thesis statement. First, the hypothesis is written as a prediction, which indicates that the researcher will conduct a study to test the claim. Additionally, it is written in the future tense, indicating that an experiment or study will take place to prove or disprove the hypothesis. The thesis statement, however, makes a claim that indicates it is already supported by evidence gathered by the researcher. A reader would expect to find persuasive evidence from sources later in the essay.

We highlight this distinction in types of claims to underscore that there is no single formula for constructing a good argument in all academic contexts. Instead, expectations for strong arguments are bound up with the expectations of particular writing communities. If you write a lab report with the kind of thesis statement that usually appears in a literary analysis, your work would likely convey the sense that you're a novice to the community of writers and researchers who expect a hypothesis statement instead of a thesis statement. One of the goals of this text is to help you develop awareness of how the expectations for good argumentation change from one academic context to the next.

Developing Reasons

When writing an academic argument that requires a thesis statement, you can choose how detailed to make that thesis statement. When we introduced thesis statements as a type of claim, we asked you to consider two possible statements on the topic of cell phone use while driving: "We should/should not support legislation to limit the use of cell phones while driving." We can also refer to these two possible forms as **simple thesis statements** because they reveal a writer's central position on a topic but do not include any reasoning as support for that position. When reasons are included as logical support, then we can think about the thesis statement as a **complex thesis statement**:

Simple Thesis:	We should support legislation to limit the use of cell phones while driving.
Reasons:	They are an unnecessary distraction.
	They increase the incidence of accidents and deaths.

When we combine the simple statement of position or belief with the reasons that support it, then we have a more complex, and fuller, thesis statement:

| **Complex Thesis:** | We should support legislation to limit the use of cell phones because they are an unnecessary distraction for drivers and because they increase needless accidents and deaths on our roadways. |

Although constructing complex thesis statements allows you to combine your statement of position with the reasons you'll use to defend that position, you may frequently encounter arguments that do not provide the reasons as part of the thesis. That is, some writers, depending on their rhetorical context, prefer to present a simple thesis and then reveal the reasons for their position throughout their argument. Others choose to write a thesis that both establishes their position and provides the reasoning for it early on. An advantage of providing a complex thesis statement is that it offers a road map to the reader for the argument that you will develop. A disadvantage is that it might provide more information about your argument than you want to or should reveal up front.

INSIDE WORK **Constructing Thesis Statements**

Generate a list of six to eight current social issues that require you to take a position. Consider especially issues that are important to your local community. Choose one or two to focus on for the other parts of this activity.

Next, explore multiple positions. Consider competing positions you can take for each of the issues you identified. Write out a simple thesis statement for those positions. Be careful not to limit your positions to pros and cons, especially if you can think of alternative positions that might be reasonable for someone to argue. Often, there are multiple sides to an issue, and we miss the complexity of the issue if we only acknowledge two sides. Then, list as many reasons as you can think of to support each of those positions. It might be helpful to connect your simple statement of thesis to your reasons using the word *because*. This activity can help you to strengthen your argument by anticipating rebuttals or counterarguments. We'll take these issues up later in the chapter.

For example:

Claim: **The U.S. Congress should support federal legislation that allows same-sex couples to marry.**

Reasons:

because _____.

because _____.

because _____.

Alternate Claim: **The U.S. Congress should not support federal legislation that allows same-sex couples to marry.**

Reasons:

because _____.

because _____.

because _____.

Alternate Claim: The decision to develop legislation allowing same-sex couples to marry should be made at the state level and not by the federal government.

Reasons:

because _____.

because _____.

because _____.

Finally, combine your simple thesis with your reasoning to construct a complex thesis for each potential position. Write out your thesis statements. ▶

Supporting Reasons with Evidence

Reasons that support a claim are not particularly powerful unless there is **evidence** to back them up. Evidence that supports an argument can take the form of any of the rhetorical appeals. Let's look again at the complex thesis from the previous section: "We should support legislation to limit the use of cell phones because they are an unnecessary distraction for drivers and because they increase needless accidents and deaths on our roadways." In order to generate the reasons, the writer relied on what he already knew about the dangers of cell phone use. Perhaps the writer had recently read a newspaper article that cited statistics concerning the number of people injured or killed in accidents as a direct result of drivers using their phones instead of paying attention to the roadways. Or perhaps the writer had read an academic study that examined attention rates and variables affecting them in people using cell phones. Maybe the writer even had some personal knowledge or experience to draw upon as evidence for her or his position. Strong, persuasive arguments typically spend a great deal of time unpacking the logic that enables a writer to generate reasons in support of a particular claim, and that evidence can take many forms.

Personal Experience You may have direct experience with a particular issue or topic that allows you to speak in support of a position on that topic. Your personal experience can be a rich resource for evidence. Additionally, you may know others who can provide evidence based on their experiences with an issue. Stories of personal experience often appeal to either ethos (drawing on the credibility of the writer's personal experience) or pathos (drawing on readers' emotions for impact). Sometimes these stories appeal to both ethos and pathos at the same time.

> Imagine the power of telling the story of someone who has been needlessly injured in an accident because another driver was distracted by talking on the phone.

Expert Testimony   Establishing an individual as an expert on a topic and using that person's words or ideas in support of your own position can be an effective way of bolstering your own ethos while supporting your central claim. However, the use of expert testimony can be tricky, as you need to carefully establish what makes the person you're relying on for evidence an actual expert on the topic or issue at hand. You must also consider your audience—whom would your audience consider to be an expert? How would you determine the expert's reputation within that community? The use of expert testimony is very common in academic argumentation. Researchers often summarize, paraphrase, or cite experts in their own discipline, as well as from others, to support their reasoning. If you've ever taken a class in which your instructor asked you to use reputable sources to support your argument, then you've probably relied on expert testimony to support a claim or reason already.

Imagine the effectiveness of citing experts who work for the National Transportation and Safety Board about their experiences investigating accidents that resulted from inattentive driving due to cell phone use.

Statistical Data and Research Findings   Statistics frequently serve as support in both popular and academic argumentation. Readers tend to like numbers, partly because they seem so absolute and scientific. However, it is important, as with all evidence, to evaluate statistical data for bias. Consider where statistics come from and how they are produced, if you plan to use them in support of an argument. Additionally, and perhaps most important, consider how those statistics were interpreted in the context of the original research reported. What were the study's conclusions?

Writers also often present the findings, or conclusions, of a research study as support for their reasons and claims. These findings may sometimes appear as qualitative, rather than just statistical, results or outcomes.

Imagine the effectiveness of citing recently produced statistics (rates of accidents) on the highways in your state from materials provided by your state's Department of Transportation.

When selecting the types and amounts of evidence to use in support of your reasons, be sure to study your rhetorical context and pay particular attention to the expectations of your intended audience. Some audiences, especially academic ones, are less likely to be convinced if you only provide evidence that draws on their emotions. Other audiences may be completely turned off by an argument that relies only on statistical data for support.

So far, we've discussed several types of evidence that are typically used in the construction of arguments—personal experience, expert testimony, statistical data and research findings. Collecting the data you need to make a strong argument can seem like a daunting task at times. It's important to keep in mind, though, that the amount of evidence you provide and the types of data your argument requires will depend entirely on the kind of argument you are constructing, as well as on the potential audience you want to persuade. Therefore, it's essential that you analyze and understand your audience's expectations when selecting support for your argument. Above all, select support that your audience will find credible, reliable, and relevant to your argument.

LaunchPadSolo

Hear criminologist Michelle Richter comment on types of research in her field.

INSIDE WORK **Analyzing Audience Expectations**

Choose any one of the complex thesis statements you constructed in the "Inside Work" activity on pages 42–43. Then identify two potential target audiences for your arguments. Freewrite for five to ten minutes in response to the following questions about these audiences' likely expectations for evidence.

- What does each audience already know about your topic? That is, what aspects of it can you assume they already have knowledge about?

- What does each audience need to know? What information do you need to make sure to include?

- What does each audience value in relation to your topic? What kinds of information will motivate them, interest them, or persuade them? How do you know?

- What sources of information about your topic might your audiences find questionably reliable? Why? ❱

Understanding Assumptions

Anytime you stake a claim and provide a reason, or provide evidence to support a reason, you are assuming something about your audience's beliefs and values, and it is important to examine your own assumptions very carefully as you construct arguments. Though assumptions are often unstated, they function to link together the ideas of two claims.

Let's consider a version of the claim and reason we've been looking at throughout this section to examine the role of assumptions: "We should support legislation to limit the use of cell phones while driving because they increase needless accidents and deaths on our roadways." In this instance, the claim and the reason appear logically connected, but let's identify the implied assumptions that the reader must accept in order to be persuaded by the argument:

Claim: We should support legislation to limit the use of cell phones while driving.

Reason: They increase needless accidents and deaths on our highways.

Implied Assumptions: We should do whatever we can to limit accidents and deaths.
Legislation can reduce accidents and deaths.

Many audiences would agree with these implied assumptions. As a result, it would likely be unnecessary to make the assumptions explicit or provide support for them. However, you can probably imagine an instance when a given audience would argue that legislating peoples' behavior does not affect how people actually behave. To such an audience, passing laws to regulate the use of cell phones while driving might seem ineffective. As a result, the audience might actually challenge the assumption(s) upon which your argument rests, and you may need to provide evidence to support the implied assumption that "legislation can reduce accidents and deaths."

A writer who is concerned that an audience may attack his argument by pointing to problematic assumptions might choose to explicitly state the assumption and provide support for it. In this instance, he might consider whether precedents exist (e.g., the effect of implementing seat belt laws, or statistical data from other states that have passed cell phone use laws) that could support his assumption that "legislation can reduce accidents and deaths."

INSIDE WORK **Considering Assumptions and Audience**

In the previous activity, you considered the most appropriate kinds of evidence for supporting thesis statements for differing audiences. This time, we ask you to identify the assumptions in your arguments and to consider whether or not those assumptions would require backing or additional support for varying audiences.

Begin by identifying the assumption(s) for each of your thesis statements. Then consider whether or not those assumptions need backing as the intended audience for your argument changes to the following:

- a friend or relative
- a state legislator
- an opinion news column editor
- a professional academic in a field related to your topic ▶

Anticipating Counterarguments

Initially, it may strike you as odd to think of counterarguments as a strategy to consider when constructing an argument. However, anticipating the objections of those who might disagree with you may actually strengthen your argument by forcing you to consider competing chains of reasoning and evidence. In fact, many writers actually choose to present **counterarguments**, or rebuttals of their own arguments, as part of the design of their arguments.

Why would anyone do this? Consider for a moment that your argument is like a debate. If you are able to adopt your opponent's position and then explain why that position is wrong, or why her reasoning is flawed, or in what ways her evidence is insufficient to support her own claim, then you support your own position. This is what it means to offer a **rebuttal** to potential counterarguments. Of course, when you provide rebuttals, you must have appropriate evidence to justify dismissing part or all of the entire counterargument. By anticipating and responding to counterarguments, you also strengthen your own ethos as a writer on the topic. Engaging counterarguments demonstrates that you have considered multiple positions and are knowledgeable about your subject.

You can also address possible counterarguments by actually conceding to an opposing position on a particular point or in a limited instance. Now you're probably wondering: Why would anyone do this? Doesn't this mean losing your argument? Not necessarily. Often, such a concession reveals that you're developing a more complex argument and moving past the pro/con positions that can limit productive debate.

Imagine that you're debating an opponent on a highly controversial issue like fracking (hydraulic fracturing). You're arguing a pro-fracking position, and your opponent makes the point that some people have experienced health issues as a result of the fracking in areas local to their homes. You might choose to concede this point by acknowledging that fracking could be a root cause of some individuals' illnesses. Though you still support fracking, you might now choose to limit the scope of your original position. That is, you could qualify your position by supporting fracking as long as it occurs, say, outside of a five-mile radius of any residence. In this case, your opponents' points are used to adjust or to **qualify** your own position, but this doesn't negate your entire argument. Your position may appear even stronger precisely because you've acknowledged the

opponents' points and refined the scope of your claim as a result, or because you've identified instances when your position might not hold true.

INSIDE WORK **Dealing with Counterarguments**

> Throughout this section, you've been working with a series of claims that you constructed. You've linked those claims to reasons as support, and you've considered the kinds of evidence most appropriate for your theses in light of particular audiences. You've also considered the likely acceptability of your assumptions, according to various potential audiences. This time, consider possible counterarguments for your thesis statements.
>
> • Who might argue against you?
>
> • What will their arguments be based on?
>
> • What might their arguments be?
>
> • How might you use a counterargument to actually support your own claim?
>
> Brainstorm a list of instances in which you might want to concede a point or two as a means of strengthening your own position. ❱

Analyzing Arguments

One way to understand the process of developing a persuasive argument is to study how others structure theirs. If you'll recall, in Chapter 2 we discussed how visual texts, like verbal ones, construct rhetorical situations. In the same way, visual texts may also seek to persuade an audience, and they may use many of the techniques explored throughout this chapter.

The following papers present arguments about visual texts. In the first, Jack Solomon, a professional writer, explores how advertisements reflect what he sees as contradictory impulses in the American character. In the second, Timothy Holtzhauser, a student writer, examines the argument strategies employed in a 1943 American war bonds ad. As you engage with their arguments, keep in mind that each writer is both making an argument and analyzing an argument simultaneously, so you'll want to consider their texts from both perspectives. Also keep in mind that their arguments are supported by evidence found in their own research. We'll explore how to conduct research in more detail in Chapter 4.

Insider Example
Professional Analysis of an Advertisement

In the following passage from "Masters of Desire: The Culture of American Advertising," Jack Solomon uses *semiotics*—a method for studying and interpreting cultural signs and symbols—to analyze the arguments made in two advertisements. As you read Solomon's argument, try to identify which elements of argument discussed in this chapter he uses in his analysis.

Excerpt from **"Masters of Desire: The Culture of American Advertising"**

JACK SOLOMON

The American dream ... has two faces: the one communally egalitarian and the other competitively elitist. This contradiction is no accident; it is fundamental to the structure of American society. Even as America's great myth of equality celebrates the virtues of mom, apple pie, and the girl or boy next door, it also lures us to achieve social distinction, to rise above the crowd and bask alone in the glory. This land is your land and this land is my land, Woody Guthrie's populist anthem tells us, but we keep trying to increase the "my" at the expense of the "your." Rather than fostering contentment, the American dream breeds desire, a longing for a greater share of the pie. It is as if our society were a vast high-school football game, with the bulk of the participants noisily rooting in the stands while, deep down, each of them is wishing he or she could be the star quarterback or head cheerleader.

For the semiotician, the contradictory nature of the American myth of equality is nowhere written so clearly as in the signs that American advertisers use to manipulate us into buying their wares. "Manipulate" is the word here, not "persuade"; for advertising campaigns are not sources of product information, they are exercises in behavior modification. Appealing to our subconscious emotions rather than to our conscious intellects, advertisements are designed to exploit the discontentments fostered by the American dream, the constant desire for social success and the material rewards that accompany it. America's consumer economy runs on desire, and advertising stokes the engines by transforming common objects—from peanut butter to political candidates—into signs of all the things that Americans covet most.

But by semiotically reading the signs that advertising agencies manufacture to stimulate consumption, we can plot the precise state of desire in the audiences to which they are addressed. In this chapter, we'll look at a representative sample of ads and what they say about the emotional climate of the country and the fast-changing trends of American life. Because ours is a highly diverse, pluralistic society, various advertisements may say different things depending on their intended audiences, but in every case they say something about America, about the status of our hopes, fears, desires, and beliefs.

Let's begin with two ad campaigns conducted by the same company that bear out Alexis de Tocqueville's observations about the contradictory nature of American society: General Motors' campaigns for its Cadillac and Chevrolet lines. First, consider an early magazine ad for the Cadillac Allanté. Appearing

Allanté Specifications

TYPE	Front-Wheel-Drive, 2-Place Roadster
WHEELBASE/CURB WEIGHT	99.4"/3494 lbs.
ENGINE	High Output, 4.1-Liter Transverse-Mounted V8
INDUCTION SYSTEM	Sequential Port Fuel Injection
HORSEPOWER (HP)	170 @ 4300
TORQUE (LB.-FT.)	236 @ 3200
COMPRESSION RATIO	8.5:1
TRANSMISSION	Four-Speed Automatic w/ Overdrive and Viscous Converter Clutch
SUSPENSION	Fully Independent/Deflected-Disc MacPherson F/R Struts
BRAKES	Bosch III Anti-Lock Braking System/Four-Wheel Discs
WHEELS/TIRES	15" x 7" Aluminum Alloy/Goodyear P225/60VR15 Radial
FUEL ECONOMY	EPA estimated 22.5 mpg combined, 16 mpg city, 24 mpg highway Not Subject to Federal Gas Guzzler Tax
TOURING RANGE*	528 mi.
MANUFACTURER'S SUGGESTED RETAIL PRICE	$54,700**

*Range based on EPA est. 24 mpg highway multiplied by gas tank capacity of 22 gallons
**Including dealer prep, tax, license, destination charge and other optional equipment additional.

Conceived and Commissioned
by America's
Luxury Car Leader—Cadillac.

Designed and
Handcrafted by
Europe's Renowned
Design Leader—Pininfarina, SpA,
of Turin, Italy.

The New Spirit of Cadillac.

as a full-color, four-page insert in *Time*, the ad seems to say "I'm special—and so is this car" even before we've begun to read it. Rather than being printed on the ordinary, flimsy pages of the magazine, the Allanté spread appears on glossy coated stock. The unwritten message here is that an extraordinary car deserves an extraordinary advertisement, and that both car and ad are aimed at an extraordinary consumer, or at least one who wishes to appear extraordinary compared to his more ordinary fellow citizens.

Ads of this kind work by creating symbolic associations between their product and what is most coveted by the consumers to whom they are addressed. It is significant, then, that this ad insists that the Allanté is virtually an Italian rather than an American car—an automobile, as its copy runs, "Conceived and Commissioned by America's Luxury Car Leader—Cadillac" but "Designed and Handcrafted by Europe's Renowned Design Leader—Pininfarina, SpA, of Turin, Italy." This is not simply a piece of product information; it's a sign of the prestige that European luxury cars enjoy in today's automotive marketplace. Once the luxury car of choice for America's status drivers, Cadillac has fallen far behind its European competitors in the race for the prestige market. So the Allanté essentially represents Cadillac's decision, after years of resisting the trend toward European cars, to introduce its own European import—whose high cost is clearly printed on the last page of the ad. Although $54,700 is a lot of money to pay for a Cadillac, it's about what you'd expect to pay for a top-of-the-line Mercedes-Benz. That's precisely the point the ad is trying to make: the Allanté is no mere car. It's a potent status symbol you can associate with the other major status symbols of the 1980s.

American companies manufacture status symbols because American consumers want them. As Alexis de Tocqueville recognized a century and a half ago, the competitive nature of democratic societies breeds a desire for social distinction, a yearning to rise above the crowd. But given the fact that those who do make it to the top in socially mobile societies have often risen from the lower ranks, they still look like everyone else. In the socially immobile societies of aristocratic Europe, generations of fixed social conditions produced subtle class signals. The accent of one's voice, the shape of one's nose, or even the set of one's chin immediately communicated social status. Aside from the nasal bray and uptilted head of the Boston Brahmin, Americans do not have any native sets of personal status signals. If it weren't for his Mercedes-Benz and Manhattan townhouse, the parvenu Wall Street millionaire often couldn't be distinguished from the man who tailors his suits. Hence, the demand for status symbols, for the objects that mark one off as a social success, is particularly strong in democratic nations—stronger even than in aristocratic societies, where the aristocrat so often looks and sounds different from everyone else.

Status symbols, then, are signs that identify their possessors' place in a social hierarchy, markers of rank and prestige. We can all think of any number of status symbols—Rolls-Royces, Beverly Hills mansions, even Shar Pei puppies (whose rareness has rocketed them beyond Russian wolfhounds as status pets and has inspired whole lines of wrinkle-faced stuffed toys)—but how do we know that something is a status symbol? The explanation is quite simple: when an object (or puppy!) either costs a lot of money or requires influential connections to possess, anyone who possesses it must also possess the necessary means and influence to acquire it. The object itself really doesn't matter, since it ultimately disappears behind the presumed social potency of its owner. Semiotically, what matters is the signal it sends, its value as a sign of power. One traditional sign of social distinction is owning a country estate and enjoying the peace and privacy that attend it. Advertisements for Mercedes-Benz, Jaguar, and Audi automobiles thus frequently feature drivers motoring quietly along a country road, presumably on their way to or from their country houses.

Advertisers have been quick to exploit the status signals that belong to body language as well. As Hegel observed in the early nineteenth century, it is an ancient aristocratic prerogative to be seen by the lower orders without having to look at them in return. Tilting his chin high in the air and gazing down at the world under hooded eyelids, the aristocrat invites observation while refusing to look back. We can find such a pose exploited in an advertisement for Cadillac Seville in which an elegantly dressed woman goes out for a drive with her husband in their new Cadillac. If we look closely at the woman's body language, we see her glance inwardly with a satisfied smile on her face but not outward toward the camera that represents our gaze. She is glad to be seen by us in her Seville, but she isn't interested in looking at us!

Ads that are aimed at a broader market take the opposite approach. If the American dream encourages the desire to arrive, to vault above the mass, it also fosters a desire to be popular, to "belong." Populist commercials accordingly transform products into signs of belonging, utilizing such common icons as country music, small-town life, family picnics, and farmyards. All of these icons are incorporated in GM's "Heartbeat of America" campaign for its Chevrolet line. Unlike the Seville commercial, the faces in the Chevy ads look straight at us and smile. Dress is casual, the mood upbeat. Quick camera cuts take us from rustic to suburban to urban scenes, creating an American montage filmed from sea to shining sea. We all "belong" in a Chevy.

Discussion Questions

1. Jack Solomon sets up an interesting contrast between "manipulate" and "persuade" at the beginning of this excerpt. How does his description of these ads mirror our understanding of arguments? In your own words, how would you describe the differences he establishes between manipulating and persuading?

2. In Solomon's analysis of the Cadillac and Chevrolet ads, where does he address the claims and reasons given by the advertisers to buy their products? Do the ads address assumptions?

3. How does Solomon characterize the appeals made by both advertisements? Where does he describe appeals to ethos? Logos? Pathos?

Insider Example
Student Analysis of an Advertisement

Timothy Holtzhauser, a student in a first-year writing class, wrote the following analysis of an advertisement as a course assignment. He used elements of rhetorical analysis and argument analysis to understand the persuasive effects of the advertisement he chose. Notice, also, that he followed Modern Language Association (MLA) style conventions, especially when citing sources within his paper and documenting them at the end of the paper. (See Chapter 4 and the Appendix for additional information on documentation styles.)

Timothy Holtzhauser

ENG 101-79

February 13, 201-

Rhetoric of a 1943 War Bonds Ad

From the front covers of magazines at the store, to the ads by Google on sidebars of websites, to the incessant commercials on television, advertisements are visible everywhere. Whether the advertisement announces or insinuates its purpose, all advertisements attempt to change the audience's manner of thinking or acting. In "Masters of Desire: The Culture of American Advertising," Jack Solomon describes the motive behind advertising as pure and simple manipulation: "'Manipulate' is the word here, not 'persuade'; for advertising campaigns are not sources of product information, they are exercises in behavior modification" (60). Even the most innocent advertisement performs this maneuver, and the

"Death Warrant . . . US War Bonds" advertisement drawn by S. J. Woolf is no different. This 1943 ad, printed in the *New York Daily News* for Bloomingdale's department store, not only encourages the purchase of U.S. war bonds by exaggerating Hitler's negative aspects, but also depicts the growing influence and activism of the United States during this era.

The main claim, or thesis

When this advertisement appeared, the United States was rapidly becoming more involved in the hostilities of World War II. While not yet engaged in the war in Europe, the United States was providing supplies and manpower for the war in the Pacific, and the government was in serious need of funds to keep the war machine rolling. The main method that the government used to obtain these funds was selling war bonds and advertising, to push the sale of these bonds. War bonds were used as a tool to raise money for the government by selling certificates that promised a return on the investment after a period of time in exchange for the investment. In New York City, publishing city of the *New York Daily News* and home of Bloomingdale's main store, there was tremendous outrage at the atrocities being committed as a result of the war. Due to this, the general public showed interest in ending the war, especially the war in the Pacific. For the most part, the city trended toward the progressive democratic mind-set and agreed with the mostly democratic-controlled government of the era (Duranti 666). While factors such as these propelled the citizens to purchase bonds as the advertisement suggests, there were other factors resisting this push as well. Particularly important was the ever-present aftermath of the Great Depression. The combination of these factors created a mixed feeling about the purchase of war bonds, but the fear of Hitler's reign continuing tended to bias the populace toward purchasing the bonds.

The next two paragraphs provide the reader with historical context for the ad and its publication. This information clarifies the rhetorical situation for readers and sets the stage for the analyses of the ad's elements that follow.

At the time of the release of this ad, the *New York Daily News* was a fairly new newspaper in New York City, as it had been initially released about twenty years beforehand. Even as a new publication, it had an extremely wide readership due to its tabloid format, which focused on images, unlike other New York papers. At the time of the printing of this ad, the *Daily News* was known to be

Drawing courtesy of S. J. Woolf

TO BRING CLOSER THE HAPPY DAY SHOWN
ABOVE—BUY MORE AND MORE WAR BONDS

BLOOMINGDALE'S
Lexington Avenue and 59th Street

slightly biased toward the democratic mind-set common among the citizens of the city ("New York Daily News"). The publishing of this advertisement at this time could be viewed as an appeal to ethos in order to push the patriotic sense of the paper. The advertisement can also be seen as an appeal to ethos by Bloomingdale's, as the company was seeking to portray itself as a patriotic firm. With that context in mind, several components of the advertisement make more sense and can be more effectively analyzed.

The analysis now focuses on specific elements of the ad. In this paragraph, the student analyzes features of Hitler's face: the bug eyes, the dropped jaw, the tufts of hair. These, he suggests, express Hitler's fear of American strength, which stems at least partially from the selling and purchasing of war bonds.

The most prominent feature in the advertisement is Hitler's face, and in particular, his facial expression. Woolf's image here uses two primary components to make the facial expression stand out: the humorously exaggerated bug-eyed stare and the dropped jaw. The effect created by these two factors is compounded by the addition of the buck teeth and the protruding ears. The bug eyes commonly serve in American imagery to express shock, and they perform that role excellently here in this advertisement. The dropped jaw is used very frequently as well, especially in cartoons, and here it strengthens the shocked expression. The buck teeth and protruding ears are two images that are used in American culture to convey the idea of a buffoon. In addition to these features, Woolf comically adds in two tufts of hair in imitation of devil horns to further enhance Hitler's evil image. When these two are added to the previous facets, it creates an image of a completely dumbfounded and baffled Hitler. The image was designed in this manner to enhance the feeling that purchasing U.S. war bonds would benefit society by eliminating the severe hindrance known as Hitler.

The next feature that stands out is the death warrant and war bond itself and Hitler's hands clutching it. Woolf draws Hitler's hands in a manner that makes them appear to be tightly gripping the paper as in anger. The paper itself shows only the words "death warrant" and "U.S. War Bonds," but one can infer from the context that the warrant is for Hitler. The fact that the warrant is printed on a war bond suggests that the U.S. government completely backs the killing of Hitler and will take action to see it through. The document appeals to the viewer's logos through the suggestion that war bonds will end the war sooner and save countless lives in the process. There is also an inherent appeal to ethos in the suggestion of the character of Bloomingdale's as a firm that strongly opposes the horrors committed by Hitler and his followers. In addition, there is an appeal to pathos, with the ad attempting to home in on the audience's moral code. This apparent encouragement of killing Hitler, coupled with the text at the bottom of the advertisement, creates a mood of vengeance directed toward Hitler.

The next major feature of the advertisement is the caption at the bottom of the image, which reads, "To bring closer the happy day shown above—buy more and more war bonds." The image shown above the text in most scenarios would not be considered a happy day for most people. The thought of death is normally enough to ruin anyone's day, but this image banks on the public having a burning vengeance that justifies the end of Hitler. The idea of vengeance is generally viewed as having serious negative repercussions, but this article portrays the idea in a positive manner by making an appeal to the audience's logos. The appeal here could best be described as sacrificing one to save millions. The caption also makes an appeal to pathos in the manner that it tries to connect with the viewer's sense of morals that Hitler has almost definitely broken in numerous ways.

The writer shifts focus to analyze the ad's caption.

The next aspect of the advertisement that stands out is the use of shading. Woolf's decision here may have been influenced by requirements of the *Daily News* at the time, but even viewed in that light it has a rhetorical effect on the advertisement. The usage of shading here creates the appearance of an unfinished image, further enhancing the idea that Hitler has just been served his death warrant hot off the press by the United States and its war bonds. It also creates a worried cast to Hitler's face through the heavy shading in the creases along his jawline. The overall image of Hitler created through the use of shading comes off as dark and sinister, representative of the common American's view on Hitler's character. In contrast, the war bond is virtually untouched by shading, leaving it nearly white. This creates the image of a beacon of hope shining through the darkness that provides a means to eliminate this terror. Additionally, the presence of a heavily shaded advertisement among the more crisp images, popular among tabloids, accents this advertisement and its message.

The final aspect of the advertisement that draws major attention is the overall construction of the image. The layout emphasizes the two key components of the advertisement: Hitler's face and the war bond. Not only does this accentuate the relationship between buying war bonds and bringing the hammer down on Hitler, but it also provides further depth to the image's rhetorical context. Hitler is posed hunched over as if to imply a deformity in his body and represent a deformity of his mind. The statement here runs on the classic American stereotype that a malformed person is either inferior or evil, a stereotype popularly used in comical representations such as this one. In addition, the hunched posture can be interpreted as the weight of the American war machine, fueled by the war bond purchases, dragging Hitler down to end his reign of terror.

With each of these analyzed aspects in mind, the advertisement can serve as an effective description of the period similar to what Jack Solomon suggests is possible in "Masters of Desire." He uses the following statement to show how advertisements are indicative of the culture of their audiences: "But by semiotically reading the signs that advertising agencies manufacture to stimulate consumption, we can plot the precise state of desire in the audiences to which they are addressed" (61). Based upon the patriotic push shown through this advertisement's attack on Hitler and visualization of handing him a death warrant, the advertisement shows the general patriotic mood of America at the time. Given the war footing of the country during this era, this patriotic pride fits well into the time frame. It also shows the growing influence of the United States across the world. Up until this point in time, America was not taken very seriously, and U.S. foreign policy was mostly designed to ignore the rest of the world and preserve America. With the serving of the death warrant to Hitler shown in this advertisement, the change in ideology is starkly apparent. Instead of the wait-and-see mentality common in America before World War II, the highly proactive and aggressive nature of America today begins to show. For a small snippet in a tabloid newspaper, this advertisement packs quite a rhetorical punch.

> Notice how the ending addresses elements of the paper's thesis statement, or how the ad "depicts the growing influence and activism of the United States during this era."

Taking into account all the elements of this advertisement, rhetorical and otherwise, the advertisement creates an astounding patriotic push for the purchase of war bonds through exaggeration and establishes the United States as a globally significant force through the implications of the death warrant for a foreign citizen. All aspects used in this advertisement work well to cleverly goad readers of the paper to purchase war bonds from Bloomingdale's, holding true to Jack Solomon's statement about advertisements not seeking to provide information, but to manipulate the audience. In the end, however, this advertisement does not convey the negative connotation often associated with manipulative advertising; rather, it uses manipulative elements to try to create a better future for the readers.

Works Cited

Bloomingdale's. Advertisement. *New York Daily News*. 1943. Print.

Duranti, Marco. "Utopia, Nostalgia, and World War at the 1939–40 New York World's Fair." *Journal of Contemporary History* 41.4 (2006): 663–83. Web. 29 Jan. 2012.

"New York Daily News." *Encyclopaedia Britannica Online*. Encyclopaedia Britannica, 2012. Web. 5 Feb. 2012.

Solomon, Jack. "Masters of Desire: The Culture of American Advertising."
*The Signs of Our Time: Semiotics: The Hidden Messages of Environments,
Objects, and Cultural Images*. Los Angeles: Jeremy P. Tarcher, 1988.
59–76. Print.

Discussion Questions

1. Where does Timothy Holtzhauser state his thesis? Why do you think he phrases his thesis in the way that he does?

2. How does Timothy use logos in his own argument? Why do you think he relies on logos to support his claim?

3. Who is the intended audience for this argument?

4. What scholarly or popular conversation(s) is Timothy joining in?

5. Which claim(s) do you find most convincing and least convincing for Timothy's rhetorical situation? Why?

WRITING PROJECT ## Composing a Rhetorical Analysis of an Advertisement

For this project, we ask you to consider the ways in which rhetorical context and appeals work together in an advertisement to create an argument.

- To begin, choose a print or online advertisement that you can analyze based on its rhetorical context and the appeals it uses to persuade the intended audience.

- Then, drawing on the principles of rhetorical analysis from Chapter 2 and the discussion of developing arguments in this chapter, compose an analysis examining the ad's use of appeals in light of the rhetorical situation the ad constructs.

RHETORICAL CONTEXT (SEE CHAPTER 2)

Central Question: How do the elements of the rhetorical context affect the way the advertisement is structured?

Author _____

Audience _____

Topic _____

Purpose _____

RHETORICAL APPEALS (SEE CHAPTER 3)

Central Question: What appeals does the advertisement use, and why?

Ethos _____

Logos _____

Pathos _____

Keep in mind that a rhetorical analysis makes an argument, so your analysis should have a central claim that you develop based on what you observed, through the frameworks of rhetorical context and rhetorical appeals, in the advertisement. Make your claim clear, and then support it with reasons and evidence from the advertisement.

tip sheet

Developing Arguments

- **Presenting an argument is different from merely stating an opinion.** Presenting and supporting an argument mean establishing a claim that is backed by reasons and evidence.

- **The unifying element of any academic argument is its primary or central claim.** A unifying claim may take the form of a thesis, a hypothesis, or a more general statement of purpose. There are numerous kinds of claims, including claims of value, definition, and policy.

- **Reasons are generated from and supported by evidence.** Evidence may take the form of inartistic proofs (including statistics and raw data) or artistic proofs, including the rhetorical appeals of ethos (appeal to credibility), logos (appeal to reason and logic), and pathos (appeal to emotion).

- **Claims presented as part of a chain of reasoning are linked by (often) unstated assumptions.** Assumptions should be analyzed carefully for their appropriateness (acceptability, believability) in a particular rhetorical context.

- **Considering and/or incorporating counterarguments is an excellent way to strengthen your own arguments.** You may rebut counterarguments, or you may concede (or partially concede) to them and modify your own argument in response.

- **Analyzing others' arguments is a good way to develop your skills at arguing,** particularly in an academic context.

Academic Research

Conducting Research

Research projects have all kinds of starting points. Sometimes we start them because a course instructor or an employer asks us to. At other times, we embark on research projects because we want to learn about something on our own. In all these cases, though, our research responds to a question or set of questions that we need to answer. These are called **research questions**, and identifying them and narrowing them down is usually the first step of starting a research project, especially in an academic context.

DEVELOPING A RESEARCH QUESTION

For many students, choosing a subject to research is incredibly difficult. The best way to start is by thinking about issues that matter to you. Writers tend to do their best work when writing about things in which they have a personal investment. Even if you're conducting research in a course with a topic that has been assigned, think about how you might approach the topic from an angle that matters to you or brings in your own unique point of view.

Another challenge that many students face is narrowing down a solid research question once they've selected an issue of interest. If a research question is too broad, then it may not be feasible to respond to it adequately in the scope of your research assignment. If it's too narrow, though, it might not be researchable; in other words, you might not be able to find enough sources to support a solid position on the issue.

As you work on drafting a research question, keep these five criteria in mind:

ANDREA TSURUMI

1. **Personal Investment**   Is this an issue you care about?
2. **Debatable Subject**   Might reasonable people looking at evidence about this issue come to different conclusions?
3. **Researchable Issue**   Is there adequate published evidence to support a position on this issue?
4. **Feasibility**   Is the scope of the research question manageable?
5. **Contribution**   Will your response to the question contribute to the ongoing conversation about the issue?

INSIDE WORK   **Writing a Research Question**

As you begin your research project, you should identify a research question that will guide your research and keep you on track. Start by brainstorming a list of possible research questions for ten minutes, and then use the five criteria below to narrow down your list to a research question that might work for you. If your answer to any of the questions is a definitive "No," then the research question might not be a good choice, or you might need to revise it to make it work for a research project.

1. **Personal Investment**   Is this an issue you care about? If the issue is too broad, is there a way you can narrow down the topic to an aspect of the issue that is of the most importance to you?

2. **Debatable Subject**   Could two reasonable people looking at evidence about this issue come to different conclusions?

3. **Researchable Issue**   Can you find adequate published evidence to support a position on this issue?

4. **Feasibility**   Is the scope of the research question manageable, given the amount of time you have to research the issue and the amount of space in which you will make your argument?

5. **Contribution**   Will your response to your question contribute to the on-going conversation about the issue? ▶

LaunchPadSolo

A political scientist emphasizes the importance of supporting evidence.

CHOOSING PRIMARY AND SECONDARY SOURCES

To respond to any research question, a writer must collect evidence to prove or disprove a hypothesis or to support a claim. Once you have identified a solid research question, you must decide whether you need to collect *primary* and/or *secondary sources* to support your research aims.

Writers can choose from among several types of sources to support their research. When considering sources to support an argument, writers must study them for information that can serve as specific *evidence* to address aspects of their claims, all the while keeping their target audience in mind.

What kind of evidence will likely be convincing to the target audience? If researchers are reviewing the existing literature on a topic or are trying to understand what has already been written about an issue before conducting a study of their own, they must search for sources that provide information about the ongoing conversation concerning that topic or issue. Then the researchers might collect data to answer a clearly defined research question that has grown out of reading those sources.

Primary sources include the results of data that researchers might collect on their own. If you're making a claim about how to interpret a work of art and you've studied the piece carefully for images and symbols that you discuss in your argument, then the work of art is your primary source. Or perhaps you've designed and conducted a survey of people's experiences with a particular phenomenon. In this case, the results you've gathered from your survey are a primary source from which you can provide evidence to answer a research question or support an argument. Other forms of primary sources include original historical documents and results from interviews you may have conducted.

Insider's View
Primary research in writing studies
MORIAH McCRACKEN, WRITING STUDIES

"I like to try to introduce my students to qualitative research in their first year, when our students have to interview a professor. Sometimes I'll help them develop survey questions and questionnaires so they can have that kind of experience, and I'll teach them about double-entry notebooks so they can do some observations in the classroom. I like to bring in qualitative methods so that students realize there are different kinds of questions to ask, and depending on my question, I'm going to have to try something a little bit different and learn how to do this kind of research in my discipline."

INSIDE WORK **Collecting Primary Evidence**

Freewrite for five to ten minutes about a time in the past when you had to collect data on your own to answer a research question.

- Why were you collecting the data? What question were you trying to answer?

- What data did you collect, and how did you collect it? Did you observe something? Conduct a survey? Interview someone?

- If you were to try to answer that research question now, what data would you collect? Would you do anything differently? Why or why not? ❱

Find additional advice on doing primary research.

Based on the scope of your argument and the expectations of your audience, you may also need to engage **secondary sources,** or research collected by and/or commented on by others. Let's say that your literature professor wants you to offer an interpretation of a poem. You study the poem carefully as your primary source and arrive at a conclusion or claim about the work.

But imagine that the assignment also requires you to use scholarly opinions to support your own position or interpretation. As a result, you spend time in the library or searching online databases to locate articles or books by scholars who provide their own interpretations or perspectives on the poem. The articles or books you rely on to support your interpretation are secondary sources because the interpretations were developed by others, commenting on the poem. Likewise, if you cite as part of your own argument the results of a survey published in an academic article, then that article serves as a secondary source of information to you. Other secondary sources include newspapers and magazines, textbooks, and encyclopedias. Many of the researched arguments you'll produce in college will require you to use both primary and secondary sources as support.

INSIDE WORK) **Using Primary and Secondary Sources**

Read Timothy Holtzhauser's ad analysis on pages 52–57 of Chapter 3. After reviewing his analysis, look at the list of works cited at the end of his essay. Then answer the following questions.

- What primary source(s) does Timothy use to support his argument? Why do you think he chooses the primary source(s) he does?

- What would the impact be if Timothy didn't use primary sources in his argument? Would his argument be more or less persuasive to his audience?

- What secondary sources does Timothy use to support his argument?

- Why do you think he chooses these particular secondary sources? What impact do they have on the development of his argument?

- If Timothy had only used primary sources and no secondary sources, what would the impact have been on the persuasiveness of his argument? ▶

SEARCHING FOR SOURCES

In Part Two, we discuss collecting primary sources to support claims in specific disciplinary areas or genres in more detail. In the rest of this chapter, though, we provide support for collecting secondary sources, which provide a foundation for research and writing in academic contexts. Even if the main evidence used to support an academic research project comes from primary sources, secondary sources can provide an overview of what other scholars have already argued with regard to a particular issue or topic. Keep in mind that academic writing and research essentially comprise a series of extended conversations about different issues, and secondary sources help you understand what part of the conversation has already happened before you start researching a topic on your own, or before you consider entering an established conversation on a topic or issue.

The school, college, or university you attend likely offers many avenues to help navigate the processes for conducting library research at your institution. Most of these processes include searching for source materials online. When you search for secondary sources online to support the development of a research study or to support a claim in an argument, it's important to consider your **search terms**, the key words and phrases you'll use while you're searching. Let's say that you're interested in understanding the effects of using cell phones while driving, a topic we explored in Chapter 2. You might begin your research with a question that reads something like this:

What are the effects of using cell phones while driving?

The first step in your research process would likely be to find out what others have already written about this issue. To start, you might rephrase your research question to ask:

What have scholars written about the effects of using cell phones while driving?

To respond, you'll need to identify the key terms of your question that will focus your search for secondary sources about the subject. You might highlight some of the key terms in the question:

What have scholars written about the effects of using cell phones while driving?

If you started your search by typing "cell phones and driving" into Google, your search would return millions of results:

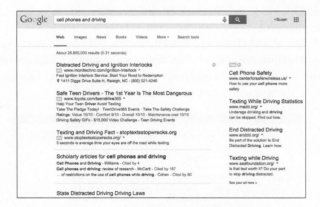

These results include links to images of people on cell phones in their cars, to news articles, and to statistics from insurance companies, to name a few. After careful evaluation, you may decide that some of these sources of data would be useful for your research, but you can also see that the results produce far too many hits to manage. There's simply no way you can comb through the millions of hits to find information that is appropriate for your purposes. As a result, you may choose to narrow your search to something that emerges as a specific issue, like "reaction time." If you narrowed your search to "cell phones and reaction time," you would see results like this:

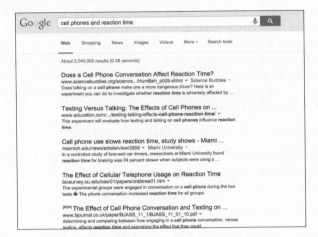

Focusing your research terms further narrows the scope of your search somewhat, but you still have far too many results to review. One concern to keep in mind, then, is that basic Google searches are not very useful in helping to locate the kinds of sources you might rely on for your research, especially in an academic context. If you want to understand what scholars have written about your topic, then you need to find scholarly or academic sources as support. A basic Google search doesn't filter different kinds of sources, so it's not generally very helpful.

Instead, you might choose to search Google Scholar to understand the ongoing conversation among scholars about your topic. Conducting a search for "cell phones and driving accidents and reaction time" in Google Scholar returns tens of thousands of results:

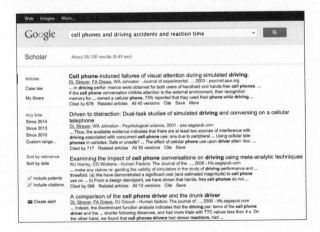

If you take a close look at the left-hand side of the screen, however, you'll notice that you can limit your search in several ways. By limiting the search to sources published since 2014, you can reduce your results significantly:

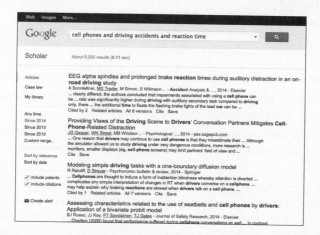

You can continue refining your search until you end up with a more manageable number of hits to comb through. Although the number is still large, thousands of results are more manageable than millions. Of course, you would likely need to continue narrowing your results. As part of this narrowing process, you are simultaneously focusing in on the conversation you originally wanted to understand: what scholars have written about your topic. Consider the criteria that would be most meaningful for your project as you refine your search by revising your search terms.

INSIDE WORK **Generating Search Terms**

Think of a controversial social issue that interests you. We chose driving while using a cell phone, but you should choose something you would potentially be interested in learning more about. Then follow these instructions, preferably working with classmates.

- Brainstorm the search terms you would use for that topic. What terms would you enter into a search engine?

- List your search terms in the box for Round 1 below, and then try doing a search using your preferred web search engine.

- How many hits did you get? Write the number in the box for Round 1.

- Switch seats with a classmate so that you can look at someone else's search terms. Should the search be narrowed? If so, revise your classmate's search terms to narrow them slightly. Write those in the box for Round 2. Try the search, and record the number of hits.

- Follow the instructions again for Rounds 3 and 4.

	Search Terms	Number of Hits
Round 1		
Round 2		
Round 3		
Round 4		

After you have finished the exercise, reflect on the following questions.

- How did your classmates narrow your search terms? What changes worked well, and what changes didn't work as well?

- If you were going to write advice for students using search engines for research, what advice would you give about search terms? ▶

Keep in mind that general search engines such as Google are not always the best places to conduct academic research, although they can often be useful starting points. Experienced researchers generally rely on more specialized databases to find the kinds of sources that will support their research most effectively.

Using Journal Databases

If you are conducting academic research, then one of the first types of sources you should look for is peer-reviewed journal articles. You may wonder why we don't recommend beginning your search by scouring your library's catalog for books. The answer is that academic books, which are often an excellent source of information, generally take much longer to make their way through the publishing process before they appear in libraries. Publishing the results of research in academic journal articles, however, is a faster method for academics to share their work with their scholarly communities. Academic journals, therefore, are a valuable resource precisely because they offer insight into the most current research being conducted in a field.

Additionally, like other scholarly work, most academic journals publish research only after it has undergone rigorous scrutiny through a peer-review process by other scholars in the relevant academic field. Work that has gone through the academic peer-review process has been sent out, with the authors' identifying information removed, and reviewed by other scholars who determine whether it makes a sufficiently significant contribution to the field to be published. Work published in a peer-reviewed academic journal has been approved not only by the journal's editor but also by other scholars in the field.

If you've ever browsed through your school's library, you've probably noticed that there are thousands of academic journals, and many are available online and easy to locate via the Internet. If you're associated with a college or university, you likely have access to a wide array of online academic journals that can be explored through databases via the library's website. You can search general library databases by refining search terms, as we discussed in the examples of using Google, but you can also find relevant resources by searching in specific disciplinary databases.

Searching for Journal Articles by Discipline

One way of searching for journal articles through your school's library is to explore the academic databases by subject or discipline. These databases usually break down the major fields of study into the many subfields that make up smaller disciplinary communities. Individual schools, colleges, and universities choose which databases they subscribe to. In the following image from the North Carolina State University's library website, you can see that agriculture is divided into various subfields: agricultural economics, animal science, crop science, and so on.

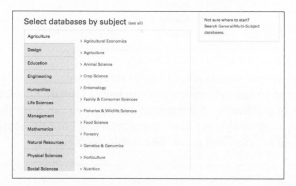

Let's say you need to find information on post-traumatic stress disorder (PTSD) among veterans of the Iraq War that began in March 2003. Consider the subfields of the social sciences where you're most likely to find research on PTSD. You might search databases in history, sociology, political science, and psychology, for instance. If you choose "Psychology," then you see a screen that lists major research databases in psychology, along with some related databases. Choosing the database at the top of the page, "PsycINFO," gains you access to one of the most comprehensive databases in that field of study.

Psychology

Databases

PsycINFO

PsycINFO, from the American Psychological Association (APA), contains more than 2 million citations and summaries of scholarly journal articles, book chapters, books, and dissertations, all in psychology and related disciplines, dating as far back as the 1800s. The database also includes information about the psychological aspects of related fields such as medicine, psychiatry, nursing, sociology, education, pharmacology, physiology, linguistics, anthropology, business, law and others. Journal coverage, which spans 1887 to present, includes international material selected from nearly 2,000 periodicals in more than 25 languages.

Selecting "PsycINFO" grants access to the PsycINFO database via a search engine—in this case, EbscoHOST. You can now input search terms such as "PTSD and Iraq war veterans" to see your results.

Notice that the search engine allows you to refine your search in a number of ways, very similar to the limitations you can use in Google Scholar: you can limit the years of publication for research articles, you can limit the search to sources that are available full-text online, you can limit the search to peer-reviewed journal articles, and more. The results look like this:

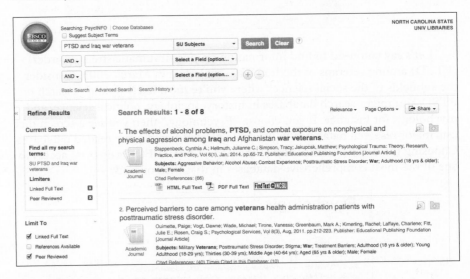

You can now access the texts of journal articles that you find interesting or that might be most relevant to your research purposes. Depending on the number and content of the results, you may choose to revise your search terms and run the search again.

EVALUATING SOURCES

Distinguishing between Scholarly and Popular Sources

As we have said, using search engines makes finding sources easy. The difficult part is deciding which sources are worth your time. If you are working on an academic paper, it is particularly useful to be able to distinguish between popular and scholarly sources.

Depending on your research and writing context, you might be able to use both scholarly and popular sources to support your research. However, in some writing situations it is most appropriate to rely on scholarly sources. For this reason, you should understand the difference between scholarly and popular sources, which comes down to a matter of audience and the publication process. **Scholarly sources** are produced for an audience of other scholars, and **popular sources** are produced for a general audience. Scholarly sources have undergone the peer-review process prior to publication, while popular sources typically have been vetted only by an editor. Generally speaking, popular sources are not very useful for supporting academic research. Let's examine a number of publication types in terms of the kind of information, scholarly or popular, they most often provide:

Examples of Scholarly Sources

- **Academic Journals** Most journal articles are produced for an audience of other scholars, and the vast majority are peer-reviewed before they are published in academic journals.

- **Books Published by Academic Presses** Academic presses publish books that also go through the peer-review process. You can sometimes identify academic presses by their names (e.g., a university press), but sometimes you need to dig deeper to find out whether a press generally publishes scholarly or popular sources. Looking at the press's website can often help answer that question.

Examples of Popular Sources

- **Newspapers** Most newspaper articles are reviewed by editors for accuracy and reliability. However, they typically provide only information that would be of interest to a general audience. They are not specifically intended for an academic audience. A newspaper might report the results of a study published in an academic journal, but it will generally not publish original academic research.

- **Magazines**   Like newspaper articles, magazine articles are typically reviewed by editors and are intended for a general reading audience, not an academic one.

Although it may seem easy to classify sources into one of these two categories, in fact it is often difficult to determine if a source is scholarly or not. Understanding the nature of scholarly and popular sources and recognizing their differences as you do your research will help you develop more effective arguments.

Scholarly works, for instance, are typically built on other sources, so they generally include references to other works that are documented in the text and listed in a complete bibliography at the end. Imagine for a moment, though, that you locate a study published on the Internet that you think would be a really good source for your research. It looks just like an article that might appear in a journal, and it has a bibliography that includes other academic sources. However, as part of your analysis of the source, you discover that the article, published only on a website, has never been published by a journal. Is this a scholarly work? It might be. Could this still be a useful scholarly work for your purposes? Perhaps. Still, as a writer and researcher, you would need to know that the article you're using as part of your own research has never been peer-reviewed or published by a journal or an academic press. This means that the validity of the work has never been assessed by other experts in the field. If you use the source in your own work, you would probably want to indicate that it has never been peer-reviewed or published in an academic journal as part of your discussion of that source.

Answering the following questions about your sources can help you evaluate their credibility and reliability:

1. Who are the authors?
2. Who is the intended audience?
3. Where is the work published?
4. Does the work rely on other reputable sources for information?
5. Does the work seem biased?

As a writer, you must ultimately make the decisions about what is or is not an appropriate source, based on your goals and an analysis of your audience. Answering the questions above can help you assess the appropriateness of sources.

INSIDE WORK   **Evaluating Sources**

For this exercise, either look at the sample essay from Timothy Holtzhauser on pages 52–57 of Chapter 3 or look at an essay that you wrote for a class in the past. Choose one of the references listed in the essay's bibliography, and write answers to the following questions.

1. Who are the authors? Do they possess any particular credentials that make them experts on the topic? With what institutions or organizations are the authors associated?

2. Who is the intended audience—the general public or a group of scholars? How do you know?

3. Where is the work published? Do works published there undergo a peer-review process?

4. Does the work rely on other reputable sources for information? What are those sources, and how do you know they are reputable?

5. Does the work seem biased? How do you know this? Is the work funded or supported by individuals or parties who might have a vested interest in the results? If so, is there a potential conflict of interest? ▶

SUMMARIZING, PARAPHRASING, AND QUOTING FROM SOURCES

Once you've located and studied the sources you want to use in a research paper, then you're ready to begin considering ways to integrate that material into your own work. There are a number of ways to integrate the words and ideas of others into your research, and you've likely already had experience summarizing, paraphrasing, and quoting from sources as part of an academic writing assignment. For many students, though, the specifics of how to summarize, paraphrase, and quote accurately are often unclear, so we'll walk through these processes in some detail.

Summarizing

Summarizing a text is a way of condensing the work to its main ideas. A summary therefore requires you to choose the most important elements of a text and to answer these questions: *What* is this work really trying to say, and *how* does it say it? Composing a summary of a source can be valuable for a number of reasons. Writing a summary can help you carefully analyze the content of a text and understand it better, but a summary can also help you identify and keep track of the sources you want to use in the various parts of your research. You may sometimes be able to summarize a source in only a sentence or two. We suggest a simple method for analyzing a source and composing a summary:

1. Read the source carefully, noting the **rhetorical context**. Who composed the source? For whom is the source intended? Where was it published? Identify the source and provide answers to these questions at the beginning of your summary, as appropriate.

2. Identify the **main points**. Pay close attention to topic sentences at the beginning of paragraphs, as they often highlight central ideas in the overall structure of an argument. Organize your summary around the main ideas you identify.

3. Identify **examples**. You will want to be able to summarize the ways the writer illustrates, exemplifies, or argues the main points. Though you will likely not discuss all of the examples or forms of evidence you identify in detail as part of your summary, you will want to comment on one or two, or offer some indication of how the writer supports his or her main points.

The following excerpt is taken from the fuller text of Jack Solomon's "Masters of Desire: The Culture of American Advertising," which appears on pages 49–52 in Chapter 3:

> Status symbols, then, are signs that identify their possessors' place in a social hierarchy, markers of rank and prestige. We can all think of any number of status symbols — Rolls-Royces, Beverly Hills mansions, even Shar Pei puppies (whose rareness and expense has rocketed them beyond Russian wolfhounds as status pets and has even inspired whole lines of wrinkle-faced stuffed toys) — but how do we know that something is a status symbol? The explanation is quite simple: when an object (or puppy!) either costs a lot of money or requires influential connections to possess, anyone who possesses it must also possess the necessary means and influence to acquire it. The object itself really doesn't matter, since it ultimately disappears behind the presumed social potency of its owner. Semiotically, what matters is the signal it sends, its value as a sign of power. One traditional sign of social distinction is owning a country estate and enjoying the peace and privacy that attend it. Advertisements for Mercedes-Benz, Jaguar, and Audi automobiles thus frequently feature drivers motoring quietly along a country road, presumably on their way to or from their country houses.

A summary of this part of Solomon's text might read something like this:

> In "Masters of Desire: The Culture of American Advertising," Jack Solomon acknowledges that certain material possessions may be understood as representations of an individual's rank or status. He illustrates this point by identifying a number of luxury automobiles that, when observed, cause us to consider the elevated economic status of the vehicles' owners (63).

You'll notice that this summary eliminates discussion of the specific examples Solomon provides. Further, it removes any discussion of the concept of semiotics. Though Solomon's ideas are clearly condensed and the writer of this summary has carefully selected the ideas to be summarized in order to further his or her own aims, the core of Solomon's idea is accurately represented.

Paraphrasing

Sometimes a writer doesn't want to summarize a source because condensing its ideas risks losing part of its importance. In such a case, the writer has to choose whether to paraphrase or quote directly from the source. **Paraphrasing** means translating the author's words and sentence structure into your own for the purpose of making the ideas clear for your audience. A paraphrase may be the same length or even longer than the part of a text being paraphrased, so the purpose of paraphrase is not really to condense a passage, as is the case for summary.

Often, writers prefer to paraphrase sources rather than to quote from them, especially if the exact language from the source isn't important, but the ideas are. Depending on your audience, you might want to rephrase highly technical language from a scientific source, for example, and put it in your own words. Or you might want to emphasize a point the author makes in a way that isn't as clear in the original language. Many social scientists and most scientists routinely paraphrase sources as part of the presentation of their own research because the results they're reporting from secondary sources are more important than the exact language used to explain the results. Quotations should be reserved for instances when the exact language of the original source is important to the point being made. Remember that paraphrasing requires you to restate the passage in your own words and in your own sentence structure. Even if you are putting the source's ideas in your own words, you must acknowledge where the information came from by providing an appropriate citation.

The following paragraph was taken from William Thierfelder's article "Twain's *Huckleberry Finn*," published in *The Explicator*, a journal of literary criticism.

> An often-noted biblical allusion in *Huckleberry Finn* is that comparing Huck to the prophet Moses. Like Moses, whom Huck learns about from the Widow Douglas, Huck sets out, an orphan on his raft, down the river. In the biblical story, it is Moses' mother who puts him in his little "raft," hoping he will be found. In the novel, Huck/Moses takes charge of his own travels. . . .

Inappropriate Paraphrase

> William Thierfelder suggests that Huckleberry is often compared to the prophet Moses. Huck, an orphan like Moses, travels down a river on a raft (194).

Although some of the language has been changed and the paraphrase includes documentation, this paraphrase of the first two sentences of Thierfelder's passage is inappropriate because it relies on the language of the original text and employs the author's sentence structure. An appropriate paraphrase that uses new language and sentence structure might look like this:

> William Thierfelder notes that numerous readers have linked the character of Huckleberry Finn and the biblical figure of Moses. They are both orphans who take a water journey, Thierfelder argues. However, Moses's journey begins because of the actions of his mother, while Huck's journey is undertaken by himself (194).

Quoting

Depending on your rhetorical context, you may find that **quoting** the exact words of a source as part of your argument is the most effective strategy. The use of quotations is much more common in some academic fields than in others. Writers in the humanities, for example, often quote texts directly because the precise language of the original is important to the argument. You'll find, for instance, that literary scholars often quote a short story or poem (a primary source) for evidence. You may also find that a secondary source contains powerful or interesting language that would lose its impact if you paraphrased it. In such circumstances, it is entirely appropriate to quote the text. Keep in mind that your reader should always be able to understand why the quotation is important to your argument. We recommend three methods for integrating quotations into your writing. (The examples below follow American Psychological Association style conventions; see "Understanding Documentation Systems" on pages 76–77 and the Appendix for more information about documentation styles.)

1. **Attributive Tags** Introduce the quotation with a tag (with words like *notes, argues, suggests, posits, maintains,* etc.) that attributes the language and ideas to its author. Notice that different tags suggest different relationships between the author and the idea being cited. For example:

   De Niet, Tiemens, Lendemeijer, Lendemei, and Hutschemaekers (2009) argued, "Music-assisted relaxation is an effective aid for improving sleep quality in patients with various conditions" (p. 1362).

2. **Further Grammatical Integration** You may also fully integrate a quotation into the grammar of your own sentences. For example:

   Their review of the research revealed "scientific support for the effectiveness of the systematic use of music-assisted relaxation to promote sleep quality" in patients (De Niet et al., 2009, p. 1362).

3. **Introduce with Full Sentence + Punctuation** You can also introduce a quotation with a full sentence and create a transitional link to the quotation with punctuation, like the colon. For example:

   The study reached a final conclusion about music-assisted relaxation: "It is a safe and cheap intervention which may be used to treat sleep problems in various populations" (De Niet et al., 2009, p. 1362).

INSIDE WORK **Summarizing, Paraphrasing, and Quoting from Sources**

Choose a source that you have found on a topic of interest to you, and find a short passage (only one or two sentences) that provides information that might be useful in your own research. Then complete the following steps and write down your responses.

1. Summarize the passage. It might help to look at the larger context in which the passage appears.

2. Paraphrase the passage, using your own words and sentence structure.

3. Quote the passage, using the following three ways to integrate the passage into your own text:
   a. attributive tags
   b. grammatical integration
   c. full sentence + punctuation

For your own research, which approach (summarizing, paraphrasing, quoting) do you think would be most useful? Consider your writing context and how you would use the source. ❱

AVOIDING PLAGIARISM

Any language and ideas used in your own writing that belong to others must be fully acknowledged and carefully documented, including in-text citations and full bibliographic documentation. Failure to include either of these when source materials are employed could lead to a charge of **plagiarism**, perhaps the most serious of academic integrity offenses. The procedures for documenting cited sources vary from one rhetorical and disciplinary context to another, so always clarify the expectations for documentation with your instructor when responding to an assigned writing task. Regardless, you should always acknowledge your sources when you summarize, paraphrase, or quote, and be sure to include the full information for your sources in the bibliography of your project.

INSIDE WORK Understanding Plagiarism

Most schools, colleges, and universities have established definitions of plagiarism and penalties or sanctions that may be imposed on students found guilty of plagiarism. You should become familiar with the definitions of plagiarism used by your institution as well as by your individual instructors.

- Locate a resource on campus (e.g., a student handbook or the website of your institution's Office of Student Conduct) that provides a definition of plagiarism from the perspective of your institution. You may discover that

Insider's View
On accidental plagiarism
KAREN KEATON JACKSON, WRITING STUDIES

"Many students come in who are already familiar with using direct quotations. But when it comes to paraphrasing and summarizing, that's when I see a lot of accidental plagiarism. So it's really important for students to understand that if you don't do the research yourself, or if you weren't there in the field or doing the survey, then it's not your own idea and you have to give credit."

Hear more on avoiding plagiarism.

in addition to defining plagiarism, your institution provides avenues of support to foster academic integrity and/or presents explanations of the consequences or penalties for violating rules of academic integrity.

- Locate a resource from one of your classes (e.g., a course website, a course syllabus) that provides a definition of plagiarism from the perspective of one of your instructors.

- Consider what is similar about the two definitions. Consider the differences between them. What do these similarities and differences reveal about your instructor's expectations and those of the larger academic community in which you participate? ▶

UNDERSTANDING DOCUMENTATION SYSTEMS

Documentation systems are often discipline-specific, and their conventions reflect the needs and values of researchers and readers in those particular disciplines. For these reasons, you should carefully analyze any writing situation to determine which documentation style to follow. You'll find examples of specific documentation systems in the disciplinary chapters in Part Two. Here are some of the most common ones:

1. **Modern Language Association (MLA)** MLA documentation procedures are generally followed by researchers in the humanities. One of the most important elements of the in-text citation requirements for the MLA documentation system is the inclusion of page numbers in a parenthetical reference. Though page numbers are used in other documentation systems for some in-text citations (as in the APA system when quoting a passage directly), page numbers in MLA are especially important because they serve as a means for readers to assess your use of sources, both primary and secondary, and are used whether you are quoting, paraphrasing, or summarizing a passage. Page numbers enable readers to quickly identify cited passages and evaluate the evidence: readers may verify that you've accurately represented a source's intent when citing the author's words, or that you've fully examined all the elements at play in your analysis of a photograph or poem. Of course, this kind of examination is important in all disciplines, but it is especially the case in the fields of the humanities, where evidence typically takes the form of words and images. Unlike some other documentation systems, the MLA system does not require dates for in-text citations, because scholars in this field often find that past discoveries or arguments are just as useful today as when they were first observed or published. Interpretations don't really expire; their usefulness remains valid across exceptionally long periods of time. Learn more about the style guides published by the Modern Language Association, including the *MLA Handbook for Writers of Research Papers* and the *MLA Style Manual and Guide to Scholarly Publishing,* along with more information about the MLA itself, at www.mla.org.

2. **American Psychological Association (APA)**   APA documentation procedures are generally followed by researchers in many areas of the social sciences and related fields. Although you will encounter page numbers in the in-text citations for direct quotations in APA documents, you're much less likely to find direct quotations overall. Generally, researchers in the social sciences are less interested in the specific language or words used to report research findings than they are in the results or conclusions. Therefore, social science researchers are more likely to paraphrase information than to quote information. Additionally, in-text documentation in the APA system requires the date of publication for research (see the examples on p. 74, and consult the Appendix for more information). This is a striking distinction from the MLA system. Social science research that was conducted fifty years ago may not be as useful as research conducted two years ago, so it's important to cite the date of the source in the text of the argument. Imagine how different the results would be for a study of the effects of violence in video games on youth twenty years ago versus a study conducted last year. Findings from twenty years ago probably have very little bearing on the contemporary social context and would not reflect the same video game content as today's games. As a result, the APA system requires including the date of research publication as part of the in-text citation. The date enables readers to quickly evaluate the currency, and therefore the appropriateness, of the research being referenced. Learn more about the *Publication Manual of the American Psychological Association* and the APA itself at its website: www.apa.org.

3. **The Council of Science Editors (CSE)**   As the name suggests, the CSE documentation system is most prevalent among disciplines of the natural sciences, although many of the applied fields of the sciences, like engineering and medicine, rely on their own documentation systems. As in the other systems described here, CSE requires writers to document all materials derived from sources. Unlike MLA or APA, however, CSE allows multiple methods for in-text citations, corresponding to alternative forms of the reference page that appears at the end of research reports. For more detailed information on CSE documentation, consult the latest edition of *Scientific Style and Format: The CSE Manual for Authors, Editors, and Publishers.* You can learn more about the Council of Science Editors at its website: www.councilscienceeditors.org.

WRITING PROJECT   **Writing an Annotated Bibliography**

The annotated bibliography is a common genre in several academic disciplines because it provides a way to compile and take notes on—that is, annotate— resources that are potentially useful in a research project. *Annotated bibliographies* are essentially lists of citations, formatted in a consistent documentation style, that include concise summaries of source material. Some annotated bibliographies include additional commentary about the sources—perhaps evaluations of their usefulness for the research project or comments about how the sources complement one another within the bibliography (perhaps by providing multiple perspectives). Annotated bibliographies are usually organized alphabetically, but longer bibliographies can be organized topically or in sections with subheadings. Each source entry gives the citation first and then a paragraph or two of summary, as in this example using MLA style:

> Carter, Michael. "Ways of Knowing, Doing, and Writing in the
> Disciplines." *College Composition and Communication* 58.3 (2007):
> 385–418. Print.
>
> In this article, Carter outlines a process for helping faculty across different academic disciplines to understand the conventions of writing in their disciplines by encouraging them to think of disciplines as "ways of doing." He provides examples from his own interactions with faculty members in several disciplines, and he draws on data collected from these interactions to describe four "metagenres" that reflect ways of doing that are shared across multiple disciplines: problem-solving, empirical inquiry, research from sources, and performance. Finally, he concludes that the metagenres revealed by examining shared ways of doing can help to identify "metadisciplines."

For this assignment, you should write an annotated bibliography that seeks to find sources that will help you respond to a specific research question. Your purpose in writing the annotated bibliography is threefold: (1) to organize and keep track of the sources you've found on your own topic, (2) to better understand the relationships among different sources that address your topic, and (3) to demonstrate knowledge of the existing research about it.

To meet this purpose, choose sources that will help answer your research question, and think about a specific audience who might be interested in the research you're presenting. Your annotated bibliography should include the following elements.

- An introduction that clearly states your research question and describes the scope of your annotated bibliography.

- As many as eight to twelve sources (depending on the scope of the sources and the number of perspectives you want to represent), organized alphabetically. If you choose a different organization (e.g., topical), explain how you have organized your annotated bibliography in the introduction.

- An annotation for each source that includes:
  - A summary of the source that gives a concise description of the main findings, focused on what is most important for responding to your research question
  - Relevant information about the authors or sponsors of the source to indicate credibility, bias, perspective, and the like

- An indication of what this source brings to your annotated bibliography that is unique and/or how it connects to the other sources
- A citation (see the Appendix) in a consistent documentation style

WRITING PROJECT ## Developing a Supported Argument on a Controversial Issue

For this writing assignment, you will apply your knowledge from Chapter 3 about developing an argument and from this chapter on finding and documenting appropriate sources. The sources you find will be evidence for the argument you develop. We ask you to make a claim about a controversial issue that is of importance to you and support that claim with evidence to persuade a particular audience of your position. As you write, you might follow the steps below to develop your argument.

- Begin by identifying an issue that you care about and likely have some experience with. We all write best about things that matter to us. For many students, choosing an issue that is very specific to their experience or local context makes a narrower, more manageable topic to write about. For example, examining recycling options for students on your college campus would be more manageable than tackling the issue of global waste and recycling.

- Once you have identified an issue, start reading about it to discover what people are saying and what positions they are taking. Use the suggestions in this chapter to find scholarly sources about your issue so that you can "listen in on" the conversations already taking place about your issue. You might find that you want to narrow your topic further based on what you find.

- As you read, begin tracking the sources you find. These sources can serve as evidence later for multiple perspectives on the issue; they will be useful both in supporting your claim and in understanding counterarguments.

- Identify a clear claim you would like to support, an audience you would like to persuade, and a purpose for writing to that audience. Whom should you talk to about your issue, and what can they do about it?

As you work to develop your argument, consider the various elements of an argument you read about in Chapter 3.

- Identify a clear central claim, and determine if it should be a simple or complex thesis statement.

- Develop clear reasons for that claim, drawn from your knowledge of the issue and the sources you have found.

- Choose evidence from your sources to support each reason that will be persuasive to your audience, and consider the potential appeals of ethos, logos, and pathos.

- Identify any assumptions that need to be explained to or supported for your audience.

- Develop responses to any counterarguments you should include in your argument.

Insider Example
Student Argument on a Controversial Issue

The following sample student argument, produced in a first-year writing class, illustrates many of the principles discussed in Chapters 3 and 4. As you read, identify the thesis, reasons, and sources used as support for the argument. Notice also that the student, Ashlyn Sims, followed MLA style conventions throughout her paper.

Ashlyn Sims

ENG 100

November 15, 201-

Project II

Condom Distribution in High School

A day rarely goes by when a teenager does not think about sex. It races back and forth in the teenage mind, sneaking its way into conversations all the time. We live in a society where sex is quickly becoming more and more common at younger ages; however, it is still considered a rather taboo topic, generating more discomfort from one generation to the next when you consider the values and beliefs of varying generations. Many teens learn things about sex through their peers because discussions of sex can be less awkward among friends, and thus a chain of risky, uninformed sex patterns can been created. Most teens will avoid talking to their parents about sex at all costs. Typically, this is because parents do not establish an open line of communication, or they make it clear that consequences will be enacted if their kids are having sex. This only keeps the cycle going, spreading sexually transmitted diseases around campuses and causing hundreds of thousands of unwanted pregnancies. So who is left to pick up the slack when parents become unapproachable to teens? Schools need to step in for the vast number of parents who do not know how to effectively educate their teens. Accessible contraceptives and sex education are necessary in schools because they can prevent sexually transmitted diseases and unwanted pregnancies while recognizing the reality that teens will inevitably have sex and steps need to be taken to ensure it is safe sex.

Sexually transmitted diseases are spreading quickly throughout high schools because teenagers do not know how to engage in safe sex practices by using condoms. Studies show that approximately one in four sexually active teens will contract an STD ("U.S. Teen Sexual Activity"). Schools need to provide condoms to students in order to slow the spread of STDs and keep their schools safer for sexually active teens. The purpose of schools is

Can you begin to identify a specific audience to whom the author is writing?

Compare the author's claim with the principles for writing a claim discussed on pages 39–41 of Chapter 3.

Why do you think the author uses this statistical data to support this reason? Where did this statistic come from? Think about whom she is writing to and what that audience might find persuasive.

to educate students and give them every tool necessary in order to succeed in the world. Sex education should be no exception. By giving students information about using some form of birth control, they can prevent the negative effects of having an STD, such as low self-esteem and self-worth, and send the strongest possible students out into the world to prosper. In more extreme cases, students can contract HIV, and it becomes a matter of life and death. Approximately half of the new cases of HIV every year occur in people under the age of twenty-five ("U.S. Teen Sexual Activity"). Although contracting HIV is not an end result for all sexually active teens, it is still a major risk factor, and the spread can be slowed with the help of condoms.

As you see places where the student has cited information from sources, think about whether she has paraphrased, summarized, or quoted. Why do you think she makes the choices she does?

Compared to older adults, adolescents are at a higher risk for acquiring STDs for a number of reasons, including limited access to contraceptives and regular health care ("U.S. Teen Sexual Activity"). When parents won't help their children practice safe sex, it becomes the schools' job to protect students and educate them accordingly. Adolescents face many obstacles to obtaining and using condoms given outside of school. Some of these obstacles include confidentiality, cost, access, transportation, embarrassment, objection by a partner, and the perception that the risks of pregnancy and infection are low (Dodd). School should be a place where students go to obtain condoms, which gives students the means to have safe sex. Because STDs are spreading at an alarming rate, schools should do their best to prevent them by distributing condoms.

Here the student reiterates the central point of the paragraph.

Pregnancies in teenagers are almost always unplanned, and they are usually the consequences of having sex without birth control. Schools need to supply students with contraceptives because a teenage pregnancy is the number one reason girls drop out of high school, and it sets them up for a life of hardships. Girls who get pregnant at an early age drop out 70% of the time (Mangal). The teenagers may not have known the importance of using contraceptives and practicing safe sex because no one ever talked to them about it. It should be the responsibility of our academic institutions to safeguard these students from pregnancies by educating them when nobody else has done so. Schools have the ability to provide contraceptives and sex education in order to prevent pregnancies and ensure that more girls will graduate and have better odds of getting a higher-paying job. The cost of a condom by the government is nothing compared to the cost it takes to raise the child of a mother who did not graduate from high school and needs welfare in order to survive. It would be absurd to spend thousands of dollars on a child when a condom costs only a few dollars.

The student offers a reason to support the distribution of condoms in schools.

The student is embedding reasons together here and developing a logical chain of reasons to support her argument.

The student's chain of reasons continues here.

Additionally, children of teen mothers are 22% more likely to have children of their own before the age of twenty (Maynard). The early childbearing could then become a cycle.

The teen years should be focused on learning everything necessary in order to succeed in life. Students need to complete their education and focus solely on making good grades and learning the skills necessary to get into college, and schools should provide anything students need in order to fulfill their greatest potential. Providing condoms is the more effective way to ensure that students can make smart decisions and focus on school, rather than raising a child.

The author makes a controversial claim here. How does she support it with her sources?

While many schools try to fight the growing numbers of STDs and pregnancies with abstinence-only classes, they are failing to face the reality that the classes do not prevent students from engaging in sex. By providing condoms for students, schools can acknowledge that students will have sex. Many schools ignore the problem and assume that if students need condoms, they can get them themselves. The reality is that many high school students cannot drive because they are under the age of sixteen or do not have a car. Others cannot afford condoms or choose to take the risk in order to avoid spending money. The difficulty in getting a condom behind parents' backs, combined with the preconceived notion that it is unlikely that one will get pregnant or an STD, creates a risky pattern of unsafe behaviors. In 1997, a study followed two thousand middle-school and elementary-aged students into high school. The study concluded that abstinence-only sex education does not keep teenagers from having sex. Neither does it increase or decrease the likelihood that if they do have sex, they will use a condom (Stepp). Changes need to be made to the programs taught in schools to best persuade students to practice safe sex. To be most effective, schools need to meet students halfway: schools will acknowledge the reality of sex among teens but will also teach them safe sex. A school that acknowledges that teens will have sex and provides condoms shows that it cares about the success and safety of its students.

The author acknowledges a potential counterargument here. How does she use her sources to refute that counterargument?

Many parents would argue that by providing access to condoms, a school is promoting the sexual behaviors of teens. Then this leads to the fear that by having more sexually active teens, the STD and pregnancy rate will increase and only produce more affected teens who would otherwise not be affected. However, at least one study has shown that a teen who is not sexually active is no more inclined to get a condom and become sexually active just because of the easy access (Kirby and Brown). Students who need condoms will be able to get them, and those who do not will know that they are available but will not have any reason to use them.

People might also argue that it is not a school's place to make decisions for the parents about whether students should have access to condoms. However, the reality is that teens will have sex, and although it is not the school's place to make these decisions, teens who have no other way to gain access will be able to protect themselves. If no more students are influenced to have sex, then the distribution of condoms is not creating any risk; it is only offering protection to the one in four teens who will contract an STD and the thousands of girls who will get pregnant. It is only giving students access to protect themselves. By providing condoms, a school does not encourage sexual activity among young adults, but rather encourages safe sex and provides options for teens who would otherwise have no options and would engage in high-risk activities anyway.

Overall, providing condoms does not encourage risky behavior; it gives high-risk students options when they cannot afford or obtain condoms. The access to condoms helps prevent sexually transmitted diseases and pregnancies. A school that does not acknowledge the high risk of teens having sex is only hurting its students. Schools need to provide condoms so that students have greater chances of fulfilling their full potential in life and do not have to work against the odds when faced with pregnancy. In order to lower the rates of STDs and pregnancies, all schools should provide condoms in the interest of the safety of sexually active students.

> The author identifies another possible counterargument. What evidence is provided to refute the counterargument?

Works Cited

Dodd, Kerri J. "School Condom Availability." *Advocates for Youth*. 1998. Web. 20 Sept. 2015. <http://www.advocatesforyouth.org/publications /449?task=view>.

Kirby, Douglas B., and Nancy L. Brown. "Condom Availability Programs in U.S. Schools." *Family Planning Perspectives* 28.5 (1996): 196–202. JSTOR. Web. 21 Sept. 2015. <http://www.jstor.org/stable/2135838>.

Mangal, Linda. "Teen Pregnancy, Discrimination, and the Dropout Rate." *American Civil Liberties Union of Washington*. ACLU, 25 Oct. 2010. Web. 21 Sept. 2015. <http://www.aclu-wa.org/blog/teen-pregnancy -discrimination-and-dropout-rate>.

> Notice what kinds of sources the author has cited. If she were to conduct additional research to support her argument, what do you think might strengthen it?

Maynard, Rebecca A. "Kids Having Kids." *The Urban Institute | Research of Record*. Web. 21 Sept. 2015. <http://www.urban.org/pubs/khk/summary.html>.

Stepp, Laura Sessions. "Study Casts Doubt on Abstinence-Only Programs." *Washington Post*. 14 Apr. 2007. Web. 26 Sept. 2015. <http://www.washingtonpost.com/wp-dyn/content/article/2007/04/13/AR2007041301003.html>.

"U.S. Teen Sexual Activity." *Kaiser Family Foundation*. Jan. 2005. Web. 21 Sept. 2015. <http://www.kff.org/youthhivstds/upload/U-S-Teen-Sexual-Activity-Fact-Sheet.pdf>.

Discussion Questions

1. Whom do you think Ashlyn Sims is targeting as her audience in this assignment? Why do you think that is her audience?

2. What is Ashlyn's thesis, and what does she provide as the reasons and evidence for her claim?

3. What assumptions connect her thesis to her reasons? Additionally, what assumptions would her audience have to accept in order to find her evidence persuasive? Really dig into this question, because this area is often where arguments fall apart.

4. What counterarguments does Ashlyn address in her essay? Why do you think she addresses these particular counterarguments? Can you think of others that she might have addressed?

5. What kinds of sources does she use in her essay? How does she integrate them into her argument, and why do you think she has made those choices?

6. What would make this essay more persuasive and effective?

tip sheet

Academic Research

- **Research typically begins with a research question, which establishes the purpose and scope of a project.** As you develop research questions, keep in mind the following evaluative criteria: personal investment, debatable subject, researchable issue, feasibility, and contribution.

- **A researcher who has established a clear focus for her research, or who has generated a claim, must decide on the kinds of sources needed to support the research focus:** primary, secondary, or both.

- **While both scholarly and popular sources may be appropriate sources of evidence in differing contexts, be sure to understand what distinguishes these types of sources** so that you can choose evidence types purposefully.

- **Primary sources are the results of data that researchers might collect on their own.** These results could include data from surveys, interviews, or questionnaires. **Secondary sources include research collected by and/or commented on by others.** These might include information taken from newspaper articles, magazines, scholarly journal articles, and scholarly books, to name a few.

- **Keep in mind that as you do research, you will likely have cause to refine your search terms.** This process involves carefully selecting or narrowing the terms you use to locate information via search engines or databases.

- **Be aware of the challenges of conducting basic searches for sources via Internet search engines** like Google. While Google Scholar may be a better means of searching for sources in the academic context, researchers often rely on more specialized research databases.

- **Peer-reviewed academic journals are an excellent source of information for academic arguments.** The publication process for journal articles is typically much shorter than for books, so using journal articles allows you access to the most current research.

- **Be aware of the strategies you can use to integrate the ideas of others into your own writing:** summarizing, paraphrasing, and/or quoting.

- **When you integrate the words or ideas of others, take care to ensure that you are documenting their words and ideas carefully to avoid instances of plagiarism,** and make sure you understand what constitutes plagiarism at your institution and/or in your individual classes. Follow appropriate rules for documenting your sources and constructing a bibliography. In academic contexts, this often means using MLA, APA, or CSE documentation systems.

Inside Academic Writing

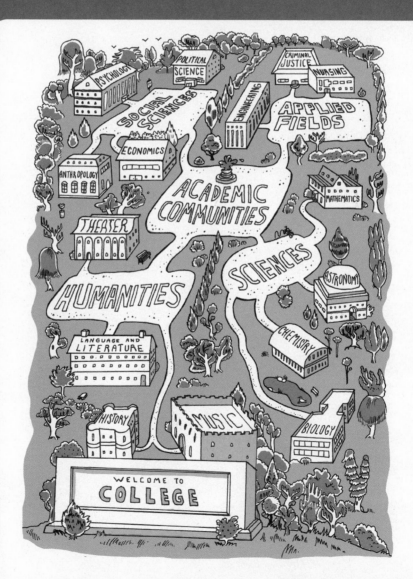

ANDREA TSURUMI

PART TWO

Inside Academic Writing

5

**Reading and Writing in
Academic Disciplines**   89

6

**Reading and Writing in
the Humanities**   108

7

**Reading and Writing in the
Social Sciences**   152

8

**Reading and Writing in the
Natural Sciences**   209

9

**Reading and Writing in the
Applied Fields**   261

Reading and Writing in Academic Disciplines

The four chapters that follow this one introduce four broad disciplinary areas in higher education: humanities, social sciences, natural sciences, and applied fields. While some differences distinguish each of these areas, certain similarities show shared values that provide ways to analyze and understand the conventions of writing and research in those areas.

To help you navigate these chapters, we have organized Chapters 6 through 8 around the same key concerns:

- **Research in the Discipline**   Every academic discipline has established conventions of research. One thing that unites them is the importance of **observation**. Whether you're a humanities scholar observing texts, or a social scientist observing human behavior, or a scientist observing the natural world, careful methods of observation are central to developing research questions and writing projects in each disciplinary area. Similarly, all disciplines rely on the concepts of **primary research** and **secondary research**. (If you gather data of your own, you're doing primary research. If you gather data by studying the research of others, you're doing secondary research.) Academic writers in a variety of disciplines engage in both primary and secondary research and find that they inform each other. For example, a social scientist studying human behavior might conduct secondary research first to learn what others have done and to develop her research questions. Then she might conduct primary research to test a hypothesis and report results.

ANDREA TSURUMI

Similarly, a humanities scholar studying historical documents might conduct secondary research to build a preliminary research question and to develop a review of literature before conducting primary research by analyzing a historical document to develop a thesis about his interpretation of that document.

- **Conventions of Writing in the Discipline** Each academic discipline has expectations about academic writing in its field. The chapters that follow this one all include sections that describe and help you analyze the *conventions* of writing in the disciplines, using the principles of rhetoric (the strategies of communication and persuasion) introduced in this chapter.

- **Genres in the Discipline** Each chapter also provides examples of *genres*, or common types of academic writing, that often cross disciplines. These *Insider Examples* of writing, not only by professionals in the disciplines but also by students entering the discipline and composing in particular genres, are annotated to reveal key features that prompt your own analysis of them.

Chapter 9 then explores the kinds of work and genres produced in a number of applied fields, including nursing, education, business, and law.

Additionally, the chapters share other common features to help you broaden your understanding of each disciplinary area: *Insider's View* excerpts of scholars discussing disciplinary writing; *Inside Work* activities that prompt you to reflect on what you've learned; *Writing Projects* that help you develop your own academic compositions; and *Tip Sheets* that summarize key information.

Throughout these chapters, we ask you to analyze and practice writing in various academic disciplines. Keep in mind, though, that we *do not* expect you to master the writing of these communities by taking just one class or by reading one book. Instead, we introduce you to the concepts associated with **disciplinary discourse**, or the writing and speaking that is specific to different disciplines. Using these concepts, you can analyze future writing situations and make choices appropriate to the rhetorical contexts. It's worth noting that such rhetorical awareness may help you enter other **discourse communities**, or groups that share

Insider's View
Writing should be different in various situations
KAREN KEATON JACKSON, WRITING STUDIES

"I think students should consider that writing has to be and should be different in various situations. Students need to go through a kind of meta-process of thinking about their own writing, one that allows them to see that the skills they learn in first-year writing can transfer. When students go into their history class or psychology class, for instance, the expectations may be different, but they'll see how they can transfer what they've learned in first-year writing to that situation."

Learn more about rhetorical situations.

common values and similar communication practices, outside of your college classes as well, socially and professionally.

Disciplinary conventions and styles are not just patterns to follow; rather, they represent shared values. In other words, there's a reason why academic texts are communicated in the way that they are: scholars in the same discipline might have similar ways of thinking about an issue, and they follow common ways of researching and investigating that represent their shared values and perspectives. The information we offer you on different academic disciplines in this book is not necessarily something to memorize, but rather something to analyze through the frame of *rhetorical context*. Ultimately, we want you to be able to look at an academic text and determine what the rhetorical context is and what conventions influence that text. As you write for different courses throughout your college career, this ability will help you determine and follow the expectations of writing for the different academic contexts you encounter. It will also help you read the assignments in your other classes because you'll understand some of the reasons that texts are written in the way that they are.

Analyzing Genres and Conventions of Academic Writing

As you know, different writing situations call for different types of writing. Different types of writing—from short items such as tweets, bumper stickers, and recipes to longer and more complex compositions such as Ph.D. dissertations, annual reports, and novels—are called *genres*. Scholars write in many different genres depending on their disciplinary areas, the kinds of work they do, and the situation in which they're writing. You have probably written in several different academic genres in your education already. You might have written a literary analysis in an English class, a lab report in a science class, a bibliography for a research paper, and maybe a personal narrative. Each of these genres has a common set of expectations that you must be familiar with in order to communicate effectively with your intended audience. In this text, you'll find information about writing in many of these genres—such as literary/artistic interpretations, rhetorical analyses, annotated bibliographies, reviews of literature, lab reports, and memos—with the ultimate goal of learning to analyze the rhetorical context so that you can determine the expected conventions of a genre in any writing situation.

Genres are not always bound by discipline, however. You'll find that the conventions of some genres are similar from one disciplinary area to another. As you read Chapters 6 through 9 on humanities, the social sciences, the natural sciences, and applied fields, pay attention to which genres are repeated and how the conventions of those genres shift or remain constant from one disciplinary context to another.

You'll notice that similar writing situations within, and even sometimes across, disciplines call for a similar genre. In other words, academics might approach a piece of writing in the same (or a similar) way even though they come from different academic disciplines.

"I think the three skills that students need to write in college settings are all tied into the rhetorical situation. If they can think about audience, purpose, and form, I think that will at least get them ready to start asking the kinds of questions they need of their professors to determine, how am I going to shape this for this particular audience, this particular discipline, this particular professor?"

Learn more about analyzing genres.

For example, you'll notice that scholars in all disciplines write reviews of literature for their research. Likewise, when reporting on the results of a research study, many academics follow the **IMRAD (Introduction, Methods, Results, and Discussion) format** or a variation of it to record and publish the results of their research, regardless of their discipline. There might be some subtle differences from one discipline or one situation to another, but common elements are evident. Literature reviews and IMRAD reports are two examples of common genres of academic writing.

As we begin to talk about specific disciplinary contexts, keep in mind these strategies to analyze the conventions of academic writing. When you read and write academic texts, you'll want to:

- understand the overall rhetorical context of the piece of writing: the author, the audience, the topic, and the purpose for writing;

- identify and understand the disciplinary area—humanities, the social sciences, the natural sciences, applied fields—and make connections to what you know about that discipline;

- consider which elements of structure, language, and reference (explained below) govern the writing situation;

- identify the genre, or category, that the writing fits into, and discover the common conventions and expectations for that genre within the rhetorical context;

- analyze the persuasive strategies used, if the author is developing an argument. (What claims are presented? How are they supported by reasons and evidence? What assumptions are in play?)

These analytical strategies will help you to approach any academic writing situation confidently and effectively.

Adapting to Different Rhetorical Contexts: An Academic Writer at Work

Even though some genres are more common in specific disciplines than others, many scholars write in more than one genre on a regular basis. Scholars write

"Aspiring scientists often don't appreciate the importance of communication skills. Science doesn't count until it's communicated to the rest of the scientific community, and eventually the public. Moreover, scientists must write all sorts of things to have a successful career, from journal articles to grant applications to press releases.

"Probably the most important thing to do well when writing as a scientist is simply to get everything right. Science is a methodology for developing reliable information about the world we live in, and getting things wrong is the surest way for scientists to lose their reputation; and for a scientist, reputation is the coin of the realm. While nearly everyone scientifically inclined finds getting things right to be an obvious and principal goal, it is also critically important to identify the audience of any particular piece of writing and address that audience in an effective way. The writing examples included in this text are all targeted for a different readership, and that represents a primary difference between them.

"Scientists write and are asked to write for all sorts of audiences. This isn't an easy task, but success in that adaptation can be the difference between a great career and failure, so it's important to treat it seriously. There isn't magic to this, and while brilliance can be challenging to achieve, competence can certainly be learned. It just takes some practice and thought."

for different rhetorical contexts all the time, and they adapt their writing to the audience, topic, and purpose of the occasion. We'd like to take an in-depth look at one scholar's writing to show you an example of how he shifts the conventions of his writing for different contexts—often academic, but sometimes more general. We've chosen to look at a scholar in a scientific field that is rarely discussed in English classes: astronomy. Mike Brotherton is an astronomer at the University of Wyoming, and we'll look at two types of writing that he does on a regular basis. Brotherton writes scholarly articles in his field to report on his research to an audience of other academics—his peers. He also sometimes writes press releases about his research, and these are intended to help journalists report news to the general public. Each piece of writing represents a different genre intended for a different audience, but together they show us the varying ways that Brotherton shares his work in the field of astronomy. Both of these rhetorical contexts call for an awareness of different conventions.

INSIDE WORK) **Reflecting on a Discipline**

In his Insider's View, "Scientists must write all sorts of things," Mike Brotherton makes several generalizations about science, scientists, and scientific writing. Which of these comments, if any, surprised you, and which ones didn't? Explain why. ❱

Using Rhetorical Context to Analyze Writing for a Non-Academic Audience

First we'll take a look at a piece of writing that Mike Brotherton composed for a non-academic audience of journalists who might be interested in research he conducted. Brotherton wrote a press release to communicate the results of his research in a genre familiar to journalists. As you read the press release, which we've annotated, keep in mind the elements of rhetorical context that are useful in analyzing all kinds of writing:

- *author* (who is the writer, and what does he or she bring to the text?)
- *audience* (for whom is the text intended?)
- *topic* (what issue is the text addressing?)
- *purpose* (why did the author write the text?)

Specifically, consider the following questions:

- How might Brotherton's position as the *author* of the press release influence the way he wrote it? What might have been different if someone else had written the press release after talking to him about his research?
- Who is the *audience* for this piece? What choices do you think Brotherton made that were specific to his audience for the press release?
- How does the *topic* of the press release affect the choices the author made? Would you have made different choices to approach the topic for a general audience? What would they be?
- What is the *purpose* for writing the press release? How might that influence Brotherton's choices as a writer? Do you think he has met that purpose? Why or why not?

Excerpt from **Hubble Space Telescope Spies Galaxy/Black Hole Evolution in Action**

MIKE BROTHERTON

Identifies the **topic** of the research study and its relevant findings

Identifies members of the research team, who are all **authors** of the study upon which the press release is based

JUNE 2ND, 2008—A set of 29 Hubble Space Telescope (HST) images of an exotic type of active galaxy known as a "post-starburst quasar" show that interactions and mergers drive both galaxy evolution and the growth of super-massive black holes at their centers. Mike Brotherton, Associate Professor at the University of Wyoming, is presenting his team's findings today at the American Astronomical Society meeting in St. Louis, Missouri. Other team members include Sabrina Cales, Rajib Ganguly, and Zhaohui Shang of the University of Wyoming, Gabriella Canalizo of the University of California at Riverside, Aleks Diamond-Stanic of the University of Arizona, and Dan Vanden Berk of the Penn State University. The result is of special interest because the images provide support for a leading theory of the evolution of massive galaxies, but also show that the situation is more complicated than previously thought.

Over the last decade, astronomers have discovered that essentially every galaxy harbors a super-massive black hole at its center, ranging from 10,000 times the mass of the sun to upwards of 1,000,000,000 times solar, and that there exists a close relationship between the mass of the black hole and properties of its host. When the black holes are fueled and grow, the galaxy becomes active, with the most luminous manifestation being a quasar, which can outshine the galaxy and make it difficult to observe.

In order to explain the relationships between galaxies and their central black holes, theorists have proposed detailed models in which both grow together as the result of galaxy mergers. This hierarchical picture suggests that large galaxies are built up over time through the assembly of smaller galaxies with corresponding bursts of star formation, and that this process also fuels the growth of the black holes, which eventually ignite to shine as quasars. Supernova explosions and their dusty debris shroud the infant starburst until the activated quasar blows out the obscuration.

Brotherton and his team turned the sharp-eyed Hubble Space Telescope and its Advanced Camera for Surveys to observe a subset of these post-starburst quasars that had the strongest and most luminous stellar content. Looking at these systems 3.5 billion light-years away, Hubble, operating without the distortions of an atmosphere, can resolve sub-kiloparsec scales necessary to see nuclear structure and host galaxy morphology.

"The images started coming in, and we were blown away," said Brotherton. "We see not only merger remnants as in the prototype of the class, but also post-starburst quasars with interacting companion galaxies, double nuclei, starbursting rings, and all sorts of messy structures."

Astronomers have determined that our own Milky Way galaxy and the great spiral galaxy of Andromeda will collide three billion years from now. This event will create massive bursts of star formation and most likely fuel nuclear activity a few hundred million years later. Hubble has imaged post-starburst quasars three and a half billion light-years away, corresponding to three and a half billion years ago, and three and a half billion years from now our own galaxy is probably going to be one of these systems.

This work is supported by grants from NASA, through the Space Telescope Science Institute and the Long-Term Space Astrophysics program, and the National Science Foundation.

Fulfills the **purpose** of a press release by stating the importance of the research project. Appears in the first paragraph to make it prominent for the audience

Provides relevant background information about the topic for the **audience**

Provides a brief overview of the study's methods

Acknowledges funding support for the research project, giving credit to funding agencies that might also be **audiences** for the journalists' news articles

The audience for a press release is very general

MIKE BROTHERTON, ASTRONOMY

"It isn't always the case that scientists write their own press releases. Often, there are writers on staff at various institutions who specialize in writing press releases and who work with scientists. I've written press releases solo (e.g., the contribution included here) and in collaboration with staff

journalists at the University of Texas, Lawrence Livermore National Laboratory, and the University of Wyoming. Press releases should be able to be run as news stories themselves and contain enough content to be adapted or cut to length. The audience for a press release is very general, and you can't assume that they have any background in your field. You have to tell them why your result is important, clearly and briefly, and little else.

"While I don't think my effort here is bad, it is far from perfect and suffers one flaw. Reporters picking up press releases want to know what single result they should focus upon. They want to keep things simple. I tried to include several points in the release, rather than focusing on a single result. Some reporters became distracted about the notion that the Milky Way and Andromeda would someday merge and might become a post-starburst galaxy, which was not a result of my research project. Even though it gave the work some relevance, in hindsight I should have omitted it to keep the focus on the results of my research."

INSIDE WORK) **Reflecting on Rhetorical Context**

In his Insider's View, "The audience for a press release is very general," Mike Brotherton explains some of the specifics of writing a press release and what he sees as the strengths and weaknesses of his own press release. Review the press release with Brotherton's comments in mind, and explain whether you agree with his assessment of it. What advice might you give him for revising the press release? ❱

Using Structure, Language, and Reference to Analyze Academic Writing

While rhetorical context provides a useful framework for analyzing a variety of types of writing, the categories of **structure**, **language**, and **reference** **(SLR)*** offer more specific help in analyzing the conventions of academic writing at a deeper level. Although discourse conventions vary from discipline to discipline, once you understand how to analyze academic writing through these

---

*The SLR concept originated in the following essay: Patricia Linton, Robert Madigan, and Susan Johnson, "Introducing Students to Disciplinary Genres: The Role of the General Composition Course," *Language and Learning Across the Disciplines* 1, no. 2 (1994): 63–78.

categories, you can determine what conventions and choices are appropriate for nearly any academic writing situation.

- **Structure, or Format and Organization** Written texts are often organized according to specific disciplinary conventions. For example, scholars in the social sciences and natural sciences usually organize experimental study reports with an introduction first, followed by a description of their research methods, then their data/results, then the analysis of that data, and finally a discussion and conclusion (IMRAD format, discussed in more detail in Chapters 7 and 8 on the social sciences and natural sciences). By contrast, scholars in the humanities tend to write and value essays that are driven by a clear thesis (or main claim: what you are trying to prove) near the beginning of the essay that indicates the direction the argument will take. Scholars in the humanities also don't tend, as much, to use headings to divide a text.

- **Language, or Style and Word Choice** The language used in academic writing follows disciplinary conventions. Consider the use of the active and passive voices. You may recall that in the active voice the subject performs the action, while in the passive voice the subject is acted upon. (Active voice: *Inez performed the experiment*; passive voice: *The experiment was performed by Inez*.) Often, the passive voice is acceptable in specific situations in the natural sciences, but it is usually not favored in the humanities. A scholar in the sciences might write, *It was determined that the two variables have a negative correlation*, a sentence that obscures the subject doing the determining (generally, the researcher or research team). Such uses of the passive voice rarely occur in the humanities, where scholars prefer the active voice. Likewise, qualifiers (words such as *might, could, likely*) are often used in the natural and social sciences to indicate the interpretive power of the data collected and to help persuade an audience to accept the results because they are not generalizing inappropriately (*The positive correlation between the variables likely indicates a strong relationship between the motivation of a student and his or her achievement of learning objectives*). When qualifiers are used in the humanities, however, they often demonstrate uncertainty and weaken an argument (*Hamlet's soliloquies in acts 2 and 4 might provide an interesting comparison because they frame the turning point of the play in act 3*).

- **Reference, or Citation and Documentation** The conventions of how scholars refer to one another's work can also shift by discipline. You might already know, for example, that many scholars in the humanities use the documentation style of the Modern Language Association (MLA), while those in the social sciences generally use the style guide published by the American Psychological Association (APA). Conventions of how often scholars quote, paraphrase, and summarize one another's work can also vary.

LaunchPadSolo

Get astronomer Mike Brotherton's take on qualifying and hedging.

In the next example of Mike Brotherton's work, we'll look at the abstract and introduction to a scholarly journal article that he wrote with several co-authors. If we consider the *structure*, *language*, and *reference conventions* used in the piece, we can gain some insight into the way such writing is structured within the sciences—and specifically in the field of astronomy.

As you read the excerpt from Brotherton's co-authored article, notice the structure, language, and reference conventions. The article contains a lot of specific scientific language, and for the purpose of your analysis right now it's not important to understand the concepts as much as it is to recognize some of the elements that make this writing unique from other writing you may have encountered in English classes in the past. Consider the following questions:

- Even though the entire article is not included, what conclusions can you draw about its **structure**? What comes first in the article, and how is it organized in the beginning?

- How would you describe the **language** that Brotherton and his co-authors choose to use in the article? What does it tell you about the audience for the article?

- What **reference conventions** does the article follow? Does the documentation style used for the parenthetical references look familiar? How often are other scholars cited, and what is the context for citing their work? What purpose do those references serve in the article?

Excerpt from **A Spectacular Poststarburst Quasar**

M. S. BROTHERTON, WIL VAN BREUGEL, S. A. STANFORD, R. J. SMITH, B. J. BOYLE, LANCE MILLER, T. SHANKS, S. M. CROOM, AND ALEXEI V. FILIPPENKO

ABSTRACT

The **language** is highly specific and technical.

We report the discovery of a spectacular "poststarburst quasar" UN J10252–0040 ($B = 19$; $z = 0.634$). The optical spectrum is a chimera, displaying the broad Mg II $\lambda 2800$ emission line and strong blue continuum characteristic of quasars, but is dominated in the red by a large Balmer jump and prominent high-order Balmer absorption lines indicative of a substantial young stellar population at similar redshift. Stellar synthesis population models show that the stellar component is consistent with a 400 Myr old instantaneous starburst with a mass of $\leq 10^{11}$ $M_{\odot}$. A deep, K_s-band image taken in $\sim 0''.5$ seeing shows a point source surrounded by asymmetric extended fuzz. Approximately 70% of the light is unresolved, the majority of which is expected to be emitted by the starburst. While starbursts and galaxy interactions have been previously associated with quasars, no quasar ever before has been seen with such an extremely luminous young stellar population.

1. INTRODUCTION

Headings indicate a particular kind of **structure**.

Is there a connection between starbursts and quasar activity? There is circumstantial evidence to suggest so. The quasar 3C 48 is surrounded by nebulosity that shows the high-order Balmer absorption lines characteristic of A-type stars (Boroson & Oke 1984; Stockton & Ridgeway 1991). PG 1700+518 shows a nearby starburst ring (Hines et al. 1999) with the spectrum of a 10^8 yr old starburst (Stockton, Canalizo, & Close 1998). Near-IR and CO mapping reveals a massive ($\sim 10^{10}$ $M_\odot$) circumnuclear starburst ring in I Zw 1 (Schinnerer, Eckart, & Tacconi 1998). The binary quasar member FIRST J164311.3+315618B shows a starburst host galaxy spectrum (Brotherton et al. 1999).

In addition to these individual objects, *samples* of active galactic nuclei (AGNs) show evidence of starbursts. Images of quasars taken with the *Hubble Space Telescope* show "chains of emission nebulae" and "near-nuclear emission knots" (e.g., Bahcall et al. 1997). Seyfert 2 and radio galaxies have significant populations of ~ 100 Myr old stars (e.g., Schmitt, Storchi-Bergmann, & Cid Fernandes 1999). Half of the ultraluminous infrared galaxies (ULIRGs) contain simultaneously an AGN and recent (10–100 Myr) starburst activity in a 1–2 kpc circumnuclear ring (Genzel et al. 1998).

The advent of *IRAS* provided evidence for an evolutionary link between starbursts and AGNs. The ULIRGs ($L_{IR} > 10^{12}$ $L_\odot$) are strongly interacting merger systems with copious molecular gas [$(0.5$–$2) \times 10^{10}$ $M_\odot$] and dust heated by both starburst and AGN power sources. The ULIRG space density is sufficient to form the quasar parent population. These facts led Sanders et al. (1988) to hypothesize that ULIRGs represent the initial dust-enshrouded stage of a quasar. Supporting this hypothesis is the similarity in the evolution of the quasar luminosity density and the star formation rate (e.g., Boyle & Terlevich 1998; Percival & Miller 1999). Another clue is that supermassive black holes appear ubiquitously in local massive galaxies, which may be out-of-fuel quasars (e.g., Magorrian et al. 1998). AGN activity may therefore reflect a fundamental stage of galaxy evolution.

Introduction **references** multiple prior studies by other scholars.

We report here the discovery of a poststarburst quasar. The extreme properties of this system may help shed light on the elusive AGN-starburst connection. We adopt $H_0 = 75$ km s^{-1} Mpc^{-1} and $q_0 = 0$.

INSIDE WORK   **Reflecting on Disciplinary Writing**

In his Insider's View "Accuracy trumps strong writing" on page 100, Mike Brotherton provides some guidelines for analyzing his scientific article through the lenses of structure, language, and reference. Write down a few points he makes about each lens that will be helpful when you approach reading a scientific article on your own.

Insider's View
Accuracy trumps strong writing
MIKE BROTHERTON, ASTRONOMY

"The audience for a scientific journal should be experts in your field but also beginning graduate students. Articles should be specific, succinct, and correct. For better or worse, in scientific articles it is necessary to use a lot of qualifications, adverbs, and modifying phrases, to say exactly what you mean even though the result is not as strong or effective.

Accuracy trumps strong writing here, although there is plenty of room for good writing. Every piece of writing, fiction or non-fiction, should tell an interesting story. The format for a scientific article is rather standard.

"There is also an abstract that gives a summary of all the parts of the paper. In many instances, the entire paper is not read but skimmed, so being able to find things quickly and easily makes the paper more useful. Audiences for scientific papers are often measured only in the dozens, if that. While popular papers can be read and used by thousands, most papers have a small audience and contribute to advancement in some niche or other, which may or may not turn out to be important.

"Some people cite heavily, and some people don't cite as heavily. And, again, you need to keep in mind your audience and what's appropriate. In writing a telescope proposal, for instance, which is not quite the same as a scientific article but has the same conventions, some reviewers want you to cite a lot of things just to prove that you know the field. This is especially true for beginning students writing proposals."

- Reread the excerpt from "A Spectacular Poststarburst Quasar" (see pp. 98–99) and reflect on any new things you notice.

- Read the excerpt again, this time with an eye to rhetorical context (author, audience, topic, and purpose for writing). Try to generalize about the usefulness of the two approaches to your reading.

- Annotate a paper you've written for another class, noting the rhetorical and SLR elements as we have in our annotations on the press release and the scholarly article. What practices about your own writing do these approaches suggest? ❯

WRITING PROJECT   ## Writing a Rhetorical Analysis of an Academic Article

For this project, you will analyze a full-length study in a discipline of your choice, published as an article in an academic journal. Your instructor may assign an article or may ask you to seek his or her approval for the article you choose to use for this project.

Using the convention categories of *structure*, *language*, and *reference*, describe the basic rhetorical features of the article you've chosen to study. In addition, try to explain why those conventions are the most appropriate for the writer in light of the goals of his or her article and for his or her intended academic audience.

The introduction to your paper should name the article you will analyze, describe the primary methods you will use to analyze it, and explain the goal of your analysis—to demonstrate and analyze features of discourse in an academic article. The body of your paper might be organized around the three convention categories—structure, language, and reference—or you might focus on one or two of the features that are of specific interest in your article. Of course, you can subdivide these categories to address specific elements of the larger categories. Under the conventions of the language category, for instance, you could address the use of qualifiers, the use of passive and active voice, and so on, providing examples from the article and commenting on their usefulness for the writer. In your conclusion, reflect on what you've found. Are there other issues still to be addressed? What other rhetorical strategies could be explored to analyze the work further? How effective are the strategies the author used, given the intended audience?

WRITING PROJECT ## Writing a Comparative Rhetorical Analysis

The goal of this writing project is to allow you to consider further the shifts in conventional expectations for writing across two disciplinary areas.

Use what you've learned about structure, language, and reference to compare and contrast the conventional expectations for writing in two different disciplines. To begin, you'll need two comparable studies: locate two articles about the same topic in academic journals representing different disciplines. For example, you might find two articles discussing the issue of increasing taxes on the wealthy to deal with the U.S. national debt. You might find one article written by an economist that addresses the impact of the national debt and projects the feasibility of different solutions, and another article written by a humanist discussing how the media has portrayed the issue.

Once you have your articles, begin by thinking about what kinds of questions the authors ask. Then examine both articles in terms of the structure, language, and reference conventions discussed in this chapter. Formulate a thesis that assesses the degree to which the rhetorical features in each category compare or contrast. Throughout your paper (which should be organized around the three areas of convention—structure, language, and reference), execute your comparisons and contrasts by illustrating your findings with examples from the texts. For example, if you find that one article (perhaps from the humanities) uses the active voice almost exclusively, then provide some examples. If the other article relies heavily on the passive voice, then provide examples of this use. End each section with a consideration of the implications of your findings: What does it say about the humanities that the writing is so characterized by active voice? Do not avoid discussing findings that might contradict your assumptions about writing in these two academic domains. Instead, study them closely and try to rationalize the authors' rhetorical decision-making.

Comparing Scholarly and Popular Articles

Choose a scholarly article and an article written for a more general audience on a common topic. You might reread the discussion of the differences between scholarly and popular articles in Chapter 4 as you're looking for articles to choose. Then use the framework for rhetorical context from Chapter 2 to conduct a rhetorical analysis of each article. In your comparison of the rhetorical contexts and decisions the authors have made, consider the questions below.

- How do the rhetorical contexts for writing compare?
- Which writing conventions are similar, and which ones are different?
- Why do you think the authors made the choices that they did in writing?

Finally, use the framework of structure, language, and reference to analyze the scholarly article. What conclusions can you draw about the conventions of the type of academic writing you're looking at by analyzing these three elements?

Translating Scholarly Writing for Different Rhetorical Contexts

At times, writing for an academic context, like Mike Brotherton's work, must be repurposed for presentation in another, more general context. Sometimes the writer does the translating, and sometimes other writers may help communicate the importance of a piece of scholarly writing to another audience.

Insider Example
Student Translation of a Scholarly Article

Jonathan Nastasi, a first-year writing student, translated a scholarly article about the possible habitability of another planet from the journal *Astronomy & Astrophysics* into a press release for a less specialized audience. He condensed the information into a two-page press release for a potential audience interested in publishing these research results in news venues. Also, he followed his writing instructor's advice to apply MLA style even though the article he summarized is scientific.

Release Date: 18 September 2014

Contact: W. von Bloh

bloh@pik-potsdam.de

Potsdam Institute for Climate Impact Research

Life May Be Possible on Other Planets

New data shows that a new planet found outside of our solar system may be habitable for life.

RALEIGH (SEPTEMBER 18, 2014)—A study from the Potsdam Institute for Climate Impact Research shows that a planet in another solar system is in the perfect position to harbor life. Additionally, the quantity of possibly habitable planets in our galaxy is much greater than expected.

An artist's rendition of Gliese 581g orbiting its star.

Gliese 581g is one of up to six planets found to be orbiting the low-mass star Gliese 581, hence its name. Gliese 581g and its other planetary siblings are so-called "Super Earths," rocky planets from one to ten times the size of our Earth. This entire system is about twenty light-years away from our Sun. W. Von Bloh, M. Cuntz, S. Franck, and C. Bounama from the Potsdam Institute for Climate Impact Research chose to research Gliese 581g because of its size and distance from its star, which make it a perfect candidate to support life.

A planet must be a precise distance away from a star in order to sustain life. This distance is referred to as the habitable zone. According to von Bloh et al., the habitable zones "are defined as regions around the central star where the physical conditions are favourable for liquid water to exist at the planet's surface for a period of time sufficient for biological evolution to occur." This "Goldilocks" zone can be affected by a number of variables, including the temperature of the star and the composition of the planet.

The actual distance of Gliese 581g from its star is known; the goal of this study was to find out if the planet is capable of supporting life at that distance. The researchers began by finding the habitable zone of the star Gliese 581—specifically, the zone that allowed for photosynthesis. Photosynthesis is the production of oxygen from organic life forms and is indicative of life. In order for the planet to harbor this kind of life, a habitable zone that allows for a specific concentration of CO_2 in the atmosphere as well as liquid water would have to be found.

The scientists used mathematical models based on Earth's known attributes and adjusted different variables to find out which scenarios yielded the best results. Some of these variables include surface temperature, mass of the planet, and geological activity. The scientists also considered settings where the surface of the planet was all-land, all-water, or a mix of both.

Considering all of these scenarios, von Bloh et al. determined that the habitable zone for Gliese 581g is between 0.125 and 0.155 astronomical units, where an astronomical unit is the distance between the Earth and the Sun. Other studies conclude that the *actual* orbital distance of Gliese 581g is 0.146 astronomical units. Because Gliese 581g is right in the middle of its determined habitable zone, the error and uncertainty in the variables that remain to be determined are negligible.

However, the ratio of land to ocean on the planet's surface is key in determining the "life span" of the habitable zone. The habitable zone can shift over time due to geological phenomena caused by a planet having more land than ocean. According to von Bloh et al., a planet with a land-to-ocean ratio similar to ours would remain in the habitable zone for about seven billion years, shorter than Gliese 581g's estimated age. In other words, if Gliese 581g has an Earth-like composition, it cannot sustain life. But if the ratio is low (more ocean than land), the planet will remain in its habitable zone for a greater period of time, thus allowing for a greater chance of life to develop.

The researchers conclude that Gliese 581g is a strong candidate for life so long as it is a "water world." According to the authors, water worlds are defined as "planets of non-vanishing continental area mostly covered by oceans."

The discovery of Gliese 581g being a strong candidate for sustaining life is especially important considering the vast quantity of planets just like it. According to NASA's *Kepler Discoveries* Web page, the Kepler telescope alone has found over 4,234 planet candidates in just five years. With the collaboration of other research, 120 planets have been deemed "habitable," according to *The Habitable Exoplanets Catalog*.

"Our results are another step toward identifying the possibility of life beyond the Solar System, especially concerning Super-Earth planets, which appear to be more abundant than previously surmised," say the authors. More and more scientists are agreeing with the idea that extraterrestrial life is probable, given the abundance of Earth-like planets found in our galaxy already. If this is true, humanity will be one step closer to finding its place in the universe.

"[W]e have to await future missions to identify the pertinent geodynamical features of Gl[iese] 581g . . . to gain insight into whether or not Gl[iese] 581g harbors life," write the researchers. The science community agrees: continued focus in researching the cosmos is necessary to confirm if we have neighbors.

The full journal article can be found at <http://www.aanda.org.prox.lib.ncsu.edu/articles/aa/full_html/2011/04/aa16534-11/aa16534-11.html>.

Astronomy & Astrophysics, published by EDP Sciences since 1963, covers important developments in the research of theoretical, observational, and instrumental astronomy and astrophysics. For more information, visit <http://www.aanda.org/>.

Works Cited

Annual Review of Astronomy and Astrophysics. Annual Reviews, 2014. Web. 17 Sept. 2014.

"Astronomy & Astrophysics (About)." *Astronomy & Astrophysics*, n.d. Web. 17 Sept. 2014.

Cook, Lynette. "Planets of the Gliese 581 System." 29 Sept. 2010. NASA. *NASA Features*. Web. 17 Sept. 2014.

The Habitable Exoplanets Catalog. Planetary Habitability Laboratory, 2 Sept. 2014. Web. 16 Sept. 2014.

Kepler Discoveries. NASA, 24 July 2014. Web. 16 Sept. 2014.

Kepler Launch. NASA, 2 Apr. 2014. Web. 16 Sept. 2014.

Von Bloh, W., M. Cuntz, S. Franck, and C. Bounama. "Habitability of the Goldilocks Planet Gliese 581g: Results from Geodynamic Models." *Astronomy & Astrophysics* 528.A133 (2011): n. pag. *Summon*. Web. 15 Sept. 2014.

Discussion Questions

1. Who was Jonathan Nastasi's audience as he wrote his press release? What cues in the writing tell you whom Jonathan views as his audience?

2. How well did he tailor his description of the research to that audience?

3. What is the purpose behind Jonathan's communication of the research findings?

4. What other genre might work for translating this research to a public audience? What would Jonathan need to do differently in that rhetorical situation?

Translating a Scholarly Article for a Public Audience

The goal of this project is to translate a scholarly article for a public audience. To do so, you will first analyze the scholarly article rhetorically and then shift the genre through which the information in your article is reported. You will produce two documents in response to this assignment:

- the translation of your scholarly article
- a written analysis of the choices you made as you wrote your translation

STEP ONE: IDENTIFYING YOUR NEW AUDIENCE AND GENRE
To get started, you'll need to identify a new audience and rhetorical situation for the information in your selected article. The goal here is to shift the audience from an academic one to a public one. You may, for instance, choose to report the findings of the article in a magazine targeted toward a general audience of people who are interested in science, or you may choose to write a newspaper article that announces the research findings. You might also choose to write a script for a news show that reports research findings to a general television audience. Notice that once you change audiences, then the form in which you report will need to shift as well. The genre you produce will be contingent on the audience you're targeting and the rhetorical situation: magazine article, newspaper article, news show script. There is an array of other possibilities for shifting your audience and genre as well.

STEP TWO: ANALYZING YOUR TARGET AUDIENCE AND GENRE EXPECTATIONS
Closely analyze an example or two of the kind of genre you're attempting to create, and consider how those genre examples fulfill the expectations of the target audience. Your project will be assessed according to its ability to reproduce those genre expectations, so you will need to explain, in detail, the rhetorical changes and other choices you had to make in the construction of your piece. Be sure that you're able to explain the rhetorical choices you make in writing your translation. Consider all four elements of rhetorical context: author, audience, topic, purpose.

STEP THREE: CONSTRUCTING THE GENRE
At this point, you're ready to begin constructing or translating the article into the new genre. The genre you're producing could take any number of forms. As such, the form, structure, and development of your ideas are contingent on the genre of public reporting you're attempting to construct. If you're constructing a magazine article, for example, then the article you produce should really look like one that would appear in a magazine. Try to mirror how the genre would appear in a real situation.

STEP FOUR: WRITING THE ANALYSIS
Once your translation is complete, compose a reflective analysis. As part of your analysis, consider the rhetorical choices you made as you constructed your translation. Offer a rationale for each of your decisions that connects the features of your translation to your larger rhetorical context. For example, if you had to translate the title of the scholarly article for a public audience, explain why your new title is the most appropriate one for your public audience.

- **You should not expect to master the writing of every academic discipline by reading one book,** even this one.

- **It's important to become familiar with key concepts of disciplinary writing in academic discourse communities:** *research* expectations; *conventions* (expectations) of writing; *genres* (types) of writing.

- **Genres are not always bound by discipline, although their conventions may vary somewhat from discipline to discipline.** For example, you can expect to write literature reviews in many different courses across the curriculum.

- **Analyzing academic writing is a multistep process.** (1) Understand the rhetorical context (author, audience, topic, purpose for writing); (2) identify the disciplinary area and what you know about it; (3) consider how expectations for features of *structure*, *language*, and *reference* govern the writing situation; (4) identify the genre of writing and the conventions that apply; (5) analyze the persuasive strategies if the writer is developing an argument.

- **Remember SLR.** The acronym for *structure*, *language*, and *reference* offers categories that can help you determine conventions and choices appropriate for most academic writing situations.

  - *Structure* concerns how texts are organized. *Example:* IMRAD— signifying Introduction, Methods, Results, and Discussion—is a common format in both the social and natural sciences.

  - *Language* encompasses conventions of style or word choice. *Example:* Active voice is typically favored in the humanities, and passive voice is more characteristic of writing in the social and natural sciences.

  - *Reference* concerns the ways writers engage source material, including their use of conventions of citation and documentation. *Example:* Many humanities scholars use MLA style; many social science scholars use APA style.

- **Academic research is important beyond the academy.** Therefore, academic writing that conveys such research often must be repurposed—translated—for different venues and audiences.

6

Reading and Writing in the Humanities

Introduction to the Humanities

An interest in exploring the meaning, or interpretation, of something and how it reflects on the human experience is one of the defining characteristics of the **humanities** that sets it apart from the social sciences, the natural sciences, and applied fields. Look at the tree at the bottom of this page, and see if you recognize any fields within the humanities with which you're already familiar.

Scholars in the humanities are interested in, and closely observe, human thought, creativity, and experience. The American Council of Learned Societies explains that humanistic scholars "help us appreciate and understand what distinguishes us as human beings as well as what unites us." Scholars in the humanities ask questions such as these:

- What can we learn about human experience from examining the ways we think and express ourselves?

- How do we make sense of the world through various forms of expression?

- How do we interpret what we experience, or make meaning for ourselves and for others?

Professor John McCurdy teaches history at Eastern Michigan University. Dr. McCurdy's research focuses on the history of early America, and he teaches courses on the colonial era and the American Revolution. In his Insider's View comments, he offers thoughts on

ANDREA TSURUMI

what humanists do and value, as well as the kind of research questions they ask. These comments come from an interview with him about his writing and about research in the humanities in general.

TEXTS AND MEANING

To understand the human condition and respond to these questions, humanists often turn to artifacts of human culture that they observe and interpret. These might be films, historical documents, comic strips, paintings, poems, religious artifacts, video games, essays, photographs, and songs. They might even include graffiti on the side of a building, a Facebook status update, or a YouTube video.

In addition to tangible artifacts, humanist writers might turn their attention to events, experiences, rituals, or other elements of human culture to develop meaning. When Ernest Hemingway wrote *Death in the Afternoon* about the traditions of bullfighting in Spain, he carefully observed and interpreted the meaning of a cultural ritual. And when historians interpret Hemingway's text through the lens of historical context, or when literary scholars compare the book to Hemingway's fiction of a later period, they are extending that understanding of human culture. Through such examination and interpretation of specific objects of study, scholars in the humanities can create artistic texts and develop theories that explain human expression and experience.

In this chapter, we'll often refer to artifacts and events that humanistic scholars study as **texts**. The ability to construct meaning from a text is an essential skill within the scholarship of the humanities. In high school English classes, students are often asked to interpret novels, poetry, or plays. You've likely written such analyses in the past, so you've developed a set of observational and interpretive skills that we'd like to build upon in this chapter. The same skills, such as the observational skills that lead you to find evidence in a literary text to develop and support an interpretation, can help you analyze other kinds of texts.

INSIDE WORK) **Thinking about Texts**

Write your responses to the following questions.

- What experiences do you already have with interpretation of texts in the humanities? Have you had to write a formal interpretation of a text before? If so, what questions did you ask?

- Imagine a text with which you are familiar. It might be a novel, a song, a painting, a sculpture, a play, a building, or a historical document. Brainstorm a list of *why* questions that you could ask about that text. ▶

OBSERVATION AND INTERPRETATION

You probably engage every day in observation of the kinds of things studied in the humanities, but you might not be doing it in the systematic way that humanistic scholars do. When you listen to music, how do you make meaning? Perhaps you listen to the words, the chord progressions, or repeated phrases. Or maybe you look to specific matters of context such as who wrote the song, what other music the artist has performed, and when it was recorded. You might consider how it is similar to or different from other songs. In order to understand the song's meaning, you might even think about social and cultural events surrounding the period when the song was recorded. These kinds of observational and interpretive acts are the very things humanists do when they research and write; they just use careful methods of observing, documenting, and interpreting that are generally more systematic than what most of us do when listening to music for enjoyment. Humanists also develop and apply theories of interpretation or build on the theories of others that help still other scholars determine how to observe and interpret texts and find meaningful connections among them. In this chapter, you will learn about some of those methods of observation and interpretation, and you will also have the opportunity to practice some of the kinds of writing and research typically seen in the humanities.

INSIDE WORK) **Observing and Asking Questions**

For this activity, pick a place to sit and observe, and bring something to write with. You might choose to do the activity in your dorm room or apartment, your workplace, a classroom, outside, in a restaurant or coffee shop, or at a gym, to name a few possibilities. For ten minutes, freewrite about all the things you see around you that could be "texts" that a humanist might interpret. Then think about the kinds of questions that a humanist might ask about those texts. Try to avoid writing about the actual activities people are engaging in; human behavior is more within the realm of the social sciences, not the humanities. Instead, think creatively about the kinds of artifacts that a humanist might analyze to understand and interpret human experience.

For example, if you observe and write in a coffee shop, you might consider the following artifacts, or texts.

- **The Sign or Logo Used for the Store**   Is there a logo? What does it include? How is it designed, and why? Is there a slogan? Whom might it relate to? What does it say about the store?

- **The Clothing of the People Working behind the Counter**   Do they have a dress code? Are they wearing uniforms? If so, what do the colors, materials, and/or style of the uniforms represent? What do they potentially tell you about the values of the business?

- **The Furniture**   Is it comfortable? New? Old? How is it arranged? What might the coffee shop be communicating to customers through that arrangement?

- **The Music Playing in the Background**   Is there music? What is playing? How loud is the music? What mood does it convey? Does it match the arrangement of the rest of the space? What emotions might the music evoke from customers?

- **The Materials Used to Serve Coffee**   Are the cups and napkins recycled? Does the store use glass or ceramic cups that can be washed and reused? Are there slogans or logos on the materials? If so, what do they say? What does the store communicate to customers through the materials used?

- **The Menu**   What kinds of items does the coffee shop serve? What language is used to describe menu items? How are the items written on the menu? Where is it displayed? Is food served? If so, what types of food are available, and what does that communicate to customers?

See how many different texts you can identify and how many questions you can generate. You might do this activity separately in the same place with a partner and then compare notes. What texts did you or your partner find in common? Which ones did you each identify that were unique? Why do you think you noticed the things you did? What was the most interesting text you identified? ❱

Research in the Humanities

The collection of information, or data, is an integral part of the research process for scholars in all academic disciplines. The data that researchers collect form the foundation of evidence they use to answer a question. In the humanities, data are generally gathered from texts. Whether you're reading a novel, analyzing a sculpture, or speculating on the significance of a cultural ritual, your object of analysis is a text and the primary source of data you collect to use as evidence typically originates from that text.

Academic fields within the humanities have at their heart the creation and interpretation of texts. A history scholar may pore through photographs of Civil

Hear more about the different kinds of texts scholars draw on in their research.

War soldiers for evidence to support a claim. An actor in a theater class might scour a script in order to develop an interpretation of a character he will perform onstage. And those who are primarily the creators of texts—visual artists, novelists, poets, playwrights, screenwriters, musicians—read widely in the field in order to master elements of style and contribute to their art in original and innovative ways. In the humanities, it's all about the text. Humanists are either creators or interpreters of texts, and often they are both.

To understand the research and writing in a specific disciplinary area, it is important to know not only what the objects of study are but also what methods scholars in that area use to analyze and study the objects of their attention. In the humanities, just as in other disciplines, scholars begin with observation. They closely observe the texts that interest them, looking for patterns, meaning, and connections that will help generate and support an interpretation. Humanists use their observations to pose questions about the human condition, to gather evidence to help answer those questions, and to generate theories about the human experience that can extend beyond one text or set of texts.

[INSIDE WORK] **Observing and Interpreting Images**

Consider each of the following images—a movie poster (A), graffiti (B), and a painting (C)—as texts that have something to say about human experience. Write your ideas in response to the following questions.

- What does the image mean?
- How do you make meaning from the image? What do you analyze to make meaning?
- What does the image make you think about?
- What emotion does the artist want you to feel? What aspect of the text do you base this on?
- Why do you think someone created this image? ❭

A. Movie Poster as Text

B. Graffiti as Text

C. Painting as Text

THE ROLE OF THEORY IN THE HUMANITIES

When scholars in the humanities analyze and interpret a text, they often draw on a specific theory of interpretation to help them make meaning. Theories in the humanities offer a particular perspective through which to understand human experience. Sometimes those perspectives are based on ideas about *how* we make meaning from a text; such theories include Formalism (sometimes called New Criticism, though it is far from new), Reader Response, and Deconstruction. Other theories, such as Feminist Theory and Queer Theory, are based more on ideas about how identity informs meaning-making. Still other theories, such as New Historicism, Postcolonialism, and Marxism, are centrally concerned with how historical, social, cultural, and other contexts inform meaning.

These are only a few of the many prominent theories of humanistic interpretation, barely scratching the surface of the theory-building work that has taken place in the humanities. Our goal is not for you to learn specific names of theories at this point, though. Rather, we want you to understand that when scholars in the humanities draw on a theory in the interpretation of a text, the theory gives them a *lens* through which to view the text and a set of questions they might ask about it. Different theories lead to different sets of questions and varying interpretations of the same text.

CLOSE READING IN THE HUMANITIES

To develop clear claims about the texts they're interpreting, scholars in the humanities must closely observe their texts and learn about them. Close observation might involve the kinds of reading strategies we discussed in Chapter 2, especially if the text is alphabetic (i.e., letter based), such as a book, a story, or a poem. One method that humanities scholars use is close reading, or careful observation of a text. It's possible to do a close reading of a story, of course, but one can also do a close reading of non-alphabetic texts such as films, buildings, paintings, events, or songs.

Most college students are highly skilled at reading for content knowledge, or for information, because that's what they're most often asked to do as students. This is what a professor generally expects when assigning a reading from a textbook. As you read such texts, you're primarily trying to figure out what the text is saying rather than thinking about how it functions, why the author makes certain stylistic choices, or how others might interpret the text. As we mentioned in Chapter 2, you might also read to be entertained, to learn, or to communicate.

Close observation or *reading* in the humanities, however, requires our focus to shift from reading for information to reading to understand how a text functions and how we can make meaning of it. Because texts are the primary sources of data used in humanistic research, it's important for those who work in the humanities to examine how a text conveys meaning to its audience. This kind of work—observing a text critically to analyze what it means and how it conveys meaning—is what we call **close reading**.

Insider Example
Professional Close Reading

In the following example of a close reading of a text, Dr. Dale Jacobs discusses how he constructs meaning from comics. He argues that comics are more complicated to interpret than texts composed only of words (e.g., a novel or short story) because graphic novel readers must also interpret visual, gestural, and spatial language at work in the panels. In doing so, Dr. Jacobs offers his own observation. Furthermore, he concludes his interpretation by calling on instructors to challenge students to think critically about how they construct meaning from texts. As you read his article, you might reflect on this question: When reading a text, how do you make meaning?

More Than Words: Comics as a Means of Teaching Multiple Literacies

DALE JACOBS

Over the last several years, comics have been an ever more visible and well-regarded part of mainstream culture. Comics are now reviewed in major newspapers and featured on the shelves of independent and chain bookstores. Major publishing houses such as Pantheon publish work in the comics medium, including books such as Marjane Satrapi's *Persepolis* and David B.'s *Epileptic*. Educational publishers such as Scholastic are also getting in on the act; in January 2005, Scholastic launched its own graphic novels imprint, Graphix, with the publication of Jeff Smith's highly acclaimed Bone series. At the NCTE Annual Convention, graphic novels and comics are displayed in ever greater numbers. School and public libraries are building graphic novels collections to try to get adolescents into the library. Comics have, indeed, emerged from the margins into the mainstream.

With all this activity and discussion surrounding comics, it is timely to consider how we as literacy teachers might think about the practice of using comics in our classrooms and how this practice fits into ongoing debates about comics and literacy. In examining these links between theory and practice, I wish to move beyond seeing the reading of comics as a debased or simplified word-based literacy. Instead, I want to advance two ideas: (1) reading comics involves a complex, multimodal literacy; and (2) by using comics in our classrooms, we can help students develop as critical and engaged readers of multimodal texts.

THE HISTORY OF ATTITUDES TOWARD COMICS AND LITERACY

Prior to their current renaissance, comics were often viewed, at best, as popular entertainment and, at worst, as a dangerous influence on youth. Such attitudes were certainly prevalent in the early 1950s when comics were at their most popular, with critics such as Fredric Wertham voicing the most strenuous arguments against comics in his 1954 book *Seduction of the Innocent* (for an extended discussion of this debate, see Dorrell, Curtis, and Rampal). Wertham baldly asserts that "[c]omic books are death on reading" (121). He goes on, "Reading troubles in children are on the increase. An important cause of this increase is the comic book. A very large proportion of children who cannot read well habitually read comic books. They are not really readers, but gaze mostly at the pictures, picking up a word here and there. Among the worst readers is a very high percentage of comic-book addicts who spend very much time 'reading' comic books. They are book-worms without books" (122). According to this thinking, children who read comic books are not really reading; they are simply looking at the pictures as a way to avoid engaging in the complex processes of learning to read. The problem, according to Wertham, is that in reading comics children focus far too much on the image to make meaning and avoid engaging with the written word, a semiotic system that Wertham clearly sees as both more complex and more important. Though he sees the visuality of comics as dangerous, Wertham shares the notion with current proponents of comics that the visual is more easily ingested and interpreted than the written. Whether the visual acts as a hindrance or a help to the acquisition of word-based literacy, the key idea remains that the visual is subservient to the written.

When I was growing up in the 1970s, I never saw comics in school or in the public library unless they were being read surreptitiously behind the cover of a novel or other officially sanctioned book. Over the last decade, however, there has been a movement to claim a value for comics in the literacy education of children. Comics have made their way into schools mainly as a scaffold for later learning that is perceived to be more difficult, in terms of both the literate practices and content involved. For example, *Comics in Education*, the online version of Gene Yang's final project for his master's degree at California State University, Hayward, embodies thinking that is typical of many educators who advocate the use of comics in the classroom. Yang, a teacher and cartoonist, claims that the educational strength of comics is that they are motivating, visual, permanent, intermediary, and popular. In emphasizing the motivational, visual permanency (in the way it slows down the flow of information), intermediacy, and the popular, such approaches inadvertently and ironically align themselves with Wertham's ideas about the relationship between word and image, even while bringing comics into the mainstream of education. Comics in this formulation are seen simply as a stepping stone to the acquisition of other, higher skills. As a teaching tool, then, comics are seen primarily as a way to motivate through their popularity and to help slow-learning students, especially in the acquisition of reading skills (see Haugaard; Koenke). While I agree with these attempts to argue for the value of comics in education, such an approach has limited value.

Libraries have also been important in the reconsideration of the place of comics as appropriate texts for children in their literacy learning and acquisition. Recently, many librarians have been arguing for the introduction of comics into library collections, usually in the form of graphic novels, as a way to get children into the library and interested in reading. The main thrust of this argument is that the presence of graphic novels will make the library seem cool and interesting, especially among the so-called reluctant readers, mainly adolescent boys, who seem to show little interest in reading or in libraries (see Crawford; Simmons). Graphic novels can compete with video games, television, and movies, giving the library the advantage it needs to get this specifically targeted demographic through the door. Many public libraries and librarians have seen the power of comics and graphic novels as a tool for drawing young people into the library, getting them first to read those comics and then building on that scaffold to turn them into lifelong readers. Again, while I agree with the inclusion of comics and graphic novels in library collections, such an approach places severe limitations on the possibilities of our uses of the medium as literacy educators.

To think through these ideas, let's assume that this strategy has some of its desired effects in drawing reluctant readers into the library and coaxing them to read. What can we then say about the effects of this approach and its conception of comics and their relation to developing literate practices? On the one hand, the use of graphic novels is seen as one strategy in teaching and encouraging literacy and literate practices; on the other hand, graphic novels are still regarded as a way station on the road to "higher" forms of literacy and to more challenging and, by implication, worthwhile texts. I'm not trying to suggest that reading comics or graphic novels exists apart from the world of word-based texts as a whole or the complex matrix of literacy acquisition. Rather, I'm simply pointing out that in the development of children's and adolescents' literacies, reading comics has almost always been seen as a debased form of word-based literacy, albeit an important intermediate step to more advanced forms of textual literacy, rather than as a complex form of multimodal literacy.

COMICS AS MULTIMODAL LITERACY: THE THEORY

If we think about comics as multimodal texts that involve multiple kinds of meaning making, we do not give up the benefits of word-based literacy instruction but strengthen it through the inclusion of visual and other literacies. This complex view of literacy is touched on but never fully fleshed out in two excellent recent articles on comics and education: Rocco Versaci's "How Comic Books Can Change the Way Our Students See Literature: One Teacher's Perspective" and Bonny Norton's "The Motivating Power of Comic Books: Insights from Archie Comic Readers." By situating our thinking about comics, literacy, and education within a framework that views literacy as occurring in multiple modes, we can use comics to greater effectiveness in our teaching at all levels by helping us to arm students with the critical-literacy skills they need to negotiate diverse systems of meaning making.

I'm going to offer an example of how comics engage multiple literacies by looking at Ted Naifeh's *Polly and the Pirates*, but first let me give a brief outline of these multiple systems of meaning making. As texts, comics provide a complex environment for the negotiation of meaning, beginning with the layout of the page itself. The comics page is separated into multiple panels, divided from each other by gutters, physical or conceptual spaces through which connections are made and meanings are negotiated; readers must fill in the blanks within these gutters and make connections between panels. Images of people, objects, animals, and settings, word balloons, lettering, sound effects, and gutters all come together to form page layouts that work to create meaning in distinctive ways and in multiple realms of meaning making. In these multiple realms of meaning making, comics engage in what the New London Group of literacy scholars calls *multimodality*, a way of thinking that seeks to push literacy educators, broadly defined and at all levels of teaching, to think about literacy in ways that move beyond a focus on strictly word-based literacy. In the introduction to the New London Group's collection, *Multiliteracies: Literacy Learning and the Design of Social Futures*, Bill Cope and Mary Kalantzis write that their approach "relates to the increasing multiplicity and integration of significant modes of meaning-making, where the textual is also related to the visual, the audio, the spatial, the behavioural, and so on.... Meaning is made in ways that are increasingly multimodal—in which written-linguistic modes of meaning are part and parcel of visual, audio, and spatial patterns of meaning" (5). By embracing the idea of multimodal literacy in relation to comics, then, we can help students engage critically with ways of making meaning that exist all around them, since multimodal texts include much of the content on the Internet, interactive multimedia, newspapers, television, film, instructional textbooks, and many other texts in our contemporary society.

Such a multimodal approach to reading and writing asserts that in engaging with texts, we interact with up to six design elements, including linguistic, audio, visual, gestural, and spatial modes, as well as multimodal design, "of a different order to the others as it represents the patterns of interconnections among the other modes" (New London Group 25). In the first two pages from

Polly and the Pirates, all of these design elements are present, including a textual and visual representation of the audio element. Despite the existence of these multiple modes of meaning making, however, the focus in thinking about the relationship between comics and education is almost always on the linguistic element, represented here by the words in the words balloons (or, in the conventions of comics, the dialogue from each of the characters) and the narrative text boxes in the first three panels (which we later find out are also spoken dialogue by a narrator present in the story).

As discussed earlier, comics are seen as a simplified version of word-based texts, with the words supplemented and made easier to understand by the pictures. If we take a multimodal approach to texts such as comics, however, the picture of meaning making becomes much more complex. In word-based texts, our interaction with words forms an environment for meaning making that is extremely complex. In comics and other multimodal texts, there are five other elements added to the mix. Thought about in this way, comics are not just simpler versions of word-based texts but can be viewed as the complex textual environments that they are.

COMICS AS MULTIMODAL LITERACY: *POLLY AND THE PIRATES* IN THE CLASSROOM

In comics, there are elements present besides words, but these elements are just as important in making meaning from the text. In fact, it is impossible to make full sense of the words on the page in isolation from the audio, visual, gestural, and spatial. For example, the first page of *Polly and the Pirates* (the first issue of a six-issue miniseries) opens with three panels of words from what the reader takes to be the story's narrative voice. Why? Partially it is because of *what* the words say — how they introduce a character and begin to set up the story — but also it is because of the text boxes that enclose the words. That is, most people understand from their experiences of reading comics at some point in their history that words in text boxes almost always contain the story's narrative voice and denote a different kind of voice than do words in dialogue balloons. What's more, these text boxes deviate in shape and design from the even rectangles usually seen in comics; instead, they are depicted more like scrolls, a visual element that calls to mind both the time period and genre associated with pirates. Not only does this visual element help to place the reader temporally and generically, but it, along with lettering and punctuation, also aids in indicating tone, voice inflection, cadence, and emotional tenor by giving visual representation to the text's audio element. We are better able to "hear" the narrator's voice because we can see what words are emphasized by the bold lettering, and we associate particular kinds of voices with the narrative voice of a pirate's tale, especially emphasized here by the shape of the text boxes. Both the visual and the audio thus influence the way we read the words in a comic, as can be seen in these three opening panels.

It seems to me, however, that the key lies in going beyond the way we make meaning from the words alone and considering the other visual elements, as well as the gestural and spatial. If I were teaching this text, I would engage students in a discussion about how they understand what is going on in the story and how they make meaning from it. Depending on the level of the class, I would stress different elements at varying levels of complexity. Here I will offer an example of how I make meaning from these pages and of some of the elements I might discuss with students.

In talking about the visual, I would consider such things as the use of line and white space, shading, perspective, distance, depth of field, and composition. The gestural refers to facial expression and body posture, while the spatial refers to the meanings of environmental and architectural space, which, in the case of comics, can be conceived as the layout of panels on the page and the relation between these panels through use of gutter space. The

© 2006 TED NAIFEH. PUBLISHED BY ONO PRESS INC. USED WITH PERMISSION.

opening panel depicts a ship, mainly in silhouette, sailing on the ocean; we are not given details, but instead see the looming presence of a ship that we are led to believe is a pirate ship by the words in the text boxes. The ship is in the center of an unbordered panel and is the only element in focus, though its details are obscured. The unbordered panel indicates openness, literally and metaphorically, and this opening shot thus acts much in the same way as an establishing shot in a film, orienting us both in terms of place and in terms of genre. The second panel pulls in closer to reveal a silhouetted figure standing on the deck of the ship. She is framed between the sails, and the panel's composition draws our eyes toward her as the central figure in the frame. She is clearly at home, one arm thrust forward while the other points back with sword in hand, her legs anchoring herself securely as she gazes across the ocean. The third panel pulls in even farther to a close-up of her face, the top half in shadow and the bottom half showing a slight smile. She is framed by her sword on the left and the riggings of the ship on the right, perfectly in her element, yet obscured from our view. Here

and in the previous panel, gestural and visual design indicate who is the center of the story and the way in which she confidently belongs in this setting. At the same time, the spatial layout of the page and the progression of the panels from establishing shot to close-up and from unbordered panels to bordered and internally framed panels help us to establish the relationship of the woman to the ship and to the story; as we move from one panel to the next, we must make connections between the panels that are implied by the gutter. Linguistic, visual, audio, gestural, and spatial elements combine in these first three panels to set up expectations in the reader for the type of story and its narrative approach. Taken together, these elements form a multimodal system of meaning making.

What happens in the fourth panel serves to undercut these expectations as we find out that the narrative voice actually belongs to one of the characters in the story, as evidenced by the shift from text box to dialogue balloon even though the voice is clearly the same as in the first three panels of the page. Spatially, we are presented with a larger panel that is visually dominated by the presence of a book called *A History of the Pirate Queen*. This book presumably details the story to which we had been introduced in the first three panels. The character holding the book is presenting it to someone and, because of the panel's composition, is also effectively presenting it to us, the readers. The gesture becomes one of offering this story up to us, a story that simultaneously becomes a romance as well as a pirate story as evidenced by the words the character says and the way she says them (with the bold emphasis on *dream* and *marry*). At this point, we do not know who this character is or to whom she is speaking, and the answers to these questions will be deferred until we turn to the second page.

On the first panel of page 2, we see three girls, each taking up about a third of the panel, with them and the background in focused detail. Both the words and facial expression of the first girl indicate her stance toward the story, while the words and facial expression of the second girl indicate her indignation at the attitude of the first girl (whom we learn is named Sarah). The third girl is looking to the right, away from the other two, and has a blank expression on her face. The next panel depicts the second and third girls, pulling in to a tighter close-up that balances one girl and either side of the panel and obscures the background so that we will focus on their faces and dialogue. The unbordered panel again indicates openness and momentary detachment from their surroundings. Polly is at a loss for words and is not paying attention to the other girl, as indicated by the ellipses and truncated dialogue balloons, as well as her eyes that are pointing to the right, away from the other girl. Spatially, the transition to panel 3 once more encloses them in the world that we now see is a classroom in an overhead shot that places the students in relation to the teacher. The teacher's words restore order to the class and, on a narrative level, name the third of the three girls and the narrative voice of the opening page. The story of the pirates that began on page 1 is now contained within the world of school, and we are left to wonder how the tensions between these two stories/worlds will play out in the remaining pages. As you can see, much more than words alone is used to make meaning in these first two pages of *Polly and the Pirates*.

CONCLUSION

My process of making meaning from these pages of *Polly and the Pirates* is one of many meanings within the matrix of possibilities inherent in the text. As a reader, I am actively engaging with the "grammars," including discourse and genre conventions, within this multimodal text as I seek to create/negotiate meaning; such a theory of meaning making with multimodal texts acknowledges the social and semiotic structures that surround us and within which we exist, while at the same time it recognizes individual agency and experience in the creation of meaning. Knowledge of linguistic, audio, visual, gestural, and spatial conventions within comics affects the ways in which we read and the meanings we assign to texts, just as knowledge of conventions within word-based literacy affects the ways in which those texts are read. For example, the conventions discussed above in terms of the grammar of comics would have been available to Naifeh as he created *Polly and the Pirates*, just as they are also available to me and to all other readers of his text. These conventions form the underlying structure of the process of making meaning, while familiarity with these conventions, practice in reading comics, interest, prior experience, and attention given to that reading all come into play in the exercise of agency on the part of the reader (and writer). Structure and agency interact so that we are influenced by design conventions and grammars as we read but are not determined by them; though we are subject to the same set of grammars, my reading of the text is not necessarily the same as that of someone else.

Reading and writing multimodal texts, then, is an active process, both for creators and for readers who by necessity engage in the active production of meaning and who use all resources available to them based on their familiarity with the comics medium and its inherent grammars, their histories, life experiences, and interests. In turn, every act of creating meaning from a multimodal text, happening as it does at the intersection of structure and agency, contributes to the ongoing process of becoming a multimodally literate person. By teaching students to become conscious and critical of the ways in which they make meaning from multimodal texts such as comics, we can also teach students to become more literate with a wide range of multimodal texts. By complicating our view of comics so that we do not see them as simply an intermediary step to more complex word-based literacy, we can more effectively help students become active creators, rather than passive consumers, of meaning in their interactions with a wide variety of multimodal texts. In doing so, we harness the real power of comics in the classroom and prepare students for better negotiating their worlds of meaning.

WORKS CITED

B., David. *Epileptic.* New York: Pantheon, 2005.

Cope, Bill, and Mary Kalantzis. "Introduction: Multiliteracies: The Beginnings of an Idea." *Multiliteracies: Literacy Learning and the Design of Social Futures.* Ed. Bill Cope and Mary Kalantzis. New York: Routledge, 2000. 3–8.

Crawford, Philip. "A Novel Approach: Using Graphic Novels to Attract Reluctant Readers." *Library Media Connection* 22.5 (Feb. 2004): 26–28.

Dorrell, Larry D., Dan B. Curtis, and Kuldip R. Rampal. "Book-Worms without Books? Students Reading Comic Books in the School House." *Journal of Popular Culture* 29 (Fall 1995): 223–34.

Haugaard, Kay. "Comic Books: Conduits to Culture?" *The Reading Teacher* 27.1 (Oct. 1973): 54–55.

Koenke, Karl. "The Careful Use of Comic Books." *The Reading Teacher* 34.5 (Feb. 1981): 592–95.

McCloud, Scott. *Understanding Comics: The Invisible Art.* New York: Harper, 1993.

Naifeh, Ted. *Polly and the Pirates* 1 (Sept. 2005): 1–2.

New London Group, The. "A Pedagogy of Multiliteracies: Designing Social Futures." *Multiliteracies: Literacy Learning and the Design of Social Futures.* Ed. Bill Cope and Mary Kalantzis. New York: Routledge, 2000. 9–37.

Norton, Bonny. "The Motivating Power of Comic Books: Insights from Archie Comic Readers." *The Reading Teacher* 57.2 (Oct. 2003): 140–47.

Satrapi, Marjane. *Persepolis.* New York: Pantheon, 2003.

Simmons, Tabitha. "Comic Books in My Library?" *PNLA Quarterly* 67.3 (Spring 2003): 12, 20.

Versaci, Rocco. "How Comic Books Can Change the Way Our Students See Literature: One Teacher's Perspective." *English Journal* 91.2 (Mar. 2001): 61–67.

Wertham, Fredric. *Seduction of the Innocent.* New York: Rinehart, 1954.

Yang, Gene. *Comics in Education.* 2003. 29 Aug. 2006 <http://www.humblecomics.com/comicsedu/index.html>.

Discussion Questions

1. In your own words, describe how Dr. Jacobs constructs meaning from the comics panels analyzed in this article.

2. What do you think he means by the phrase *multimodal text*?

3. Study one of the comics panels for a minute, and consider how you make meaning from it. Freewrite for five minutes about your own process for making sense of what the comic means.

4. Freewrite for five minutes discussing something you were asked to interpret in the past: perhaps a painting, a novel, a poem, or something else. How did you make meaning of what you were observing and interpreting?

STRATEGIES FOR CLOSE READING AND OBSERVATION

For most of us, when we observe a printed text closely, we highlight, underline, and take notes in the margins. If we're analyzing a visual or aural text, we might take notes on our thoughts, observations, and questions. We might keep a separate notebook or computer file in which we expand on our notes or clarify meaning. As with any skill, the more you practice these steps, the better you'll become at interpretation. We encourage you to take detailed notes, underline passages if applicable, and actively engage with a text when conducting your observation.

We recommend two specific data-collection steps for humanistic inquiry. First, we suggest that you take notes in the margins for a printed text or on a separate sheet of paper as you read, view, or listen to a text to be interpreted. These notes will draw your attention to passages that may serve as direct evidence to support points you'll make later. Additionally, you can elaborate in more detail when something meaningful in the text draws your attention. Jotting down page numbers, audio/video file time markers, and paragraph numbers is often a helpful step for cataloging your notes. The key is to commit fully to engaging with a text by systematically recording your observations.

Second, we recommend developing a **content/form-response grid** to organize the essential stages of your interpretation. The "content" is what happens in the text, and the "form" is how the text's creator structures the piece. In the case of a painting, you might comment on the materials used, the artist's technique, the color palette and imagery choice, or the historical context of the piece. In the case of a religious or political text, you might examine style, language, and literary devices used. The "response" is your interpretation of what the elements you've identified might mean.

Now read the opening paragraphs from "The Story of an Hour," a very brief short story by Kate Chopin published in 1894 that is now recognized as a classic work of American literature. The excerpt includes a student's notes in the margins followed by a content/form-response grid. Notice the frequency of notes the student takes in the margins and the kinds of questions she asks at this early stage. She offers a fairly equal balance of questions and claims. Pay attention to how she follows the two steps of humanistic inquiry mentioned above:

1. Examine the text and take careful notes. Try keeping marginal notes (if appropriate) and/or separate notebook or sheets of paper to expand on your notes.

2. Complete a content/form-response grid based on the notes you collect.

Excerpt from **The Story of an Hour**

KATE CHOPIN

Heart trouble? I wonder what kind of trouble.

The news of her husband's death is delivered by her sister.

Knowing that Mrs. Mallard was afflicted with a heart trouble, great care was taken to break to her as gently as possible the news of her husband's death. It was her sister Josephine who told her, in broken sentences; veiled hints that revealed in half concealing. Her husband's friend Richards was there, too, near her. It was he who had been in the newspaper office when intelligence of the railroad disaster was received, with Brently Mallard's name leading the list of "killed." He had only taken the time to assure himself of its truth by a second telegram, and had hastened to forestall any less careful, less tender friend in bearing the sad message.

Why would she act differently from other women hearing the same kind of news?

Interesting comparison. The storm-like quality of her grief.

She did not hear the story as many women have heard the same, with a paralyzed inability to accept its significance. She wept at once, with sudden, wild abandonment, in her sister's arms. When the storm of grief had spent itself she went away to her room alone. She would have no one follow her.

Why is she "exhausted"? Interesting word choice.

There stood, facing the open window, a comfortable, roomy armchair. Into this she sank, pressed down by a physical exhaustion that haunted her body and seemed to reach into her soul.

There are lots of images of life here. This really contrasts with the dark news of the story's opening.

She could see in the open square before her house the tops of trees that were all aquiver with the new spring life. The delicious breath of rain was in the air. In the street below a peddler was crying his wares. The notes of a distant song which some one was singing reached her faintly, and countless sparrows were twittering in the eaves.

This student's annotations can be placed into a content/form-response grid that helps her keep track of the ideas she had as she read and observed closely, both for information (*what*) and for ways the text shaped her experience of it (*how*). Notice that the student uses the Content/Form section to summarize the comments from her annotations, and then she reflects on her annotations in the Response section:

Content/Form Notes (*what* and *how*)	Response (What effect does it have on me?)
Heart trouble? I wonder what kind of trouble.	*There's a mystery here. What's wrong with Mrs. Mallard's heart?*
The news of her husband's death is delivered by her sister.	*Interesting that a female relative is chosen to deliver the news. A man would be too rough?*
Why would she act differently from other women hearing the same kind of news?	*I wonder what is special about Mrs. Mallard that causes her reaction to be different. Is she putting on a show? Story says her reaction was "sudden" and "wild."*
Why is she "exhausted"? Interesting word choice.	*Maybe this has to do with her heart condition or with how physically draining her mourning is.*
There are lots of images of life here. This really contrasts with the dark news of the story's opening.	*This is a sudden change in feeling. Everything is so calm and pleasant now. What happened?*

The purpose of this activity is to construct meaning from the text based on the student's close observation of it. This is an interpretation. We can already see that major complexities in the story are beginning to emerge in the student's response notes—such as the importance of the story's setting and the change that occurs in Mrs. Mallard.

Because content/form-response grids like the one above allow you to visualize both your ideas and how you arrived at those ideas, we recommend using this activity anytime you have to observe a text closely in order to interpret its meaning. For a non-alphabetic text, start with the content/form-response grid and use it to log your initial notes as you observe; then reflect later. In the end, such an activity provides a log of details that can help explain how you arrived at a particular conclusion or argument about the text.

INSIDE WORK   **Annotating a Text**

> Use this activity as an opportunity to practice close reading. Read the whole text of Kate Chopin's "The Story of an Hour" on pages 126–28, and then annotate the text as you read, paying particular attention to the following elements.
>
> - **Content:** what is being said (the facts, the events, and who the characters are)
>
> - **Form:** how it is being said (the style, language, literary techniques, and narrative perspective)

A follow-up activity at the conclusion of the story asks you to draw a content/form-response grid like the example above. It's important to take extensive marginal notes (perhaps one or two comments per paragraph) and highlight and underline passages as you read the story. These notes will help shape your content/form-response grid and will strengthen your interpretation. We encourage you to expand on your notes on a separate sheet of paper while you read the story. ◗

The Story of an Hour

KATE CHOPIN

Knowing that Mrs. Mallard was afflicted with a heart trouble, great care was taken to break to her as gently as possible the news of her husband's death.

It was her sister Josephine who told her, in broken sentences; veiled hints that revealed in half concealing. Her husband's friend Richards was there, too, near her. It was he who had been in the newspaper office when intelligence of the railroad disaster was received, with Brently Mallard's name leading the list of "killed." He had only taken the time to assure himself of its truth by a second telegram, and had hastened to forestall any less careful, less tender friend in bearing the sad message.

She did not hear the story as many women have heard the same, with a paralyzed inability to accept its significance. She wept at once, with sudden, wild abandonment, in her sister's arms. When the storm of grief had spent itself she went away to her room alone. She would have no one follow her.

There stood, facing the open window, a comfortable, roomy armchair. Into this she sank, pressed down by a physical exhaustion that haunted her body and seemed to reach into her soul.

She could see in the open square before her house the tops of trees that were all aquiver with the new spring life. The delicious breath of rain was in the air. In the street below a peddler was crying his wares. The notes of a distant song which some one was singing reached her faintly, and countless sparrows were twittering in the eaves.

There were patches of blue sky showing here and there through the clouds that had met and piled one above the other in the west facing her window.

She sat with her head thrown back upon the cushion of the chair, quite motionless, except when a sob came up into her throat and shook her, as a child who has cried itself to sleep continues to sob in its dreams.

She was young, with a fair, calm face, whose lines bespoke repression and even a certain strength. But now there was a dull stare in her eyes, whose gaze was fixed away off yonder on one of those patches of blue sky. It was not a glance of reflection, but rather indicated a suspension of intelligent thought.

There was something coming to her and she was waiting for it, fearfully. What was it? She did not know; it was too subtle and elusive to name. But she felt it, creeping out of the sky, reaching toward her through the sounds, the scents, the color that filled the air.

Now her bosom rose and fell tumultuously. She was beginning to recognize this thing that was approaching to possess her, and she was striving to beat it back with her will—as powerless as her two white slender hands would have been.

When she abandoned herself a little whispered word escaped her slightly parted lips. She said it over and over under her breath: "free, free, free!" The vacant stare and the look of terror that had followed it went from her eyes. They stayed keen and bright. Her pulses beat fast, and the coursing blood warmed and relaxed every inch of her body.

She did not stop to ask if it were or were not a monstrous joy that held her. A clear and exalted perception enabled her to dismiss the suggestion as trivial.

She knew that she would weep again when she saw the kind, tender hands folded in death; the face that had never looked save with love upon her, fixed and gray and dead. But she saw beyond that bitter moment a long procession of years to come that would belong to her absolutely. And she opened and spread her arms out to them in welcome.

There would be no one to live for during those coming years; she would live for herself. There would be no powerful will bending hers in that blind persistence with which men and women believe they have a right to impose a private will upon a fellow-creature. A kind intention or a cruel intention made the act seem no less a crime as she looked upon it in that brief moment of illumination.

And yet she had loved him—sometimes. Often she had not. What did it matter! What could love, the unsolved mystery, count for in face of this possession of self-assertion which she suddenly recognized as the strongest impulse of her being!

"Free! Body and soul free!" she kept whispering.

Josephine was kneeling before the closed door with her lips to the keyhole, imploring for admission. "Louise, open the door! I beg, open the door—you will make yourself ill. What are you doing, Louise? For heaven's sake open the door."

"Go away. I am not making myself ill." No; she was drinking in a very elixir of life through that open window.

Her fancy was running riot along those days ahead of her. Spring days, and summer days, and all sorts of days that would be her own. She breathed a quick prayer that life might be long. It was only yesterday she had thought with a shudder that life might be long.

She arose at length and opened the door to her sister's importunities. There was a feverish triumph in her eyes, and she carried herself unwittingly like a goddess of Victory. She clasped her sister's waist, and together they descended the stairs. Richards stood waiting for them at the bottom.

Some one was opening the front door with a latchkey. It was Brently Mallard who entered, a little travel-stained, composedly carrying his grip-sack and umbrella. He had been far from the scene of accident, and did not even know there had been one. He stood amazed at Josephine's piercing cry; at Richards' quick motion to screen him from the view of his wife.

But Richards was too late.

When the doctors came they said she had died of heart disease—of joy that kills.

INSIDE WORK **Preparing a Content/Form-Response Grid**

Based on your annotations and notes, construct a content/form-response grid modeled after the example on page 125. Be sure to include your responses to the items you identify in the Content/Form column. Remember that in this case "content" relates to what happens in the story, and "form," in the context of a literary text, relates to how the writer makes the story function through style, narrative perspective, and literary techniques.

Once you've completed your close reading, you might pair up with a classmate or two and share your content/form-response grids. When doing so, consider the following questions as part of your discussion.

1. What facts or events did you note about the story?

2. What did you notice about the ways Chopin shapes your experience of the story? What style or literary techniques did you note?

3. What patterns do you see in the notes you've taken in the Form column? What repeated comments did you make, or what elements strike you in a similar way? How would you explain the meaning of those patterns? ❱

RESPONDING TO THE INTERPRETATIONS OF OTHERS

LaunchPadSolo

Learn more about incorporating sources into your writing.

Before, during, and after observing a text, humanistic scholars also draw on the work of other scholars to build and support their interpretations. If you were interpreting Chopin's story, for example, you might review the notes you made in your content/form-response grid, search for interesting patterns, and then see if other scholars have noticed the same things. You might look for an element of the story that doesn't make sense to you and see if another scholar has already offered an interpretation. If you agree with the interpretation, you might cite it as support for your own argument. If you disagree, you might look for evidence in the story to show why you disagree and then offer your own interpretation.

As in other disciplines, scholars in the humanities draw on the work of others to make sure they're contributing something new to the ongoing conversation about the artifact, event, or phenomenon they're studying. They also read the work of others to determine if they agree or disagree with an interpretation. Because of the importance of specific language and detail in the humanities, scholars in the humanities quote one another's exact words often, and they also quote directly from their primary sources. We'll discuss some of the reasons for these conventions, and others, in the next section.

Conventions of Writing in the Humanities

Some writing conventions are shared across different fields in the humanities. Because the kinds of texts humanistic scholars examine can vary so much, though, there are also sometimes distinctions in writing conventions among its various fields. One of the challenges of learning the conventions of a disciplinary discourse community is figuring out the specific expectations for communicating with a specific academic audience. In this section, we turn our attention from *research in the humanities* to examine and interpret artifacts themselves, to *strategies of rhetorical analysis* that help us examine how scholars in the humanities write about those artifacts.

Many scholars learn about disciplinary writing conventions through imitation and examination of articles in their fields. Recall that in Chapter 5 we introduced a three-part method for analyzing an academic text by examining the conventions of structure, language, and reference. Applying this analytical framework to professional writing in the various humanities fields can help you further understand conventions appropriate for any given subfield. An awareness of the conventions for writing in any academic context may facilitate your success in writing in those contexts.

Dr. Shelley Garrigan teaches Spanish language and literature at North Carolina State University. As Dr. Garrigan describes in her Insider's View, scholars learn conventions of writing in their field through a variety of means, including learning from peers.

Insider's View
Peer-mentoring can play a role in understanding disciplinary conventions

SHELLEY GARRIGAN, SPANISH LANGUAGE AND LITERATURE

COURTESY OF SHELLEY GARRIGAN

"I learned [about the conventions of writing in my discipline] by trial and error. In graduate school, the papers that we wrote were expected to be publishable according to the academic standards of literary analysis, and yet I can recall no specific guidelines, rubrics, or feedback from professors geared toward teaching me to shape my writerly approach to the material. In fact, I remember that the feedback on a final paper that I received back from one professor in particular contained little more than a congratulations for so actively "seeking my voice." This effort was evidently enough to earn me an A– on the project, and yet I had no idea specifically what he meant. Nor was I sure that I should feel happy about being on the right track or bothered that I wasn't quite there yet.

"Peer-mentoring probably played the most significant role in the development of my professional writerly voice during graduate school. With a small group of fellow students, we regularly made informal arrangements with one another to read each other's papers. The praise and constructive criticism that we offered one another was a fundamental factor in my own development as a writer."

STRUCTURAL CONVENTIONS

From your experience in high school, you might already be familiar with common structural features of writing in the humanities. Arguments in the humanities are generally "thesis-driven"; that is, they make an interpretive claim about a text and then support that claim with specific evidence from the text and sometimes with material from other sources that support their interpretation. By contrast, arguments in the social sciences and the natural sciences are usually driven by a hypothesis that must be tested to come to a conclusion, which encourages a different structure (see Chapters 7 and 8). First we'll talk about how humanistic scholars develop research questions and thesis statements. Then we'll turn our attention to a common structure that many students learn in secondary school to support their thesis statements with evidence, which is loosely based on the structure of the thesis-driven argument, and we'll compare it with published scholarship in the humanities.

Insider's View
The research is going to support your own ideas
KAREN KEATON JACKSON, WRITING STUDIES

"When we talk about what the paper should look like, I let them know that the research part of your paper is not the longest part. I always say the longest part of your paper is this brainchild, your program that you're coming up with. And I say that purposely because I don't want the research running your paper. This is your paper, your voice. The research is going to support your own ideas.

"I think this sends the message that there's more to it than this; you can be more creative and not just rely on the research."

 LaunchPadSolo

Get expert advice on incorporating research.

DEVELOPING RESEARCH QUESTIONS AND THESIS STATEMENTS

An important part of the interpretation process is using observations to pose questions about a text. From these close observations, humanists develop *research questions* that they answer through their research. A research question in the humanities is the primary question a scholar asks about a text or set of texts. It is the first step in interpretation because questions grow out of our observations and the patterns or threads that we notice. A *thesis statement* is an answer to a research question and is most persuasive when supported by logical evidence. Thesis statements are discussed in more detail in Chapter 3 as the central claim of an argument. It's important to note that developing a research question works best when it is generated prior to writing a thesis statement. Novice writers can sometimes overlook this crucial step in the writing process and attempt to make a thesis statement without formulating a well-realized research question first.

As John McCurdy mentions earlier in this chapter, some of the most important questions for humanists begin by asking, "Why?" Why does George befriend Lenny in *Of Mice and Men*? Why did Pablo Picasso begin experimenting with cubism in his paintings in the early 1900s? Why did President Lincoln frequently use religious imagery and language in public discourse? To answer such questions, humanistic scholars must collect evidence to support their claims, and in the humanities, evidence often originates from texts.

Many students confess to struggling with the process of writing a good thesis statement. A key to overcoming this hurdle is to realize that a good thesis statement comes first from asking thoughtful questions about a text and searching for answers to those questions through observation.

Examples of Research Questions and Corresponding Thesis Statements

© TECH GADGETS/ ALAMY

Research Question: Why does F. Scott Fitzgerald use the adjective *great* to describe Gatsby in *The Great Gatsby*?

Thesis Statement: The adjective *great* is used both ironically and derisively throughout F. Scott's Fitzgerald's novel *The Great Gatsby*, as evidenced by the use of Nick Carraway as the narrator and the carnival-like depictions of Gatsby's home and parties.

Research Question: Why did Georges-Pierre Seurat experiment with pointillism in the mid-1800s?

Thesis Statement: Georges-Pierre Seurat drew upon the scientific research of Ogden Rood and other color theorists to create paintings with minute brushstrokes in a style now called pointillism, which Seurat believed unified optically to make colors more vivid than in traditional painting styles of the time.

SUNDAY AFTERNOON ON THE ISLAND OF LA GRANDE JATTE, 1884–86 (OIL ON CANVAS), SEURAT, GEORGES-PIERRE (1859–91)/THE ART INSTITUTE OF CHICAGO, IL, USA/BRIDGEMAN IMAGES

Once you have carefully observed a text, gathered thorough notes, and developed a content/form-response grid as discussed earlier in the chapter, you're in a great position to begin brainstorming and drafting research questions. Recall that we encourage open-ended questions (*who, what, when, where, why,* and *how*) as opposed to closed, *yes/no* questions (questions that can be answered with a *yes* or *no*) as a pivotal step before drafting a thesis statement. Scholars in the humanities often start by asking questions that begin with *why*, but you might also consider questions of *what* and *how*.

INSIDE WORK   **Developing *Why*, *What*, and *How* Questions**

The process of asking questions after conducting a close reading of a text is part of interpretation, and it can help you generate effective research questions to guide the development of a thesis. In this activity, we walk you through developing potential research questions from your notes on "The Story of an Hour." You could easily follow these steps after observing another kind of text as well.

1. Review your notes on "The Story of an Hour," and develop three questions about the story's content and form using *Why* as a starter word.

2. Next, develop three questions using *What* as your starter word. Try to focus your questions on different aspects of the story's characters, language, style, literary techniques, or narrative perspective.

3. Then use *How* as a starter word to develop three more questions. Again, write your questions with a different aspect of the story as the central focus for each. That is, don't just repeat the same questions from your *What* or *Why* list, inserting *How* instead. Think of different questions that can help address the story's meaning.

Try sharing your questions with a fellow student, and discuss which ones might lead to promising thesis statements to ground an extended interpretation. Effective research questions have the following characteristics.

- They can be answered with specific evidence from the text and from your notes: an effective research question can be answered with evidence and not just feelings or opinions.

- They can be answered in more than one way (i.e., they might require you to make a claim as opposed to being questions of fact): an effective research question is debatable. ▶

DEVELOPING EFFECTIVE THESIS STATEMENTS

The thesis statement, or the central claim, asserts *what* the author intends to prove, and it may also provide insight into *how* it will be proven. Providing both of these elements in a thesis allows writers to establish a blueprint for the structure of their entire argument—what we describe as a complex thesis statement in Chapter 3. Based on the thesis alone, a reader can determine the central claim and see how the writer intends to go about supporting it.

In the following example, Sarah Ray provides a thesis for her interpretation of Chopin's "The Story of an Hour." Notice that she includes clues as to how she will prove her claim in the thesis statement itself:

Blueprint for how   —— Through Mrs. Mallard's emotional development and the concomitant juxta-
Sarah will prove her   position of the vitality of nature to the repressive indoors, Chopin exposes the
claim   role of marriage in the oppression of one's true self and desires.
Sarah's interpretation ——
of the story, provided
as a clear claim

Although it's not uncommon for thesis statements in humanistic scholarship to remain implied, as opposed to being stated explicitly, most interpretations explicitly assert a claim close to the beginning of the argument, often in the introductory paragraph (or, in a longer piece, paragraphs). Thesis statements may appear as single-sentence statements or may span multiple sentences.

Notice, for example, how Zenia Kish, a professor of American studies, states her claim at the end of the introductory section to her article "'My FEMA People': Hip-Hop as Disaster Recovery in the Katrina Diaspora." In the full text of the article, Kish builds up to this statement through several paragraphs of explanation, which all contribute to her thesis statement, shown here:

> I will examine how both national and local New Orleans artists identify with and rebel against the forces of marginalization that produced different senses of being a refugee, and also how they exploit marginality and the hustle as strategies to return home, however different or new that home may be. Providing listeners with an affective mapping of the social, economic, and discursive contradictions that produced the Katrina diaspora as refugees, post-Katrina hip-hop is a critical site for interrogating the ongoing tragedy of African American bodies that don't matter. (p. 673)

Blueprint for how Kish will prove her claim

Reasons provided for Kish's claim

Clear statement of Kish's claim

INSIDE WORK   Drafting Thesis Statements

Review the questions and responses you drafted in the "Developing *Why*, *What*, and *How* Questions" Inside Work activity. Some scholars use "I" in thesis statements, like the example from Zenia Kish, while others avoid using "I." Make sure you pay attention to requirements for the particular type of writing you're doing in your discipline. (Don't hesitate to ask your professor if "I" statements are acceptable.) You can always edit the thesis statement later to take out "I" if needed, but sometimes it helps when figuring out what you want to say to include yourself in the statement. So, for now, consider structuring your responses to your two selected questions as separate thesis statements, using an "I" statement in the following form.

By examining _____ (a, b, c, etc.—the evidence you have found), I argue that _____ (your claim).

Example Thesis Statement: **By examining Mrs. Mallard's emotional development and the juxtaposition of the vitality of nature to the repressive indoors in the story, I argue that Chopin exposes the role of marriage in the story to show the oppression of a person's true self and desires.**

Now test the appropriateness of your claim by asking the following questions about it.

- **Is the thesis debatable?** Claims in the humanities are propositions, not statements of fact. For example, the assertion that "The Story of an Hour" deals with a wife's response to the news of her husband's death is a fact. It is not, therefore, debatable and will not be a very useful thesis. If, however, we assert that the wife's response to her husband's death demonstrates some characteristic of her relationship with her husband and with the institution of marriage, then we're proposing a debatable claim. This is a proposition we can try to prove, instead of a fact that is already obviously true.

- **Is the thesis significant?** Claims about texts should offer substantial insight into the meaning of the artifacts. They should account for as much of the artifacts as possible and avoid reducing their complexity. Have you paid attention to all of the evidence you collected, and have you looked at it in context? Are you considering all of the possible elements of the text that might contribute to your interpretation?

- **Does the thesis contribute to an ongoing scholarly conversation?** Effective thesis statements contribute to an ongoing conversation without repeating what others have already said about the text. How does the claim extend, contradict, or affirm other interpretations of the text?

Once you've analyzed Chopin's story and constructed two separate thesis statements, consider sharing them with a classmate, identifying strengths and weaknesses in both. How is your claim both argumentative and significant? How many direct quotes from the story would help support your points? Which of the two thesis statements offers a more significant insight into the story's meaning? ▶

FIVE-PARAGRAPH ESSAYS AND OTHER THESIS-DRIVEN TEMPLATES

Many students learn to write academic arguments following a template taught in primary and secondary school as the **five-paragraph essay.** This template places a thesis, or claim, at the front of the argument (often at the end of an introductory paragraph), devotes the body of the essay to supporting the thesis, and then offers a final paragraph of conclusion that connects all the parts of the argument by summarizing the main points and reminding readers of the argument's overall significance.

LaunchPadSolo

See more on the transition into college writing.

While the premise behind this structure is based on some conventions of the humanities, following the template too closely could get you into trouble. Not every thesis has three points to prove, for example, giving you three body paragraphs in which to present evidence. And sometimes an introduction needs to be longer than one paragraph—as in the case of Zenia Kish's article " 'My FEMA People': Hip-Hop as Disaster Recovery in the Katrina Diaspora," which originally appeared in the academic journal *American Quarterly.* The elements of the template that tend to be consistent in scholarship in the humanities, though, are these:

- Thesis statements generally appear toward the beginning of the argument in an introduction that explains the scope and importance of the topic.

- The body of the argument presents evidence gathered from the text to support the thesis.

- The conclusion connects the parts of the argument together to reinforce the thesis, summarizing the argument's important elements and reminding readers of its overall significance.

A template such as this one can provide a useful place to start as you organize your argument, but be careful not to allow a template to restrict your argument by oversimplifying your understanding of how humanistic scholars structure their writing.

OTHER STRUCTURAL CONVENTIONS IN THE HUMANITIES

There are other structural features conventional of writing in the humanities that you should consider when you begin a project in the discipline.

Title

Scholars in the humanities value the artistic and creative use of language, and titles of their work often reflect that value. In contrast to articles in the social sciences and the natural sciences, which often have descriptive titles that directly state the topic of study, articles in the humanities tend to have titles that play with language in creative ways, sometimes using quotations from the text in interesting ways. Humanistic scholars are also notorious for their love of subtitles. Here are a few examples:

- *Burlesque West: Showgirls, Sex, and Sin in Postwar Vancouver*
- " 'The Fault of Being Purely French': The Practice and Theory of Landscape Painting in Post-Revolutionary France"
- "Reforming Bodies: Self-Governance, Anxiety, and Cape Colonial Architecture in South Africa, 1665–1860"
- "Resident Franchise: Theorizing the Science Fiction Genre, Conglomerations, and the Future of Synergy"

Paragraphs and Transitions

In arguments in the humanities, paragraphs tend to link back to the thesis by developing a reason and providing evidence. The paragraphs are often connected through **transitional words or phrases** (e.g., *similarly, in addition, in contrast, for example*) that guide readers by signaling shifts between and among the parts of an argument. These words and phrases help the reader understand the order in which the reasons are presented and how one paragraph connects to the preceding one.

LANGUAGE CONVENTIONS IN THE HUMANITIES

Writing in the humanities generally follows several conventions of language use that might sound familiar because they're often taught in English classes. Keep in mind, though, that even though these conventions are common in the humanities, they aren't necessarily conventional in other disciplinary areas.

Descriptive and Rhetorical Language

Writers in the humanities often use language that is creative or playful, not only when producing artistic texts but sometimes also when writing interpretations of texts. For example, you might notice that writing in the humanities uses figurative language and rhetorical devices (similes, metaphors, and alliteration, for example) more often than in other disciplines. Because writers in the humanities are studying texts so closely, they often pay similarly close attention to the text they're creating, and they take great care to choose precise, and sometimes artistic, language. In many cases, the language not only conveys information; it also engages in rhetorical activity of its own.

Active Voice

Writing in the humanities tends to privilege the use of the active voice rather than the passive voice. Sentences written in the **active voice** clearly state the subject of the sentence, the agent, as the person or thing doing the action. By contrast, the **passive voice** inverts the structure of the sentence, obscuring or eliminating mention of the agent. Let's look at three simple examples.

> **Active Voice:** The girl chased the dog.
>
> **Passive Voice (agent obscured):** The dog was chased by the girl.
>
> **Passive Voice (agent not mentioned):** The dog was chased.

In the first example, the girl is the subject of the sentence and the person (the agent) doing the action — chasing. In the second sentence, the girl is still there, but her presence is less prominent because the dog takes the subject's position at the beginning of the sentence. In the final sentence, the girl is not mentioned at all.

Now let's look at an example from a student paper in the humanities to understand why active voice is usually preferred. In Sarah Ray's interpretation of "The Story of an Hour" (printed in full on pp. 143–49), she writes this sentence in the introduction, using active voice:

> **Active Voice:**   Kate Chopin presents a completely different view of marriage in "The Story of an Hour," published in 1894.

If Sarah were to write the sentence in the passive voice, eliminating the agent, it would look like this:

Passive Voice: A completely different view of marriage is presented in "The Story of an Hour," published in 1894.

In this case, the active voice is preferred because it gives credit to the author, Kate Chopin, who created the story and the character. Scholars in the humanities value giving credit to the person doing the action, conducting the study, or creating a text. Active voice also provides the clearest, most transparent meaning—another aspect of writing that is valued in the humanities. In Chapters 7 and 8, we'll discuss why the passive voice is sometimes preferable in the social sciences and the natural sciences.

Hedging

In the humanities, writers sometimes hedge the claims that they make when interpreting a text, even though they are generally quite fervent about defending their arguments once established. In fact, the sentence that you just read contains not one but three **hedges**, or qualifiers. Take a look:

> In the humanities, writers tend to hedge the claims that they make when interpreting a text.

Each highlighted phrase limits the scope of the claim in a way that is important to improve accuracy and to allow for other possibilities. In contrast, consider the next claim:

> Writers hedge the claims that they make.

If we had stated our claim that way, not only would it not be true, but you would immediately begin to think of exceptions. Even if we had limited the claim to writers in the humanities, you still might find exceptions to it. As the original sentence is written, we've allowed for other possibilities while still identifying a predominant trend in humanities writing.

Humanistic scholars hedge their claims for several reasons. The disciplines of the humanities don't tend to claim objectivity or neutrality in their research (for more detail, see Chapters 7 and 8), so they allow for other interpretations of and perspectives on texts. As an example, take a look at the first sentence of Dale Jacobs's Conclusion from his article printed earlier in the chapter:

> My process of making meaning from these pages of *Polly and the Pirates* is one of many meanings within the matrix of possibilities inherent in the text. (par. 16)

In this example, Jacobs not only hedges the interpretation he has offered, but he explicitly states that there are many possible meanings in the text he has just analyzed.

REFERENCE CONVENTIONS IN THE HUMANITIES

Scholars in the humanities frequently cite the work of others in their scholarship, especially when supporting an interpretation of a text. They often quote the language from their primary sources exactly instead of summarizing or paraphrasing, because the exact words or details included in the primary source might be important to the argument.

Engagement with Other Scholars

When humanistic scholars cite the work of other scholars, they show how their research contributes to ongoing conversations about a subject—whether they're agreeing with a previous interpretation, extending someone else's interpretation, or offering an alternative one. These citations can strengthen their own argument and provide direct support by showing that another scholar had a similar idea or by demonstrating how another scholar's ideas are incorrect, imprecise, or not fully developed.

As we mentioned in Chapter 4, you can integrate the work of others into your writing by paraphrasing, summarizing, or quoting directly. Scholars in the humanities use all these options, but they quote directly more often than scholars in other disciplines because the exact language or details from their primary sources are often important to their argument.

Take a look at this example from Zenia Kish's article "'My FEMA People': Hip-Hop as Disaster Recovery in the Katrina Diaspora." She situates her argument about the message of hip-hop music after Hurricane Katrina within the work of another scholar, Hazel Carby, who had written about the cultural meaning of the blues. Although Carby was writing about a genre that preceded hip-hop, Kish makes a connection between Carby's interpretation of the blues and her own interpretation of the message of hip-hop at a particular point in history:

> Where the early blues served to "sp[ea]k the desires which were released in the dramatic shift in social relations that occurred in a historical moment of crisis and dislocation," as Hazel Carby observes (36), I would argue that the post-Katrina moment is the first time that mainstream American hip-hop has taken up the thematic of contemporary black migration as a mass phenomenon in any significant way. (p. 674)

Establishing Focus/Stance

Most scholars in the humanities include references to the work of others early in their writing to establish what the focus and stance of their own research will be. Because abstracts appear in humanities scholarship less frequently than in social sciences and natural sciences research, the introduction to an article in the humanities provides a snapshot of how the researcher is positioning himself or herself in the ongoing conversation about an object of study.

As you read scholarship in the humanities, notice how frequently the text references or cites secondary sources in the opening paragraphs. Look at this example from the second page of Dale Jacobs's article on teaching literacy through the use of comics, on page 115 of this chapter. Jacobs situates his work historically among work published about comics in the 1950s, and he also references the research of other scholars who had already written about that history in more detail:

> Prior to their current renaissance, comics were often viewed, at best, as popular entertainment and, at worst, as a dangerous influence on youth. Such attitudes were certainly prevalent in the early 1950s when comics were at their most popular, with critics such as Fredric Wertham voicing the most strenuous arguments against comics in his 1954 book *Seduction of the Innocent* (for an extended discussion of this debate, see Dorrell, Curtis, and Rampal). (par. 3)

In these two sentences, Jacobs positions his work within that of other scholars, showing how it's connected to and distinct from it. Also, by citing the work of Dorrell, Curtis, and Rampal, Jacobs doesn't have to write a lengthy history about a period that's tangentially related to his argument but not central to it.

DOCUMENTATION

A few documentation styles are prevalent in the humanities, and those styles tend to highlight elements of a source that are important in humanistic study. Many scholars in the humanities, especially in literature and languages, follow the documentation style of the Modern Language Association (MLA). Scholars in history and some other disciplines of the humanities follow the *Chicago Manual of Style* (CMS). When using CMS, scholars can choose between two kinds of citations. In the humanities, researchers generally use the footnote style of documentation.

The values of the humanities are most prevalent in the in-text citations of both MLA and CMS. In MLA, in-text citations appear in parenthetical references that include the author's last name and a page number, with no comma in between (Miller-Cochran et al. 139). The page number is included regardless of whether the cited passage was paraphrased, summarized, or quoted from—unlike in other common styles like APA, where page numbers are usually given only for direct quotations. One reason for including the page number in the MLA in-text citation is that humanistic scholars highly value the original phrasing of an argument or passage and might want to look at the original source. The page number makes searching easy for the reader, facilitating the possibility of examining the original context of a quotation or the original language of something that was paraphrased or summarized.

CMS style also supports looking for the information in the original source by giving the citation information in a footnote on the same page as the referenced material. Additionally, CMS allows authors to include descriptive details in a footnote that provides more information about where a citation came from in a source.

INSIDE WORK) **Analyzing Scholarly Writing in the Humanities**

Answer the following questions about a scholarly article in the humanities. You might choose to focus on Zenia Kish's article, referenced earlier in this chapter, or find another article on a topic that interests you more.

A. Structural Elements

- **Title** Does the title of the interpretation seek to entertain, to challenge, or to impress the reader somehow? Does the title reveal anything about the writer and his or her relationship to the intended audience?

- **Thesis** Can you identify a clear statement of thesis? Where is it located? Does the thesis preview the stages of the claim that will be discussed throughout the paper? In other words, does the thesis explicitly or implicitly provide a "blueprint" for guiding the reader through the rest of the paper? If so, what is it?

- **Paragraphs and Transitions** Look closely at four successive body paragraphs in the paper. Explain how each paragraph relates to the paper's guiding thesis. How does the writer transition between each of the paragraphs such that his or her ideas in each one stay linked together?

B. Language Elements

- **Descriptive and Rhetorical Language** Is the language of the text meant only to convey information, or does it engage in rhetorical activity? In other words, do similes, metaphors, or other rhetorical devices demonstrate attempts to be creative with language? If so, what are they?

- **Voice** Is the voice of the text primarily active or passive?

- **Conviction and Hedging** Is the writer convinced that his or her interpretation is correct? If so, in what way(s) does specific language convey that conviction? Alternatively, if the writer doesn't seem convinced of the certainty of his or her argument, is there evidence of hedging? That is, does the writer qualify statements with words and phrases such as *tend*, *suggest*, *may*, *it is probable that*, or *it is reasonable to conclude that*? What is the significance of hedging?

C. Reference Elements

- **Engagement with Other Scholars** Choose two or three examples from the article showing the author's use of another scholar's words or ideas, if appropriate. Explain how the writer uses the words and ideas of another to support his or her own argument. Keep in mind that a writer may use another's word or ideas as direct support by showing that another scholar has the same or similar ideas, or by demonstrating how another scholar's ideas are incorrect, imprecise, or not fully developed. Also, does the writer use block quotations? Does he or she fully integrate others' words and ideas in his or her own sentences? Further, notice the writer's attitude toward other scholars: Does he or she treat other scholars' ideas fully and respectfully? Is there praise for others' ideas? Or are their ideas quickly dismissed? Is there any evidence of hostility in the writer's treatment of other voices?

- **Establishing Focus/Stance**   How frequently does the text reference or cite secondary source materials in the opening paragraphs? What function do such citations or references serve in the article's overall organization?

- **Documentation**   Look closely at examples of internal documentation as well as the writer's Works Cited or References page. What form of documentation applies? Why might the chosen documentation system be appropriate for writing about texts in the humanities? ❱

Genres of Writing in the Humanities

The disciplines included under the umbrella of the humanities vary widely, but several genres occur frequently across disciplines. In her Insider's View response to interview questions, Dr. Shelley Garrigan, an associate professor of Spanish at North Carolina State University, describes the kind of academic writing that she does most frequently.

Similar to scholars in the social sciences and the natural sciences, scholars in the humanities often present their research at conferences and publish their work in journal articles and books. In some fields of the humanities, books are highly valued, and scholars here tend to work individually more frequently than scholars in the social sciences and the natural sciences. Also, many scholars in the humanities engage in creative work and might present it at an art installation, reading, or exhibit.

TEXTUAL INTERPRETATION

One of the primary genres that humanities researchers write is an interpretation of a text or set of texts. The research methods and activities outlined in this chapter provide support for

Insider's View
Academics often write for other academics
SHELLEY GARRIGAN, SPANISH LANGUAGE AND LITERATURE

COURTESY OF SHELLEY GARRIGAN

"I write academic articles and am currently editing a book-length manuscript. The articles that I have are peer-reviewed and published in academic journals, in which the readership is largely limited to other specialists in my field or in fields that touch upon what I study. Although the book has the possibility of inviting a wider range of readers, it is contracted with an academic press, and so the reading public that it may attract will most likely also be associated with or limited to academia."

interpretations of texts in a variety of fields in the humanities. A **textual interpretation** makes a clear claim about the object of study and then supports that claim with evidence from the text, and often with evidence drawn from the interpretations of other scholars.

WRITING PROJECT **Interpreting a Text**

In this Writing Project, you'll complete a close reading and offer an interpretation of a text for an audience of your peers. Begin by selecting a text that you find particularly interesting. You may choose from a host of categories, including the ones listed here.

paintings	advertisements
photographs	short stories
sculptures	poems
buildings	music videos or recordings

As a model for reading closely, follow the procedures outlined earlier in this chapter for creating a content/form-response grid. As you read, view, listen to, and/or study the text and make notes, consider the ways you are interacting with the text by creating a form-function diagram: *What* are you learning, and *how* is the text itself shaping your experience of it?

Once your close reading is complete, formulate a thesis (or a claim) about the text. You'll need to provide evidence to support your thesis from the text itself. You might also include evidence from secondary sources as support. (See Chapter 3 for more information on developing a clear thesis and Chapter 4 for gathering secondary sources.) Remember that depending on the scope of your thesis, your interpretation may or may not require you to do additional research beyond your close reading of the text. As you compose your interpretation, also keep in mind the conventions of structure, language, and reference that typically appear in scholarship in the humanities. Integrate them into your interpretation as appropriate.

Insider Example
Student Interpretation of a Text

In the following essay, "Till Death Do Us Part: An Analysis of Kate Chopin's 'The Story of an Hour,'" Sarah Ray offers an interpretation of Chopin's story that relies on close observation of the text for support. Read her essay below, and pay particular attention to her thesis statement and to her use of evidence. Note how her thesis responds to the question, "How does Mrs. Mallard's marriage function in the story?" Sarah didn't use outside scholars to support her interpretation, so you could also consider how secondary sources might have provided additional support for her claim.

Sarah Ray

ENG 101

10 April 201-

Till Death Do Us Part: An Analysis of Kate Chopin's

"The Story of an Hour"

    The nineteenth century saw the publication of some of the most renowned romances in literary history, including the novels of Jane Austen and the Brontë sisters, Charlotte, Emily, and Anne. While their stories certainly have lasting appeal, they also inspired an unrealistic and sometimes unattainable ideal of joyful love and marriage. In this romanticized vision, a couple is merely two halves of a whole; one without the other compromises the happiness of both. The couple's lives, and even destinies, are so intertwined that neither individual worries about what personal desires and goals are being forsaken by commitment to the other. By the end of the century, in her "The Story of an Hour" (1894), Kate Chopin presents a completely different view of marriage. Through the perspective of a female protagonist, Louise Mallard, who believes her husband has just died, the author explores the more challenging aspects of marriage in a time when divorce was rare and disapproved of. Through Mrs. Mallard's emotional development and the concomitant juxtaposition of the vitality of nature to the repressive indoors, Chopin explores marriage as the oppression of one's true self and desires.

    "The Story of an Hour" begins its critique of marriage by ending one, when the news of Brently Mallard's death is gently conveyed to his wife, Louise. Chopin then follows Mrs. Mallard's different emotional stages in response to her husband's death. When the news is initially broken to Louise, "[s]he did not hear the story as many women have heard the same, with a paralyzed inability to accept its significance"

FORM: Ray uses a common line from marriage vows to indirectly indicate that she focuses on the role of marriage in her interpretation.

CONTENT: Ray clearly states her thesis and provides a preview about how she will develop and support her claim.

CONTENT: In this paragraph, Ray develops the first part of her thesis, the stages of Mrs. Mallard's emotional development.

(Chopin par. 3). She instead weeps suddenly and briefly, a "storm of grief" that passes as quickly as it had come (par. 3). This wild, emotional outburst and quick acceptance says a great deal about Louise's feelings toward her marriage. "[S]he had loved [her husband]—sometimes" (par. 15), but a reader may infer that Louise's quick acceptance implies that she has considered an early death for her spouse before. That she even envisions such a dark prospect reveals her unhappiness with the marriage. She begins to see, and even desire, a future without her husband. This desire is expressed when Louise is easily able to see past her husband's death to "a long procession of years to come that would belong to her absolutely" (par. 13). Furthermore, it is unclear whether her "storm of grief" is genuine or faked for the benefit of the family members surrounding her. The "sudden, wild abandonment" (par. 3) with which she weeps almost seems like Louise is trying to mask that she does not react to the news as a loving wife would. Moreover, the display of grief passes quickly; Chopin devotes only a single sentence to the action. Her tears are quickly succeeded by consideration of the prospects of a future on her own.

Chopin uses the setting to create a symbolic context for Louise's emotional outburst in response to the news of her husband's death. Louise is informed of Brently's death in the downstairs level of her home: "It was her sister Josephine who told her, in broken sentences; veiled hints that revealed in half concealing" (par. 2). No mention is made of windows, and the only portal that connects to the outside world is the door that admits the bearers of bad news. By excluding a link to nature, Chopin creates an almost claustrophobic environment to symbolize the oppression Louise feels from her marriage. It is no mistake that this setting plays host to Mrs. Mallard's initial

FORM: Ray primarily uses active voice to clarify who is doing the action in her sentences.

emotional breakdown. Her desires have been suppressed throughout her relationship, and symbolically, she is being suffocated by the confines of her house. Therefore, in this toxic atmosphere, Louise is only able to feel and show the emotions that are expected of her, not those that she truly experiences. Her earlier expression of "grief" underscores this disconnect, overcompensating for emotions that should come naturally to a wife who has just lost her husband, but that must be forced in Mrs. Mallard's case.

Chopin continues Mrs. Mallard's emotional journey only after she is alone and able to process her genuine feelings. After her brief display of grief has run its course, she migrates to her upstairs bedroom and sits in front of a window looking upon the beauty of nature. It is then and only then that Louise gives in not only to her emotions about the day's exploits, but also to those feelings she could only experience after the oppression of her husband died with him—dark desires barely explored outside the boundaries of her own mind, if at all. They were at first foreign to her, but as soon as Louise began to "recognize this thing that was approaching to possess her . . . she [strove] to beat it back with her will" (par. 10). Even then, after the source of her repression is gone, she fights to stifle her desires and physical reactions. The habit is so engrained that Louise is unable to release her emotions for fear of the unknown, of that which has been repressed for so long. However, "her bosom rose and fell tumultuously . . . When she abandoned herself a little whispered word escaped her slightly parted lips. She said it over and over under her breath: 'free, free, free!' . . . Her pulses beat fast, and the coursing blood warmed and relaxed every inch of her body" (pars. 10, 11). When she's allowed to experience them, Louise's feelings and desires provide a glimpse into a possible joyous

FORM: Ray uses transitions between paragraphs that indicate her organization and connect different ideas.

future without her husband, a future where "[t]here would be no powerful will bending hers in that blind persistence with which men and women believe they have a right to impose" (par. 14). Her marriage is over, and Louise appears finally to be able to liberate her true identity and look upon the future with not dread but anticipation.

The author's setting for this scene is crucial in the development of not only the plot but also her critique of marriage. Chopin sought to encapsulate the freedom Louise began to feel in her room with this scene's depiction of nature. For example, Chopin describes the view from Louise's bedroom window with language that expresses its vitality: "She could see in the open square before her house the tops of trees that were all aquiver with the new spring life" (par. 5). She goes on to say, "The delicious breath of rain was in the air. In the street below a peddler was crying his wares . . . and countless sparrows were twittering in the eaves" (par. 5). The very adjectives and phrases used to describe the outdoors seem to speak of bustling activity and life. This is in stark contrast to the complete lack of vivacity in the description of downstairs.

The language used in the portrayal of these contrasting settings is not the only way Chopin strives to emphasize the difference between the two. She also uses the effect these scenes have on Mrs. Mallard to convey their meaning and depth. On the one hand, the wild, perhaps faked, emotional outburst that takes place in the stifling lower level of the house leaves Louise in a state of "physical exhaustion that haunted her body and seemed to reach into her soul" (par. 4). On the other hand, Louise "[drank] in a very elixir of life through that open window" (par. 18) of her bedroom through which nature bloomed. Because the author strove to symbolize Mrs. Mallard's marriage with the oppressive downstairs

FORM: When making assumptions about the author's intentions, Ray sometimes uses hedging words—in this case, "seem to."

and her impending life without her husband with the open, healing depiction of nature, Chopin suggests that spouses are sometimes better off without each other because marriage can take a physical toll on a person's well-being while the freedom of living for no one but one's self breathes life into even the most burdened wife. After all, "[w]hat could love, the unsolved mystery, count for in face of this possession of self-assertion" (par. 15) felt by Mrs. Mallard in the wake of her emancipation from oppression?

Chopin goes on to emphasize the healing capabilities and joy of living only for one's self by showing the consequences of brutally taking it all away, in one quick turn of a latchkey. With thoughts of her freedom of days to come, "she carried herself unwittingly like a goddess of Victory. She clasped her sister's waist, and together they descended the stairs" (par. 20). Already Chopin is preparing the reader for Mrs. Mallard's looming fate. Not only is she no longer alone in her room with the proverbial elixir of life pouring in from the window, but also she is once again sinking into the oppression of the downstairs, an area that embodies all marital duties as well as the suffocation of Louise's true self and desires. When Brently Mallard enters the house slightly confused but unharmed, the loss of her newly found freedom is too much for Louise's weak heart to bear. Chopin ends the story with a hint of irony: "When the doctors came they said she had died of heart disease—of joy that kills" (par. 23). It may be easier for society to accept that Mrs. Mallard died of joy at seeing her husband alive, but in all actuality, it was the violent death of her future prospects and the hope she had allowed to blossom that sent Louise to the grave. Here lies Chopin's ultimate critique of marriage: when there was no other viable escape, only death could provide freedom from an oppressive marriage.

By killing Louise, Chopin solidifies this ultimatum and also suggests that even death is kinder when the only other option is the slow and continuous addition of the crushing weight of marital oppression.

In "The Story of an Hour," Kate Chopin challenges the typical, romanticized view of love and marriage in the era in which she lived. She chooses to reveal some of the sacrifices one must make in order to bind oneself to another in matrimony. Chopin develops these critiques of marriage through Louise Mallard's emotional responses to her husband's supposed death, whether it is a quick, if not faked, outburst of grief, her body's highly sexualized awakening to the freedoms to come, or the utter despair at finding that he still survives. These are not typical emotions for a "grieving" wife, and Chopin uses this stark contrast as well as the concomitant juxtaposition of nature to the indoors to further emphasize her critique. Louise Mallard may have died in the quest to gain independence from the oppression of her true self and desires, but now she is at least "[f]ree! Body and soul free!" (par. 16).

CONTENT: Ray provides a broad summary of her argument in the concluding paragraph.

CONTENT: In her last sentence, Ray reveals a portion of the significance of the story to an understanding of marital oppression.

Work Cited

Chopin, Kate. "The Story of an Hour." Ann Woodlief's Web
Study Texts. Web. <http://www.vcu.edu/engweb
/webtexts/hour/>. 10 Apr. 2013.

FORM: Ray cites her
source using MLA
format.

Discussion Questions

1. Describe how Sarah Ray's thesis is both debatable and significant.

2. How does the author use evidence from the text to support her
   interpretation?

3. How has she organized her interpretation?

4. How could it help Sarah's interpretation if she looked at the work of
   other scholars who have studied Chopin's story?

ARTISTIC TEXTS

Many scholars in the humanities are creators of artistic texts. It has been said
about artistic texts that when you create them, they're the arts, and when you
study them, they're the humanities. This formulation oversimplifies somewhat,
but it's helpful as shorthand for thinking about the relationship between arts
and humanities. Artistic texts can occur in many different forms and media.
Some of the more common artistic texts that students create include the
following:

paintings	songs	stories
sculptures	pottery	video games
poems	models	short films

The process that you follow to create an artistic text will vary according to the
type of text you create. In a writing class, an instructor might ask you to create
an artistic text and then reflect on the process of creating it. Additionally, he or
she might ask you to interpret your own text or that of another student.

In this three-part project, you'll create a text, reflect on the process of creating it, and then develop a preliminary interpretation of the text. Your assessment will be based primarily on your reflection on and close reading of your text. We encourage you to try something new; indeed, you might discover a talent you didn't realize you had, or you might understand something new about the creative process by trying an art form you haven't experimented with before.

PART 1

Choose an art form that you'd like to experiment with for this activity. You might try something that you've done before, or you might want to experiment with something new. Some possibilities are listed below.

- sketching or painting a figure or a landscape
- composing a poem or a song
- using a pottery wheel or sculpting with clay
- writing a short story
- creating an advertisement or Public Service Announcement for an issue important to you
- designing a video game
- directing a (very) short film

PART 2

After completing the creative portion of this project, respond to the following prompts for reflection about the process of creating the text.

- First reflect on the process of creating your text and what you learned from it.
- What was the most challenging part of the project for you?
- What was the most enjoyable part of the project?
- What did you discover about yourself as you participated in this activity?
- Did you find yourself trying to imitate other examples you've seen, heard, or experienced, or were you trying to develop something very different?
- What inspired you as you were working?

PART 3

Once you've reflected on the process of creating your text, examine the text closely and take notes regarding the elements of it that you see as important to its meaning. Once you've developed notes, do the following.

1. Complete a content/form-response grid to highlight the notes you see as most important for constructing meaning from the text. Be sure to articulate responses about why you see each note as important and relevant toward interpreting meaning.

2. Brainstorm a list of *how*, *what*, and *why* questions regarding various aspects of the text related to its meaning(s).

3. Select one or two questions that seem most promising to try and answer. You should be able to draw direct evidence from the text (and your notes) that supports your answer.

4. Select and rewrite the best question that has evidence, and then write a thesis statement.

You should construct the remainder of your interpretation of the text based on the thesis statement. Try to develop an interpretation that's organized with clear reasons and evidence (see Chapter 3). Use examples actually taken from your text as evidence.

tip sheet

Reading and Writing in the Humanities

- **In the humanities, scholars seek to understand and interpret human experience.** To do so, they often create, analyze, and interpret texts.

- **Scholars in the humanities often conduct close readings of texts** to interpret and make meaning from them, and they might draw on a particular theoretical perspective to ask questions about those texts.

- **Keeping a content/form-response grid can help you track important elements of a text** and your response to them as you do a close reading.

- **Writing in the humanities also draws on the interpretations of others,** either as support or to position an interpretation within other prior scholarship.

- **Arguments in the humanities generally begin with a thesis statement** that asserts *what* the author intends to prove, and it may also provide insight into *how* the author will prove it. Each section of the argument should provide support for the thesis.

Reading and Writing in the Social Sciences

Introduction to the Social Sciences

S ocial scientists study human behavior and interaction along with the systems and social structures we create to organize our world. Professionals in the fields of the **social sciences** help us understand why we do what we do as well as how processes (political, economic, personal, etc.) contribute to our lives. As the image at the bottom of this page shows, the social sciences encompass a broad area of academic inquiry that comprises numerous fields of study. These include sociology, psychology, anthropology, communication studies, and political science, among others.

Maybe you've observed a friend or family member spiral into addictive or self-destructive behavior and struggled to understand how it happened. Maybe you've spent time wondering how cliques were formed and maintained among students in your high school, or how friends are typically chosen. Perhaps larger social issues like war, poverty, or famine concern you the most. If you've ever stopped to consider any of these kinds of issues, then you've already begun to explore the world of the social sciences.

Social scientist Kevin Rathunde, who teaches at the University of Utah, shares his perspective on the work and writing of social scientists in Insider's View features in this chapter. Excerpts from Dr. Rathunde's paper entitled "Middle School Students' Motivation and Quality of Experience: A Comparison of Montessori and Traditional School Environments," which he wrote and published with a colleague, Mihaly

ANDREA TSURUMI

Csikszentmihalyi, in the *American Journal of Education*, also appear throughout this chapter. Rathunde and Csikszentmihalyi's study investigated the types of educational settings that contribute to the best outcomes for students. Specifically, they compared traditional public school environments with those of Montessori schools to assess how students learn, interact, and perceive the quality of their experiences in these differing environments.

As a social scientist, you might study issues like therapy options for autism, the effects of substance abuse on families, peer pressure, the dynamics of dating, social networking websites, stress, or the communication practices of men and women. You might study family counseling techniques or the effects of divorce on teens. Or perhaps you might wonder (as Rathunde and Csikszentmihalyi do) about the effects of differing educational environments on student satisfaction and success.

Whatever the case may be, if you're interested in studying human behavior and understanding why we do what we do, you'll want to consider further how social scientists conduct research and how they present their results in writing. As in all the academic domains, progress in the social sciences rests upon researchers' primary skills at making observations of the world around them.

Insider's View
Social scientists care about the conditions that allow people to connect
KEVIN RATHUNDE, SOCIAL SCIENCES

COURTESY OF KEVIN RATHUNDE

"There are many branches of social science. In general, as the name 'social science' implies, the main focus of scientific action and dialogue is on people and social processes. My training was in an interdisciplinary program on human development at the University of Chicago. As a result, my perspective on social science tends to reach across disciplinary boundaries. I also work in an interdisciplinary department at the University of Utah. The professional conversations I have with colleagues—both within and outside of my department—are wide-ranging. If there is a common denominator to them, it might be the well-being of individuals, families, and society. Social scientists care about the conditions that allow people to connect with others, participate in the lives of their communities, and reach their full potential."

INSIDE WORK **Observing Behavior**

For this activity, pick a place to sit and observe people. You can choose a place that you enjoy going to regularly, but make sure you can observe and take notes without being interrupted or distracted. For example, you might observe people in your school's library or another space on campus. Try to avoid places where you could feel compelled to engage in conversation with people you know.

For ten minutes, freewrite about the people around you and what they're doing. Look for the kinds of interactions and engagements that characterize their behavior. Then draft some questions that you think a social scientist observing the same people might ask about them. For example, if you wrote about behaviors you observed in a college classroom or lecture hall, you might consider questions like the ones listed here.

- How are students arranged around the room? What does the seating arrangement look like? What effect does the room's arrangement have on classroom interaction, if any?
- What are students doing? Are they taking notes? Writing? Sleeping? Typing? Texting? Listening? Doing something else?
- Are students doing different things in different parts of the room, or are the activities uniform throughout the room? Why?
- What is the instructor doing in the classroom? Where is he or she positioned? How are students responding?
- Are students using technology? If so, what kinds of technology? What are they using the technology to do?
- If people are interacting with one another in the classroom, what are they talking about? How are they interacting? How are they positioned when they interact? Are numerous people contributing to the conversation? Is someone leading the conversation? If so, how?

See how many different behaviors, people, and interactions you can observe and how many questions you can generate. You might do this activity in the same place with a partner and then compare notes. What did you or your partner find in common? What did you each observe that was unique? Why do you think you noticed the things you did? What was the most interesting thing you observed? ▶

Research in the Social Sciences

As we've indicated, the social sciences comprise a diverse group of academic fields that aim to understand human behavior and systems. But it may be difficult to see the commonalities among these disciplines that make it possible to refer to them as social sciences. One of the ways we can link these disciplines and the values they share, beyond their basic concern for why and how people do things, is by considering how social scientists conduct and report their research.

THE ROLE OF THEORY

Unlike in the natural sciences, where research often takes place in a laboratory setting under controlled conditions, research in the social sciences is necessarily "messier." The reason is fairly simple: human beings and the systems they organize cannot generally be studied in laboratory conditions, where variables are controlled. For this reason, social scientists do not generally establish fixed laws or argue for absolute truths, as natural scientists sometimes do. For instance, while natural scientists are able to argue, with certainty, that a water molecule contains two atoms of hydrogen and one of oxygen, social scientists cannot claim to know the absolute fixed nature of a person's psychology (why a person does what she does in any particular instance) or that of a social system or problem (why homelessness persists, for instance).

Much social science research is therefore based on **theories of human behavior and human systems**, which are propositions that scholars use to explain specific phenomena. Theories can be evaluated on the basis of their ability to explain why or how or when a phenomenon occurs, and they generally result from research that has been replicated time and again to confirm their accuracy, appropriateness, and usefulness. Still, it's important to understand that theories are not laws; they are not absolute, fixed, or perfect explanations. Instead, social science theories are always being refined as research on particular social phenomena develops. The Rathunde and Csikszentmihalyi study we highlight in the Insider's View boxes with Dr. Rathunde, for instance, makes use of goal theory and optimal experience theory as part of the research design to evaluate the type of middle school environment that best contributes to students' education.

Insider Example
Exploring Social Science Theory

Read the following excerpt from Kalervo Oberg's "Cultural Shock: Adjustment to New Cultural Environments," and then reflect on his theory by answering the questions that follow the selection. Oberg (1901–1973) was a pioneer in economic anthropology and applied anthropology, and his foundational work in this study has been cited hundreds of times by sociologists and anthropologists who are interested in the phenomenon. Oberg himself coined the term *culture shock*.

Excerpt from **Cultural Shock: Adjustment to New Cultural Environments**

KALERVO OBERG

Culture shock is precipitated by the anxiety that results from losing all our familiar signs and symbols of social intercourse. These signs or cues include the thousand and one ways in which we orient ourselves to the situations of daily life: when to shake hands and what to say when we meet people, when and how to give tips, how to give orders to servants, how to make purchases, when to accept and when to refuse invitations, when to take statements seriously and when not. Now these cues which may be words, gestures, facial expressions, customs, or norms are acquired by all of us in the course of growing up and are as much a part of our culture as the language we speak or the beliefs we accept. All of us depend for our peace of mind and our efficiency on hundreds of these cues, most of which we do not carry on the level of conscious awareness.

Now when an individual enters a strange culture, all or most of these familiar cues are removed. He or she is like a fish out of water. No matter how broad-minded or full of good will you may be, a series of props have been knocked from under you, followed by a feeling of frustration and anxiety. People react to the frustration in much the same way. First they *reject* the environment which causes the discomfort: "the ways of the host country are bad because they make us feel bad." When Americans or other foreigners in a strange land get together to grouse about the host country and its people—you can be sure they are suffering from culture shock. Another phase of culture shock is *regression*. The home environment suddenly assumes a tremendous importance. To an American everything American becomes irrationally glorified. All the difficulties and problems are forgotten and only the good things back home are remembered. It usually takes a trip home to bring one back to reality.

SYMPTOMS OF CULTURE SHOCK

Some of the symptoms of culture shock are: excessive washing of the hands; excessive concern over drinking water, food, dishes, and bedding; fear of physical contact with attendants or servants; the absent-minded, far-away stare (sometimes called "the tropical stare"); a feeling of helplessness and a desire for dependence on long-term residents of one's own nationality; fits of anger over delays and other minor frustrations; delay and outright refusal to learn the language of the host country; excessive fear of being cheated, robbed, or injured; great concern over minor pains and irruptions of the skin; and finally, that terrible longing to be back home, to be able to have a good cup of coffee and a piece of apple pie, to walk into that corner drugstore, to visit one's relatives, and, in general, to talk to people who really make sense.

Individuals differ greatly in the degree in which culture shock affects them. Although not common, there are individuals who cannot live in foreign countries. Those who have seen people go through culture shock and on to a satisfactory adjustment can discern steps in the process. During the first few weeks most individuals are fascinated by the new. They stay in hotels and associate with nationals who speak their language and are polite and gracious to foreigners. This honeymoon stage may last from a few days or weeks to six months depending on circumstances. If one is a very important person he or she will be shown the show places, will be pampered and petted, and in a press interview will speak glowingly about progress, good will, and international amity, and if he returns home he may well write a book about his pleasant if superficial experience abroad.

But this Cook's tour type of mentality does not normally last if the foreign visitor remains abroad and has seriously to cope with real conditions of life. It is then that the second stage begins, characterized by a hostile and aggressive attitude towards the host country. This hostility evidently grows out of the genuine difficulty which the visitor experiences in the process of adjustment. There is maid trouble, school trouble, language trouble, house trouble, transportation trouble, shopping trouble, and the fact that people in the host country are largely indifferent to all these troubles. They help but they just don't understand your great concern over these difficulties. Therefore, they must be insensible and unsympathetic to you and your worries. The result, "I just don't like them." You become aggressive, you band together with your fellow countrymen and criticize the host country, its ways, and its people. But this criticism is not an objective appraisal but a derogatory one. Instead of trying to account for conditions as they are through an honest analysis of the actual conditions and the historical circumstances which have created them, you talk as if the difficulties you experienced are more or less created by the people of the host country for your special discomfort. You take refuge in the colony of your countrymen and its cocktail circuit, which often becomes the fountain-head of emotionally charged labels known as stereotypes. This is a peculiar kind of invidious shorthand which caricatures the host country and its people in a negative manner. The "dollar-grasping American" and the "indolent Latin American" are samples of mild forms of stereotypes. The use of stereotypes may salve the ego of someone with a severe case of culture shock but it certainly does not lead to any genuine understanding of the host country and its people. This second stage of culture shock is in a sense a crisis in the disease. If you overcome it, you stay; if not, you leave before you reach the stage of a nervous breakdown.

If the visitor succeeds in getting some knowledge of the language and begins to get around by himself, he is beginning to open the way into the new cultural environment. The visitor still has difficulties but he takes a "this is my cross and I have to bear it" attitude. Usually in this stage the visitor takes a superior attitude to people of the host country. His sense of humor begins to exert itself. Instead of criticizing he jokes about the people and even cracks jokes about his or her own difficulties. He or she is now on the way to recovery. And there is also the poor devil who is worse off than yourself whom you can help, which in turn gives you confidence in your ability to speak and get around.

In the fourth stage your adjustment is about as complete as it can be. The visitor now accepts the customs of the country as just another way of living. You operate within the new milieu without a feeling of anxiety although there are moments of strain. Only with a complete grasp of all the cues of social intercourse will this strain disappear. For a long time the individual will understand what the national is saying but he is not always sure what the national means. With a complete adjustment you not only accept the foods, drinks, habits, and customs, but actually begin to enjoy them. When you go on home leave you may even take things back with you and if you leave for good you generally miss the country and the people to whom you have become accustomed.

Discussion Questions

1. In your own words, define what you think Kalervo Oberg means by *culture shock*.
2. What are the four stages of culture shock, according to Oberg?
3. Oberg's essay was written more than half a century ago. In what ways does it seem dated? In what ways does it strike you as still valid or relevant?

INSIDE WORK **Tracing a Theory's Development**

As we indicated, theories in the social sciences exist to be developed and refined over time, based on our developing understandings of a social phenomenon as a result of continued research. Conduct a search (using the web or your academic database access) to determine if you can make a rough estimate as to how often Oberg's theory of culture shock has been cited in published research. You might even make a timeline, or another visual representation, of what you find. As you look at the research, identify any evidence or indicators that the theory has been updated or altered since its first appearance. In what ways has the theory been refined? ❯

RESEARCH QUESTIONS AND HYPOTHESES

As we've noted throughout this book, research questions are typically formulated on the basis of observations. In the social sciences, such observations focus on human behavior, human systems, and/or the interactions between the two. Observations of a social phenomenon can give rise to questions about how a phenomenon operates or what effects it has on people or, as Rathunde suggests, how it could be changed to improve individuals' well-being. For example, in their social science study, "'Under the Radar': Educators and Cyberbullying in Schools," W. Cassidy, K. Brown, and M. Jackson (2012) offer the following as guiding research questions for their investigation:

> Our study of educators focused on three research questions: Do they [educators] consider cyberbullying a problem at their school and how familiar are they with the extent and impact among their students? What policies and practices are in place to prevent or counter cyberbullying? What solutions do they have for encouraging a kinder online world? (p. 522)

Research that is designed to inform a theory of human behavior or to provide data that contributes to a fuller understanding of some social or political structure (i.e., to answer a social science research question) also often begins with the presentation of a *hypothesis*. As we saw in Chapter 3, a hypothesis is a testable proposition that provides an answer or predicts an outcome in response to the research question(s) at hand. It's important to note that not all social science reports include a statement of hypothesis. Some social science research establishes its focus by presenting the questions that guide researchers' inquiry into a particular phenomenon instead of establishing a hypothesis. C. Kern and K. Ko (2010) present the following hypothesis, or predicted outcome, for their social science study, "Exploring Happiness and Performance at Work." The researchers make a prediction concerning what they believed their research would show before presenting their findings later in their research report:

> The intent of this analysis was to review how happiness and performance related to each other in this workplace. It is the authors' belief that for performance to be sustained in an organization, individuals and groups within that organization need to experience a threshold level of happiness. It is difficult for unhappy individuals and work groups to continue performing at high levels without appropriate leadership intervention. (p. 5)

Hypotheses differ from *thesis statements*, which are more commonly associated with arguments in the humanities. While thesis statements offer researchers' final conclusions on a topic or issue, hypothesis statements offer a predicted outcome. The proposition expressed in a hypothesis may be either accepted or rejected based on the results of the research. For example, an educational researcher might hypothesize that teachers' use of open-ended questioning increases students' level of participation in class. However, the researcher wouldn't be able to confirm or reject such a hypothesis until the end of his or her research report.

INSIDE WORK   Developing Hypotheses

1. For five minutes, brainstorm *social science* topics or issues that have affected your life. One approach is to consider issues that are causing you stress in your life right now. Examples might include peer pressure, academic performance, substance abuse, dating, or a relative's cancer treatment.

2. Once you have a list of topics, focus in on two or three that you believe have had the greatest impact on you personally. Next, generate a list of possible *research questions* concerning the topics that, if answered, would offer you a greater understanding of them. Examples: *What triggers most people to try their first drink of alcohol? What types of therapies are most effective for working with children on the autism spectrum? What kinds of technology actually aid in student learning?*

3. When you've reached the stage of proposing a possible answer to one or more of your questions, then you're ready to state a hypothesis. Try proposing a *hypothesis*, or testable proposition, as an answer to one of the research questions you've posed. For example, if your research question is *What triggers most people to try their first drink of alcohol?* then your hypothesis might be *Peer pressure generally causes most people to try their first drink of alcohol, especially for those who try their first drink before reaching the legal drinking age.* ❱

METHODS

Research in the diverse fields of the social sciences is, as you probably suspect, quite varied, and social scientists collect data to answer their research questions or test their hypotheses in several different ways. Their choice of methods is directly influenced by the kinds of questions they ask in any particular instance, as well as by their own disciplinary backgrounds. In his Insider's View on page 161, Kevin Rathunde highlights the connection between the kinds of research questions a social scientist asks and the particular methods the researcher uses to answer those questions.

We can group most of the research you're likely to encounter in the fields of the social sciences into three possible types: quantitative, qualitative, and mixed methods. Researchers make choices about which types of methods they'll employ in any given situation based on the nature of their line of inquiry. A particular research question may very well dictate the methods used to answer that question. If you wanted to determine the number of homeless veterans in a specific city, for instance, then collecting numerical, or quantitative, data would likely suffice to answer that question. However, if you wanted to know what factors affect the rates of homelessness among veterans in your community, then you would need to do more than tally the number of homeless veterans. You'd need to collect a different type of data to help construct an answer — perhaps responses to surveys or interview questions.

Quantitative Methods

Quantitative studies include those that rely on collecting numerical data and performing statistical analyses to reveal findings in research. Basic statistical data, like those provided by *means* (averages), *modes* (most often occurring value), and *medians* (middle values), are fundamental to quantitative social science research. More sophisticated statistical procedures commonly used in professional quantitative studies include correlations, chi-square tests, analysis of variance (ANOVA), and multivariate analysis of variance (MANOVA), as well as regression model testing, just to name a few. Not all statistical procedures are appropriate in all situations, however, so researchers must carefully select procedures based on the nature of their data and the kinds of findings

they seek. Researchers who engage in advanced statistical procedures as part of their methods are typically highly skilled in such procedures. At the very least, these researchers consult or work in cooperation with statisticians to design their studies and/or to analyze their data.

You may find, in fact, that a team of researchers collaborating on a social science project often includes individuals who are also experienced statisticians. Obviously, we don't expect you to be familiar with the details of statistical procedures, but it's important that you be able to notice when researchers rely on statistical methods to test their hypotheses and to inform their results.

Also, you should take note of how researchers incorporate discussion of such methods into their writing. In the following example, we've highlighted a few elements in the reporting that you'll want to notice when reading social science studies that make use of statistical procedures:

- **Procedure**   What statistical procedures are used?
- **Variables**   What variables are examined in the procedures?
- **Results**   What do the statistical procedures reveal?
- **Participants**   From whom are the data collected, and how are those individuals chosen?

In their study, "Middle School Students' Motivation and Quality of Experience: A Comparison of Montessori and Traditional School Environments,"

Variables examined, participants or populations involved in the study, and statistical procedure employed—MANCOVA, or a multivariate analysis of covariance—are identified.

Results of the statistical procedure are identified.

Rathunde and Csikszentmihalyi report on the statistical procedures they used to examine different types of schools:

> The first analysis compared the main motivation and quality-of-experience variables across school type (Montessori vs. traditional) and grade level (sixth vs. eighth) using a two-way MANCOVA with parental education, gender, and ethnic background as covariates. Significant differences were found for school context (Wilks's lambda = .84, $F(5, 275)$ = 10.84, $p < .001$), indicating that students in the two school contexts reported differences in motivation and quality of experience. After adjusting for the covariates, the multivariate eta squared indicated that 17 percent of the variance of the dependent variables was associated with the school context factor. The omnibus test for grade level was not significant (Wilks's lambda = .99, $F(5, 275)$ = .68, p = .64), indicating that students in sixth and eighth grade reported similar motivation and quality of experience. Finally, the omnibus test for the interaction of school context x grade level was not significant (Wilks's lambda = .97, $F(5, 275)$ = 2.02, p = .08). None of the multivariate tests for the covariates—parental education, gender, and ethnic background—reached the .05 level. (p. 357)

Qualitative Methods

Qualitative studies generally rely on language, observation, and reporting of individual human experiences to reveal findings in research. Research reports often communicate these methods through the form of a study's results, which rely on in-depth narrative reporting. Methods for collecting data in qualitative studies include interviews, document analysis, surveys, and observations.

We can see examples of these methods put into practice in Barbara Allen's "Environmental Justice, Local Knowledge, and After-Disaster Planning in New Orleans" (2007), published in the academic social science journal *Technology and Society*. In this example, we've highlighted a few elements in the reporting that you'll want to notice when reading qualitative research methods:

- **Method** What method of data collection is used?
- **Data** What data is gathered from that method?
- **Results** What are the results? What explanation do the researchers provide for the data, or what meaning do they find in the data?
- **Participants** From whom is the data collected, and how are these individuals chosen?

Participants

Data-collection method: interview

Data, followed by explanation or meaning of data

Six months after the hurricane I contacted public health officials and researchers, many of whom were reluctant to talk. One who did talk asked that I did not use her name, but she made some interesting observations. According to my informant, health officials were in a difficult position. Half a year after the devastation, only 25% of the city's residents had returned; a year after the storm, that number rose to about 40%. Negative publicity regarding public health issues would deter such repatriation, particularly families with children who had not returned in any large numbers to the city. The informant also told me to pursue the state public health websites where the most prominent worries were still smoking and obesity, not Hurricane Katrina. While the information on various public health websites did eventually reflect concerns about mold, mildew, and other contamination, it was never presented as the health threat that independent environmental scientists, such as Wilma Subra, thought it was. (pp. 154–55)

— Data

. . .

About five months after Hurricane Katrina, I received an e-mail from a high school student living in a rural parish west of New Orleans along the Mississippi River (an area EJ advocates have renamed Cancer Alley). After Hurricane Katrina, an old landfill near her house was opened to receive waste and began emitting noxious odors. She took samples of the "black ooze" from the site and contacted the Louisiana Department of Environmental Quality, only to be told that the landfill was accepting only construction waste, and the smell she described was probably decaying gypsum board. I suspect her story will be repeated many times across south Louisiana as these marginal waste sites receive the debris from homes and businesses ruined by the hurricane. The full environmental impact of Hurricane Katrina's waste and its hastily designated removal sites will not be known for many years. (p. 155)

— Participant

— Explanation or meaning of data

Mixed Methods

Studies that make use of both qualitative and quantitative data-collection techniques are generally referred to as **mixed-methodology studies**. Rathunde and Csikszentmihalyi's study, "Middle School Students' Motivation and Quality of Experience: A Comparison of Montessori and Traditional School Environments," used mixed methods: the authors report findings from both qualitative and quantitative data. In this excerpt, they share results from qualitative data they collected as they sought to distinguish among the types of educational settings selected for participation in their study:

> After verifying that the demographic profile of the two sets of schools was similar, the next step was to determine if the schools differed with respect to the five selection criteria outlined above. We used a variety of qualitative sources to verify contextual differences, including observations by the research staff; teacher and parent interviews; school newsletters, information packets, mission statements, and parent teacher handbooks; summaries from board of education and school council meetings; and a review of class schedules and textbook choices discussed in strategic plans. These sources also provided information about the level of middle grade reform that may or may not have been implemented by the schools and whether the label "traditional" was appropriate. (p. 64)

However, Rathunde and Csikszentmihalyi's central hypothesis, "that students in Montessori middle schools would report more positive perceptions of their school environment and their teachers, more often perceive their class-mates as friends, and spend more time in collaborative and/or individual work rather than didactic educational formats such as listening to a lecture" (p. 68), was tested by using quantitative methods:

> The main analyses used two-way multivariate analysis of covariance (MANCOVA) with school type (Montessori vs. traditional) and grade level (sixth vs. eighth) as the two factors. Gender, ethnicity, and parental education were covariates in all of the analyses. Overall multivariate F tests (Wilks's lambda) were performed first on related sets of dependent variables. If an overall F test was significant, we performed univariate ANOVAs as follow-up tests to the MANCOVAs. If necessary, post hoc analyses were done using Bonferroni corrections to control for Type I errors. Only students with at least 15 ESM signals were included in the multivariate analyses, and follow-up ANOVAs used students who had valid scores on all of the dependent variables. (p. 68)

Addressing Bias

A political scientist weighs in on avoiding bias.

Because social scientists study people and organizations, their research is considered more valuable when conducted within a framework that minimizes the influence of personal or researcher bias on the study's outcome(s). When possible, social scientists strive for **objectivity** (in quantitative research) or **neutrality** (in qualitative research) in their research. This means that researchers undertake all possible measures to reduce the influence of biases on their research. Bias is sometimes inevitable, however, so social science research places a high value on honesty and transparency in the reporting of data. Each of the methods outlined above requires social scientists to engage in rigorous procedures and checks (e.g., ensuring appropriate sample sizes and/or using multiple forms of qualitative data) to ensure that the influence of any biases is as limited as possible.

INSIDE WORK **Considering Research Methods**

In the previous activity, we asked you to consider possible hypotheses, or testable propositions, to the research questions you posed. Now choose one of your hypothesis statements, and consider the types of methods that might be appropriate for testing the hypothesis. Think about the kinds of data you'll generate from the different methods.

- Would quantitative, qualitative, or mixed research methods be the most appropriate for testing your hypothesis? Why?

- What specific methods would you use—statistical procedures, surveys, observations, interviews? Why?

- Who would you want to have participate in your research? From whom would you need to collect your data in order to answer your research question? ❯

THE IRB PROCESS AND USE OF HUMAN SUBJECTS

All research, whether student or faculty initiated and directed, must treat its subjects, or participants, with the greatest of care and consider the ethical implications of all its procedures. Although institutions establish their own systems and procedures for verifying the ethical treatment of subjects, most of these include an **institutional review board (IRB)**, or a committee of individuals whose job is to review research proposals in light of ethical concerns for subjects and applicable laws. Such proposals typically include specific forms of documentation that identify a study's purpose; rigorously detail the research procedures to be followed; evaluate potential risks and rewards of a study, especially for study participants; and ensure (whenever possible) that participants are fully informed about a study and the implications of their participation in it.

We encourage you to learn more about the IRB process at your own institution and, when appropriate, to consider your own research in light of the IRB policies and procedures established for your institution. Many schools maintain informational, educational, and interactive websites. You'll notice similarities in the mission statements of institutional review boards from a number of research-intensive universities:

> **Duke University:** To ensure the protection of human research subjects by conducting scientific and ethical review of research studies while providing leadership and education for the research community.

> **The George Washington University:** To support [the] research community in the conduct of innovative and ethical research by providing guidance, education, and oversight for the protection of human subjects.

> **University of New Mexico:** To promote the safety and protection of individuals involved in human research by providing support, guidance, and education to facilitate ethical and scientifically sound research.

Conventions of Writing in the Social Sciences

In light of the variety of research methods used by social scientists, it's not surprising that there are also a number of ways social scientists report their research findings. In this section, we highlight general conventional expectations of *structure*, *language*, and *reference* that social scientists follow to communicate their research to one another. Understanding these conventions, we believe, can help foster your understanding of this academic domain more broadly.

Aya Matsuda is a linguist and social science researcher at Arizona State University, where she studies the use of English as an international language, the integration of a "World Englishes" perspective into U.S. education, and the ways bilingual writers negotiate identity. In her Insider's View, Dr. Matsuda explains that she learned the conventions of writing as a social scientist, and more particularly as a linguist, "mostly through writing, getting feedback, and revising."

As Dr. Matsuda also suggests, reading can be an important part of understanding the writing of a discipline. Furthermore, reading academic writing

with a particular focus on the rhetorical elements used is a powerful way to acquire insight into the academic discipline itself, as well as a way to learn the literacy practices that professional writers commonly follow in whatever academic domain you happen to be studying.

STRUCTURAL CONVENTIONS AND IMRAD FORMAT

Structural conventions within the fields of the social sciences can vary quite dramatically, but the structure of a social science report should follow logically from the type of study conducted or the methodological framework (quantitative, qualitative, or mixed-methods) it employs. The more quantitative a study is, the more likely its reporting will reflect the conventions for scientific research, using IMRAD format. Qualitative studies, though, sometimes appear in other organizational forms that reflect the particular qualitative methods used in the study. But just as numerous fields within the social sciences rely on quantitative research methods, so too do many social scientists report their results according to the conventional form for scientific inquiry: *IMRAD (Introduction, Methods, Results, and Discussion) format.*

Introduction

The introduction of a social science report establishes the context for a study, providing appropriate background on the issue or topic under scrutiny. The introduction is also where you're likely to find evidence of researchers' review of previous scholarship on a topic. As part of these reviews, researchers typically report what's already known about a phenomenon or what's relevant in the current scholarship for their own research. They may also situate their research goals within some gap in the scholarship—that is, they explain how their research contributes to the growing body of scholarship on the phenomenon under investigation. If a theoretical perspective drives a study, as often occurs in more qualitative studies, then the introduction may also contain an explanation of the central tenets or the parameters of the researchers' theoretical lens. Regardless, an introduction in the social sciences generally builds to a statement of specific purpose for the study. This may take the form of a hypothesis or thesis, or it may appear explicitly as a general statement of the researchers' purpose, perhaps including a presentation of research questions. The introduction to Rathunde and Csikszentmihalyi's study provides an example:

> The difficulties that many young adolescents encounter in middle school have been well documented (Carnegie Council on Adolescent Development 1989, 1995; Eccles et al. 1993; U.S. Department of Education 1991). During this precarious transition from the elementary school years, young adolescents may begin to doubt the value of their academic work and their abilities to succeed (Simmons and Blyth 1987; Wigfield et al. 1991). A central concern of many studies is motivation (Anderman and Maehr 1994); a disturbingly consistent finding associated with middle school is a drop in students' intrinsic motivation to learn (Anderman et al. 1999; Gottfried 1985; Harter et al. 1992).
>
> Such downward trends in motivation are not inevitable. Over the past decade, several researchers have concluded that the typical learning environment in middle school is often mismatched with adolescents' developmental needs (Eccles et al. 1993). Several large-scale research programs have focused on the qualities of classrooms and school cultures that may enhance student achievement and motivation (Ames 1992; Lipsitz et al. 1997; Maehr and Midgley 1991). School environments that provide a more appropriate developmental fit (e.g., more relevant tasks, student-directed learning, less of an emphasis on grades and competition, more collaboration, etc.) have been shown to enhance students' intrinsic, task motivation (Anderman et al. 1999).
>
> The present study explores the issues of developmental fit and young adolescents' quality of experience and motivation by comparing five Montessori middle schools to six "traditional" public middle schools. Although the Montessori educational philosophy is primarily associated with early childhood education, a number of schools have extended its core principles to early adolescent education. These principles are in general agreement with the reform proposals associated with various motivation theories (Anderman et al. 1999; Maehr and Midgley 1991), developmental fit theories (Eccles et al. 1993), as well as insights from various recommendations for middle school reform (e.g., the Carnegie Foundation's "Turning Points" recommendations; see Lipsitz et al. 1997). In addition, the Montessori philosophy is consistent with the theoretical and practical implications of optimal experience (flow) theory (Csikszentmihalyi and Rathunde 1998). The present study places a special emphasis on students' quality of experience in middle school. More specifically, it uses the Experience Sampling Method (ESM) (Csikszentmihalyi and Larson 1987) to compare the school experiences of Montessori middle school students with a comparable sample of public school students in traditional classrooms. (pp. 341–42)

Provides an introduction to the topic at hand: the problem of motivation for adolescents in middle school. The problem is situated in the scholarship of others.

Reviews relevant scholarship: the researchers review previous studies that have bearing on their own aims—addressing the decline in motivation among students.

Identifies researchers' particular areas of interest

Although the introductory elements of Rathunde and Csikszentmihalyi's study actually continue for a number of pages, these opening paragraphs reveal common rhetorical moves in social science research reporting: establishing a topic of interest, reviewing the scholarship on that topic, and connecting the current study to the ongoing scholarly conversation on the topic.

Methods

Social science researchers are very particular about the precise reporting of their methods of research. No matter what the type of study (quantitative, qualitative, or mixed-methods), researchers are very careful not only to identify the methods used in their research but also to explain why they chose certain ones, in light of the goals of their study. Because researchers want to reduce the influence of researcher bias and to provide enough context so others might replicate or confirm their findings, social scientists make sure that their reports thoroughly explain the kinds of data they have collected and the precise procedures they used to collect that data (interviews, document analysis, surveys, etc.). Also, there is often much discussion of the ways the data were interpreted or analyzed (using case studies, narrative analysis, statistical procedures, etc.).

An excerpt from W. Cassidy, K. Brown, and M. Jackson's study on educators and cyberbullying provides an example of the level of detail at which scholars typically report their methods:

Provides highly specific details about data-collection methods, and emphasizes researchers' neutral stance

> Each participant chose a pseudonym and was asked a series of 16 in-depth, semi-structured, open-ended questions (Lancy, 2001) and three closed-category questions in a private setting, allowing their views to be voiced in confidence (Cook-Sather, 2002). Each 45- to 60-minute audiotaped interview was conducted by one of the authors, while maintaining a neutral, nonjudgmental stance in regards to the responses (Merriam, 1988).

Provides detailed explanation of procedures used to support the reliability of the study's findings

> Once the interviews were transcribed, each participant was given the opportunity to review the transcript and make changes. The transcripts were then reviewed and re-reviewed in a backward and forward motion (Glaser & Strauss, 1967; McMillan & Schumacher, 1997) separately by two of the three researchers to determine commonalities and differences among responses as well as any salient themes that surfaced due to the frequency or the strength of the response (Miles & Huberman, 1994). Each researcher's analysis was then compared with the other's to jointly determine emergent themes and perceptions.

Connects the research to the development of theory

> The dominant themes were then reviewed in relation to the existing literature on educators' perceptions and responses to cyberbullying. The approach taken was "bottom-up," to inductively uncover themes and contribute to theory, rather than apply existing theory as a predetermined frame for analysis (Miles & Huberman, 1994). (p. 523)

You'll notice that the researchers do not simply indicate that the data were collected via interviews. Rather, they go to some lengths to describe the kinds of interviews they conducted and how they were conducted, as well as how those interviews were analyzed. This level of detail supports the writers' ethos, and it further highlights their commitment to reducing bias in their research. Similar studies might also report the interview questions at the end of the report in an appendix. Seeing the actual questions helps readers interpret the results on their own and also provides enough detail for readers to replicate the study or test the hypothesis with a different population, should they desire to do so. Readers of the study need to understand as precisely as possible the methods for data collection and analysis.

Results

There can be much variety in the ways social science reports present the results, or findings, of a study. You may encounter a section identified by the title "Results," especially if the study follows IMRAD format, but you may not find that heading at all. Instead, researchers often present their results by using headings and subheadings that reflect their actual findings. As examples, we provide here excerpts from two studies: (1) Rathunde and Csikszentmihalyi's 2005 study on middle school student motivation, and (2) Cassidy, Brown, and Jackson's 2012 study on educators and cyberbullying.

In the Results section of their report, Rathunde and Csikszentmihalyi provide findings from their study under the subheading "Motivation and Quality-of-Experience Differences: Nonacademic Activities at School." Those results read in part:

> Follow-up ANCOVAs were done on each of the five ESM variables. Table 3 summarizes the means, standard errors, and significance levels for each of the variables.

Table 3

Univariate F-Tests for Quality of Experience in Nonacademic Activities at School by School Context

| ESM Measure | School Context | | F-test | p |
	Montessori ($N = 131$)	Traditional ($N = 150$)		
Flow (%)	11.0 (1.7)	17.3 (1.6)	7.19	.008
Affect	.32 (.05)	.14 (.05)	6.87	.009
Potency	.22 (.05)	.16 (.05)	1.90	NS
Motivation	−.03 (.05)	−.12 (.05)	1.70	NS
Salience	−.38 (.04)	−.19 (.04)	11.14	.001

Means are z-scores (i.e., zero is average experience for the entire week) and are adjusted for the covariates gender, parental education, and ethnicity. Standard errors appear in parentheses. Flow percent indicates the amount of time students indicated above-average challenge and skill while doing nonacademic activities.

Consistent with the relaxed nature of the activities, students in both school contexts reported higher levels of affect, potency, and intrinsic motivation in nonacademic activities, as well as lower levels of salience and flow (see table 2). In contrast to the findings for academic work, students in both groups reported similar levels of intrinsic motivation and potency. In addition, students in the traditional group reported significantly more flow in nonacademic activities, although the overall percentage of flow was low.

— Result

— Result

— Result

Result

Similar to the findings for academic activities, the Montessori students reported better overall affect, and despite the fact that levels of salience were below average for both student groups, the traditional students reported that their activities were more important. (pp. 360–61)

You'll notice that in this section, the researchers remain focused on reporting their findings. They do not, at this point, go into great detail about what those findings mean or what the implications are.

Cassidy, Brown, and Jackson also report their findings in a Results section, and they subdivide their findings into a number of areas of inquiry (identified in the subheadings) examined as part of their larger study. Only the results are presented at this point in the article; they are not yet interpreted:

RESULTS

Familiarity with technology

Results

Despite the district's emphasis on technology, the educators (except for two younger teachers and one vice-principal) indicated that they were not very familiar with chat rooms and blogs, were moderately familiar with YouTube and Facebook and were most familiar with the older forms of communication — email and cellular phones.

Cyberbullying policies

Result

We asked respondents about specific cyberbullying policies in place at their school and their perceived effectiveness. Despite the district's priorities around technology, neither the school district nor either school had a specific cyberbullying policy; instead educators were supposed to follow the district's bullying policy. When VP17-A was asked if the district's bullying handbook effectively addressed the problem of cyberbullying, he replied: "It effectively addresses the people that are identified as bullying others [but] it doesn't address the educational side of it . . . about what is proper use of the Internet as a tool."

P14-B wanted to see a new policy put in place that was flexible enough to deal with the different situations as they arose. VP19-B thought that a cyber-bullying policy should be separate from a face-to-face bullying policy since the impact on students is different. He also felt that there should be a concerted district policy regarding "risk assessment in which you have a team that's trained at determining the level of threat and it should be taken very seriously whether it's a phone threat, a verbal threat, or a cyber threat." Participants indicated that they had not considered the idea of a separate cyberbullying policy before the interview, with several commenting that they now saw it as important. (pp. 524, 526–27)

Result

Visual Representations of Data The Results section of a report may also provide data sets in the form of charts and/or figures. Figures may appear as photos, images, charts, or graphs. When you find visual representations of data in texts, it's important that you pause to consider these elements carefully. Researchers typically use *tables* when they want to make data sets, or

Table 1

Comparison of Montessori and Traditional Middle School Samples on Various
Background Variables

Background Variable	School Context	
	Montessori	Traditional
Ethnicity (%):		
European American	72.6	74.9
Asian American	10.2	7.8
Latino	1.9	3.4
African American	12.7	12.6
Other	2.6	1.2
Parental education	5.5	5.4
Home resources	29.6	29.5
School-related:		
Parental discussion	2.41	2.49
Parental involvement	2.11	2.10
Parental monitoring	1.69	1.66
Number of siblings	1.8	2.0
Mother employment (%)	71.6	74.1
Father employment (%)	83.7	88.1
Intact (two-parent) family (%)	81.0	84.0
Grade point average	1.97	1.93

Note. None of the differences reported in the table was statistically significant.

raw data, available for comparisons. These tables, such as the one Rathunde
and Csikszentmihalyi include in "Middle School Students' Motivation and
Quality of Experience: A Comparison of Montessori and Traditional School
Environments," present variables in columns and rows, as seen above.

In this instance, the "background variable[s]" used to describe the student populations are listed in the column, and the rows identify two "school
context[s]," Montessori and Traditional schools, for comparison. The table's
title reveals its overall purpose: to compare "Montessori and Traditional
Middle School Samples on Various Background Variables." Rathunde and
Csikszentmihalyi describe the contents of their table this way:

> Table 1 summarizes this comparison. The ethnic diversity of the samples was
> almost identical. Both shared similar advantages in terms of high parental
> education (baccalaureate degree or higher), high rates of two-parent families,

high family resources, and other indicators of strong parental involvement in their children's education. Although only one-third of the Montessori students received grades, *t*-tests indicated that both samples were comprised of good students (i.e., they received about half As and half Bs). (p. 356)

Researchers use *figures* when they want to highlight the results of research or the derived relationships between data sets or variables. *Graphs*, a type of figure, contain two axes — the horizontal x-axis and the vertical y-axis. The relationship between variables on these axes is indicated by the cells of overlap between the two axes in the body of the figure. Conventionally, the *x-axis* identifies an independent variable, or a variable that can be controlled; by contrast, the *y-axis* identifies the dependent variable, which is dependent on the variable identified in the x-axis. Here's a figure from Rathunde and Csikszentmihalyi's study:

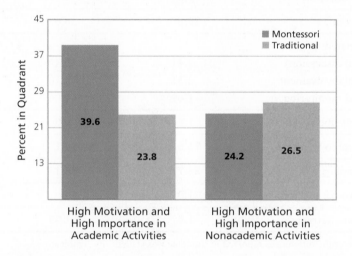

Figure 2. Percentage of undivided interest in academic and nonacademic activities

As with tables, the titles of figures reveal their overall purpose. In this case, the researchers demonstrate the "[p]ercentage of undivided interest in academic and nonacademic activities." Reading the figure, in this instance, comes down to identifying the percentage of "undivided interest" that students in Montessori and traditional middle schools (revealed in different colors, as the legend indicates) expressed in the quadrants "High Motivation and High Importance in Academic Activities" and "High Motivation and High Importance in Nonacademic Activities." Colored cells in the body of the graph reveal the percentages. Rathunde and Csikszentmihalyi note about this figure: "[O]n the key variable undivided interest, students in the traditional group reported a slightly higher percent of high-motivation and high-importance activities; this noteworthy change from academic activities is illustrated in figure 2" (p. 361).

Whenever you see charts or figures in social science reports, you should take time to do the following:

- study the titles carefully
- look for legends, which provide keys to understanding elements in the chart or figure
- identify the factors or variables represented, and understand how those factors or variables are related, as well as how they are measured
- look closely for possible patterns

Discussion

This section of a social science report explains the significance of the findings in light of the study's aims. This is also where researchers reflect on the study more generally, highlight ways their study could be improved (often called "limitations"), and/or identify areas of further research that the study has brought to light. Researchers sometimes lay out the groundwork for continued research, based on their contribution, as part of the ongoing scholarly conversation on the topic or issue at hand. A few excerpts from the Discussion section of Rathunde and Csikszentmihalyi's study reveal their adherence to these conventional expectations:

DISCUSSION

Given the well-documented decline in students' motivation and engagement in middle school, and the ongoing emphasis on middle school reform (Cross 1990; Eccles et al. 1993; Lipsitz et al. 1997), an increasing number of studies have explored how to change classroom practices and school cultures in ways that provide a healthier fit for young adolescents (Ames 1992; Eccles et al. 1993; Felner et al. 1997; Maehr and Midgley 1991). The present study adds to this area of research by comparing the motivation and quality of experience of students from five Montessori middle schools and six traditional middle schools. (p. 362)

Reveals why their study is important to the ongoing conversation on this topic

. . .

Results from the study showed that while engaged in academic work at school, Montessori students reported higher affect, potency (i.e., feeling alert and energetic), intrinsic motivation (i.e., enjoyment, interest), and flow experience than students from traditional middle schools. (p. 363)

Discusses important findings

. . .

The present study did not look at whether such experiential differences translated into positive achievement and behavioral outcomes for the students. This is an important topic for future research. (p. 363)

Identifies limitations in the study and an area for possible future research

Conclusion

On occasion, researchers separate out coverage of the implications of their findings (as part of a Discussion section) from other elements in the Discussion.

When this occurs, these researchers typically construct a separate Conclusion section in which they address conventional content coverage of their study's limitations, as well as their findings' implications for future research.

Following are some additional structural conventions to consider when you are reading or writing in the fields of the social sciences.

OTHER STRUCTURAL CONVENTIONS

Titles

Research reports in the social sciences, as in the natural sciences, tend to have rather straightforward titles that are concise and that contain key words highlighting important components of the study. Titles in the social sciences tend not to be creative or rhetorical, although there is a greater tendency toward creativity in titles in qualitative studies, which are more typically language driven than numerically driven. The title of Barbara Allen's study reported in the academic journal *Technology in Society*, for instance, identifies the central issues her study examined as well as the study location: "Environmental Justice, Local Knowledge, and After-Disaster Planning in New Orleans." Similarly, the title of Rathunde and Csikszentmihalyi's article is concise in its identification of the study's purpose: "Middle School Students' Motivation and Quality of Experience: A Comparison of Montessori and Traditional School Environments."

Abstracts

Another structural feature of reports in the social sciences is the abstract. **Abstracts** typically follow the title of the report and the identification of the researchers. They provide a brief overview of the study, explaining the topic or issue under study, the specific purpose of the study and its methods, and offering a concise statement of the results. These elements are usually summarized in a few sentences. Abstracts can be useful to other researchers who want to determine if a study might prove useful for their own work or if the methods might inform their own research purposes. Abstracts thus serve to promote collaboration among researchers. Though abstracts appear at the beginning of research reports, they're typically written after both the study and the research report are otherwise completed. Abstracts reduce the most important parts of a study into a compact space.

The following example from Rathunde and Csikszentmihalyi illustrates a number of the conventions of abstracts:

The study's purpose is identified.

Methods are briefly outlined.

This study compared the motivation and quality of experience of demographically matched students from Montessori and traditional middle school programs. Approximately 290 students responded to the Experience Sampling Method (ESM) and filled out questionnaires. Multivariate analyses showed that the Montessori students reported greater affect, potency (i.e., feeling energetic), intrinsic motivation, flow experience, and undivided interest (i.e., the combination of high intrinsic motivation and high salience or importance) while engaged in academic activities at school. The traditional middle school students reported higher salience while doing academic work; however, such responses were often accompanied by low intrinsic motivation. When engaged in informal, nonacademic activities, the students in both school contexts reported similar experiences. These results are discussed in terms of current thought on motivation in education and middle school reform.

— Results are provided.

— Implications of the research findings are noted.

Acknowledgments

Acknowledgment sections sometimes appear at the end of social science reports. Usually very brief, they offer a quick word of thanks to organizations and/or individuals who have helped to fund a study, collect data, review the study, or provide another form of assistance during the production of the study. This section can be particularly telling if you're interested in the source of a researcher's funding. Barbara Allen's "Environmental Justice, Local Knowledge, and After-Disaster Planning in New Orleans" contains the following Acknowledgments section:

ACKNOWLEDGMENTS

I would like to thank Carl Mitcham, Robert Frodeman, and all the participants of the Cities and Rivers II conference in New Orleans, March 21–25, 2006. The ideas and discussions at this event enabled me to think in a more interdisciplinary manner about the disaster and its impact as well as about my own assumptions regarding environmental justice and citizen participation in science.

In addition, I would like to thank the American Academy in Rome for giving me the time to think and write about this important topic. Conversations with my colleagues at the academy were invaluable in helping me to think in new ways about historic preservation and rebuilding. (p. 159)

References

The documentation system most often used in the social sciences is the style regulated by the American Psychological Association, which is referred to as **APA format**. (For more details about APA style conventions, see p. 77 of Chapter 4 and the Appendix.) Studies in the social sciences end with a References page that follows APA guidelines—or the formatting style used in the study, if not APA.

Appendices

Social science research reports sometimes end with one or more appendices. Items here are often referenced within the body of the report itself, as appropriate. These items may include additional data sets, calculations, interview questions, diagrams, and images. The materials typically offer context or support for discussions that occur in the body of a research report.

INSIDE WORK Observing Structural Conventions

Although we've discussed a number of structural expectations for reports in the social sciences, we need to stress again that these expectations are conventional. As such, you'll likely encounter numerous studies in the social sciences that rely on only a few of these structural features or that alter the conventional expectations in light of the researchers' particular aims. For this activity, we'd like you to do the following.

- Select a social science topic.

- Locate two articles published in peer-reviewed academic journals that address some aspect of your selected topic.

- Compare and contrast the two articles in terms of their structural features. Note both (1) instances when the articles follow the conventional expectations for social science reporting as explained in this chapter, and (2) instances when the articles alter or diverge from these expectations. Speculate as to the authors' reasoning for following the conventional expectations or diverging from them. ▶

LANGUAGE CONVENTIONS

As with structural conventions, the way social scientists use language can vary widely with respect to differing audiences and/or genres. Nevertheless, we can explore several language-level conventional expectations for writing in the social sciences. In the following sections, we consider the use of both active and passive voice, as well as the use of hedging (or hedge words) to limit the scope and applicability of assertions.

Active and Passive Voice

Many students have had the experience of receiving a graded paper back from an English teacher in high school and discovering that a sentence or two was marked for awkward or inappropriate use of the passive voice. This problem occurs fairly often as students acclimate their writing to differing disciplinary communities. As we discussed in Chapter 6, the passive voice usually appears with less frequency in the fields of the humanities, while writers in the social sciences and natural sciences use it more frequently, and with good purpose. (For a fuller discussion and examples of the differences between active and passive voice constructions, see pp. 136–37 in Chapter 6.)

You may wonder why anyone would want to add words unnecessarily or remove altogether the actor/agent from a sentence. The passive voice is often preferable in writing in the social sciences and natural sciences because, although it may seem wordy or unclear to some readers in some instances, skillful use of the passive voice can actually foster a sense that researchers are acting objectively or with neutrality. This does not mean that natural or social scientists are averse to the active voice. However, in particular instances, the passive voice can go a long way toward supporting an ethos of objectivity, and its use appears most commonly in the Methods sections of social science reports. Consider these two sentences that might appear in the Methods section of a hypothetical social science report:

Active Voice: We asked participants to identify the factors that most influenced their decision.

Passive Voice: Participants were asked to identify the factors that most influenced their decision.

With the agent, *we*, removed, the sentence in passive voice deemphasizes the researchers conducting the study. In this way, the researchers maintain more of a sense of objectivity or neutrality in their report.

Hedging

Another language feature common to writing in the social sciences is hedging. Hedging typically occurs when researchers want to make a claim or propose an explanation but also want to be extremely careful not to overstep the scope of their findings based on their actual data set. Consider the following sentences:

Participants seemed to be anxious about sharing their feelings on the topic.

Participants were anxious about sharing their feelings on the topic.

When you compare the two, you'll notice that the first sentence "hedges" against making a broad or sweeping claim about the participants. The use of *seemed to be* is a hedge against overstepping, or saying something that may or may not be absolutely true in every case. Other words or phrases that are often used to hedge include the following, just to name a handful:

probably	perhaps
some	possibly
sometimes	might
likely	it appears that
apparently	partially

Considering that social scientists make claims about human behavior, and that participants in a study may or may not agree with the conclusions, it's perhaps not surprising that writers in these fields often make use of hedging.

INSIDE WORK Observing Language Features

Use the two articles you located for the previous Inside Work exercise, in which you compared and contrasted their structural conventions.

- This time, study the language of the articles for instances of the two language conventions we've discussed in this section. Try to determine in what sections of the reports passive voice and hedging occur most frequently.

- Offer a rationale for your findings. If you find more instances of the use of passive voice in the Methods sections than in the Results sections, for instance, attempt to explain why that would be the case. Or, if you find more instances of verbal hedging in the Results sections than in the Methods sections, what do you think explains those findings? ▶

REFERENCE CONVENTIONS

The style guide for writing followed in most (but not all) social science fields is the *Publication Manual of the American Psychological Association* (APA). Many referencing conventions of the social sciences are governed by the APA, and some are worth examining in more detail.

In-Text Documentation

One of the distinguishing features of the APA method for documenting sources that are paraphrased, summarized, or cited as part of a report is the inclusion of a source's year of publication as part of the parenthetical notation in or at the end of a sentence in which a source is used. We can compare this to the MLA documentation system described in Chapter 6 through the following examples:

MLA: The study reports that "in some participants, writing block appears to be tied to exhaustion" (Jacobs 23).

APA: The study reports that "in some participants, writing block appears to be tied to exhaustion" (Jacobs, 2009, p. 23).

Although these examples by no means illustrate all the differences between MLA and APA styles of documentation, they do highlight the elevated importance that social sciences fields place on the year of a source's publication. Why? Imagine that you're reading a sociological study conducted in 2010 that examines the use of tobacco products among teenagers. The study references the finding of a similar study from 1990. By seeing the date of the referenced study in the in-text citation, readers can quickly consider the usefulness of the 1990 study for the one being reported on. Social scientists value recency, or the most current data possible, and their documentation requirements reflect this preference.

Summary and Paraphrase

Another reference distinction among the academic domains concerns how writers reference others' ideas. You've probably had experience writing papers for teachers who required you to cite sources as support for your ideas. You may have done this by copying the language directly from a source. If so, then you noted that these words belonged to another person by putting quotation marks around them and by adding a parenthetical comment identifying the source of the cited language. These practices hold true for writers in the social sciences as well.

However, as you become more familiar with the reference practices of researchers in these fields, you'll discover that social scientists quote researchers in other fields far less frequently than scholars in the humanities do. Why is this so? For humanist scholars, language is of the utmost importance, and how someone conveys an idea can seem almost inseparable from the idea being conveyed. Additionally, for humanists, language is often the "unit of measure"—that is, *how* someone says something (like a novelist or a poet) is actually *what* is being studied. Typically, this is not the case for social science researchers (with the exception of fields such as linguistics and communication, although they primarily address how study participants say something and not how prior research reported its findings). Instead, social scientists tend to be much more interested in other researchers' methodology and findings than they are in the language through which those methods or finding are conveyed. As a result, social scientists are more likely to summarize or paraphrase source materials than to quote them directly.

INSIDE WORK **Observing Reference Features**

In this section, we've suggested that two areas of conventional reference features in social science writing are (1) the elevated position of year of publication in the internal documentation of source material, and (2) the preference among social scientists for summarizing and paraphrasing sources.

- Use the same two studies that you examined for the last two Inside Work activities.

- Based on the principle that social scientists are concerned with the recency of research in their areas, examine the References page (the ending bibliography) for each study. How does the form of entries on the References page reflect the social science concern with the recency of sources?

- Look more closely at the introductions of the two articles, and note the number of times in each article another source is referenced. Count the number of times these sources are paraphrased, summarized, or quoted directly. Based on your findings, what can you conclude about the ways social scientists reference source material? ▶

COURTESY OF AYA MATSUDA

"My writing is mostly in the form of research papers that are published as articles in scholarly journals or chapters in scholarly books. I also review other applied linguists' manuscripts and write evaluation reports on them, usually to help journal editors decide whether or not to publish manuscripts in their journals. I also write book reviews that are published in scholarly journals. But because of the 'real-life' nature of the kinds of questions my field addresses, there are many other kinds of writing that applied linguists do. Textbooks, articles in newspapers and general magazines, policies, consultation reports, and public education materials (e.g., brochures) are some examples of other types of writing that my colleagues do. Grant writing is also an important kind of writing that researchers in my field do."

Genres of Writing in the Social Sciences

Scholars in the social sciences share the results of their research in various ways. As Dr. Matsuda reveals in her Insider's View, social scientists write in a variety of forms for differing venues. They might, for instance, present their work at a conference or publish their research results in a journal or a book.

In this section, we offer descriptions of, and steps for producing, two of the most common types of writing, or genres, required of students in introductory-level courses in the social sciences. These are the literature review and the theory-response paper. As genres, literature reviews and responses to social science theories sometimes appear as parts of other, longer works. Sometimes, though, they stand alone as complete works.

THE LITERATURE REVIEW

The literature review (also referred to as a review of scholarship) is one of the most common genres you will encounter in academic writing. Though this chapter is dedicated to writing in the social sciences, and the literature review genre occurs quite frequently in the social sciences, you can find evidence of reviews of scholarship in virtually every academic field—including the humanities, the natural sciences, and applied fields. The skills required for this genre are thus important to the kinds of inquiry that occur across all the academic disciplines.

At its core, the **literature review** is an analysis of published resources related to a specific topic. The purposes of a literature review may vary: students and researchers may conduct a review of scholarship simply to establish what research has already been conducted on a topic, or the review may make a case for how new research can fill in gaps or advance knowledge about a topic. In the former situation, the resulting literature review may appear as a freestanding piece of writing; in the latter, a briefer review of scholarship may be embedded at the start (usually in the introduction) of a research study.

In fact, most published scholarly articles include a review of literature in the first few pages. Besides serving as a means to identify a gap in the scholarship or a place for new scholarship, a literature review helps to establish researchers' credibility by demonstrating their awareness of what has been discovered about a particular topic or issue. It further respectfully acknowledges the hard work of others within the community of scholarship. Equally as important, the literature review illustrates how previous studies interrelate. A good literature review may examine how prior research is similar and different, or it may suggest how a group of researchers' work developed over several years and how scholars have advanced the work of others.

Insider Example
An Embedded Literature Review

Read the first two paragraphs to "Happiness in Everyday Life: The Uses of Experience Sampling," a social science study reported by Mihaly Csikszentmihalyi and Jeremy Hunter, as an example of a review of scholarship that is embedded within a larger study report. As you read, consider the purposes of a literature review to which it responds, including:

- reviewing what is known on a topic or issue
- identifying a gap in scholarship
- establishing the researchers' ethos

Excerpt from **Happiness in Everyday Life: The Uses of Experience Sampling**

MIHALY CSIKSZENTMIHALYI AND JEREMY HUNTER

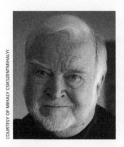

INTRODUCTION

Current understanding of human happiness points at five major effects on this emotion. These are, moving from those most impervious to change to those that are most under personal control: genetic determinants, macro-social conditions, chance events, proximal environment, and personality. It is not unlikely that, as behavioral geneticists insist, a "set level" coded in our chromosomes accounts for perhaps as much as half of the variance in self-reported happiness (Lykken & Tellegen, 1996; Tellegen et al., 1988). These effects are probably mediated by temperamental traits like extraversion, which are partly genetically determined and which are in turn linked to happiness (Myers, 1993). Cross-national

This section of the study's introduction establishes what is known about the topic at hand. It reviews the scholarship of others.

comparisons suggest that macro-social conditions such as extreme poverty, war, and social injustice are all obstacles to happiness (Inglehart & Klingemann, 2000; Veenhoven, 1995). Chance events like personal tragedies, illness, or sudden strokes of good fortune may drastically affect the level of happiness, but apparently these effects do not last long (Brickman et al., 1978; Diener, 2000). One might include under the heading of the proximal environment the social class, community, family, and economic situation—in other words, those factors in the immediate surroundings that may have an impact on a person's well-being. And finally, habits and coping behaviors developed by the individual will have an important effect. Hope, optimism, and the ability to experience flow can be learned and thus moderate one's level of happiness (Csikszentmihalyi, 1997; Seligman, 2002).

In this paper, we present a method that allows investigators to study the impact of momentary changes in the environment on people's happiness levels, as well as its more lasting, trait-like correlates. Research on happiness generally considers this emotion to be a personal trait. The overall happiness level of individuals is measured by a survey or questionnaire, and then "happy" people—those who score higher on a one-time response scale—are contrasted with less happy ones. Whatever distinguishes the two groups is then assumed to be a condition affecting happiness. This perspective is a logical outcome of the methods used, namely, one-time measures. If a person's happiness level is measured only once, it is by definition impossible to detect intra-individual variations. Yet, we know quite well that emotional states, including happiness, are quite volatile and responsive to environmental conditions.

WRITING A LITERATURE REVIEW

The scope of a freestanding literature review can vary greatly, depending on the knowledge and level of interest of the investigator conducting the review. For instance, you may have very little knowledge about autism, so your review of the scholarship might be aimed at learning about various aspects of the condition and issues related to it. If this is the case, your research would cast a pretty wide net. However, let's say you're quite familiar with certain critical aspects of issues related to autism and are interested in one aspect in particular—for example, the best therapies for addressing autism in young children. If this is the case, then you could conduct a review of scholarship with a more focused purpose, narrowing your net to only the studies that address your specific interest. Regardless of the scope of your research interest, though, literature reviews should begin with a clear sense of your topic. One way to narrow the focus of your topic is by proposing one or more research questions about it. (See Chapter 4 for more support for crafting such research questions.)

Once you've clearly established your topic, the next step is to conduct your research. The research you discover and choose to read, which may be quite

How does this review of previous scholarship affect your view of the writers? What does it say about them?

Reveals the researchers' purpose in the context of the review of scholarship. Identifies a space, or gap, in the scholarship for investigation.

substantial for a literature review, is chosen according to the scope of your research interest. (For help in narrowing a search based on key terms in your research question, see Chapter 4.) Here are some tips to conducting research:

- As you search for and review possible sources, pay particular attention to the *abstracts* of studies, as they may help you quickly decide if a study is right for your purposes.

- Unless your review of scholarship targets the tracing of a particular thread of research across a range of years, you should probably focus on the most current research available.

- After you've examined and gathered a range of source materials, determine the best way to keep track of the ideas you discover. Many students find this is a good time to produce an annotated bibliography as a first step in creating a literature review. (See Chapter 4, pp. 77–79, for more help on constructing annotated bibliographies.)

Another useful strategy for organizing your sources is a **source synthesis chart**. We recommend this as a way to visualize the areas of overlap in your research, whether for a broad focus (*What are researchers studying with regard to autism?*) or a more narrow one (*What are the best therapies for addressing autism in young children?*). Here's an abbreviated example of a source synthesis chart for a broad review of scholarship on autism:

| Authors of Study | Topics We Expect to Emerge in Scholarship | | | |
	Issues of Diagnosis	*Treatments*	*Debate over Causes*	*Wider Familial Effects*
Solomon et al. (2012)	pp. 252–55 Notes: emphasizes problems families face with diagnosis	pp. 257–60 Notes: examines and proposes strategies for family therapists	p. 253 Notes: acknowledges a series of possible contributing factors	
Vanderborght et al. (2012)		pp. 359–67 (results) Notes: examines use of robot for storytelling		
Grindle et al. (2012)		pp. 208–313 (results) Notes: school-based behavioral intervention program (ABA)		p. 229 Notes: home-based therapy programs
Lilley (2011)	pp. 135–37 Notes: explores the roles of mothers in diagnosis processes	pp. 143–51 Notes: explores rationales and lived experiences of ABA and non-ABA supporters		

In this case, the studies that we read are named in the column under "Authors of Study." The topics or issues that we anticipated would emerge from our review of the sources are shown in the top row. Based on our reading of a limited number of studies, four at this point, we can already discern a couple of areas of overlap in the scholarship: the diagnosis of autism in children, and intervention programs for children with autism. We can tell which researchers talked about what issues at any given time because we've noted the areas (by page number, along with some detail) where they addressed these issues. The empty cells in the synthesis chart reveal that our review of the sources, thus far at least, suggests there is less concern for those topics. We should note, however, that our review of sources is far from exhaustive. If you're able to create a visual representation of your research such as this one, then you're well on your way to creating a successful literature review. Keep in mind that the more detailed you can make your synthesis chart, the easier your process may be moving forward.

The last step before writing is perhaps the most challenging. You must synthesize the sources. **Synthesizing sources** is the process of identifying and describing the relationships between and among researchers' ideas or approaches: What trends emerge? Does the Grindle et al. study say something similar to the Lilley study about behavioral interventions? Something different? Do they share methods? Do they approach the issue of behavioral interventions similarly or differently? Defining the relationships between the studies and making these relationships explicit is critically important to your success. As you read the sources, you'll likely engage in an internal process of comparing and contrasting the researchers' ideas. You might even recognize similarities and differences in the researchers' approaches to the topic. Many of these ideas will probably be reflected in your synthesis chart, and you might consider color-coding (or highlighting in different colors) various cells to indicate types of relationships among the researchers you note.

A quick review of the abstract to "The Experience of Infertility: A Review of Recent Literature," a freestanding literature review published in the academic journal *Sociology of Health and Illness*, demonstrates the areas of synthesis that emerged from the professionals' examination of recent research on infertility:

Four synthesis points: (1) more recent studies approach the topic of infertility differently; (2) there remains a focus on examining infertility from a clinical viewpoint; (3) there are still questions about research methods, but there have also been "important improvements" in methods; (4) two trends emerged from these scholars' review of the current research.

About 10 years ago Greil published a review and critique of the literature on the socio-psychological impact of infertility. He found at the time that most scholars treated infertility as a medical condition with psychological consequences rather than as a socially constructed reality. This article examines research published since the last review. More studies now place infertility within larger social contexts and social scientific frameworks, although clinical emphases persist. Methodological problems remain, but important improvements are also evident. We identify two vigorous research traditions in the social scientific study of infertility. One tradition uses primarily quantitative techniques to study clinic patients in order to improve service delivery and to assess the need for psychological counseling. The other tradition uses primarily qualitative research to capture the experiences of infertile people in a sociocultural context. We conclude that more attention is now being paid to the ways in which the experience of infertility is shaped by social context. We call for continued progress in the development of a distinctly sociological approach to infertility and for the continued integration of the two research traditions identified here.

Presents conclusions reached as a result of the literature review project

Another example, this one a brief excerpt from the introduction to Csikszentmihalyi and Hunter's "Happiness in Everyday Life: The Uses of Experience Sampling," demonstrates the kind of synthesis that typically appears in reviews of scholarship when they're embedded as part of a larger study:

> Cross-national comparisons suggest that macro-social conditions such as extreme poverty, war, and social injustice are all obstacles to happiness (Inglehart & Klingemann, 2000; Veenhoven, 1995). Chance events like personal tragedies, illness, or sudden strokes of good fortune may drastically affect the level of happiness, but apparently these effects do not last long (Brickman et al., 1978; Diener, 2000).

The writers indicate that there is agreement between researchers: both Inglehart & Klingemann (2000) and Veenhoven (1995) have confirmed the finding in "cross-national comparisons."

Again, the writers indicate there is agreement between researchers: both Brickman et al. (1978) and Diener (2000) have confirmed this finding.

WRITING PROJECT **Writing a Literature Review**

Your goal in this writing project, a freestanding literature review, is to provide an overview of the research that has been conducted on a topic of interest to you.

THE INTRODUCTION

The opening of your literature review should introduce the topic you're exploring and assess the state of the available scholarship on it: What are the current areas of interest? What are the issues or elements related to a particular topic being discussed? Is there general agreement? Are there other clear trends in the scholarship? Are there areas of convergence and divergence?

THE BODY

Paragraphs within the body of your literature review should be organized according to the issues or synthesized areas you're exploring. For example, based on the synthesis chart shown earlier, we might suggest that one of the body sections of a broadly focused review of scholarship on autism concern issues of diagnosis. We might further reveal, in our topic sentence to that section of the literature review, that we've synthesized the available research in this area and that it seems uniformly to suggest that although many factors have been studied, no credible studies establish a direct link between any contributing factor and the occurrence of autism in children. The rest of that section of our paper would explore the factors that have been examined in the research to reiterate the claim in our topic sentence.

Keep in mind that the body paragraphs should be organized according to a claim about the topic or ideas being explored. They should not be organized merely as successive summaries of the sources. Such an organization does not promote effective synthesis.

THE CONCLUSION
Your conclusion should reiterate your overall assessment of the scholarship. Notify your readers of any gaps you've determined in the scholarship, and consider suggesting areas where future scholarship can make more contributions.

TECHNICAL CONSIDERATIONS
Keep in mind the conventions of writing in the social sciences that you've learned about throughout this chapter. Use APA documentation procedures for in-text documentation of summarized, paraphrased, and cited materials, as well as for the References page at the end of your literature review.

Insider Example
Student Literature Review

William O'Brien, a first-year writing student who had a particular interest in understanding the effects of sleep deprivation, composed the following literature review. As you read, notice how William's text indicates evidence of synthesis both between and among the sources he used to build his project. Notice also that he followed APA style conventions in his review.

Effects of Sleep Deprivation: A Literature Review

William O'Brien

North Carolina State University

Effects of Sleep Deprivation: A Literature Review

Introduction

The writer establishes the general topic, sleep deprivation, in the opening paragraph.

Everybody knows the feeling of having to struggle through a long day after a night of poor sleep, or sometimes even none at all. You may feel groggy, cloudy, clumsy, or unable to think of simple things. Sometimes you may even feel completely fine but then get angry or frustrated at things that normally would not affect you. No matter how you deal with it on that particular day, the reality is that even slight sleep deprivation can have extremely negative effects on mental ability. These effects are amplified when poor sleep continues for a long period of time. In a society with an ever-increasing number of distractions, it is becoming harder for many people to get the recommended amount of sleep. Sleep issues plague the majority of the U.S. population in one way or another. The Centers for Disease Control recognizes insufficient sleep as a public health epidemic.

Synthesis point: scholars agree on the negative effects of short-term sleep deprivation.

Synthesis point: questions remain about the effects of long-term sleep deprivation.

A lot of research is being conducted relating to sleep and sleep deprivation, and for good reason. Most researchers seem to agree that short-term sleep deprivation has purely negative effects on mental functioning in general. However, the particular types of effects caused by poor sleep are still being debated, as are the long-term implications of sleep deprivation. The questions for researchers, then, are under what circumstances do these negative effects begin to show, to what extent do they show, and most significant, what exactly are these negative effects?

Short-Term Effects of Sleep Deprivation

Focuses on scholarship that uses experimental studies to examine the effects of short-term sleep deprivation

In order to examine the direct and immediate effects of sleep deprivation, numerous researchers rely on experimentation, to control for other variables, for results. Research by Minkel et al. (2012) identified a gap in the research relating to how sleep deprivation affects the stress response (p. 1015). In order to test how inadequate sleep affects the stress response, the researchers divided healthy adults into two groups. Participants in the first group acted as the control and were allowed a 9-hour sleeping opportunity during the night. The second group was not allowed to sleep at all during that night. The next day, the participants completed stressful mental tasks (primarily math) and were asked to report their stress levels and mood via visual scales (Minkel et al., 2012, pp. 1016-1017). The researchers hypothesized that insufficient sleep would increase the stress response to each stressor as compared to the rested group, and that sleep loss would increase the stress response in proportion to the severity of the stressor (p. 1016). Their findings, however, showed that while the negative response to stressors was more profound for the sleep-deprived group, the differences in stress response between groups were not significant for the high-stressor condition. Still, the research clearly showed that sleep-deprived people have "significantly greater subjective stress, anger, and anxiety" in response to low-level stressors (p. 1019).

Research by Jugovac and Cavallero (2012) also focused on the immediate effects of sleep deprivation on attention. This study's purpose was to research the effects of sleep deprivation on attention through three attentional networks: phasic alerting, covert orienting, and executive control (Jugovac & Cavallero, 2012, p. 115). The study tested 30 young adults using the Attention Network Test (ANT), the Stanford Sleepiness Scale (SSS), and the Global Vigor-Affect Scale (GVA) before and after a 24-hour sleep deprivation period (p. 116). (All participants were subjected to sleep deprivation, because the tests before the sleep deprivation served as the control.)

Links the two studies reviewed according to their similar focus on short-term effects of sleep deprivation

The findings built upon the idea that sleep deprivation decreases vigilance and that it impairs the "executive control" attentional network, while appearing to leave the other components (alerting and orienting) relatively unchanged (pp. 121-122). These findings help explain how one night of missed sleep negatively affects a person's attention, by distinguishing the effects on each of the three particular attentional networks.

The writer links this study to the continuing discussion of short-term effects of sleep deprivation but also notes a difference.

Research by Giesbrecht, Smeets, Leppink, Jelicic, and Merckelbach (2013) focused on the effects that short-term sleep deprivation has on dissociation. This research is interesting and different from the other research in that it connects sleep deprivation to mental illness rather than just temporarily reduced mental functioning. The researchers used 25 healthy undergraduate students and kept all participants awake throughout one night. Four different scales were used to record their feelings and dissociative reactions while being subjected to two different cognitive tasks (Giesbrecht et al., 2013, pp. 150-152). The cognitive tasks completed before the night of sleep deprivation were used to compare the results of the cognitive tasks completed after the night of sleep deprivation. Although the study was small and the implications are still somewhat unclear, the study showed a clear link between sleep deprivation and dissociative symptoms (pp. 156-158).

This paragraph provides a summative synthesis, or an overview of the findings among the sources reviewed.

It is clear that sleep deprivation negatively affects people in many different ways. These researchers each considered a different type of specific effect, and together they form a wide knowledge base supporting the idea that even a very short-term (24-hour) loss of sleep for a healthy adult may have multiple negative impacts on mental and emotional well-being. These effects include increased anxiety, anger, and stress in response to small stressors (Minkel et al., 2012), inhibited attention—the executive control attentional network more specifically (Jugovac & Cavallero, 2012)—and increased dissociative symptoms (Giesbrecht et al., 2013).

Long-Term Effects of Sleep Deprivation

Although the research on short-term effects of sleep deprivation reveals numerous negative consequences, there may be other, less obvious, implications that studies on short-term effect cannot illuminate. In order to better understand these other implications, we must examine research relating to the possible long-term effects of limited sleep. Unfortunately, long-term sleep deprivation experiments do not seem to have been done and are probably not possible (due to ethical reasons and safety reasons, among other factors). A study by Duggan, Reynolds, Kern, and Friedman (2014) pointed out the general lack of previous research into the long-term effects of sleep deprivation, but it examined whether there was a link between average sleep duration during childhood and life-long mortality risk (p. 1195). The researchers analyzed data from 1,145 participants in the Terman Life Cycle Study from the early 1900s, which measured bedtime and wake time along with year of death. The amount of sleep was adjusted by age in order to find the deviations from average sleep time for each age group. The data were also separated by sex (Duggan et al., 2014, pp. 1196-1197). The results showed that, for males, sleeping either more or less than the regular amount of time for each age group correlated with an increased life-long mortality risk (p. 1199). Strangely, this connection was not present for females. For males, however, this is a very important finding. Since we can surmise that the childhood sleep patterns are independent of and unrelated to any underlying health issues that ultimately cause the deaths later on in life, it is more reasonable to assume causation rather

The writer shifts to an examination of the long-term effects of sleep deprivation and acknowledges a shift in the methods for these studies.

Establishes one of the study's central findings related to long-term effects of sleep deprivation

than simply correlation. Thus, the pattern that emerged may demonstrate that too little, or too much, sleep during childhood can cause physiological issues, leading to death earlier in life, which also reaffirms the idea that sleep is extremely important for maintaining good health.

While this study examined the relationship between sleep duration and death, a study by Kelly and El-Sheikh (2014) examined the relationship between sleep and a slightly less serious, but still very important, subject: the adjustment and development of children in school over a period of time. The study followed 176 third grade children (this number dropped to 113 by the end of the study) as they progressed through school for five years, recording sleep patterns and characteristics of adjustment (Kelly & El-Sheikh, 2014, pp. 1137-1139). Sleep was recorded both subjectively through self-reporting and objectively though "actigraphy" in order to assess a large variety of sleep parameters (p. 1137). The study results indicated that reduced sleep time and poorer-quality sleep are risk factors for problems adjusting over time to new situations. The results also indicate that the opposite effect is true, but to a lesser extent (p. 1146).

From this research, we gain the understanding that sleep deprivation and poor sleep quality are related to problems adjusting over time. This effect is likely due to the generally accepted idea that sleep deprivation negatively affects cognitive performance and emotional regulation, as described in the Kelly and El-Sheikh article (2014, pp. 1144-1145). If cognitive performance and emotional regulation are negatively affected by a lack of sleep, then it makes sense that the sleep-deprived child would struggle to adjust over time as compared to a well-rested child. This hypothesis has important implications. It once again affirms the idea that receiving the appropriate amount of quality sleep is very important for developing children. This basic idea does not go against the research by Duggan et al. (2014) in any way; rather, it complements it. The main difference between each study is that the research by Duggan et al. shows that too much sleep can also be related to a greater risk of death earlier in life. Together, both articles provide evidence that deviation from the appropriate amount of sleep causes very negative long-term effects, including, but certainly not limited to, worse adjustment over time (Kelly & El-Sheikh, 2014) and increased mortality rates (Duggan et al., 2014).

Conclusion

This research provides great insight into the short-term and long-term effects of sleep deprivation. Duggan et al. (2014) showed increased mortality rates among people who slept too much as well as too little. This result could use some additional research. Through the analysis of each article, we see just how damaging sleep deprivation can be, even after a short period of time, and thus it is important to seriously consider preventative measures. While sleep issues can manifest themselves in many different ways, especially in legitimate sleep disorders such as insomnia, just the simple act of not allowing oneself to get enough sleep every night can have significant negative effects. Building on this, there seems to be a general lack of discussion on *why* people (who do not have sleep disorders) do not get enough time to sleep. One possible reason is the ever-increasing number of distractions, especially in the form of electronics, that may lead to overstimulation. Another answer may be that high demands placed on students and adults through school and work, respectively, do not give them time to sleep enough. The most probable, yet most generalized, answer, however, is that people simply do not

Provides a summative synthesis that examines relationships between the sources and considers implications of findings

Conclusion acknowledges what appears as a gap in the scholarship reviewed

appropriately manage their time in order to get enough sleep.
People seem to prioritize everything else ahead of sleeping,
thus causing the damaging effects of sleep deprivation to
emerge. Regardless, this research is valuable for anyone who
wants to live a healthy lifestyle and function at full mental
capacity. Sleep deprivation seems to have solely negative
consequences; thus, it is in every person's best interests to get
a full night of quality sleep as often as possible.

References

Duggan, K., Reynolds, C., Kern, M., & Friedman, H. (2014). Childhood sleep duration and lifelong mortality risk. *Health Psychology, 33*(10), 1195-1203. doi:10.1037/hea0000078

Giesbrecht, T., Smeets, T., Leppink, J., Jelicic, M., & Merckelbach, H. (2013). Acute dissociation after one night of sleep loss. *Psychology of Consciousness: Theory, Research, and Practice, 1*(S), 150-159. doi:10.1037/2326-5523.1.S.150

Jugovac, D., & Cavallero, C. (2012). Twenty-four hours of total sleep deprivation selectively impairs attentional networks. *Experimental Psychology, 59*(3), 115-123. doi:10.1027/1618-3169/a000133

Kelly, R., & El-Sheikh, M. (2014). Reciprocal relations between children's sleep and their adjustment over time. *Developmental Psychology, 50*(4), 1137-1147. doi:10.1037/a0034501

Minkel, J., Banks, S., Htaik, O., Moreta, M., Jones, C., McGlinchey, E., Simpson, N., & Dinges, D. (2012). Sleep deprivation and stressors: Evidence for elevated negative affect in response to mild stressors when sleep deprived. *Emotion, 12*(5), 1015-1020. doi:10.1037/a0026871

THEORY RESPONSE ESSAY

Faculty in the fields of the social sciences often ask students to apply a social science theory to their own experiences. Psychology, sociology, and communication professors may ask students to use a psychological, sociological, or communication theory as a lens through which to explain their own or others' behaviors. Assignments like these involve writing a **theory response essay**. These assignments are popular for a number of reasons: (1) they allow students to engage with the fundamental elements of social sciences (theories); (2) they allow students to attend to the basic processes of data collection that are common in the social sciences; and (3) they are often quite engaging for faculty to read and are among the most interesting for students to write.

Whether you're using elements of Freud's dream theories to help understand your own dreams or you're using an interpersonal communication theory to understand why people so easily engage with you, the theory you're working with provides the frame for your analysis of some event or action. The theory is the core of any theory response.

Precisely because the theory is the core of such a writing project, it's crucial that in the beginning stage of such a project, you work with a theory that is actually applicable to the event, action, or phenomenon you want to understand better. You also want to choose a theory that genuinely interests you. Luckily, theories of human behavior and human system interactions abound. If you aren't assigned a theory for the project, then consider the places where you might go about locating a workable theory. Textbooks in the social sciences frequently make reference to theories, and numerous academic websites maintain lists and explanations of social science theories. Here are a few categories of theories that students often find interesting:

birth order theories   friendship theories

parenting style theories   stage theories of grieving

addiction theories

If you're unable to locate a workable theory that's "ready-made" for application to some experience(s), then consider building a theory based on your reading of a social science study. Though this certainly makes completing the assignment challenging, it is not without rewards.

Personal Experience

Regardless of whether you're working with a particular theory or constructing a theory of behavior based on one or more studies, consider making a list of the "moments" or events in your life that the theory might help you understand further. Your next step might be to write out detailed descriptions of those events as you see or remember them. Capture as much detail as you can, especially if you're writing from memory. Then apply the theory (all of its component parts) to your event or moment to see what it can illuminate for you: Where does it really help you understand something? Where does it fail to help? How might the theory need to change to account for your experiences?

Others' Experiences

Some instructors might ask you to collect and analyze the experiences of others. If you're assigned to do this, then you'll need to consider a data-collection method very carefully and ask your instructor if there are specific procedures at your institution that you should follow when collecting data from other people. We recommend, for now, that you think about the methods most commonly associated with qualitative research: observations, interviews, and open-ended surveys. These rich data-producing methods are most likely to provide the level of detail about others' experiences needed to evaluate the elements of your theory. Trying to understand others' experiences in light of the theory you're working with means considering the same analytical questions that you applied to your own experiences: Where does the theory really help you understand something? Where does it fail to help? How might the theory need to change to account for the experiences of those in your study?

WRITING PROJECT **Writing a Theory Response**

The goal of this writing project is to apply a theoretical framework from an area of the social sciences to your own experiences. The first step is to choose a theoretical framework that has some relevance to you, providing ample opportunity to reflect on and write about your own experiences in relation to the theory.

THE INTRODUCTION

The introduction to your study should introduce readers to the theory and explain all of its essential elements. You should also be clear about whether you're applying the theory to your own experiences or the experiences of others, or to both. In light of the work you did applying the theory, formulate a thesis that assesses the value of the theory for helping to understand the "moments," events, or phenomena you studied.

THE BODY

The body can be organized in a number of ways. If your theory has clear stages or elements, then you can explain each one and apply it to relevant parts of your experiences or those of others. If the theory operates in such a way that it's difficult to break into parts or stages or elements, then consider whether or not it's better to have subheadings that identify either (1) the themes that emerged from your application, or (2) your research subjects (by pseudonym). In this case, your body sections would be more like case studies. Ultimately, the organization strategy you choose will depend on the nature of the theory you're applying and the kinds of events you apply it to. The body of your project should establish connections among the theory's component elements.

THE CONCLUSION
The conclusion of your study should assert your overall assessment of the theory's usefulness. Reiterate how the theory was useful and how it wasn't. Make recommendations for how it might need to be changed in order to account for the experiences you examined in light of the theory.

TECHNICAL CONSIDERATIONS
Keep in mind the conventions of writing in the social sciences that you've learned about throughout this chapter. Use APA documentation procedures for in-text documentation of summarized, paraphrased, and cited materials, as well as for the References page at the end of your study.

Insider Example
Student Theory Response Paper

Matt Kapadia, a first-year writing student, was interested in understanding the ways people rationalize their own successes and failures. In the following paper, he analyzes and evaluates a theory about the social science phenomenon of attribution (as described at changingminds.org) through the lenses of both his own and others' experiences. As you read Matt's paper, pay close attention to the moments when he offers evaluation of the theory. Ask yourself if his evaluation in each instance makes sense to you, based on the evidence he provides. Notice also that he followed APA style conventions in his paper.

Evaluation of the Attribution Theory
Matt Kapadia
North Carolina State University

Evaluation of the Attribution Theory

In an attempt to get a better sense of control, human beings are constantly attributing cause to the events that happen around them (Straker, 2008). Of all the things people attribute causes to, behavior is among the most common. The attribution theory aims to explain how people attribute the causes of their own behaviors compared to the behaviors of those around them. Behaviors can be attributed to both internal and external causes. Internal causes are things that people can control or are part of their personality, whereas external causes are purely circumstantial and people have no control over the resulting events (Straker, 2008). The attribution theory uses these internal and external causes to explain its two major components: the self-serving bias and the fundamental attribution error. The self-serving bias evaluates how we attribute our own behaviors, whereas the fundamental attribution error evaluates how we attribute the behaviors of those around us (Straker, 2008). This paper evaluates how applicable the attribution theory and its components are, using examples from personal experience as well as data collected from others. Based on the findings of this evaluation, I believe the attribution theory holds true on nearly all accounts; however, the category of the self-serving bias might need revision in the specific area dealing with professionals in any field of study or in the case of professional athletes.

Attribution Theory: An Explanation

The foundation of the attribution theory is based in the nature of the causes people attribute behaviors to, whether it be internal or external. A person has no control over an external cause (Straker, 2008). An example would be a student failing a math test because the instructor used the

The writer establishes a thesis that includes an evaluation of the theory's usefulness in various contexts.

In this paragraph and the next two, the writer reviews and exemplifies the component parts of the theory. That is, the writer offers an explanation of the theory, with examples to illustrate points, as appropriate.

wrong answer key. In this case, the student had no control over the grade he received, and it did not matter how much he had studied. A bad grade was inevitable. A person can also attribute behavioral causes to internal causes. Internal causes are in complete control of the person distributing the behavior and are typically attributed to part of the individual's personality (Straker, 2008). An example would be a student getting a poor grade on his math test because he is generally lazy and does not study. In this case, the student had complete control of his grade and chose not to study, which resulted in the poor grade. These two causes build up to the two major categories within the attribution theory.

The first major category of the attribution theory is that of self-serving bias. This category explores how people attribute causes to their own behaviors. It essentially states that people are more likely to give themselves the benefit of the doubt. People tend to attribute their poor behaviors to external causes and their good behaviors to internal causes (Straker, 2008). An example would be a student saying he received a poor grade on a test because his instructor does not like him. In this case, the student is attributing his poor behavior, making a poor grade on the test, to the external cause of his instructor not liking him. However, following the logic of the theory, if the student had made a good grade on the test, then he would attribute that behavior to an internal cause such as his own good study habits.

The second category of the attribution theory, the fundamental attribution error, states the opposite of the self-serving bias. The fundamental attribution error talks about how people attribute cause to the behaviors of those around them. It states that people are more likely to attribute others' poor behaviors to internal causes and their good behaviors to external causes (Straker, 2008). An example would be a student saying his friend got a better grade on the math test than him because the instructor likes his friend more. The student jumps to the conclusion that his friend's good grade was due to the external cause of the instructor liking the friend more. Moreover, if his friend had done poorly on the test, the student would most likely attribute the poor grade to an internal factor, such as his friend not studying for tests.

Personal Experiences

A situation from my personal experiences that exemplifies the ideas of the attribution theory is my high school golfing career. For my first two years of high school, I performed relatively poorly on the golf course. My team consistently placed last in tournaments, and I ranked nowhere near the top golfers from neighboring high schools. I blamed my performance on factors such as the wind and flat-out bad luck. At the same time, I attributed my teammates' poor performances to factors such as not practicing hard enough to compete in tournament play. In doing this, I became no better a golfer because I was denying that the true cause of my poor scores was the fact that I was making bad swings and not putting in the hours of work needed to perform at a higher level. I finally recognized this during my junior year of high school. I started to realize that blaming everything but myself was getting me nowhere and that the only way to improve was to take responsibility for my own play. I started practicing in areas where my game needed improvement and putting in hours at the driving range to improve my swing memory. In doing this, I became a much better player; by the time my senior season came around, I was ranked one of the top golfers in my conference and one of the best amateur players in the state of North Carolina. However, my team still did not perform

The writer details a particular personal experience that he'll later analyze through the lens of the theory.

well due to my teammates' performance, which I continued to attribute to their poor practice habits.

This experience reflects the attribution theory in several ways. I displayed self-serving bias in my early years of high school golf. I attributed all of my poor performances to external causes, such as the wind, that I could not control. At the same time, I was displaying the fundamental attribution error in attributing my teammates' poor performances to internal causes such as not practicing hard enough. Throughout my high school golf career, I displayed the ideas of the attribution theory's category of the fundamental attribution error. However, during my junior and senior seasons my attributions moved away from the attribution theory's category of the self-serving bias. I began to attribute my poor performance to internal causes instead of the external causes I had previously blamed for my mishaps.

I believe that this is generally true for any athlete or professional seeking improvement in his or her prospective field. If a person continues to follow the ideas discussed in the category of the self-serving bias, he is not likely to improve at what he is trying to do. If Tiger Woods had constantly attributed his bad play to external causes and not taken responsibility for his actions as internal causes, he would have never become the best golfer in the world. Without attributing his poor behaviors to internal causes, he would have never gained the motivation to put in the hours of work necessary to make him the best. This observation can be applied to any other professional field, not only athletics. Personal improvement is only likely to take place when a person begins to attribute his or her poor behaviors to internal causes. I believe athletes and professionals represent problem areas for the theory of self-serving bias. However, the ideas of the fundamental attribution error generally hold true.

In this section, the writer analyzes his experiences through the lens of the theory.

Experiences of Others

The writer provides some insight into his methods for collecting data on the experiences of others.

To evaluate the attribution theory, I conducted an experiment to test both the fundamental attribution error and the self-serving bias. The test subjects were three friends in the same class at North Carolina State University: MEA101, Introduction to Geology. The students were asked to write down if their grades were good or bad on the first test of the semester ("good" meant they received an 80 or higher on the test, and "bad" meant they received below an 80). After the three students had done this for themselves, they were asked to attribute the grades of the others to a cause. This activity provided a clear sample of data that could test the validity of the self-serving bias and the fundamental attribution error. The reason I chose a group of friends versus a group of random strangers was that when people know each other they are more likely to attribute behavioral causes truthfully, without worrying about hurting anyone's feelings.

In this section, the writer provides the results of his data collection.

For the purposes of this experiment, the test subjects will be addressed as Students X, Y, and Z to keep their names confidential. The results of the experiment were as follows. The first student, Student X, received a "bad" grade on the test and attributed this to the instructor not adequately explaining the information in class and not telling the students everything the test would ultimately cover. However, Students Y and Z seemed to conclude that the reason Student X got a "bad" grade was because he did not study enough and is generally lazy when it comes to college test taking. Student Y received a "good" grade on the test and attributed this to studying hard the night before and to the fact that the test was relatively easy if one studied the notes. Students X and Z seemed to conclude that Student Y is a naturally smart student who usually receives good grades on tests regardless of how much he or she studies. Finally, Student Z received a "bad" grade on the test and attributed this to the instructor not covering the material on the test well enough for students to do well, a similar response to Student X. However, Students X and Y attributed Student Z's poor grade to bad study habits and not taking the class seriously.

These results tend to prove the ideas of both of the attribution theory's categories. Student X attributed his poor grade to the external cause of the instructor not covering the material well enough, demonstrating the self-serving bias. Students Y and Z attributed Student X's poor grade to the internal cause of Student X not studying hard enough and being a generally lazy college student, exemplifying the ideas of the fundamental attribution error. Student Y attributed her good grade to the internal cause of good study habits, also exemplifying the self-serving bias. However, Students X and Z felt that the reason for Student Y's success was the external cause of being a naturally good student who does well with or without studying, reflecting the ideas of the fundamental attribution error. Student Z's results also hold true to the theory. Student Z attributed his poor grade to the external cause of the instructor not covering the material adequately, a belief shared by Student X. Also holding true to the fundamental attribution error, both Students X and Y attributed Student Z's failure to the internal cause of poor study habits. Based on the findings of this experiment, I can say that both the fundamental attribution error and the self-serving bias hold true on all accounts.

Conclusion

Overall, I believe the attribution theory's categories of the self-serving bias and the fundamental attribution error are very applicable to everyday life. Based on the data gathered

In this section, the writer discusses the implications of his findings for his overall evaluation of the theory.

The writer concludes his response paper by reviewing his overall evaluation of the theory in light of his own and others' experiences he analyzed.

through personal experiences and the experiences of others through the experiment described in this analysis, I believe the theory holds true in the vast majority of situations where people attribute causes to behaviors and/or actions. The only area needing revisions is the self-serving bias when applied to the specific situations of professionals in a field of study or in the case of professional athletes. In both situations, improvement must occur in order to become a professional, and the only way this is likely to happen is by accepting internal fault for poor behaviors. By accepting internal fault, a person gains the motivation to put in the hours of work necessary to learn and improve at what he or she is trying to do. Without this improvement and learning, the ability to reach the professional level is slim to none. This displays the exact opposite of the attribution ideas that are described in the self-serving bias. With the exception of this small niche of situations that falsify the self-serving bias, the validity of the attribution theory is confirmed on all accounts.

Reference

Straker, D. (2008). *Attribution theory*. Retrieved from
changingminds.org: http://changingminds.org
/explanations/theories/attribution_theory.htm

tip sheet

Reading and Writing in the Social Sciences

- **Observation plays a critical role in the social sciences.** The academic fields of the social sciences, including sociology, psychology, anthropology, communication studies, and political science, among others, make observations about human behavior and interactions, as well as the systems and social structures we create to organize the world around us.

- **Social science research rests on theories of human behavior and human systems.** These are propositions that are used to explain specific phenomena. Social science research contributes to the continual process of refining these theories.

- **Researchers in the social sciences typically establish a hypothesis,** or a testable proposition that provides an answer or predicts an outcome in response to the research question(s) at hand, at the beginning of a research project.

- **Social science researchers must make choices about the types of methods they use** in any research situation, based on the nature of their line of inquiry and the kind of research question(s) they seek to answer. They may use a quantitative, qualitative, or mixed-methods research design to collect data for analysis.

- **Social scientists must guard against bias in their research.** As such, they rely on rigorous procedures and checks (e.g., ensuring appropriate sample sizes and/or using multiple forms of qualitative data) to ensure that the influence of any biases is as limited as possible.

- **IMRAD format—Introduction, Methods, Results, and Discussion—is a common *structure* used for the organization of research reports in the social sciences.** Although research reports in the social sciences may appear in any number of forms, much of the scholarship published in these fields appears in the IMRAD format.

- **The passive voice and hedging are uses of *language*** that characterize, for good reason, social scientific writing.

- **APA style is the most common documentation style used for *reference*** in the fields of the social sciences.

- **The genres of the literature review and the theory response paper are often produced in the fields of the social sciences.**

Reading and Writing in the Natural Sciences

Introduction to the Natural Sciences

Each of us has likely observed something peculiar in the natural world and asked, "Why does it do that?" or "Why does that happen?" Perhaps you've observed twinkling stars in the night sky and wanted to know why such distant light seems to move and pulse. Or perhaps you've wondered why, as you drive, trees closer to your car appear to rush by much faster than trees in the distance. Maybe you can recall the first time you looked at a living cell under a microscope in a biology course and wondered about the world revealed on the slide.

For most scientists, observation of natural phenomena is the first step in the process of conducting research. Something in the natural world captures their attention and compels them to pose questions. Some moments of scientific observation are iconic—such as Newton's observation of an apple falling from a tree as inspiration for his theory of gravity.

We interviewed Sian Proctor, a geologist at South Mountain Community College in Phoenix, Arizona, where she teaches classes in physical, environmental, and historical geology. Dr. Proctor has participated in several unique research team experiences, including the Hawaii Space Exploration Analog and Simulation (HI-SEAS) Mars habitat, the NASA Spaceflight and Life Sciences Training Program (she was a finalist for the 2009 NASA Astronaut Program), and the PolarTREC (Teachers and Researchers Exploring and Collaborating) program in Barrow, Alaska. Her work has taken her out of the college/university setting many

ANDREA TSURUMI

209

Geologists work out in the field, in labs, in educational institutions, and in the corporate world

SIAN PROCTOR, GEOLOGY

COURTESY OF SIAN PROCTOR

"Geology is an extremely diverse discipline encompassing specialties such as planetary geology, geochemistry, volcanology, paleontology, and more. The goal of a general geologist is to develop understanding of Earth processes such as the formation of mineral or energy resources, the evolution of landscapes, or the cause of natural disasters. Geologists work out in the field, in labs, in educational institutions, and in the corporate world. They collect data, analyze samples, generate maps, and write reports. Geology instructors teach students how to conceptualize all the information and processes mentioned above. It is our job to get students to think like a geologist (if you are teaching majors) or gain an appreciation for the Earth and Earth processes (if you are teaching non-majors)."

times. In her Insider's View, she describes the varied places in which scientists conduct observations and collect data as part of their work to understand the natural world.

As Dr. Proctor's description of her field reveals, those who work in the **natural sciences** study observable phenomena in the natural world and search for answers to the questions that spark researchers' interests about these phenomena. The disciplines of the natural sciences include a wide array of fields of academic research, including those in agricultural and life sciences, as well as physical sciences. As Dr. Proctor's own life experiences suggest, the search for understanding of natural phenomena can take scientists to many different places, and there is much variety in the ways they engage in research. One aspect that holds this diverse group of disciplines together, though, is a set of common values and procedures used in conducting research. You're probably already familiar with or at least have heard about the **scientific method**, a protocol for conducting research in the sciences that includes the following elements, or steps:

1. Observe.
2. Ask a research question.
3. Formulate a hypothesis.
4. Test the hypothesis.
5. Explain the results.

In this chapter, we describe the process of writing activities involved in scientific research. We present this strategy, the **scientific writing process**, in terms of a four-step process that maps onto the elements of the scientific method. The process begins with careful observation of natural phenomena and leads to the development of research questions. This step is followed by an investigation that culminates in the reporting or publication of the research:

1. Observe and describe.
2. Speculate.
3. Experiment.
4. Report.

The following table illustrates how the elements of the scientific method map onto the scientific writing process:

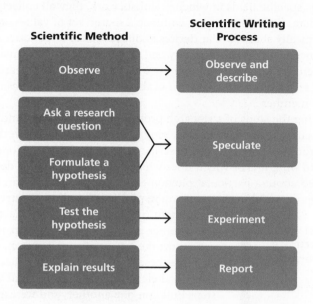

Before we delve too deeply into the research and writing practices of students and scholars of the sciences and how they connect, though, let's consider some of the areas of inquiry that make up the natural sciences.

Astronomy, biology, chemistry, earth science, physics, and mathematics are some of the core disciplinary areas within the natural sciences. Each area of inquiry includes numerous areas of specialty, or fields. For example, quantum physics, acoustics, and thermodynamics are three fields of physics. Conservation biology and marine science are fields of biology. Ecology (the study of organisms and their relationships to their environments) also operates under the umbrella of biology.

Interdisciplinary research is quite common in the natural sciences. An **interdisciplinary field** is an area of study in which different disciplinary perspectives or methods are combined into one. In such instances, methods for data collection often associated with one field may be used within another field of study. Consider biochemistry and biophysics, two interdisciplinary fields. In biochemistry, methods often associated with chemistry research are useful in answering questions about living organisms and biological systems. A biochemist may study aspects of a living organism such as blood alkalinity and its impact on liver function. Likewise, researchers in biophysics may use methods typical of physicists to answer research questions about biological systems. Biophysicists, for instance, might use the methodology of physics to unlock the mysteries of human DNA.

Research in the Natural Sciences

No matter the specific fields in which scientists work, they all collect, analyze, and explain data. Scientists tend to embrace a shared set of values, and as a result they typically share similar desires about how best to conduct research. The importance of any scientific study and its power to explain a natural phenomenon, then, are largely based on how well a researcher or research team designs and carries out a study in light of the shared values and desires of the community's members.

Completing the steps of a research project in a logical order and reporting the results accurately are keys to mastering research and writing in the natural sciences. You must observe and describe an object of study before you can speculate as to what it is or why it does what it does. Once you've described and speculated about a particular phenomenon, and posed a research question and a hypothesis about it, then you're positioned well to construct an experiment (if appropriate) and collect data to test whether your hypothesis holds true. When you report the results of your research, you must describe these steps and the data collected accurately and clearly. These research and writing steps build on one another, and we explore each step in more detail moving forward.

We interviewed biomedical scientist Paige Geiger, who teaches in the Department of Molecular and Integrative Physiology at the University of Kansas Medical Center, where she conducts experimental research in a laboratory on the effects of exercise and age on muscle metabolism and insulin resistance in Type II diabetes. In her Insider's View, she describes the kind of work that natural scientists do in her field and the importance of conducting careful, thorough data collection in the sciences.

Natural scientists collect evidence through systematic observation and experimentation, and they value methods that are quantifiable and replicable. In some instances, the natural sciences are described as "hard" sciences and the social sciences as "soft." This distinction stems from the tendency for natural scientists to value quantitative methods over qualitative methods, whereas social scientists often engage in both forms of data collection and sometimes combine quantitative and qualitative methods in a single

Insider's View

We value innovation, ideas, accurate interpretation of data, and scientific integrity

PAIGE GEIGER, MOLECULAR AND INTEGRATIVE PHYSIOLOGY

COURTESY OF PAIGE GEIGER

"A biomedical scientist performs basic research on questions that have relevance to human health and disease, biological processes and systems. We design scientific studies to answer a particular research question and then report our results in the form of a manuscript for publication. Good science is only as good as the research study design itself. We value innovation, ideas, accurate interpretation of data, and scientific integrity. There is an honor system to science that the results are accurate and true as reported. Manuscripts are peer-reviewed, and there is inherent trust and belief in this system."

study. (See Chapter 7, pp. 160–64, for more discussion of quantitative and qualitative methods.) Natural scientists value experiments and data collection processes that can be repeated to achieve the same or similar results, often for the purposes of generalizing their findings. Social scientists acknowledge the fluidity and variability of social systems and therefore also highly value qualitative data, which helps them to understand more contextual experiences.

INSIDE WORK) Considering a Natural Science Topic

> Generate a list of natural science topics or issues that interest you. Include any you may have read about or heard about recently, perhaps in a magazine or blog or from a television news report. Then select one for further consideration. Try to focus on a topic in which you're genuinely interested or for which you have some concern. If you're currently taking a natural science course or studying in one of the fields of the natural sciences, you might consider a topic that has emerged from your classroom or laboratory experiences. Answer the following questions.
>
> - What is the topic?
> - What do you think scientists are currently interested in discovering about this topic? What would you like to know about the topic?
> - Could the topic be addressed by researchers in more than one field of the sciences? Is the topic multidisciplinary in nature? What fields of the natural sciences are currently exploring or could potentially explore the topic?
> - How do or could scientists observe and collect data on some aspect of the topic?
> - In a broader sense, how does the topic connect with you personally? ▶

OBSERVATION AND DESCRIPTION IN THE NATURAL SCIENCES

Observing in the natural world is an important first step in scientific inquiry. Indeed, the first step of the scientific method is observation, as we show in the table on page 211. Beyond simple observation, though, researchers in the natural sciences conduct **systematic observations** of their objects of study. A systematic approach to observation requires a researcher to follow a regular, logical schedule of observation and to conduct focused and *neutral* observations of the object of study. In other words, the researcher tries to minimize or eliminate any bias about the subject matter and simply records everything he or she experiences, using the five senses. These observations, when written up to share with others as part of a research report, form the basis of description of the object of study. In order to move from observation to description, researchers must keep careful notes about their systematic observations. We discuss one method of tracking those observations, an observation logbook, on pages 227–28.

INSIDE WORK Thinking about Systematic Observation in the Sciences

Read student Kedric Lemon's account of his observations (on pp. 229–39) of various batteries, which he completed between October 11 and October 19, 2013, as part of his observation logbook. Then answer the following questions.

- What do you know about who the author is, based on the language used in this description? Provide at least two specific examples of how the language suggests something about the author's background, knowledge, or frame of reference.

- What can you determine about the observation schedule that the author—the researcher—followed to write this description?

- What kinds of details must the researcher have noted when observing to write this description?

- Did you find any language that seems to reveal bias on the part of the researcher? If so, make a note of this language.

- Based on your answers to the previous questions, what kind of plan for systematic observation would you recommend for the topic you chose in the previous Inside Work activity? ❱

MOVING FROM DESCRIPTION TO SPECULATION

The distinction between description and speculation is a subtle but important one to understand as it relates to scientific inquiry. As we've seen, descriptive writing in the sciences is based on observations. Of course, descriptive writing in the sciences isn't only applicable to a physical space or a stored energy device. A researcher could use similar observational methods to describe, say, the movements of an ant crawling along a sidewalk or tidal erosion along a section of a beach. **Descriptive writing**, then, is the action outcome associated with the first step of the scientific method—observation.

Speculative writing, in contrast, seeks to explain *how* or *why* something behaves the way that it does, and it is most commonly associated with asking a research question and formulating a hypothesis—the second and third steps of the scientific method. In order to speculate about how or why something exists or behaves as it does, a researcher must first observe and describe. Developing a thorough observational strategy and completing a descriptive writing process will help you to lay a solid foundation for speculating about your object of study so that you can later develop a clear research question and formulate a credible hypothesis worthy of testing through experimentation.

To understand the difference between description and speculation, compare the following two zoo memos written by middle school students.* Which

* From "Revitalizing Instruction in Scientific Genres: Connecting Knowledge Production with Writing to Learn in the Sciences," *Science Education* 83, no. 2 (1999), 115–30.

one is the better example of descriptive writing? Which one engages more fully in speculative writing?

Middle School Students' Science Memo #1 (12-year-old girls)

On Monday, July 17, DC and I observed the Muntjac. We learned that this animal comes from Asia. And that they eat the bottom part of the grass because it is fresher. We also learned that Muntjacs are very secretive animals. We also observed the difference between a male and female. The male has a [*sic*] earring in his left ear and he has horns. To urinate they stand on three legs. They like to disappear into the bushes. Their habbitat [*sic*] is bushy land.

Another behavior that we observed was the adult Muntjac often moved toward the fence and sniffed. We believe he was sniffing for food. He also rolled back his ears and stuck out his neck. We think he is always alert to protect his family from danger. On one occasion, the male Muntjac came toward the fence. KT [another student] held her shirt toward him. He ran away quickly.

In conclusion, we can say that the Muntjac constantly hunts for food, but is always alert to protect itself and its family.

Middle School Students' Science Memo #2 (13-year-old boys)

Today we went to the Atlanta zoo, where we looked at different animals such as zebras, giraffes, gorilas [*sic*], monkeys, and orangatangs [*sic*]. From my observations of the giraffe I found out that they are rather slow and are always eating. They do many strange things, such as wagging their tails, wiggling their ears, and poking out their tounges [*sic*]. They are very large and I read that they weigh more than a rhinoserous [*sic*], which is close to 2 or 2½ tons, and their necks extend out 7 ft. long. Their tails are 3 ft. long and are sometimes used for swating [*sic*] flies. At times the giraffes will stand completely motionless.

Discussion Questions

1. What similarities and differences do you notice between the two samples?
2. Which sample engages in speculative writing more fully, and which one adheres to mostly descriptive writing?

The process of articulating an explanation for an observed phenomenon and speculating about its meaning is an integral part of scientific discovery.

By collecting data on your own and then interpreting it, you're engaging in the production of knowledge even before you begin testing a proposed hypothesis. In this respect, scientific discovery is similar to writing in the humanities and the social sciences. Scientists interpret data gained through observation, modeling, or experimentation much in the same way that humanists interpret data collected through observation of texts. The ability to *observe systematically* and *make meaning* is the common thread that runs through all academic research.

Descriptive writing seeks to define an object of study, and it functions like a photograph. Speculative writing engages by asking *how* or *why* something behaves the way that it does, and in this sense it triggers a kind of knowledge production that is essential to scientific discovery. Following a writing process that moves a researcher from describing a phenomenon to considering *how* or *why* something does what it does is a great strategy for supporting scientific inquiry.

To this end, we encourage you to collect original data as modeled in the writing projects presented at the end of this chapter—the observation logbook (p. 228), the research proposal (p. 241), and the lab report (p. 248). Your view on the natural world is your own, and the data you collect and how you interpret that data are yours to decide. The arguments you form based on your data and your interpretation of that data can impact your world in small or very large ways.

INSIDE WORK **Practicing Description and Speculation**

For this activity, you should go outdoors and locate any type of animal (a squirrel, bird, butterfly, frog, etc.) as an object of study. Decide beforehand the amount of time you'll spend observing your subject (five minutes may be enough), and write down in a notebook as many observable facts as possible about your subject and its behavior. Consider elements of size, color, weight, distance traveled, and interaction with other animals or physical objects. If you're able to make a video or take a picture (e.g., with a cell phone camera), please do so.

After you've collected your notes and/or video, return to your classroom and write two paragraphs about your subject. Label the first paragraph "Description" and the second paragraph "Speculation," and use the following writing prompt.

Writing Prompt: The director of your local wildlife management agency needs a written report detailing the behaviors that you observed while watching your animal. Be sure to use your notes or video for accuracy. In the first paragraph, write a *description* of the subject and its behavior. Limit your description to observable facts; resist explaining why the subject appears the way it does or behaves the way it does. In the second paragraph, *speculate* about why the animal appears or behaves the way it does. Limit your speculation to the subject's behavior (or appearance) based on the observable data you wrote in your description. Finally, consider writing questions at the end of the second paragraph that might be answered in future research but that cannot be answered on the basis of your observations alone. ◗

Once you've conducted observations and collected data, you can move to speculation, which involves writing research questions and formulating a hypothesis, consistent with the second and third steps of the scientific method. Writing research questions and hypotheses in the natural sciences is a similar process to those activities in the social sciences (see Chapter 7). Devoting time to several days of focused observation, collecting data, and writing and reflecting on your object of study should trigger questions about what you're observing.

As you write research questions, you might consider the difference between open-ended and closed-ended research questions. A **closed-ended question** can be answered by *yes* or *no*. By contrast, an **open-ended question** provokes a fuller response. Here are two examples:

Closed-Ended Question: Is acid rain killing off the Fraser fir population near Mount Mitchell in North Carolina?

Open-Ended Question: What factors contribute to killing off the Fraser fir population near Mount Mitchell in North Carolina?

Scientists use both open-ended and closed-ended questions. Open-ended questions usually begin with *What*, *How*, or *Why*. Closed-ended questions can be appropriate in certain instances, but they can also be quite polarizing. They often begin with *Is* or *Does*. Consider the following two questions:

Closed-Ended Question: Is global warming real?

Open-Ended Question: What factors contribute to global warming?

Rhetorically, the closed-ended question divides responses into *yes* or *no* answers, whereas the open-ended question provokes a more thoughtful response. Neither form of question is better per se, but the forms do function differently. If you're engaging in a controversial subject, a closed-ended research question might serve your purpose. If you're looking for a more complete answer to a complex issue, an open-ended question might serve you better.

Once you've established a focused research question, informed by or derived on the basis of your observation and speculation about a natural science phenomenon, then you're ready to formulate a hypothesis. This will be a testable proposition that provides an answer or that predicts an outcome in response to the research question(s) at hand.

INSIDE WORK **Developing Research Questions and a Hypothesis**

Review the observation notes and the descriptions and explanations you produced in the Inside Work activity on page 216. What potential research questions emerged? For example, in an observation logbook about house finches and nesting practices written by one of the authors of this textbook, a question that remained unanswered was why two eggs from the initial brood of five were removed from the nest. Potential research questions for a study might include the one shown here.

> **Research Question:** **Do female house finches remove eggs from their own nests?**

From such a question, we can formulate a hypothesis.

> **Hypothesis:** **Our hypothesis is that female house finches do remove eggs from their own nests. Furthermore, our observational data supports other scholars' claims that female house finches cannibalize their brood on occasion.**

Now you try it. Write down at least two research questions that emerged from your observations, and then attempt to answer each question in the form of a hypothesis. Finally, discuss your hypotheses with a classmate or small group, and make the case for which one most warrants further study. Freewrite for five minutes about the evidence you have or additional evidence you could collect that would support your chosen hypothesis. ▶

DESIGNING A RESEARCH STUDY IN THE NATURAL SCIENCES

As we've noted, research in the natural sciences most often relies on quantitative data to answer research questions. While there are many ways to collect and analyze quantitative data, most professional scientists rely on complex statistical procedures to test hypotheses and generate results.

We interviewed Michelle LaRue, a research fellow at the Polar Geospatial Center, a research group based at the University of Minnesota. Her doctorate is in conservation biology, and her research has focused mainly on large-mammal habitat selection and movement—in particular, the phenomenon of potential recolonization of cougars in the American Midwest. In her Insider's View excerpt, Dr. LaRue describes the kinds of questions she asks as a scientist and the kinds of data collection and analysis she typically undertakes as part of her efforts to answer her research questions.

In the previous two sections, we discussed how to conduct systematic observation that leads to description of a phenomenon, and then we explored processes for speculating about what you observed in order to construct a research question and a hypothesis. One way to test a hypothesis is to engage in a systematic observation of the target of your research phenomenon. Imagine that you're interested in discovering factors that affect the migration patterns of bluefin tuna, and you've hypothesized that water temperature has some effect on those patterns. You could then conduct a focused observation to test your hypothesis. You might, for instance, observe bluefin tuna in their migration patterns and measure water temperatures along the routes.

Another way to test a hypothesis, of course, is to design an experiment. Experiments come in all shapes and sizes, and one way to learn about the experimental methods common to your discipline is by reading the Methods sections of peer-reviewed scholarly articles in your field. Every discipline has slightly different approaches to experimental design. Some disciplines, such as astronomy, rely almost exclusively on non-experimental systematic observation, while others rely on highly controlled experiments. Chemistry is a good example of the latter.

One of the most common forms of experimental design is the **comparative experiment**. In a comparative experiment, a researcher tests two or more types of objects and assesses the results. For example, an engineering student may want to test different types of skateboard ball bearings. She may design an experiment that compares a skateboard's distance rolled when using steel versus ceramic bearings. She could measure distances rolled, speed, or the time it takes to cover a preset distance when the skateboard has steel bearings and when it has ceramic bearings.

In some disciplines of the natural sciences, it's common practice to test different objects against a control group. A **control group** is used in a comparative experimental design to act as a baseline with which to compare other objects. For example, a student researcher might compare how subjects score on a memorization test after having consumed (a) no coffee, (b) two cups of decaf coffee, or (c) two cups of caffeinated coffee. In this example, the group of subjects consuming no coffee would function as a control group.

Hear more about the prewriting process from a professional mathematician.

Regardless of a study's design, it is important to realize that academic institutions have very clear policies regarding experimental designs that involve human subjects, whether that research is being conducted by individuals in the humanities, the social sciences, or the natural sciences. Both professional and student researchers are required to submit proposals through an institutional review board, or IRB. In the United States, *institutional review boards* operate under federal law to ensure that any experiment involving humans is ethical. This is often something entirely new to undergraduate students, and it should be taken seriously. No matter how harmless a test involving human subjects may seem, you should determine if you must submit your research plans through an IRB. This can often be done online. Depending on the nature and scope of your research, though, the processes of outlining the parameters of your research for review may be quite labor-intensive and time-consuming. You should familiarize yourself with the protocol for your particular academic institution. An online search for "institutional review board" and the name of your school should get you started. (For more on the role of institutional review boards, see Chapter 7.)

INSIDE WORK **Freewriting about an Experiment**

Start this activity by writing, in one sentence, what your initial research goal was when you began an observation about a phenomenon that interested you. You might draw on your writing from earlier Inside Work activities to start.

Example: **My goal was to study a bird's nest I discovered on my front porch.**

For many students beginning their inquiry in the sciences, learning about a topic may be the extent of their initial objective. For more advanced students, however, starting an observation from a strong knowledge base may sharpen the objective. The example below draws on prior knowledge of the object of study.

Example: **My goal was to determine whether a female house finch eats her own eggs.**

Once you've written down what your initial objective was, then freewrite for five minutes about what you now know. What are the most important things you learned about your object of study?

Most important, what hypothesis can you make about your object of study?

Hypothesis: **My observational data suggest that female house finches often remove eggs from their nest and may occasionally cannibalize their brood.**

After developing a hypothesis, the next step in the scientific method is to test the hypothesis. Keep in mind data in the sciences to support a hypothesis come from either a systematic observation or an experiment.

Freewrite for five minutes about how you could collect data that would test your hypothesis. As you write, consider feasible methods that you could follow soon, as well as methods that might extend beyond the current semester but that you could develop into a larger project for later use in your undergraduate studies. Consider whether an experiment or a systematic observation would be more useful. Most important, use your imagination and have fun. ▶

After observing and describing, speculating and hypothesizing, and conducting an experimental study or systematic observation, scientists move toward publishing the results of their research. This is the final step of the scientific method and the final stage of the scientific writing process that we introduced at the beginning of the chapter: scientists explain their results by reporting their data and discussing its implications. There are multiple forms through which scientists report their findings, and these often depend on the target audience. For instance, a scientist presenting his research results at an academic conference for the consideration of his peers might report results in the form of a poster presentation. Research results can also be presented in the form of an academic journal article. A scientist who wants to present her results to a more general audience, though, might issue a press release. In the next two sections of this chapter, we discuss conventions for reporting results in the natural sciences and provide examples of common genres that researchers in the natural sciences produce as a means of reporting their results.

Conventions of Writing in the Natural Sciences

Although the different fields of study that make up the natural sciences have characteristics that distinguish them from one another, a set of core values and conventions connect these areas of inquiry. The values shared among members of the scientific community have an impact on the communication practices and writing conventions of professionals in natural science fields:

- objectivity
- replicability
- recency
- cooperation and collaboration

In this section, we examine each of these commonly held values in more detail. And we suggest that these values are directly linked to many of the conventions that scientists follow when they write, or to the ways scientists communicate with one another more generally.

COURTESY OF MICHELLE LaRUE

"I learned the conventions of science writing through literature review, imitation, and a lot of practice: this often included pages and pages of

feedback from advisors and colleagues. Further, reading wildlife and modeling articles helped me focus on the tone, writing style, and format expected for each journal. After that, it was all about practicing my writing skills.

"I also learned the KISS principle during my undergraduate career: Keep It Simple, Stupid. This mantra reminds me to revise my writing so it's clear, concise, and informative. It is my opinion that science writing can be inherently difficult to understand, so it's important to keep the message clear and straightforward.

"I find that as I progress and hone my writing and research skills, sitting down to write gets easier, and I have been able to move up in the caliber of journal in which I publish papers. Writing is a skill that is never perfected; striving for the next best journal keeps me focused on improvement."

OBJECTIVITY

In her Insider's View, Michelle LaRue notes the importance of maintaining clarity in the presentation of ideas in science writing. Of course, clarity is a general expectation for all writing, but the desire for clarity in science writing can also be linked to the community's shared value of objectivity. As we noted earlier, **objectivity** (or neutrality) in observation and experimentation are essential to the research that scientists do. Most researchers in the natural sciences believe that bias undermines the reliability of research results. When scientists report their results, therefore, they often use rhetorical strategies that bolster the appearance of objectivity in their work. (Note that our marginal annotations below indicate which parts of the SLR model apply—structure, language, and reference; see Chapter 5.)

Rhetorical Features That Convey Objectivity

Titles may be considered a **language** and/or a **structural** feature of a text.

- **Titles**   Scientists tend to give their reports very clear titles. Rarely will you find a "creative" or rhetorical title in science writing. Instead, scientists prefer non-rhetorical, descriptive titles, or titles that say exactly what the reports are about.

The IMRAD format is a common **structure** used in scientific writing.

- **IMRAD**   Researchers in the sciences generally expect research reports to appear in the IMRAD format (for more detail, see Chapters 5 and 7):

  Introduction

  Methods

  Results

  Discussion

Notice how the structure of IMRAD parallels the ordered processes of the scientific writing process (observe and describe, speculate, experiment, and report). This reporting structure underscores the importance of objectivity because it reflects the prescribed steps of the scientific method, which is itself a research process that scientists follow to reduce or eliminate bias.

- **Jargon**   Scientists often communicate in highly complex systems of words and symbols that hold specific meaning for other members of the scientific community. These words and symbols enable scientists to communicate their ideas as clearly as possible. For example, a scientific researcher might refer to a rose as *Rosa spinosissima*. By using the Latin name, she communicates that the specific type of rose being referenced is actually the one commonly referred to as the Scotch rose. The use of jargon, in this instance, is actually clarifying for the intended audience. Using jargon is a means of communicating with precision, and precision in language is fundamental to objective expression.

  > Jargon is a **language** feature.

- **Numbers**   Scientific reports are often filled with charts and figures, and these are often filled with numbers. Scientists prefer to communicate in numbers because unlike words, which can inadvertently convey the wrong meaning, numbers are more fixed in terms of their ability to communicate specific meaning. Consider the difference between describing a tree as "tall" and giving a tree's height in feet and inches. This represents the difference between communicating somewhat qualitatively and entirely quantitatively. The preference for communicating in numbers, or quantitatively, enables members of the scientific community to reduce, as much as possible, the use of words. As writers use fewer words and more numbers in scientific reports, the reports appear to be more objective.

  > Numbers and other symbol systems function in much the same way as words, so they may be understood as a **language** feature.

INSIDE WORK Looking for Conventions of Objectivity

Although we've discussed a number of writing expectations related to objectivity in the sciences, we need to stress again that these expectations are conventional. As such, you'll likely encounter numerous studies in the sciences that rely on only a few of these features or that alter the conventional expectations in light of a study's particular aims.

- Choose a scientific topic of interest to you, and locate a research article on some aspect of that topic in a peer-reviewed academic journal article.
- Once you've found an appropriate article, look at the features of the article that reflect the writers' desire for objectivity in science reporting. Note evidence of the following in particular:
  - straightforward, descriptive titles
  - IMRAD
  - jargon
  - numbers

- Take notes on instances where the article follows conventional expectations for science reporting as explained in this chapter, as well as instances where the article alters or diverges from these expectations. Speculate as to the authors' reasoning for their decisions to follow the conventional expectations or to diverge from them. ◗

REPLICABILITY

Like objectivity, the **replicability** of research methods and findings is important to the production and continuation of scientific inquiry. Imagine that a scientific report reveals the discovery that eating an orange every day could help prevent the onset of Alzheimer's disease. This sounds great, right? But how would the larger scientific community go about verifying such a finding? Multiple studies would likely be undertaken in an attempt to replicate the original study's finding. If the finding couldn't be replicated by carefully following the research procedures outlined in the original study, then that discovery wouldn't contribute much, if anything at all, to ongoing research on Alzheimer's disease precisely because the finding's veracity couldn't be confirmed.

Several conventional aspects of writing in the natural sciences help ensure the replicability of a study's findings and underscore replicability as an important value shared by members of the scientific community:

Detail may be considered a **language** or a **structural** feature.

- **Detail**   One of the conventional expectations for scientific writing involves the level of detail and specificity, particularly in certain areas of research reporting (e.g., Methods sections). Scientists report their research methods in meticulous detail to ensure that others can replicate their results. This is how scientific knowledge builds. Verification through repeated testing and retesting of results establishes the relative absolute value of particular research findings. It's not surprising, then, that the Methods sections of scientific research reports are typically highly detailed and specific.

Hypotheses are a **structural** feature.

- **Hypotheses**   Hypothesis statements predict the outcome of a research study, but the very nature of a prediction leaves open the possibility of other outcomes. By opening this "space" of possibility, scientists acknowledge that other researchers could potentially find results that differ from their own. In this way, scientists confirm the importance of replicability to their inquiry process.

Precision is a **language** feature of scientific writing.

- **Precision**   Scientific communication must be precise. Just as researchers must choose words and numbers with attention to accuracy and exactness, so too must they present their findings and other elements of scientific communication with absolute precision. As you engage with scientific discourse, you should be able to develop a sense of the precise nature of scientific description and explanation.

RECENCY

Scientific research is an ongoing process wherein individual studies or research projects contribute bits of information that help fill in a larger picture or research question. As research builds, earlier studies and projects become the bases for additional questioning and research. As in other fields, like the social sciences, it's important that scientific researchers remain current on the developments in research in their respective fields of study. To ensure that their work demonstrates **recency**—that is, it is current and draws on knowledge of other recent work—researchers in the sciences may follow numerous conventions in their writing, including those listed here:

Learn about putting your research in context.

The purposeful selection of resources is a **reference** feature.

- **Reference Selection** Scientific writers typically reference work that has been published recently on their topic. One way to observe the importance of recency is to examine the dates of studies and other materials referenced in a recent scientific publication. If you do this, then you'll likely discover that many studies referenced are relatively recent. By emphasizing recent research in their reports, scientists convey the importance of remaining on top of the current state of research in their areas of expertise. Knowledge production in the natural sciences is highly methodical and builds slowly over time. It's not surprising, then, that the recency of research is important to members of this community.

- **Documentation** The importance of recency is also evident in the methods of documentation most often employed in the fields of the natural sciences, like APA (American Psychological Association), CSE (Council of Science Editors), and others. Unlike MLA, for instance, where only page numbers appear next to authors' names in parenthetical citations—as in (Jacobs 1109)—the APA system requires a date next to authors' names, both for in-text references to research and, often, in parenthetical remarks when this is not provided in text—as in (Jacobs, 2012, pp. 198–199). The fact that the APA method generally requires a date highlights scientists' concern for the recency of the research they reference and on which they build their own research.

Scientific documentation systems of **reference** are often APA or CSE, but they are frequently also specific to the journal in which an article is published.

INSIDE WORK **Looking for Conventions of Replicability and Recency**

Start with the same article that you used in the previous Inside Work activity to search for writing conventions that demonstrate objectivity. If you don't already have an article selected, search for an academic article published in a peer-reviewed journal on a scientific topic of interest to you.

- Look for at least one example of the researchers' use of the following conventions that might demonstrate how much they value replicability and recency. Note evidence of the following:

- details
- precision
- timely reference selection
- choice of documentation style

- Take notes on instances where the article follows conventional expectations for science reporting as explained in this chapter and instances where the article alters or diverges from these expectations. Speculate as to the authors' reasoning for their decisions to follow the conventional expectations or to diverge from them. ◗

COOPERATION AND COLLABORATION

Unlike the clichéd image of the solitary scientist spending hours alone in a laboratory, most scientists would probably tell you that research in their fields takes place in a highly cooperative and collaborative manner. In fact, large networks of researchers in any particular area often comprise smaller networks of scholars who are similarly focused on certain aspects of a larger research question. These networks may work together to refine their research goals in light of the work of others in the network, and researchers are constantly sharing—through publication of reports, team researching, and scholarly conferences—the results of their work. Several common elements in scientific writing demonstrate this value:

The presentation of researchers' names is a **structural** feature.

- **Presentation of Researchers' Names** As you examine published research reports, you'll find that very often they provide a list, prominently, of the names of individuals who contributed to the research and to the reporting of that research. This information usually appears at the top of reports just after the title, and it may also identify the researchers' institutional and/or organizational affiliations. Names typically appear in an order that identifies principal researchers first. Naming all the members of a research team acknowledges the highly cooperative nature of the researching processes that many scientists undertake.

How researchers in the natural sciences treat one another is a feature of **reference**.

- **Treatment of Other Researchers** Another feature you might notice is the way science professionals treat one another's work. In the humanities, where ideas are a reflection of the individuals who present them, researchers and writers often direct commentary toward individuals for their ideas when there's cause for disagreement or dissatisfaction with other researchers' ideas. Conventionally, however, science researchers treat others in their field more indirectly when objections to their research or findings come up. Instead of linking research problems to individuals, scientists generally direct their dissatisfaction with others' work at problems in the research process or design. This approach highlights the importance of cooperation and collaboration as shared values of members of the scientific community.

Genres of Writing in the Natural Sciences

Once again we interviewed Paige Geiger, whom you met earlier in this chapter. She teaches in the Department of Molecular and Integrative Physiology at the University of Kansas Medical Center. In the following Insider's View, she describes two important genres of writing in her discipline.

In this section, we provide descriptions of, and steps for producing, three of the most common genres that writers in the natural sciences produce: an observation logbook, a research proposal, and a lab report. The observation logbook provides a location for carefully recording systematic observations at the beginning of a research process. The research proposal forms the basis for the important grant proposals that Dr. Geiger describes, and it might draw on information gathered during initial observations. It also incorporates other elements such as a careful review of the literature on a subject. Lab reports are the final results of research, and they reflect the form in which a scientist might ultimately publish a scholarly journal article.

AN OBSERVATION LOGBOOK

Systematic and carefully recorded observations can lay a solid foundation for further exploration of a subject. These observations might take place as an initial step in the scientific writing process, or they might be part of the data collection that occurs when testing a hypothesis.

Insider's View
Two different forms serve very different purposes

PAIGE GEIGER, MOLECULAR AND INTEGRATIVE PHYSIOLOGY

COURTESY OF PAIGE GEIGER

"There are two kinds of writing in my discipline—writing manuscripts for publication and writing grant applications. The two different forms serve very different purposes. We must write grant applications to obtain funding to perform our research. The applications are usually for three to five years of funding and are very broad in scope. These applications describe what you plan to do and the results you expect to see. This requires a comprehensive assessment of the literature, an explanation of what is known and what is unknown regarding the specific research question. You must describe how you will design the studies, how you will collect and analyze data, and how you will handle problems or unexpected results. This kind of writing is considered an art form. It is something that you improve upon throughout your career.

"Writing manuscripts for publication is quite different. A manuscript deals with a very specific research question, and you report the direct results of your investigation. There is some background information to place the study in a greater context, but the focus is on the data and the interpretation of the data from this one study. This form of writing is very direct, and overinterpretation of the data is frowned upon. In addition to these two forms of writing, scientists also write review articles and textbook chapters on their area of expertise."

One way to focus and record your observations of a phenomenon is to keep an **observation logbook**. The tools that we discuss over the next few pages parallel the kind of systematic observation that's needed to undertake scientific inquiry, and the observation logbook functions as both a data collection tool and a reflective strategy that becomes useful later in research writing and reporting stages. The observation logbook is a foundational part of the research process that precedes the construction of a formal lab report.

Sometimes observation logbooks include speculation in addition to description, but the two types of writing should be clearly separated from each other to ensure that the more objective observations are not confused with any speculation. Speculation, you'll remember, occurs at the stage of formulating research questions and a hypothesis.

WRITING PROJECT **Keeping an Observation Logbook**

For this project, you'll need to decide on a particular object of study and collect at least five days of observations about it. We encourage you to develop a multi-modal data collection process that includes digital photos and videorecorded evidence. For each daily entry, begin with description before moving into speculation. A natural outgrowth of descriptive writing should include brainstormed research questions that could be answered with further experiments, research, or observation.

For each day, you should do the following.

1. Collect and include photographic evidence.
2. Write a description of your object of study and its status.
3. Generate questions for future research.

At the conclusion of five days, answer the following questions.

1. What did I learn about my object of study?
2. What claims can I now make regarding my object of study?
3. What evidence could I use from my observational logbook to support those claims?

Finally, write a one- to two-page paper that includes two sections.

1. Description
2. Speculation

For the **Description** section, write a description of your object of study. Refrain from explaining or speculating about behavior in this section; simply write the observations that are most important to give a clear picture of what you studied and how you studied it. Make use of time measurements and physical measurements such as weight, size, and distance. For the **Speculation** section, assert suggestions as to why certain behaviors emerged in your object of study. You might begin by deciding which behaviors most surprised you or seem most interesting to you.

You might also use the Speculation section as a place to begin thinking about future questions that could be explored as a follow-up to your observations.

Insider Example
Student Observation Logbook

In the following observation logbook, written using APA style conventions, student Kedric Lemon catalogs his observations concerning the efficiency of several types of batteries over a five-day period. His observations form the basis for his experimental study, which appears later on pages 249–59. You'll notice that he carefully separates his observations and description from any speculation about why he observed what he did.

Comparing the Efficiency of Various Batteries
Being Used over Time
Kedric Lemon
North Carolina State University

Comparing the Efficiency of Various Batteries Being Used over Time

Logbook

Introduction

The purpose of this study is to see if some batteries can hold their charge for longer periods of time than others. Also, this observational study will determine if there is an overwhelming difference between generic brand and the top name-brand batteries, or if people are really just paying for the name. I will perform this study by first recording all of the batteries' initial voltages, and then each day I will allow each of the batteries to go on for an hour and a half and then again check the voltage. It is important that I test the voltage immediately after the batteries come out of the flashlight. Otherwise, results could vary. Before putting in the second set of batteries, I will allow the flashlight to cool down for an hour because after being in use for an hour and a half they are likely hot, and I am unsure if this can affect how fast the other batteries will be consumed. I will look first at how much charge was lost over the duration that they were used in the flashlight. Then I will compare them to one another to determine which one has lost the most over a day, and second, which of the batteries still holds the highest voltage. I hypothesize that the Duracell battery will decrease at the slowest rate and that it will have the highest initial voltage.

Establishes the purpose of the study, and outlines an observational protocol

Outlines methods

Establishes a hypothesis

Friday, October 11, 2013

Begins a report on systematic observation of the phenomenon

Today was the first day that I observed results from my batteries. I believe that the first thing is to state the initial voltages of all three types of batteries. (Also, it is important to note that these are the averages of the batteries, as the flashlight demands two AA batteries.)

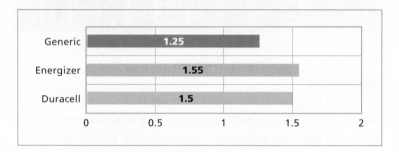

So from these initial observations the Energizer battery has the highest initial voltage.

After allowing all of the batteries to run for an hour and a half, I again took the voltages of the batteries and found this:

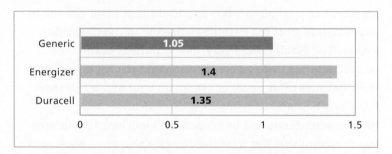

Energizer and Duracell both appear to be decreasing at approximately the same rates thus far in the observation, whereas the generic brand has already dropped much faster than the other two types of batteries. From this observation I have raised the question: What is the composition of the

Observations leading to questions

Duracell and Energizer batteries that allows them to hold a better initial charge than the generic brand of batteries?

Sunday, October 13, 2013

Today I again put the three sets of batteries into the flashlight, in the same order as the trial prior, to allow them all to have close to the same time between usages, again to try and avoid any variables. Today my data showed similar results after allowing all of the batteries to run in the flashlight for an hour and a half:

Provides evidence of the researcher's attempt to remain systematic in his observations

After this day of observing the results I found that the generic brand of batteries did not decrease as significantly as it did after the first trial. This day the generic brand lost close to the same voltage as the other two types of batteries. Another interesting observation I found was that Energizer and Duracell had the same voltages.

Tuesday, October 15, 2013

On this day of observation I again put the batteries into the flashlights for the trial time. The data I found for this day was as follows:

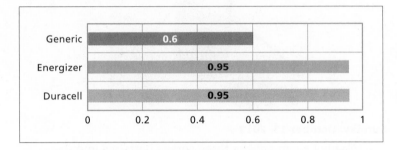

On this day I found that again the generic brand decreased by an amount similar to the other two batteries. Also I found that the generic brand's intensity has begun to decrease. However, both the other two batteries still give off a strong light intensity. This observation raises the question: At what voltage does the light intensity begin to waver? Another question is: Will the other two batteries begin to have lower light intensity at approximately the same voltage as the generic, or will they continue to have a stronger light intensity for longer? The figures below show the change of light intensity of the generic brand of batteries from the beginning until this day's observation.

Figure 1. Before   *Figure 2.* After

Student's observations continue to raise questions

Thursday, October 17, 2013

Today is my fourth day of observation. The readings for the voltages for this day were:

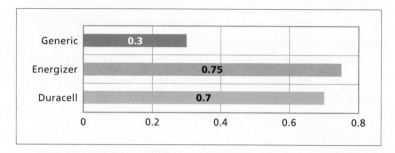

The generic brand is losing even more intensity when it is in the flashlight. It is obvious that it is getting near the end of its battery charge. Today was also the biggest decrease in charge for the generic brand of batteries. This is interesting because it is actually producing less light than before, so why does it lose more voltage toward the end of its life? Also, another thing I observed for this day was that again the Energizer brand holds more voltages than the Duracell, like before. There is still no change in light intensity for the two name brands.

Saturday, October 19, 2013

Today is my final day of observation. This is the data I collected for this day:

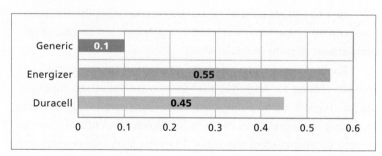

Today the generic battery hardly produced any light out of the flashlight by the end of the time period, although it still didn't drop to 0 voltage, so there are clearly still some electrons flowing in the current throughout the battery. Also, I observed that the Duracell battery has clearly dropped well below the Energizer now. The Duracell has shown a slight decrease in the light intensity compared to when the observational study first started. So what is the composition of the Energizer battery that makes it outlast the Duracell battery?

Narrative

Description

The narrative description provides a summary of the student's systematic observation.

Five days of observations were conducted over an eight-day period. It did not matter what day of the week I took these observations nor the conditions of the environment around my object of study at the time of the observations. The only thing that I made sure that was constant environmentally for all of the batteries in the study was the temperature because more heat results in higher kinetic energy, which causes electrons to move faster. I had to decide on the types of batteries that I wanted to study for the observational study. The batteries I decided on were: Duracell, Energizer, and a generic brand from Wal-Mart. Before I took my first observation I tested each of the batteries that were to be used with the voltmeter to know the initial charge of the battery. Doing this gave me an idea from the beginning of which battery is typically the most powerful and also how much the batteries would be losing in comparison to their initial charge.

Each of these battery types was tested for the same amount of time for each day that they were observed. Since the flashlight took two batteries to run properly I was planning on taking the average of the two batteries, but I found them to be very similar in all of the trials. I believe that this occurrence is a result of the entire circuit acting at the same time, causing equal electron transfer between the two batteries to occur, thus causing them to have equal voltages.

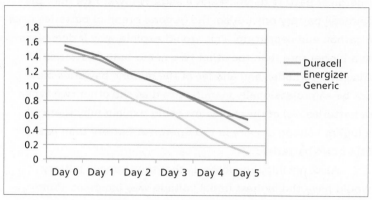

Final Graph from Five Days of Observations

The graph above shows the change in voltage over the five-day period that I took the observations. As you can see, Duracell and Energizer are very similar to one another, with Energizer performing slightly higher than the Duracell brand. The generic has a lower initial voltage than the other two batteries and continues to decrease at a faster rate than the other two batteries. Another thing you can see from this graph is how quickly the generic brand lost its voltage toward the end of its life, whereas the other two batteries seemed to continue to decrease at approximately the same rate throughout.

Speculation

My initial hypothesis that the Duracell battery would decrease at the slowest rate was not supported by this data. I have done a little bit of research on the composition of the cathodes of the Duracell and Energizer batteries. I found that

Evaluates initial hypothesis (speculation) in light of the data the Duracell battery uses a copper tip on the cathode, whereas the Energizer uses a combination of lithium with the copper tip to allow longer battery life. This would explain why the Energizer battery decreases at a slightly lower rate than the Duracell battery does. Also, the generic brand of batteries uses a carbon and copper tip. This would explain why it decreases at a higher rate than the other two name-brand batteries. Also, the cathodes and anodes of the generic batteries may not be as professionally manufactured as the other two types of batteries. All of these reasons could explain why there is a higher voltage density in the Energizer battery than in the other two batteries.

Also, my initial hypothesis that the Duracell battery would have the highest initial voltage was incorrect. From the research that I have gathered, the only explanation for the higher initial voltage in the Energizer battery would be the presence of the alkaline metals that the manufacturer puts into its batteries, whereas the Duracell manufacturer does no such thing. However, there is little information on the Internet about the generic brand of batteries that I used for the experiment, but I was able to find that the reason it has such a lower initial voltage than the other two types of batteries is because it is not packed as well. It takes special equipment to make all the electrons store properly, and the equipment used is not as powerful as the ones that Duracell and Energizer use for their batteries. These ideas all make up my understanding of why there is such a major difference in the rates at which the batteries lose their charge.

For further research into this topic I would recommend using a larger sample, because I used only two batteries for each type of battery. Also, I would recommend looking into the new rechargeable batteries, as that is what a lot of people

Further speculates about factors that contributed to rejection of the hypothesis

Provides suggestions for future research on the subject

are turning to more recently. Another thing that I would try is leaving the batteries on longer because from some of the research that I have done, Duracell does better than Energizer over continuous usage. This means that maybe there is something in the Energizer batteries that causes them to speed up reactions over long periods of use that will cause them to decrease faster over this period. A study like that would be very interesting to compare to my own.

Another interesting topic to follow up on would be the cost of each of the batteries and which battery would be the most cost-effective for users. A lot of people today are buying the generic brand of batteries because they think that this is saving them money. Yes, the generic brand is sold at a lower price, but it is also being used up faster than the other two types of batteries.

RESEARCH PROPOSAL

The research proposal is one of the most common genres of academic writing in the natural sciences. Professional scholars use the **research proposal** to plan out complex studies, to formulate their thoughts, and to submit their research designs to institutional review boards or to grant-funding agencies. The ability to secure grant funding (i.e., to write an effective research proposal and connect it to a realistic, clear budget) is a highly sought-after skill in a job candidate for many academic, government, and private industry positions. In many cases, an effective proposal results from practice with and knowledge of the conventions expected for the genre. No doubt, much of the work of science could not get done without the research proposal, because it is such an important vehicle for securing the funding and materials necessary to conduct research.

Most research proposals include the following sections:

- Title page
- Introduction (and literature review)
- Methods
- References

The *title page* should include (1) the title of your proposal, (2) your name and the names of any co-authors/researchers, and (3) the name of your academic institution. Your instructor may require additional information such as a running header, date, or author's note. Be sure to ask your instructor what documentation and formatting style to use and what information is required in any specific writing context.

The *introduction* of a research proposal explains the topic and purpose of the proposed research. Be sure to include your research question and/or your proposed hypothesis. Additionally, your introduction should contextualize your research by reviewing scholarly articles related to your topic and showing how your proposed research fills a gap in what is already known about the topic. Specifically, the introduction should explain how other researchers have approached your topic (or a closely related one) in the past, with attention to the major overlapping findings in that research. An effective introduction incorporates a literature review that demonstrates your knowledge of other scholars' research. As such, it builds your credibility to conduct your proposed research. (See Chapter 7, pp. 182–85, for more information about writing a literature review.)

The *Methods section* of a research proposal explains exactly what you will do to test your hypothesis (or answer your research question) and how you will do it. It differs from the Methods section of a lab report in several ways: (1) it should be written in future tense, and (2) it should include more detail about your plans. Further, the Methods section should address how long your study will take and should specify how you will collect data (in a step-by-step descriptive manner).

The *references list* for a research proposal is essentially the same as the references list for a lab report or any other academic project. You'll need to include the full citation information for any work you used in your literature review or in planning or researching your topic.

WRITING PROJECT **Developing a Research Proposal**

Drawing on a topic of interest to you, develop a research proposal that outlines a specific research question and/or hypothesis, and describe how you would go about answering the question or testing the hypothesis. Keep in mind that successful research proposals include the elements listed below.

- Title page
- Introduction (and literature review)
- Methods
- References

You might try drawing on the observations you collected while completing an observation logbook to develop your research question and/or hypothesis.

Insider Example
Research Proposal

In the following example of a professional research proposal by Gary Ritchison, a biologist at Eastern Kentucky University, note how the Introduction section begins with a brief introduction to the topic (par. 1) and then proceeds to review the relevant literature on the topic (pars. 1 and 2). As you read, consider how a potential funding entity would likely view both the content and the form in which that content is presented. Also note that the references list is titled "Literature Cited." Minor variations like this are common from discipline to discipline and in various contexts. Here, Ritchison has followed CSE style conventions in his proposal.

Hunting Behavior, Territory Quality, and Individual
Quality of American Kestrels
(*Falco sparverius*)

Gary Ritchison

Department of Biological Sciences
Eastern Kentucky University

Introduction

American Kestrels (*Falco sparverius*) are widely distributed throughout North America. In Kentucky, these falcons are permanent residents and are most abundant in rural farmland, where they hunt over fields and pastures (Palmer-Ball 1996). Although primarily sit-and-wait predators, hunting from elevated perches and scanning the surrounding areas for prey, kestrels also hunt while hovering (Balgooyen 1976). Kellner (1985) reported that nearly 20% of all attacks observed in central Kentucky were made while kestrels were hovering. Habitats used by hunting kestrels in central Kentucky include mowed and unmowed fields, cropland, pastures, and plowed fields (Kellner 1985).

Several investigators have suggested that male and female American Kestrels may exhibit differences in habitat use during the non-breeding period, with males typically found in areas with greater numbers of trees, such as wooded pastures, and females in open fields and pastures (Stinson et al. 1981; Bohall-Wood and Collopy 1986). However, Smallwood (1988) suggested that, when available, male and female kestrels in south-central Florida established winter territories in the same type of habitat. Differential habitat use occurred only because migratory female kestrels usually arrived on wintering areas before males and, therefore, were more likely to establish territories in the better-quality, more open habitats before males arrived (Smallwood 1988).

In central Kentucky, many American Kestrels are residents. As a result, male and female kestrels would likely have equal opportunity to establish winter territories in the higher-quality, open habitats. If so, habitat segregation should be less apparent in central Kentucky than in areas further south, where wintering populations of kestrels are largely

Establishes the topic and provides background information on American Kestrels

Reveals evidence of a review of previous scholarship

Establishes a local context for research

migratory. In addition, territory quality should be correlated with individual quality because higher-quality resident kestrels should be able to defend higher-quality territories.

The objectives of my proposed study of American Kestrels will be to examine possible relationships among and between hunting behavior, territory quality, and individual quality in male and female American Kestrels. The results of this study will provide important information about habitat and perch selection by American Kestrels in central Kentucky in addition to the possible role of individual quality on hunting behavior and habitat use.

Methods

Field work will take place from 15 October 2000 through 15 May 2001 at the Blue Grass Army Depot, Madison Co., Kentucky. During the study period, I will search for American Kestrels throughout accessible portions of the depot. Searches will be conducted on foot as well by automobile.

An attempt will be made to capture all kestrels observed using bal-chatri traps baited with mice. Once captured, kestrels will be banded with a numbered aluminum band plus a unique combination of colored plastic bands to permit individual identification. For each captured individual, I will take standard morphological measurements (wing chord, tarsus length, tail length, and mass). In addition, 8 to 10 feathers will be plucked from the head, breast, back, and wing, respectively. Plumage in these areas is either reddish or bluish, and the quality of such colors is known to be correlated with individual quality (Hill 1991, 1992; Keyser 1998). Variation in the color and intensity of plumage will be determined using a reflectance spectrometer (Ocean Optics S2000 fiber optic spectrometer, Dunedin, FL), and these values will be used as a measure of individual quality. To confirm that plumage

Reveals research purposes and identifies significance of the proposed research

This section provides a highly detailed description of proposed research procedures, or methods.

color and intensity are dependent on condition, we will use tail feather growth rates as a measure of nutritional condition during molt. At the time of capture, the outermost tail feathers will be removed and the mean width of daily growth bars, which is correlated with nutritional condition (Hill and Montgomerie 1994), will be determined.

References established methods, or those used by other researchers, to support his own method design

Each focal American Kestrel (N = at least 14; 7 males and 7 females) will be observed at least once a week. Observations will be made at various times during the day, with observation periods typically 1 to 3 hours in duration. During focal bird observations, individuals will be monitored using binoculars and spotting scopes. Information will be recorded on a portable tape recorder for later transcription. During each observation, I will record all attacks and whether attacks were initiated from a perch or while hovering. For perches, I will note the time a kestrel lands on a perch and the time until the kestrel either initiates an attack or leaves for another perch (giving up time). If an attack is made, I will note attack distances (the distance from a perch to the point where a prey item was attacked) and outcome (successful or not). If successful, an attempt will be made to identify the prey (to the lowest taxonomic category possible).

The activity budgets of kestrels will also be determined by observing the frequency and duration of kestrel behaviors during randomly selected 20-min observation periods (i.e., a randomly selected period during the 1- to 3-hour observation period). During these 20-minute periods, the frequency of occurrence of each of the following behaviors will be recorded: capturing prey, preening, engaging in nonpreening comfort movements (including scratching, stretching wing or tail, shaking body plumage, cleaning foot with bill, and yawning), vocalizing, and flying. The context in which flight occurs, including pounces on prey, and the duration of flights and of preening bouts will also be recorded.

Territories will be delineated by noting the locations of focal kestrels, and the vegetation in each kestrel's winter territory will be characterized following the methods of Smallwood (1987). Possible relationships among hunting behavior (mode of attack, perch time, attack distance and outcome [successful or unsuccessful], and type of prey attacked), territory vegetation, time budgets, sex, and individual quality will be examined. All analyses will be conducted using the Statistical Analysis System (SAS Institute 1989).

Literature Cited

Balgooyen TG. 1976. Behavior and ecology of the American Kestrel in the Sierra Nevada of California. Univ Calif Publ Zool 103:1-83.

Bohall-Wood P, Collopy MW. 1986. Abundance and habitat selection of two American Kestrel subspecies in north-central Florida. Auk 103:557-563.

Craighead JJ, Craighead FC Jr. 1956. Hawks, owls, and wildlife. Harrisburg (PA): Stackpole.

Hill GE. 1991. Plumage coloration is a sexually selected indicator of male quality. Nature 350:337-339.

Hill GE. 1992. Proximate basis of variation in carotenoid pigmentation in male House Finches. Auk 109:1-12.

Hill GE, Montgomerie R. 1994. Plumage colour signals nutritional condition in the House Finch. Proc R Soc Lond B Biol Sci 258:47-52.

Kellner CJ. 1985. A comparative analysis of the foraging behavior of male and female American Kestrels in central Kentucky [master's thesis]. [Richmond (KY)]: Eastern Kentucky University.

Keyser AJ. 1998. Is structural color a reliable signal of quality in Blue Grosbeaks? [master's thesis]. [Auburn (AL)]: Auburn University.

Mengel RM. 1965. The birds of Kentucky. Lawrence (KS): Allen Press. (American Ornithologists' Union monograph; 3).

Palmer-Ball B. 1996. The Kentucky breeding bird atlas. Lexington (KY): Univ. Press of Kentucky.

SAS Institute. 1989. SAS user's guide: statistics. Cary (NC): SAS Institute.

Smallwood JA. 1987. Sexual segregation by habitat in American Kestrels wintering in southcentral Florida: vegetative structure and responses of differential prey availability. Condor 89:842-849.

Smallwood JA. 1988. The relationship of vegetative cover to
       daily rhythms of prey consumption by American Kestrels
       wintering in southcentral Florida. J Raptor Res 22:77-80.
Stinson CH, Crawford DL, Lauthner J. 1981. Sex differences in
       winter habitat of American Kestrels in Georgia. J. Field
       Ornithol 52:29-35.

LAB REPORT

Lab reports are the formal reporting mechanism for research in the sciences. When a scientist publishes an article that reports the results of a research study, it is generally in the form of a lab report. Lab reports include information reported in IMRAD format, and the sections of the lab report are often listed exactly in that order:

- Introduction
- Methods
- Results
- Discussion

Be sure to read through the section on pages 166–74 of Chapter 7 that describes the different kinds of information typically presented in each of these sections.

If a group of researchers writes a research proposal before writing a lab report, they've already completed the first two sections of the lab report and only need to revise the report to reflect what they actually accomplished in the study (instead of what they planned to do). The Results and Discussion sections report new information about the data they gathered and what they offer as explanations and interpretations of what those results might mean. The Discussion section might also include suggestions for future research, demonstrating how research in the sciences is always building upon prior research.

Composing a Lab Report

The final writing project for this chapter is a lab report. You might report results from either experimentation or systematic observation. Your research could take place in an actual laboratory setting, or it could just as easily take place in the wider environment around you. Regardless, be sure to check with your instructor about whether your lab report should be based on formal observation or experimentation.

Since lab reports use IMRAD organizational format, your report should include the following sections:

- Introduction
- Methods
- Results
- Discussion

As you report your results and discuss their significance, you might include elements of visual design to help communicate the results to your audience. These might include tables or figures. Also, you might include an abstract, and you'll need to include a reference list that cites all sources used in your report. (See Chapter 7 for more information on writing tables and figures, and more information on abstracts.)

Insider Example
Student Lab Report

In the following sample lab report, Kedric Lemon revisits the question of which battery type is most effective. He draws on the information gathered in his observation logbook (pp. 229–39) to design a research study that allows him to conduct further investigation to answer his research question.

The researcher provides a descriptive, non-rhetorical title.

Which Type of Battery Is the Most Effective

When Energy Is Drawn Rapidly?

Kedric Lemon

North Carolina State University

Which Type of Battery Is the Most Effective
When Energy Is Drawn Rapidly?

Introduction

Today batteries are used in many of the products that we use every day, from the TV remote to the car we drive to work. AA batteries are one of the most widely used battery types, but which of these AA batteries is the most effective? Almeida, Xará, Delgado, and Costa (2006) tested five different types of batteries in a study similar to mine. They allowed each of the batteries to run the product for an hour. The product they were powering alternated from open to closed circuit, so the batteries went from not giving off energy to giving off energy very quickly. The researchers then measured the pulse of the battery to determine the charge. The pulse test is a very effective way of reading the battery because it is closed circuit, meaning it doesn't run the battery to find the voltage, and it is highly accurate. They found that the Energizer battery had the largest amount of pulses after the experiment. The energizer had on average 20 more pulses than the Duracell battery, giving the Energizer battery approximately a half hour longer in battery life when being used rapidly. Booth (1999) also performed his experiment using the pulse test. However, this experiment involved allowing the batteries to constantly give off energy for two hours, and then Booth measured the pulse. So his experiment is more comparable to my observational study because it was constantly drawing energy from the battery. In this experiment he found that the Duracell battery was the most effective. The Duracell battery had over 40 more pulses per minute than the Energizer battery, which means that the battery could last for an hour longer than the Energizer battery would.

The report follows the conventional IMRAD format.

The researcher establishes a focus for his research by positing a research question.

Reviews previous research, and connects that research to the current research project

However, in today's market, rechargeable batteries are becoming increasing popular. Zucker (2005) compared 16 different types of rechargeable batteries. Most of these batteries were Nickel Metal Hydride, but a couple of them were the more traditional rechargeable AA battery, the Nickel Cadmium. In his study Zucker was testing how these batteries faired on their second charge after being discharged as closely as they could; rechargeable batteries are not allowed to go to 0 volts because then they cannot be recharged. In the end Zucker found that all but four of the batteries came back up to at least 70% of their initial charge, two of which did not even recharge at all. He found that, not surprisingly, the two most effective rechargeable batteries were Duracell and Energizer, which both came back to 86% of the first charge. However, the Energizer rechargeable battery had the higher initial charge, so Zucker concluded that the Energizer battery was the most effective rechargeable battery. Yu, Lai, Yan, and Wu (1999) looked at the capacity of three different Nickel Metal Hydride (NiMH) rechargeable batteries. They first took three different types of NiMH batteries and found the electrical capacity through a voltmeter. After, they measured the volume of each of the batteries to discover where it fell in the AA battery range of 600 to 660 mAh/cm3. They used this to test the efficiency of the NiMH batteries, as there are slightly different chemical compositions inside the batteries. In the end they concluded that the NiMH battery from the Duracell brand was the most efficient.

Li, Daniel, and Wood (2011) looked at the improvements being made to lithium ion AA batteries. The lithium ion AA batteries are extremely powerful, but in recent years they have become increasingly more popular for studying by many researchers. Li et al. tested the voltage of the lithium ion AA rechargeable battery and found that the starting voltage was

Prominence of dates points to the researcher's concern for the recency of source materials

Continues review of previous scholarship on this topic

on average 3.2 volts. That is more than the average onetime-use AA battery. They further found that what makes modern lithium ion batteries so much more powerful is the cathodes. Research into cathode materials has significantly increased the rate of reactions for lithium ion batteries.

The objective of this study is to determine which brand of batteries is the most efficient and to compare a generic rechargeable battery to these regular AA batteries. My original research question for my logbook was Which brand of AA batteries is the most effective over extended usage? However, for my final study I wanted to look at how batteries reacted when they were being used very quickly, so I formed two research questions for this study: Which type of battery is the most effective for rapid uses? How do regular AA batteries compare to a generic AA rechargeable battery? My hypothesis for this experiment is that the Energizer battery will be the most effective battery when energy is being taken from the battery rapidly.

Establishes specific research questions on the basis of previous observations

Hypothesis

Method

Observation Logbook

In my observation logbook I looked at how different types of batteries compared when they were being tested through a flashlight. The batteries I observed were Duracell, Energizer, and a generic brand. I allowed the flashlight to run for an hour with the set of batteries inside. I did this step for all three types of batteries that I observed in that study. After the hour was up I tested the voltage with a voltmeter. I continued to do this for five consecutive days. For each of the tests I made sure that the temperature was the same for each of the batteries while they were being tested. I also allowed the flashlight to remain off for an hour to let it cool down. These steps were taken to avoid any unknown variables.

Reports on research previously conducted

For my follow-up study, I decided to look at how batteries compare when they are being used in quick bursts, meaning that they quickly change from using no energy to using a lot of energy rapidly. In order to test the battery this way I had to change the flashlight to a strobe light so that it quickly turns on and off automatically. I also decided to add a rechargeable battery to my tests since this is an increasingly popular item today. I found my data by attaching the batteries to a voltmeter immediately after they were taken out of the strobe light. Each of the set of batteries was in the strobe light for 20 minutes.

Variables that I made sure remained constant for this experiment were the temperature of the room as well as the temperature of the strobe light. For this reason I allowed the strobe light a 30-minute cooldown before I put the next set of batteries into it.

Limitations

One of the limitations that I faced in this study was an inability to get the thermocouple that I wanted to measure the temperature of the battery. Also I had a small sample size, so if I had taken more samples, then my results would have been more valid. I could improve on these by getting a thermocouple that would measure the temperature. This would allow me to compare the expected voltage of the battery through the thermocouple and the voltmeter. After

Provides a detailed account of research procedures

The researcher uses technical language, or jargon.

the battery got out of the strobe light I would hook it up to the thermocouple and then measure the voltage by looking at the voltmeter. I could tell what the voltage of the battery is through the thermocouple using a graph that one of my secondary sources provided. Another limitation that I faced in this experiment was that I lacked better equipment that could have made my results more accurate—like a pulse reader or a better voltmeter, as I was using a fairly inexpensive one.

Results

My results from my logbook provided me with primarily quantitative data. For each of the types of batteries I found these results.

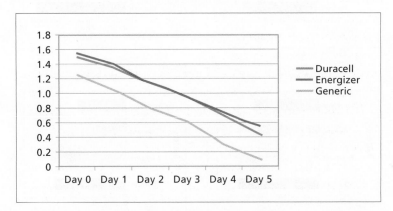

For the Energizer battery I found that it started off with the largest initial charge of 1.55 volts. On average the Energizer battery lost .16 volts for every hour. The Duracell battery had an initial charge of 1.5 volts and lost an average of .18 volts per hour. Last, the generic brand of battery had an initial voltage of 1.25 volts and lost on average .23 volts every hour.

In this experiment I found that the Energizer battery again had the highest starting charge and highest ending charge. The Duracell AA battery was close behind the

The researcher notes limitations he encountered with the methods.

Outlines the major findings of the study. A number of results are also presented visually, in the form of graphs and figures.

The researcher frequently presents results in tables and charts.

Energizer. The generic brand of batteries came next, followed by the rechargeable battery.

This experiment showed similar results to what I had found in my logbook. The Duracell and Energizer batteries were both very similar, while the generic brand lagged behind.

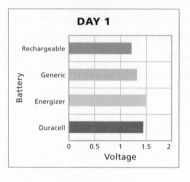

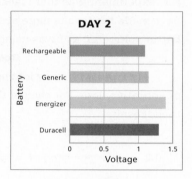

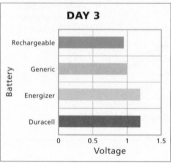

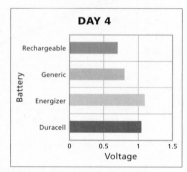

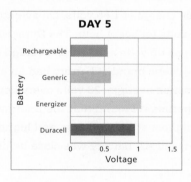

Battery	Initial voltage (volts)	Final voltage (volts)	Average volts lost (volts/20 min)
Energizer	1.60	1.10	0.10
Duracell	1.55	0.95	0.12
Generic	1.40	0.60	0.16
Rechargeable	1.20	0.55	0.13

The table shows that the Energizer battery had the best results in all categories. If I had taken more samples, then I may have found that some of the batteries performed better or worse than they did here, because I could have taken the average of many tests rather than looking at only one. Using a pulse test reader would have been an even more informative way of exploring this experiment because that instrument can estimate the battery life with high precision.

Discussion

Through this experiment I found that the Energizer battery is the most effective battery when used in rapid bursts. Also I found that the rechargeable battery had very bad ratings. Despite the poor ratings, however, it is rechargeable, being a potential reason for its failure. The rechargeable battery is not able to commit as many of its chemicals to solely providing the maximum amount of energy; it has to provide some of the chemicals to the battery's capabilities of recharging. Based on this, the rechargeable battery could be the most effective battery. I found that other studies with similar methods (Booth 1999; Yu, Lai, Yan, & Wu 1999) determined that the Duracell battery was the most effective. However, these studies were conducted years ago.

If I had had more days to conduct this experiment, I could have more accurately represented the usefulness of

Provides an overview of the implications of major findings in light of previous scholarship the rechargeable battery, because after it exhausted its first charge it came back completely recharged for the next day. Another limitation that I faced in this experiment was that I overestimated how fast the battery voltages would decrease in the strobe light, so I was unable to see how the batteries acted near the end of their charge. An area of study for further research would be to compare different types of rechargeable batteries. For instance, I already know that the lithium ion AA rechargeable batteries carry more volts than regular AA batteries, and they are rechargeable.

If I had had more time to perform this experiment or had allowed the batteries to be in the strobe light for a longer time, I think that I would have found that the rechargeable battery would be ahead of the generic battery in terms of the average voltage lost. Also I think that the gap would have been larger between the Duracell battery and the Energizer battery because looking at my results from the observation logbook shows that the Energizer battery does a lot better than the Duracell battery toward the end of its life. This being said, I think that the Duracell battery does not handle the rapid uses as well as the extended uses.

These results show that the Energizer battery is the most effective battery for rapid use and, from my observation logbook, the most effective for extended use. The rechargeable battery used in this experiment is hard to compare to these regular AA batteries because I wasn't able to exploit its sole advantage, recharging. However, this was just a generic brand of rechargeable batteries, so it would be interesting to see how the Duracell and Energizer rechargeable batteries compare to their regular batteries.

Discusses limitations of the study overall

References

Almeida, M. F., Xará, S. M., Delgado, J., & Costa, C. A. (2006). Characterization of spent AA household alkaline batteries. *Waste Management, 26*(5), 466-476. doi:10.1016/j.wasman.2005.04.005

Booth, S. A. (1999). High-drain alkaline AA-batteries. *Popular Electronics, 16*(1), 5.

Li, J., Daniel, C., & Wood, D. (2011). Materials processing for lithium-ion batteries. *Journal of Power Sources, 196*(5), 2452-2460. doi:10.1016/j.jpowsour.2010.11.001

Yu, C. Z., Lai, W. H., Yan, G. J., & Wu, J. Y. (1999). Study of preparation technology for high performance AA size Ni–MH batteries. *Journal of Alloys and Compounds, 293*(1-2), 784-787. doi:10.1016/S0925-8388(99)00463-6

Zucker, P. (2005). AA batteries tested: Rechargeable batteries. *Australian PC User, 17*(6), 51.

Provides a list of sources used in the construction of the lab report

- **Systematic observation plays a critical role in the natural sciences.** The disciplines of the natural sciences rely on methods of observation to generate and answer research questions about how and why natural phenomena act as they do.

- **Many natural scientists work in interdisciplinary fields of study.** These fields, such as biochemistry and biophysics, combine subject matter and methods from more than one field to address research questions.

- **Scientists typically conduct research according to the steps of the scientific method:** observe, ask a research question, formulate a hypothesis, test the hypothesis through experimentation, and explain results.

- **The scientific writing process follows logically from the steps of the scientific method:** observe and describe, speculate, experiment, and report.

- **To test their hypotheses, or their proposed answers to research questions, natural scientists may use multiple methods.** Two common methods are systematic observation and experimentation.

- **Scientific research proposals are typically vetted by institutional review boards (IRB).** Committees that review research proposals are charged with the task of examining all elements of a scientific study to ensure that it treats subjects equitably and ethically.

- **Conventional rhetorical features of the scientific community reflect the shared values of the community's members.** Some of these values are objectivity, replicability, recency, and cooperation and collaboration.

- **Members of the scientific community frequently produce a number of genres.** These include the observation logbook, the research proposal, and the lab report.

Reading and Writing in the Applied Fields

Introduction to the Applied Fields

In this chapter, we explore some of the applied fields that students often encounter or choose to study as part of their college experience. Throughout the chapter, we also look at some of the genres through which writers in these fields communicate to various audiences.

WHAT ARE APPLIED FIELDS?

Applied fields are areas of academic study that focus on the production of practical knowledge and that share a core mission of preparing students for specific careers. Often, that preparation includes hands-on training. Examples of applied fields that prepare students for particular careers include nursing, business, law, education, and engineering, but a somewhat more complete list appears below.

Some Applied Fields

Sports psychology	Counseling
Business	Statistics
Law	Engineering
Education	Speech pathology
Nursing	Public administration
Applied physics	Architecture
Applied linguistics	Broadcast journalism
Social work	

ANDREA TSURUMI

Research in the applied fields typically attempts to solve problems. An automotive engineering team, for example, might start with a problem like consumers' reluctance to buy an all-electric vehicle. The team must first observe and acknowledge that there is a problem, and then it would need to define the scope of the problem. Why does the problem exist? What are the factors contributing to consumers' reluctance to buy an all-electric vehicle? Once a problem has been identified and defined, the team of researchers can then begin to explore solutions to overcome the problem.

Examples of large-scale problems that require practical applications of research are issues such as: racial inequality in the American criminal justice system, the lack of clean drinking water in some non-industrialized nations, obesity and heart disease, and ways to provide outstanding public education to children with behavioral problems. These are all real-world problems scholars and practitioners in the applied fields are working to solve this very moment.

INSIDE WORK **Defining and Solving Problems**

> Describe a time when you conducted research to solve a problem. Start by defining the problem and explaining why you needed to solve it. When did you first identify the problem? What caused you to seek solutions to it? How did you research and understand the problem? What methods did you use to solve it? ❱

Professionals in applied fields often work in collaboration with one another, or in teams, to complete research and other projects, and professors who teach in these areas often assign tasks that require interaction and cooperation among a group of students to create a product or to solve a problem. In the field of business management, for example, teams of professionals often must work together to market a new product. Solid communication and interpersonal skills are necessary for a team to manage a budget, design a marketing or advertising campaign, and engage with a client successfully all at the same time. As such, the ability to work cooperatively — to demonstrate effective interpersonal and team communication skills — is highly valued among professionals in the applied fields. You shouldn't be surprised, then, if you're one day applying for a job in an applied field and an interviewer asks you to share a little about your previous experiences working in teams to successfully complete a project. As you learn more about the applied fields examined in this chapter, take care to note those writing tasks completed by teams, or those moments when cooperation among professionals working in a particular field are highlighted by the content of the genres we explore.

Our purpose in this chapter is to offer a basic introduction to a few of the many applied fields of study and to explore some of the kinds of writing that typically occur in these fields. Because the applied fields vary so much, we've chosen to focus on specific disciplines as examples since we cannot generalize conventions across applied fields. The rest of the chapter examines specific applied fields and examples of writing through a rhetorical approach.

Considering Additional Applied Fields

Visit your college or university's website, and locate a listing of the majors or concentrations offered in any academic department. In light of the definition of an *applied field* proposed above, consider whether any of the majors or concentrations identified for that particular discipline could be described as applied fields. Additionally, spend some time considering your own major or potential area of concentration: Are you studying an applied field? Are there areas of study within your major or concentration that could be considered applied fields? If so, what are they, and why would you consider them applied fields? ▶

Rhetoric and the Applied Fields

Because applied fields are centrally focused on preparing professionals who will work in those fields, students are often asked to engage audiences associated with the work they'll do in those fields after graduation. Imagine that you've just graduated from college with a degree in business management and have secured a job as a marketing director for a business. What kinds of writing do you expect to encounter in this new position? What audiences do you expect to be writing for? You may well be asked to prepare business analyses or market reports. You may be asked to involve yourself in new product management or even the advertising campaign for a product. All these activities, which call for different kinds of writing, will require you to manage information and to shape your communication of that information into texts that are designed specifically for other professionals in your field—such as boards of directors, financial officers, or advertising executives. As a student in the applied field of business management, you therefore need to become familiar with the audiences, genres, conventions, and other expectations for writing specific to your career path that extend beyond academic audiences. Being mindful of the rhetorical situation in which you must communicate with other professionals is essential to your potential success as a writer in an applied field.

As with more traditional academic writing, we recommend that you analyze carefully any writing situation you encounter in an applied field. You might begin by responding to the following questions:

1. **Who is my audience?** Unlike the audience for a lab report for a chemistry class or the audience for an interpretation of a poem in a literature class, your audience for writing in an applied field is just as likely to be non-academic as academic. Certainly, the writing most students will do in their actual careers will be aimed at other professionals in their field, not researchers or professors in a university. In addition to understanding exactly who your audience is, be sure to consider the specific needs of your target audience.

LaunchPadSolo

Criminal justice instructor Michelle Richter discusses the role of audience.

2. **In light of my purpose and the audience's needs, is there an appropriate genre that I should rely on to communicate my information?** As in the more traditional academic disciplines, there are many genres through which professionals in applied fields communicate. Keeping your purpose for writing in mind, you'll want to consider whether the information you have to share should be reported in a specific genre: Should you write a memorandum, a marketing proposal, or an executive summary, for instance? Answering this question can help you determine if there is an appropriate form, or genre, through which to communicate your information.

3. **Are there additional conventional expectations I should consider for the kind of writing task I need to complete?** Beyond simply identifying an appropriate genre, answering this question can help you determine how to shape the information you need to communicate to your target audience. If the writing task requires a particular genre, then you're likely to use features that conventionally appear as part of that genre. Of course, there are many good reasons to communicate information in other ways. In these situations, we recommend that you carefully consider the appropriateness of the structural, language, and reference features you employ.

Genres in Selected Applied Fields

In the sections that follow, we offer brief introductions to some applied fields of study and provide examples of genres that students and professionals working in these fields often produce. We explore expectations for these genres by highlighting conventional structure, language, and reference features that writers in these fields frequently rely on.

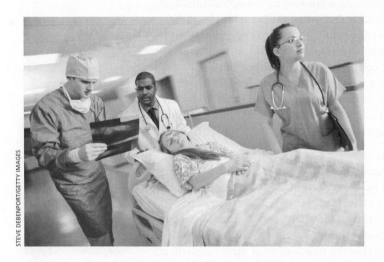

NURSING

Most of us have had experiences with nurses, who, along with physicians and other medical professionals, serve on the front lines of preventing and treating illness in our society. In addition to their hands-on engagement with individuals in clinical and community settings, nurses spend a good deal of their time writing—whether documenting their observations about patients in medical charts, preparing orders for medical procedures, designing care plans, or communicating with patients. A student of nursing might

STEVE DEBENPORT/GETTY IMAGES

encounter any number of additional forms of writing tasks, including nursing care plans for individuals, reviews of literature, and community or public health assessment papers, just to name a few. Each of these forms of communication requires that nurses be especially attuned to the needs of various audiences. A nurse communicating with a patient, for example, might have to translate medical jargon such that the individual can fully understand his or her treatment. Alternatively, a nurse who is producing a care plan for a patient would likely need to craft the document such that other nurses and medical professionals could follow methodically the assessments and recommendations for care. Some nurses, especially those who undertake advanced study or who prepare others to become nurses, often design, implement, or participate in research studies.

We interviewed Dr. Janna Dieckmann, a registered nurse and clinical associate professor in the School of Nursing at the University of North Carolina at Chapel Hill. In her Insider's View, she offers valuable insights into the writing and researching practices of the nursing community.

As Dr. Dieckmann notes, many nurses, especially those working to prepare other nurses, may also participate in various kinds of scholarly research endeavors. In the section that follows, we provide an excerpted look at a 2005 research study published in *Newborn and Infant Nursing Reviews*, a journal of nursing, along with an example of discharge instructions. The latter is a genre of writing that nurses who work in a clinical setting often produce for patients.

Insider's View

Nurses and nursing consider many different areas of research and interest

JANNA DIECKMANN, NURSING

"Research in nursing is varied, including quantitative research into health and illness patterns, as well as intervention to maximize health and reduce illness. Qualitative research varies widely, including research in the history of nursing, which is my focus. There is a wide variety of types of writing demanded in a nursing program. It is so varied that many connections are possible. Cross-discipline collaborations among faculty of various professional schools are valued at many academic institutions today. One of my colleagues conducted research on rats. Another looked at sleep patterns in older adults as a basis for understanding dementia onset. One public health nursing colleague conducts research on out-of-work women, and another examines crosscultural competence. These interests speak to our reasons for becoming nurses—our seeking out of real life, of direct experience, of being right there with people, and of understanding others and their worlds."

Scholarly Research Report

Some nurses are both practitioners and scholars of nursing. As practitioners, they assess and care for patients in cooperation with other medical professionals. As scholars, they may, as Dr. Dieckmann indicates, conduct research on a host of issues, including the history and best practices of nursing. In addition to producing scholarship that advances the field of nursing, these nurses typically work in colleges or universities with programs that prepare individuals for careers in nursing. Such nurses, then, may assume multiple roles as researchers and educators, and as practitioners.

Insider Example
Professional Research Report in Nursing

As you read the following research report, pay particular attention to the structure, language, and reference parallels between the form of the report and those you've encountered already in the fields of the natural sciences and the social sciences. Keep in mind that the text presented here is made up of a series of excerpts from a much lengthier and more substantial research report.

Rural African-American Mothers Parenting Prematurely Born Infants: An Ecological Systems Perspective

MARGARET SHANDOR MILES, PhD, FAAN; DIANE HOLDITCH-DAVIS, PhD, FAAN; SUZANNE THOYRE, PhD; LINDA BEEBER, PhD

The abstract provides an overview of the report, including a description of the study's purpose, its methods, and its central findings.

ABSTRACT

This qualitative descriptive study describes the concerns and issues of rural African-American mothers with prematurely born infants. Mothers were part of a larger nurse-parent support intervention. The 18 mothers lived in rural areas in the Southeast, and their infants were younger than 35 weeks gestational age at birth and at high risk for developmental problems because they either weighed less than 1500 grams at birth or required mechanical ventilation. Field notes written by the intervention nurses providing support to the mothers after discharge from the hospital were analyzed using methods of content analysis. Concerns of the mothers related to the infant's health and development, the maternal role in parenting the infant, personal aspects of their lives, and relationship issues particularly with the fathers. Findings support the importance of an ecological systems perspective when designing research and caring for rural African-American mothers with prematurely born children.

The review of the literature begins with a synthesis point: mothers experience a period of transitioning. Both McHaffie and May confirm this conclusion.

REVIEW OF THE LITERATURE

Although mothers are excited about taking the preterm infant home, a number of studies have noted that they are also anxious during this important transition. McHaffie[1] found mothers insecure and lacking in confidence at first, followed by a period of accommodation as they learned about the infant's behavioral cues and needs. During this period, mothers became overwhelmed with responsibilities, and fatigue resulted. As the infants settled into their new surroundings and the mothers felt the rewards of caregiving, they became confident in their maternal role. May[2] also found that mothers went through a process of learning about the added responsibilities of caregiving, and this resulted in strains on their time and energy. Mothers were vigilant about looking for changes in the infant's status and for signs of progress through improved physical health and development. During this process, they looked for signs that their child was normal and sought support from others....

METHOD

This study used a qualitative descriptive design[3] to identify the concerns and issues of the mothers based on field notes written by the intervention nurses providing support to the mothers after discharge from the hospital.[4] The Nursing Support Intervention was an 18-month in-person and telephone intervention provided by master's-prepared nurses starting around the time of discharge of the infant and ending when the infants were around 18 months old corrected for prematurity. The nurses helped the mothers to process the mothering experience and resolve emotional distress that is caused by prematurity, identify and reduce parenting and other life stresses, develop relationships with their infants, and identify and use acceptable resources to meet needs of the infant and the mother....

Qualitative research methods are explained.

RESULTS

The concerns and issues raised by the mothers with the intervention nurses fell into four major categories: infant health and development, parenting, personal concerns, and relationship issues (Table 1). —————————————

Results of the study, or categories of concerns identified among mothers, are presented in the form of a summary table. The researchers explore these results in more detail in a number of additional paragraphs.

Table 1.
Maternal concerns of rural African-American mothers in parenting prematurely born infants

Infant health and development	Establishing feeding and managing gastrointestinal tract distress
	Managing medical technologies
	Preventing and managing infections
	Establishing sleep patterning
	Learning developmental expectations
Parenting	Learning the infant's needs
	Establishing daily patterns
	Balancing roles
Personal concerns	Coping with financial problems
	Managing stressful jobs while securing appropriate childcare
	Losing and trying to regain educational opportunities toward a better life
	Working toward securing a home of one's own
	Managing depressive symptoms
Relationship issues	Working through relationship with infant's father

The study's Discussion section connects findings to potential changes in support that could improve outcomes for mothers and their children.

DISCUSSION

Findings from this study provide insight into the needs of mothers of prematurely born infants after discharge from the hospital. In the early months after discharge, support is needed related to caring for the infant. As their infants grow, mothers may need help in identifying and getting resources for developmental problems. Agencies that provide services to mothers need to consider the complex lives of the mothers, especially those who are single and living in poverty. Of utmost importance is helping the mothers to manage issues related to finding a job, managing work, and care of their infant. Finding acceptable day care is a particularly important need. Furthermore, community programs are needed to help the mothers achieve their dreams of furthering their education and finding acceptable homes for themselves and their children.

REFERENCES

1. McHaffie HE. Mothers of very low birthweight babies: how do they adjust? J Adv Nurs. 1990;15:6–11.

2. May KM. Searching for normalcy: mothers' caregiving for low birthweight infants. Pediatr Nurs. 1997;23:17–20.

3. Sandelowski M. Whatever happened to qualitative description? Res Nurs Health. 2000;23: 334–340.

4. Holditch-Davis D. A nursing support intervention for mothers of preterm infants. Grant funded by the National Institute of Nursing Research (NR05263). 2001.

Discharge Instructions

If you've ever been hospitalized, then you probably remember the experience quite vividly. It's likely that you interacted with a nurse, who perhaps assessed your health upon arrival. You were also likely cared for by a nurse, or a particular group of nurses, during your stay. Nurses also often play an integral role in a patient's discharge from a hospital. Typically, before a patient is released from a hospital, a nurse provides, in written form, and explains to the patient (and perhaps a family member or two, or another intended primary caregiver) a set of instructions for aftercare. This constitutes the **discharge instructions**.

This document, or series of documents, includes instructions for how to care for oneself at home. The instructions may focus on managing diet and medications, as well as caring for other needs, such as post-operative bandaging procedures. They may also include exercise or diet management plans recommended for long-term recovery and health maintenance. Often presented in bulleted series of items or statements, these lists are usually highly generic; that is, the same instructions frequently apply for patients with the same or similar health conditions. For this reason, discharge instruction forms may include spaces for nurses or other healthcare professionals to write in more specific information relating to a patient's individual circumstances. As well, discharge instructions frequently include information about a patient's follow-up care with his or her doctor or primary caregiver. This could take the form of a future appointment time or directions to call for a follow-up appointment or to consult with another physician. An additional conventional element of discharge instructions is a list of signs of a medical emergency and directions concerning when and how to seek medical attention immediately, should certain signs or symptoms appear in the patient. Finally, discharge instructions are typically signed and dated by a physician or nurse, and they are sometimes signed by the patient as well.

Many patients are in unclear states of mind or are extremely vulnerable at the time of release from a hospital, so nurses who provide and explain discharge instructions to patients are highly skilled at assessing patients' understanding of these instructions.

Insider Example
Discharge Instructions

The following text is an example of a typical set of discharge instructions. As you read the document, consider areas in the instructions that you think a nurse would be more likely to stress to a patient in a discharge meeting: What would a nurse cover quickly? What would he or she want to communicate most clearly to a patient?

FIRST HOSPITAL
Where Care Comes First

Patient's Name: John Q. Patient
Healthcare Provider's Name: First Hospital
Department: Cardiology
Phone: 617-555-1212
Date: Thursday, May 8, 2014
Notes: **Nurses can write personalized notes
to the patient here.**

Discharge Instructions for Heart Attack

A heart attack occurs when blood flow to the heart muscle is interrupted. This deprives
the heart muscle of oxygen, causing tissue damage or tissue death. Common treatments
include lifestyle changes, oxygen, medicines, and surgery.

Steps to Take

Home Care
- Rest until your doctor says it is okay to return to work or other activities.
- Take all medicines as prescribed by your doctor. Beta-blockers, ACE inhibitors,
  and antiplatelet therapy are often recommended.
- Attend a cardiac rehabilitation program if recommended by your doctor.

Diet
Eat a heart-healthy diet:
- Limit your intake of fat, cholesterol, and sodium. Foods such as ice cream, cheese,
  baked goods, and red meat are not the best choices.
- Increase your intake of whole grains, fish, fruits, vegetables, and nuts.
- Consume alcohol in moderation: one to two drinks per day for men, one drink per
  day for women.
- Discuss supplements with your doctor.
Your doctor may refer you to a dietician to advise you on meal planning.

Physical Activity
The American Heart Association recommends at least 30 minutes of exercise daily, or at
least 3–4 times per week, for patients who have had a heart attack. Your doctor will let
you know when you are ready to begin regular exercise.
- Ask your doctor when you will be able to return to work.
- Ask your doctor when you may resume sexual activity.
- Do not drive unless your doctor has given you permission to do so.

Medications
The following medicines may be prescribed to prevent you from having another heart
attack:
- Aspirin, which has been shown to decrease the risk of heart attacks
  - Certain painkillers, such as ibuprofen, when taken together with aspirin, may
    put you at high risk for gastrointestinal bleeding and also reduce the effective-
    ness of aspirin.
- Clopidogrel or prasugrel
  - Avoid omeprazole or esomeprazole if you take clopidogrel. They may make
    clopidogrel not work. Ask your doctor for other drug choices.
- ACE inhibitors
- Nitroglycerin
- Beta-blockers or calcium channel blockers

- Cholesterol-lowering medicines
- Blood pressure medicines
- Pain medicines
- Anti-anxiety or antidepressant medicines

If you are taking medicines, follow these general guidelines:

- Take your medicine as directed. Do not change the amount or the schedule.
- Do not stop taking them without talking to your doctor.
- Do not share them.
- Ask what the results and side effects are. Report them to your doctor.
- Some drugs can be dangerous when mixed. Talk to a doctor or pharmacist if you are taking more than one drug. This includes over-the-counter medicine and herbal or dietary supplements.
- Plan ahead for refills so you do not run out.

Lifestyle Changes and Prevention

Together, you and your doctor will plan proper lifestyle changes that will aid in your recovery. Some things to keep in mind to recover and prevent another heart attack include:

- If you smoke, talk to your doctor about ways to help you quit. There are many options to choose from, like using nicotine replacement products, taking prescription medicines to ease cravings and withdrawal symptoms, participating in smoking cessation classes, or doing an online self-help program.
- Have your cholesterol checked regularly.
- Get regular medical check-ups.
- Control your blood pressure.
- Eat a healthful diet, one that is low in saturated fat and rich in whole grains, fruits, and vegetables.
- Have a regular, low-impact exercise program.
- Maintain a healthy weight.
- Manage stress through activities such as yoga, meditation, and counseling.
- If you have diabetes, maintain good control of your condition.

Follow-Up

Since your recovery needs to be monitored, be sure to keep all appointments and have exams done regularly as directed by your doctor. In addition, some people have feelings of depression or anxiety after a heart attack. To get the help you need, be sure to discuss these feelings with your doctor.

Schedule a follow-up appointment as directed by your doctor.

Call for Medical Help Right Away If Any of the Following Occurs

Call for medical help right away if you have symptoms of another heart attack, including:

- Chest pain, which may feel like a crushing weight on your chest
- A sense of fullness, squeezing, or pressure in the chest
- Anxiety, especially feeling a sense of doom or panic without apparent reason
- Rapid, irregular heartbeat
- Pain, tingling, or numbness in the left shoulder and arm, the neck or jaw, or the right arm
- Sweating
- Nausea or vomiting
- Indigestion or heartburn
- Lightheadedness, weakness, or fainting
- Shortness of breath
- Abdominal pain

If you think you have an emergency, call for medical help right away.

Directions are provided in as few words as possible.

Provides directions for how to "follow up" with medical provider(s).

Identifies emergency indicators

In Table 1 on page 267, the authors of the qualitative research report "Rural African-American Mothers Parenting Prematurely Born Infants: An Ecological Systems Perspective" identify a number of "concerns and issues" among rural mothers with premature infants. Choose one of these "concerns and issues," and develop a discharge plan for a mother and child in response. Using "Discharge Instructions for Heart Attack" as a model for your own set of discharge instructions, complete the following.

- Provide a brief introduction in which you offer a quick overview of the concern or issue.

- Provide supporting instructions for patients in three central areas: Steps to Take, Follow-Up, and Emergency Response. Note that many, or all, of the directives or recommendations that make up your instructions may be non-medical treatments, interventions, or therapies. You may consult additional sources for support, as needed.

- Authorize the discharge orders by signing and dating your document.

Once you've completed the discharge instructions, spend some time reflecting on the challenges you faced in the process of devising your instructions: What were the least and most challenging parts of writing the instructions? ▶

EDUCATION

When your teachers tell you that writing is important, they're probably conveying a belief based on their own experiences. Professional educators do a lot of writing. As students, you're aware of many contexts in which teachers write on a daily basis. They have project assignment sheets to design, papers

to comment on and grade, websites to design, and e-mails to answer, just to name a few. However, educators also spend a great deal of time planning classes and designing lesson plans. Though students rarely see these written products, they are essential, if challenging and time-consuming, endeavors for teachers. We provide examples and discussion of two forms of writing frequently produced by professionals in the various fields of education: the lesson plan and the Individualized Education Plan (IEP).

When designing a **lesson plan**, teachers must consider many factors, including their goals and objectives for student learning, the materials needed to execute a lesson, the activities students will participate in as part of a lesson, and the methods they'll use to assess student learning. Among other considerations, teachers must also make sure their lesson plans help them meet prescribed curricular mandates.

Insider Example
Student Lesson Plan

The following lesson plan for a tenth-grade English class was designed by Dr. Myra Moses, who at the time of writing the plan was a doctoral candidate in education. In this plan, Dr. Moses begins by identifying the state-mandated curricular standards the lesson addresses. She then identifies the broader goals of her lesson plan before establishing the more specific objectives, or exactly what students will do to reach the broader learning goals. As you read, notice that all the plan's statements of objectives begin with a verb, as they identify actions students will take to demonstrate their learning. The plan ends by explaining the classroom activities the teacher will use to facilitate learning and by identifying the methods the instructor will use to assess student learning. These structural moves are conventional for the genre of a lesson plan.

Educational Standard → Goals → Objectives → Materials → Classroom Activities → Assessment

Lesson Plan

Overview and Purpose

This lesson is part of a unit on Homer's *Odyssey*. Prior to this lesson students will have had a lesson on Greek cultural and social values during the time of Homer, and they will have read the *Odyssey*. In the lesson, students will analyze passages from the *Odyssey* to examine author's and characters' point of view. Students will participate in whole class discussion, work in small groups, and work individually to identify and evaluate point of view.

Education Standards Addressed

This lesson addresses the following objectives from the NC Standard Course of Study for Language Arts: English II:

1.02 Respond reflectively (through small group discussion, class discussion, journal entry, essay, letter, dialogue) to written and visual texts by:

Identifies the state-mandated curricular elements, or the educational objectives, the lesson addresses. Notice that these are quite broad in scope.

- relating personal knowledge to textual information or class discussion.
- showing an awareness of one's own culture as well as the cultures of others.
- exhibiting an awareness of culture in which text is set or in which text was written.

1.03 Demonstrate the ability to read, listen to, and view a variety of increasingly complex print and non-print expressive texts appropriate to grade level and course literary focus, by:

- identifying and analyzing text components (such as organizational structures, story elements, organizational features) and evaluating their impact on the text.
- providing textual evidence to support understanding of and reader's response to text.
- making inferences, predicting, and drawing conclusions based on text.
- identifying and analyzing personal, social, historical, or cultural influences, contexts, or biases.

5.01 Read and analyze selected works of world literature by:

- understanding the importance of cultural and historical impact on literary texts.

Teacher identifies specific goals for the lesson. These goals fit well within the broader state-mandated curricular standards.

Objectives identify what students will do as part of the lesson. Notice that the statements of objectives begin with verbs.

Goals

1. To teach students how to identify and evaluate an author's point of view and purpose by examining the characters' point of view.
2. To teach students to critically examine alternate points of view.

Objectives

Students will:

1. Identify point of view in a story by examining the text and evaluating how the main character views his/her world at different points in the story.
2. Demonstrate that they understand point of view by using examples and evidence from the text to support what they state is the character's point of view.
3. Apply their knowledge and understanding of point of view by taking a passage from the text and rewriting it from a supporting character's point of view.

4. Evaluate the rationality of a character's point of view by measuring it against additional information gathered from the text, or their own life experience.

Materials, Resources

Identifies materials needed for the lesson

- Copies of *The Odyssey*
- DVD with video clips from television and/or movies
- Flip chart paper
- Markers
- Directions and rubric for individual assignment

Activities

Outlines classroom procedures for the two-day lesson plan

Session 1

1. Review information from previous lesson about popular cultural and social views held during Homer's time (e.g., Greek law of hospitality). This would be a combination of a quiz and whole class discussion.
2. Teacher-led class discussion defining and examining point of view by viewing clips from popular television shows and movies.
3. Teacher-led discussion of 1 example from *The Odyssey*. E.g., Examine Odysseus's point of view when he violates Greek law of hospitality during his encounter with the Cyclops, Polyphemus. Examine this encounter through the lens of what Homer might be saying about the value Greeks placed on hospitality.
4. In small groups the students will choose 3 places in the epic and evaluate Odysseus's point of view. Students will then determine what Odysseus's point of view might reflect about Homer's point of view and purpose for that part of the epic.
5. Groups will begin to create a visual using flip chart paper and markers to represent their interpretations of Odysseus's point of view to reflect about Homer's point of view and purpose.

Session 2

1. Groups will complete visual.
2. Groups will present their work to the rest of the class.
3. The class will discuss possible alternate interpretations of Homer's point of view and purpose.
4. Class will review aspects of point of view based on information teacher provided at the beginning of the class.

5. Beginning during class and finishing for homework, students will individually take one passage from the epic that was not discussed by their groups and do the following:

    - write a brief description of a main character's point of view
    - write a response to prompts that guide students in evaluating the rationality of the main character's point of view based on information gathered from the text, or the students' own life experience
    - rewrite the passage from a supporting character's point of view

Identifies how the teacher will assess students' mastery of the concepts and material covered in the lesson

Assessment

- Evaluate students' understanding of Greek cultural/social values from Homer's time through the quiz.
- Evaluate group's understanding of point of view by examining the visual product — this artifact will not be graded, but oral feedback will be provided that should help the students in completing the independent assignment.
- Evaluate the written, individual assignment.

Individualized Education Program (IEP)

Professional educators are often required to design education plans that address the specific needs of individual students who, according to federal definitions, are identified with a disability. These are **individualized education programs (IEP)**. IEP development most often results from cooperation among educational professionals (teachers, school administrators, guidance counselors, etc.) and parents as they plan a student's educational course in light of his or her individual disability and needs. IEPs, like general lesson plans, are guided by the identification of goals and objectives for individual students, taking into account the student's disability or disabilities.

Insider Example
Student IEP

The sample IEP that follows indicates both an academic goal and a functional goal for the student. The academic goal relates to the student's desired academic achievement, while the functional goal specifies a desired behavioral outcome. These goals are followed by statements of objectives that represent steps the student will take to achieve the specified goals. Both sections end with descriptions of how the student's progress toward the desired goals will be measured or assessed.

Student Description for IEP

Joey Smith is a 16-year-old 11th grader. He has a learning disability in reading, and he also has attention deficit hyperactivity disorder.

Joey generally works well with others and has a good sense of humor. He likes to be helpful and is good at encouraging others. He tries hard when assigned tasks, but gets extremely frustrated and gives up quickly when he has difficulty completing a task as easily or quickly as he thinks he should. He responds well to being asked to try again if someone can work with him individually to get him started on the task again. Sometimes he acts up in class, usually in a joking manner. This tends to result in him frequently being off-task, as well as affecting the students around him. He displays the classic characteristics of a student with attention deficit hyperactivity disorder, including losing focus easily, needing to move around frequently, exhibiting difficulty paying attention to details, and continually blurting out inappropriate comments, or talking at inappropriate times.

Check Purpose:
- ☐ Initial
- ☒ Annual Review
- ☐ Reevaluation
- ☐ Addendum
- ☐ Transition Part C to B

INDIVIDUALIZED EDUCATION PROGRAM (IEP)

Duration of Special Education and Related Services: From: 06/05/2008 To: 06/04/2009

Student: Joey Smith   **DOB: 08/21/1992**

School: ABC High School   **Grade: 10**

Primary Area of Eligibility* Learning Disability
Secondary Area(s) of Eligibility (if applicable): Other Health Impairment
(*Reported on Child Count)

Student Profile

Student's overall strengths:

Joey works hard to complete assignments and accomplish his goals. He interacts well with others, including his peers. He is very helpful and often encourages his peers when they are trying to accomplish their own goals. Joey has a good sense of humor and is good at entertaining others.

Summarize assessment information (e.g., from early intervention providers, child outcome measures, curriculum based measures, state and district assessments results, etc.), and review of progress on current IEP/IFSP goals:

Overall, Joey is making significant progress on his IEP goals. He continues to do well with improving his reading skills. He still struggles with implementing strategies consistently to help him remain focused and committed to completing his tasks; however, he continues to make progress.

Parent's concerns, if any, for enhancing the student's education:

Parent had no concerns at this time.

Parent's/Student's vision for student's future:

Joey will learn to motivate himself to complete tasks and learn to rely less on external motivation from others. He will complete high school and then attend community college.

INDIVIDUALIZED EDUCATION PROGRAM (IEP)

Duration of Special Education and Related Services: From: 06/05/2008 To: 06/04/2009

Student: Joey Smith   **DOB: 08/21/1992**

School: ABC High School   **Grade: 10**

Consideration of Transitions

> If a transition (e.g., new school, family circumstances, etc.) is anticipated during the life of this IEP/IFSP, what information is known about the student that will assist in facilitating a smooth process?   ☒ N/A
>
> The student is age 14 or older or will be during the duration of the IEP.
>   ☒ Yes   ☐ No

Consideration of Special Factors (Note: If you check yes, you must address in the IEP.)

> Does the student have behavior(s) that impede his/her learning or that of others?
>   ☒ Yes   ☐ No
>
> Does the student have Limited English Proficiency?   ☐ Yes   ☒ No
>
> If the student is blind or partially sighted, will the instruction in or use of Braille be needed?   ☐ Yes   ☐ No   ☒ N/A
>
> Does the student have any special communication needs?   ☐ Yes   ☒ No
>
> Is the student deaf or hard of hearing?   ☐ Yes   ☒ No
> ☐ The child's language and communication needs.
> ☐ Opportunities for direct communications with peers and professional personnel in the child's language and communication mode.
> ☐ Academic level.
> ☐ Full range of needs, including opportunities for direct instruction in the child's language, and
> ☐ Communication mode.
> (Communication Plan Worksheet available at www.ncpublicschools.org/ec/policy /forms.)
>
> Does the student require specially designed physical education?   ☐ Yes   ☒ No

Present Level(s) of Academic and Functional Performance
Include specific descriptions of what the student can and cannot do in relationship to this area. Include current academic and functional performance, behaviors, social/ emotional development, other relevant information, and how the student's disability affects his/her involvement and progress in the general curriculum.

> Joey consistently reads at grade level. He can answer comprehension questions accurately if given additional time. He does well on tests and assignments that require reading if given additional time and if allowed to be in a separate setting with minimized distractions during longer tests.

INDIVIDUALIZED EDUCATION PROGRAM (IEP)

Duration of Special Education and Related Services: From: 06/05/2008 To: 06/04/2009

Student: Joey Smith   **DOB: 08/21/1992**

School: ABC High School   **Grade: 10**

Annual Goal

☒ Academic Goal   ☐ Functional Goal

> Joey will continue to learn and demonstrate functional reading skill at grade level.

The academic goal for the student is identified here.

Does the student require assistive technology devices and/or services?   ☐ Yes   ☒ No
If yes, describe needs:

(Address after determination of related services.) Is this goal integrated with related service(s)?   ☐ Yes*   ☒ No
*If yes, list the related service area(s) of integration:

Competency Goal

Required for areas (if any) where student participates in state assessments using modified achievement standards.
Select Subject Area: ☐ Language Arts   ☐ Mathematics   ☐ Science
List Competency Goal from the *NC Standard Course of Study*:
(Standard must match the student's assigned grade.)

Note: Selected Grade Standard Competency Goals listed are those identified for specially designed instruction. In addition to those listed, the student has access to grade-level content standards through general education requirements.

Benchmarks or Short-Term Objectives (if applicable)
(Required for students participating in state alternate assessments aligned to alternate achievement standards)

> 1) Joey will recognize and use vocabulary appropriate for grade level with 90% accuracy.
> 2) Joey will recognize the author's point of view and purpose with 85% accuracy.
> 3) Joey will apply decoding strategies to comprehend grade-level text with 85% accuracy.

The IEP identifies specific objectives the student will achieve toward reaching the academic goal.

Describe how progress toward the annual goal will be measured

> Progress toward this annual goal will be measured by work samples and tests or quizzes.

The IEP identifies ways the student's progress will be measured.

INDIVIDUALIZED EDUCATION PROGRAM (IEP)

Duration of Special Education and Related Services: From: 06/05/2008 To: 06/04/2009

Student: Joey Smith   **DOB:** 08/21/1992

School: ABC High School   **Grade:** 10

Present Level(s) of Academic and Functional Performance

Include specific descriptions of what the student can and cannot do in relationship to this area. Include current academic and functional performance, behaviors, social/emotional development, other relevant information, and how the student's disability affects his/her involvement and progress in the general curriculum.

> Joey does well getting back on task with assistance and when he implements attention-focusing strategies. He needs to improve working on his ability to self-monitor and keep himself on task.

Annual Goal

☐ Academic Goal   ☒ Functional Goal

The functional goal for the student is identified here.

> Joey will continue learning to identify situations where he is more likely to lose focus. He will learn to identify and apply appropriate attention-focusing strategies in a variety of situations.

Does the student require assistive technology devices and/or services? ☐ Yes ☒ No
If yes, describe needs:

>

(Address after determination of related services.) Is this goal integrated with related service(s)? ☐ Yes* ☒ No
*If yes, list the related service area(s) of integration:

>

Competency Goal

> **Required for areas (if any) where student participates in state assessments using modified achievement standards.**
> **Select Subject Area:** ☐ Language Arts ☐ Mathematics ☐ Science
> **List Competency Goal from the *NC Standard Course of Study*:**
> *(Standard must match the student's assigned grade.)*
>
> *Note: Selected Grade Standard Competency Goals listed are those identified for specially designed instruction. In addition to those listed, the student has access to grade-level content standards through general education requirements.*

INDIVIDUALIZED EDUCATION PROGRAM (IEP)

Duration of Special Education and Related Services: **From: 06/05/2008 To: 06/04/2009**

Student: <u>Joey Smith</u>   **DOB: 08/21/1992**

School: <u>ABC High School</u>   **Grade: <u>10</u>**

Benchmarks or Short-Term Objectives (if applicable)
(Required for students participating in state alternate assessments aligned to alternate achievement standards)

1) Joey will be able to articulate how he feels when he becomes frustrated when work gets difficult on 4 trials over a 2-week period as evaluated by structured observations every 6 weeks.
2) By January, Joey will independently request a break from work when he needs it to prevent class disruptions and allow himself to refocus.

The IEP identifies specific objectives the student will achieve toward reaching the functional goal.

Describe how progress toward the annual goal will be measured

Progress will be monitored through documented teacher observation, student self-monitoring checklist, and anecdotal logs.

The IEP identifies ways that the student's progress will be measured.

Teacher for a Day

For this exercise, imagine that you've just taken a job teaching in your major area of study. Identify a specific concept or skill you can see yourself teaching to a group of students. Consider the background and previous knowledge of your target audience. Then, with the concept or skill in mind, design a single-day lesson plan that addresses each of the following elements of a typical lesson plan.

- **Goal(s)** State the specific goal(s) for the skill you want to teach.
- **Objectives** Identify what students will do to better understand the concept or learn the target skill.
- **Materials** Identify the materials needed to carry out the lesson plan successfully.
- **Classroom Activities** Outline the procedures, in chronological order, for the day's lesson.
- **Assessment** Explain how you will assess your students' mastery of the concept or skill. ▶

BUSINESS

Communication in businesses takes many forms, and professionals writing in business settings may spend substantial amounts of time drafting e-mails and memos, or writing letters and proposals. In some instances, businesses may hire individuals solely for their expertise in business communication practices. Such individuals are highly skilled in the analysis and practice of business communication, and their education and training are often aimed at these purposes. Still, if your experiences lead you to employment in a business setting, you're likely to face the task of communicating in one or more of the genres frequently used in those settings. It's no surprise, then, that schools of business, which prepare students to work in companies and corporations, often require their students to take classes that foster an understanding of the vehicles of communication common to the business setting. In the following section, we provide some introductory context and annotated examples of a couple of the more common forms of communication you're likely to encounter in a business setting: the memorandum and the business plan.

Memorandum

The **memorandum**, or memo, is a specialized form of communication used within businesses to make announcements and to share information among colleagues and employees. Although memos serve a range of purposes, like sharing information, providing directives, or even arguing a particular position, they are not generally used to communicate with outside parties, like other companies or clients. While they may range in length from a couple of

paragraphs to multiple pages, they're typically highly structured according to conventional expectations. In fact, you'd be hard pressed to find an example of a professional memo that didn't follow the conventional format for identifying the writer, the audience, the central subject matter, and the date of production in the header. Also, information in memos typically appears in a block format, and the content is often developed from a clear, centralized purpose that is revealed early on in the memo itself.

Insider Example
Student Memorandum

The following is an example of a memo produced by a student in a professional writing class. His purpose for writing was to share his assessment of the advantages and drawbacks of a particular company he's interested in working for in the future. As you read, notice how the information in the opening paragraphs forecasts the memo's content, along with how the memo summarizes its contents in the concluding passages. We've highlighted a number of the other conventional expectations for the memo that you'll want to notice.

MEMO

To: Jamie Larsen
          Professor, North Carolina State University

From: James Blackwell
          Biological Engineering, North Carolina State University

Date: September 2, 2014

Subject: Investigative Report on Hazen and Sawyer

I plan on one day using my knowledge gained in biological engineering to help alleviate the growing environmental problems that our society faces. Hazen and Sawyer is a well-known environmental engineering firm. However, I need to research the firm's background in order to decide if it would be a suitable place for me to work. Consequently, I decided to research the following areas of Hazen and Sawyer engineering firm:

• Current and Past Projects
• Opportunities for Employment and Advancement
• Work Environment

The purpose of this report is to present you with my findings on Hazen and Sawyer, so that you may assist me in writing an application letter that proves my skills and knowledge are worthy of an employment opportunity.

Current and Past Projects

Founded in 1951, Hazen and Sawyer has had a long history of providing clean drinking water and minimizing the effects of water pollution. The company has undertaken many projects in the United States as well as internationally. One of its first projects was improving the infrastructure of Monrovia, Liberia, in 1952. I am interested in using my knowledge of environmental problems to promote sustainability. Designing sustainable solutions for its clients is one of the firm's main goals. Hazen and Sawyer is currently engaged in a project to provide water infrastructure to over one million people in Jordan. Supplying clean drinking water is a problem that is continuously growing, and I hope to work on a similar project someday.

Opportunities for Employment and Advancement

Hazen and Sawyer has over forty offices worldwide, with regional offices in Raleigh, NC, Cincinnati, OH, Dallas, TX, Hollywood, FL, Los Angeles, CA, and its headquarters in New York City. The company currently has over thirty job openings at offices across the United States. I would like to live in the Raleigh area following graduation, so having a regional office here in Raleigh greatly helps my chances of finding a local job with the company. Hazen and Sawyer also has offices in Greensboro and Charlotte, which also helps my chances of finding a job in North Carolina. I am interested in finding a job dealing with stream restoration, and the Raleigh office currently has an opening for a Stream Restoration Designer. The position requires experience with AutoCAD and GIS, and I have used both of these programs in my Biological Engineering courses.

In addition to numerous job openings, Hazen and Sawyer also offers opportunities for professional development within the company. The Pathway Program for Professional Development is designed to keep employees up-to-date on topics in their fields and also stay educated to meet license requirements in different states. Even if I found a job at the Raleigh office, I would most likely have to travel out of state to work on projects, so this program could be very beneficial. I am seeking to work with a company that promotes continuous professional growth, so this program makes me very interested in Hazen and Sawyer.

Work Environment

Hazen and Sawyer supports innovation and creativity, and at the same time tries to limit bureaucracy. I am seeking a company that will allow me to be creative and assist with projects while not being in charge initially. As I gain experience and learn on the job, I hope to move into positions with greater responsibility. The firm offers a mentoring program that places newly hired engineers with someone more experienced. This program would help me adapt to the company and provide guidance as I gain professional experience. I hope to eventually receive my Professional Engineering license, so working under a professional engineer with years of experience would be a great opportunity for me. Hazen and Sawyer supports positive relationships among its employees, by engaging them in social outings such as sporting events, parties, picnics, and other activities.

References

Hazen and Sawyer—Environmental Engineers and Scientists. Web. 2 Sept. 2014.
<http://www.hazenandsawyer.com/home/>.

Many people dream of being their own bosses. One avenue for achieving this dream is to create a successful business, or to own and operate a service or company. Anyone undertaking such a task in the economy today will need a solid business background that includes knowledge of the many forms of written communication required to start and continue the operation of a successful business. Two very important genres for these purposes are the business plan and the business proposal. If you're a business owner looking to raise capital, or if you've got a good idea or product that you want to sell to potential investors, then you're going to need a solid **business plan**, a document that clearly and efficiently describes your business and its essential operations, analyzes your market competition, and assesses the expected expenses and potential for profit. Let's say that you've got a great idea for a new lawn care service, but you need capital to purchase the necessary equipment and to advertise your services to potential customers. To obtain that capital, you're likely going to need a business plan that others can read when deciding whether to invest in your business.

By contrast, the **business proposal** is a form of communication through which a company proposes a relationship of some sort with another entity—often another company. Companies frequently receive unsolicited business proposals. A photocopying company, for instance, may design a proposal to begin a relationship that involves installing and maintaining all the photocopiers owned by a particular city or municipality. At other times, companies request business proposals. Imagine that you're the president of a landscaping service, for example, and you've decided to outsource all work that involves tree removal. To determine whom you want to hire for those jobs, you call for proposals from those companies or individuals to determine whose services best match your needs. In the world of business, effective communication means making money.

Insider Example
Student Business Plan

The following business plan was produced by a student in a writing class that addressed the communication needs of his major. As you read, notice how the student shaped the plan to satisfy the needs of the target audience, a bank, as a potential source of funding.

The Electricity Monitor Company

Daniel Chase Mills

The annotations in the left margin read:

The cover page for the plan highlights the name of the proposed company, along with the author of the plan.

The author identifies a specific audience for the plan—in this case a potential source of funding. More than a generic plan, then, this document is crafted specifically for the purpose of seeking start-up capital.

Identifies the writer/ company submitting the plan for consideration, along with appropriate contact information

The Electricity Monitor Company

This document is a request for a start-up business loan for a company that will design, manufacture, and sell an electricity-monitoring product that will answer customers' demands for a solution to high power bills.

To: Ms. Jane Harmon Bausch, President

First National Bank

10 Money Street

Raleigh, North Carolina 27695

Prepared By:

Daniel Chase Mills

The Electricity Monitor Company

100 Satellite Lane

City, North Carolina 20000

Email: dcmills@ncsu.edu

Phone: (919) 555-2233

November 21, 2014

In the executive summary, the writer provides a general overview of the plan: identifies a problem, briefly describes the company's unique product and market, and highlights potential customers. The section ends by noting the dollar amount requested from the bank.

In what way is an executive summary like an abstract?

Executive Summary

The Electricity Monitor Company

Prepared by Daniel Chase Mills, November 21, 2014

This document is a start-up business proposal for the Electricity Monitor Company and a request for an investment from First National Bank of Raleigh, North Carolina. The Company will design, manufacture, and sell the Electricity Monitor. Families with a traditional circuit-breaker box often struggle with high power bills, due to their inability to monitor their electricity usage. The Electricity Monitor is a device that will answer this pain point. This device is an adapter that attaches to any existing breaker box with installation simple enough for consumers to perform on their own. The device monitors current electricity usage and determines ways to reduce energy consumption. The device is superior to alternatives in the market in that it is cheaper, easier to install, and more effectively solves the problem of not knowing how much electricity is being used. The overall purpose of the

Electricity Monitor Company is to develop a high-quality product that can generate excitement in the electricity monitor market and turn a profit for its business owners and investors. The total loan request from First National Bank is three hundred and fifty-four thousand dollars ($354,000.00).

Table of Contents

Title Page	ii
Executive Summary	iii
Table of Contents	iv
List of Tables and Figures	iv
Introduction to the Electricity Monitor Company	1
A. Purpose	1
B. Problem: High Power Bills	2
C. Current Alternatives to High Power Bills	2
D. The Electricity Monitor	2
E. Market for This Product	3
Plan of Business	4
A. Overview	4
B. Cost Analysis	4
C. Summary	6
Conclusion	6
Bibliography	6
Attachments	7
A. Cost Breakdown	7

Notice the ordering of elements of the plan. How would you describe the order of these elements?

List of Tables and Figures

Figure 1, Price Comparison	3
Figure 2, Market Breakdown	4
Table 1, Design Expense	4
Table 2, Manufacturing Expense	5
Table 3, Marketing Expense	5
Table 4, Total Cost Analysis	5

Introduction to the Electricity Monitor Company

A. Purpose

The purpose of this document is to request funding from First National Bank for a start-up business called the Electricity Monitor Company. This

Briefly identifies the general purpose of the document and offers a preview of the document's contents

document will contain an overview of the problem that the company will address in the market, how the Electricity Monitor will solve this problem, and a plan for this business.

Explains a problem that consumers face

B. Problem: High Power Bills

In twenty-first century America, and in most first world countries, electricity is a necessity. In the home, electricity is used for a variety of devices. Due to the vast number of devices that use electricity, and no good way of knowing how much power they are consuming on a daily basis, families with a traditional circuit-breaker box often struggle with using too much electricity. The problem is high power bills.

Provides a brief market analysis, and identifies a gap in the market

C. Current Alternatives to High Power Bills

How is this section of the report similar to or different from a review of scholarship?

There are three currently available solutions to measuring home energy usage in an attempt to lower power bills: Plug-in Meters, Energy Meter Monitors, and Home Energy Monitors. Plug-in Meters are devices that plug in to individual outlets to measure energy usage of a single device. An Energy Meter Monitor attaches to an electricity meter, measures total energy consumption of a home, and estimates what the power bill will be for the month. Neither device is effective in determining energy usage of the entire home across multiple devices. The Home Energy Monitors contain multiple channels to measure energy usage across multiple devices in the home, but these devices are extremely expensive and require detailed installation that increases the cost of the products. Three Home Energy Monitoring Devices are the TED 5000, eGuage, and EnviR, with respective prices of $239, $494, and $129. I have determined that the current solutions in this market are too expensive and do not adequately provide families with an affordable way to monitor their electricity usage. I have developed a better solution to this pain point.

Stresses reasons that support the business's potential for success

D. The Electricity Monitor

The Electricity Monitor is a device that can solve the pain point of high power bills by measuring the electricity usage of each device in the home. This device can easily attach to any existing breaker box. Installation of the device can be performed by any customer with the instructions provided with the device. At a price of $75, this device will be much cheaper than current solutions to monitoring power usage. A price comparison is shown in Figure 1 below. By measuring electricity usage of each device in the home, the Electricity Monitor will be able to accurately estimate the power bill for the month (within 1% error) and update daily with changes to electricity usage trends in the home. All data will be transmitted to a monitoring display. This device is also superior to the competition in that it makes suggestions as to how to decrease energy consumption and provides information on which devices in the home are using the most energy. Using the data from the Electricity Monitor, families will finally have the tool they need to save money on their power bill.

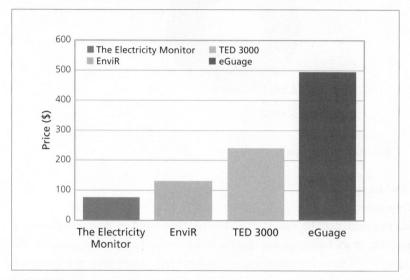

Fig. 1. Price comparison

Charts and figures appear commonly in business documents for clarification of ideas or to explain relationships between variables.

E. Market for This Product

Performs a more detailed market analysis

Industry market research from the IBIS World database shows small household appliance manufacturing to have $3.1 billion in annual revenue with $77.9 million in annual profit. This number alone shows the vastness of this market. In addition, IBIS World estimates 38.4% of this market to account for small household devices similar to the Electricity Monitor. Figure 2 below from IBIS World shows the market breakdown. The main demographic for this product will be families of three or more who are unhappy with their current power bill. The United States Census Bureau estimated there to be 4.4 million households with families of three or more people, accounting for 39% of all households in 2011. IBIS World describes the technology change in this market to be "Medium." This leads me to believe that a new product in this market could really shake the market and attract interest from consumers. Assuming that the current trend for revenue and profit in the small household appliance industry performs as predicted, the market for the Electricity Monitor will be large.

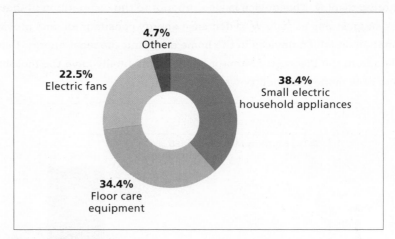

Fig. 2. Market breakdown

Explains governance and operating procedures of the proposed company

Plan of Business

A. Overview

I plan to construct the Electricity Monitor Company to hold complete ownership of all business sectors for the Electricity Monitor product. The Company will have an engineering department responsible for the design of the product, a manufacturing facility where the product will be built, and a marketing department responsible for the marketing and selling of the product. The overall cost for the start-up is analyzed below. This breakdown of cost can also be found in the Attachments section of this document.

Offers a detailed analysis of costs associated with the business start-up

B. Cost Analysis

Table 1
Design Expense

Design Expense	Description	Total Cost
Building	Rented office space	$ 5,000.00
Software	CAD modeling and FEA software license	$ 4,000.00
Total		$ 9,000.00

Table 1 is an analysis of the cost for designing the product. The requested loan will need to cover the first month of rent for an office and also a license for software that will be used to design the product. The labor is not included in the cost here because I will be designing the product myself.

Table 2
Manufacturing Expense

Manufacturing Expense (First 500 Products)	Description	Total Cost
Building	Small manufacturing facility	$ 100,000.00
Manufacturing equipment	Laser cutting machine, etc.	$ 200,000.00
Tools	Screwdrivers, socket wrenches, Allen wrenches, etc.	$ 5,000.00
Materials	First 500 monitors (avg cost $20/monitor)	$ 10,000.00
Labor	$25/hr with five employees @ 40 hours a week	$ 20,000.00
Total		$ 335,000.00

Table 2 is an analysis of the cost for manufacturing the product. The building and manufacturing equipment are one-time costs for the initial start-up. The materials and labor will be ongoing costs, but the loan request is only enough to cover the first 500 products manufactured. Five hundred products have been estimated as enough to cover the first month of sales and will allow my company to be self-sufficient after selling the first 500 products.

Table 3
Marketing Expense

Marketing Expense	Description	Total Cost
Commercial	Television ad	$ 5,000.00
Web search	Google AdWords	$ 5,000.00
Total		$ 10,000.00

Table 3 is an analysis of the total marketing expense. I will additionally market this product to retail stores that could also sell this product, but cost for labor of this marketing is not included here because I will do it myself.

Table 4
Total Cost Analysis

Business Sector	Total Cost
Design	$ 9,000.00
Manufacturing	$ 335,000.00
Marketing	$ 10,000.00
Total	$ 354,000.00

Table 4 is a summary of the total cost analysis for this product. The highlighted cell in Table 4 represents the total start-up cost for the Electricity Monitor Company. This is also the total requested loan amount from First National Bank.

C. Summary

The total cost for this start-up was analyzed in Tables 1 through 4 above. The cost of materials was estimated from current market cost of materials and is subject to change with the market. However, my request for the bottom-line loan amount for this start-up is three hundred and fifty-four thousand dollars ($354,000.00), and this request will not change with cost of materials. A sound business plan has been constructed that will allow the Electricity Monitor Company to become self-sufficient after one month. In order for this business plan to work, the product must be successful in attracting customers quickly as projected by the market research.

The conclusion reiterates the proposed product's unique characteristics and potential for success in hopes of securing the capital investment.

Conclusion

The overall purpose of the Electricity Monitor start-up business is to develop a high-quality product that can generate excitement in the electricity monitor market and turn a profit for its business owners and investors. This product will benefit not only its investors, but also its consumers in that it will solve their pain point of not being able to affordably measure their current energy consumption. In comparison to other products in the market that attempt to solve the problem of high power bills, the Electricity Monitor is superior in price, ease of installation, and overall ability to solve the problem. There is nothing quite like this product currently in the market, and this is why it will be successful. The market research has proven that there is a large potential market and that current technology change is not very high. I am excited about starting the Electricity Monitor Company, the potential of this product, and the benefits for all parties involved. Please grant the requested loan amount of three hundred and fifty-four thousand dollars ($354,000.00) and help me make unnecessarily high power bills a thing of the past.

Documents sources consulted in the preparation of the business document

Bibliography

Entrepreneur. "TV Ads." Web. <http://www.entrepreneur.com/article /83108>.

IBIS World. "Vacuum, Fan, & Small Household Appliance Manufacturing in the US." Web. <http://clients1.ibisworld.com.prox.lib.ncsu.edu/reports /us/industry/ataglance.aspx?indid=786>.

Kreider, Rose M. "America's Families and Living Arrangements: 2012."
United States Census Bureau. Web. <https://www.census.gov/prod
/2013pubs/p20-570.pdf>.

Thornton Oliver Keller Commercial Real Estate. "Rental Rate Calculations."
Web. <http://tokcommercial.com/MarketInformation/LearningCenter
/RentalRateCalculations.aspx>.

Attachments

A. Cost Breakdown

Design Expense	Description	Total Cost
Building	Rented office space	$ 5,000.00
Software	CAD modeling and FEA software license	$ 4,000.00
Total		**$ 9,000.00**

Compiles the costs associated with the business start-up. See the reference to the attachment on page 290.

Manufacturing Expense (First 500 Products)	Description	Total Cost
Building	Small manufacturing facility	$ 100,000.00
Manufacturing equipment	Laser cutting machine, etc.	$ 200,000.00
Tools	Screwdrivers, socket wrenches, Allen wrenches, etc.	$ 5,000.00
Materials	First 500 monitors (avg cost $20/monitor)	$ 10,000.00
Labor	$25/hr with five employees @ 40 hours a week	$ 20,000.00
Total		**$ 335,000.00**

Marketing Expense	Description	Total Cost
Commercial	Television ad	$ 5,000.00
Web search	Google AdWords	$ 5,000.00
Total		**$ 10,000.00**

Business Sector	Total Cost	
Design	$ 9,000.00	
Manufacturing	$ 335,000.00	
Marketing	$ 10,000.00	
Total	**$ 354,000.00**	

For this exercise, imagine that you're the chief financial officer for a company, Music Studio Emporium. Your company has twenty employees, and you've been charged with the task of notifying ten of them that they'll be receiving a 2 percent annual pay increase, effective immediately, based on their sales records. Unfortunately, you must also notify your other ten employees that they will not be receiving raises. Draft a brief memo to each group of employees—one for those receiving raises and one for those who aren't—in which you explain the company's decisions regarding your employees' compensation. Feel free to provide additional reasoning for those decisions, as you see fit.

Refer to the memo on page 284 as a model of the structural features you'll want to employ in constructing your memo. Once you're done, consider how the nature of the news you had to convey to each audience influenced the way you delivered that news. What did you do the same for each of your audiences? What did you do differently in constructing the two memos? ❱

LAW

Most of us probably have clichéd understandings of the law at work. Many of these likely originated from television shows and movies. In these scenarios, there's almost always lots of drama as the lawyers battle in court, parse witnesses' words, and attempt to sway a judge or jury to their side of a case.

In real life, the practice of law may not always be quite as dramatic or enthralling as it appears on the screen. In fact, many lawyers rarely, or maybe never, appear in court. A criminal defense attorney may regularly appear before a judge or jury in a courtroom setting, but a corporate lawyer may spend the majority of her time drafting and analyzing business contracts. This difference is directly related to the field of law an individual specializes in, be it criminal law, family law, tax law, or environmental law, just to name a few.

Regardless of an attorney's chosen specialization, though, the study of law remains fundamentally concerned with debates over the interpretation of language. This is because the various rules that govern our lives—statutes, ordinances, regulations, and laws, for example—are all constructed in language. As you surely recognize, language can be quite slippery, and rules can often be interpreted in many different ways. We need only briefly to consider current debates over free speech issues or the "right to bear arms" or marriage equality to understand how complicated the business of interpreting laws can become. In the United States, the U.S. Supreme Court holds the authority to provide the final interpretation on the meaning of disputed laws. However, there are lots of legal interpretations and arguments that lower courts must make on a daily basis, and only a tiny portion of cases are ever heard by the U.S. Supreme Court.

As in the other applied fields, there are many common forms of communication in the various fields of law, as lawyers must regularly communicate with different kinds of stakeholders, including clients, other lawyers, judges, and law enforcement officials. For this reason, individuals working in the legal professions are generally expert at composing e-mail messages, memos, letters to clients, and legal briefs, among other genres. The following examples provide a glimpse into two types of writing through which lawyers frequently communicate.

Legal Brief

One of the first forms of writing students of law are likely to encounter in their academic study is the **legal brief**. Briefs can serve any number of functions, but their primary purpose is to outline the critical components of a legal argument to a specified audience. They may be descriptive or argumentative. A typical assignment for a student in law school might include writing a legal brief that describes a particular court's decision and explains how the court reached that decision. Cases that appear before the U.S. Supreme Court are usually accompanied by numerous legal briefs that are written and filed with the Court by parties who are interested in the outcomes of those cases. Many of these briefs are argumentative. Students of law, then, must be familiar with the basic structural components, or the structural conventions, of the legal brief. And law schools regularly instruct their students to produce legal briefs using the generalized form known as **IRAC**—an acronym for **Introduction, Rule, Application, and Conclusion**—as a means to describe past court decisions and/or to present written arguments to a court:

- **Identify the Legal Issue(s) in the Case**

    Introduction   Legal cases can be very complicated. It is a lawyer's task to explore the facts of a case, along with its legal history, to determine which facts are actually relevant and which are irrelevant as they pertain to a legal question or dispute.

- **Identify and Explain the Relevant Law(s) to the Case**

    Rule   Often, many different statutes, regulations, laws, or other court precedents are applicable and need exploration as part of a legal dispute. A lawyer must identify the applicable rules of law and explain their relevance to the legal question or dispute at hand.

- **Apply the Relevant Rules to the Facts of the Case**

  Application   The facts of the case are explored through the lens of relevant rules. Arguments are presented in these sections of a brief.

- **Argue for a Particular Decision or Outcome**

  Conclusion   Based on the application of relevant rules to the facts of the case, a lawyer makes a recommendation that the judge or court should reach a particular conclusion.

Insider Example
Professional Legal Brief

The following excerpts are from a 55-page legal brief that was filed with the U.S. Supreme Court on behalf of the University of Texas at Austin, et al., which was sued by an applicant after being denied admission to the university. In arguing their case, attorneys writing on behalf of the respondents, or the university, defended its decision to deny admission to the complainant, or the petitioner, Abigail Fisher. As you read the excerpted sections below, try to identify parts of the brief that correspond to the elements of the IRAC structure for presenting legal arguments: Introduction, Rule, Application, and Conclusion.

No. 11-345

In the
Supreme Court of the United States

ABIGAIL NOEL FISHER,
Petitioner,

v.

UNIVERSITY OF TEXAS AT AUSTIN, ET AL.,
Respondents.

ON WRIT OF CERTIORARI TO THE
UNITED STATES COURT OF APPEALS
FOR THE FIFTH CIRCUIT

BRIEF FOR RESPONDENTS

PATRICIA C. OHLENDORF
*Vice President for
Legal Affairs*

GREGORY G. GARRE
Counsel of Record
MAUREEN E. MAHONEY

THE UNIVERSITY OF
   TEXAS AT AUSTIN
Flawn Academic Center
2304 Whitis Avenue
Stop G4800
Austin, TX 78712

DOUGLAS LAYCOCK
UNIVERSITY OF VIRGINIA
   SCHOOL OF LAW
580 Massie Road
Charlottesville, VA 22903

J. SCOTT BALLENGER
LORI ALVINO McGILL
KATYA S. GEORGIEVA
LATHAM & WATKINS LLP
555 11th Street, NW
Suite 1000
Washington, DC 20004
(202) 637-2207
gregory.garre@lw.com

JAMES C. HO
GIBSON, DUNN &
   CRUTCHER LLP
2100 McKinney Avenue
Suite 1110
Dallas, TX 75201-6912

Counsel for Respondents

INTRODUCTION

After considering largely the same objections raised by petitioner and her amici here, this Court strongly embraced Justice Powell's controlling opinion in *Regents of the University of California v. Bakke*, 438 U.S. 265 (1978), and refused to prohibit the consideration of race as a factor in admissions at the Nation's universities and graduate schools. *Grutter v. Bollinger*, 539 U.S. 306 (2003); *see id.* at 387 (Kennedy, J., dissenting). And although the Court has made clear that any consideration of race in this context must be limited, it has been understood for decades that "a university admissions program may take account of race as one, non-predominant factor in a system designed to consider each applicant as an individual, provided the program can meet the test of strict scrutiny by the judiciary." *Id.* at 387 (Kennedy, J., dissenting) (citing *Bakke*, 438 U.S. at 289-91, 315-18 (Powell, J.)); *see id.* at 322-23. The University of Texas at Austin (UT)'s highly individualized consideration of race for applicants not admitted under the State's top 10% law satisfies that demand, and meets strict scrutiny under any conception of that test not designed simply to bar the consideration of race altogether.

> Identifies the critical issue at stake, and lays out the respondents' position

That conclusion follows *a fortiori* from existing precedent. UT's admissions plan was modeled on the type of plan upheld in *Grutter* and commended by Justice Powell in *Bakke*. Moreover, UT's plan lacks the features criticized in *Grutter* by Justice Kennedy—who agreed with the majority that *Bakke* is the "correct rule." *Id.* at 387 (dissenting). Justice Kennedy concluded that Michigan Law School's admissions plan used race "to achieve numerical goals

> Reviews relevant precedents, or earlier conclusions reached by the Court

indistinguishable from quotas." *Id.* at 389. Here, it is undisputed that UT has not set any "target" or "goal" for minority admissions. JA 131a. Justice Kennedy stressed that Michigan's "admissions officers consulted . . . daily reports which indicated the composition of the incoming class along racial lines." *Grutter*, 539 U.S. at 391 (dissenting). Here, it is undeniable that no such monitoring occurs. JA 398a. And Justice Kennedy believed that race was "a predominant factor" under Michigan's plan. *Grutter*, 539 U.S. at 393 (dissenting). Here, petitioner argues (at 20) that UT's consideration of race is too "minimal" to be constitutional. That paradoxical contention not only overlooks the indisputably meaningful impact that UT's plan has on diversity, *infra* at 36-38, it turns on its head Justice Powell's conception of the appropriately nuanced and modest consideration of race in this special context.

Presents the complainant's central claims, and offers response

Because petitioner cannot dispute that UT's consideration of race is both highly individualized and modest, she is forced to take positions directly at odds with the record and existing precedent. Her headline claim that UT is engaged in "racial balancing" (Pet. Br. 6-7, 19, 27-28, 45-46) is refuted by her own concession that UT has *not* set any "target" for minority admissions. JA 131a. Her argument that the State's top 10% law bars UT from considering race in its holistic review of applicants not eligible under that law is foreclosed by *Grutter*'s holding that percentage plans are not a complete, workable alternative to the individualized consideration of race in full-file review. 539 U.S. at 340. And her argument that, in 2004, UT had already achieved all the diversity that the Constitution allowed is based on "a limited notion of diversity" (*Parents Involved in Cmty. Schs. v. Seattle Sch. Dist. No. 1*, 551 U.S. 701, 723 (2007)) rejected by this Court—one that crudely lumps together distinct racial groups and ignores the importance of diversity among individuals *within* racial groups.

Identifies stakes for the outcome of the decision, and reasserts the respondents' position

In the end, petitioner really is just asking this Court to move the goal posts on higher education in America—and overrule its precedent going back 35 years to *Bakke*. Pet. Br. 53-57. *Stare decisis* alone counsels decisively against doing so. Petitioner has provided no persuasive justification for the Court to reexamine, much less overrule, its precedent, just nine years after this Court decided *Grutter* and eliminated any doubt about the controlling force of Justice Powell's opinion in *Bakke*. And overruling *Grutter* and *Bakke* (or effectively gutting them by adopting petitioner's conception of strict scrutiny) would jeopardize the Nation's paramount interest in educating its future leaders in an environment that best prepares them for the society and workforce they will encounter. Moreover, the question that petitioner herself asked this Court to decide is the constitutionality of UT's policy under *existing* precedent, including *Grutter. See* Pet. i; Pet. Br. i. Because the court of appeals correctly answered that question, the judgment below should be affirmed.

STATEMENT OF THE CASE

. . .

E. Petitioner's Application for Admission

Petitioner, a Texas resident, applied for admission to UT's Fall 2008 freshman class in Business Administration or Liberal Arts, with a combined SAT score of 1180 out of 1600 and a cumulative 3.59 GPA. JA 40a-41a. Because petitioner was not in the top 10% of her high school class, her application was considered pursuant to the holistic review process described above. JA 40a. Petitioner scored an AI of 3.1, JA 415a, and received a PAI score of less than 6 (the actual score is contained in a sealed brief, ECF No. 52). The summary judgment record is uncontradicted that—due to the stiff competition in 2008 and petitioner's relatively low AI score—petitioner would not have been admitted to the Fall 2008 freshman class even if she had received "a 'perfect' PAI score of 6." JA 416a.

<aside>Provides background facts about the case concerning the student's application to UT–Austin</aside>

Petitioner also was denied admission to the summer program, which offered provisional admission to some applicants who were denied admission to the fall class, subject to completing certain academic requirements over the summer. JA 413a-14a. (UT discontinued this program in 2009.) Although one African-American and four Hispanic applicants with lower combined AI/PAI scores than petitioner's were offered admission to the summer program, so were 42 Caucasian applicants with combined AI/PAI scores identical to or lower than petitioner's. In addition, 168 African-American and Hispanic applicants in this pool who had combined AI/PAI scores identical to or *higher* than petitioner's were *denied* admission to the summer program.[1]

---

[1]These figures are drawn from UT's admissions data and are provided in response to petitioner's unsupported assertion (at 2) that her "academic credentials exceeded those of many admitted minority applicants." Petitioner presented a subset of this data (admitted minority students) to the district court as Plaintiffs' Exhibits 26 and 27 at the preliminary injunction hearing (the court later returned the exhibits). *See* W.D. Tex. Record Transmittal Letter (July 27, 2012), ECF No. 136. UT summarized additional data in a sealed letter brief after the hearing. ECF No. 52; JA 20a (discussing data and explaining that petitioner had not requested data regarding the applicants "who were *not* admitted to UT"). In denying a preliminary injunction, the district court stated (without citation) that 64 minority applicants with lower AI scores than petitioner were *admitted* to Liberal Arts. *Fisher v. Texas*, 556 F. Supp. 2d 603, 607 & n.2 (W.D. Tex. 2008). That statement is not binding at the merits stage. *University of Texas v. Camenisch*, 451 U.S. 390, 395 (1981). Although the district court did not specify whether it was referring to admissions to the fall class or the summer program, that figure can only encompass admits to the summer program. As explained in the unrebutted summary judgment record, with her AI score, petitioner could not "have gained admission through the fall review process," even with a "perfect" PAI score. JA 415a-16a. Petitioner has submitted no contrary evidence (and UT is aware of none). That leaves the now-defunct summer program. The district court's statement that minority applicants with lower AI scores than petitioner were admitted does not establish that race was a factor in petitioner's

UT did offer petitioner admission to the Coordinated Admissions Program, which allows Texas residents to gain admission to UT for their sophomore year by completing 30 credits at a participating UT System campus and maintaining a 3.2 GPA. JA 414a. Petitioner declined that offer and enrolled at Louisiana State University, from which she graduated in May.

F. Procedural History

Provides a brief history of the case in the courts, explaining decisions by lower courts

Petitioner and another applicant—"no longer involved in this case," Pet. Br. ii—filed suit in the Western District of Texas against UT and various University officials under 42 U.S.C. § 1983, alleging, *inter alia*, that UT's 2008 full-file admissions procedures violate the Equal Protection Clause. JA 38a. They sued only on their own behalf (not on behalf of any class of applicants) and sought a declaratory judgment and injunctive relief barring UT's consideration of race and requiring UT to reconsider their own applications in a race-blind process. JA 39a. They also sought a "refund of [their] application fees and all associated expenses incurred . . . in connection with applying to UT." *Id.*; *see* App. 3a-4a.

The district court denied petitioner's request for a preliminary injunction. The parties filed cross-motions for summary judgment and supporting statements of fact (JA 103a-51a, 363a-403a). Applying strict scrutiny (App. 139a), the court granted judgment to UT, holding that UT has a compelling interest in attaining a diverse student body and the educational benefits flowing from such diversity, and that UT's individualized and holistic review process is narrowly tailored to further that interest. App. 168-69a.

The Fifth Circuit affirmed. Like the district court, the court of appeals found that "it would be difficult for UT to construct an admissions policy that more closely resembles the policy approved by the Supreme Court in *Grutter*." App. 5a. And the court likewise took it as "a given" that UT's policy "is subject to strict scrutiny with its requirement of narrow tailoring." App. 35a. While acknowledging that *Bakke* and *Grutter* call for some deference to a university's "educational judgment," the court emphasized that "the scrutiny triggered by

---

denial from the summer program, because (as noted above) many more minority applicants (168) with identical or *higher* AI/PAI scores were *denied* admission to the summer program. It is thus hard to see how petitioner could establish any cognizable injury for her § 1983 damages claim—the only claim still alive in this case—or, for that matter, standing to maintain that claim. *See Texas v. Lesage*, 528 U.S. 18, 19, 21 (1999) (per curiam); *Lujan v. Defenders of Wildlife*, 504 U.S. 555, 562 (1992). (Petitioner's claims for injunctive relief dropped out of the case at least once she graduated from a different university in May 2012, making this issue pertinent now.) And that is just one apparent vehicle—if not jurisdictional—defect with this case. *See* Br. in Opp. 6-22; *see also* Adam D. Chandler, *How (Not) to Bring an Affirmative-Action Challenge*, 122 Yale L. J. Online (forthcoming Sept. 2012), *available at* http://ssrn.com/abstract_id=2122956 (discussing vehicle defects stemming from, among other things, the unusual manner in which this case was framed).

racial classification 'is no less strict for taking into account' the special circumstances of higher education." App. 34a, 36a. Applying strict scrutiny, the court upheld UT's admissions policy. App. 71a.

Judge Garza concurred. He recognized that the court's opinion was "faithful" to *Grutter*, but argued that *Grutter* was wrongly decided. App. 72a-73a.

SUMMARY OF ARGUMENT

Presents a summary of arguments in defense of the respondents' position in light of the facts of the case

UT's individualized consideration of race in holistic admissions did not subject petitioner to unequal treatment in violation of the Fourteenth Amendment.

I. Racial classifications are subject to strict scrutiny, including in the higher education context. But ever since Justice Powell's opinion in *Bakke*, this Court has recognized that universities have a compelling interest in promoting student body diversity, and that a university may consider the race of applicants in an individualized and modest manner—such that race is just one of many characteristics that form the mosaic presented by an applicant's file.

UT's holistic admissions policy exemplifies the type of plan this Court has allowed: race is only one modest factor among many others weighed; it is considered only in an individualized and contextual way that "examine[s] the student in 'their totality,'" JA 129a; and admissions officers do not know an applicant's race when they decide which "cells" to admit in UT's process. At the same time, UT's policy *lacks* the features that Justice Kennedy found disqualifying in *Grutter*: it is undisputed that UT has not established any race-based target; race is not assigned any automatic value; and the racial or ethnic composition of admits is not monitored during the admissions cycle.

II. Petitioner's arguments that she was nevertheless subjected to unequal treatment in violation of the Fourteenth Amendment are refuted by both the record and existing precedent.

. . .

III. The Court should decline petitioner's far-reaching request to reopen and overrule *Bakke* and *Grutter*. That request is outside the scope of the question presented, which asks the Court to review UT's policy under *existing* precedent, including *Grutter*. In any event, petitioner has failed to identify any special justification for taking the extraordinary step of overruling *Grutter*, just nine years after this Court decided *Grutter* and unequivocally answered any doubt about the validity of Justice Powell's opinion in *Bakke*. Abruptly reversing course here would upset legitimate expectations in the rule of law—not to mention the profoundly important societal interests in ensuring that the future leaders of America are trained in a campus environment in which they are exposed to the full educational benefits of diversity.

. . .

Concludes by asserting
the decision that
respondents believe
the Court should reach

CONCLUSION

The judgment of the court of appeals should be affirmed.

Respectfully submitted,

PATRICIA C. OHLENDORF
Vice President for
Legal Affairs
THE UNIVERSITY OF
TEXAS AT AUSTIN
Flawn Academic Center
2304 Whitis Avenue
Stop G4800
Austin, TX 78712

DOUGLAS LAYCOCK
UNIVERSITY OF VIRGINIA
SCHOOL OF LAW
580 Massie Road
Charlottesville, VA 22903

GREGORY G. GARRE
Counsel of Record
MAUREEN E. MAHONEY
J. SCOTT BALLENGER
LORI ALVINO McGILL
KATYA S. GEORGIEVA
LATHAM & WATKINS LLP
555 11th Street, NW
Suite 1000
Washington, DC 20004
(202) 637-2207
gregory.garre@lw.com

JAMES C. HO
GIBSON, DUNN &
CRUTCHER LLP
2100 McKinney Avenue
Suite 1110
Dallas, TX 75201-6912

AUGUST 2012

Counsel for Respondents

E-Mail Correspondence

As you might expect, technological advances can have a profound impact on the communication practices of professionals. There may always be a place for hard copies of documents, but e-mail communication has no doubt replaced many of the letters that used to pass between parties via the U.S. Postal Service. Like most professionals these days, those employed in the legal fields often spend a lot of time communicating with stakeholders via e-mail. These professionals carefully assess each rhetorical situation for which an e-mail communication is necessary, both (1) to make sure the ideas they share with stakeholders (the explanations of legal procedures, or legal options, or applicable precedents, etc.) are accurate, and (2) to make sure they communicate those ideas in an appropriate fashion (with the appropriate tone, clarity, precision, etc.).

Insider Example
E-Mail Correspondence from Attorney

The following example is an e-mail sent from a practicing lawyer to a client. In this instance, the lawyer offers legal advice concerning a possible donation from a party to a foundation. As you read the lawyer's description of the documents attached to his **e-mail correspondence** with the client, pay attention to the ways the attorney demonstrates an acute awareness of his audience, both in terms of the actual legal advice he provides and in terms of the structure and language of his message.

Dear _____

As promised, here are two documents related to the proposed gift of the ABC property to the XYZ Foundation (the "Foundation"). The first document summarizes the recommended due diligence steps (including the creation of a limited liability company) that should take place prior to the acceptance of the property, accompanied by estimated costs associated with each such step. The second document contains a draft "pre-acceptance" agreement that the Foundation could use to recover its documented costs in the event that either the donor or the Foundation backs out of a gift agreement following the due diligence process.

> Establishes the level of familiarity and tone

> Provides transactional advice, explaining what procedure needs to occur between the two parties involved: a donor and a receiving foundation

You will note that we have limited the Foundation's ability to recover costs in the event that the Foundation is the party that "pulls the plug." In such a scenario, the Foundation could recover costs only if it reasonably determines that either (i) the property would create a risk of material exposure to environmentally related liabilities or (ii) the remediation of environmental issues would impose material costs on the Foundation. We realize that even in light of this limiting language, the agreement represents a fairly aggressive approach with the donor, and we will be glad to work with you if you wish to take a softer stance.

> Provides additional advice to protect the interests of the parties in the event that either party decides to back out of the transaction

> Explains more specific details included in the attached legal documents to protect the interests of the Foundation

Please don't hesitate to call me with any questions, concerns, or critiques. As always, we appreciate the opportunity to serve you in furthering the Foundation's good work.

> Communicates a willingness to continue the relationship with the client

Best regards,

Joe

Joseph E. Miller, Jr.
Partner
joe.miller@FaegreBD.com
Direct: +1 317 237 1415
FaegreBD.com Download vCard
FAEGRE BAKER DANIELS LLP
300 N. Meridian Street
Suite 2700
Indianapolis, IN 46204, USA

> Provides standard identification and contact information for communication between and among professionals

INSIDE WORK   **Lawyer for a Day**

Imagine that you're an attorney, and you've just been hired as a consultant by the Board of Governors of a local college that's in the process of designing new guidelines for student admissions. As part of that process, the Board has asked you to review legal briefs presented on behalf of various stakeholders in *Fisher v. University of Texas at Austin, et al.* Additionally, the Board wants you to provide a summary of UT–Austin's response to the charge that its admissions procedures violated the petitioner's rights under the Fourteenth Amendment to the U.S. Constitution.

Read again the section of the legal brief filed with the U.S. Supreme Court entitled "Summary of Argument" (on p. 301), and then draft an e-mail correspondence to your client (the Board of Governors) in which you offer an overview of UT–Austin's response to its possible violation of a prospective student's constitutional rights. As part of your summary, offer your client an assessment of the likely effectiveness of UT–Austin's argument. Be clear and precise in your presentation of UT–Austin's argument in defense of its position. Keep your audience and your relationship to that audience in mind as you compose your e-mail. ▶

WRITING PROJECT   **Discovering Genres of Writing in an Applied Field**

In this chapter, you've read about some of the conventions of writing in the applied fields of nursing, education, business, and law. You might be interested in a field that's not represented in this chapter, though. For this assignment, you will conduct research to discover more about the kinds of writing that are common within a particular applied field—ideally, one you're interested in. You might conduct either primary or secondary research to respond to this assignment. However, you should focus on collecting examples of the kinds of writing done in the field. Consider following the steps below to complete this assignment.

1. Collect examples of the kinds of writing done in the field.

2. Describe the different genres and how they relate to the work of that applied field.

3. Look for comparisons and contrasts across those genres. Do any commonalities point to conventions shared across genres? Are there differences that are important to notice? What do the patterns across the genres tell you about the work and values of that applied field?

Variation: Imagine that your audience is a group of incoming students interested in the same field of study you've researched for this project. Your task is to write a guide for those students about the conventions of writing expected in this applied field. Depending on what you have found, you may need to identify what conventions are appropriate for specific genres of writing.

- **The applied fields focus on the practical application of knowledge and career preparation.** Many applied fields also focus on problem-solving as part of the practical application of knowledge.

- **When beginning a writing task in applied fields, carefully analyze the rhetorical situation.** Consider your purpose and your audience carefully, and assess the appropriateness of responding in a particular genre.

- **Much of the writing in applied fields follows conventional expectations for structure, language, and reference appropriate to the fields.** Regardless of your writing task, you should be aware of these conventional expectations.

- **Students and professionals in applied fields often communicate information through field-specific genres.** Nurses, for example, often construct discharge directions, just as students and professionals in the fields of law often compose legal briefs.

Entering Academic Conversations

Readings and Case Studies

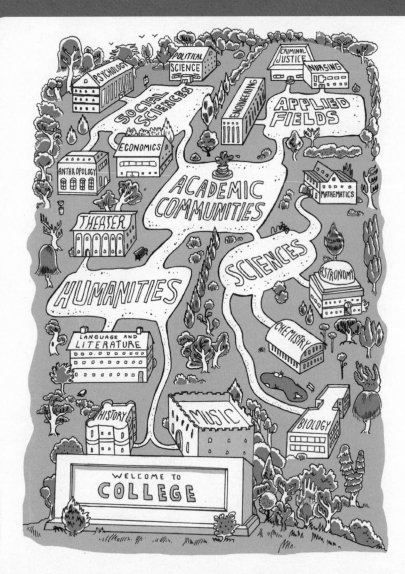

PART THREE

Entering Academic Conversations

Readings and Case Studies

10

Love, Marriage, and Family 309

ACADEMIC CASE STUDY: PERSPECTIVES ON LOVE 336

11

Crime, Punishment, and Justice 381

ACADEMIC CASE STUDY: CAPITAL PUNISHMENT 396

12

Food, Sustainability, and Class 451

ACADEMIC CASE STUDY: GENETICALLY MODIFIED FOOD 478

13

Global Climate Change and Natural Catastrophes 545

ACADEMIC CASE STUDY: HURRICANE KATRINA 565

Love, Marriage, and Family

The readings in this chapter provide a glimpse into various aspects of love, marriage, and family. Bringing together a wide variety of sources, the chapter presents multiple views on these topics, ranging from insights drawn from large survey data to interviews about individual experiences.

The chapter begins with a reading that explores the cultural influences that have shaped the current state of marriage in the United States. The text that follows examines the relationships between parents and children, focusing on the relatively recent phenomenon of "helicopter parents," or parents who are overly involved in their children's lives. Other readings in the chapter focus on two types of families that have historically been excluded from, or have faced significant challenges with attaining, social acceptance and legal legitimacy: same-sex families and multi-racial families. In addition to reviewing general trends in the way others perceive these types of families, these final readings focus on the experiences of being marginalized or excluded and on the ways in which families cope with those experiences.

As you read selections from the chapter, we hope you will consider the relationships between your own experiences and those presented in the popular and academic readings offered. We encourage you to consider critically the issues they raise and to pose your own questions about those issues. These might include the following:

- What constitutes a marriage, a family?
- How have definitions of "family" changed over time?
- How are individuals included and excluded from social legitimacy as a family? How are those lines drawn in our society?
- How do individuals negotiate their own family identities in times of trial or change?
- How do your own family experiences align with those described in the readings?

The academic case study for this chapter focuses on love. It comprises readings that explore the topic from a range of scholarly perspectives:

- **Humanities**   How have dominant notions of love and marriage been challenged historically?
- **Social Sciences**   Who falls in love first, men or women?
- **Natural Sciences**   How does our body chemistry change when we experience love?
- **Applied Fields**   How do men and women market themselves online in the quest for love?

How American Family Life Is Different

ANDREW CHERLIN

Andrew Cherlin is a professor of sociology at Johns Hopkins University, specializing in families and public policy. He publishes regularly in both scholarly and popular venues on topics such as marriage and divorce, children's well-being, intergenerational relations, family policy, and welfare policy. The following excerpt is from *The Marriage-Go-Round: The State of Marriage and the Family Today* (2009), a popular text informed by scholarship that places the American family within an international context to demonstrate how American families differ from families in other wealthy countries. In this excerpt, Cherlin argues that it is America's contradictory emphasis on marriage and individualism that differentiates it from other countries.

THE CONTRADICTIONS OF AMERICAN CULTURE

There are many similarities, of course, between the United States and other Western nations. All have industrialized in similar ways, and all are making the transition from factory work to office work. All are being affected by the globalizing economy. Moreover, all of the Western nations are democracies, and they share a common cultural heritage. The United States has even more in common with Great Britain than with the rest of Europe, including a language, a legal system, and a colonial past. All of these similarities reflect important characteristics of Western societies, but they won't help us to explain distinctive American family patterns. To do that, we have to look for differences, not similarities, between the United States and other countries.

One difference lies in the realm of culture: the contradictory emphases on marriage and individualism found only in the United States. People tend to think of a nation's culture as consistent and unified—a set of values and expectations that fit together to create a coherent whole. We learn this culture in childhood, it is commonly thought, from parents, teachers, and the media, and each of us applies it the same way as adults. But this understanding is simplistic. Culture often contains multiple, inconsistent ways of viewing the same reality, and individuals choose, sometimes without even realizing it, which view to adopt. We have more culture in our heads than we use, in other words, and not all of it coheres. To use an earlier metaphor, culture is a vast tool kit, and people reach into this kit to select the tools they need to organize their lives. In the kit are sets of tools I will call cultural models—frameworks for interpreting common situations we encounter. Cultural models are habits of thought, taken-for-granted ways of interpreting the world that we draw upon in everyday life. But sometimes there is more than one cultural model—more than one set of tools—that we can apply to a given situation. That is the case with intimate partnerships, where Americans can draw upon both a cultural model of marriage and a cultural model of individualism.

In a similar vein, Karla B. Hackstaff wrote a book about the "contesting ideologies" of a marriage culture and a divorce culture in contemporary American society. The marriage culture, she maintained, has three bases. First, marriage is a given: you have to marry, it's something everyone does, it's the only proper way to live your adult life. Second, marriage is forever. Third, divorce is a last resort. I think that fifty or sixty years ago marriage was indeed a given in American culture. But I don't think it's a given anymore. You can choose not to marry and still live a socially acceptable life. Nevertheless, marriage continues to be the most desired and most prestigious way to have a family.

Consequently, I would amend Hackstaff's definition to say that marriage is no longer a given but is still the preferred way to live one's personal life. I agree with her that people still think of marriage as lasting forever and of divorce as a last resort. Everyone, of course, is aware that these days marriages often end in separation or divorce. Yet most people still think that marriage *should* last forever and that divorce should be avoided. For instance, Americans were asked in a national survey whether they agreed or disagreed with this statement: "Marriage is a lifetime relationship that should never be ended except under extreme circumstances." Seventy-six percent agreed, 13 percent said they neither agreed nor disagreed, and only 11 percent said they disagreed. Moreover, when people marry, almost all of them intend for their own marriage to last forever. When a journalist interviewed sixty people whose marriages had ended within five years, she found that every one of them expected at first that their marriages would

last forever. Nor are these expectations limited to the middle class. Low-income, unmarried mothers in the Philadelphia area told two sociologists that they would marry only if they were sure the relationship would last forever. A twenty-year-old Puerto Rican mother said, "If I get married, I wanna be with this person for the rest of my life. I don't wanna just get married and then our relationship goes wrong, and then I have to go and get a *divorce!*"

This tendency to draw a line between other people's 5 families (lots of marriages fail these days) and your own (my marriage will last forever) can be seen in other opinions about family life. For instance, in another national survey, people were asked, "In general, do you think that because of such things as divorce, more working mothers, or single parents, etc., family ties in the U.S. are breaking down—or don't you think so?" Seventy-six percent responded that they thought family ties were breaking down. Yet their responses were very different to the follow-up question "What about your own family? Are family ties breaking down, or not?" Eighty-two percent said that their own family ties were *not* breaking down. Some may call it denial, but people think their own family is in good shape even though they think the family in general is in decline. Similarly, they are optimistic that their own marriage will last forever—at least when they start it—although they know that many other marriages will not.

Americans also believe that spouses should be sexually faithful to each other. In fact, over the past few decades, people have become *more* disapproving of extramarital sex. The number of Americans who answered "always wrong" to the question "What is your opinion about a married person having sexual relations with someone other than the marriage partner—is it always wrong, almost always wrong, wrong only sometimes, or not wrong at all?" increased from 70 percent in 1973 to 82 percent in 2004. This trend is all the more notable since, during the same period, people have become much more tolerant of sex before marriage, with close to a majority now saying that premarital sex is not wrong at all.

Overall, then, I would suggest that the American cultural model of marriage contains the following elements today:

- Marriage is the best way to live one's family life.
- A marriage should be a permanent, loving relationship.
- A marriage should be a sexually exclusive partnership.
- Divorce should be a last resort.

There may be other elements, but these are the ones that matter for the argument I am making. Despite the decline in the percentage of people who ever marry, the rise of cohabitation, and the increase in divorce, Americans still have this set of tools in their kit.

The cultural model of marriage is stronger in the United States than in most other Western countries. In 2006, the U.S. Congress debated the wisdom of a federal constitutional amendment stating, in part, "Marriage in the United States shall consist only of the union of a man and a woman." In his weekly radio address two days before the senatorial debate, President George W. Bush, a supporter of the amendment, told the nation, "Marriage cannot be cut off from its cultural, religious, and natural roots without weakening this good influence on society." No political observers expected this amendment to be approved by Congress, because a two-thirds majority is required, and indeed it was defeated. But a simple majority of senators and representatives voted for it.

In another sign of support for heterosexual marriage, Congress, in early 2006, enacted a law providing $150 million per year for research and demonstration projects that promote "healthy marriage and responsible fatherhood." These funds can be used for activities such as relationship skills training for young couples who want to marry or married couples who want to avoid divorce, public advertising campaigns on the value of marriage, and education programs in high school that promote marriage. The advertisements that I saw on the sides of buses in Baltimore saying "Marriage works" were privately funded, but they were a prototype of what the healthy marriage funds may support.

These government interventions on behalf of marriage have no counterpart in other Western nations, because nowhere else is the meaning and function of marriage such a contested issue. No other government provides funds for promoting marriage. Just north of the border in 2004, Paul Martin, the prime minister of Canada, announced plans to introduce legislation that would legalize same-sex marriage. He told reporters he expected the measure to pass because "I've always thought Canada is the most postmodern country," an assertion one cannot imagine an American president making. By 2005 Canada and a few other Western countries (Belgium, the Netherlands, Spain) allowed same-sex marriage. Many European countries, including Britain and France, had enacted national, civil union–like statuses for same-sex partners. A British legal scholar, John Eekelaar, wrote, "The Civil Partnership Act of 2004 has cleverly created an institution for England and Wales for same-sex partners that is equivalent to marriage with hardly a murmur of protest." Such a measure in the United States would cause a cacophony of protest. Only in the United States is marriage so central a value that conservatives and liberals battle fiercely over its definition and over providing government support.

How Americans' beliefs about marriage compare to other nations can also be seen in the World Values Surveys, conducted in more than sixty countries, including all members of the European Union, Canada, and the United States, between 1999 and 2002. Adults in each country were asked whether they agreed or disagreed with the statement "Marriage is an outdated institution." Fewer Americans agreed (10 percent)—that is, fewer endorsed the idea that marriage is outdated—than in any other Western country, including Italy (17 percent), Sweden (20 percent), Canada (22 percent), Great Britain (26 percent), or France (36 percent). Americans are more likely to think that marriage is still appropriate for the times.

There's not much written about the strength of the cultural model of marriage because many observers mistakenly think that marriage is fading away. But the literature on the cultural model of individualism today is vast. The rise of individualism, historians and social commentators have argued, has been one of the master trends in the development of Western society over the past few centuries. And most would agree that an individualistic outlook on family and personal life has become more important since the mid-twentieth century. Robert Bellah and his colleagues, in an influential book on individualism and commitment in American life, distinguished between two types of individualism. They called the older form "utilitarian individualism." Think of the utilitarian individualist as the self-reliant, independent entrepreneur pursuing material success, such as a high position in a corporation or a senior partnership in a law firm. The great German social theorist Max Weber, in a classic book, suggested that there is a link between a similar concept, which he called "the Protestant ethic," and the economic development of the West. He noted that Calvinists (including the group that became known as the Puritans in England and America) believed that some individuals had been predestined by God for earthly success. This doctrine encouraged people to work hard so that they could prove to others (and themselves) that they were among the elect. Weber used the writings of Benjamin Franklin, a prototype of the utilitarian individualist, to illustrate this spirit of industriousness. "Early to bed and early to rise," Franklin advised in one of his famous aphorisms, "makes a man healthy, wealthy, and wise."

The newer form of individualism, which Bellah and his colleagues called "expressive individualism," germinated in the late nineteenth and early twentieth centuries and flowered in the second half of the twentieth. It is a view of life that emphasizes the development of one's sense of self, the pursuit of emotional satisfaction, and the expression of one's feelings. Until the past half century, individuals moved through a series of roles (student, spouse, parent, housewife or breadwinner) in a way that seemed more or less natural. Choices were constrained. In mill towns, two or three generations of kin might work at the same factory. Getting married was the only acceptable way to have children, except perhaps among the poor. Young people often chose their spouses from among a pool of acquaintances in their neighborhood, church, or school. But now you can't get a job in the factory where your father and grandfather worked because overseas competition has forced it to close, so you must choose another career. You get little help from relatives in finding a partner, so you sign on to an Internet dating service and review hundreds of personal profiles. As other lifestyles become more acceptable, you must choose whether to get married and whether to have children. You develop your own sense of self by continually examining your situation, reflecting on it, and deciding whether to alter your behavior as a result. People pay attention to their experiences and make changes in their lives if they are not satisfied. They want to continue to grow and change throughout adulthood.

This kind of expressive individualism has flourished as prosperity has given more Americans the time and money to develop their senses of self—to cultivate their own emotional gardens, as it were. It suggests a view of intimate partnerships as continually changing as the partners' inner selves develop. It encourages people to view the success of their partnerships in individualistic terms. And it suggests that commitments to spouses and partners are personal choices that can be, and perhaps should be, ended if they become unsatisfying.

The World Values Surveys asked about expressive individualism using a cluster of questions that contrast "survival versus self-expression" values. The answers to these questions suggest that the level of expressive individualism among Americans is high but not out of line for a wealthy Western nation: a little below that in Sweden and the Netherlands, comparable to the levels in Norway and West Germany, and greater than in Britain, Canada, or France. One question in this cluster asked people to place themselves on a scale of 1 to 10, where 1 means that they think the actions they take have no real effect on what happens to them (which indicates survival values) and 10 means they think they have completely free choice and control over their lives (self-expression values). More Americans placed themselves at the free choice end than did people in any other Western country, but some of the other countries were close: 82 percent of Americans chose 7, 8, 9, or 10, compared to

77 percent of Canadians, 74 percent of Swedes, and 73 percent of Germans.

The cultural model of individualism, then, holds that self-development and personal satisfaction are the key rewards of an intimate partnership. Your partnership must provide you with the opportunity to develop your sense of who you are and to express that sense through your relations with your partner. If it does not, then you should end it.

Cohabiting relationships, especially those without children, come closest to this kind of partnership. They are held together solely by the voluntary commitments of the partners, and should either party become dissatisfied with the relationship, it is expected that she or he will end it. The rise of cohabitation reflects the growing influence of the cultural model of individualism on personal and family life. Living together provides a way of obtaining the emotional rewards of a partnership while minimizing the commitment to it.

Even among married couples, we have seen the rise of what Barbara Whitehead calls "expressive divorce." Beginning in the 1960s people began to judge the success of their marriages not by their material standard of living or how well they raised children but rather by whether they felt their personal needs and desires were being fulfilled. They turned inward and examined whether their marriages restricted their personal development. They were more likely to turn to psychotherapists for help in seeking out the causes of their unhappiness with their marriages. And if they perceived that their marriages were personally unfulfilling, they considered leaving. According to this logic, if a person finds that he or she has changed since marriage in a direction different from the one his or her spouse has taken, then that person is justified in leaving the marriage in order to express this newer, fuller sense of self. It's too bad, the feeling goes, especially if the couple is raising children, but to stay in a marriage that constrains the partners' sense of who they are would be worse.

Concerning family life, then, the cultural model of individualism in the United States today emphasizes these elements:

- One's primary obligation is to oneself rather than to one's partner and children.

- Individuals must make choices over the life course about the kinds of intimate lives they wish to lead.

- A variety of living arrangements are acceptable.

- People who are personally dissatisfied with marriages and other intimate partnerships are justified in ending them.

As a twenty-first-century individual, you must choose your style of personal life. You are allowed to—in fact, you are almost required to—continually monitor your sense of self and to look inward to see how well your inner life fits with your married (or cohabiting) life. If the fit deteriorates, you are almost required to leave. For according to the cultural model of individualism, a relationship that no longer fits your needs is inauthentic and hollow. It limits the personal rewards that you, and perhaps your partner, can achieve. In this event, a breakup is unfortunate, but you will, and must, move on.

In practice, few Americans use just the cultural 20 tools of the marriage model or just the tools of the individualism model. Rather, most Americans draw upon both. As a result, our actual marriages and cohabiting relationships typically combine them. People may rely on both sets of tools at the same time, or they may move from one to the other over time as their assessment of their personal lives changes. Moreover, they may not realize that they are combining two inconsistent models.

For instance, let's return to the national survey in which people were asked whether they thought marriage was a lifetime relationship that shouldn't be ended except under extreme circumstances. You'll recall that 76 percent agreed. The great majority, then, answered in a way consistent with the cultural model of marriage. Just a few pages farther along in the questionnaire they were asked whether they agreed or disagreed with this statement: "When a marriage is troubled and unhappy, it is generally better for the children if the couple stays together." It, too, reflects the marriage model, because the troubled and unhappy individual, by staying in the marriage, subordinates his or her personal satisfaction to the greater goal of raising the children well. It would seem logical, therefore, that most of the people who agreed that marriage is for life would also agree that it's better if the couple stays together. But they don't. Only 25 percent of the people who said marriage is for life also said that the couple should stay together. Forty percent disagreed and 35 percent said they neither agreed nor disagreed. How can it be that a few minutes after they all agreed that marriage is for life, only one-fourth agreed that unhappy people should stay in marriages for the sake of the children? These respondents, like many Americans, are drawing from two different cultural models simultaneously. When people think about the way marriage should be, they tend to say that it should be for life. But when people think about individual satisfaction, they tend to give others wide latitude to leave unhappy living arrangements. Cue them in one direction, and you get one picture; cue them in another, and you get a different picture. Both pictures, contradictory as they may be, are part of the way that Americans live their family lives. Together they spin the American merry-go-round of intimate partnerships.

Reading Questions

1. How does Cherlin define *cultural model*? What metaphor does he adopt to help his readers understand cultural models?

2. How does Cherlin amend Hackstaff's definition of *marriage culture*? What evidence does he use to support his amendment?

3. What is the difference between "utilitarian individualism" and "expressive individualism"?

4. In what ways are the cultural models of marriage and individualism contradictory?

Rhetoric Questions

5. Cherlin relies heavily on survey data to support his claims about marriage and individualism. What other types of evidence could be used to support, refute, or amend his claims?

6. How would you describe Cherlin's style of presenting ideas from other academics? How does this style affect the overall tone of the piece?

Response and Research Questions

7. Cherlin writes that the United States stands out from other nations in that the meaning and function of marriage are constantly contested here. Other than discussions surrounding government intervention in marriage, what national debates might signify disagreement about the meaning and function of marriage?

8. According to Cherlin, survey data reveals that most people believe marriage in general is breaking down in the United States, yet they also believe that their own marriage is in good shape. What might explain this contradiction?

9. Cherlin proposes Benjamin Franklin as a model of "utilitarian individualism." What prominent figure could serve as a model for "expressive individualism"? Explain your choice.

The Myth of the Helicopter Parent

SUSAN KRAUSS WHITBOURNE

Susan Krauss Whitbourne is a professor of psychology at the University of Massachusetts–Amherst. She publishes regularly in both scholarly and popular outlets on topics of adult development and aging. Whitbourne is the author of several books, including *The Search for Fulfillment* (2010). Additionally, she writes a popular blog for *Psychology Today* entitled "Fulfillment at Any Age" and contributes to the *Huffington Post*. In the article below, written for *Psychology Today*, Whitbourne explores the effects of "helicopter parenting" on both children and parents. Specifically, she asks, "Will indulgent parents hurt their children—and themselves? Or will helicoptering young adult children benefit all concerned?" Drawing on scholarship from the discipline of psychology, Whitbourne tailors her answers for a non-technical audience.

So-called "helicopter parents" are roundly criticized by everyone from teachers to media experts for smothering [their children] with too much loving. If you want to "land your kids in therapy," according to psychotherapist Lori Gottlieb writing in *Atlantic* magazine, then by all means give them everything under the sun. If you want them to become productive members of society with reasonably normal lives, then keep the hugs and kisses to a minimum and even deny them things once in a while. "Well-meaning parents can ruin their children," so the claim goes.

These observations led University of Texas psychologist Karen Fingerman and her colleagues (2012) to put the claims to the empirical test. They believed that today's children, especially when they're young adults, need more support than ever from their parents—ranging from advice to financial help. Today's young adults don't necessarily expect support from parents. Given the stretching out of adolescence, and particularly "emerging adulthood" (ages 18–29; Arnett, 2000), such expectations, if not hope, are not out of the question. Parents today may worry that they're providing more help than they "should" based on the social norms of their own youth. Therefore, they may fear violating social norms for parental support. On the other hand, research based on the Longitudinal Study of Generations (Byers, Levy, Allore, Bruce, & Kasl, 2008) suggests that parents of young adults report fewer depressive symptoms when they are heavily involved with their kids. Providing

tangible and emotional support helps people feel that they are part of the lives of their children by making them feel they "matter."

So which will it be? Will indulgent parents hurt their children—and themselves? Or will helicoptering young adult children benefit all concerned? Fingerman and team had at their disposal a sample of 399 parents (reporting on 886 children) and 592 children (reporting on 1,158 parents) living in the greater Philadelphia area who completed a computer-assisted telephone interview. They were asked questions from the Intergenerational Support Index, a measure in which parents and children indicate the extent to which parents provide support ranging from advice and listening to financial and practical help. Both parents and children rated the intensity of support parents provided: "too little" to "more than you would like" with the middle point being "about right." This was the measure of intense support. Children answered questions about their own adjustment and life satisfaction, and parents rated their life satisfaction as well.

The children ranged in age from 19 to 41 years old, with a mean of 24. They lived from 0 to 5,000 miles away from their parents, with an average distance of 172 miles. [Moreover,] 30% of them actually lived with their parents, 24% had children of their own, and 35% were full-time students.

A substantial number of children (about one-fifth) 5 reported that their parents in fact provided them with intense support, but more felt this came from their mothers (27%) than from their fathers (15%). These numbers corresponded closely to what parents said about the support they felt they provided. In fact, parents and children were remarkably consistent in reporting the areas of their relationship in which parents provided intense support. Parents provided the most support in the emotional areas that included listening, emotional help, and advice; and less in the areas of practical, financial, and socializing. However, parents did not provide support equally to all of their children. About 30% of parents provided support to only one child (for those who had more than one child). Those children most likely to receive support tended to be younger, to live with their parents, or to have children of their own, and mothers were more likely than fathers to provide intense support.

How did these helicoptered children fare? According to the findings presented by Fingerman and her group, the children whose parents provided them with intense support experienced better outcomes. Helicoptered children actually had higher life satisfaction and more clearly defined goals. However, helicoptering parents had many self-doubts as indicated by their lower life satisfaction.

Helicopter parenting, at least for grown children, seems to have its benefits. Parents who are involved and supportive across a wide range of areas produce young adult children who have a clearer sense of self and are more satisfied with their lives. However, parents who felt that their children need too much support were themselves lower in life satisfaction.

Parental support to grown children isn't a one-size-fits-all affair. The adult children who seemed to benefit the most from the involvement of their parents in their lives tended to be younger, lived with their parents, and had children of their own. It is possible that the reason they found this support so helpful was that they were in a life stage when the continued help of their parents could ease their adjustment into adulthood. Parents and children characterized by these intense support bonds may be feeling some pangs of guilty pleasure. They enjoy their relationship, and the children seem to do well as a result. However, because

they hear so much in the media about the dangers of over-involved parents, they feel that there's something wrong with them for being in this type of relationship.

You might be thinking, and you'd be right, that as a correlational study, we can't conclude that intense parenting causes better outcomes in grown children. Perhaps parents provide more intense support for children who they see as "worthy" of investment. Furthermore, parents who are dissatisfied with their lives may also rate their children as less successful or needier. It's also possible that parents and children who have better relationships feel more satisfied with their lives in general and may even be mentally healthier.

Nevertheless, the findings lead to a new understanding of parent-child support in the years of emerging adulthood. For parents, having your 20-something (or even 30-something) kids depend on you for everything from advice to a little financial help now and then doesn't mean you've failed. For grown children, you don't have to break yourself off entirely from your parents in order to be considered successful or mature.

Another piece of good news from this study is that there are many ways for parents and children to stay connected. Even if you don't live with or near your family, email, Facebook, and other social media can allow you to provide support at many levels. To be a successful helicopter parent, just listening can help your kids navigate the sometimes rocky years of early adulthood. And kids, it's not a bad idea to listen to your parents. It may be good for your mental health!

REFERENCES

Arnett, J. J. (2000). Emerging adulthood: A theory of development from the late teens through the twenties. *American Psychologist, 55,* 469–480. doi:10.1037/0003-066X .55.5.469

Byers, A. L., Levy, B. R., Allore, H. G., Bruce, M. L., & Kasl, S. V. (2008). When parents matter to their adult children: Filial reliance associated with parents' depressive symptoms. *Journals of Gerontology: Series B: Psychological Science and Social Sciences, 63,* P33–P40.

Fingerman, K. L., Cheng, Y. P., Wesselmann, E. D., Zarit, S., Furstenberg, F., & Birditt, K. S. (2012). Helicopter parents and landing pad kids: Intense parental support of grown children. *Journal of Marriage and Family, 74,* 880–896.

Reading Questions

1. How does Whitbourne define *helicopter parents*? What debate concerning helicopter parents is Whitbourne addressing?

2. What research methods were used to collect data in the Fingerman et al. study? What specific demographics did the study draw from?

3. What conclusions about helicopter parents (and their children) does Whitbourne draw from the Intergenerational Support Index?

Rhetoric Questions

4. Whitbourne writes that "as a correlational study, we can't conclude that intense parenting causes better outcomes in grown children" (par. 9). How does Whitbourne hedge her claims throughout the article and anticipate her audience's questions?

5. Throughout the article, Whitbourne both summarizes and analyzes data. How does she transition between summary and analysis? How might you use one or more of these techniques in your own writing?

6. Analyze the structure of Whitbourne's article. Specifically, note what each paragraph in the article is meant to accomplish. Then compare Whitbourne's article to a similar one in *Psychology Today*. Note any structural patterns you're able to see.

Response and Research Questions

7. What connections can you make between your own life experiences (as a child and/or as a parent) and the ideas Whitbourne explores in her work?

8. Locate the original Fingerman et al. study using your library's journal database. What techniques does Whitbourne use to make sense of academic scholarship for a non-technical audience?

Changing Counts, Counting Change: Toward a More Inclusive Definition of Family

BRIAN POWELL, CATHERINE BOLZENDAHL, CLAUDIA GEIST, AND LALA CARR STEELMAN

As a team of researchers and writers, Brian Powell, Catherine Bolzendahl, Claudia Geist, and Lala Carr Steelman utilize their collective experience and training in the field of sociology to explore various definitions of family that circulate in American culture. This excerpt from *Counted Out: Same-Sex Relations and Americans' Definitions of Family* (2010) draws on survey data collected from more than 1,500 people in 2003 and 2006. These surveys asked respondents to explain their views about marriage, adoption, cohabitation, and many other issues related to family. In the passage below, the authors explore attitudes toward same-sex marriage as a way to understand Americans' perception of family more generally.

Family counts. Few would dispute this statement. Family is assigned a great many responsibilities and in turn is afforded a great number of benefits. It has a profound influence on our lives. But "family" counts too. How "family" is defined determines which living arrangements are expected to perform these responsibilities, which are granted these benefits, and upon which social legitimacy is conferred. Definitions of family—and especially whether same-sex couples should be seen as family—currently lie at the heart of passionate scholarly and public controversy and debate. Whether same-sex couples are counted in or out of this definition, we argue, is a crucial touchstone for understanding family more generally and accordingly is intertwined with views regarding a host of family issues—among them, the relative influence of parenting versus genetic inheritance, gender and parenting, and marital naming practices. Yet we have known little about the boundaries that Americans erect between family and nonfamily—that is, which living arrangements they include as family and which ones they do not. The unique and comprehensive approach taken in this book, however, narrows this gap by explicitly canvassing Americans' views on the definition of family.

In this closing chapter, we revisit the key patterns and themes that emerged from our interviews and discuss what these patterns may indicate about family in American society now and into the future. Despite their disagreements regarding whether same-sex couples should be seen as family and accorded, by extension, marital and other familial rights, "pro-family" and gay rights activists do agree about the centrality of the question of same-sex couples for our understanding of family. The conservative commentator Maggie Gallagher, for example, observes that "gay marriage is not some sideline issue, it *is* the marriage debate" (Gallagher 2003). Since the very first interviews we conducted in 2003, there have been remarkable changes surrounding the debate about same-sex couples and their actual legal status. These changes have not followed a predictably linear path. Rather, they have swung back and forth so much that they have triggered everything from

unbridled optimism to devastating despair among both advocates of the extension of family rights to same-sex couples and critics apprehensive about the possible loss of "traditional" families. We have seen gains—or losses, in the view of certain "pro-family" groups—in the rapidly shifting legal and political landscape where the rights of same-sex couples have been advanced. Among these gains are court-initiated legalization of same-sex marriage in Massachusetts, Connecticut, Iowa, and, for a short period of time, California; legislatively approved same-sex marriage in Vermont, New Hampshire, Washington, D.C., and, temporarily, Maine; a publicly supported vote (Referendum 71) in Washington State in favor of expansion of domestic partnership rights and protections for same-sex couples, as well as for senior heterosexual couples;[1] and, at the time of the writing of this chapter, attempts by political leaders to at least tread softly toward extension of some familial rights to same-sex couples (for example, President Barack Obama's executive order granting hospital visitation rights to same-sex couples) or sometimes to more boldly follow the lead of these states' leads.

At the same time, we have experienced losses—or gains according to traditional "pro-family" groups. Some sharply divided courts, including those with fairly liberal traditions (such as New York's), declined to overturn the long-standing prohibition against same-sex marriage in their states. Often these courts justify their ruling by deferring to the legislature and the will of the people. More than twenty states—representing a cross-section of this nation and wide divergence in political views and geographical locations—have put forth ballot initiatives to outlaw same-sex marriage. Some political commentators contend that this flurry of initiatives played a nontrivial role in the 2004 presidential election and increased support for Republican candidates in state elections: in fact, some pundits maintain that the ballot initiatives in swing states (such as Ohio) were a cynical ploy to secure George W. Bush's reelection. All but one effort passed—many of them decisively. And in Arizona, the one exception, the success was short-lived: voters opposed Proposition 107 ("protection of marriage") in 2006, but in

2008 they cast ballots in favor of Proposition 102, which amended the state constitution to define marriage as a union between one man and one woman. Even in California, one of the most socially liberal states—indeed, a state that several of our respondents labeled as overly liberal or far removed from the American mainstream—voters jettisoned the previously discussed breakthrough court decision when they narrowly voted in favor of Proposition 8, which revised the state constitution to restrict marital status to heterosexual couples.[2] These setbacks often extend beyond the debate regarding marriage. In Arkansas, legislation mainly designed to bar same-sex couples from adopting children or offering a home to foster children also passed.[3]

It is tricky to make predictions about the future of same-sex families, especially given the sheer fluidity of the situation and the intensified public reaction to the debate and to issues regarding sexuality more broadly. Even traditional forms of American entertainment are engaging this issue—from television personalities who advocate for or against same-sex marriage, to contestants in beauty pageants who are asked their views on same-sex marriage, to bloggers who gossip over whether a reality show contestant is gay. Currently, and somewhat surprisingly, some pundits and spokespersons for political parties and advocacy groups act as if the debate is over and proponents of same-sex marriage have prevailed with the American public, or shortly will do so (Waldman 2009). Neither the numbers from our data nor actual votes on initiatives are anywhere near the sufficient magnitude to support the idea that the public is ready to embrace same-sex couples with open arms.[4] To be sure, there still are many Americans who are—in their own words—"appalled," "disgusted," and "repelled" by the very idea of same-sex families and the extension of rights to these groups. Nevertheless, we remain confident that the resistance to same-sex partnerships will dissipate in the not-too-distant future.

Social scientists typically are more comfortable making claims about the past and present, while shying away from forecasting the future. Yet, if we tie together the various pieces of evidence that stand out in the previous chapters, we can make some admittedly cautious but empirically based predictions. We began by identifying and deciphering three distinguishable categories of Americans who vary in the lines that they draw between family and nonfamily: inclusionists, moderates, and exclusionists. These categories have provided a recurring baseline throughout the book that, in turn, is connected to other views about the family. At one end of the spectrum, exclusionists are restrictive in whom they welcome into the realm of family, while at the other end inclusionists are more receptive to living arrangements that exclusionists routinely reject. Moderates may be the most interesting group—or at least most important in terms of the future of American attitudes and beliefs. Moderates are at the very least open to new ways of defining family, but remain more guarded than inclusionists when it comes to granting family status to same-sex couples.

CHANGING COUNTS AND RECOUNTS

It is telling that even in a short period of time—just three years—we experienced a notable decrease in the percentage of exclusionists and a corresponding increase in the percentage of inclusionists. By 2006 a very clear majority (over three-fifths) of Americans had come to include same-sex couples with children and/or childless same-sex couples under the rubric of "family." This change is all the more impressive given that during that three-year period—from 2003 to 2006—anti-gay-marriage and, more broadly, anti-same-sex-relationships rhetoric reached perhaps its most heated level and arguably was also at its most effective. Although one might question whether this change is merely a blip in one particular data set, the corresponding open-ended comments provided by respondents convinced us that these changes are quite real. Moreover, these patterns are corroborated by a recently added and, in our opinion, most welcome question regarding same-sex marriage provided in the National Opinion Research Center's General Social Survey. Interviewees in the General Social Survey were asked their view regarding same-sex marriage in 2004, 2006, and 2008.[5] Between 2004 and 2006, the percentage of Americans who agreed that "homosexuals should have the right to marry" rose from 29.8 percent to 35.3 percent. Our own survey did not go beyond 2006, but the 2008 General Social Survey suggests that support for same-sex marriage increased further, up to 39.3 percent. Admittedly, these figures fall below any threshold that signals an irreversible tipping point, and therefore they challenge the idea promoted by some pundits that the debate is over. But these figures do indicate that the patterns we report throughout the book are not idiosyncratic to our data. These figures also signify that there is good reason to be confident that views of family and family rights will continue to expand, perhaps with increasing speed.

Had we not listened to the comments that Americans gave to explain the boundaries that they make between family and nonfamily, we might not be as optimistic. The quantitative data give us a picture of the boundaries, but the qualitative data animate the struggles that Americans face in defining family—struggles that should compel them to reevaluate their definitions of family. We do not see much struggle, however, among inclusionists. They believe that love and commitment make a family and bind it together. They embrace a broad definition of family that not only privileges love and commitment but also recognizes the various instrumental and expressive purposes of family and further defers to others' self-definitions of their own living situation. Inclusionists are unambiguous in their views and seem to be impervious to the arguments proffered by those who endorse narrower definitions of family. In fact, we are hard-pressed to envision a scenario in which a large segment of the inclusionist group would reverse itself and rein in its broad-ranging definition of family.

Most exclusionists also do not struggle with their definition of family. Or more precisely, they typically do not wrestle over the question of same-sex couples, although they do face challenges in their views regarding cohabiting heterosexual couples, especially those with children. Regarding same-sex couples, however, exclusionists do not show much potential for change in their views. Exclusionists insist upon heterosexuality, censure homosexuality (sometimes with palpable hostility), rely on interpretations of biblical text that putatively condemn same-sex unions, and emphasize the importance of biological parents—or "blood" relations. These frames may be so powerful that they counteract any attempts to broaden the definition of family, therefore rendering exclusionists unlikely candidates for change.

Still, we see some opportunities for movement even among some exclusionists. Although most exclusionists believe that the structure of families—notably, the presence of marriage—trumps the functions that families provide, some do not. This latter group may be receptive to entreaties to expand the definition of family to those living arrangements in which the needs and functions of family are met by its members regardless of legal documents or sexual orientation. Ironically, the focus on structure—more specifically, the legally endorsed familial structure—may ultimately be an effective strategy to relax exclusionists' resistance to same-sex couples. From our interviews, it is apparent that several exclusionists saw legal marriage as the key ingredient of family status and, in fact, as the only requirement to warrant that status. If legal definitions carry weight with exclusionists who respect legal tradition above all else, then legalization of same-sex marriage in various states may be sufficient to push some exclusionists toward a more moderate, if not inclusionist, stance. Thus, while our overall assumption is that definitions of family precipitate changes in views regarding the extension of legal rights to nontraditional living arrangements, for this group a change in the law might simultaneously shape both their views about same-sex marriage and the line of demarcation they draw between family and nonfamily. Legal changes in the status of same-sex couples, then, may move some exclusionists incrementally toward acceptance of same-sex couples as family.

We see much greater potential for movement [10] among moderates, who—more so than either inclusionists or exclusionists—appear to genuinely struggle as they try to reconcile their traditionalism with their openness to change. This group, however, does not waver on the issue of children: if there is a child in the household, moderates deem the living arrangement to be a family. Given the pivotal role that moderates as a bloc may play in the future of same-sex marriage (and in the extension of other rights to nontraditional family forms), campaigns that emphasize the positive effect that marital rights have on children of same-sex couples may be a winning formula. Moreover, with sophisticated and ever-changing reproductive technologies and increased opportunities for adoption, the number and visibility of same-sex couples residing with their children certainly may increase. From a political standpoint, framing the equality of same-sex couples in terms of "the best interests of the child" may prove to be a successful gateway that, when opened, fosters greater acceptance of same-sex households, along with equal rights and protections.

Still, moderates are hesitant to define childless same-sex couples—and childless heterosexual cohabiting couples—as family. But even here we foresee this reluctance eventually being transformed into steadier or even unwavering support. Surely, we see little evidence that moderates will become more restrictive in their definitions of family. In fact, the arguments that appear most persuasive to exclusionists—for example, pronouncements regarding the immorality of homosexual relations and reliance on biblical text (or particular interpretations of biblical text)—carry little weight among moderates. In contrast, arguments that appeal to inclusionists ultimately may also convert moderates. Given that so many moderates stipulate that the presence of children signals commitment among same-sex and heterosexual partners, the increasing visibility of other signals of commitment may also become a persuasive wellspring of change.

Among these signals is the length of time spent living together—as demonstrated by the sizable number of moderates who agree that a childless same-sex couple who have lived together for ten years constitute a family. Another signal, however, is detected from the functions that partners perform as a unit.

Moderates are fully aware that families comprise members who are interdependent in accomplishing shared goals. The more moderates are aware of or actually witness people in loving nontraditional living arrangements carrying out the various emotional and instrumental functions of family, the more receptive they should become to a more expansive definition of family. And this awareness is indeed likely to expand, given the growing number of media representations of loving same-sex families and the greater openness of same-sex couples themselves in schools, work settings, and communities. As moderates reexamine their views regarding same-sex families, social scientists might need to take a fresh look at their own views regarding functional approaches to family.[6] Although functionalism was once the mainstay of much sociological thought, recently it has been summarily dismissed by many social scientists as mere rationalization of the status quo and therefore an unremitting source of conservatism. But our interviews suggest an alternative interpretation: when the functions of families were brought up in our interviews, this topic tended, perhaps counterintuitively, to liberalize individual viewpoints.

Moderates' cognizance of their ambivalence and the inconsistencies in their responses makes us even more convinced of future changes in the boundaries that Americans make between family and nonfamily. In our interviews, moderates often realized that their emphasis on love and commitment, as well as on meeting familial needs, was at odds with their initial exclusion of childless same-sex and cohabiting heterosexual couples from the definition of family. Upon acknowledging their contradictory responses, some asked to change their responses—almost always in the direction of more inclusion. Others did not make this request but clearly felt uneasy with the dissonance in their responses. Some even volunteered that their views might switch or at least soften in the near future. The response of a fifty-year-old moderate woman from Georgia personifies the kind of ambivalence that might give way to a more inclusive view:

> I don't...I don't know if...I don't know, between my religious upbringing and my traditional upbringing,

I don't know. I'm still working on this one for myself, and I still don't have one answer. . . . We're not adamant against it [same-sex couples], but like I said, I mean, process is changing. If you call me next year, I might change my mind.

She continued by describing her upbringing and the ongoing process by which she was evaluating her own views:

Well, you know, it's just traditional southern upbringing, where it's not like we knew homosexuals. But you know, it's just, I don't know, it's just . . . it's hard to explain. With my age group we're still learning to consider other—I can't think of the word. I can't think of the word: goodness, it's like once I hit fifty, I forget things! I was brought up one way, but I am slowly changing and considering other options. But I'm not totally, you know, I haven't totally changed some of the things. So, I'm, that's why some of my answers have been like flip-flopping, 'cause I'm not adamant about some of the things. So like I said, this is one of the areas that I am still thinking about. . . . It might be that under the right circumstances I could be convinced that it would be okay.

This respondent might have been apologetic about her lack of clarity or consistency, but her comments spoke volumes about what we believe is an inevitable pull toward greater acceptance of same-sex living arrangements. She exemplifies the many moderates who are poised to ultimately embrace a broader definition of family. A climate of acceptance is encouraging for those who advocate the extension of familial rights to same-sex couples—and to cohabiting heterosexual ones—but conversely, it is alarming to opponents and may further gird their resistance. Some commentators on this subject suggest that defenders of "traditional marriage" realize that there remains only a small window of time in which they can proactively prevent the extension of familial rights to nontraditional living arrangements. This realization could well be the precipitating factor behind the flurry of anti-gay-marriage initiatives that were advanced in the past few years. To the dismay of inclusionists, these initiatives have been enormously successful. But even among some exclusionists, we hear resigned recognition that these successes are likely to be short-lived: "In the end I believe all will prevail for the gay community. I will never agree with it. But that will be something I will have to live and die with."

CHANGING DIVISIONS

This sense of resignation may be due in large measure 15 to exclusionists' appreciation of the vast generational cleavages in definitions of family. Exclusionists realize that youths are no longer living in, as one person puts it, "the *Leave It to Beaver* world anymore." Older respondents were especially attuned to generational differences; in fact, they mentioned these differences more frequently than did younger Americans. The patterns are clear: the younger generation is strikingly more expansive in their definition of family than are their elders, especially those age sixty-five or older. Over 75 percent of adults under the age of thirty view some types of same-sex couples as family, while over 60 percent of adults sixty-five years of age or older refuse to acknowledge any living arrangement involving gay men or lesbians as family.

Some commentators speculate that youths will outgrow their more liberal views about family. We are less convinced. Instead, generations matter. For example, the members of the baby boom generation espouse more liberal views regarding family than would ordinarily be expected, breaking the otherwise smooth linear relationship between age and conservative views on family. This departure in the pattern highlights the powerful influence that a historical climate of tolerance has on individuals as they approach adulthood. Our younger respondents came of age—or are coming of age—at a time when gay issues have been more widely discussed and certainly gays have been less stigmatized. Some mass media have been at the cutting edge in presenting nontraditional families—showing, for example, single-parent and step-parent households at times when out-of-wedlock childbearing and divorce were not generally accepted. The same is true today for media images of gays and lesbians. Contemporary media and other conduits of information are more open about same-sex relations and overall are less heterosexist than they were even just a decade ago. Ironically, even the most virulently negative characterizations of gays and lesbians in public discourse may have the unintended consequence of making a taboo topic less taboo. While one can rightfully critique some images of gays and lesbians in the media (Gamson 1998; Walters 2001), the increased visibility of gays and lesbians in the public domain may be pivotal to the receptiveness of younger adults to a broader definition of family. If trends continue on the same path that they appear to favor, then the replacement of older cohorts by younger ones should invariably reshape the boundaries between family and nonfamily.

Educational differences should create a similar demographic pull toward inclusivity. As also confirmed in past scholarship about social attitudes, Americans with higher levels of education typically are more cosmopolitan in their views. Compared to their peers with lower levels of education, they report greater receptivity to including same-sex couples in their definitions of family. Such increased liberalism is not unexpected. College exposes youths to new ideas and experiences that challenge the often more insular viewpoints they might have had upon entering college. Moreover, college students may know and have contact with gay peers, a pattern that might soften once staunchly held exclusionist positions.[7]

Contact with gay men and lesbians is not limited, however, to the college-educated. Having a gay friend or relative in one's network or even just knowing someone who is gay is related quite strongly to the acceptance of same-sex living arrangements as family. The notable increase between 2003 and 2006 in the percentage of Americans who reported having a gay friend or relative suggests two things. First, gay and lesbian Americans are becoming more open about their sexuality to their friends, relatives, and acquaintances—even during or perhaps because of the heightened negative rhetoric about same-sex couples that took place between 2003 and 2006. Second, heterosexual Americans increasingly acknowledge the presence of gays and lesbians in their personal and professional social networks. These changes parallel the greater visibility of gay and lesbian public figures and, importantly, show no sign of abating. Additionally, current forms of communication (such as blogs,

Twitter, and email) all encourage dialogue and openness about sexuality rather than denial of it. In the business world, many companies already offer same-sex benefits and programs, thus perhaps making employees feel more comfortable informing their colleagues about their sexual preference. Taken together, these trends insinuate more openness by the gay community, increasing recognition of gays and lesbians by others, and, in turn, greater receptivity to a broader conceptualization of family.

Earlier in this book, we identified other sociodemographic factors that also are implicated in Americans' definition of family. Regarding gender, women cast a wider net than do men when making decisions about who counts as family. This pattern also foretells a shift toward greater acceptance of various living arrangements as family. Women remain the primary caretakers of children and thus may hold greater sway over what their children come to believe. In a country where divorce and single-parenthood rates remain high, the effects of mothers' views may be especially pronounced. Consequently, children may learn from the example set by their mothers to be more open-minded about other types of families. Women also are as likely as men to vote, if not more so (Carroll and Fox 2006). Thus, as a voting bloc, women may have great sway over future elections and ballot initiative outcomes. Of course, not all women are inclusionists and not all men are exclusionists, but the average pattern is suggestive. Should the majority of women favor a more expansive vision of family, then politicians' hesitation to endorse the same may correspondingly lessen.

This is not to say that men are impervious to change. On the contrary, increased education and contact with gay friends and relatives are at least as liberalizing for men as they are for women. Younger generations of men, not unlike the women of their age cohorts, also are more receptive to inclusionist definitions of family than are their older counterparts. Young men often are portrayed as unrelentingly homophobic, presumably because homosexuality challenges hegemonic* ideas of masculinity. But the patterns

*hegemonic: the dominant social or political perspective.

found in our data challenge the idea that young men constitute the group most resistant to inclusionist visions of family. The patterns also suggest room for future change among men, especially if we listen to how men talk about family. The different frames that men and women use to define family may be useful in campaigns that target male voters. For example, appeals to the responsibilities that are met in the family may provide a winning strategy for gay rights advocates in gaining support among men.

Spatial boundaries also figure into the boundaries that individuals draw between family and nonfamily. Urban-rural and regional schisms in Americans' definitions of family suggest that change will be uneven—with fairly rapid steps taken toward inclusivity in certain areas and nontrivial pushback in others. These differences to some degree explain why, for example, some Americans living in urban areas in the Northeast are so perplexed by strong hostility to same-sex marriage—and more broadly to the idea that a same-sex couple constitutes a family—when they consider it a non-issue, while other Americans living in rural areas of the South are baffled by and even fearful of the acknowledgment of the rights of same-sex couples that is perhaps inexorably under way.

What we already know about attitudes toward interracial couples also may be instructive here. The reader may recall that [in a previous chapter] we not only showed that age (cohort) and education affect Americans' current definitions of family (that is, whether they are exclusionist) but also noted that these factors closely parallel the age and educational differences in Americans' views regarding interracial marriage several decades ago. The very same survey—the General Social Survey—confirms a huge gap between urban and rural dwellers in 1972, the first year of the survey. In that year, over half (57.4 percent) of rural Americans favored "laws against marriages between (Negroes/Blacks/African Americans) and whites," while over three-fourths (78.9 percent) of respondents living in large cities were opposed to such discriminatory mandates. Although the rural-urban gap never entirely disappeared, over time rural Americans' views drifted closer to those of urban Americans (in other words, became more

tolerant). By the mid-1990s, more than three-fourths of rural Americans also expressed opposition to miscegenation laws (76.2 percent in 1994). The very same changes transpired among southerners, although stubborn pockets of resistance in some southern states lingered. These patterns are not atypical: scholars have confirmed that social attitudes—especially innovative and liberal ones—typically spread in the United States from urban to rural areas and from nonsouthern to southern states (Fischer 1978; Firebaugh and Davis 1988). Urban-rural and regional gaps may not entirely disappear, but rural and southern views are more likely to move in the direction of urban and nonsouthern views than the other way around.

Currently, one might characterize the social and political climate regarding familial definitions as one in which pockets of acceptance are scattered. That is, in a small number of states, individuals are more receptive to a broadened definition of family that includes same-sex couples and ultimately promotes the extension of rights and benefits to these couples. The number of such states is small, but if the regional and urban-rural changes in attitudes toward interracial marriage are any indication, the number will continue to grow. Although such growth is likely to encounter additional resistance, this opposition will diminish to the point where only pockets of resistance remain—as we have witnessed with respect to attitudes toward interracial marriage.

Most sociodemographic trends seem to propel us in the direction of a more inclusive definition of family. One influence, however, may stand in the way. Religious ideology and identity—measured in several ways, but most notably by interpretations of the Bible as literal—are powerfully entwined with some Americans' definitions of family. Homosexuality and same-sex relationships are often couched by exclusionists in terms of violating biblical doctrine—as flouting "God's law," "the biblical standard," and "*the* rules." For Americans who resolutely hold on to these positions, it is difficult to envision much movement toward greater inclusivity. The use of these religious frames is so powerful that the greater adherence of some Americans to religious orthodoxy—at least compared to the rest of the Western world—may be a major stumbling block that stands in the way of acceptance of nontraditional groups as families.

Should the number of Americans who subscribe 25 to religiously orthodox or fundamentalist views increase in the future, then we might expect a slowing down or even a reversal in the trend toward a more inclusive definition of family. Whether religious conservatism and fundamentalism in the United States will increase, however, has been widely debated. Some scholars contend that fundamentalism has reached its peak in popularity and is now noticeably on the decline. Instead, they forecast, Americans will become more and more secularized, as indicated by the rise in the number of Americans who indicate that they are agnostic, atheist, or unaffiliated with any particular religion. Others do not deny that religion remains important in the everyday lives of Americans, but they believe that the absolutism associated with fundamentalism is being supplanted by a more expansive religious worldview—an expansiveness that is manifested, for example, in greater concern over global warming and poverty in the developing countries (Bolzendahl and Brooks 2005). The possibility that this greater liberalism will extend to views regarding same-sex relationships is certainly not out of the question. After all, religious messages can and do shift dramatically over time—as witnessed, for example, in the civil rights movement. Many messages in religious texts encourage tolerance above and beyond other values. Relying on these messages, some denominations explicitly welcome gays and lesbians, such as the United Church of Christ and the Episcopal Church (in the United States). Casting religion as an insurmountable and unalterable bulwark holding back the extension of familial definitions and of civil liberties to include gay citizens therefore may itself be too rigid a view.

CHANGING ACCOUNTS

The invocation of "God's will" takes a surprising twist when used to explain the etiology of sexual preference. Ordinarily, we might expect religious reasoning—or, at least, the insertion of "God's will" into causal explanations—to behave in conservative ways. Yet Americans who believe that "God's will" is the principal factor determining sexual preference are surprisingly liberal in their definitions of family. Also unexpected is the age profile of the Americans who are most likely to subscribe to this account: younger adults. These two perhaps jarring patterns do not necessarily imply that religious views per se now automatically convert into liberalism or are on the rise. But they do suggest that some Americans see sexuality as determined not by the individual or the environment, but instead by forces that exist well beyond our understanding. In other words, it is possible to use the concept of "God's will" in a way that reinforces the immutability of sexuality and challenges claims that sexual preference can be changed. Importantly, as comments by the interviewees clarify, this frame may simultaneously appeal to those who are religious and supportive of same-sex families and to those who do not necessarily see themselves as religious (atheists, agnostics, and spiritualists). Just as appeals to "God's will" have been successfully employed in various progressive social causes, the use of this apparent religious frame may be called upon to justify equality for same-sex couples.

Religion and science typically are not thought of as natural allies. Instead, they often are pitted against each other and as such are portrayed as promoting incompatible accounts of human behavior. But here we see a clear exception. Ostensibly religious ("God's will") and scientific (genetic inheritance) explanations of sexual preference share a great deal in common. Paralleling "God's will" explanations, genetic accounts are robustly coupled with a more inclusive definition of family. When Americans attribute sexual preference to genetics—or to "God's will"—they in essence reject the idea that homosexuality is a "lifestyle" choice and therefore is reversible or, in the parlance of gay reparative therapy, "curable." Instead, adherents of genetic accounts—like those who endorse "God's will" explanations—view sexual preference not as a choice, but rather as an intrinsic and immutable trait of individuals.

This view is becoming increasingly popular—as indicated by the growing number of Americans between 2003 and 2006 who selected genetic or "God's will" explanations in the closed-ended questions and correspondingly the declining number who placed responsibility on parenting and parenting practices. Open-ended remarks, especially regarding the extension of marital and other rights to same-sex couples, further demonstrate the resonance of explanations that underscore the genetic or fixed nature of sexual preference. In 2003, the notion that the origins of sexual preference are beyond the realm of individual control rarely appeared in Americans' comments. By 2006, however, Americans had begun to employ this line of reasoning as a compelling factor behind their support of, among other things, gay marriage. Clearly, Americans are hearing and sharing the message promoted by many—but certainly not all—gay rights activists that individuals should not be disparately treated because of a trait that is beyond their control. Should increasing reliance on genetic and "God's will" accounts follow the growth that was witnessed between 2003 and 2006, then support for a more inclusive vision of family should correspondingly accelerate.

These patterns may simultaneously hearten and unsettle social scientists. They certainly should be encouraging to social scientists who advocate expanding familial definitions because they suggest a likely and perhaps unavoidable movement toward inclusivity. But these same patterns also may be disquieting to those social scientists who express serious reservations about the use of genetic accounts of human or social behavior—reservations predicated to a large extent on the historical usage of genetic differences to rationalize racial and gender discrimination. Despite a recent upswing in scholarly ventures that explore the joint influence of social and biological or genetic factors on human behavior, a very large contingency of social scientists remains intransigently opposed to such endeavors, dismissing them as a contemporary rationalization for inequality and unequal treatment.[8] Yet equating genetic frames with a reactionary position is a dangerous oversimplification. As we can

see from the responses that Americans give, genetic explanations need not be inherently conservative. Instead, they can be a source of liberalism in some cases. Just as Americans are reevaluating their beliefs about family, many social scientists will need to reconsider their assumptions regarding "nature" and "nurture"—especially in the case of sexual preference, where "nature" currently yields the more liberal response while "nurture" produces the more conservative one.

UNCHANGING BARRIERS

The most exclusionist definitions of family come from Americans who believe that parents and parenting practices are primarily accountable for sexual preference. This group sees few limits to parenting—even, or especially, when it comes to sexuality, which they believe can and should be controlled. In listening to Americans' comments regarding the optimal living situation for girls and boys in single-parent households, we come to appreciate how intertwined Americans' views on sexual preference and gender really can be. Americans who believe that boys are better off living with their fathers and girls are better off living with their mothers also are more likely to believe that sexual preference is due to parents and, more importantly, are more likely to take a strongly exclusionist stance when defining the boundaries between family and nonfamily. They do not believe in same-sex couples, but they do believe in the importance of a same-sex parent: fathers for boys and mothers for girls. The same-sex parent is seen as the front-line role model who instills in boys appropriate and desirable masculine traits and behaviors and in girls requisite feminine traits and behaviors. The marked sex differentiation endorsed by Americans may be surprising given the assertions made by many social commentators that gender divisions have loosened greatly. Yet remarks by Americans who highlight the merits of same-sex role models—especially the importance of a male figure in a boy's life as a means to counteract the feminizing influence of women—echo similar arguments made over a century ago. These arguments suggest a sustained fear, disdain, or loathing of feminine qualities in boys—which appears to be coupled with a continuing fear, disdain, or loathing of homosexuality.

But the ongoing durability of gender stereotypes and the power of gender expectations also are seen in the comments by Americans who presume that both boys and girls would be better off living with their mother. This group of Americans is skeptical about fathers' ability to parent and instead perhaps overstates the unique qualifications that women possess in this arena. Clearly, they hold distinct gendered stereotypes regarding parents. Nevertheless, their focus on nurturance and their less rigid differentiation between boys and girls may be critical factors in their greater willingness to include same-sex couples with children as family and may be influential in moving them to even greater inclusivity in the future. That inclusivity may eventually approach that of the group of Americans who believe that a parent's gender and a child's gender are less consequential than the actual quality of the parent-child relationship. Tellingly, members of this group constitute a much smaller percentage than the other two—further evidence of the tenacity of gendered expectations and the wide-ranging effects of these expectations, most notably on definitions of family.

The resiliency of certain gendered assumptions amid a sea of other social changes is clearly on display when Americans discuss their views about marital name change. Nearly three-fourths of Americans agree that it is better for a woman to change her name at marriage, while one-half concur that women should be legally required to change their name at marriage, and almost one-half believe that it is unacceptable for a man to take the name of his wife. These responses not only tell us about Americans' views regarding name practices but also reveal a great deal about their understanding of gender in family life, their openness to a variety of gendered identities, and their receptiveness to a broader definition of family. Despite a clear correspondence between liberal views regarding marital name change and expansive definitions of family, it appears that the rate of change in the latter is much more rapid than in the former. This disparity, we believe, is due mostly to the intensified public attention to the issue of same-sex relations (even in such a short period as 2003 through 2006), in contrast to the virtual absence of public dialogue over marital name change. This pattern also suggests that, ironically, despite the current inextricable link between views regarding gender and sexuality, changes in Americans' views regarding the definition of family may liberalize so swiftly that they may well be decoupled from at least some views regarding gender in the future.

CHANGING BOUNDARIES

Throughout this book, we have found persuasive evidence that Americans are moving toward a more encompassing definition of family that includes same-sex households. In other words, the boundary between family and nonfamily is being redrawn. For most proponents of equality for same-sex families, this is good news. Still, moving the boundary does not eliminate it. The boundary is simply repositioned. Placing same-sex couples within the category of family does not deny that other living arrangements will continue to be counted out—such as friends living together, nonromantic relationships, and non-exclusive partnerships. Although many of the Americans we interviewed challenged some heteronormative conceptions of "the family," there were limits. For example, over 90 percent—including most inclusionists—categorically dismissed housemates as nonfamily. Would this response have shifted had we focused on the functions of this living arrangement rather than on its form? It is possible, especially for some inclusionists who in their open-ended comments suggested that families can come in a variety of packages that perform familial functions. Still, an unintentional consequence of efforts to include same-sex couples as family—and correspondingly, to recognize same-sex marriage—might be further marginalization of other living arrangements, or "chosen families," that do not enjoy legal recognition and the rights and benefits attendant with such a status.

Two legal scholars, Martha Fineman and Nancy Polikoff, both make arguments along these lines.

Fineman (1995, 2004) proposes a more narrow model—or legal definition—of family that expressly privileges relationships between a dependent and his or her caretaker.[9] She also believes that the intimate nature of horizontal relationships between adults should be left out of the question of family and that state-sanctioned marriage should be replaced by private contracts between adult partners. Mirroring Fineman's line of reasoning, Polikoff (2008) critiques the use of marriage as a means of conveying legal and social status. She grants the advantages that legal marital status would provide to same-sex couples, but also is troubled that same-sex marriage would create and strengthen boundaries between the married and nonmarried (see also Ettelbrick 2001; Walters 2001; Warner 1999). According to Polikoff, compelling couples to marry in order to obtain benefits and legal status necessarily results in the exclusion of a number of familial (biological or not) forms that need and deserve protection and benefits under the law, such as adult children taking care of parents, couples who choose not to marry, and cohabiting friends who share a long-standing (though nonsexual) economic and emotional interdependence. Polikoff proposes that marriage be converted to a merely cultural or religious ceremony and that family laws be based on the choices that people make in forming their own family. We bring up Fineman's and Polikoff's positions not because they represent the modal viewpoint currently held among scholars, gay rights activists, or gay men and lesbians (for a detailed description of the various debates within the gay community regarding same-sex marriage, see Hull 2006). But their comments remind us that when efforts to define same-sex couples as family—and relatedly, to legalize same-sex marriage—are successful, the battleground regarding the definition of family will shift, just as it shifted after other barriers to family or marital status were broken.

COUNTING CHANGE

The United States includes a rich diversity of families 35 whether or not they are officially recognized as such. In fact, "the family," although still invoked far too often in public and scholarly venues, is an increasingly untenable and obsolete concept. Many nontraditional or hitherto transgressive living arrangements—single-parent households, voluntarily childless couples, divorced homes—no longer carry strongly negative connotations or elicit highly judgmental reactions, as in the past. The idea of the legal recognition of interracial marriage, for example, at one time was unthinkable in most parts of the United States. Decades after the Supreme Court ordered the removal of antimiscegenation laws, interracial relations are tolerated, accepted, or even embraced by most Americans.[10]

Despite resistance in some communities to acknowledging a similarity between interracial and same-sex couples, the parallels between the two as highlighted throughout this book are impossible to ignore. The very same sociodemographic cleavages that distinguished supporters and vehement opponents of interracial marriage have reemerged to differentiate between advocates of an inclusive definition of family and critics who take a more exclusionist stance. The discomfort with same-sex couples and, more broadly, contact with gays and lesbians that Americans express closely resembles the discomfort with interracial couples and contact with other races. Arguments to resist the inclusion of same-sex couples as family echo the arguments that were advanced against interracial couples: for example, that these couples are abhorrent, unnatural, and against the law of God. By the same token, the reasons currently offered on behalf of an inclusive vision of family are strikingly similar to the reasons given to support interracial marriage: for example, that love and commitment define the family regardless of its members, that one cannot choose one's sexual preference just as one cannot choose one's race, and that whom one falls in love with cannot be controlled.

But today the fact that interracial relations were legally prohibited not so long ago seems unfathomable, beyond the pale of possibility. Given the cumulative and compelling evidence presented in this book, we envisage a day in the near future when same-sex families also will gain acceptance by a large plurality of the public, the denial of similar rights to same-sex couples will be nothing more than an antiquated memory, and same-sex couples will no longer be counted out.

NOTES

1. Referendum 71 offers expanded domestic partner rights to heterosexual couples when at least one of the partners is sixty-two years old or older.

2. At the time of the writing of this chapter, the constitutionality of Proposition 8 has been challenged before the California Supreme Court.

3. Although a state judge overturned the law, some "pro-family" groups have indicated that they likely will appeal this judicial decision.

4. Even in New York, surely among the most consistently liberal states, Governor David Paterson's attempts to bring forth a vote in the New York Senate to legalize same-sex marriage initially were met with a tepid reaction—and in some cases vehement opposition—by New York legislators from both the Democratic and Republican Parties who were leery of reactions from constituents. Although advocates of same-sex marriage were able to bring a marriage equality bill to a full vote, they did not succeed in getting the bill passed.

5. This question also was asked in 1988.

6. For discussions of how an emphasis on familial functions need not bolster conservative visions of family and instead can undercut them, see Fineman (1995, 2004).

7. The liberalizing effect of education has not gone unnoticed by college students. In our undergraduate classes, we routinely ask students to complete the same set of closed-ended questions and to write their open-ended personal definitions of family. Their responses confirm not only a strikingly large percentage who see same-sex couples as family but also an appreciation of the powerful role played in their inclusive conceptualization of family by college and, in particular, their contact with a diverse group of students.

8. Similarly, some gay activists worry that, taken to the extreme, the position that sexuality is fixed and beyond an individual's control could justify disparate treatment of bisexuals, transsexuals, those who change sexual identities later in life, and others who choose not to identify as either "gay" or "straight."

9. Fineman's preferred typology of family is shared by very few Americans who were interviewed in the Constructing the Family Survey. Only 3 percent indicated that only households in which there is a parent-child relationship count as a family. Fineman's definitions of family may be more attractive in other countries, however. After hearing the results of the Constructing the Family Survey, David Reimer, Cornelia Hausen, Irena Kogan, and Markus Gangl from the University of Mannheim and Mannheim Centre for European Social Research led a data collection effort in 2005 in which more than nine hundred Germans who lived in or near Mannheim, an urban area with a strong manufacturing base, were presented with ten living arrangements (the same as those asked in the Constructing the Family Survey, with the exception of housemates) and asked to indicate which living arrangements they believed count as family. Among this German sample, the most common pattern was to define family solely on the basis of the presence of children. Whereas marriage by itself is a decisive factor among Americans, Germans grant more weight to living arrangements that include children—so much weight, in fact, that married couples without children are less likely than same-sex couples with children to be deemed a family. That said, Germans also are less likely than Americans to privilege single-parent households, perhaps because there is a fairly low proportion of single-parent households and because Germany's public policies and institutional practices especially encourage a two-parent—and in particular, a breadwinner-homemaker—arrangement.

10. This is not to deny the continued disavowal of interracial relationships among a certain segment of the population. Media representations of interracial couples still provoke strongly visceral reactions by some. The cover story in a recent edition of the *St. Louis Post-Dispatch* (Moore 2009), for example, featured an interracial couple kissing, prompting thousands of comments, mostly complaints:

> Haven't read the story but don't like to see blacks and whites kissing.

> …The reality here is that the silent majority does not accept interracial [*sic*] behavior and views it as unnatural. Most responsible parents do not allow cross-relationships such as these and for valid reasons.

The parallel with same-sex couples was explicitly brought up by several readers:

> Next year it will be two people of the same sex. Not that there's anything wrong with that….

> It should be two men kissing because those are the morals that the media wants the public to adopt and if you're offended, the liberals tell you it's because only their morals matter and what you want doesn't matter because they're in control and you're a mentally unstable hater.

REFERENCES

Bolzendahl, Catherine I., and Clem Brooks. 2005. "Polarization, Secularization, or Differences as Usual? The Denominational Cleavage in U.S. Social Attitudes since the 1970s." *Sociological Quarterly* 46(1): 47–78.

Carroll, Susan J., and Richard Logan Fox, eds. 2006. *Gender and Elections: Shaping the Future of American Politics.* New York: Cambridge University Press.

Ettelbrick, Paula L. 2001. "Domestic Partnership, Civil Unions, or Marriage: One Size Does Not Fit All." *Albany Law Review* 64(3): 905–14.

Fineman, Martha Albertson. 1995. *The Neutered Mother, the Sexual Family, and Other Twentieth-Century Tragedies.* New York: Routledge.

Fineman, Martha Albertson. 2004. *The Autonomy Myth: A Theory of Dependency.* New York: New Press.

Firebaugh, Glenn, and Kenneth E. Davis. 1988. "Trends in Antiblack Prejudice, 1972–1984: Region and Cohort Effects." *American Journal of Sociology* 94(2): 251–72.

Fischer, Claude S. 1978. "Urban-to-Non-Urban Diffusion of Opinions in Contemporary America." *American Journal of Sociology* 94(2): 251–72.

Gallagher, Maggie. 2003. "The Stakes." *National Review Online* (July 14). Available at: http://article.nationalreview.com/269352/the-stakes/maggie-gallagher (accessed May 18, 2010).

Gamson, Joshua. 1998. *Freaks Talk Back: Tabloid Talk Shows and Sexual Nonconformity.* Chicago: University of Chicago Press.

Hull, Kathleen E. 2006. *Same-Sex Marriage: The Cultural Politics of Love and Law.* Cambridge: Cambridge University Press.

Polikoff, Nancy D. 2008. *Beyond (Straight and Gay) Marriage: Valuing All Families under the Law.* Boston: Beacon Press.

Waldman, Paul. 2009. "We've Already Won the Battle over Gay Marriage." *The American Prospect* (April 14). Available at: http://www.prospect.org/cs/articles?article-weve_already_won_the_battle_over_gay_marriage (accessed May 3, 2010).

Walters, Susana Dunata. 2001. *All the Rage: The Story of Gay Visibility in America.* Chicago: University of Chicago Press.

Warner, Michael. 1999. *The Trouble with Normal: Sex, Politics, and the Ethics of Queer Life.* New York: Free Press.

Reading Questions

1. How do the authors define *inclusionists*, *moderates*, and *exclusionists*?

2. The authors draw a parallel between changing attitudes about same-sex marriage and attitudes about interracial marriage. What patterns do the authors identify? What does this history of interracial marriage suggest about same-sex marriage?

Rhetoric Questions

3. Identify moments of forecasting and previewing in the structure of the text. Where are these paragraphs located within the essay, and why?

4. Choose two passages in which the authors rely heavily on survey data to support their claims. How do they integrate data within these passages? What phrases or key words do they use?

Response and Research Questions

5. Writing about their methodology, the authors note that "quantitative data give us a picture of the boundaries, but the qualitative data animate the struggles that Americans face in defining family" (par. 7). Choose and explain an instance from the text when the authors demonstrate the ideas expressed in this statement.

6. The authors write that their data suggest an "alternative interpretation" (12) to those typically proposed in the field of sociology. Think about a topic that you're writing about or might choose to write about in the future. Explain how you might determine if there is room for change, refinement, and/or redefinition of what others have written on the topic.

In Strangers' Glances at Family, Tensions Linger

SUSAN SAULNY

A national correspondent for the *New York Times*, Susan Saulny has written about a wide array of topics for popular audiences. From politics to gun control to race, Saulny crafts compelling news stories that are both informative and persuasive for readers. In the article below, published in the *New York Times* in October 2011, Saulny describes the experiences of two generations of a multiracial family, the Greenwoods and the Dragans. At times heartbreaking, this article relays anecdotes to convey each family's struggles as they are met with confusion by the outside world and the ways they make sense of these experiences.

TOMS RIVER, N.J. — *"How come she's so white and you're so dark?"*

The question tore through Heather Greenwood as she was about to check out at a store here one afternoon this summer. Her brown hands were pushing the shopping cart that held her babbling toddler, Noelle, all platinum curls, fair skin, and ice-blue eyes.

The woman behind Mrs. Greenwood, who was white, asked once she realized, by the way they were talking, that they were mother and child. "It's just not possible," she charged indignantly. "You're so . . . dark!"

It was not the first time someone had demanded an explanation from Mrs. Greenwood about her biological daughter, but it was among the more aggressive. Shaken almost to tears, she wanted to flee, to shield her little one from this kind of talk. But after quickly paying the cashier, she managed a reply. "How come?" she said. "Because that's the way God made us."

The Greenwood family tree, emblematic of a growing number of American bloodlines, has roots on many continents. Its mix of races — by marriage, adoption, and other close relationships — can be challenging to track, sometimes confusing even for the family itself.

For starters: Mrs. Greenwood, 37, is the daugh- 5 ter of a black father and a white mother. She was adopted into a white family as a child. Mrs. Greenwood married a white man with whom she has two daughters. Her son from a previous relationship is half Costa Rican. She also has a half brother who is white, and siblings in her adoptive family who are biracial, among a host of other close relatives — one from as far away as South Korea.

The population of mixed-race Americans like Mrs. Greenwood and her children is growing quickly, driven largely by immigration and intermarriage. One in seven new marriages is between spouses of different races or ethnicities, for example. And among American children, the multiracial population has increased almost 50 percent, to 4.2 million, since 2000.

But the experiences of mixed-race Americans can be vastly different. Many mixed-race youths say they feel wider acceptance than past generations, particularly on college campuses and in pop culture. Extensive interviews and days spent with the Greenwoods show that, when they are alone, the family strives to be colorblind. But what they face outside their home is another story. People seem to notice nothing but race. Strangers gawk. Make rude and racist comments. Tell offensive jokes. Ask impolite questions.

The Greenwoods' experiences offer a telling glimpse into contemporary race relations, according to sociologists and members of other mixed-race families.

It is a life of small but relentless reminders that old tensions about race remain, said Mrs. Greenwood, a homemaker with training in social work.

"People confront you, and it's not once in a while, 10 it's all the time," she said. "Each time is like a little paper cut, and you might think, 'Well, that's not a big deal.' But imagine a lifetime of that. It hurts."

Jenifer L. Bratter, an associate sociology professor at Rice University who has studied multiracialism, said that as long as race continued to affect where people live, how much money they make, and how they are treated, then multiracial families would be met with double-takes. "Unless we solve those issues of inequality in other areas, interracial families are going to be questioned about why they'd cross that line," she said.

According to Census data, interracial couples have a slightly higher divorce rate than same-race couples—perhaps, sociologists say, because of the heightened stress in their lives as they buck enduring norms. And children in mixed families face the challenge of navigating questions about their identities.

"If we could just go about whatever we're doing and not be asked anything about our family's colors," Mrs. Greenwood said, "that would be a dream."

A FAMILY'S STORY

The colors that strangers find so intriguing when they see the Greenwood family are the result of two generations of intermixing.

Their story begins with Mrs. Greenwood's adoptive parents, Dolores and Edward Dragan, of Slovak and Polish descent, veterans of Woodstock and the March on Washington, who always knew they wanted to adopt. They were drawn to children who were hardest to place in permanent homes. In the early 1970s, those children were mixed race. [15]

Mrs. Dragan, a retired art teacher, remembers telling her adoption agency that she and her husband, then a principal, would take "any child, any color," at a time when most people like themselves were looking for healthy white infants.

They adopted two mixed-race children within two years. The family seemed complete until Mr. Dragan came home from school one day and joked to his wife, "I'm in love with another woman." It was the sprightly 6-year-old Heather, a student. She had been living with foster parents and was up for adoption.

"Holy cow, she just brought the energy into our home," Mrs. Dragan recalled of their early days together in Flemington, N.J.

As the children grew, the Dragans tried to infuse their world with African-American culture. There were family trips to museums in Washington, as well as beauty salons in Philadelphia, where Mrs. Dragan learned black hairstyling skills.

However, the children were not particularly interested, and do not remember race being a big part of their identities when they were younger. "We were happy to be whoever we thought we were at that time," Mrs. Greenwood said. [20]

But as she moved into adulthood, she began to identify herself as a black woman of mixed heritage. She also felt more of a connection with whites and Latinos, and had a son, Silas Aguilar, now 18, with a Costa Rican boyfriend. She later married Aaron Greenwood, a computer network engineer who is a descendant of Quakers. A few years ago, they bought a split-level ranch house in Toms River and started a bigger family.

STINGING INSULTS

The shoulder shrugs about being mixed race within the family are in stark contrast to insults outside the home—too many for the Dragans and the Greenwoods to recount.

But some still sting more than others. On one occasion, a boy on the school bus called young Heather a nigger, and she had no idea what the word meant, so Mrs. Dragan, now 69, got the question over homework one night: "Mom, what's a nigger?"

Once, on a beach chair at a resort in Florida years ago, a white woman sunning herself next to Mrs. Dragan bemoaned the fact that black children were running around the pool. "Isn't it awful?" Mrs. Dragan recalled the woman confiding to her.

Within minutes, Mrs. Dragan, ever feisty despite [25] her reserved appearance, had her brood by her side. "I'd like to introduce you to my children," she told the woman. Awkward silence ensued.

"You know what? She deserved it," Mrs. Dragan recalled during an interview at her home in Lambertville, N.J. "I figured, why miss an opportunity to embarrass someone if they needed it?"

Sometimes, the racism directed toward the Dragans seemed similar to what a single-race minority family might experience.

When the children were still young, a real estate agent in Flemington warned prospective buyers in her neighborhood about the Dragan household, saying that "there are black people living there, and I feel it's my duty to let you know." The people bought the house anyway, and later told the Dragans about the incident, once they had become friends.

"We weren't blind to the reality of racism," Mr. Dragan explained, "yet when you get into a situation where it's your family, it really takes on a different dimension."

Mrs. Dragan said her life came to revolve around 30 shielding the children: "I was always on my A-game. My antennas were always up. I was aware all the time."

Fast-forward 30 years, and Mrs. Dragan sees her daughter, Mrs. Greenwood, going through similar episodes with her own children — all because mother and child are not the same color.

"She gets the same stares I got when I was a young mother in the supermarket, with three African-American kids hanging off the cart," said Mrs. Dragan, whose wisps of blond hair frame a fair-skinned face.

"You sort of put it out of your mind once your children are grown and you think, I just want to relax, that part's over for now," she continued. "But I've gotten a little more agitated lately."

She does not like what she is hearing from her daughter these days. A typical story: On the boardwalk at the shore over the summer, Noelle scampered toward the carousel, her parents in tow. Even at 21 months, Noelle is a regular customer, so the ride operator, Risa Ierra, felt free to have a little fun.

"You know this little one isn't really theirs, right?" 35 Ms. Ierra joked to the other people in line. "Must have been switched at the hospital."

Since Mr. and Mrs. Greenwood are friendly with her, they said later that they were not offended. But the exchange was typical of remarks Mrs. Greenwood hears often, even from people who seem well-meaning.

"Oh my God! Are they yours? Or are you their nanny?" she said she was often asked. (By contrast, her mother, Mrs. Dragan, was often asked if she was hosting inner-city children as part of a charitable effort.)

"That's the most common thing I get," Mrs. Greenwood said of the nanny question. "But I don't want to go there. I don't want to justify me being their mother to strangers."

HUMOR AND STRENGTH

The family has always used humor to cope, but sometimes that is not enough.

When the Dragan children were young, for in- 40 stance, the family stopped at a restaurant near Disney World and people seemed to drop their forks when they walked in. "Yes, it's true!" one of the Dragan children yelled. "These folks aren't from around here!"

At least the family laughed, if no one else did.

Of the constant confrontations, Mrs. Dragan said, "I don't always feel successful. I feel like I could have thrown my hands up a number of times, with the kids and other people."

Often, she found the energy to fight. "Other times," she said, "I locked myself in the house."

The Dragans concede that at times they felt a strain on their relationship. "There is a lot of stress when people are looking at you and scrutinizing and judging," Mr. Dragan said. "You might not hear it but you feel it. We felt it. That is stressful for a marriage. You do have to help and reinforce each other. Humor has really gotten us through a lot of heartache."

Mrs. Greenwood uses the same strategy. She likes 45 T-shirts with messages. She has one that she wears on St. Patrick's Day: "This is what Irish looks like," it says, a reference to her biological mother's lineage. She is thinking about having one made that says, "Yes, I'm the mom."

Mrs. Greenwood is not ready to have a conversation about race with Sophia, now 7. But Sophia is starting to notice the stares, the jokes, the questions. Mrs. Greenwood feels as though the world is forcing race into her home, which has been a respite from race ever since she was a little girl herself.

"I actually don't know what to tell Sophia and Noelle when they start asking me, 'Am I black?'" she said.

"If they look in the mirror or to society, they're not going to be black," she said, worried about what sort of internal conflicts this might cause.

"I'm afraid she's going to start questioning who she is, and she shouldn't have to," Mrs. Greenwood added.

Mr. Greenwood has already tried something. "I've told Sophia that she is a perfect mix of her mommy and daddy," he said, "but we're going to have to talk more."

Silas, Mrs. Greenwood's half-Latino son from a previous relationship, started to ask race questions around age 7.

"I went up to my mom and said, 'What am I?'" Silas recalled. "And, 'What are you? Are we the same thing?' I was just shooting questions. It was like a brain mash. I looked at my family and thought, 'What is going on here?' I was just lost. But after a really long explanation, I eventually understood."

He paused, adding later, "I think my little sisters will be fine."

Race is not something Silas says he spends a lot of time worrying about. He learned long ago about the family tree, and that he is part black, that his grandmother is Slovakian, his cousin is Asian, and so on — and hardly any of that matters to him.

"Barriers are breaking down," he said.

For the moment, the matter seems simple enough for Sophia, too. She responds confidently when asked what race she is. "Tan!" says the second-grade student. "Can't you tell by just looking?"

Reading Questions

1. Drawing on sociological work on multiracialism, what social issues does Saulny suggest our society needs to address?

2. According to Saulny, what are some contributing factors to the rise in the number of multi-racial families in America?

3. How does the Dragan family cope with negative responses to their racial identity?

Rhetoric Questions

4. At the end of the article, Saulny focuses primarily on Silas and Sophia's understandings of race. How do the children's understandings of race differ from that of their parents? What is the rhetorical effect of ending the article in this way?

5. Identify three instances in the text that rely on an emotional response from the reader. How does the text elicit this response in each instance?

Response and Research Questions

6. Despite the thirty-year differences between Mrs. Dragan and her daughter, Heather Greenwood, Saulny reports that they received much the same reactions to their interracial family. Does this surprise you? Why or why not?

7. In paragraph 7, Saulny writes, "People seem to notice nothing but race." What is your reaction to such an assertion? Does this notion fit in the context of your own experiences?

8. Think of a time when your own racial identity was made apparent to you. How did your response compare to the Dragan family's?

The Strategies of Forbidden Love: Family across Racial Boundaries in Nineteenth-Century North Carolina

WARREN E. MILTEER JR.

Warren E. Milteer Jr. completed his PhD in history at the University of North Carolina–Chapel Hill in 2014. In this article, which appeared in the Spring 2014 edition of the *Journal of Social History*, Milteer explores "forbidden love" and makes the case that "free women of mixed ancestry and white men developed relationships that mimicked legally sanctioned marriages" in nineteenth-century North Carolina. His argument, which relies heavily on primary document analysis, explores the wider implications for these seemingly impossible historical constructs.

ABSTRACT

This article contends that although local beliefs and legal edicts attempted to discourage sexual and familial relationships between women of color and white men in North Carolina, free women of mixed ancestry and white men developed relationships that mimicked legally sanctioned marriages. These unions often produced children who maintained frequent interaction with both parents. In nineteenth-century Hertford County, North Carolina, free women of mixed ancestry and their white partners developed creative strategies to deal with the legal limitations inherent in their situation. Women and men in these relationships found ways to secure property rights for women and children and developed methods to prevent legal scrutiny of their living arrangements.

By the early to mid-nineteenth century, Hertford County, located in the tobacco- and cotton-growing intercoastal plain of North Carolina, had developed a reputation throughout the eastern seaboard as a place where free women of mixed ancestry lived outside of marriage with white men.[1] In 1853, William D. Valentine, a prominent organizer in the Hertford County Whig Party, wrote in reference to the practice: "So common has it long been that I apprehend it is tolerated by married men in this locality. They too indulge. The whites are more blamable than the low degraded colored."[2] Calvin Scott Brown heard similar tales of sexual encounters across racial boundaries as he traveled toward Hertford County to begin his

work as an administrator of a new school for people of color during the 1880s: "I remember on my way here for the first time from Franklin, Virginia, a man on the boat asked me where I was going...I told him I was going to Winton." The man responded that the inhabitants of Hertford County "were the most degraded people upon the face of the earth." He said that mulatto women "lived with white men and that white men came from as far as Baltimore to have the mulatto girls."[3]

Historical records, including accounts from children produced from relationships between free women of mixed ancestry and white men, support these rumors of sexual exploitation in nineteenth-century Hertford County. Mollie Cherry Hall Catus remembered that her white father, Albert Vann,

> would come in at bed-time and even before his wife died he would come and stay with my mother [Sallie Ann Hall] all night and get up and go to his house the next morning. His children despised us and I despised them and all their folks, and I despised him....He had plenty of property but didn't give mother one thing.[4]

Many non-white women, both enslaved and free, lived under similar conditions as Sallie Ann Hall, and many of their children had the same attitudes about their white fathers' actions. However, the historical record demonstrates that not all free women of mixed ancestry served their white partners as concubines. In several instances, relationships between free women of mixed ancestry and white men took the form of long-term dedicated partnerships.[5]

This study focuses on long-term monogamous relationships between free women of mixed ancestry and white men who probably would have married if legal and social circumstances had been different. North Carolina law banned marriage between whites and non-whites for most of the nineteenth century, yet many free women of mixed ancestry and white men still built lifetime partnerships. Legal restrictions alone could not dissuade these men and women from sharing their lives together. Although historical sources reveal relatively few relationships of this type in contrast with the often-cited situations of concubinage, scholars must acknowledge that some whites and non-whites in the nineteenth century, just as people today, desired to share their lives together regardless of the lack of legal recognition and social approval. Because the law did not permit these unions, evidence of their existence is at best hidden and sometimes does not appear at all in surviving documents. These unions' lack of legal recognition coupled with destruction of the majority of Hertford County's pre–Civil War court records preclude an exact count of how many of these relationships existed at any particular time. Yet the surviving evidence still allows scholars to understand how free women of mixed ancestry and white men navigated through a society that refused to publicly approve their relationships.[6]

This article contends that although local beliefs and legal edicts discouraged sexual and familial relationships between women of color and white men, some free women of mixed ancestry actively developed relationships with white men that often resembled legally sanctioned marriages. These illegal unions often produced children who maintained frequent interaction with both parents. Free women of mixed ancestry and their white partners developed creative strategies to deal with the legal limitations inherent in any unrecognized union. Even as state lawmakers banned and illegitimated their relationships, women and men in these relationships found ways to secure property rights for women. They developed creative

strategies to pass on wealth to their children, who by law were illegitimate and therefore not entitled to their fathers' estates. These couples even found ways to obscure the illegality of their living arrangements in an era when an unmarried couple living in the same house constituted fornication and adultery, which courts treated as a single crime in North Carolina.

Although contemporary observers suggested that Hertford County had an unusual propensity for unions between non-white women and white men, a closer examination of family histories and surviving documents from other areas would likely reveal that couples across the United States sought solutions for similar domestic issues. Through much of the nineteenth century, the majority of states prohibited marriages between whites and non-whites.[7] Free non-white women and white men in these parts of the nation undoubtedly used many of the same strategies employed by couples in Hertford County to overcome legal obstacles and social stigmas. They along with couples composed of white women and non-white men, both without the legal protections of marriage, would have needed to seek out special arrangements to protect and pass down family assets, provide care to children, and shield themselves from public scrutiny and legal prosecution.

Since 1715, North Carolina law had either discouraged or banned marriage between whites and non-whites. The first law to address marriage fined any white man or woman who intermarried with "any Negro, Mulatto or Indyan Man or Woman" fifty pounds. The General Assembly updated this law in 1741 by levying the same fine on any white man or woman who married "an Indian, negro, mustee, or mulatto man or woman, or any person of mixed blood to the third generation, bond or free."[8] Neither of these laws actually prohibited intermarriage between whites and non-whites but simply discouraged marriages by imposing heavy fines. Both laws also fined clergy and other officials who married whites to non-whites. These laws appear to have discouraged the issuances of legal marriage bonds to mixed couples in Hertford County and many other parts of the state. Nevertheless, in 1830 the General Assembly passed an act banning "any free negro or free person of color" from marrying "a white person."[9] In 1875, a state convention added a similar intermarriage ban to the North Carolina Constitution.[10]

For the past generation, historians have endeavored to understand relationships between non-white women and white men in the United States through the laws governing marriage in the colonial and national periods. Historians have reviewed court cases at the municipal, state, and federal levels in order to understand how different localities treated people living in unlawful mixed unions. Past scholars have focused on the exploitative nature of many of these relationships, in which white men extracted sexual favors from women of color, most of whom had no form of recourse in a society that ignored the sexual indiscretions of offending white men. However, more than a generation of new scholarship has clearly demonstrated that white planters, politicians, and plebeians* also took part in liaisons with women of color that were more mutually beneficial and often long-term.[11]

Yet only the most recent scholarship has begun to uncover the intricacies of daily life for women of color, white men, and their families. Scholars have shown that familial relationships between whites and non-whites existed despite legal prohibitions, but much work still needs to be completed in order to understand how women of color and white men managed family life in communities that refused to give legal recognition to their unions. Even less is understood about the unique position of free women of color involved in illicit unions with white men. Slave status placed limitations on women that caused relationships between enslaved women and white men to be inherently skewed in the favor of white men, whether those white men intended to treat those women as long-term partners or brief subjects of their sexual aggression. However, freedom offered women of color a greater variety of possible relationships with white men, which scholars have yet to fully explore. Free women of color had choices far beyond those available to enslaved women. These women, like white women, had the option to marry free men of their own race, engage in contracts, and own and sell property. When they chose to engage in relationships with white men, free women of color had greater freedom than enslaved women to determine and shape their familial relations and could reap greater benefits from those interactions. Most importantly, these couples helped to develop the rationale for such relationships and the guidelines for how free women of color and white men carried out their relationships in public and private spaces.

The free women of mixed ancestry who chose to develop life-long relationships with white men in nineteenth-century Hertford County came from a variety of family backgrounds, but most were not wealthy. Louisiana Weaver's father, Charles Weaver, was a poor and sickly man of color who struggled to provide for his family and often depended on the labor of his wife, Delilah, and their children in order to make ends meet. Celia Garnes, the daughter of Daniel and Betsey Garnes, grew up in a household in which her parents had trouble supporting their children and were almost forced by the courts to bind out* several of their sons. Sallie Yeates Bizzell was the daughter of Velia Bizzell, a free-born woman of mixed ancestry, who toiled in local fisheries as a fish cleaner, making only half what her male counterparts made for the same day's work. Whoever Sallie's father was, he did not provide for the family. Mary Jane and Susan Chavis also grew up under tough circumstances. Both girls were the daughters of Emmaline Chavis, a free woman of color; however, they had different fathers. Mary Jane was the daughter of Samuel Powell, a white man, who left her mother alone with six children after he was shot and killed in a brawl. Susan was reportedly the daughter of Nathaniel Turner, a free man of color, who was between marriages at the time of Susan's birth. Strong tensions appear to have existed between Susan's parents, as Turner brought larceny charges against Emmaline Chavis for stealing bacon from his storehouse. These women who chose

*plebeians: members of lower social classes.

*bind out: to apprentice, or place someone in service to another.

to build relationships with white men sought better adult lives than those they experienced as children and did not find legal husbands who could help them reach that goal.[12]

Financial mobility likely played a significant role in the choices of free women of mixed ancestry. In an era in which women in general had limited opportunities for work and faced significant wage discrimination, free women of mixed ancestry had to consider the financial security and social standing of potential mates. For a poor woman looking to move up financially, a relationship with a well-established white man who was willing to build a long-term relation was a promising opportunity. A white man could not directly pass on the benefits of whiteness to a woman of color and her children as he could for a white woman and her children. White enforcement of racial boundaries limited free people of color's access to certain exclusively white networks, therefore limiting a white man's ability to extend his social connections. However, a white man could convey property obtained through connections to these networks and, as long as he lived, he could pass on some of the intangible benefits of being part of middle- and upper-class white social circles.

The second-class social and political position of non-white men in North Carolina's social hierarchy may have influenced women's companion choices. During much of the nineteenth century, the law and social customs granted white men privileges, which men of color, especially slaves, could not enjoy. White superiority, in effect, was not simply an ideology, but in many instances a social reality. Free women of mixed ancestry may have taken this reality into consideration and used it to rationalize their mate selections. Calvin Scott Brown recalled, "When I first came here [to Hertford County] I often heard mulatto women say that they would rather be a white man's concubine than a nigger's wife."[13] Brown's statement suggests that at least some women of mixed ancestry in Hertford County viewed certain non-whites as the inferiors of white men. Historians have found non-white women in other societies including much of Latin America and the Caribbean who used

similar logic to support their choices to embrace illicit arrangements with white men over legally sanctioned marriages to non-whites.[14] As in other slave or former slave societies, Hertford County residents drew significant distinctions between different groups of non-white people. Free people of color were politically and legally distinct from enslaved people, who had no civil rights in American slave societies. After emancipation, people continued to draw meaningful distinctions between the old free people of color and newly emancipated slaves and their descendants. In Hertford County, social divisions between "mulattoes," which included almost all of the old free population of color, and "blacks" reinforced these lines of distinction. Women of mixed ancestry in Hertford County may have taken these distinctions into consideration when choosing marriage partners. A woman's choice of a partner had long-term implications for both her and any children that she might have. Associations with a man of lower social status would have ultimately diminished the social standing of a woman of higher social position.

Basic feelings of love, admiration, and affection versus purely economic and social motivations may have driven relationships between free women of mixed ancestry and white men. Examples exist from all time periods and areas of the world where people with different social statuses, ancestral origins, economic positions, and belief systems have crossed socially constructed boundaries in order to build loving relationships. At least some free women of mixed ancestry and white men likely moved beyond the social constructions that attempted to order their world to fulfill their desires for love and acceptance from another human being whom they found attractive and desirable. The racial categories used to divide people with different ancestries, appearances, and community positions could not always overcome natural attraction. Laws against marriage between whites and non-whites attempted to curb the influences of attraction and affection and make unions across racial boundaries socially unacceptable. The people who engineered marriage laws attempted to impose their beliefs about appropriate behavior through granting or denying the privilege of marriage. However, their attempts could not convince every couple to deny their own feelings in order to conform to the societal norm.

Although love and attraction likely played an important part in the development of relationships between free women of mixed ancestry and white men, the social and economic realities still carried considerable weight in the rationale of relationships. Social and economic status of the participants in these relationships could determine the feasibility of living in a socially unacceptable manner. Free women of mixed ancestry who chose white mates usually selected men of high standing in the community. Christian Wiggins partnered with Noah Cotton, a planter and descendant of a long-established Hertford County family. Louisiana Weaver established a family with James Kiff, the county tax collector and a businessman. Sallie Yeates Bizzell developed a long-term relationship with Richard Henry Shield, a well-respected doctor. Mary Jane Chavis's partner was James Norfleet Holloman, a successful merchant and active participant in local Democratic Party politics.[15] Most free women of mixed ancestry who had white partners chose men of wealth and prestige. Free women of mixed ancestry made their mate selections just as carefully as women who contracted in legal marriage with the hope of securing economic stability.

For non-white women, associations with men of high social position were imperative to social mobility as well as immunity from legal prosecution for fornication and adultery. Hertford County's courts never brought white men of high status into court for committing fornication and adultery with women of color. The elite white power structure that controlled the local judiciary was generally unwilling to shame publicly members of its own group by placing well-to-do white male fornicators on trial. Social respectability resulting from birth into well-established families, economic success, or connections to important white-only social networks protected these men from legal prosecution. Only the relationships of white men who lacked these attributes faced prosecution.

The backgrounds of two white men prosecuted for fornication and adultery with women of color during the March 1854 term of Hertford County Court illustrate this class-based legal double standard. The court charged two couples, William Futrell and Frusa Reid and Wiley Ezell and Celia Garnes, with fornication and adultery. William Futrell appears to have come from a poor farming family. The 1850 Census lists the Futrell family as owners of real estate worth only $48. Wiley Ezell owned a modest amount of real property, but the circumstances of his birth as the son of an unwed mother likely stained his reputation in the community. At their trials, both couples pled not guilty, and in the end the jury found only Futrell and Reid guilty of fornication and adultery. The jury acquitted Ezell and Garnes of all charges, although their cohabitation and children should have served as enough evidence to find the couple in the wrong. The Hertford County court records do not explain how Ezell and Garnes won their case; however, the list of jurors contains a possible clue. Starkey Sharpe Harrell, one of the jurors in the Ezell and Garnes case, carried on a relationship with Emma Butler, a free woman of color, and may have sympathized with Ezell. Records from a later period suggest that Harrell and Ezell maintained a close relationship, and Ezell named Harrell the executor of his estate. Ezell came from a lower-class background, but at the time of trial may have begun to surround himself with people of wealth and good reputation. Cases like the *State v. Futrell and Reid* and the *State v. Ezell and Garnes* were a rarity in Hertford County, appearing on the court docket usually no more than once every five or ten years. The second of these cases shows that of those white men and women of color brought into court, only a few actually ended with a guilty verdict and punishment for the couples.[16]

Even though relations between free women of mixed ancestry and white men usually went unprosecuted, couples took precautions to limit the public visibility of their unlawful arrangements. In the antebellum period, some free women of mixed ancestry openly lived with their white partners, but most white men, attempting to maintain a façade to protect their respectability, kept two separate houses. One house, usually the main family quarters, served as the primary residence of the woman and her children. Another house, sometimes larger and sometimes smaller, was the permanent residence of the white father. This was the arrangement that Sallie Yeates Bizzell and Richard Henry Shield set up for their family. In the 1850s, Shield purchased a piece of property to maintain as his own residence. Then Bizzell purchased a small five-acre tract beside Shield, which served as her regular residence.[17] Jesse Rob Weaver remembered that his mother, Louisiana Weaver, and father, James Kiff, set up a similar situation for their family in the 1870s and 1880s. Weaver stated, "My father provided a good large farm. One part was [my mother's] through his efforts.... He had one farm and house joining our field and he with our help worked both farms."[18]

When mothers and fathers maintained separate residences, children and both parents still often came together in one or the other of these physical spaces for family time. Jesse Rob Weaver recalled going back and forth between his mother's and father's houses as a youngster. A Hertford County teacher recollected that one of the daughters of Mary Jane Chavis and James Norfleet Holloman, who grew up at the turn of the century, told this teacher that "her father used to come see her mother every day and every night. He would sit around the fire with the whole family and talk just like any other father."[19] Although many free women of mixed ancestry and white men attempted to create an illusion of physical separation, their families experienced a life more similar to those headed by two parents than those headed by only a single parent. These families' façades were formalities, not realistic attempts to hide illicit relationships. As shown in the example of the teacher, people in the neighborhood knew the reality of their neighbors' situations.

Inside these households, free women of mixed ancestry and their white partners negotiated the operations of daily life for their families. Women engaged in long-term relationships with white partners could maintain significant power in family decision making. They ruled the domestic realm of their households and worked side by side with their white partners to make decisions about other family matters such as finances.

Clarence Chavis, son of Mary Jane Chavis and James Norfleet Holloman, remembered that his father was "very attentive" to his mother and stated, "What was produced on the farm he and she agreed mutually as to how best to dispose of it. He always consulted her about how was best to spend the money."[20] Jesse Rob Weaver recalled that his mother "handled" the money that his father brought home.[21] Cooperation between women and men in these mixed-status relationships was imperative to their survival. Neither the woman nor man was bound by law to maintain their partnership. Unlike the relationships of married couples, the state had not sanctioned their relationship, so the law could not require court or legislative approval if the woman and man chose to dissolve their union. Of course the woman was less likely than the man to walk away from a relationship that provided financial security, but unlike some enslaved women, a free woman of color did have a choice. A long-term relationship with a white man was not her only option.

Like most legally recognized couples, free women of mixed ancestry and white men living in long-term relationships produced children, who often became the focus of these couples' energies and affections. Although the law did not acknowledge the relationship between white fathers and their mixed children, fathers in long-term partnerships with those children's mothers typically played an important role in their children's support and development. An acquaintance of the Chavis family recalled that one of James Norfleet Holloman's daughters

> said that her father was a merchant and would often go to Baltimore and Norfolk and buy things and would never come home without bringing all of them something, from dolls to suits of clothes. She said she felt proud that he was her father. She said that although in public they called him Mr. H[olloman], at home they called him daddy, and he was as sweet and loving to them as any father.... I have known this family all my life and know most of these things were true.

Holloman's daughter Bessie added that her father would allow his children to borrow his horses and buggies. Clarence Chavis remembered that his father "paid the children's school bills."[22]

Wiley Ezell recognized his children by Celia Garnes in a similar manner by providing for their needs. Even when they were adults, Ezell helped his children financially. Ezell ran an account with the merchants Knight and Barham on behalf of his son Joseph Garnes. Purchases on the account included essential items such as shoes and clothing. Ezell also aided his son Albert Garnes and son-in-law Henry T. Lassiter, husband of his daughter Delia Ann, by purchasing corn on their behalves through his own credit account.[23]

James Kiff supported his children as many of his contemporaries in the same situation did. His son Jesse Rob Weaver recalled that Kiff

> would come to our house every morning and every night. He would eat there sometimes. He would tell us what to do each day.... He arranged for us to have gifts and things as any father would do. I stayed with him mostly till he died. I would stay at nights and sleep with him.

Kiff also provided his children with many other essential needs, including sending them to school and helping them to maintain their mother's farm.[24] Although the law denied recognition to families like the Kiff-Weaver family, they still found ways to carve out spaces where members could live like the legally recognized families around them. White fathers' contributions to their non-white families reveal their desires to create the kind of family experience for themselves and their children that their married neighbors had. By failing to grant white men and non-white women the right to marry, the law placed a handicap on attempts to create a legitimate household. However, the dedication of white fathers who bypassed legally and socially imposed obstacles in order to care for their loved ones elucidates the complicated nature of respectability in nineteenth-century Southern society. Social norms and North Carolina law required fathers to take care of their children if both parties were free. However, those same social norms and laws created obstacles for white fathers to provide for non-white children.

Deep ties to extended family across the color line further highlight the determination of couples to enjoy an unbounded family life. Wiley Ezell went beyond simply helping his children. In 1851, he extended a loan to his partner's brother, Noah Garnes, for $18.68, which Ezell never collected.[25] James Kiff's sister, Penny Hedgepath, played an important role in the lives of his children. Jesse Rob Weaver retained very fond memories of his aunt, whom he helped to take care of after the death of his father. He remembered, "I thought she could cook the best food I ever ate. She was good to all of us and would give us some of anything she had to eat."[26] These examples demonstrate that racial divisions and lack of legal recognition sometimes failed to overcome the social significance given to common ancestry and extended kinship. Lawmakers sought to define the family as a racially uniform unit by prohibiting marriage across the color line, but people on the ground, at least occasionally, rejected this notion.[27]

Women of mixed ancestry, when they spent many years in close unions with white men, worked with their partners to set up some form of financial security for themselves and their children. White men used a number of legally enforceable options in order to provide for their families at the time of their deaths. Wills, promissory notes, and property transfers before death were all methods to provide financial security to partners and children with no legally recognized familial relationship. During the nineteenth century, several white men left wills in the hands of trusted friends who promised to take care of children and partners. Before his death in 1815, Noah Cotton dictated a will leaving all his property to his nine children and partner, Christian Wiggins, whom some people in the community recognized as "Christian Cotton." John Vann, the executor of the will, made a conscious effort to obtain shelter, food, and education for Noah's and Christian's children. Using funds from Noah's estate sale and receipts from the rental of his plantation and two slaves, Vann paid the monthly bills for the children's upkeep.[28]

Many years later, Richard W. Knight followed the example of men like Noah Cotton and used a will to protect the future interests of his family. Sometime in the late nineteenth century, Knight had begun a long-term relationship with Susan Chavis, which produced three daughters. Desiring to pass on his wealth to them, Knight wrote his will in 1908 leaving all of his property, "real, personal, and mixed," to Susan Chavis. He requested that at Susan's death, all of his property be divided among the couple's three daughters, Mary S. Roberts, Mattie J. Chavis, and Hattie F. Graves. Knight appointed James Norfleet Holloman, the partner of Mary Jane Chavis, Susan's half-sister, as the executor of his estate. In 1913, two witnesses supported the authenticity of the will at the probate court after Knight's death. There is no evidence to suggest that Susan and her children did not ultimately receive the property left to them.

Wiley Ezell attempted to create a similar situation for his partner Celia Garnes and their children. In his will, Ezell left his home place to his children with the prerequisite that they care for their mother for the rest of her life. Ezell made Starkey Sharpe Harrell, the juror from the 1854 fornication and adultery case, his executor.[29] Unlike the cases of Noah Cotton and Richard Knight, however, several people challenged Ezell's last wishes. Soon after Ezell's death in 1879, Harrell sent notice to the court renouncing his right as executor of the Ezell estate. The court then replaced Harrell with John F. Newsome. Newsome moved quickly after his appointment and began the process of settling Ezell's numerous debts, including several notes on behalf of Celia Garnes and her sons, Joseph, Daniel, and Albert. While Newsome was in the process of settling the estate, Ezell's niece, C. Elizabeth Futrell, and her husband Amos filed a suit against Celia Garnes and her four children claiming that the will devising all of Ezell's property to the Garneses was not Ezell's true last will and testament. Benjamin B. Winborne, the lawyer for the Futrells, argued that Elizabeth, as the sole daughter of Ezell's only sister, was her uncle's only heir at law. The probate judge ruled in favor of the Futrells, but Newsome refused to surrender the assets of the estate to them. Failing to gain Newsome's cooperation, the Futrells sued Newsome as the administrator of the estate and in 1882 won a judgment in their favor.

Wills were imperfect means to transfer property to loved ones. When legitimate heirs challenged the rights of children and partners with no legally recognized connection to a man, the law could be swayed against the wishes of the progenitor. Celia Garnes and her children never collected all that Ezell intended for them to have from his estate. However, the Garneses successfully procured some of Ezell's assets through other means. Daniel, Albert, and Celia Garnes collected debts from the estate for various sorts of work. Whether the Garneses actually performed this work or Ezell simply gave them notes to collect against his estate for fear that someone might challenge his will is not clear. The Garneses also took possession of much of Ezell's personal property, including the contents of his house by purchasing them at his estate sale. Celia Garnes and her children failed to gain all that Ezell intended to leave to them, but under the circumstances, the outcome could have been much worse.[30]

Some white men relied solely on promissory notes to convey wealth to their partners and progeny. Before their deaths, men would issue these notes to their partners and children. Upon their deaths, the women and children could use the notes to make claims against the estates of the white progenitors. This was the arrangement made between Sallie Yeates Bizzell and Richard Henry Shield. In 1867, Shield gave Bizzell a promissory note for $1,500 with interest. In the note, he specifically stated that he, his heirs, and executors guaranteed this debt to Bizzell. After Shield's death in 1870, Sallie collected the value of the note from the executor of his estate.[31] Surviving sources do not explain Shield's reasoning for leaving Bizzell a promissory note versus leaving a will with instructions. Shield probably understood that while wills could be contested, promissory notes were collectible no matter who was the bearer.

Although promissory notes were a safer method for white men to pass on wealth to their partners and children, legal heirs still challenged the exchange of notes. James Kiff left his children "notes or mortgages amounting to $18,000," as his son Jesse Rob Weaver remembered. Just days before his death in 1882, Kiff gave the notes to his son Samuel Weaver. James may have suspected that his brother, William Kiff, would try to block his wishes. Indeed, William qualified as administrator of his brother's estate and then attempted to claim all of his brother's property, including the notes. William sued James's children for the notes, taking the case all the way to the North Carolina Supreme Court. Jesse Rob explained that his uncle "tried to get everything from us but he failed. My father had things so fixed that he couldn't get it."[32] After each of William Kiff's appeals, the courts sided with the defendants and secured the Weavers' rights to their father's property.[33]

Promissory notes were the most effective means of passing property posthumously on to illegitimate children whose inheritance rights could be challenged by legal heirs, such as siblings or nieces and nephews. The Kiff and Weaver case demonstrates that many participants in mixed relationships were well aware of the dissatisfaction of close family members in regards to their relationships. They knew that if they set up the executions of their estates carefully, the legal system was bound to back their actions. Into the 1880s, at least some courts were unwilling to challenge the exchange of notes, even when people of color were involved. A ruling against the Weaver children would have represented a ruling for chicanery. In the Weaver case, the courts were unwilling to create a precedent with such disastrous potential.

While promissory notes were more reliable than wills, making real estate property transfers through deeds during the man's lifetime was the most secure way to transfer property to his family. Unlike with wills and promissory notes, men could personally prevent challenges to their wishes by guaranteeing that the register of deeds recorded the deeds in the county records. In 1870, James Kiff made his first land transfer to his partner, Louisiana Weaver. The deed states that Kiff sold Weaver several tracts of land for $498.33. Two subsequent deeds also state that Weaver paid Kiff for real estate. The facts that Kiff and Weaver were engaged in an intimate relationship and that single women in nineteenth-century Hertford County had little ability to accrue large sums of money suggest that an actual exchange of money between Kiff and Weaver was very unlikely. But Kiff knew that a deed of sale was much stronger than a deed of gift, the method often chosen to exchange property through relatives. He likely chose a deed of sale because creditors and other parties could challenge deeds of gift.[34]

Other partners and fathers used deeds of sale to transfer land to their families. Soon after the birth of his last child, James Norfleet Holloman deeded his partner, Mary Jane Chavis, a tract of land adjoining his other properties. The deed of sale states that Mary Jane Chavis paid Holloman $200. Almost twenty years later, Holloman transferred the cemetery lot where the family had recently buried Mary Jane Chavis to his son, Clarence Chavis. The deed for this land transfer implied that Clarence Chavis paid his father for the small cemetery plot. Richard W. Knight used similar tactics to grant land to his daughter, Mattie J. Chavis. In 1906, shortly before his death, Knight transferred a lot in the town of Union to his daughter under the supposition that Mattie J. Chavis paid him $130 for the property.[35] None of these men used the more contestable deeds of gift to transfer property to their families. As long-time buyers and sellers of land, they were cognizant of the possible implications of one type of land transfer over another. In the cases of Kiff, Holloman, and Knight, the historical record clearly demonstrates that all of these men knew one another and operated within some of the same social circles. Similarities in the methods used by white men to convey real estate to their non-white families suggest that these men may have shared strategies for the secure transfer of property.

Free women of mixed ancestry and their white partners worked with ingenuity to create environments for their families to thrive despite living in a state that denied their partnerships and children legal recognition. The material circumstances of the women of mixed ancestry involved in long-term partnerships with white men improved drastically over their lives. All of the women in this article grew up poor, but by the time of their deaths most owned their own homes and sometimes additional properties. At her death in 1914, Louisiana Weaver was one of the wealthiest women of color in her locality. Weaver owned several tracts of land and in her will bequeathed $100 in gold to each of her five sons. The children of these women enjoyed much more comfortable lives than their mothers experienced in their early years. Most of the children of these couples married, established families, owned property, and generally enjoyed financial success. Some of the children and grandchildren of these couples intermarried and others married the children of other successful families.[36] Although the law discouraged or prevented women of mixed ancestry from marrying their white partners, these women clearly demonstrated that inconsistencies in the law could be exploited to their benefit and that of their children.

These conclusions should not imply that free women of mixed ancestry built long-term partnerships with white men only for financial gain. While the historical record has a difficult time revealing love between human beings, the examples cited in this paper reveal that at least in some situations, relationships between free women of mixed ancestry and white men were bound together by mutual respect. Furthermore, some neighbors and friends recognized the bonds between free women of mixed ancestry, white men, and their children, and went to great lengths to respect those bonds even when the law granted those bonds no such respect.

Peggy Pascoe's work has shown that communities[35] continued to debate the extent to which these laws should be enforced against white men even as lawmakers and judges attempted to strengthen white supremacy through tougher enforcement of laws banning relationships between whites and non-whites. Scholars have demonstrated that stronger enforcement of marriage restrictions and the proliferation of extralegal activities to punish and discourage sex between whites and non-whites came about during and after the Civil War. However, Pascoe noted that lawmakers and judges sought to target with increased persecution a particular type of relationship, those between white women and non-white men. She argues that not until the 1890s did the desire to uphold white supremacy make officials, judges, and juries more likely to subject white men "to the full range of the disabilities of miscegenation law." Even past this

period up to the *Loving v. Virginia* decision, which found state miscegenation laws unconstitutional, the rights of white men continued to threaten the full enforcement of marriage and cohabitation restrictions.[37] The examples in this article show that even into the first decade of the twentieth century, the white power structure in Hertford County, at least in some cases, decided to uphold the rights of white men to choose their partners over widespread demands to prosecute white-non-white relationships.

The relationships discussed in this article reveal the limitations of race as a method to stratify society. Many people in the nineteenth century argued that the separation of races was a product of nature or even divine provenance. However, long-term partnerships between free women of mixed ancestry and white men demonstrate that such arguments were more political in nature than grounded in biological science or biblical scripture. The relationships in this study suggest that had such faulty argumentation not dominated nineteenth-century law and society, many mixed couples would have sought legal recognition. Their determination to build strong families, secure property rights, and uphold a public image of respectability supports the supposition that given the choice, they would have selected marriage. Free women of mixed ancestry and their white partners did not want to live on the edge of society; they simply hoped—and strived—to define their own relationships and build their own families.

ENDNOTES

I completed the research for this article with support from the Center for the Study of the American South and North Caroliniana Society. I would like to thank Kathleen DuVal, Susannah Loumiet, and the two anonymous reviewers for the *Journal of Social History* for their thoughtful comments and suggestions. Participants at the Thinking Gender Conference at UCLA and Virginia Tech's Bertoti Conference also provided valuable feedback on earlier versions of this article. I would also like to acknowledge the staffs of the State Archives of North Carolina, the Moorland-Spingarn

Center, and the Southern Historical Collection for helping me procure primary source materials. Finally, I would like to express my gratitude to the descendants of the families discussed in this article for their friendship and support. Address correspondence via email: wemilteer@hotmail.com.

1. "Women of mixed ancestry" in this context refers to women with various combinations of European, Native American, and African ancestry. Throughout the nineteenth century, Hertford County residents drew important distinctions between slaves and their descendants, who locals generally categorized as black, and free people of color, most who usually fell under the mulatto category. In nineteenth-century North Carolina, the term *mulatto* was not used exclusively to refer to people of African descent. People descended from native peoples and Europeans also fell under the mulatto category. "Women of mixed ancestry" reinforces this ambiguity. See William D. Valentine Diary, Volume 12, 164–65, Southern Historical Collection (hereafter SHC); *State v. William Chavers* (Dec. 1857), Supreme Court Cases, State Archives of North Carolina (hereafter SANC).

2. William D. Valentine Diary, Volume 13, 85, South Historical Collection.

3. E. Franklin Frazier Papers Box 131–92, Folder 7; Manuscript Division, Moorland-Spingarn Research Center, Howard University (hereafter EFFP Box 131–92, Folder 7, MDMSRCHU).

4. EFFP Box 131–92, Folder 7, MDMSRCHU.

5. For further discussion of the contrast between concubinage and long-term relationships between free women of color and white men, see Kenneth Aslakson, "The 'Quadroon-Plaçage' Myth of Antebellum New Orleans: Anglo-American (Mis)interpretations of French-Caribbean Phenomenon," *Journal of Social History* 3 (2012): 709–34.

6. *Guide to Research Materials in the North Carolina State Archives: County Records* (Raleigh, 2002), 177. For further discussion of marriage as a public institution, see Nancy Cott, *Public Vows: A History of Marriage and the Nation* (Cambridge, 2000).

7. Peggy Pascoe, *What Comes Naturally: Miscegenation Law and the Making of Race in America* (New York, 2009), 42–43.

8. Walter Clark, ed., *The State Records of North Carolina*, vol. 23 (Goldsboro, 1904), 65, 160. For further discussion of the impacts of these laws in colonial North Carolina, see Kirsten Fischer, *Suspect Relations: Sex, Race, and Resistance in Colonial North Carolina* (Ithaca, 2002).

9. *Acts Passed By the General Assembly of the State of North Carolina at the Session of 1830–1831* (Raleigh, 1831), 9–10.

10. *Amendments to the Constitution of North Carolina, Proposed by the Constitutional Convention of 1875 and the Constitution As It Will Read As Proposed to Be Amended* (Raleigh, 1875), 65.

11. For general studies of mixed marriages in the United States, see Gary B. Nash, *Forbidden Love: The Secret History of Mixed-Race America* (New York, 1999); Peter Wallenstein, *Tell the Court I Love My Wife: Race, Marriage, and Law—An American History* (New York, 2002). For further discussion of relations between enslaved women and white men see Deborah Gray White, *Ar'n't I a Woman: Female Slaves in the Plantation South* (New York, 1985); Kent Anderson Leslie, *Woman of Color, Daughter of Privilege: Amanda America Dickson 1849–1893* (Athens, 1995); Jean Fagan Yellin, *Harriet Jacobs: A Life* (New York, 2004); Annette Gordon-Reed, *The Hemingses of Monticello: An American Family* (New York, 2008). For further discussion of relations between free women of color and white men, see Adele Logan Alexander, *Ambiguous Lives: Free Women of Color in Rural Georgia, 1789–1879* (Fayetteville, 1991); Victoria E. Bynum, *Unruly Women: The Politics of Social and Sexual Control in the Old South* (Chapel Hill, 1992); Joan Martin, "Plaçage and the Louisiana Gens de Couleur Libre: How Race and Sex Defined the Lifestyles of Free Women of Color" in *Creole: The History and Legacy of Louisiana's Free People of Color*, ed. Sybil Kein (Baton Rouge, 2000); Joshua D. Rothman, *Notorious in the Neighborhood: Sex and Families across the Color Line in Virginia, 1787–1861* (Chapel Hill, 2003); Amrita Chakrabarti Myers, *Forging Freedom: Black Women and the Pursuit of Liberty in Antebellum Charleston* (Chapel Hill, 2011).

12. Richard R. Weaver Pension File, National Archives and Records Administration; Hertford County County Court Minutes, Volume 1, May 1832, SANC; Letter J. A. Anderson to Chesson and Armstead, John B. Chesson Papers, Box 1, Chesson Papers Miscellaneous, SANC; William D. Valentine Diary, Volume 13, 188, SHC; State v. Emmy Chavers, Hertford County Civil and Criminal Action Papers, Box 1, Civil and Criminal Cases 1864, SANC; Death Certificate of Susan Chavis, SANC.

13. EFFP Box 131–92, Folder 7, MDMSRCHU. The context of Calvin Scott Brown's statement appears to suggest that the term "nigger" may have referred specifically to people recognized in the community as "black" and would not have included "mulattoes" or people recognized as being of mixed ancestry.

14. Mavis Christine Campbell, *The Dynamics of Change in a Slave Society: A Sociopolitical History of the Free Coloreds of Jamaica, 1800–1865* (London, 1976), 51; David Brion Davis, *Inhuman Bondage: The Rise and Fall of Slavery in the New World* (New York, 2006), 180.

15. Benjamin B. Winborne, *The Colonial and State Political History of Hertford County* (Raleigh, 1906), 235, 333.

16. Hertford County County Court Minutes, Volume 3, March 1854, SANC; 1850 United States Federal Census,

Hertford County, North Carolina, Northern District, 291a, 309a; EFFP Box 131–92, Folder 7, MDMSRCHU. The 1850 Census lists two men named William Futrell living in the same Hertford County household. Which of these men was involved in the case with Frusa Reid is unclear.

17. Hertford County Record of Deeds, Volume A, 653, SANC.

18. EFFP Box 131–92, Folder 7, MDMSRCHU. The 1870 Census confirms the proximity between Louisiana Weaver's house and James Kiff's place as described by Jesse Rob Weaver. See 1870 United States Federal Census, Hertford County, North Carolina, Winton Township, 54.

19. EFFP Box 131–92, Folder 7, MDMSRCHU.

20. EFFP Box 131–92, Folder 7, MDMSRCHU.

21. EFFP Box 131–92, Folder 7, MDMSRCHU.

22. EFFP Box 131–92, Folder 7, MDMSRCHU.

23. Hertford County Estates Records, Box 13, Ezell, Wiley, SANC.

24. EFFP Box 131–92, Folder 7, MDMSRCHU.

25. Hertford County Estates Records, Box 13, Ezell, Wiley, SANC.

26. EFFP Box 131–92, Folder 7, MDMSRCHU.

27. For further discussion of the way lawmakers attempted to define family through marriage laws, see Cott, *Public Vows*, 24–55.

28. Will of Noah Cotton 1815, John Vann Papers, Box 4, SANC; Estate of Noah Cotton, John Vann Papers, Box 3, SANC.

29. Hertford County Record of Wills, Volume C, 222, SANC.

30. Hertford County Estates Records, Box 13, Ezell, Wiley, SANC.

31. Hertford County Estates Records, Box 40, Shields, Richard H., SANC.

32. EFFP Box 131–92, Folder 7, MDMSRCHU.

33. North Carolina Supreme Court ruled that Samuel Weaver was entitled to his father's notes after the settlement of all of James Kiff's debts. See *William Kiff Admr. v. Samuel Weaver et al.* 94 NC 274 (Feb 1886), Supreme Court Cases, SANC.

34. Hertford County Record of Deeds, Volume B, 50–51, SANC; Hertford County Record of Deeds, Volume F, 548–549, SANC; Hertford County Record of Deeds, Volume H, 196–97, SANC.

35. Hertford County Record of Deeds, Volume V, 172–73, SANC; Hertford County Record of Deeds, Volume 50, 172, SANC; Hertford County Record of Deeds, Volume 32, 88, SANC.

36. Hertford County Record of Wills, Volume D, 324–26, SANC. Examples of intermarriages between families include the marriage of Louisiana Weaver's and James Kiff's son to Sallie Yeates Bizzell's and R. H. Shield's daughter and the marriage between Mary Jane Chavis's and J. N. Holloman's son, to Sallie Yeates Bizzell's and R. H. Shield's granddaughter. See Hertford County Marriage Register and Hertford County Marriage Licenses in the State Archives of North Carolina for further examples.

37. Pascoe, *What Comes Naturally*, 10–11. For further discussion of changes in the regulation of relationships between white and non-whites after the Civil War, see Martha Hodes, *White Women, Black Men: Illicit Sex in the Nineteenth-Century South* (New Haven, 1997).

Reading Questions

1. Milteer acknowledges a number of difficulties that attend the kind of historical research presented in the article. What are they?

2. According to Milteer, what is a likely financial justification for mixed free women choosing to develop long-term relationships with white men? What evidence does he provide for this?

3. What, according to Milteer, seems to be the role of love in mate selection for the mixed free women he discusses in the article?

4. Why were certain white men unlikely to face legal or social scrutiny for developing relationships with mixed free women?

5. Why were promissory notes "a safer method for white men to pass on wealth to their partners and children" (par. 29)? What, according to Milteer, was the most secure way to transfer property to partners and children?

Rhetoric Questions

6. What is the primary form of evidence that Milteer uses to support his conclusions?

7. The article's introduction includes testimony from a number of individuals. What is the effect of the use of personal testimony on you as a reader?

8. Milteer spends a great deal of time interpreting historical documents and records as part of his argument. Did you find any of his interpretations particularly strong? Weak? Explain why.

Response and Research Questions

9. Milteer writes, "Lawmakers sought to define the family as a racially uniform unit by prohibiting marriage across the color line, but people on the ground, at least occasionally, rejected this notion" (23). Do you see evidence of individuals rejecting lawmakers' definitions of marriage or family in society today? Explain.

10. What does Milteer mean when he writes, "The relationships discussed in this article reveal the limitations of race as a method to stratify society" (36)? In what ways does Milteer's article reveal these limitations?

ACADEMIC CASE STUDY • PERSPECTIVES ON LOVE   SOCIAL SCIENCES

Women and Men in Love: Who Really Feels It and Says It First?

MARISSA A. HARRISON AND JENNIFER C. SHORTALL

Marissa A. Harrison is currently an associate professor of psychology at Pennsylvania State University. She has published multiple articles on topics concerning human behavior, including sexuality. "Women and Men in Love: Who Really Feels It and Says It First?" was written with co-author Jennifer C. Shortall, a graduate student at Duquesne University at the time of the article's 2011 publication in the *Journal of Social Psychology*. The article explores attitudes toward love and romance among men and women, concluding that "women may not be the greater 'fools for love' that society assumes."

ABSTRACT

A widely held belief exists that women are more romantic and tend to fall in love faster than men. Responses from 172 college students indicated that although both men and women believe that women will fall in love and say "I love you" first in a relationship, men reported falling in love earlier and expressing it earlier than women reported. Analyses also showed no sex differences in attitudinal responses to items about love and romance. These results indicate that women may not be the greater "fools for love" that society assumes and are consistent with the notion that a pragmatic and cautious view of love has adaptive significance for women.

Love has been called "the deepest and most meaningful of sentiments" (Rubin, 1970), although what constitutes "love" can have a myriad of meanings, ranging from concepts involving an initial state of attraction, to falling in love, to being/staying in love (Aron et al.,

2008). Yet even though it is difficult to define *falling in love*, and the consideration of such may not ever rise entirely above subjectivity (Hendrick & Hendrick, 1986; Sternberg & Weis, 2006), researchers have commented that almost everyone can relate to being or falling in love (Esch & Stefano, 2005; Stefano & Esch, 2007).

How love is expressed and experienced may differ between women and men. With respect to the expression of love, surprisingly little research has focused on the locution "I love you," even though these three small words appear to be a critical delineation in relationships (Owen, 1987), as such expressions of affection are thought to be decisive moments for the advancement of romantic relationships (Baxter & Braithewaite, 2008). Researchers have indicated that cross-culturally, females tend to use the locution "I love you" more than males (Wilkins & Gareis, 2006). This is not surprising, since evidence suggests that women and men differ in their expression of emotions and in their descriptions of related cognitions (Barbara, 2008). Women tend to be more expressive in relationships, and women are *expected* by others to be more expressive (Rubin, 1970; Hess, Adams, & Kleck, 2007), particularly in instances of romantic love (Durik et al., 2006). Interestingly, women appear to enjoy a neurological advantage in terms of processing multisensory, emotional experiences (Collignon et al., 2010); this is likely one reason why women are faster at perceiving others' emotions (Hampson, van Anders, & Mullin, 2006) and have more confidence than do men when expressing affection, liking, and love to the opposite sex (Blier & Blier-Wilson, 1989). In contrast, due to their "inexpressiveness and restrictive emotionality" (Blier & Blier-Wilson, 1989, p. 287) men may experience intimacy, parenting, and relationship problems (Dosser, 1982; Balswick, 1988).

Despite men's purported emotional restriction, however, a few older studies have shown that men report saying "I love you" first in a relationship (Owen, 1987; Brantley, Knox, & Zusman, 2002). Owen (1987) posited that this transpires because men are socialized to take the initiative in relationships, and

that this verbal declaration may prompt women to reciprocate this iteration and commit prematurely to a relationship. Brantley, Knox, and Zusman (2002) interpreted this through an evolutionary lens, positing that men use this locution first in a relationship as an inroad to sexual access. In support of Brantley and colleagues' theory, Tucker, Marvin, and Vivian (1991) noted that women listed their partners' expressions of "I love you" in their top 10 romantic acts, but men did not. If men possess knowledge that women find "I love you" to be romantic, men may communicate what their partners want to hear so as to advance a relationship sexually and/or emotionally. This makes sense evolutionarily, as women in our ancestral environment, who have few gametes compared to men, would have benefitted from pair-bond assurance more than would males (Symons, 1979) and saying "I love you" appears to communicate a commitment. Moreover, men place a greater premium on sex than women do (Buss, 2004, 2006), and this is theorized to be the case because of the reproductive advantage that sex with multiple women confers to men, who have a virtually unlimited supply of sperm. Thus, any strategy serving as the means to a sexual end would be beneficial to men, including declarations of love. With this in mind, then, one might wonder if the public's perception of women as the more romantic sex (Hatfield & Walster, 1978; Hyde & Delamater, 2009) might simply be due to the fact that men report being and are perceived as more sexual than are women, and are therefore viewed as *less* romantic.

It should be noted, however, that men may have a 5 different sexual attitude toward long-term, committed partners than they do toward short-term, sex-only partners. Evidence shows that men and women report similar preferences for a long-term partner who is kind, intelligent, and understanding, and one who loves them in return (Buss, 2007).

In terms of romance, a widely held stereotype in our society contends that women are more romantic than are men, although older data from college students show men to have a greater number of romantic attitudes than women do (Knox & Sporakowski, 1968). Further, researchers have reported that men fall in love earlier than do women (Kanin, Davidson, & Schreck, 1970; Rubin, Peplau, & Hill, 2004). Even adolescent boys seem to fall in love earlier than do adolescent girls (Montgomery & Sorrell, 1998), and these individuals are at an age when passionate love is thought to be more intense (Hatfield & Sprecher, 1986). Although at what age we fall in love for the first time has been the topic of scientific scrutiny (e.g., Montgomery & Sorrell, 1998; Reagan, Durvasula, Howell, Ureno, & Rea, 2004), the exact *time frame* of falling in love (e.g., hours, days, weeks, months into a relationship) is difficult to study empirically because of the retrospective nature of the question. Perhaps this is why this not been extensively explored in previous studies.

Much of the seminal research of "love" was conducted more than a generation ago (e.g., 1960s, 1970s). The present study used a contemporary sample of college students in an attempt to determine if there has been a social change in this phenomenon. Our study attempts to replicate, integrate, and extend upon previous work on which sex falls in love first, when they fall in love, and who says, "I love you" first. This study also sought to examine if women's perceptions of love and romance are really that different from men's perceptions by asking questions about these phenomena, thus attempting to dispel the popular notion that women are hopeless romantics and support the notion that women are careful, comparison shoppers in terms of relationships.

METHOD

All procedures were approved by the local Institutional Review Board. A 28-item Internet-based instrument was created to assess similarities and differences between men's and women's attitudes, expectations, and experiences with respect to love and relationships. As researchers have reported that first- and second-year college students have an expected high incidence of falling in love (Aron, Paris, & Aron, 1995), the choice of a college sample was appropriate for the purposes of this study. We attempted to obtain a diverse sample by recruiting participants from the

subject pool of a mid-sized university and by recruiting volunteer respondents from a large community college in a major metropolitan city in the northeastern United States. Of the 188 participants who responded to the questionnaire, 10 did not indicate their sex and were excluded from analysis. Although of interest, the sample of homosexual and bisexual respondents was not large enough for analysis, and therefore the data from seven individuals (6 men and 1 woman) who reported preferring to date and have sex with men and women equally, mostly the same sex, or only the same sex were excluded from the analysis to control for error variance. The resulting sample of 171 heterosexual individuals consisted of 72 men and 99 women with a mean age of 20.28 (SD = 5.25). Ethnicities reported were: 77.1% White, 13.0% Asian, 5.3% Black, 3.5% Hispanic, and 1.1% Other.

RESULTS

Analyses revealed that 61 men (84.72%) and 88 (90.90%) women reported they had been involved in a committed, romantic relationship at some point in their lives, with no sex difference, $X^2(1, N = 171)$ = 1.54, p > .214, N.S. Additionally, 27 men (38.02%) and 56 women (56.57%) reported that they were *currently* involved in a committed, romantic relationship and this sex difference was significant, $X^2(1, N = 170)$ = 5.69, p < .017. Of people who were currently in relationships, most men (91.30%) and women (98.21%) reported being "in love" with their partner, with no sex difference in frequency, $X^2(1, N = 76)$ = 2.13, p > .144.

As this study was interested in relationship dynam- 10 ics, only responses from those with previous relationship experience were included in subsequent analyses. Participants were asked, "In your most recent romantic relationship, how long did it take you to realize you were in love?" Answer choices were: 1 = "*I am not in love,*" 2 = "*Immediately,*" 3 = "*A few days,*" 4 = "*A few weeks,*" 5 = "*A few months,*" 6 = "*A year,*" and 7 = "*More than a year.*" Men (M = 4.47, SD = 1.23) reported falling in love more quickly than women (M = 5.01, SD = .99) reported falling in love, $t(127)$ = 2.74,

$p < .007$, $d = .48$. In addition, in response to the question, "In your most recent committed, romantic relationship, who said 'I love you' FIRST?" only 12.10% reported that neither partner did. Among those for whom this was expressed, there was a relationship to sex, with 64% of men compared to 18.51% of women reporting they said "I love you" to their partners first, $X^2(1, N = 131) = 27.80$, $p < .000$.

Participants were also asked, "Who falls in love first in a relationship, a man or a woman?" Interestingly, 87.78% of participants believed that a woman falls in love first in a relationship, $X^2(1, N = 131) = 74.82$, $p < .000$, and this response was unrelated to sex, $X^2(1, N = 131) = .939$, $p > .332$. Participants were further asked, "Do you think a man or a woman is more likely to say 'I love you' first in a relationship?" Results showed that 75.20% of participants believed that a woman is more likely to express this sentiment first, $X^2(1, N = 125) = 31.75$, $p < .000$, and there was no relationship to sex, $X^2(1, N = 125) = 2.04$, $p > .153$.

Participants were asked, "About how far into a relationship would you be able to tell you were in love?" and "About how far into a relationship would you be able to tell your partner was in love?" Answer choices were presented on a Likert-type scale: 1 = "Immediately"; 2 = "A few days"; 3 = "A few weeks"; 4 = "A few months"; 5 = "A year"; and 6 = "More than a year." Women anticipated knowing they were in love with a partner ($M = 4.00$, $SD = .67$) later than men anticipated knowing they were in love ($M = 3.62$, $SD = 1.14$), $t(148) = 2.54$, $p < .012$, $d = .41$, and women anticipated being able to tell their partner was in love with them later ($M = 4.09$, $SD = .80$) than men anticipated being able to tell ($M = 3.70$, $SD = .99$), $t(147) = 2.63$, $p < .009$, $d = .43$. However, both sexes reported anticipating they would know they were in love with a partner the same time they knew their partners were in love with them [women: $t(87) = 1.82$, $p = .072$; men: $t(60) = .820$, $p = .416$]. Participants were also asked, "How far into a committed, romantic relationship would you want to have sex with a partner?" The same scale reported above was used for responses. Women reported a desire to wait longer

to have sex ($M = 3.83$, $SD = 1.14$) than men reported ($M = 3.42$, $SD = 1.18$), $t(147) = 2.15$, $p < .034$, $d = .35$ Additional analyses showed that men's responses indicated that they anticipated wanting to have sex at the same time they would know they were in love, $t(59) = 1.01$, $p < .318$, and that their partners were in love, $t(59) = 1.61$, $p < .112$. Women's responses indicated they also anticipated wanting to have sex at the same time they would know they were in love, $t(87) = 1.39$, $p < .167$, and their responses indicated they would want to have sex before knowing their partners were in love, $t(86) = 2.19$, $p < .031$, but a Bonferroni correction to alpha for multiple comparisons renders this result non-significant.

Participants were then presented with a series of statements about love, dating, romance, sex, and physical attraction, and were asked to report on a scale the degree to which they agreed with each statement, with again, 1 = "Totally disagree"; 2 = "Slightly disagree"; 3 = "Neither agree nor disagree"; 4 = "Slightly agree"; and 5 = "Totally agree." When employing a Bonferroni correction to alpha for multiple comparisons, there were no sex differences in responses to any questions about love and romance. Results are presented in Table 1.

DISCUSSION

In our contemporary college sample, nearly 9 out of 10 people who have had relationship experience expressed that it is likely a woman who will fall in love first in a relationship. Further, 7 out of 10 people believed that a woman will say "I love you" first. However, our data showed that men reported falling in love sooner and that three times as many men as women said "I love you" first to their partners. These results show no change from those in older studies (e.g., Dion & Dion, 1973) in that men report falling in love and saying it first. This suggests that women tend to be more pragmatic about love than society tends to believe, i.e., not rushing fool-heartedly into a relationship. The emergence of the locution "I love you" in relationship vocabulary is important, as emotional narration can offer a window into the speaker's

Table 1
Men's and Women's Responses to Items about Love and Romance

Item	Men (*n* = 72) M (SD)	Women (*n* = 100) M (SD)	*t(df)*	*p*
Romantic love is a biological trick to get you to reproduce.	2.53 (1.32)	2.04 (1.07)	2.69 (170)	.008
You really need to get to know someone's personality before you can be in love with them.	4.32 (.80)	4.57 (.66)	2.20 (169)	.029
Love at first sight exists.	3.08 (1.20)	3.08 (1.20)	.015 (167)	.988
Love is a waste of time.	1.85 (1.10)	1.39 (.82)	3.10 (169)	.029
My being in love is important to me.	3.76 (1.04)	3.89 (1.14)	.758 (169)	.450
Physical attraction fades over time.	2.90 (1.20)	2.61 (1.08)	1.67 (170)	.096
Being in love fades over time.	2.46 (1.17)	2.32 (1.10)	.791 (170)	.430
I am a fool for love.	2.86 (1.25)	3.20 (1.28)	1.74 (169)	.084
I become more and more in love with the person I am attracted to.	3.88 (.96)	3.98 (.91)	.73 (170)	.467
I become more and more physically attracted to the person I love.	4.08 (1.12)	4.31 (.84)	1.47 (167)	.143

Notes. No differences were significant after employing a Bonferroni correction to alpha for multiple comparisons. Answers were given on a 5-point Likert-type scale where 1 = "*Totally disagree*"; 2 = "*Slightly disagree*"; 3 = "*Neither agree nor disagree*"; 4 = "*Slightly agree*"; and 5 = "*Totally agree.*"

affective state (Barbara, 2008). It can be argued that men's falling in love and exclaiming this love first may be explained as a byproduct of men equating love with sexual desire, as evidence suggests that men are more interested in sex than are women (see Buss, 2006). However, researchers have proposed that passionate love and sexual desire are distinctly different mechanisms (see Reis & Aron, 2008), and our data showed that men and women showed equivocal agreement that they become increasingly physically attracted to someone with whom they are in love, indicating an understanding of the difference. Again, evidence does suggest that people in North American culture (from which our sample was obtained) can relate to what it means to fall in love (Aron et al., 2008).

Our results indicated that when asked to speculate, women reported anticipating they would know they were in love with a partner in about a few months and that they would also know the feeling was mutual within a few months. This was significantly later than the timeline indicated by men, who reported anticipating knowing they were in love and knowing their partner's mutual feelings in about a few weeks to a few months. These findings are novel and provide support that women do not rush into a romance before men do. Additionally, neither sex indicated an expected temporal difference between realizing one's own and one's partner's feelings. This further indicates that women are not hopeless romantics engulfed in unrequited or unsure love any more or less than are men.

Most men and women in our study reported being involved in a committed relationship before, and almost all who were in romantic relationships at the time of participation reported being in love with their partners. As in previous research, men's reports of when they fell in love with their partners indicated that they did so sooner than women's reports indicated they did. However, unlike previous studies, our data highlighted a timeline, whereby men reported falling in love with their most recent, committed partner in about a few weeks to a few months, and women reported falling in love in about a few months. These findings corroborate our data, as mentioned above, that show men are more likely than women to say "I love you" first to their partners.

Not surprisingly, women in our study reported a preference to engage in first sex later in a new relationship (a few months into it) than men's reported preference (a few weeks to a few months into it), but both sexes reported a desire to have sex at the same time they were certain of their own and their partner's feelings. This suggests that women, relative to men, are making more careful assessments of their partners before committing sexually and emotionally to a relationship.

Interestingly, other than the above, our data indicated no significant differences between the sexes, revealing that women's general viewpoints (including cynical beliefs, e.g., "Love is a waste of time") about love, dating, and romance are not different than those of men. These data reveal a trend for women which apparently goes against the popular belief that women are more romantic and idealistic about love than are men. There were no sex differences in agreement to statements such as "Love at first sight exists," "My being in love is important to me," "Physical attraction fades over time," "Being in love fades over time," and "I am a fool for love." These data show that women are *not* greater fools for love than are men as is the common societal stereotype, and are not, as Heiss (2005) reported, "handicapped in the competition" (p. 575). In fact, these data arguably show that both sexes are equally as pragmatic and as foolish about love.

It is curious why the belief that women are fools for love persists, as the notion that women should logically and realistically view love and commitment follows evolutionary theory that women need to be discriminative in their mate choices due to their relatively limited reproductive capabilities (Symons, 1979). That is, it is reproductively advantageous for a woman to be tentative and not simply jump into a sexual or romantic relationship until she is sure of her partner's intent to commit, as this would have assured resources and protection in the ancestral environment which was likely not very female-friendly.

Still, alternative explanations may exist for such [20] beliefs and therefore our findings. Who says what to whom and at what time in a relationship may simply be learned from others as appropriate or inappropriate. Personal perceptions and cognitions of sex roles likely lead men and women to behave in love relationships as they feel they are expected to behave. For example, it may be part of a man's gender schema (Bem, 1981) to be the one to facilitate the solidification of a relationship by stating "I love you" first. Likewise, it may be enmeshed in a woman's gender schema to wait for the man in a relationship to make such a move first. Societal expectations may dictate and place pressure upon men and women to act accordingly as well, likely beginning very early in life, and messages on how men and women "typically" behave as their respective genders are presented though the family, school, friends, and media (for discussion, see Macionis, 2004, p. 250). As beliefs can be culturally transmitted, however, they can create selection pressures for behavioral adaptations (Confer et al., 2010). With respect to interpreting the findings of the present study through an evolutionary framework, perhaps it is men who expressed love to their partners first that left more descendants than men who did not, and likewise, perhaps it is women who waited for men to make the first move left more descendants. It seems plausible that both evolutionary and cultural theory can come into play when interpreting the results presented herein.

There are admitted limitations to the present study. First, participants' responses, as is the case with any self-report research, may reflect inaccuracies due to social desirability, difficulties with estimates, and problems with retrospective judgments (Hyde & DeLamater, 2009). Future studies might involve longitudinal assessments of individuals who have recently become romantically involved, recording progression of love experiences and expressions. For example, a diary study would allow fairly accurate determination of the time frame and expression of love feelings. In addition, the love and romance experiences of college men and women from the northeastern United States may not represent the psychology of men and women in all cultures. As such, additional research may wish to replicate these findings in other countries.

In conclusion, our data show that women tend to be more cautious about love and the expression thereof than what is commonly believed. Perhaps women are perceived as less rational about love compared to men because women have a greater capacity for processing emotional experiences (Collignon et al., 2010) and have a more emotionally expressive nature than do men (Rubin, 1970; Hess, Adams, & Kleck, 2007; Barbara, 2008). If this is the case, then the stereotype of women as hopeless romantics compared to men will likely persist even in the face of scientific evidence to the contrary.

REFERENCES

Aron, A., Fisher, H., Strong, G., Acevedo, B., Riela, S., & Tsapelas, I. (2008). Falling in love. In S. Sprecher, A. Wenzel, & J. Harvey (Eds.), *Handbook of relationship initiation* (pp. 315–336). New York, NY: Psychology Press.

Aron, A., Paris, M., & Aron, E. (1995). Falling in love: Prospective studies of self-concept change. *Journal of Personality and Social Psychology, 69*, 1102–1112.

Balswick, J. (1988). *The inexpressive male*. Lexington, MA: Lexington Books.

Barbara, G. (2008). Gender differences in verbal expression of love schema. *Sex Roles, 58*, 814–821.

Baxter, L., & Braithewaite, D. (2008). *Engaging theories in interpersonal communication: Multiple perspectives*. Thousand Oaks, CA: Sage.

Bem, S. (1981). Gender schema theory: A cognitive account of sex typing. *Psychological Review, 88*, 354–364.

Blier, M., & Blier-Wilson, L. (1989). Gender differences in self-rated emotional expressiveness. *Sex Roles, 21*, 287–295.

Brantley, A., Knox, D., & Zusman, M. (2002). When and why gender differences in saying "I love you" among college students. *College Student Journal, 36*, 614–615.

Buss, D. (2004). *The evolution of desire*. New York, NY: Basic Books.

Buss, D. (2006). The evolution of love. In R. Sternberg & K. Weis (Eds.), *The new psychology of love* (pp. 65–86). New Haven, CT: Yale University Press.

Buss, D. (2007). The evolution of human mating. *Acta Psychologia Sinica, 39*, 502–512.

Collignon, O., Girard, S., Gosselin, F., Saint-Amour, D., Lepore, F., & Lassonde, M. (2010). Women process multisensory emotion expressions more efficiently than men. *Neuropsychologia, 48*, 220–214.

Confer, J., Easton, J., Fleischman, D., Goetz, C., Lewis, D., Perilloux, C., & Buss, D. (2010). Evolutionary psychology: Controversies, questions, prospects, and limitations. *American Psychologist, 65*, 110–126. doi: 10.1037/a0018413

Dion, K., & Dion, K. (1973). Correlates of romantic love. *Journal of Consulting and Clinical Psychology, 41*(1), 51–56.

Dosser, D. (1982). Male expressiveness behavioral intervention. In K. Solomon & M. Levy (Eds.), *Men in transition: Theory and therapy*. New York, NY: Plenum.

Durik, A., Hyde, J., Marks, A., Roy, A., Anaya, D., & Schultz, G. (2006). Ethnicity and gender stereotypes of emotion. *Sex Roles, 54*, 429–445.

Esch, T., & Stefano, G. (2005). The neurobiology of falling in love. *Neuroendocrinology Letters, 26*, 175–192.

Hampson, E., van Anders, S., & Mullin, L. (2006). A female advantage in the recognition of emotional facial expressions: Test of an evolutionary hypothesis. *Evolution and Human Behavior, 27*, 401–416.

Hatfield, E., & Sprecher, S. (1986). Measuring passionate love in intimate relationships. *Journal of Adolescence, 9*, 383–410.

Hatfield, E., & Walster, W. (1978). *A new look at love*. Lanham, MD: University Press of America.

Heiss, J. (2005). Gender and romantic love roles. *Sociological Quarterly, 32*, 575–591.

Hendrick, C., & Hendrick, S. (1986). A theory and method of love. *Journal of Personality and Social Psychology, 50*, 392–402.

Hess, U., Adams, R., & Kleck, R. (2007). When two do the same it might not mean the same: The perception of emotional expressions shown by men and women. In U. Hess & P. Phillipot (Eds.), *Group dynamics and emotional expression: Studies in emotion and social interaction, 2nd series* (pp. 33–50). New York, NY: Cambridge University Press.

Hyde, J., & DeLamater, J. (2009). *Understanding human sexuality* (10th ed.). New York, NY: McGraw-Hill.

Kanin, E., Davidson, K., & Schreck, S. (1970). A research note on male-female differentials in the experience of heterosexual love. *Journal of Sex Research, 6*, 64–72.

Knox, D., & Sporakowski, M. (1968). Attitudes of college students toward love. *Journal of Marriage and the Family, 30*, 638–642.

Macionis, J. (2004). *Society: The basics* (7th ed.). Upper Saddle River, NJ: Pearson Education.

Montgomery, M., & Sorrell, G. (1998). Love and dating experience in early and mid adolescence: Grade and gender comparisons. *Journal of Adolescence, 21*, 677–689.

Owen, W. (1987). The verbal expression of love by women and men as a critical communication event in personal relationships. *Women's Studies in Communication, 10*(1), 15–24.

Reagan, P. C., Durvasula, R., Howell, L., Ureno, O., & Rea, M. (2004). Gender, ethnicity, and the developmental timing of first sexual and romantic experiences. *Social Behavior and Personality, 32*, 667–676.

Reis, H., & Aron, A. (2008). Love: What is it, why does it matter, and how does it operate? *Perspectives on Psychological Science, 3*(1), 80–86.

Rubin, Z. (1970). Measurement of romantic love. *Journal of Personality and Social Psychology, 16*, 265–273.

Rubin, Z., Peplau, L., & Hill, C. (2004). Loving and leaving: Sex differences in romantic attachments. *Sex Roles, 7*, 821–835.

Stefano, G., & Esch, T. (2007). Love and stress. *Activitas Nervosa Superior, 49*(3–4), 112–113.

Sternberg, R., & Weis, K. (2006). *The new psychology of love.* New Haven, CT: Yale University Press.

Symons, D. (1979). *The evolution of human sexuality.* New York, NY: Oxford University Press.

Tucker, R., Marvin, M., & Vivian, B. (1991). What constitutes a romantic act? An empirical study. *Psychological Reports, 69*, 651–654.

Wilkins, R., & Gareis, E. (2006). Emotional expression and the locution "I love you": A cross-cultural study. *International Journal of Intercultural Relations, 30*, 51–75.

Reading Questions

1. The researchers note that "a few older studies have shown that men report saying 'I love you' first in a relationship" (par. 4). Based on the authors' review of scholarship, what are two possible reasons for this?

2. The researchers outline at least three main areas of inquiry for their study. What are these areas?

3. The researchers report excluding data from analysis from a number of their respondents. Why were these particular individuals excluded from the study?

4. Based on the researchers' findings, who reported falling in love more quickly, men or women? Who tended to believe that women would fall in love first in a relationship?

5. What evidence does the research provide to support the idea that "women do not rush into a romance before men do" (15)?

Rhetoric Questions

6. What does the table on page 352 ("Men's and Women's Responses to Items about Love and Romance") add to the study's effectiveness?

7. Read the study's concluding paragraph again. How would you assess the researchers' tone and attitude in this moment? What is the effect of that tone on you as a reader?

Response and Research Questions

8. The researchers note the limitations associated with using self-reported data in their research. Do you see any additional limitations in their study?

9. As they suggest, the researchers' work assumes that people tend to believe that women are more romantic and less cautious about falling in love. Do you agree or disagree with this notion? Why?

10. Do you find the study's results at all surprising? Why or why not? What might your answer reveal about some of your own beliefs and attitudes?

Hormonal Changes When Falling in Love

DONATELLA MARAZZITI AND DOMENICO CANALE

Donatella Marazziti is a professor of psychiatry and the director of the laboratory of psychopharmacology at the University of Pisa, Italy. She has researched and published widely on the subjects of love and biochemistry, and she is author of the best seller *The Nature of Love* (2002), among other scholarly texts. In this study, co-written with Domenico Canale, the researchers examine hormone changes in individuals who have recently fallen in love. They conclude that the hormone changes identified are "reversible, state-dependent, and probably related to some physical and/or psychological features typically associated with falling in love." The study was published in the journal *Psychoneuroendocrinology* in 2004.

SUMMARY

To fall in love is the first step in pair formation in humans and is a complex process which only recently has become the object of neuroscientific investigation. The little information available in this field prompted us to measure the levels of some pituitary, adrenal, and gonadal hormones in a group of 24 subjects of both sexes who had recently (within the previous six months) fallen in love, and to compare them with those of 24 subjects who were single or were part of a long-lasting relationship. The following hormones were evaluated by means of standard techniques: FSH, LH, estradiol, progesterone, dehydroepiandrosterone sulphate (DHEAS), cortisol, testosterone, and androstenedione.

The results showed that estradiol, progesterone, DHEAS, and androstenedione levels did not differ between the groups and were within the normal ranges. Cortisol levels were significantly higher amongst those subjects who had recently fallen in love, as compared with those who had not. FSH and testosterone levels were lower in men in love, while women of the same group presented higher testosterone levels. All hormonal differences were eliminated when the subjects were re-tested from 12 to 24 months later. The increased cortisol and low FSH levels are suggestive of the "stressful" and arousing conditions associated with the initiation of a social contact. The changes of testosterone concentrations, which varied in opposite directions in the two sexes, may reflect changes in behavioral and/or temperamental traits which have yet to be clarified. In conclusion, the findings of the present study would indicate that to fall in love provokes transient hormonal changes, some of which seem to be specific to each sex.

1. INTRODUCTION

The formation of pair bonding is relevant in several animal species, and particularly in mammals since, in some cases, it ensures not only that a new couple is formed which can thus generate offspring, but also that a safe and stable environment is set up wherein the newborn can receive sufficient care to enable them to mature and become capable of surviving alone (Bowlby, 1969; Kleiman, 1977; Carter et al., 1997a, 1997b).

The process of pair bonding in humans begins with the subjective experience of falling in love, which sometimes leads to the establishment of long-lasting relationships: for this reason, its function exceeds that of reproduction alone and, given its relevance to the survival of the species, it would not be surprising if it were regulated by precise and long-standing neural mechanisms (Uvnäs-Moberg, 1997, 1998; Carter, 1998). Indirect evidence of the biological process involved in falling in love is provided by cross-cultural studies which suggest that it is present in virtually all societies and is, perhaps, genetically determined (Jankoviak and Fischer, 1992). Furthermore, common features of this process can be identified in studies from all over the world and include: perception of an altered mental state, intrusive thoughts and images of the other, sets of behavioral patterns aimed at eliciting a reciprocal response, and a definite course and predictable outcome (Leckman and Mayes, 1999).

One of the first biological hypotheses with regard 5 to falling in love associates this state to increased levels of phenylethylamine, on the basis of the similarities between the chemical structure of this neurotransmitter and that of amphetamines which provoke mood changes resembling those typical of the initial stage of a romance; however, no empirical data have been gathered to support this theory (Liebowitz, 1983). The strong suggestion is that different mechanisms may be involved (Panksepp, 1982; Jankoviak, 1986; Hazan and Shaver, 1987; Fisher, 1992; Porges, 1998; Insel and Young, 1997), and it has been recently demonstrated that the intrusive thoughts of the early, romantic phase of falling in love are underlaid by a decreased functionality of the serotonin transporter (Marazziti et al., 1999).

The complexity of the process would seem, therefore, to be understood better when we consider falling in love as a basic emotion, such as anxiety or fear, due to the activation of the amygdala and related circuits and neurotransmitters (Bartels and Zeki, 2000; LeDoux, 2000). Consistent with this hypothesis is the observation that stress and threatening situations may facilitate the onset of new social bonds and intimate ties (Bowlby, 1973; Reite, 1985; Kraemer, 1992; Panksepp et al., 1994). The review of animal data is beyond the scope of this paper; however, it should perhaps be noted also that stress and corticosterone have been demonstrated to promote pair bonding formation in different species (DeVries et al., 1995, 1996; Hennessy, 1997; Levine et al., 1997; Mendoza and Mason, 1997). Furthermore, these elements induce the synthesis and release of neuropeptides, such as oxytocin, which are involved in the subsequent processes, including sexual and maternal behaviors and, more in general, positive social contacts, which reduce anxiety (McCarthy et al., 1992; Numan, 1994; Carter, 1998). The literature relevant to humans in this regard is meager, albeit in agreement with animal findings, and suggests that the activation of the hypothalamic-pituitary-adrenal (HPA) axis due to stressful experiences or, more in general, to arousal, may trigger the development of different kinds of social attachment, possibly also that which begins with falling in love (Milgram, 1986; Chiodera et al., 1991; Simpson and Rhole, 1994).

Given the paucity of data in this field and the unexplored questions regarding the possible role of gonadal hormones, our study aimed at evaluating the levels of some pituitary, adrenal, and gonadal hormones in a homogenous group of subjects of both sexes who were in the early, romantic phase of a loving relationship, and to compare them with those of subjects who were single or were already in a long-lasting relationship.

2. SUBJECTS AND METHODS

2.1. Subjects

Twenty-four subjects (12 male and 12 female, mean age ± SD: 27 ± 4 years) who declared that they had recently fallen in love were recruited from amongst residents (17) and medical students (7), by means of advertisement. They were selected according to the criteria already applied in a previous study (Marazziti et al., 1999), in particular: the relationship was required to have begun within the previous 6 months (mean ± SD: 3 ± 1 months) and at least four hours a day spent in thinking about the partner (mean ± SD: 9 ± 3 hours), as recorded by a specifically designed questionnaire.

Twenty-four subjects (12 female and 12 male, mean age ± SD: 29 ± 3), belonging to the same environment and with similar educational levels, with either a long-lasting (mean ± SD: 67 ± 28 months) or no relationship, served as the control group.

No subject had a family or personal history of [10] any major psychiatric disorder or even subthreshold symptoms, or had ever taken psychotropic drugs, except for three who occasionally took benzodiazepines because of difficulties in sleeping at night, as assessed by a detailed psychiatric interview conducted by one of the authors (DM). In addition, all subjects had undergone the following rating scales: the Hamilton Rating Scale for Depression (Hamilton, 1960), the Hamilton Rating Scale for Anxiety (Hamilton, 1959), and the Yale-Brown Obsessive-Compulsive Rating Scale (Goodman et al., 1986), with the results that all total scores fell within the normal range.

All subjects, except for four singles (three women and one man), were indulging in normal and regular sexual activity, as assessed by self-report questionnaires and, during the psychiatric interview, no differences were noted between the romantic lovers and the control subjects.

The women had regular menstrual cycles and were not taking contraceptive pills. Their blood samples were drawn in the early follicular phase (between the third and the fifth day of the menses); the men had no history of genital disease or hypogonadism. All subjects were free of physical illness, were neither heavy cigarette smokers nor belonged to high-risk HIV individuals, and all underwent a general and detailed check-up, carried out by one of the authors (DC).

All gave their informed written consent to their inclusion in the study.

2.2. Hormonal measurements

Venous blood (10 ml) was collected between 8 and 9 a.m. from fasting subjects and centrifuged at low-speed centrifugation (200 × g, for 20 min, at 22°C) to obtain serum which was stored at −20°C until the assays, which were performed within a few days.

The following hormones were evaluated by means [15] of standard techniques in duplicate for each point, by biologists who were blind to each subject's conditions: FSH, LH, estradiol, progesterone (chemiluminescent immuno-assay, CMIA, Architect, Abbott, Abbott Park, USA), dehydroepiandrosterone sulphate (DHEAS) (Spectria, Orion Diagnostic, Essoo, Finland), cortisol (CMIA, DPC, Immulite, Los Angeles, USA), testosterone, and androstenedione (RIA, Testo-CTK, Diasorin Biomedica, Saluggia, Italy).

2.3. Statistics

The differences in hormone levels between subjects of the two sexes who recently had or had not fallen in love were measured by means of the Student t-test (unpaired, two-tailed). The possible effects of the length of the relationship or of the time devoted to thinking about the partner on the hormonal levels were assessed according to Pearson's analysis. All analyses were carried out using the SSPS version 4.0, by means of personal computer programs (StatView V) (Nie et al., 1998).

3. RESULTS

Table 1 shows that cortisol levels (ng/ml) were significantly higher in the subjects who had recently fallen in love, as compared with control subjects (239 ± 39 vs 168 ± 31, $p < 0.001$), with no difference between women and men.

The levels of LH, estradiol, progesterone, DHEAS, and androstenedione did not differ between the groups and were within normal ranges according to the sex and the follicular phase of the women.

On the other hand, testosterone levels (ng/ml) in men who had recently fallen in love were significantly lower than in singles or individuals with a long-lasting relationship (4.1 ± 1.0 vs 6.8 ± 2.1, $p > 0.003$); the results in women were the opposite, that is, higher levels in the women from the first group, as compared with those from the second (1.2 ± 0.4 vs 0.6 ± 0.2, $p < 0.001$).

Table 1

Hormonal Levels in Subjects in the Early Stage of Falling in Love and in Control Subjects

	Subjects in love		Control subjects	
	M	F	M	F
FSH	3.2 ± 1.1^	8.1 ± 4.2	9.3 ± 3.8	9.1 ± 3.1
LH	6.9 ± 2.3	12.3 ± 3.4	7.1 ± 2.8	10 ± 4.3
Estradiol	<50	170 ± 23	<50	145 ± 32
Progesterone	<0.2	0.57 ± 0.3	<0.2	0.55 ± 0.3
Testosterone	4.1 ± 1.0*	1.2 ± 0.4**	6.8 ± 2.1	0.6 ± 0.2
DHEAS	2736 ± 1122	2232 ± 986	2450 ± 1000	2315 ± 980
Cortisol	224 ± 21°	243 ± 41°°	165 ± 21	172 ± 44
Androstenedione	2.0 ± 1.0	2.1 ± 0.7	2.1 ± 0.7	1.9 ± 0.7

M, male; F, female.

^Significant: $p < 0.0001$; *Significant: $p < 0.003$; **Significant: $p < 0.001$; °Significant: $p < 0.001$; °°Significant: $p < 0.0001$.

FSH levels were significantly lower in men who [20] had fallen in love than in those from the control group ($p < 0.0001$).

When the cortisol, testosterone, and FSH levels were re-tested in 16 out of the total of 24 subjects in love, from 12 to 28 months later, no differences from control subject levels were detected. Hormonal measurements were also repeated in 15 out of the total of 24 control subjects after the same time interval, but no significant differences from those of the first assessment were noted (data not shown).

The length of the relationship and the time spent in thinking about the partner did not affect hormonal levels.

Singles or subjects with a long-lasting relationship did not differ in any of the parameters evaluated.

4. DISCUSSION

The main bias of this study is probably represented by the criteria used for selecting the subjects who had fallen in love since, despite our best efforts, no definite indication was available. Since the altered mental state associated with falling in love seems to have a precise time course, with an average duration of between 18 months and 3 years (Tennov, 1979; Marazziti et al., 1999), we chose the length of the relationship as one criterion which, furthermore, can easily be recorded. The other main criterion adopted was the time spent in thinking about the partner which, according to various authors, represents a core feature of this phase (Tesser and Paulhus, 1976; Tennov, 1979; Shea and Adams, 1984). One might perhaps infer that the subjects who are in love suffer from a moderate form of OCD, or have an obsessive-compulsive personality, a positive family history of OCD or even obsessive-compulsive subthreshold symptoms; however, we excluded all these possibilities by means of the psychiatric interview and specific questionnaires. It might also be judged questionable that our hormonal evaluation was performed on a single sample; however, this could represent a bias for LH measurement only, for which a pulsatile pattern is well recognized.

However, in spite of this limitation, our study led to some intriguing and innovative findings, in particular that healthy subjects of both sexes who had recently fallen in love did show some hormonal changes.

The first finding was that the cortisol levels were higher in subjects in love, as compared with those from the control group. This condition of "hypercortisolemia" is probably a non-specific indicator of some changes which occur during the early phase of a relationship, reflecting the stressful conditions or arousal associated with the initiation of a social contact which helps to overcome neophobia.* Such conditions appear to be fundamental, as a moderate level of stress has been demonstrated to promote attachment and social contacts in both animals and humans (DeVries et al., 1995, 1996; Hennessy, 1997; Levine et al., 1997; Mendoza and Mason, 1997). In addition, different data indicate an association between HPA activation following stressful experiences and the development of social attachment which, in turn, promotes physiological states which reduce anxiety and related negative sensations (Hinde, 1974; Milgram, 1986; Simpson and Rhole, 1994; Legros, 2001). We observed no difference in cortisol levels between women and men, but this is perhaps not surprising, given indications that they represent rather an unspecific reaction to different triggers.

On the other hand, while LH, estradiol, progesterone, DHEAS, and androstenedione levels did not differ between men and women, the testosterone concentrations showed some sex-related peculiarities: in both men and women who were at the early stage of a relationship, they were lower and higher, respectively, than those in men and women from the control group. Although none reached pathological levels, all subjects presented this finding, as if falling in love tended temporarily to eliminate some differences between the sexes, or to soften some male features in men and, in parallel, to increase them in women. It is tempting to link the changes in testosterone levels to changes in behaviors, sexual attitudes, or, perhaps, aggressive traits which move in different directions in

*neophobia: fear of new things.

the two sexes (Zitzmann and Nieschlag, 2001); however, apart from some anecdoctal evidence, we have no data substantiating this which would justify further research. Similarly, we have no explanation for the decreased level of FSH in male subjects who were in love, apart from the suggestions that it may represent another marker of hypothalamic involvement in the process of falling in love.

It is noteworthy that when we measured the cortisol, testosterone, and FSH levels for a second time, 12–18 months later, in those 16 (out of the total of 24) subjects who had maintained the same relationship but were no longer in the same mental state to which they had referred during the first assessment and now reported feeling calmer and no longer "obsessed" with the partner, the hormone levels were no different from those of the control group. This finding would suggest that the hormonal changes which we observed are reversible, state-dependent, and probably related to some physical and/or psychological features typically associated with falling in love.

In conclusion, our study would suggest that falling in love represents a "physiological" and transient condition which is characterized (or underlaid) by peculiar hormonal patterns, one of which, involving testosterone, seems to show a sex-related specificity.

Studies are now in progress to establish whether the noted hormonal changes may be related to the modifications of specific behaviors, such as aggression or sexual or attachment attitudes.

ACKNOWLEDGMENTS

We thank Prof. Lucia Grasso and the technical staff of the Hormone laboratory of the "Dipartimento di Endocrinologia" of the University of Pisa for performing the hormone assay. We express our gratitude to Prof. Aldo Pinchera and Prof. Enio Martino of the same Department for the fruitful discussion during the preparation of the manuscript, and to Dr. Elena Di Nasso from the "Dipartimento di Psichiatria, Neurobiologia, Farmacologia e Biotecnologie," who was helpful in selecting the subjects included in the study.

REFERENCES

Bartels, A., Zeki, S., 2000. The neural basis of romantic love. Neuroreport 11, 3829–3838.

Bowlby, J., 1969. Attachment and Loss. Attachment. vol. 1. Basic Books, New York.

Bowlby, J., 1973. Attachment and Loss. Separation: anxiety and anger. vol. 2. Basic Books, New York.

Carter, C.S., 1998. Neuroendocrine perspectives on social attachment and love. Psychoneuroendocrinol 23, 779–818.

Carter, C.S., DeVries, A.C., Taymans, S.E., 1997a. Peptides, steroids and pair bonding. Ann NY Acad Sci 807, 260–268.

Carter, C.S., Lederhendler, I.I., Kilpatrick, B. (eds)., 1997b. The integrative neurobiology of affiliation. Ann NY Acad Sci 807.

Chiodera, P., Salvarani, C., Bacchi-Modena, A., Spallanzani, R., Cigarini, C., Alboni, A., Gardini, E., Coiro, V., 1991. Relationship between plasma profiles of oxytocin and adrenocorticotropic hormone during suckling or breast stimulation in women. Horm & Res 35, 119–123.

DeVries, A.C., DeVries, M.B., Taymans, S.E., Carter, S.C., 1995. The modulation of pair bonding by corticosteroids in female prairie voles. Proc Natl Acad Sci USA 92, 7744–7748.

DeVries, A.C., DeVries, M.B., Taymans, S.E., Carter, S.C., 1996. The effects of stress on social preferences are sexually dimorphic in prairie voles. Proc Natl Acad Sci USA 93, 11980–11990.

Fisher, H., 1992. Anatomy of Love. Fawcett Columbine, New York.

Goodman, W.K., Price, L.H., Rasmussen, S.A., 1986. The Yale Brown Obsessive-Compulsive Scale I: Development, use and reliability. Arch Gen Psychiatry 46, 1006–1011.

Hamilton, M., 1959. The assessment of anxiety state by rating. Br J Med Psychol 32, 50–55.

Hamilton, M., 1960. A rating scale for depression. J Neurol Neurosurg Psychiatry 23, 56–62.

Hazan, C., Shaver, P., 1987. Romantic love conceptualized as an attachment process. J Personal Soc Psychol 52, 511–524.

Hennessy, M.B., 1997. Hypothalamic-pituitary-adrenal responses to brief social separation. Neur Biobehav Rev 21, 11–29.

Hinde, R.A., 1974. Biological Bases of Human Social Behavior. McGraw-Hill, New York.

Insel, T.R., Young, L.J., 1997. The neurobiology of attachment. Nature Rev 2, 129–136.

Jankoviak, W.R., 1986. A psychobiological theory of love. Psychol Rev 93, 119–130.

Jankoviak, W.R., Fischer, E.F., 1992. A cross-cultural perspective on romantic love. Ethol 31, 149–155.

Kleiman, D., 1977. Monogamy in mammals. Quart Rev Biol 52, 39–69.

Kraemer, G.W., 1992. A psychobiological theory of attachment. Behav Brain Sci 15, 493–520.

Leckman, J.F., Mayes, L.C., 1999. Preoccupations and behaviors associated with romantic and parental love. Perspectives on the origin of obsessive-compulsive disorder. Child & Adol Psychiatry Clin North Am 1, 635–665.

LeDoux, J.E., 2000. Emotion circuits in the brain. Ann Rev Neurosci 2, 155–184.

Legros, J.J., 2001. Inhibitory effects of oxytocin on corticotrope function in humans: are vasopressin and oxytocin ying-yang neurohormones? Psychoneuroendocrinol 26, 649–655.

Levine, S., Lyons, D.M., Schatzberg, A.F., 1997. Psychobiological consequences of social relationships. Ann NY Acad Sci 807, 210–218.

Liebowitz, M.R., 1983. The Chemistry of Love. Little, Brown and Company, Boston.

Marazziti, D., Akiskal, H.S., Rossi, A., Cassano, G.B., 1999. Alteration of the platelet serotonin transporter in romantic love. Psychol Med 29, 741–745.

McCarthy, M.M., Kow, L.M., Pfaff, D.W., 1992. Speculations concerning the physiological significance of central oxytocin in maternal behavior. Ann NY Acad Sci 652, 70–82.

Mendoza, S.P., Mason, W.A., 1997. Attachment relationships in New World primates. Ann NY Acad Sci 807, 203–209.

Milgram, N.A., 1986. Stress and Coping in Time of War: Generalizations from the Israeli Experiences. Brunner Mazel, New York.

Nie, N.H., Hull, C.H., Steinbrenner, K., Bent, D.H., 1998. Statistical Package for the Social Science (SPSS), 4th ed. McGraw-Hill, New York.

Numan, M., 1994. Maternal behavior. In: Knobil, E., Neill, I. (Eds.), The Physiology of Reproduction. Raven Press, New York, pp. 221–302.

Panksepp, J., 1982. Toward a psychobiological theory of emotions. Behav Brain Res 5, 407–467.

Panksepp, J., Nelson, E., Silvy, S., 1994. Brain opioids and mother-infant social motivation. Acta Pediatr Suppl 397, 40–46.

Porges, S.W., 1998. Love and emotions. Psychoneuroendocrinol 23, 837–861.

Reite, M., 1985. The Psychobiology of Attachment and Separation. Academic Press, New York.

Shea, J.A., Adams, G.R., 1984. Correlates of romantic attachment: a path analysis study. J Youth Adol 13, 27–31.

Simpson, J.A., Rhole, W.A., 1994. Stress and secure base relationships in adulthood. Adv Pers Relat 5, 181–204.

Tennov, D., 1979. Love and Limerence. The Experience of Being in Love. Stein and Day, New York.

Tesser, A., Paulhus, D.L., 1976. Toward a causal model of love. J Pers & Soc Psychol 34, 1095–1103.

Uvnäs-Moberg, K., 1997. Physiological and endocrine effects of social contact. Ann NY Acad Sci 807, 146–163.

Uvnäs-Moberg, K., 1998. Oxytocin may mediate the benefit of positive social interaction and emotions. Psychoneuroendocrinol 23, 819–835.

Zitzmann, M., Nieschlag, E., 2001. Testosterone levels in healthy men and the relation to behavioural and physical characteristics: facts and constructs. Eur J Endocrinol 144, 183–197.

Reading Questions

1. The study's introduction explicitly establishes the researchers' goals for their study. What are those goals?

2. Based on what criteria do the researchers select study participants for their experimental group—those who had recently fallen in love?

3. Following analysis of blood samples, what statistical procedure is used to compare differences in hormone levels between subjects who had or had not recently fallen in love?

4. What central limitation, or bias, are the researchers concerned with, based on the study's Discussion section?

Rhetoric Questions

5. How does the introduction establish the significance or importance of the researchers' work for their audience?

6. Closely analyze the structure of the study's Discussion section. Based on your analysis, what do you see as the section's organizational logic? In other words, what do you believe the researchers set out to achieve in this section of the study?

7. Identify areas in the study where the researchers first acknowledge and then offer response to the effects of possible limitations to their study's methods or findings. Do these areas strengthen or weaken their report? Explain your response.

8. How does the Acknowledgments section affect the researchers' ethos?

Response and Research Questions

9. The researchers write that falling in love "tended temporarily to eliminate some differences between the sexes, or to soften some male features in men and, in parallel, to increase them in women" (par. 27). Consider a time when you've fallen in love or when you've witnessed what you thought was someone falling in love. Do your experiences support the researchers' conclusion in this instance?

10. Do you have any anecdotal evidence, based on personal experiences, that might support or challenge any of the researchers' central findings? If so, what are they? Explain your answers.

Looking for Love on Craigslist: An Examination of Gender Differences in Self-Marketing Online

CARA O. PETERS, JANE B. THOMAS, AND RICHARD MORRIS

Cara O. Peters is a professor of marketing at Winthrop University in South Carolina. The following study, conducted with her colleagues Jane B. Thomas and Richard Morris, also of Winthrop University, examines differences in the ways men and women represent, or market, themselves online in Craigslist advertisements for relationships. According to the authors, their study provides "unique insight into differences between males and females that can be used when creating marketing messages from a managerial perspective." The article appeared in the *Journal of Marketing Development and Competitiveness* in 2013.

The purpose of this research is to examine the self-marketing occurring among heterosexual men and women who are advertising for a prospective date on the social media site Craigslist. Qualitative and quantitative analysis of 1,200 posts was conducted. The findings offer unique insight into differences between males and females that can be used when creating marketing messages. The results illustrate that language is an imprecise form in how people read and understand the written and spoken word. It is important for marketers to understand the criteria that consumers are searching for and the language that they use in self-marketing.

INTRODUCTION

Those in the popular press have begun to assert that men and women use social media differently. For example, some have argued that certain social media sites, like Pinterest, are only utilized by women (Conaway, 2013a). Others contend that women, when compared to men, are more likely to use Facebook and other social media to foster and reinforce social connections (Bond, 2009; Joinson, 2008). Furthermore, some researchers have found that women are more likely to have a public Facebook profile, put up more photos of family and friends, frequently update their own profile photos, and post more often about their ongoing activities (Bond, 2009; Strano, 2008). In contrast, recent research reports that women are less likely to report their detailed, personal information

(such as phone numbers) on social media sites when compared to men (Conaway, 2013b). While these studies have begun to identify the different ways men and women use social media, they only present part of the picture. There is virtually no examination to date of how men and women present and "market" themselves differently via social media.

Given that studies show men and women use social media differently and the fact that academics have known for quite some time that the two genders communicate differently (cf. Lakoff & Bucholtz, 2004), it seems important for marketers to understand the differences in communication used by males and females in social media and how these language differences assist in the development of an online identity that is packaged and presented to others. Marketers could better communicate with potential target audiences if they had a stronger understanding of the language utilized by the different genders. Moreover, knowing more about gendered language also helps understand online consumer behavior, not only for social media sites (like Pinterest) but also for other websites that are selling goods and services (like eHarmony.com and Match.com).

In both the popular press and among academics, there is a small but growing literature around the idea of "self-marketing" (a.k.a., "personal branding") in which individual consumers carefully construct a personal identity, much like a brand image, that is presented to others (McCaffrey, 1983; Montoya & Vandehey, 2008; Peters, 1997; Shepherd, 2005). "Self-marketing" appears to happen in a variety of contexts, ranging from functional to social reasons, such as in search of employment, promotion, self-expression, social connections (i.e., familial relationships and friendships), and romantic relationships (i.e., dating) (Labrecque, Markos, & Milne, 2011). Furthermore, many assert that much of self-marketing takes place online via social media (Chase, 2011; Elmore, 2010; Greer, 2010; Hearn, 2008; Hyatt, 2010).

As explained in our literature review below, e-dating [5] is the ultimate form of "self-marketing," which presents a unique opportunity to explore differences in the language used by men and women in social media. Self-marketing via Craigslist.com served as the focus of the current study because this website is one of the most well-known online communities that is public (i.e., no fee required). In the United States alone, more than 50 million people use Craigslist, and the site has 30 billion page views per month (http://www.craigslist.org/about/factsheet). Craigslist provides more than 100 topical forums that contain more than 200 million user postings at any given time. One of Craigslist's topical forums is "personal advertisements." These advertisements are a unique blend of content that mirrors traditional newspaper personal ads with online dating. However, unlike traditional newspaper ads and e-dating websites, personal ads on Craigslist require no fees, no contracts, no limits on text, and provide for more real-time communication between interested individuals. Within these personal ads on Craigslist, individuals are using self-marketing to communicate with prospective partners, who then decide to make connections based on information provided in the online post.

The purpose of this research is to examine the self-marketing occurring among heterosexual men and women who are advertising for a prospective date/partner on the popular social media site Craigslist. The central aim of this study is to review the content of these online ads and then explore how men and women communicate differently as they self-market online. This paper makes a unique contribution to the literature, as research in self-marketing via social media has yet to delve into gender differences. Little is known about how men and women market and present themselves differently via social media sites. Findings from this study also provide insights for understanding gendered language and developing marketing communication for online communities, social media, and other marketing activities. Following is the theoretical foundation, methodology, findings, and discussion.

LITERATURE REVIEW

Schau and Gilly (2003) argue that consumers consciously construct online identities, using a combination of words and pictures. Although they were studying web pages and not social media per se, these authors seem to have planted the early seeds of the online self-marketing literature that is currently growing into a field of study on its own. Although self-marketing has been around for quite some time in the popular press (McCaffrey, 1983; Peters, 1997), the literature has flourished among practitioners (cf. Chase, 2011; Elmore, 2010; Greer, 2010; Hyatt, 2010; Montoya & Vandehey, 2008) and is beginning to take hold among academics as well. From an academic perspective, Shepherd (2005) defines self-marketing as "those activities undertaken by individuals to make themselves known in the market place" (p. 590). Shepherd suggests that individuals are continually reinventing themselves in an effort to remain desirable to others. Lair, Sullivan, and Cheney (2005) similarly describe self-marketing as efforts by individuals to create and position the self as a package that is presented to others. Hearn (2008) also examined self-marketing, although from the perspective of consumer culture theory. She states that in marketing themselves online, people purposefully direct messages outward and this self-production is "narrated, marked by visual codes of mainstream culture industry, and subject to extraction value" (p. 197).

One of the few academic studies of self-marketing to date that actually includes data collection, as opposed to being conceptual in nature, is Labrecque, Markos, and Milne's (2011) examination of twelve individuals' online profiles. These researchers found that individuals purposefully craft and post material on social media to project a personal identity. Through interviews, Labrecque et al. found that most of the informants had a "branding strategy" and were "consciously aware" of what they were posting. The twelve individuals attempted to highlight their positive attributes that they believed were of value to the target audience (and were also ways to differentiate themselves from others). After interviewing the informants, the researchers then conducted "brand audits" of these online profiles, inviting HR professionals and undergraduate students to judge the content of these profiles. The results of these brand audits suggested that at times the audience did not fully comprehend the positioning of the informants and authenticity was often important in posting and interpreting the content of the profiles.

The literature on e-dating suggests that in their efforts to find prospective partners/dates, consumers are practicing self-marketing online. E-dating consists of a set of "activities such as subscribing to a dating website, posting a personal ad, and/or replying to dating messages online" (Close & Zinkhan, 2004, p. 153). The primary means for communicating with others in the e-dating process is via an online personal ad that lists the person's personal data, self-description, and states what they are looking for (Malchow-Moller, 2003). Because these online personal ads communicate what is "valuable" about the person in order to attract prospective partners, several researchers have argued that these online personal ads are self-marketing (Arvidsson, 2006; Coupland, 1996; Patterson & Hodgson, 2006).

Malchow-Moller (2003) found that when posting 10 e-dating personal ads, consumers experience tension as they balance highlighting their positive attributes against presenting their authentic or true selves. While the mediation in e-dating allows for greater control over the presentation of self and can create opportunities for misrepresentation, it also allows for consumers to be more open in the self-disclosure

process (Malchow-Moller, 2003). Malchow-Moller (2003) actually found that consumers present themselves how they want to be perceived, as opposed to how they actually are, which could lead to the tension described by Ellison et al. (2006). Another factor that weighs into what consumers post about themselves in the e-dating process is that prospective daters use subtle cues in the posts to make judgments about the content of the post and whether he/she wants to reply to the e-dater (Malchow-Moller, 2003). For example, Rosen, Cheever, Cummings, and Felt (2008) found that the amount of emotionality and self-disclosure in the personal ad were key factors that affected a person's perception of a potential e-dating partner. Posts with more emotional language (like excited or wonderful) had a more positive effect on the reader, but the amount of self-disclosure needed to be more moderate because too much self-disclosure led to negative perceptions.

There is a small but growing literature on gender differences in e-dating personal ads, but these studies tend to focus more on traditional media, as there are only a few that examine gender differences in an online context. Butler-Smith, Cameron, and Collins (1998) examined personal ads from the Sunday newspaper and found that content typically fell along lines of gendered stereotypes. Men more often sought younger partners and offered financial security, when compared to women. Women specified that men must have financial security more frequently than men. These researchers did not find gender differences among a host of other variables, including relationship commitment (i.e., fling versus long term), declared age, divorced, and family status (i.e., children). In a follow-up study, Cameron and Collins (1999) analyzed personal ads from the newspaper and found that women's declaration of wealth and divorced status had a positive impact on the demand for male looks. In other words, when women reported being wealthy, they were more likely to be seeking an attractive male. In addition, Cameron and Collins (1999) found that older women were less likely to require attractiveness in a prospective partner.

Jagger (1998), like Butler-Smith et al. (1988), analyzed newspaper ads and found that the content mirrored gendered stereotypes. Men offered financial status and sought physical attractiveness in prospective partners, while women offered physical attractiveness and sought men with financial resources. However, what was unique to Jagger's study was that she also found that both men and women equally marketed their bodies as a primary selling point. In fact, both genders marketed their bodies more frequently than their other resources. Jagger suggests that this may be the case because lifestyle choices may be displacing financial resources as identity markers for men in today's society. However, despite these findings, more recent studies examining newspaper personal ads have continued to reinforce the assertion that content of personal ads follows typical gender stereotypes. For example, Tither (2000) found that females were more likely to offer weight and seek financial security, while men were more likely to offer height, stipulate weight, and prefer to date someone younger.

There are a few studies that examine personal ads online. Specifically, Dawson and McIntosh (2006) analyzed Internet dating ads for attractiveness, income, physical attributes, and other positive personal characteristics (i.e., personality, lifestyle, interests). These researchers found that when men stated that they had wealth and were attractive, they were less likely to place emphasis on positive personal characteristics. For women, when they placed emphasis on their physical attractiveness, they too were less likely to emphasize other positive personal characteristics. These findings put a new twist on the previous literature on gender differences in personal advertisements. Simply put, Dawson and McIntosh's findings support the assertion that personal ad content is largely consistent with gender stereotypes (in that men seek physical attractiveness in women and women seek financial resources in men), but their findings also support previous research in that they suggest when these factors are not prominent in the personal advertiser, he/she will then emphasize other

positive attributes such as lifestyle, personality, and interests. Interestingly, Gallant, Williams, Fisher, and Cox (2011) analyzed photos posted in e-dating sites and found that, while women emphasized reproductive fitness in their photos, the men's photos did not emphasize the ability to provide resources.

Bond (2009) appears to have provided one of the few studies to date that specifically examines gendered self-marketing on social media. While Bond does not explicitly examine e-dating per se, he surveyed 137 college students with respect to the amount and content of their self-disclosure on social media. Bond found that women, when compared to men, were more likely to include images and information related to friends, family, romantic partners, holidays, school, and alcohol. (The only variable where men disclosed more than women was sports.) The content of the posts was also analyzed for sexual expressiveness, but females were only marginally more sexually expressive when compared to men (i.e., the finding was not statistically significant). While Bond's study was important, it merely proves that there may be differences among men and women in self-marketing via social media. Studies have yet to uncover the specific gender differences that exist when women and men self-market via social media. Toward that end, the methodology is presented next.

METHODOLOGY

Craigslist.org was selected for data collection because it is one of the most popular self-advertising websites in the world. This online community is the 15th most viewed site on the Internet in the United States (http://www.craigslist.org/about/factsheet). Craigslist's platform does not require a set time a posting has to be up, which gives users the ability to post whenever they want, leave it up for an extended time, and take it down when needed. This site does not require consumers to use a template when creating an advertisement. This provides users more freedom of self-expression than traditional e-dating sites, which require fees and use of an existing template. Thus,

Table 1

Sampling Process

Region	Cities with largest number of posts	Categories selected*
Southeast	Jacksonville	Men seeking women
	Memphis	Women seeking men
Upper Midwest	Chicago	Men seeking women
	Milwaukee	Women seeking men
Northeast	New York City	Men seeking women
	Philadelphia	Women seeking men
Southwest	Los Angeles	Men seeking women
	Phoenix	Women seeking men
Lower Midwest	Houston	Men seeking women
	San Antonio	Women seeking men
Northwest	Portland	Men seeking women
	Seattle	Women seeking men

*The first fifty posts were selected from each of these categories.

Craigslist.com was chosen for the current study since self-expression was less restrictive.

The sampling process utilized methods employed by Kroft and Pope (2008) in their research on the matching efficiency for job and apartment postings on Craigslist and Thomas, Peters, and Tolson (2007) in their research on Myspace.com. To obtain the sample data from Craigslist.org, the United States was divided into six different regions (Northeast, Southeast, etc.) and the two cities with the largest number of posts were selected from each region. Table 1 presents a summary of the sampling process. It should be noted that the cities with the largest number of posts also had substantial population bases, allowing for greater diversity among those who posted. Data was selected from the Craigslist "personal advertisements" section. The personal advertisements section had eight sub-categories: strictly platonic, women seeking women, women seeking men, men seeking women, men seeking men, miscellaneous romance, casual encounters, and missed connections. Because this study focused on differences between heterosexual men and women, data were drawn from two of the eight sub-categories, women seeking men and men seeking women. For each selected city, the first fifty posts within these two sub-categories were extracted and saved as a Word document. This resulted in a total of 1,200 posts in the data set.

A two-step process was used to examine the self-marketing occurring among men and women on Craigslist. This two-step approach provided a more holistic view of the data and clearer insights into how men and women differ in regards to gender and self-marketing. Categories from the data were first explored from a heterosexual cohort viewpoint (i.e., the two categories men seeking women and women seeking men were analyzed for common themes). This process was then followed by examination of the differences by gender (i.e., men seeking women and women seeking men were separated and compared).

For the first phase of the study, content analysis was selected as the method for analyzing the 1,200 posts because it provides a well-accepted, objective, systematic, and scientific process for analyzing communication (Kassarjian, 1977, pp. 8–9). Each of the two authors participating in the study (who are trained, qualitative researchers) printed hard copies of data. Utilizing the transcripts, the authors then followed an emergent coding process as described by Stemler (2001). To identify the categories for classification, the two authors independently reviewed the transcripts, noting the general categories of content as they read through the data. The authors then met and shared their independent classification schemes. After discussing the commonalities and differences in the classification schemes, the authors identified a set of common categories for purposes of classification. After independently returning to transcripts and coding each of the individual posts until all the data had been accounted (Stemler, 2001), the authors got back together and shared their independent coding of the data. Inter-rater reliability was computed using the number of agreements divided by the total number of observations (Hartman, 2006). The authors had 98.4% agreement and discrepancies were reviewed and resolved via debate and discussion. The frequency of occurrence for each category is reported in Table 2. In addition to tabulating the frequency of occurrence, each category of data was interpreted for its specific meaning. Finally, exemplary verbatim quotes were drawn from the data to be incorporated into the interpretation presented in the findings.

For the second phase of the study, the authors conducted a quantitative analysis comparing the frequency of occurrence by gender. The frequency and percentage of each category and subtopic of discussion was calculated for men and then women. This step was followed with a Chi-square test of the proportions to uncover statistically significant differences in the topics discussed by men and women. Table 3 presents the frequency and percentage of occurrence by gender. Because of the exploratory nature of the study, the authors utilized the 2-tailed p-value when interpreting the significance of the z-scores (i.e., $p \leq .05$ was used as the significance level).

FINDINGS

The categories that emerged from the data and the analysis of differences by gender are presented together in order to provide for a comprehensive understanding of the themes utilized in self-marketing and also allow for a parceling out of the differences that may exist between the self-marketing of men and women. Furthermore, this approach also provides a clearer understanding of how marketers and advertisers can use these findings when marketing to men and women. Four general categories emerged from the data: types of interaction, criteria for partner, self-disclosure, and tone (see Table 2). Within each of these general categories there was a subset of four to seven items that comprised the category. It should be noted that the total number of responses for these four categories was much greater than 1,200 (i.e., the total number of posts selected for the sample) because more than one category could have been represented in a given post. In other words, a consumer's post could contain information that fell into more than one category. In addition, Craigslist provides the consumer with a number when posting on the site and thus all data was treated anonymously and no identifying markers (such as name or email address) are reported below.

Types of Interaction

Data included in this category provide insight into what a person is seeking from the relationship. When reading the posts, it appeared that many of the participants specified the type of interaction that they were seeking. The types of interaction sought represented a range of sexual to non-sexual interactions, including kinky, sex, dating, long-term relationship (LTR), friend, and other (see Table 2). While a small number of the posts contained lewd comments, most of the content reflected posters who were seeking those types of interactions that would commonly occur in traditional, offline dating situations.

Table 2
Content of the Ads

	Frequency	Percentage
1. Types of Interaction		
a. Kinky	53	0.0654085
b. Sex	71	0.088476
c. Dating (Friend to More)	282	0.3644395
d. LTR (Long-Term Relationship)	141	0.1848945
e. Friend/New to Area/Bored	117	0.149766
f. Other	114	0.1470145
Sub-total:	778	
2. Criteria for Partner		
a. Relationship Status	113	0.1402915
b. STD-Free/Drug-Free	83	0.106293
c. Demographics (Race, Religion, Employed)	193	0.2442595
d. Physical Characteristics (Age, Weight, Height)	374	0.509156
Sub-total:	763	
3. Self-Disclosure		
a. Physical Characteristics (Age, Weight, Height)	492	0.2754425
b. Personality (Shy, Outgoing)	279	0.1558555
c. Hobbies/Interests	332	0.185488
d. Sex Life (Desire)	40	0.0224245
e. Family Structure (Divorced, Kids, Pets)	205	0.11458
f. Demographics (Race, Religion, Professional, Employed)	328	0.1834985
g. Non-Smoking/Disease-Free/Non-Drinking/Drug-Free	112	0.06271
Sub-total:	1788	
4. Tone		
a. Sales Pitch	30	0.0652505
b. Wordy	72	0.156796
c. Honesty (Real/Not Real)	101	0.2196915
d. Picture for Picture	258	0.558262
Sub-total:	461	
Total:	3697	

Table 3
Gender Differences in Self-Marketing by Category

	Frequency (%)			2-tailed
	Women	**Men**	**z-score**	**p-value**
1. Types of Interaction				
a. Kinky	9 (0.025)	44 (0.106)	−4.486	0.000★
b. Sex	17 (0.047)	54 (0.130)	−4.025	0.000★
c. Dating (friend to more)	143 (0.394)	139 (0.335)	1.708	0.087
d. LTR	87 (0.240)	54 (0.130)	3.957	0.000★
e. Friend/New to Area/Bored	51 (0.140)	66 (0.159)	−0.722	0.472
f. Other	56 (0.154)	58 (0.140)	0.571	0.569
2. Criteria for Partner				
a. Relationship Status	82 (0.169)	31 (0.112)	2.154	0.032★
b. STD-Free/Drug-Free	56 (0.115)	27 (0.097)	0.783	0.435
c. Demographics (Race, Religion, Employed)	134 (0.276)	59 (0.212)	1.959	0.050★
d. Physical Characteristics (Age, Weight, Height)	213 (0.439)	161 (0.579)	−3.722	0.000★
3. Self-Disclosure				
a. Physical Characteristics (Age, Weight, Height)	211 (0.234)	281 (0.316)	−3.882	0.000★
b. Personality (Shy, Outgoing)	165 (0.183)	114 (0.128)	3.202	0.001★
c. Hobbies/Interests	193 (0.214)	139 (0.157)	3.149	0.002★
d. Sex Life (Desire)	13 (0.014)	27 (0.030)	−2.282	0.023★
e. Family Structure (Divorced, Kids, Pets)	113 (0.126)	92 (0.104)	1.457	0.144
f. Demographics (Race, Religion, Professional, Employed)	158 (0.176)	170 (0.191)	−0.868	0.384
g. Non-Smoking/Disease-Free/Non-Drinking/Drug-Free (vice versa)	47 (0.052)	65 (0.073)	−1.830	0.067
4. Tone				
a. Sales Pitch	14 (0.059)	31 (0.138)	−2.868	0.004★
b. Wordy	32 (0.135)	27 (0.121)	0.465	0.638
c. Honesty (Real/Not Real)	47 (0.198)	59 (0.263)	−1.660	0.097
d. Picture for Picture	144 (0.608)	161 (0.719)	−2.521	0.012★

★$p \leq .05$ significance level

The most frequently mentioned type of interaction was dating (n = 282, 36%) and the least frequent type of interaction discussed was kinky (n = 53, 6%). Dating involved individuals stating that they were looking for someone to start out as friends, go out on a few dates (like to lunch or the theater), with the idea that the relationship could potentially turn into a romantic [one] if both parties agree. The second most frequently discussed type of interaction was long-term relationship (n = 141, 18%). In contrast to dating, which was based more on friendship with the potential (but no expectation of) a relationship, the long-term relationship posters clearly stated that they were looking for an exclusive, committed relationship for an extended period of time. For example, a woman in New York City wrote an advertisement that began with a description of her physical appearance and a clear statement that she is seeking a long-term relationship.

> I am a very attractive full-figured Black and Puerto Rican woman. I am very voluptuous with a great shape. I work out so I am getting my body tight. I have body and face shots as well. I have no children, crazy ex-boyfriends, or stalkers in my life. I am college educated with a great career. I love sports, including WWE wrestling (yes I know it is fake). I love going dancing because I am a good dancer. I like going to museums especially art museums. I like going away on vacations even though the restrictions for flying are a bit tedious. I like playing video games and just staying home to relax. I work very hard and sometimes I have to travel for business so if you can be understanding about my career, then we will have no problems. I will make every effort to make for a relationship. I have a good career, however no one special in my life. Race is not important. I am not looking for someone over forty-five. Please be employed, attractive, and looking to be in a relationship. I am not interested in men with children. I have no children so I am seeking someone with no children as well. I don't smoke so please be a non-smoker as well. I like to laugh and have a good time. If you are seeking someone who has no drama and wants to be in a committed relationship, then please respond back. Take care!

In contrast to dating or long-term relationship posts, the friend types of interactions (n = 117, 15%) consisted of someone who was bored or lonely (many of which were new to the area) and were looking for platonic relationships. This man from San Antonio,

who is new to the area, creates a short post that clearly explains what he wants.

> I have a good job and am self sustaining. I just moved to the San Antonio area for my job and would love to get to know the area. I hear there is much to see, I only need someone to see it with. I would like you to have a job as well.

The least-discussed types of interaction were sexual (n = 71, 9%) and kinky (n = 53, 6%) interactions. These types of interactions sought consisted of one-night stands where the poster is asking someone to fulfill his/her sexual or physical fantasies, with little expectation of a friendship or long-term relationship coming from the interaction. Sexual posts merely stated that the person was looking for sex, while kinky posts stated that the person was looking for a more erotic type of physical interaction (like sexual fetishes). For example, the following post from a man in Chicago is written similar to a job description. In this post he describes the type of woman he is seeking for this "full time position."

> Am accepting applications and reviewing resumes for the full time position with extreme benefits for a sexy young lady to play the role of "Spoiled Sex Princess." As Hiring Manager, I require that you submit the following documentation: 1. Resume, 2. Photograph (Clothing is optional; extra bonus points for lingerie shots), 3. Work Experience, 4. Talents. The hiring manager (who just happens to be the person you will be reporting to) is an upper managerial type, advanced degreed with stylish wavy hair, hazel eyes, smart, intelligent, passionate, romantic with stylish clothes, stylish shoes, smart, sensual and very sexual. Duties include, but not limited to, serious role playing so a flair for the dramatic will be handy. "Boss after work with sexy Secretary." "Teacher keeping Naughty Girl After School for Discipline," and my personal favorite—"Catholic School Girl Gone Bad." Physically, must be able to withstand extended sessions of foreplay. Serious spoiling, pampering and pleasing available. Whatever your beautiful heart desires . . . within reason. Lingerie showings are on the itinerary as well as mutually pleasurable "oral activities." Physically must be able to withstand extended sessions of foreplay and be able to simulate a variety of different positions for the extreme sessions of intercourse. For the intelligent, open minded, college educated and extremely sexual young woman only. Serious Inquiries from seriously sexually advanced women only.

With respect to differences in the types of interactions sought, the analysis did reveal some statistically significant differences by gender (see Table 3). Men (n = 54, 13%) were more likely to state that they were interested in sex when compared to women (n = 17, 4%). Moreover, men (n = 44, 11%) were more likely to be seeking kinky interactions than women (n = 9, 2%). However, women (n = 87, 24%) were more likely to be seeking a long-term relationship, when compared to men (n = 54, 13%). These findings suggest that men seem to seek out more one-time, sexual encounters while women may be seeking more long-term, committed relationships, which is consistent with previous research (Dawson & McIntosh, 2006; Gallant et al., 2011). From a marketing perspective, this finding suggests that men and women utilize somewhat traditional norms (i.e., men seek sex and women seek relationships) when specifying what they want from e-dating on Craigslist.

Criteria for a Partner

The criteria for a partner category was defined as the characteristics that are required for a potential date/partner to be considered suitable. Four criteria were identified in the data: physical characteristics, demographics, relationship status, and drug/sexually transmitted disease (STD; see Table 2). The most frequently discussed criteria for a prospective partner was preferred physical characteristics. More than half of the posts clearly articulated preferences for the physical characteristics of a partner, including age, weight, and height (n = 374, 51%). For example, a female from San Antonio not only describes her criteria for a partner, but also comments that she offers a complete package to a potential suitor.

> Yes, like most other women, I am looking for the whole package, but I feel that I can because I offer the whole package in return :) I want someone who is attractive, smart, funny, great personality, responsible/mature, up for random fun and who is open to a more serious relationship if things worked out well between the two of us. I must admit I'm not looking to be someone's hookup or casual friend. Taller than 5'7", average body type or better, somewhere between 25 and 35, race is of no issue to me—I've dated across the board. Also, I don't have children and would prefer that you don't as well.

The second most frequently discussed topic related to criteria for a partner was related to demographics, such as race, religion, and professional status (n = 193, 24%, Table 2). The following post from a 35-year-old male musician in Houston, Texas, demonstrates how self-marketing is used when describing the criteria for a partner.

> I am looking for a 24 to 43, fit, non-smoker, not yet spoiled, able to have fun and be happy no matter what the event is, educated with employable skills. You should like: music (including hard rock), kids, cats, good conversation, motorcycles, going out for dinner and drinks, concerts.

Less frequently discussed criteria for a partner included preferred relationship status (n = 113, 14%) and drug/alcohol/STD-free status (n = 83, 11%). For some posters it was important that they state up front that they were looking for someone to date who was not already in an existing relationship or married. In addition, a minority of the posts also clearly articulated that a person who answers the ad must not have a sexually transmitted disease or any issues with alcohol and drugs.

With respect to statistically significant gender differences (see Table 3), women (n = 213, 44%) tended to specify preferred physical characteristics when compared to men (n = 161, 58%). This difference could be attributed to the absence of a face-to-face encounter, but the lack of interpersonal interaction exists for both genders. To the extent that gender is a contributing factor, the results are counter-intuitive when compared to previous research on personal ads. Past research on personal ads in newspapers suggests that men are more likely to specify preferred physical characteristics when compared to women (Jagger, 1998; Tither, 2000). The findings of the present study are different in the context of self-marketing on Craigslist.

In addition, when compared to men (n = 59, 21%), women were more likely to create personal advertisements that specified preferences on demographics (n = 134, 28%). In contrast to the findings on preferred physical characteristics, the finding on demographics is consistent with previous research on personal ads in newspapers. Research on personal ads in newspapers found women, who are seeking resources, are likely to prefer partners that are professional and employed in contrast to men (Butler-Smith et al., 1998; Dawson & McIntosh, 2006; Gallant et al., 2011; Jagger, 1998).

Finally, the data also suggest that women (n = 82, 17%) were more likely to specify the preferred relationship status of a prospective partner when compared to men (n = 31, 11%). This finding is consistent with the literature on e-dating as some studies have found that authenticity can be an issue in this context. Men, more often than women, misreport their relationship status (i.e., claim they are single when actually married) when participating in online dating activity (Close & Zinkhan, 2004).

Self-Disclosure

Self-disclosure is the essence of self-marketing. It is through the process of self-disclosure that participants in the Craigslist personal ads revealed as much or as little as they wanted the other person to know about themselves. Furthermore, self-disclosure is required to establish trust and mutual understanding in interpersonal relationships (Derlega, 1979; Ellison et al., 2006). Seven key pieces of personal information were revealed in the data: physical characteristics, personality, hobbies/interests, desire for a sex life, family structure, demographics, and smoker/drug-free/disease-free (see Table 2). Consumers utilized these seven pieces of information to carefully construct an image of themselves for a prospective dater.

Individuals most frequently offered information about their physical characteristics (n = 492, 27%), hobbies/interests (n = 332, 19%), and demographics (n = 328, 18%). Personality (n = 279, 16%) characteristics and family structure (n = 205, 11%) were also disclosed frequently in the posts. And while discussed less frequently, non-smoking/drug-free/disease-free (n = 112, 6%) and desire for a sex life (n = 40, 2%) were also present in the data. The following post from a woman in Chicago illustrates how she discloses her physical characteristics and hobbies/interests.

> More about me—Height/Weight proportionate, 5'3, 110 lbs., blue eyes, brown hair, I'm spiritual but not religious. I enjoy reading, watching movies, hanging out, dining out, drinking, live music, dance clubbing, communing with nature, going on impulsive adventures, and just walking the beach can be a work out.

It is interesting that while individuals were seeking partners that met specific criteria (see criteria for partner above), they were also not afraid to disclose their personal information. This finding was not necessarily surprising because, in some ways, e-dating allows individuals a forum for less inhibited self-expression when compared to face-to-face communication (Malchow-Moller, 2003; Rosen et al., 2008).

At the same time, authenticity is important, and individuals often project their ideal (as opposed to actual selves) online (Close & Zinkhan, 2004; Malchow-Moller, 2003). Consumers, after all, are self-marketing in looking for a prospective date on Craigslist. Individuals seeking online for a date or partner understand the importance of these personal facts and use this information to help them form a complete image of the other person. Similar to how consumer brands are recognized by their trademark, self-marketing provides cues such as physical characteristics and hobbies that are used to help others determine whether or not the person is a fit for them (Arvidsson, 2006; Hearn, 2008; Patterson & Hodgson, 2006). It could be that much of what consumers put in the posts was in response to what they see in preferred criteria for a partner. This may be why consumers self-disclosed on items like family structure, being drug/disease-free, and their desire for a sex life, as shown in the example below from a woman in Memphis.

> I am a single parent of one and am really frustrated right now because I don't have any friends who I can call on in my time of need. I have been single for 4 yrs. Men seem to play so many games and that has led me to Craigslist. I'm sexy, smart, independent, fun, have paperwork to prove I'm STD FREE and still that's not enough I guess. I am not trying to get over on anyone but I am really frustrated right now due to some recent circumstances that may lead to some bad things that I need someone to help me avoid. We can talk about the specific things later. I have my own apt, car, and job but it's still a strain especially when you don't have anyone to have your back and vice versa. I really would like to just meet a knight in shining armor to take away some of my stress that may need a good girl to cook, clean, or be there for them as a companion and see where things go. I'm tired of stressing and would love to just be

happy for a while to just enjoy someone but that's not the case. I am serious about life especially since I have a son to raise alone so please ONLY the mature and sincere apply.

The data analysis revealed gender differences in four of the seven items that comprised the self-disclosure category (see Table 3). Men were more likely to reveal information about their physical characteristics (n = 281, 32%), when compared to women (n = 211, 23%). This finding is somewhat counterintuitive in light of previous research on newspaper personal ads. Previous research by Jagger (1998), Dawson & McIntosh (2006), and Gallant et al. (2011) suggests women would be more likely to advertise their physical characteristics. However, men (n = 27, 3%) were also more likely to self-disclose their preferences for a certain type of sex life than women (n = 13, 1%), which is somewhat consistent with sexual strategies theory (Dawson & McIntosh, 2006; Gallant et al., 2011). It is interesting that while women were less likely to disclose their physical characteristics and sex life preferences, they were more likely to describe their personality (n = 165, 18%) and hobbies/interests (n = 193, 21%) in their self-marketing, when compared to men (n = 114, 13%; and n = 139, 16%, respectively). Thus, gender differences do appear to exist in self-marketing related to utilizing personality and hobbies/interests in attempting to attract a prospective date.

Tone

The tone of the personal ad conveyed the overall feeling and approach that the individual was using for the self-marketing. The tone of the post is important because the language selected for use in the post becomes the subtle cues utilized by others in judging the content (Rosen et al., 2008). If the post is deemed too wordy or the individual is believed to be dishonest, her personal advertisement may be ignored. Four sub-categories were identified related to the tone: sales pitch, wordy, honesty, and picture for picture (see Table 2).

Picture for picture (n = 258, 56%) and honesty (i.e., "Keeping things real") (n = 101, 22%) were the most frequent tone utilized in the ads. These findings

are supported by previous research that says authenticity can be important in e-dating (Close & Zinkhan, 2004). Because of the mediated nature of e-dating, there is a tendency for the consumer to not always be completely accurate in his/her post and may tend to project their ideal (as opposed to real) self (Malchow-Moller, 2003). The tone of the ads asking for honesty and asking to exchange current photos suggests that the posters want to be forthright and are looking for frank information in return. This post from a woman in Jacksonville illustrates the importance of honesty.

> Keep it real and no one gets hurt. Just be yourself unless you're one of "those kind of guys." A façade living out a charade. Then umm yea; buh-bye.

The other tones that appeared to emerge from the data were extreme wordiness (n = 72, 16%) and a sales pitch (n = 30, 7%). The wordiness could have been the fact that the poster did not plan out his/her advertisement and, instead, wrote the ad in a "stream of consciousness." Furthermore, wordiness could also have been due to the fact that he/she was nervous and unsure exactly what to post, so he/she put down everything that came to mind when typing up the ad. Although less frequent, there were also ads that had a tone that appeared to mirror a sales pitch for a consumer good. This man from Chicago utilized a sales tone.

> I am a masculine, yet boyish, sexy American white boy. 34, that's me in the body, blond hair, hazel eyes, and super smooth with a great body. Discreet, personable, sane, healthy, d/d free. Looking for an attractive woman, and most importantly, someone with a good attitude and an open mind. Contact me for more. Yes the ad is real!!!!!!!! . . . Lastly—no hassles, no drama, no b/s, no attitudes, and no wasting of each other's time.

Utilizing a tone with a sales pitch when writing a personal ad suggests that the consumer realizes that the post for a date is truly a form of self-marketing, where the poster is trying to attract a potential partner into the exchange, as suggested by previous research (Arvidsson, 2006; Patterson & Hodgson, 2006).

When examining gender differences by the type of tone, the data also suggested differences exist among men versus women. While there was no difference on the two genders with respect to preference for honesty and wordiness, men were more likely than women to request a picture for a picture (n = 31, 14% for men; n = 14, 6% for women) and to utilize the sales pitch (n = 171, 72% for men; n = 144, 61% for women) in their self-marketing. Men asking for a current photo is consistent with previous research. Close and Zinkhan (2004) found that authenticity can be an issue in e-dating. While men tend to misreport their relationship status (i.e., they say that they are single when really married), women tend to misrepresent their age and weight. If they share a photo, it can even be from many years ago (Close & Zinkhan, 2004). To the extent this is a common occurrence in the context of e-dating, men may be more likely to request an updated photo from women, as found in the data from the present study.

DISCUSSION

The findings from this study reinforce some of what is already known in the e-dating and personal ads literature. And yet, some of the findings are innovative, making a contribution to both of these literatures, as well as the literature on self-marketing. In fact, no study to date has examined gender differences in self-marketing. The present study not only extends the literature on e-dating and personal ads, but it also unpacks how men and women market themselves differently in the context of personal ads on Craigslist.

To begin, the results of this study support some of the existing findings in previous research on e-dating. Specifically, this study suggests that authenticity in the context of e-dating is an issue for both men and women. There was no difference in gender with respect to honesty (i.e., "keep it real"). However, in our sample, women were more likely to state a preferred relationship status for a prospective dater when compared to men. This is a significant finding related to authenticity because previous research has indicated men are more likely (than women) to misreport being involved in a relationship when participating in e-dating (Close & Zinkhan, 2004). Similarly, the present study found that men were more likely to

articulate that they wanted to exchange photos with a prospective dater when compared to the women in the sample. This also reinforces existing findings by Close and Zinkhan (2004), who found women were more likely to share old photos and not disclose current age and weight when interacting with a prospective e-dater.

The results of this study also reinforce existing findings in the literature on personal ads. This study's findings show that much of the content of online personal ads in the context of Craigslist is based on traditional gender stereotypes, such as men want sex and women are seeking long-term relationships. Furthermore, the findings also show that women, when compared to men, are more likely to state preferred demographics (such as employment status) in their online personal ads. This finding also suggests that women are seeking men that can provide resources, as suggested by previous research.

And yet, this study's findings also make some novel 45 contributions to the literature on personal ads and e-dating. For example, the content of the Craigslist ads showed a range of types of relationships sought. Not all interactions sought were romantic in nature, nor were they all based on the idea of an extended relationship. Some relationships sought were more platonic in nature (i.e., new to the area and looking for a friend) and others were more one-time, discrete interactions (i.e., a one-night stand). In addition, criteria for a partner, such as relationship status and being disease/drug-free, are new to the literature on personal ads. It is possible that these things have always been important to dating via personal ads, but the free-form and unlimited space available on Craigslist could have brought these issues to the forefront of the advertising content.

This study also makes a contribution to the literature on self-marketing in that it begins to unpack gender differences that exist as consumers begin to market and brand themselves online. One interesting finding from this study was that men utilized a tone of a sales pitch more often than women. Why this is the case has yet to be determined. Do men view e-dating more as a form of self-marketing than women? Or are men more comfortable selling and marketing themselves than women? Clearly, this gender difference merits future research. Other gender differences that occurred in self-marketing included that men pitched more of their physical characteristics in the ads, while women pitched more of their personality characteristics and hobbies/interests. Again, this was a counter-intuitive finding in that sexual strategies theory suggests that women should want to sell their physical characteristics (in order to attract more prospective partners), while men should want to sell their ability to produce resources (i.e., their demographics). This was not the case in the data. Future research needs to unpack these gender differences to determine the extent to which consumers plan out what kind of content they build into a personal ad in order to maximize their chance at obtaining a potential date. Finally, the results of this study also showed that women were more likely than men to specify preferred physical characteristics of prospective partners. This finding also suggests that future studies are needed to understand why, given that men want to attract fertile females, women are more likely to specify what they want with respect to the physical attractiveness of a man.

The findings of this study also offer unique insight into differences between males and females that can be used when creating marketing messages from a managerial perspective. In advertising consumer products, crafting the right message and using the right person to deliver the message is crucial for the success of the campaign. The present study suggests that the same premises are true in self-marketing on Craigslist. Online dating is replete with obvious marketing tactics where the presentation of the self is consciously sales oriented. The types of interaction, criteria for partner, self-disclosure, and tone of the post suggest that online self-marketing is carefully constructed and communicated. Thus, the findings of this study provide insight into how gendered identities are constructed, which is insightful for those creating marketing messages. For example, consumers often try a product because they like the package and/ or remember a slogan or brand message. In much the same way, when online self-marketing is effective, an individual might connect with someone whose post matches his/her personal views. Thus, it is important when creating marketing messages to understand what types of messages would appeal to the target market. Should the message be about building a relationship with the consumer or about benefits offered by the product? What selection criteria are important to members of the target market? Is the criteria more fact based (i.e., like demographics) or is it related to emotions? Finally, how should the marketing message be constructed? Answers to these questions can assist marketers in crafting a message and improving positioning of brands. And answers to these types of questions should also be studied among consumers who are self-marketing online as well.

Another interesting implication of this study is that the Internet is an important space for finding and exhibiting one's self because it is free from the immediate bias often present in face-to-face communication (McKenna and Bargh, 2000). According to Arvidsson (2006), Internet dating sites are the perfect branding tool where communication and interaction are based on the brand image (i.e., self-marketing) that is created and accepted. Marketers are encountering an untapped resource with social media tools, like Craigslist. Information from online communities represents an important source of marketing information that can be acquired at minimal cost. Our findings illuminate opportunities for marketers to expand their understanding of how the genders self-market and what they are looking for in heterosexual relationships. Not only is this information useful for a host of online dating companies (like eHarmony. com), but it is also relevant for media companies (like VH1, Cosmopolitan, Playboy, Facebook) and consumer product companies, like fashion designers (i.e., Abercrombie & Fitch), beauty products (i.e., Calvin Klein), and other product categories that are marketed via appeals to identity and sex.

Finally, the results of this study also illustrate that language is an imprecise form in how people read and understand the written and spoken word. It is important for marketers, especially advertisers, to understand the criteria that consumers are searching for and the language that they use to describe the criterion. In the case of self-marketing via Craigslist, words are used to motivate another person to get in touch with the poster in the hope that the first encounter (i.e., an e-mail hopefully followed by a face-to-face meeting) will lead to something more. The same scenario happens in advertising. The advertising message is carefully crafted to encourage the consumer to desire an experience with the product. The message is a strategic combination of words and sometimes pictures that provide a reason to believe. And yet, no matter how right the copywriter "gets" the words, it is the picture that may often seal the deal. In Craigslist, a thoughtfully crafted personal ad may attract someone's attention, but it might be a picture-for-a-picture exchange that generates the next level of interest.

REFERENCES

Arvidsson, A. (2006). "Quality singles": Internet dating and the work of fantasy. *New Media and Society, 8*(4), 671–690.

Bond, B. J. (2009). He posted, she posted: Gender differences in self-disclosure on social network sites. *Rocky Mountain Communication Review, 6*(2), 29–37.

Butler-Smith, P., Cameron, S., & Collins, A. (1998). Gender differences in mate search effort: An exploratory economic analysis of personal advertisements. *Applied Economics, 30*(10), 1277–1285.

Cameron, S., & Collins, A. (1999). Looks unimportant? A demand function for male attractiveness by female personal advertisers. *Applied Economics Letters, 6*(6), 381.

Chase, L. (2011). The power of personal branding. *American Salesman, 56*(6), 7.

Close, A., & Zinkhan, G. M. (2004). Romance and the Internet: The e-mergence of e-dating. *Advances in Consumer Research, 31*, 153–157.

Conaway, C. (2013a). Are men more risky with social media? May 1. Retrieved from http://goodmenproject.com/good-feed-blog/are-men-more-risky-with-social-media/

Conaway, C. (2013b). Pinterest is for girls, Gentlemint is for boys, February 26. Retrieved from http://cameronconaway.com/pinterest-is-for-girls-gentlemint-is-for-boys/

Coupland J. (1996). Dating advertisements: Discourses of the commodified self. *Discourse & Society, 7*(2), 187–207.

Dawson, B., & McIntosh, W. D. (2006). Sexual strategies theory and Internet personal advertisements. *Cyberpsychology & Behavior, 9*(5), 614–617.

Derlega, V. (1979). Appropriateness of self-disclosure. In Gordon J. Chelune (Ed.), Self-disclosure: Origins, patterns, and implications of openness in interpersonal relationships (pp. 151–176). San Francisco: Jossey-Bass.

Ellison, N., Heino, R., & Gibbs, J. (2006). Managing impressions online: Self-presentation processes in the online dating environment. *Journal of Computer-Mediated Communication, 11*(2), 415–441.

Elmore, L. (2010). Personal branding 2.0. *Women in Business, 62*(1), 12.

Gallant, S., Williams, L., Fisher, M., & Cox, A. (2011). Mating strategies and self-presentation in online personal advertisement photographs. *Journal of Social, Evolutionary, and Cultural Psychology, 5*(1), 106–121.

Greer, J. (2010). The art of self-marketing online. *U.S. News & World Report, 147*(5), 30.

Hartman, K. (2006). Television and movie representations of salespeople: Beyond Willy Loman. *Journal of Personal Selling & Sales Management, 26*(3), 283–292.

Hearn, A. (2008). "Meat, mask, burden": Probing the contours of the branded self. *Journal of Consumer Culture, 8*(2), 197–217.

Hyatt, J. (2010). Building your brand (and keeping your job). *Fortune, 162*(3), 70–76.

Jagger, E. (1998). Marketing the self, buying another: Dating in a postmodern, consumer society. *Sociology, 32*(4), 795–814.

Joinson, A. N. (2008). Looking at, looking up, or keeping up with people? Motives and uses of Facebook. *CHI 2008 Proceedings*, 1027–1036.

Kassarjian, H. H. (1977). Content analysis in consumer research. *Journal of Consumer Research, 4*(1), 8–18.

Kroft, K., & Pope, D. (2008). *Does online search crowd out traditional search and improve matching efficiency? Evidence from Craigslist.* Working paper.

Labrecque, L. I., Markos, E., & Milne, G. R. (2011). Online personal branding: Processes, challenges, and implications. *Journal of Interactive Marketing, 25*(1), 37–50.

Lair, D., Sullivan, K., & Cheney, G. (2005). Marketization and the recasting of the professional self: The rhetoric and ethics of personal branding. *Management Communications Quarterly, 18*(3), 307–343.

Lakoff, R. T., & Bucholtz, M. (2004). *Language and woman's place: Text and commentaries.* New York, NY: Oxford University Press.

Malchow-Moller, A. (2003). Internet dating. A focus group investigation of young Danes' and Frenchmen's attitudes towards the phenomenon. *Kontur, 7*, 11–20.

McCaffrey, M. (1983). *Personal marketing strategies: How to sell yourself, your ideas, & your services.* Englewood Cliffs, NJ: Prentice Hall.

McKenna, K. A., & Bargh, J. A. (2000). Plan 9 from cyberspace: The implication of the Internet for personality and social psychology. *Personality & Social Psychology Review* (Lawrence Erlbaum Associates), *4*(1), 57–75.

Montoya, P., & Vandehey, T. (2008). *The brand called you: Create a personal brand that wins attention and grows your business.* New York, NY: McGraw-Hill.

Patterson, A., & Hodgson, J. (2006). A speeddating story: The lover's guide to marketing excellence. *Journal of Marketing Management, 22*(5/6), 455–471.

Peters, T. (1997). The brand called you. *Fast Company, 10,* 83–88.

Rosen, L. D., Cheever, N. A., Cummings, C., & Felt, J. (2008). The impact of emotionality and self-disclosure on online dating versus traditional dating. *Computers in Human Behavior, 24*(5), 2124–2157.

Schau, H., & Gilly, M. C. (2003). We are what we post? Self-presentation in personal web space. *Journal of Consumer Research, 30*(3), 385–404.

Shepherd, I. H. (2005). From cattle and Coke to Charlie: Meeting the challenge of self-marketing and personal branding. *Journal of Marketing Management, 21*(5/6), 589–606.

Stemler, S. (2001). An overview of content analysis. *Practical Assessment, Research, and Evaluation, 7*(17).

Strano, M. (2008). User descriptions and interpretations of self-presentation through Facebook profile images. *Cyberpsychology: Journal of Psychosocial Research on Cyberspace, 2*(2), Retrieved from http://www.cyberpsychology .eu/view.php?cisloclanku=2008110402&article=(search in Issues)

Thomas, J., Peters, C., & Tolson, H. (2007). An exploratory investigation of the virtual community MySpace.com: What are consumers saying about fashion? *Journal of Fashion Marketing & Management, 11*(4), 587–603.

Tither, J. M. (2000). Selling yourself and procuring another: Investigating gender differences in NZ dating advertisements. *New Zealand English Journal, 14,* 66–74.

Reading Questions

1. The authors of this study identify a gap in the scholarship as part of their introduction. According to the authors, what is that gap?

2. In your own words, explain how the researchers selected the cities they focused on for their collection of Craigslist postings.

3. According to Table 2, what was the most frequent criterion for a partner identified in the content of the ads?

4. Based on their examination of self-disclosure in the ads, the researchers suggest that "gender differences do appear to exist in self-marketing related to utilizing personality and hobbies/interests in attempting to attract a prospective date" (par. 36). What specific findings do the researchers use to support this conclusion?

Rhetoric Questions

5. Based on the article's (unlabeled) abstract, who are the researchers' intended audiences? What evidence does the abstract provide to support your conclusions?

6. In the Methodology section, the authors describe the two phases of their research "used to examine the self-marketing occurring among men and women on Craigslist" (17). Contrast the authors' descriptions of these two phases in terms of length and level of detail. What accounts for the differences in the two descriptions?

7. Describe the authors' strategy, or the organizational principle, for reporting their findings.

8. To whom are the final paragraphs of the study directed? How do you know this?

Response and Research Questions

9. What do you see as the potential advantages or drawbacks of attempting to find love by self-marketing online?

10. In the Discussion section, the authors note that "[o]ne interesting finding from this study was that men utilized a tone of a sales pitch more often than women." They then pose the following questions: "Do men view e-dating more as a form of self-marketing than women? Or are men more comfortable selling and marketing themselves than women?" (46). Based on your own life experiences, how would you answer the researchers' questions?

11. Imagine for a moment that you're on a quest to find love online. Construct a brief Craigslist ad in which you describe yourself and your ideal partner. Once you're done, reflect on the strategies you used to "market" yourself. What did you include or choose to leave out? What do you see as most effective about your self-marketing?

WRITING PROJECT   Contributing to a Scholarly Conversation

For this assignment, choose a family-related topic and compose an academic essay that contributes to the scholarly conversation surrounding that topic in a field or discipline of your choice. For example, in "Changing Counts, Counting Change," Brian Powell et al. position themselves within the scholarly conversation in the field of sociology regarding the functional view of families. Arguing that scholars need to take a "fresh look," the authors use their own survey data to provide an alternative interpretation. In other words, by understanding the scholarly conversations about the topic and conducting their own research, the authors were able to help others understand the topic in a new way.

Using the readings in this chapter as a model, you might choose a topic related to how "family" is defined within different cultures or how definitions of marriage have historically shifted over time. Additionally, you might investigate how gender roles and expectations are perceived by diverse groups of people. No matter what topic you choose, think about how particular disciplinary perspectives might ask questions about the topic and how those questions can inform your research.

One of your first steps will therefore be to explore others' ideas by conducting research into your topic. Using the research skills you developed in Chapter 3, remember to think about research not just as gathering supporting evidence for your own argument. Think about research also as tracing out a conversation among scholars:

- What are others saying about your topic?
- Is there room for change, refinements, or redefinition in what they are saying about your topic?
- How might you contribute to this conversation?

Depending on your instructor and the expectations of your disciplinary perspective, you may choose to conduct research by designing a study, collecting data, and analyzing your results. Follow appropriate disciplinary and genre expectations in structuring your argument, providing evidence for your claims, and citing your sources.

WRITING PROJECT **Writing a Comparative Analysis of Research Methodologies**

In this chapter, the writers draw on a wide variety of research methodologies to explore their research questions. For example, Warren Milteer Jr. relies heavily on analysis of historical documents to explore racial boundaries in nineteenth-century North Carolina, whereas Brian Powell et al. rely on a mixed methodology that includes the use of survey data to understand shifting perspectives on same-sex marriage.

Drawing on the readings in the academic case study in this chapter, compose a descriptive analysis of the methods utilized in two differing academic disciplines. You might begin by identifying the following for each research report:

- **Research Question(s)**   What phenomenon are the researchers studying, and what do they want to know about it?

- **Research Methods**   What research methods are used to find answers to the research question(s)?

As you describe the researchers' methods, be sure to engage in analysis as well. In other words, consider why the researchers use the methods they do and how those methods compare to others. Conclude your descriptive analysis by highlighting any similarities or differences in the two disciplines' methods.

Crime, Punishment, and Justice

This chapter includes a number of popular and academic texts aimed at examining various aspects of crime, punishment, and justice in American society. The opening selections present perspectives from a number of popular sources. The first identifies some of the highly controversial implications for criminal prosecution and punishment that have resulted from recent advances in the fields of neuroscience and neuroimaging. The second selection presents a series of statistics about our criminal justice system as evidence of its bias in the treatment of people of color. The third article traces the journey of an adolescent who was charged and punished as an adult, raising questions about the appropriate treatment of youthful offenders in our criminal justice system. The last work, also intended for a popular audience, tells the story of a successful financial planner who spent four months incarcerated at Rikers Island, New York, one of the most notoriously violent prisons in America, after being convicted of a white-collar crime.

We hope these readings will foster your own further consideration of a few of the many complex issues related to the topics of crime, punishment, and justice in America:

- Is criminal behavior biologically driven? If so, then how do we punish individuals for criminal behavior?

- Is our criminal justice system color-blind? Does it treat people equitably, regardless of race?

- Should adolescents be charged, prosecuted, and punished as adults?

- Are white-collar criminals punished appropriately?

- What is life in jail or prison really like? Does punishment in America need to change? If so, in what ways?

Beyond the typical lines of inquiry directed at the topic of the death penalty in America (e.g., Does it act as a deterrent? Can it be fairly applied? Does it constitute "cruel or unusual" punishment?), the academic case study for this chapter explores capital punishment from a number of perspectives that reveal, collectively, wide variety in the kinds of inquiry that characterize distinct disciplinary approaches:

- **Humanities** What meaning can be found in the last-meal requests of individuals facing execution?

- **Social Sciences** How do movies affect viewers' moods about and attitudes toward the death penalty?

- **Natural Sciences** Does the current execution drug cocktail work as it was intended? Is it constitutional?

- **Applied Fields** What do criminal justice practitioners themselves think of capital punishment?

Inside a Psychopath's Brain: The Sentencing Debate

BARBARA BRADLEY HAGERTY

Barbara Bradley Hagerty is a former National Public Radio (NPR) religion correspondent. She is also the author of the *New York Times* best-selling book *Fingerprints of God: The Search for the Science of Spirituality* (2009). In the following article, published on NPR's website in June 2010 as the second part of a three-part series entitled *Inside the Criminal Brain*, Hagerty reports on the implications of emerging technologies in neuroscience and neuroimaging for the prosecution of crimes and for the punishment of criminals.

Kent Kiehl has studied hundreds of psychopaths. Kiehl is one of the world's leading investigators of psychopathy and a professor at the University of New Mexico. He says he can often see it in their eyes: There's an intensity in their stare, as if they're trying to pick up signals on how to respond. But the eyes are not an element of psychopathy, just a clue.

Officially, Kiehl scores their pathology on the Hare Psychopathy Checklist, which measures traits such as the inability to feel empathy or remorse, pathological lying, or impulsivity.

"The scores range from zero to 40," Kiehl explains in his sunny office overlooking a golf course. "The average person in the community, a male, will score

about 4 or 5. Your average inmate will score about 22. An individual with psychopathy is typically described as 30 or above. Brian scored 38.5 basically. He was in the 99th percentile."

"Brian" is Brian Dugan, a man who is serving two life sentences for rape and murder in Chicago. Last July, Dugan pleaded guilty to raping and murdering 10-year-old Jeanine Nicarico in 1983, and he was put on trial to determine whether he should be executed. Kiehl was hired by the defense to do a psychiatric evaluation.

In a videotaped interview with Kiehl, Dugan de- 5 scribes how he only meant to rob the Nicaricos' home. But then he saw the little girl inside.

"She came to the door and...I clicked," Dugan says in a flat, emotionless voice. "I turned into Mr. Hyde from Dr. Jekyll."

On screen, Dugan is dressed in an orange jumpsuit. He seems calm, even normal—until he lifts his hands to take a sip of water and you see the handcuffs. Dugan is smart—his IQ is over 140—but he admits he has always had shallow emotions. He tells Kiehl that in his quarter century in prison, he believes he's developed a sense of remorse.

"And I have empathy, too—but it's like it just stops," he says. "I mean, I start to feel, but something just blocks it. I don't know what it is."

Kiehl says he's heard all this before: All psychopaths claim they feel terrible about their crimes for the benefit of the parole board.

"But then you ask them, 'What do you mean, you 10 feel really bad?' And Brian will look at you and go, 'What do you mean, what does it mean?' They look at you like, 'Can you give me some help? A hint? Can I call a friend?' They have no way of really getting at that at all," Kiehl says.

Kiehl says the reason people like Dugan cannot access their emotions is that their physical brains are different. And he believes he has the brain scans to prove it.

BRAIN SCANNING IN A MOBILE MRI

On a crystal clear June morning at Albuquerque's Youth Diagnostic and Development Center, juveniles who have been convicted of violent offenses march by, craning their necks as a huge trailer drives through the gates. This is Kiehl's prize—a $2 million mobile MRI provided by the Mind Research Network at the University of New Mexico. Kiehl transports the mobile MRI to maximum-security prisons around the state, and over the past few years, he has scanned the brains of more than 1,100 inmates, about 20 percent of whom are psychopaths.

For ethical reasons, Kiehl could not allow me to watch an inmate's brain being scanned, so he asked his researchers to demonstrate.

After a few minutes of preparation, researcher Kevin Bache settles into the brain scanner, where he can look up and see a screen. On the screen flash three types of pictures. One kind depicts a moral violation: He sees several hooded Klansmen setting a cross on fire. Another type is emotional but morally ambiguous: a car that is on fire but you don't know why. Another type of photo is neutral: for example, students standing around a Bunsen burner.

The subjects rate whether the picture is a moral 15 violation on a scale of 1 to 5. Kiehl says most psychopaths do not differ from normal subjects in the way they rate the photos: Both psychopaths and the average person rank the KKK with a burning cross as a moral violation. But there's a key difference: Psychopaths' brains behave differently from that of a nonpsychopathic person. When a normal person sees a morally objectionable photo, his limbic system lights up. This is what Kiehl calls the "emotional circuit," involving the orbital cortex above the eyes and the amygdala deep in the brain. But Kiehl says when psychopaths like Dugan see the KKK picture, their emotional circuit does not engage in the same way.

"We have a lot of data that shows psychopaths do tend to process this information differently," Kiehl says. "And Brian looked like he was processing it like the other individuals we've studied with psychopathy."

Kiehl says the emotional circuit may be what stops a person from breaking into that house or killing that girl. But in psychopaths like Dugan, the brakes don't work. Kiehl says psychopaths are a little like people with very low IQs who are not fully responsible for their actions. The courts treat people with low IQs differently. For example, they can't get the death penalty.

"What if I told you that a psychopath has an emotional IQ that's like a 5-year-old?" Kiehl asks. "Well, if that was the case, we'd make the same argument for individuals with low emotional IQ—that maybe they're not as deserving of punishment, not as deserving of culpability, etc."

IMPLICATIONS OF THE DIAGNOSIS

And that's exactly what Dugan's lawyers argued at trial last November. Attorney Steven Greenberg said that Dugan was not criminally insane. He knew right from wrong. But he was incapable of making the right choices.

"Someone shouldn't be executed for a condition 20 that they were born with, because it's not their fault," Greenberg says. "The crime is their fault, and he wasn't saying it wasn't his fault, and he wasn't saying, give [me] a free pass. But he was saying, don't kill me because it's not my fault that I was born this way."

This argument troubles Steven Erickson, a forensic psychologist and legal scholar at Widener University School of Law. He notes that alcoholics have brain abnormalities. Do we give them a pass if they kill someone while driving drunk?

"What about folks who suffer from depression? They have brain abnormalities, too. Should they be entitled to [an] excuse under the law?" he asks. "I think the key idea here is the law is not interested in brain abnormalities. The law is interested in whether or not someone at the time that the criminal act occurred understood the difference between right and wrong."

At trial, Jonathan Brodie, a psychiatrist at NYU Medical School who was the prosecution's expert witness, went further. Even if Dugan's brain is abnormal, he testified, the brain does *not* dictate behavior.

"There may be many, many people who also have psychopathic tendencies and have similar scans, who don't do antisocial behavior, who don't rape and kill," Brodie says.

Moreover, Brodie told the jury, Dugan's brain 25 scan in 2009 says nothing about what his brain was like when he killed Jeanine Nicarico.

"I don't know with Brian Dugan what was going on in his brain" when he committed his crime, Brodie says. "And I certainly don't know what was going on from a brain scan that was taken 24 years later."

The jury seemed to zero in on the science, asking to reread all the testimony about the neuroscience during 10 hours of deliberation. But in the end, they sentenced Dugan to death. Dugan is appealing the sentence.

In the meantime, this case signals the beginning of a revolution in the courtroom, Kiehl says.

"Neuroscience and neuroimaging is going to change the whole philosophy about how we punish and how we decide who to incapacitate and how we decide how to deal with people," he says, echoing comments of a growing number of leading scholars across the country, including Princeton and Harvard.

Just like DNA, he believes brain scans will even- 30 tually be standard fare. And that, he and others say, could upend our notions of culpability, crime, and punishment.

Reading Questions

1. Why does Kiehl believe that psychopaths like Dugan, a self-confessed murderer and rapist, cannot access their emotions in the same way the average person can?

2. What do MRI results reveal about psychopaths' limbic systems that separate them from non-psychopathic individuals?

3. What appears to be the defense strategy of Dugan's attorneys at trial? What is their argument with regard to his guilt or innocence?

4. What are psychiatrist Jonathan Brodie's objections to the Dugan defense strategy?

5. Kiehl says that the Dugan case "signals the beginning of a revolution in the courtroom" (par. 28). How does this position make sense in light of the jury's verdict in the Dugan case?

Rhetoric Questions

6. This part of the NPR series *Inside the Criminal Brain* is presented in three sections. Consider the structural design of the text, and provide a brief explanation for the writer's decision to divide the text as she does.

7. Choose any one of the three sections in this article, and determine the average number of sentences per paragraph in the section. As well, calculate the average number of quotations per paragraph. Why do you suppose Hagerty makes such language and reference decisions?

8. If possible, read the other two parts of the series of reports included in *Inside the Criminal Brain*. Describe the relationship of Part Two, "Inside a Psychopath's Brain: The Sentencing Debate," to the other two parts. Why is it positioned as the second report in the series?

Response and Research Questions

9. According to forensic psychologist Steven Erickson, "the law is not interested in brain abnormalities" (22). Should it be? Why or why not?

10. Kiehl suggests that neuroscience and neuroimaging are going to change the way society thinks about how it punishes criminal behavior. Do you agree with this suggestion? What kinds of potential changes might we anticipate?

The Top 10 Most Startling Facts about People of Color and Criminal Justice in the United States: A Look at the Racial Disparities Inherent in Our Nation's Criminal-Justice System

SOPHIA KERBY

Sophia Kerby is a special assistant to the Center for American Progress's *Progress 2050* project, which provides support for the development of progressive ideas in response to the nation's increasingly diverse population. Kerby's report was published online at the Center for American Progress's website in March 2012. The report presents a series of statistics as evidence to suggest that "eliminating the racial disparities inherent to our nation's criminal-justice policies and practices must be at the heart of a renewed, refocused, and reenergized movement for racial justice in America."

This month the United States celebrates the Selma-to-Montgomery marches of 1965 to commemorate our shared history of the civil rights movement and our nation's continued progress toward racial equality. Yet decades later a broken criminal-justice system has proven that we still have a long way to go in achieving racial equality.

Today people of color continue to be disproportionately incarcerated, policed, and sentenced to death at significantly higher rates than their white counterparts.

Further, racial disparities in the criminal-justice system threaten communities of color—disenfranchising thousands by limiting voting rights and denying equal access to employment, housing, public benefits, and education to millions more. In light of these disparities, it is imperative that criminal-justice reform evolves as the civil rights issue of the 21st century.

Below we outline the top 10 facts pertaining to the criminal-justice system's impact on communities of color.

1. *While people of color make up about 30 percent of the United States' population, they account for 60 percent of those imprisoned.* The prison population grew by 700 percent from 1970 to 2005, a rate that is outpacing crime and population rates. The incarceration rates disproportionately impact men of color: 1 in every 15 African American men and 1 in every 36 Hispanic men are incarcerated in comparison to 1 in every 106 white men.

2. *According to the Bureau of Justice Statistics, one in three black men can expect to go to prison in their lifetime.* Individuals of color have a disproportionate number of encounters with law enforcement, indicating that racial profiling continues to be a problem. A report by the Department of Justice found that blacks and Hispanics were approximately three times more likely to be searched during a traffic stop than white motorists. African Americans were twice as likely to be arrested and almost four times as likely to experience the use of force during encounters with the police.

3. *Students of color face harsher punishments in school than their white peers, leading to a higher number of youth of color incarcerated.* Black and Hispanic students represent more than 70 percent of those involved in school-related arrests or referrals to law enforcement. Currently, African Americans make up two-fifths and Hispanics one-fifth of confined youth today.

4. *According to recent data by the Department of Education, African American students are arrested far more often than their white classmates.* The data showed that 96,000 students were arrested and 242,000 referred to law enforcement by schools during the 2009–10 school year. Of those students, black and Hispanic students made up more than 70 percent of arrested or referred students. Harsh school punishments, from suspensions to arrests, have led to high numbers of youth of color coming into contact with the juvenile-justice system and at an earlier age.

5. *African American youth have higher rates of juvenile incarceration and are more likely to be sentenced to adult prison.* According to the Sentencing Project, even though African American juvenile youth are about 16 percent of the youth population, 37 percent of their cases are moved to criminal court and 58 percent of African American youth are sent to adult prisons.

6. *As the number of women incarcerated has increased by 800 percent over the last three decades, women of color have been disproportionately represented.* While the number of women incarcerated is relatively low, the racial and ethnic disparities are startling. African American women are three times more likely than white women to be incarcerated, while Hispanic women are 69 percent more likely than white women to be incarcerated.

7. *The war on drugs has been waged primarily in communities of color where people of color are more likely to receive higher offenses.* According to the Human Rights Watch, people of color are no more likely to use or sell illegal drugs than whites, but they have higher rates of arrests. African Americans comprise 14 percent of regular drug users but are 37 percent of those arrested for drug offenses. From 1980 to 2007 about one in three of the 25.4 million adults arrested for drugs was African American.

8. *Once convicted, black offenders receive longer sentences compared to white offenders.* The U.S. Sentencing Commission stated that in the federal system black offenders receive sentences that are 10 percent longer than white offenders for the same crimes. The Sentencing Project reports that African Americans are 21 percent more likely to receive mandatory-minimum sentences than white defendants and are 20 percent more likely to be sentenced to prison.

9. *Voter laws that prohibit people with felony convictions to vote disproportionately impact men of color.* An estimated 5.3 million Americans are denied the right to vote based on a past felony conviction. Felony disenfranchisement is exaggerated by racial disparities in the criminal-justice system, ultimately denying 13 percent of African American men the

right to vote. Felony-disenfranchisement policies have led to 11 states denying the right to vote to more than 10 percent of their African American population.

10. *Studies have shown that people of color face disparities in wage trajectory following release from prison.* Evidence shows that spending time in prison affects wage trajectories with a disproportionate impact on black men and women. The results show no evidence of racial divergence in wages prior to incarceration; however, following release from prison, wages grow at a 21 percent slower rate for black former inmates compared to white ex-convicts. A number of states have bans on people with certain convictions working in domestic health-service industries such as nursing, child care, and home health care — areas in which many poor women and women of color are disproportionately concentrated.

These racial disparities have deprived people of color of their most basic civil rights, making criminal-justice reform the civil rights issue of our time. Through mass imprisonment and the overrepresentation of individuals of color within the criminal justice and prison system, people of color have experienced an adverse impact on themselves and on their communities from barriers to reintegrating into society to engaging in the democratic process. Eliminating the racial disparities inherent to our nation's criminal-justice policies and practices must be at the heart of a renewed, refocused, and reenergized movement for racial justice in America.

There have been a number of initiatives on the state and federal level to address the racial disparities in youth incarceration. Last summer Secretary of Education Arne Duncan announced the Schools Discipline Initiative to bring increased awareness of effective policies and practices to ultimately dismantle the school-to-prison pipeline. States like California and Massachusetts are considering legislation to address the disproportionate suspensions among students of color. And in Clayton County, Georgia, collaborative local reforms have resulted in a 47 percent reduction in juvenile-court referrals and a 51 percent decrease in juvenile felony rates. These initiatives could serve as models of success for lessening the disparities in incarceration rates.

Reading Questions

1. According to Kerby, what are three negative effects on communities of color caused by the racial disparities in the treatment of people of color by the criminal justice system?

2. The article reports that people of color make up what percentage of the prison population in the United States?

3. What percentage of African American men have lost the right to vote as a result of a felony conviction, according to Kerby's reporting?

4. What evidence is there to suggest that women of color are treated differently from white women in the criminal justice system?

5. According to the U.S. Sentencing Commission, as reported in Kerby's article, how much longer are sentences imposed on African American offenders than sentences given to white offenders for the same crime?

Rhetoric Questions

6. Kerby presents the core content of her piece in a numbered list. Is this an effective strategy in light of her audience and goals?

7. Spend some time learning more about the Center for American Progress. With what political organizations or beliefs is it associated? Do these associations have any impact on your evaluation of the information presented in Kerby's report, or on the writer's ethos? Why or why not?

Response and Research Questions

8. Kerby provides evidence to suggest that the American criminal justice is broken. Do you agree that it is broken? Why or why not?

9. Kerby's final paragraph mentions the "school-to-prison pipeline." What is this, and what role might it play in the unequal treatment of people of color by the criminal justice system?

10. Choose any one of the statistical findings, as reported by Kerby, presented in the piece. Locate a reputable source that either substantiates or challenges that finding.

Should Juvenile Criminals Be Sentenced Like Adults?

CLARK MERREFIELD

Clark Merrefield is a reporter for the *Daily Beast*, a website that offers both news and opinions. In the article "Should Juvenile Criminals Be Sentenced Like Adults?" Merrefield shares the story of a young man who was sentenced to ten years in prison following his prosecution as an adult offender for robbery. In addition to the question in its title, the story raises a number of other questions about the appropriateness of charging and treating adolescents as adults in our criminal justice system. The article was posted on the *Daily Beast* in November 2012.

In August 2006, Sean Shevlino pulled on a hoodie, went to a Piggly Wiggly near his house, waited until the coast was clear, and hopped the counter.

Sean's friend's older brother worked at the Piggly Wiggly and had told Sean that when the lady behind the service counter went for a smoke break, all Sean had to do was jump over and snag some cash from the safe. It wouldn't be locked.

Sure enough, it wasn't. Sean opened the safe, grabbed a Ziploc bag of cash, stuffed it under his hoodie, and ran to a friend's house. He was 16.

Before then, Sean had seemed to be a typical American kid from Mount Pleasant, S.C., a politically conservative, affluent suburb outside Charleston. He was the quiet, introverted brother between Seamus and Alex. His mother, April, was a schoolteacher; his father, Peter, is a Navy veteran who leases shipping containers. Peter and April provided what they felt was a comfortable, college-bound track for the boys. Life seemed as normal as it gets.

But when Sean turned 15, "things quickly went 5 downhill," April said. "He started acting terrible to us. He just seemed very angry."

Sean was couch surfing with friends before the robbery and had been looking for a quick way to pay his friends back for their hospitality.

When Sean told them about the idea to rob the Piggly Wiggly, they told him he was crazy. But when Sean got an idea in his head, it stuck.

"When I got all the money, [my friends'] minds changed a little bit," Sean said.

And then Sean and his buddies had another idea: if he could get that much money again, maybe even more, they could get their own apartment. A few of the friends were 18 and could sign a lease. Sean would still go to school and finish his education, but he'd live on his terms.

The Food Lion just off Highway 17 was bigger 10 than the Piggly Wiggly. It would have more money. Easy money, part two.

But the boys soon realized that the Food Lion had more fail-safes; it wouldn't be as simple as hopping a counter. Someone—Sean doesn't remember who—suggested using a toy gun to stick up the place. Sean thought about it for half a second. "Yeah, why not?" he said. "We can do that."

With the last of the Piggly Wiggly cash, the teens bought their supplies: an orange ski mask, a pair of motorcycle gloves, a pellet gun, four walkie talkies, and a pair of goggles.

Just before 11 p.m. on Aug. 26, the plan coalesced.

Sean—whose code name was "Butch Cassidy"—crouched below a big window near the Food Lion's entrance. Christopher Cousins, 16, who worked at the store, said over the radios, "Butch is about to do it."

As the last customer left the store, Sean recalled, 15 Chris said, "If you're gonna do it, Sean, you gotta do it right now."

Sean could hear doubt in Chris's voice. "Nobody really thought we were going to go through with this thing," Sean said. "I heard that and I had this thought—I didn't really want to do it—but I had all these expectations riding on my shoulders. I had gotten them all involved in it up to this point."

Nobody backed down.

Sean entered the Food Lion. He found a manager who was buying a package of Goldfish crackers and pulled the pellet gun on him.

"He was terrified," Sean said. "And that's when it hit me. Like, Oh my God, I just scared the crap out of this guy."

With the pellet gun pointed at him the manager 20 opened the safe. Sean packed a black gym bag with as much cash as he could grab, and then he and the lookouts bolted across the parking lot to the getaway car, a blue-green Toyota RAV4.

"Haul ass!" Sean told the driver, Graham Stolte.

Stolte pulled onto Highway 17 and blue lights appeared out of the darkness. The police were flying toward the Food Lion.

"Holy shit," Sean thought as the cop cars streaked by in the opposite direction. "I just did something serious right here. I shouldn't have done that."

When the cash was counted there was nowhere near enough for Sean to get an apartment, and the money soon ran out. About a week later—after another robbery and a BMW joyride—the police caught up with Sean. Eleven teenagers in all, including the starting quarterback at the local high school, were involved to varying degrees with the two-week crime spree.

Sitting in an interrogation room, Peter Shevlino 25 asked his son if he had really stolen a car. He knew Sean had been acting out, but he never expected anything like this.

"Yeah," Sean said. "I did."

Peter ran his hands through his hair and looked at Sean without speaking.

"When he didn't yell at me that's when I knew I had really messed up," Sean said.

Sean, now 22, spoke to the *Daily Beast* by phone from MacDougall Correctional Institution in Ridgeville, S.C., five years into a 10-year sentence for armed robbery. Under South Carolina law, Sean, who was 16 at the time of his crimes, was charged as an adult.

Increasingly, social scientists, law-enforcement authorities, lawyers, and judges are questioning the wisdom of charging juveniles as adults.

It is only in the last few years that the law has begun to recognize what science has long known: that adolescent brain development takes more time than previously thought.

"While some teenagers can be astonishingly mature and others inconceivably childish, middle adolescence—roughly, ages 14 to 18—might be the worst time in a person's life for rational decision making," says Laurence Steinberg, an adolescent psychologist at Temple University. Research has repeatedly shown that during these years, pleasure centers are at full throttle, and foresight is lacking, particularly in young men.

"Among all American boys, about 75 percent violate the law at some point," Steinberg says. "For some it might be as minor as possession of marijuana and for others it could be as serious as armed robbery, but in either case they're breaking the law. The question we ask is why some stop and others don't. Our sense is most stop because they just grow up."

During pre- and early-adolescence, the brain becomes more efficient and logical, and dopamine activity increases. Things like sex, drugs, and adrenaline thrills feel really good, and when teens are in groups they are even more likely to go for the thrill.

But as teens approach adulthood, the pathways between the brain's CEO and the limbic system—the emotional center—increase substantially, allowing for greater impulse control. According to some studies, brain development is not complete until the mid-20s.

Steinberg is concerned that harsh punishment of juveniles often doesn't fit the crime. "If it were just a process of normal maturation, then I think it's important that we don't sanction them in a way that's going to mess up their lives."

Sean's original prosecutor offered him the 10-year sentence—in an adult prison—as part of a plea deal. But the Shevlinos resisted, hoping that if Sean could demonstrate an ability to change, maybe the new prosecutor, Scarlett Wilson, would reduce the charges and offer a youthful offender sentence.

The plan was that Sean would hold off on accepting the plea for as long as possible. In the meantime he would go to Three Springs, a now-defunct Outward Bound–style program in middle-of-nowhere Pittsboro, N.C. He'd learn how to control his anger and defiance. (After a battery of psychological tests, Sean had been diagnosed with oppositional defiant disorder.)

In early October 2006 Sean spent his first night at Three Springs. He had to prove that even though his actions belied a simmering anger, he wasn't one of the violent ones. More than that, Sean had to show he could lead among his regiment of 12 boys.

Sean moved swiftly through the military-style hierarchy, and by the end of his time was performing the work of paid counselors. The Three Springs program certainly wasn't a cure-all for every young man, but for some, like Sean, it seemed to work. It helped him learn to manage his ODD and prepare to reenter society.

But in the heart of tough-on-crime country, there was a public perception that an example had to be made. Wilson, the prosecutor, explained that she ultimately decided the 10-year plea deal was appropriate for Sean and one of the other teens—the two "ringleaders."

Sean had to make a choice: go to trial and face decades in prison, or take the plea. Sean accepted the plea in January 2008. With good behavior he would be out of adult prison in eight and a half years.

According to one frequently quoted statistic, a quarter-million teenagers under 18 pass through the adult justice system each year. Howard Snyder, a researcher with the Bureau of Justice Statistics, is developing a more statistically rigorous estimate using a sampling of court cases from 2012. But right now, even he isn't exactly sure how many juveniles encounter the adult system each year.

What Snyder does know is that 40 percent of 17-year-olds in America do not have any chance to be tried as a juvenile, and the available research shows that prosecuting young people as adults does not rehabilitate them or deter future crimes. A U.S. Department of Justice review of several large-scale studies found that, excluding arrests for nonviolent property or drug offenses, young people tried in adult

criminal court generally have greater recidivism*
rates than those tried in juvenile court.

However, recent Supreme Court cases and new
state legislation indicate a changing attitude toward
how we treat our youngest wrongdoers.

In 2005 the court outlawed the death penalty for
those who had committed their crimes before the age
of 18, relying in large part on the emerging science
of brain development. The court went a step further
last summer, prohibiting mandatory sentences of life
without parole for juveniles. Also since 2005, several
states have raised the adult criminal bar to age 18,
either for some or all offenses. A state task force in
North Carolina, one of two states where the age of
criminal responsibility is 16, has recommended that
for minor crimes, teens under 18 remain in the juvenile system.

The benefits of keeping juveniles out of the adult
system are also financial. If the age were raised to 18
for misdemeanors and nonviolent felonies, North Carolina would net $52.3 million a year over the long run,
according to an analysis by the Vera Institute of Justice.

Sean Shevlino is now an adult, but he spent the
last years of his youth in the same prison where he
now sits. The experience has no doubt affected him
deeply and has changed his father's views on criminal
justice too.

"I never believed in my wildest dreams that children were treated like this in this country," Peter Shevlino said. "You would have called me a hard-right,
conservative Republican. The people in that camp—
even after this, very good friends that we have—they
still cling to the idea that this is sort of a one-off. It's
hard for people to accept that, no, it's not; we have a
severely broken system. It's hard to accept that everything we've been doing for the past 40 to 50 years has
been wrong."

Even Scarlett Wilson explained by email that while
she has no control over legislation, she believes "it is
better when juveniles are housed in prison separately
from adults."

After Sean accepted his 10-year sentence, he was
taken by bus to Kirkland maximum security prison
in Columbia, S.C. He looked up at the sentry towers
dotting the campus as the bus entered Kirkland. He
couldn't believe what was happening.

"You get to Kirkland and you get stripped naked
and they wash you down and you're with all these
people—like 50 or 60 guys—and I'm the youngest
one there by far," Sean said. "I'm just looking around
like, There's no way I could ever do 10 years here in
prison. That's not going to happen."

Sean had to fight other inmates, especially early
on, but the work he did at Three Springs and consistent contact with his family have helped him maintain
perspective and adapt to prison.

"I've seen a lot of young guys like me who didn't
have a head on their shoulders and didn't know how
to handle the pressure," he said. "Back here it's survival of the fittest."

Reading Questions

1. According to Temple University psychologist Laurence Steinberg, what is the
   toughest time for adolescents, and why is this time the most difficult in terms of
   adolescents' rational decision-making abilities?

2. According to the report, what are two reasons the Shevlinos decided to send Sean
   to Three Springs?

3. What important decisions did the U.S. Supreme Court make in 2005 that have
   affected the prosecution and punishment of individuals under the age of eighteen?

4. To what does Sean give credit for his ability to adapt to imprisonment at the
   correctional facility?

*recidivism: going back to a previous behavior, in this case a criminal behavior.

Rhetoric Questions

5. What is the effect of the reporter telling Sean's story at the beginning of the piece and then returning to it at the end? Could the piece just as easily have started at another point? Why or why not?

6. Outline the article briefly by identifying four clear sections or movements. How would you label each of those four sections? Where does each section begin and end?

7. The reporter addresses the possible financial savings that states could experience if they did not treat juveniles as adults. Why does the writer raise this issue, given the larger context of the piece? Does it work? Why or why not?

Response and Research Questions

8. The report cites a U.S. Department of Justice review that found that "excluding arrests for nonviolent property or drug offenses, young people tried in adult criminal court generally have greater recidivism rates than those tried in juvenile court" (par. 44). Why do you think this happens? In other words, why do you suppose young offenders repeat patterns of negative behavior, even after experiencing punishment?

9. Do you believe that incarcerated juvenile offenders should be housed separately from adult offenders? Why or why not?

I Survived Prison: What Really Happens behind Bars

ABIGAIL PESTA (REPORTING)

Abigail Pesta is an award-winning investigative and features reporter who has published articles in a number of national and international venues, including the *Wall Street Journal*, the *New York Times*, the *Atlantic*, and *Newsweek*. In "I Survived Prison: What Really Happens behind Bars," which appeared in *Marie Claire* online in March 2009, Pesta relates the experience of a highly successful financial planner, Jennifer Wilkov, who was sentenced to four months in jail at Rikers Island, New York, following her conviction for a white-collar crime. Pesta reports the experience from Wilkov's point of view.

I'm rolling up to Rikers Island, a notoriously violent prison in New York City, on a bus with about a dozen other women. My wrist is handcuffed to a lifelong drug addict whose stomach is distended from fibroids, she tells me. One of the ladies clearly hasn't bathed for weeks, and the smell is unbearable.

Simply boarding this bus was a feat in itself. If you think it sounds challenging to round up a group of hyperactive third-graders for a field trip, you should've seen the guards trying to get a bunch of loud-mouthed, drugged-out, furious female convicts to shut up, stand in line, and get on the bus.

A plain, redbrick building looms before me. I'm about to become a prisoner in a massive penitentiary, and I feel an overwhelming sense of dread. I'm surrounded by people who have been here before, who know the system, who know how to work the guards. But I know nothing. I'm thinking, I have to get through this. I have to stay safe. Stay alive. I tell myself that maybe someone in this prison needs me; perhaps that's the reason life has thrown me this curveball. For a moment, I think I hear a distant voice calling for help.

As the bus pulls to a stop, I try for about the millionth time to wrap my head around how I got here.

Just a couple of years ago, I was working as a Cer- 5 tified Financial Planner for American Express Financial Advisors and living with my cat, Figaro, in a leafy Brooklyn neighborhood. The trouble started when a relative recommended an investment opportunity in California—an operation that was buying foreclosed homes, fixing them up, then reselling them at a profit. He'd invested himself, and I followed suit.

At the same time, some of my clients started inquiring about real-estate opportunities, and I asked the compliance officer at American Express if I could mention this one. He said AmEx didn't deal with "hard property" real estate but that I could refer people independently if I filled out the proper securities forms. I did so, then told a few people about the investment, while advising them to do their own homework.

About a year later, in August 2005, I launched my own financial-planning business. Things went swimmingly for the first year, until investors—including members of my family and me—stopped getting any returns on that real-estate deal. So an attorney and I paid a visit to the owners of the California company. After our meeting, the attorney deemed the operation a scam and said I should report it to the authorities.

I did so immediately, in October 2006. A month later, several plainclothes officers confronted me on my street. "You're gonna let us in your apartment, or we're gonna beat the door down," one of them snarled. They confiscated my cell phone, computer, and files, while another set of police cleared out my office nearby. I was stunned, but I thought my stuff might help them nail the crooks.

Eight months later, when I was sitting in my office one morning in a favorite outfit—Ralph Lauren top, white pants, white heels—the police returned. I was arrested and accused of being part of a $1.6 million real-estate fraud, since I'd recommended the investment and had received standard referral fees. (Of course my family and I had lost a substantial amount of money in the con ourselves, but that didn't seem to matter.) After I answered a slew of questions from an assistant district attorney, my criminal-defense lawyer—who, by the way, was from the firm that had unsuccessfully defended Martha Stewart—advised me to agree to a deal with the DA. If I pleaded guilty, I'd get sentenced to six months in jail but could be out in four. "Four months is better than four years, which is what you could get if you go to trial and lose," my lawyer said. I hated the idea of making that deal, but since I was new to the legal field, I took his advice and signed the papers. That was January 2008.

For the next few months, while I awaited my sen- 10 tencing, I moved my belongings into storage and stayed with friends, as I'd put my apartment on the market prior to the legal nightmare. I worked as a book consultant, since I'd written and published three finance books myself. I tried to do some research on Rikers, but Googling turned out to be a mistake. What popped up were reports of abuse, injustice, and rape, along with news of guards running an alleged prison fight club, in which inmates were forced to beat each other to a pulp. Nonetheless, any New York City dweller sentenced to less than a year on state charges gets sent there.

Terrified, I started preparing for hell. I sought advice from self-defense experts, and enlisted them to shout insults in my face so I could practice my response. I cut my hair and donated it to charity, because I'd been warned that prisoners could yank it, hard. I talked to my mom constantly. She believed I was innocent, as did my friends—at least, my true friends, who even wrote letters to the judge about me. A few people couldn't cope and dropped out of my life. Meanwhile, a tsunami of unflattering stories about me hit the media—the *New York Times*, *New York Daily News*, the Associated Press. The headlines were infuriating, and humiliating. I felt increasingly angry about pleading guilty.

In June 2008, I went to a criminal courthouse in downtown Manhattan to be formally sentenced. The courtroom looked like something straight out of *Law & Order*, with old-fashioned wood-paneled walls, wooden pews, and a sign above the judge's head that said "In God We Trust." I stood before the judge and asked her if I could withdraw my guilty plea. The answer: No.

That same day, I said good-bye to my family, my cell phone, my normal life. Then I was handcuffed and escorted to a dingy basement room called "the bridge," where I waited with a bunch of prostitutes and drug addicts for the bus to Rikers.

When I replay it all in my mind, it seems like a bad movie or a nightmare—not anything real. But the reality sets in as soon as I step off the bus at Rikers, where the indignities begin promptly. For starters, I'm told to strip naked and squat—the idea being that any contraband I might be hiding inside me will tumble out. Then the guards make me sit in a computerized chair called the B.O.S.S.; the chair seems to be doing an X-ray of my insides to detect anything I might have swallowed in order to conceal it. I tell myself not to take any of this personally, but it's hard not to let it mess with my mind. I feel like I'm in a foreign country where I don't know the language or the rules, and no one wants to help. Anything I say can be misinterpreted. I'm afraid to ask even the simplest questions. Guards and inmates are staring at me; they know I'm new here. I have to stay alert.

I undergo a series of medical tests (for tuberculosis, HIV) for the next six hours. Then I put on a dark-green jumpsuit and head to my new home: a minuscule, private cinder-block cell (about eight feet by three feet) that contains a metal cot with a block of foam on top and a sheet but no pillow. There's a white porcelain toilet and sink right out in the open; I'm handed a towel, a bar of scratchy white soap that's more like bleach, and half a roll of toilet paper. No hot water. A tiny window looks out onto a parking lot.

I sit on the cot, take a deep breath, and thank God I'm alive; I've made it this far. I think, *Whatever I'm supposed to do here, let me do it well.* I remind myself that I can survive by becoming invisible: I will not act superior, or fearful. I'll follow directions, and I won't ask any questions of anyone. By this time, it's 4 in the morning, and I've been up for more than 24 hours. Breakfast will be served in one hour. I lie awake, not sure if I'm allowed to sleep; I'm afraid of getting in trouble if I miss breakfast.

After a week marked by entire days of keeping mostly to myself, I move to a dorm with 50 other women. The beds are crowded onto an open floor surrounded by tan Sheetrock walls. Most of the women here have aligned themselves with people from the housing projects they come from, so there are Latin factions, African-American ones, and so forth. I keep my head down, and pray.

There are regular confrontations. One woman randomly decides she doesn't want me to use the phone and tries to pick fights with me in front of the guards when I call my mother. One day she says, unprovoked, "Did you call me an idiot?" I reply that I don't say that type of thing, and luckily, the situation doesn't escalate. I know I have to stand up for myself and not show fear.

One evening, I witness a fight just before dinner. We're all assembling in the dormitory, with the guards barking at us to "shut up and line up," as usual. Suddenly, one woman flies at another, punching her everywhere—in the face, the gut. I've never seen a fistfight in real life, with two people trying to kill each other. Another woman jumps in, and the trio turns into a tornado, careening around the room. The guards gradually isolate them, ordering everyone else out. I imagine that the women were sent to solitary confinement in a dreaded place known as "the bin."

The most threatening person is a brute of a woman who leers at me menacingly one night in the communal showers. I know she wants to rape me; I've been warned of the signs. Rumor has it that another woman was recently raped by three female inmates in the high-security wing, which is a heavily patrolled area, so presumably the guards knew what was happening. In my case, a fellow inmate comes and stands defiantly by my side in the shower, and the bully backs off.

I lose 14 pounds in the first six weeks, due to stress and also to the fact that I've been an organic vegetarian for years. I have Crohn's disease, a serious digestive disorder, and my diet has helped me keep it under control. But there is hardly anything green or even remotely fresh served in jail. Meals mostly consist of slices of bread and turkey patties or fried chicken quarters, which the prisoners like to refer to as "seagull meat." I don't eat much, to the delight of my fellow inmates, who constantly ask for my leftovers. There's also a commissary, which is stocked with cookies, candy, and Kool-Aid packets that inmates can purchase once a week. Only a prison dietitian knows of my condition. Her advice? "You have to find a way to survive here."

Our days are extremely regimented; we're counted several times by guards changing shifts so they can make sure we're present, and alive. There's a law library and an outdoor area for exercise, such as jump rope. A TV blasts shows like *Jerry Springer* and *Maury Povich* in a common room. We're allowed to make the occasional cup of tea, but only if the entire dorm is clean, which is a regular source of friction. Religious services are popular, with prisoners frequently spouting, "Only God can judge." All of us have jobs; I make 39 cents an hour working in the prison garden, as part of a training program provided by the Horticultural Society of New York. Nighttime is a cacophony of raucous arguments among all the wound-up women who have been consuming sugar and starch all day, with the guards threatening to flip on the fluorescent lights if people don't pipe down.

As time creeps by, what keeps me sane is the continuing belief that I'm here for a reason, that I might be able to help someone. Gradually, I do. I manage to teach a woman from Trinidad to read, and I show others how to do yoga. I hold poetry readings with the woman who bunks next to me, an African-American Muslim who has been homeless at times. When I describe how I'd once heard someone calling for help, she says it was her.

On the final day of my ordeal, in October 2008, my mother and a dear friend escort me out into a bright, brisk fall afternoon. At this point, I've contracted a full-body yeast infection called candida, but I've never felt better—or freer—in my life. With my 40th birthday just around the corner, I feel oddly proud of myself. I'm tougher than I realized, and now I know I can win the respect of people from worlds very different from my own. I can keep a positive outlook in the worst of circumstances. Ironically, I have my experience at Rikers to thank for that knowledge. As one of the guards once said to me, "If you can survive this place, you can survive anything."

Reading Questions

1. What specific fears related to her impending stay at Rikers Island does Wilkov express on the bus ride to the prison?

2. What is the crime to which Wilkov pleads guilty? What is her punishment?

3. Wilkov mentions food a number of times throughout her story. How is food used as both a punishment and a reward in her prison experience?

4. Wilkov raises the issue of privacy frequently. In what ways is her privacy seemingly violated by the experience of prison?

5. To what belief does Wilkov credit her ability to maintain her sanity while in prison?

Rhetoric Questions

6. What purpose does Wilkov have in telling her story? What purpose do you think *Marie Claire* had in publishing it? What do you see as the story's intended effects on the magazine's readers?

7. How would you describe the tone of Pesta's work overall? How does her work establish that tone? What impact does the tone have on you as a reader?

8. In what ways does Pesta's piece follow conventional expectations for a news article?

Response and Research Questions

9. Regardless of her actual guilt or innocence, do you think the punishment Wilkov receives fits the white-collar crime for which she was convicted? Why or why not?

10. Wilkov reports that immediately following her sentencing, she was "handcuffed and escorted to a dingy basement room called 'the bridge,' where [she] waited with a bunch of prostitutes and drug addicts for the bus to Rikers" (par. 13). How would you describe Wilkov's attitude toward the other criminals?

11. Wilkov says, at the end of her experience in prison, that she felt "proud" of herself. Why does she feel proud? Do you think she has reason to be proud?

ACADEMIC CASE STUDY • CAPITAL PUNISHMENT   HUMANITIES

Dining on Death Row: Last Meals and the Crutch of Ritual

MICHAEL OWEN JONES

Michael Owen Jones is retired from the University of California–Los Angeles, where he spent more than forty years teaching courses in folklore. He is a widely published scholar, with more than 100 articles and three books to his credit. In "Dining on Death Row: Last Meals and the Crutch of Ritual," which appeared in the *Journal of American Folklore* in 2014, Jones considers the ritual of the last meal as it is experienced by individuals facing capital punishment. He explores implications of the ritual for our society by investigating its various social, political, and ceremonial meanings.

This essay examines last meal requests by those facing execution. After surveying food and beverage selections, I explore how culinary choices are marked by ethnicity, region, class, and gender, as well as inflected by memories, the longing for certain sensory experiences, and the intent to make a moral, political, or philosophical statement. I also consider which last suppers and comments have inspired movies, TV shows, musical compositions, and advertising; why the public desires information about the food requested by those facing death; how the condemned's meals have become politicized, feeding arguments by both those for and those against the death penalty; what the origin of the last meal ritual is; and why the custom is perpetuated. Possessing varied meanings for different participants in the drama of execution, the ceremonial last meal is one of the most powerful symbolic elements within a larger phenomenon laden with rituals and symbols.

A fascination with the final meals of condemned inmates pervades American popular culture and consciousness. News articles concerning those just executed often mention final repasts. Several books on the subject have appeared over the past dozen years, such as *Last Suppers* (Treadwell and Vernon 2001), *Last Meal* (Black 2003), *Meals to Die For* (Price 2004b), and *Their Last Suppers* (Caldwell 2010). For $20, the maximum cost of a final meal permitted by several states, a Canadian company called Last Meals Delivery Service will provide clients in Toronto "a replica of the 'last meal' consumed by someone executed in the United States" (http://pauljkneale.com/lastmeals.html; website is no longer accessible). Since 2003, the highly popular weblog *Dead Man Eating* (http://deadmaneating.blogspot.com/) has posted end-of-life meals in prisons throughout the United States. Numerous websites list the more extravagant orders; some bloggers also ask readers to ponder: What would you request as *your* last meal?

Few scholarly works, though, consider final repasts. They are limited to an article dwelling on theories of penology (LaChance 2007), a paper on the Internet regarding the meaning of execution that focuses more on last words than last meals (Meyer 2008), a student report concerning the media's attention to end-of-life meals (Jeung 2009), an unpublished piece (Gordon 2006) discussing some of the moral issues about capital punishment raised by Bigert and Bergström's film *Last Supper* (2005), a lengthy review of this film by folklorist LuAnne Roth (2011), and an article on the caloric content of last meals (Wansink, Kniffin, and Shimizu 2012).

Over the past half-century, folklorists have contributed extensively to foodways study beginning with the seminal work of Don Yoder at the University of Pennsylvania (Long 2009). Much of this literature deals with research methods (e.g., Anderson 1971; Camp 1978; Kalčik 1984; Long 1998; Rikoon 1982; Yoder 1972) and the traditions of various immigrant and ethnic groups, among them Italians (Cicala 1995; Magliocco 1993; Theophano 1991), Jews (Kirshenblatt-Gimblett 1986; Siporin 1994), and Pennsylvania Germans (Yoder 1961, 1962). Often employing fieldwork, folklorists have documented diverse regional customs and symbolism related to food, such as festivals and celebrations (Humphrey and Humphrey 1988), Cincinnati chili (Lloyd 1981), pasties in Michigan's Upper Peninsula (Lockwood and Lockwood 1991), clambakes in New England (Neustadt 1992), and crawfish consumption among Louisiana Cajuns (Gutierrez 1992). They have considered the role of commercially prepared foods in domestic rituals and routines, including Spam and ramen noodles (Kim and Livengood 1995) as well

as Jell-O (Newton 1992), and they have investigated rumors of contamination of institutional and fast food (Fine 1980; Rich and Jacobs 1973; Turner 1987, 1993). Despite interest in a wide range of populations and settings, however, folklorists have largely overlooked eating behind bars, and particularly the last meals of prisoners about to be executed. Even the detailed ethnographic research of Bruce Jackson and Diane Christian among those on death row contains few references to food.[1] For logistical, legal, and ethical reasons, the topic does not lend itself to interviewing and observing individuals taking their last bite of food as they confront that "existential precipice, the very end of life" (O'Neill 2001:1192). The absence of scholarship about dining on death row and unsuitability of fieldwork methods necessitate the use of other sources of information on the Internet and in media reports, biographies, and popular culture products in order to address a range of questions that will help delimit this area of inquiry, one that is no less compelling for its neglect in academe.

"When you lose so much of your freedom," said the 5 prisons operations manager for Oregon's Department of Corrections, "things like food take on tremendous importance" (Rose 2005). Many desirable items are scarce or non-existent in prison. Meals are repetitive, hot food often arrives cold, and the quality of preparation depends on the skills of inmate cooks. Food costs are frequently trimmed by state legislatures. In 2008, the average daily expense of feeding a Michigan prisoner was $2.48 (prison food costs accounted for 20 percent of the state's general fund; see "Prison Food Service Costs" 2008). In 2005, California's county jails allocated $2.25 per day per inmate, and the state prisons spent $2.45, while federal penitentiaries allotted $2.78 (Pringle 2005). The Oregon Department of Corrections managed to cut the cost from $2.88 in 2001 to $2.30 by bargain hunting and bulk shopping (Rose 2005). Typically menus are established on a cycle of a month or six weeks, and then repeated ad nauseam. As Darris Adams, sentenced to life plus 14 years for kidnapping and carjacking, said about the food at New Folsom, a maximum security prison in Represa, California, "If I don't eat, I don't survive, but it's not like I look forward to it. After so many years you get immune to it. You just swallow" (Pringle 2005).

In 2002, a row over the declining quality of sandwiches caused a deadly prison riot in England (Rose 2005). In mid-June 1960, 17 men on death row in San Quentin mounted a hunger strike demanding better meals. They complained that the food was cold, vegetables were watery, the desserts monotonous. They insisted on receiving steak, not roast beef, and some of the same items afforded those on the main line. The warden defended the menu, the irony in his remark probably unintended, stating that tamale pies, fried hominy, and meringue desserts were deliberately withheld from the condemned because "these things are fattening and the men do not get as much exercise as other prisoners" ("Want Better Meals: Condemned Inmates" 1960:3-B). Improvement in conditions, including food, was a factor in the inmate riot in 1971 that took 43 lives at New York's Attica prison (Bernstein 2010). Poor food service as well as allegations of food contaminated with hair balls, rocks, cardboard, bread ties, worms, and human feces precipitated a riot in Northpoint Training Center in central Kentucky in August 2009, causing a fiery melee and damage to six buildings (Schreiner 2010).

Given the importance of food in prison, particularly when a meal will be the last one, several questions arise. What food and beverage do inmates ask for as their final repast? To what extent and in what ways are culinary choices of prisoners marked by ethnicity, region, class, or gender as well as inflected by memories, the longing for certain sensory experiences, or the intent to make a moral, political, or philosophical statement? Why is there such widespread fascination by the general public with traditional last meals? How has the end-of-life meal become politicized and referred to in arguments by both those for and those against the death penalty? What are the origins of providing a special meal to the condemned? Why is the custom perpetuated? Addressing these questions contributes to the literature in folkloristics concerning several topics, such as marginalized groups, food customs, and the role of ritual and symbolism in people's lives, particularly when they confront death.

A FEAST BEFORE DYING

Food is never just something to eat.
— Margaret Visser (1986:12)

Texas has carried out the death sentence with the greatest zeal, accounting for about one-third of the executions since the death penalty resumed in 1976 (deathpenaltyinfo.org). Between December 7, 1982, and September 10, 2003, 245 of 310 Texas inmates on the eve of execution ordered special last meals. French fries headed the inventory of items at 48 percent of requests. At 35 percent, burgers were second in popularity, often cheeseburgers and frequently with double meat patties. Chicken, almost always deep fried, was included in 19 percent. Steak occurred in 18 percent of orders. Ice cream, including shakes, appeared in 29 percent. Pie (usually pecan), cake (most often chocolate or white with white icing), cheesecake, peach cobbler, banana pudding ("with real bananas"), and cookies, cinnamon rolls, and doughnuts figured in 29 percent of orders. Seven inmates ordered multiple desserts. Sodas (typically Coke or Dr Pepper) were included in 30 percent of the requests.[2] Although the last meal in Texas is served at 4 p.m., two hours before execution, 21 percent of the inmates ordered breakfast, mostly eggs, sausage (occasionally bacon, steak, or pork chops), and hash browns, sometimes with biscuits and gravy; the exception was one man who asked for two boxes of Frosted Flakes and a pint of milk.

Certain items turned up infrequently. Only 16 percent of meals contained salad, and 12 percent included milk. Other than deep-fried potatoes and onion rings, vegetables were evident mainly by their absence, found in only 4 percent of meal requests; these included carrots, peas, green beans, cauliflower, broccoli with cheese topping, corn on the cob, and fried okra.

Many last meal orders sought beverages, food, 10 and preparations that rarely appear on prison menus. Milk tends to be available only at breakfast but not every day in some facilities; for instance, in 2010, Alabama cut milk from seven to three days and fruit from twice weekly to once, saving the state $700,000 a year (Reutter, Hunter, and Sample 2010). Water, an artificial fruit drink, or a beverage resembling Kool-Aid is provided at other meals. Casseroles, goulash, and soy-stretched chicken dishes are common on daily menus, with pudding or Jell-O for dessert (Grace 2003). In order to boost calories while cutting costs, meat is often extended through grinding and adding Textured Vegetable Protein. Increasingly, cold cuts are served at lunch, which cost Georgia three cents per inmate in 1999, netting the state a savings of $438,000 (*FoodService Director* 1999). In 2005, Michigan abolished coffee because it lacks nutritional value, and thereby reduced expenses by half a million dollars a year. Some prisons have banished fried foods, thus eliminating the cost of cooking fat, decreasing equipment maintenance costs, and lessening sewage and drain problems (*FoodService Director* 1999) as well as attempting to reduce medical expenses in a system with increasingly longer prison sentences and an aging population (Riell 2001). Meals have been trimmed in some prison systems from three to two on weekends and holidays, or to days when inmates are not working, a cutback that led to a dramatic increase in prisoner assaults in Georgia in 2009 (Reutter, Hunter, and Sample 2010).

An emphasis on sensory experiences, particularly in circumstances of deprivation, looms large in food choice among condemned prisoners who miss the taste and texture of savory fried chicken, juicy burgers, and sugar-laden pies, cakes, and sodas. Brian Price, an inmate at the Walls Unit in Huntsville, Texas, who prepared about two hundred last meals over a 10-year period, said he seasoned burgers with Worcestershire sauce, garlic powder, salt, and pepper. "[T]hen I'd grill the onions right there beside it and toast the buns with butter. I did the best I could with what I had and I'd always use fresh lettuce and tomato to garnish it with" (quoted in Hannaford 2004). Many orders were quite specific regarding number of items or manner of preparation; for instance, Toronto Patterson requested "[s]ix pieces of crispy fried chicken, four jalapeno peppers, four buttered buttermilk biscuits, chef salad (with bacon bits, black olives, ham, and Italian dressing), six Sprites, and white cake with white icing," while Frank McFarland specified a heaping portion of lettuce, a sliced tomato, a sliced cucumber, four celery stalks, four sticks of American or Cheddar cheese, two bananas, and two cold half pints of milk. "He added that he wanted all the vegetables to be washed prior to serving, and that the cheese sticks be 'clean'" (Price 2004b:235), whether out of fastidiousness or perhaps distrust of the kitchen. The first last meal that Price cooked was Lawrence Buxton's request for steak, pineapple upside-down cake, tea, punch, and coffee. He was touched when the inmate sent word back about how much he enjoyed the meal: "I gave this guy a little bit of pleasure—just something to distract him for a brief moment before his execution. It's a very humbling and emotional experience and I always prayed over each meal" (quoted in Hannaford 2004).

As indicated in a nationwide poll by *Food & Wine* magazine in 2003, a burger and fries—death row inmates' most requested meal—is "the quintessential American food" (Shaw 2004), a reputation aided and abetted by the proliferation of fast food and chain restaurants. Tito Valdez Jr., serving 25 years to life for conspiracy/solicitation to commit murder, said, "I remember the days when I could eat whatever I wanted: Denny's Grand Slam for breakfast, a cold Subway pastrami sandwich for lunch, a juicy Carl's hamburger with crispy fries for dinner" (Valdez n.d.). What he fondly recalled after being imprisoned for many years is what most inmates in Texas have ordered as a final meal.

A number of prisoners combined two, three, or even four types of meat in a meal order, and also asked for multiple sodas and pastries. If a single helping of meat, starch, and sweet represents the "normal" meal—for example, the burger, fries, and banana pudding given to Billy Woods at his behest, or the chili dogs, baked beans, corn, and peanut butter cookies served to Clifton Russell Jr., who asked for whatever was on the menu for other prisoners that day—then 73 of 245 meals (30 percent) of Texas prisoners involved excessive amounts of food. Robert Drew, for instance, wanted "[s]teak (cooked rare), ham, two hamburgers, two pieces of fish and chocolate milk shake." Kia Johnson specified "[f]our fried chicken breasts, onion rings, fried shrimp, French fries, fried catfish, double-meat cheeseburger with grilled onions, strawberry fruit juice, and pecan pie." Hilton Crawford ordered "[t]welve beef ribs, three enchiladas, chicken fried steak with cream gravy, crisp bacon sandwich, ketchup, a loaf of bread, cobbler, three Cokes, three root beers, French fries, and onion rings." Robert Lee Willie, an inmate in Louisiana who was macho to the end, amended his vow not to accept favors from prison officials, that is, "everything but fried seafood," writes Prejean (1993:204). "He *loves* fried seafood." A guard brought him trays of fried shrimp, oysters, and fish as well as a salad and fried potatoes, which he ate while handcuffed. "Robert...picks up a fried shrimp with his fingers, smells it with obvious delight, and eats. And eats and eats and talks and eats, and it is hard for me to realize that this is his last meal." Several websites note that Thomas Grasso in Oklahoma sent for a dozen steamed clams, two dozen steamed mussels, six barbecued spareribs with sweet and sour sauce, a cheeseburger, a can of SpaghettiOs, a strawberry milk shake, and half a pumpkin pie. "I did not get my SpaghettiOs. I got spaghetti," he complained. "I want the press to know this" (Campos 2003; Collins 2010; Yglesias 1995). Grasso's grievance and the orders for large amounts of fare, particularly meat and fried food, reveal further the importance of the sensory in regard to food selection.

Final meal requests, however, are subject to cost and availability restrictions, which vary: $20 in Texas and limited to what is maintained in the kitchen or butcher shop (never lobster, and not steak since 1993, according to Price 2004a), $40 in Florida using ingredients that are present locally, $40 in Indiana and the meal may be ordered from one of a half-dozen restaurants in town, and $50 in California. A prisoner on death row in San Quentin scheduled for execution in late fall asked for fresh strawberries. When told that "[w]e can't get fresh strawberries in November," the inmate replied "I'll wait" (Shaw 2004). Sometimes the prison chaplain or other officials have bent the rules to provide inmates with items "from the free world" (Price 2004a), including fruit (Shaw 2004), Häagen-Dazs instead of ice cream from the commissary (Verhovek 1998), and a special sauce (Hickey 2001). On several occasions, writes inmate cook Brian Price (2004b:15), officials brought him food items to prepare that they had purchased: "Venison, liver, shrimp, bacon, fresh tomatoes, lettuce, and even a 'blooming onion' appeared suddenly on the day of execution."

Because of restrictions, orders for large quantities of food may be pared down. Texas inmate David Allen Castillo requested 24 soft-shell tacos; he received four. He also wanted six tostados, but was given two; two cheeseburgers, which were refused him; and two whole onions, five jalapenos, one chocolate shake, and a quart of milk, which were granted (Price 2004a). Substitutions occur. When Pedro Muniz in Texas asked for salad and shrimp, which were not available, he received a cheeseburger, fries, and cola. If nothing particular is requested, then a Georgia inmate is served steak and eggs, while a Texas prisoner is provided with whatever is scheduled that day for the general prison population (Hickey 2001). The "Final Meal Requests" link on the website of the Texas Department of Criminal Justice issues the caveat that "[t]he final meal requested may not reflect the actual meal served," something overlooked or ignored by many who utilize food choice as a basis for pro–death penalty sentiments. Even Brian Price (2004a), who prepared last meals for a decade, said he initially assumed that a death row prisoner received what he ordered.

A second factor of social class based on education and income likely has salience in explaining meal selection. An examination of 196 bios of prisoners executed in Texas reveals that 21 individuals (11 percent) had seven years or less of schooling, 50 (26 percent) made it through middle school, 30 (15 percent) graduated from high school, 17 (9 percent) had some junior college experience, five (2.6 percent) went to a four-year college but not all graduated, and the largest number at 68 (35 percent) dropped out of school in the 10th or 11th grade, that is, by age 16 when they were no longer legally compelled to attend. Two-thirds (135) committed murder for financial gain, or in some fashion benefitted materially.[3] Often amounts seem paltry: $250 from a feed and farm supply; $140 from a laundry; a pistol, purse, and $8 from a home; a $2.70 six-pack of beer from a store clerk (Price 2004b:311, 320, 337; Serrill 1983). Given their underprivileged backgrounds and underclass status, they likely chose the kind of food as a last meal—burgers, french fries, fried chicken—that had been readily obtainable and familiar before incarceration. Moreover, steak, lobster, and shrimp have long been considered prestige or luxury items owing to price, and they are certainly not part of ordinary prison fare, which probably accounts for their presence in many last meal requests.

In addition to certain sensory qualities and the possible impact of social class, food choice sometimes is influenced by ethnicity and regional upbringing. Of 245 meal requests in Texas, 16 were for tacos, burritos, quesadillas, enchiladas, or simply "Mexican platter" or "Mexican lunch," five inmates asked for tortillas with their meal, and 28 specified the addition of jalapenos, *picante* sauce, salsa, red pepper, or chili powder to their food. Not all of these prisoners bore a Latino identity, but many grew up in Texas, and hence were familiar with these foods and condiments and their flavor principles (Rozin 1982). The five requests for chicken fried steak, usually with "country gravy" or "white gravy," two for fried okra, two others for a "big bowl of grits," nine for barbecued beef, ribs, or chicken, one for mustard greens and spiced beets, and another for "½ pound of chitterlings" likewise indicate regional influence from different areas of the South.

According to one reporter (Hannaford 2004), Brian Price, who prepared last meals, "says inmates generally choose food unique to their culture. Mexican guys want Mexican food. The black guys generally want everything from 'chitlins' [stuffed pig intestines] to fried chicken and watermelon." Actual counts of the 187 last meals that he prepared indicate that this might be overstated (of the 212 inmates he

identifies, 17 Caucasians, 17 African Americans, and eight Latinos declined a final serving of food). Among the 57 African Americans requesting a final meal, only four asked for something that can be construed as "soul" food, of which barely one fits the stereotype: "½ pound of chitterlings, fried chicken (dark meat), 10 slices of bacon, 1 raw onion, fried shrimp, peach cobbler, 1 pitcher of whole milk" (the inmate was not served the chitterlings, however: Price 2004b:309). Twenty-one blacks asked for burgers, steak, or chicken—much like their white counterparts—nine requested other foods, two wanted fajitas or enchiladas, and three specified hot sauce, a bowl of chili, or jalapeno peppers as part of their meal. Of the 23 Latinos, three stipulated Mexican cuisine exclusively. Seven other Latinos specified meals consisting of both Mexican and American foods, two preferred only ice cream, one wanted venison steak, and one indicated shrimp but was given a cheeseburger instead. Just one person requested watermelon, a Latino. The lone Asian, born in South Vietnam and raised in Texas, ordered steak, french fries, beans, and water. Perhaps more than ethnicity, the data indicate that regional association or upbringing in a particular geographical area affects food choice.

Dietary restrictions owing to religious beliefs and practices seem to have played no part in last meal requests, at least not in Texas. Is gender a factor? In provisioning mythology, red meat is masculine while the more delicate chicken and fish, along with fruit, vegetables, and salad, tend toward the feminine. Males select fried food; females prefer baked. Men eat heartily; women daintily (Adler 1981; Fakazis 2011; Heisley 1990; Jones 2007). While they account for 10 percent of murder arrests, only 1 percent of women have been executed since capital punishment resumed (deathpenaltyinfo.org). Hence, gender disparities in the criminal justice system (along with racial inequalities) make comparing male and female food preference somewhat problematic.

Of the dozen women executed in seven states since 1976, seven declined a final meal (Allen, Barfield, Beets, Block, Newton, Plantz, Wuornos), but one of these women (Barfield) did have a bag of Cheez

Doodles and a soft drink, and another (Wuornos) was given a cup of coffee and ate some snack food (for particulars, see http://deathpenaltyinfo.org/women -and-death-penalty). One moderate meal was for salad, pickled okra, pizza, strawberry shortcake, and cherry limeade (Riggs), and another consisted of sweet peas, fried chicken, Dr Pepper, and apple pie (Lewis). Two other selections epitomized feminine food preference: Buenoano requested steamed broccoli and asparagus salad, strawberries, and a cup of tea, and Tucker asked for a banana, peach, and garden salad with ranch dressing, which she did not eat (Hannaford 2004). In contrast, Lois Nadean Smith—who earned the sobriquet in high school of "Mean Nadean" ("Oklahoma Executes Third Woman" 2001)—stipulated barbecued ribs, onion rings, strawberry banana cake, and cherry lemonade.

In sum, 58 percent of the 12 women in the United States, including three in Texas, declined a meal, in contrast to 21 percent of men in Texas, one woman demanded a masculine plate of barbecued ribs and fried onion rings, and four women (33 percent) preferred restrained servings of mainly feminine cuisine. More than 90 percent of these 12 women, then, chose nothing or female foods in moderate amounts, in contrast to men in Texas who ordered substantial portions of meat and fried food but little fruit, salad, or fresh vegetables. (A mere 12 of 243 men requested meals without red meat; seven orders were for fruit, salad, and/or vegetables, while five others involved fish, eggs, and/or cheese.) Studies of "comfort food" preferences, often selected during times of stress, suggest that men tend to choose foods that are whole meals and such items as steak, casseroles, and soup, in contrast to women who often opt for salads, fruit, and snack food. The male choices possess a nostalgic quality associated with meals prepared by others in their youth, while the female selections exhibit convenience, indulgence, and perhaps in some instances an implicit rejection of the traditional role of homemaker (Locher et al. 2005; Wansink, Cheney, and Chan 2003).

Several inmates, both male and female, asked for only a beverage such as Coke, freshly squeezed orange juice, or coffee. Perhaps because of anxiety, others nibbled on snack food, ate sparingly, or requested little: an apple, a plain cheese sandwich, a flour tortilla, and water. John Ramos, on death row until the Florida Supreme Court reversed the conviction, said, "I thought about my last meal....I was gonna tell them, 'Just feed me the same s—. It's disgusting of you to offer me the best food when I'm gonna puke it back in your face'" (quoted in Freedberg 1999). According to a death-watch log, at 11:50 a.m. on Sunday, three days before his execution in Arkansas, Earl Van Denton refused to order a last meal. At 4:46 a.m. on Monday, he refused breakfast. At 8:37 p.m., Tuesday, "Denton got up and vomited in [sic] commode." At 2:02 a.m. on Wednesday, execution day, he vomited, and again at 10:17 that morning. At 3:00 p.m., last meals were served to the other two prisoners to be executed that night; despite the prison nurse's urging, Denton took no food (Kuntz 1997). Since 1995, a condemned prisoner in Indiana is served a "special meal," as it is called (Hickey 2001), at least two days before the execution because many inmates told officials they were not hungry in the 24 hours before their death; on the last day they are given regular prison fare (VanSickle 2003). Hence, when Joseph Trueblood in Indiana refused a special last meal as a means of "protesting what the state is getting ready to do," he was given the same dinner as other inmates: a bologna sandwich, a cheese sandwich, fruit, and cookies, which he did not eat (Tan 2003; VanSickle 2003).

Do most of the condemned consume their last meal? The jury is still out. Several prison spokespersons contend that inmates eat a good part of their final meal—including the steak they have to saw through with plastic knives or that is pre-cut and eaten with a plastic spoon or "spork" (see reports in Hickey 2001; Poltilove 2009; and Verhovek 1998). Other accounts indicate that while a few eat heartily, most do not. McClary (2007) writes: "On Thursday evening, however, [Claude H.] Ryan was so nervous he couldn't eat his last meal and, as his final hour approached, he suffered a near breakdown. He refused all religious rites, but asked Reverend Arvid C. Ohrnell, the prison chaplain, to accompany him to the gallows." In addition, Crowder (2004) informs readers that "[p]rison officials described [David Kevin] Hocker as antsy but upbeat the day of his death. He asked a lot of questions about the execution procedure and talked about his religious beliefs. Hocker had no breakfast or lunch Thursday. He requested a last meal of frankfurters, French fries, American cheese and chocolate cake, but he did not eat it, prison spokesman Brian Corbett said." At least four in Texas (Derrick, Kelly, Jernigan, and Tucker) ordered final meals, but once they were delivered, declined to eat them. In the documentary film *Last Supper*, a former prison warden from Bangkok, Thailand, explains that, in the words of the film's reviewer (Roth 2011:107), "the last supper is often *not* consumed by the condemned, who is too nervous to eat. Instead it is given to Buddhist monks as an offering." Wilbert Rideau, in prison for 44 years after stabbing a woman to death, contends that a prisoner's last meal is often ordered for and eaten by his friends: "Condemned men usually lost their appetites" (quoted in Garner 2010). "I wouldn't be able to eat," said former warden Donald Cabana, "and I've never seen very many who do except to push the food around" (quoted in Dow 2002:188–89). Finally, Robert Johnson in *Death Work* (1990:91) maintains that most prisoners "eat little or nothing at all." He quotes an officer who said that "[f]ood is the last thing they got on their minds." Johnson also described to a reporter his having watched a condemned man kneel in his cell, the Styrofoam container on his bed, and attempt to eat the steak he had requested: "He ate a bite or two, and that was it." The last meal, noted Johnson, is usually ordered the day before execution when the condemned still harbor the hope of reprieve; by the time the meal arrives, however, "your appetite goes with your hope" ("Last Meal" 1991).

In sum, it would appear that a number of prisoners consume part of the meal while others order nothing or eat nothing they ordered. Yet other inmates request hearty meals, even inordinate amounts of food. There seems to be no general trend, however, no direct correlation between size of meal and kinds of food ordered on the one hand, and on the other, expressions of remorse, insistence on innocence, unbridled contentiousness, or manifestations of bravado.

A few prisoners have utilized the occasion to make political or moral statements. In North Carolina, Ricky Lee Sanderson explained: "I didn't take [the last meal] because I have very strong convictions about abortion and the 33 million babies that have been aborted in this country. Those babies never got a first meal and that's why I didn't take the last in their memory" ("Last Words on Death Row" 2007). On the card for setting forth the final meal request, one inmate in Texas wrote "Justice, Temperance, with Mercy." Another penciled "God's saving grace, love, truth, peace and freedom." A third indicated "Justice, Equality, World Peace." Lawrence Russell Brewer, a white supremacist gang member executed on September 21, 2011, for chaining an African American man to the back of a pickup truck and dragging him to his death, asked for an enormous meal of steaks, triple bacon cheeseburger, barbecued meat, omelet, pizza, fried okra, ice cream, fudge, and root beer. He did not eat any of whatever food he actually received (Graczyk 2011; Oremus 2011; Reuters 2011). An outraged state legislator said that the Texas inmate had ordered the meal in an attempt to "make a mockery out of the process" (Fernandez 2011), that is, he exploited the meal request as a subversive act. In Tennessee, Philip Workman asked that his final meal be a vegetarian pizza donated to any homeless person near the prison. The state refused. A local woman called friends; together they bought 150 pizzas for $1,200, which were delivered to a rescue mission. "I just felt like I had to do something positive," she said. The president of the People for Ethical Treatment of Animals (PETA) added another 15 veggie pies, and a Minneapolis radio station sent 17 pizzas to a center that helps teens in crisis (Fantz 2007).

"Some of the condemned prefer to fast," observes the inmate cook Brian Price (2004b:21). "Others order favorite foods from their childhood, recalling happier times to somewhat comfort themselves." This is the final factor in food choice, likely the most important one and implied in the previous discussion of other influences. An account on the Prison Talk blog conveys the sense of comfort and past memories that food may conjure up for prisoners. Bookgirl writes (June 7, 2002) that at Christmas she took her husband some homemade biscuits, "not because I can bake good biscuits but because he asked me to try. They turned out...different." He shared his Christmas food with others who had received none, including an elderly man with no teeth who consumed nothing but the biscuits. No one else liked them. Asked if he thought they were good, the man replied: "Every morning when I was a little boy, my mama baked biscuits for breakfast. When I came to prison, she still baked biscuits for me every Christmas. My mama died a few years ago, and I ain't had any homemade biscuits since then. Your wife's biscuits taste just like my mama's—God rest her soul, that woman never could bake a decent biscuit! They taste awful, but they remind me of my mama." Concludes Bookgirl: "That's the sweetest insult I've ever had."

In *My Last Supper* (Dunea 2007), photographer Melanie Dunea asked 50 of the world's top chefs what they would have for their final meal. The majority described simple foods: scrambled eggs, a cheeseburger, and a steak; a tuna sandwich with bacon, a Krispy Kreme doughnut, and a Corona beer; or just fried chicken, a hot dog, or a big bowl of spaghetti. One picked a roast, reminiscing to the book's reviewer (Stein 2007) about his family's Sunday lunch in Scotland when he was growing up. The reviewer writes that "when it comes to our deepest desires, it turns out that food isn't just about taste. It's tied right into memory and the longing for the sensations of when we felt happiest or most loved." He quotes a restaurant owner: "If someone can hand us those memories...it's the culinary equivalent of a big hug." Another chef remarked about answers to the question of the last meal: "There's always a return to childhood....The word Mom comes up at least a third of the time" (Stein 2007).

Texas inmate Kenneth Gentry asked for a final meal of a bowl of butter beans in addition to biscuits, mashed potatoes, onions, tomatoes, chocolate cake, and Dr Pepper with ice. The lima beans, said Brian Price, are "difficult to prepare, but it was something

his mum made him when he was a kid and I knew it would take him back to a time when it was peaceful. So I cooked them real slow" (quoted in Hannaford 2004; see also Price 2004b:41). "No food can ever mean as much to you as that food [which you grew up with]," writes John Lancaster in *The New Yorker* (2011:68). It is comfort food, "designed to remind us of familiar things, to connect us with our personal histories and our communities and our families. That has always been true and it always will be true."

Only the notion of physical and emotional comfort as well as pleasant memories triggered by the taste, texture, aroma, and mouth feel of food can account for the overwhelming presence of cakes and pie and ice cream and milk shakes in so many final repasts, or breakfast served late afternoon a couple of hours before execution. How else to explain an order for "an old-fashioned cheeseburger," smothered chicken and rice, Cool Whip and cherries, "one cup of hot tea (from tea bags) and six chocolate chip cookies," a birthday cake, a strawberry shake and cheesecake, a meal topped off with bubble gum, salmon croquettes with scrambled eggs and biscuits, a bag of Jolly Ranchers candy, or even liver and onions? Indiana granted a death row inmate's last request for his mother to be allowed to prepare his two favorite meals, which she cooked on-site with ingredients provided by the prison and then shared with her inmate son and several other relatives as well as his spiritual adviser (Hickey 2001). The comforting physical sensations of warm, easily eaten, filling foods and the emotional association of food with particular individuals and pleasurable events provide relief of distress for many inmates facing their execution; this factor dominates in explaining culinary selection among the condemned.[4]

FOOD, CRIMES, AND SYMBOLS

Like an additional flavor, meanings are carried with food. —David Mas Masumoto (1987:113)

The public has long been attracted to executions as 30 well as inquisitive about the crimes and final actions of condemned prisoners. From the Middle Ages onward, executions were popular amusements attended by hundreds, sometimes thousands, in all ranks of society. Reasons varied, including perhaps the satisfaction of witnessing the restoration of law and order through ritualized retribution, catharsis in escaping from resentful or deprived lives, feelings of pleasure in the excitement of being in a crowd, morbid curiosity, sympathy with the condemned, or the need for strategies of defense against the fear of death (Banner 2000; Gatrell 1994; Johnson 1990; McLynn 1989). As the barrister, inveterate diarist, and frequent execution watcher James Boswell (1740–95) wrote about his "impulse to be present at every execution": "I can account for this curiosity in a philosophical manner, when I consider that death is the most aweful [sic] object before every man, whoever directs his thoughts seriously towards futurity" (quoted in McLynn 1989:268).

England banned public executions in 1868, and they ceased in America by the 1930s. The lives and deaths of criminals continue to intrigue, however, as evident in the mass media. Known as the "pick-ax murderer" whose conversion to Christianity gained worldwide publicity, Karla Faye Tucker is celebrated in song by four bands in addition to being the subject of two plays, several documentaries, and an interview on *Larry King Live* as well as inspiring the movies *Last Dance* (1996) and *Crossed Over* (2002). Aileen Wuornos has had two documentary films, one comic book, a song, an opera, and a movie about her (Kassab 2002; KRT 2002; Word 2002). Charlize Theron won a Golden Globe and an Academy Award Oscar for her portrayal in *Monster* (2003), said to be based on the life of Wuornos, a Daytona Beach prostitute who became a serial killer. Eating Krispy Kreme donuts helped the actress gain 30 pounds for her role (Stossel 2004). Convicted of robbing and murdering a gas station attendant one night and a motel manager the next evening, 32-year-old Gary Gilmore was executed by firing squad in Utah, a method that he chose. His last meal consisted of steak, potatoes, milk, and coffee although he consumed only the beverages along with contraband whiskey. His last request was for his eyes to be used

for transplants (two people received corneas). His last words: "Let's do it!" (see Ramsland n.d.). Norman Mailer won a Pulitzer Prize for *The Executioner's Song* based on Gilmore's story, and Tommy Lee Jones garnered an Emmy for his portrayal of Gilmore in a television movie. Five weeks before his execution, the cast of *Saturday Night Live* sang a medley of Christmas songs with altered lyrics entitled "Let's Kill Gary Gilmore for Christmas" (snltranscripts.jt.org). *Playboy* published a lengthy interview with him that appeared shortly after his death. He is celebrated in song by two musical groups, The Adverts and The Police. In a *Seinfeld* episode, Jerry finally decides to buy a particular jacket and says to Elaine: "Well, in the immortal words of Gary Gilmore, 'Let's do it.'" Dan Wieden, one of the founders of the ad agency for Nike, credits the inspiration for his "Just Do It" to "Let's do it" (Greene 2010).

A last supper industry has emerged, replete with official and unofficial websites reporting final meal requests and last words, displaying a last meals trivia game, and offering Dead Man Eating T-shirts, underwear, and coffee mugs. Why does the public hunger for information about prisoners' last meals? In papers and print, pundits refer to a "morbidly curious public," "voyeuristic fascination," and "macabre enjoyment," but never quite answer the question. Clues to understanding the intrigue about last meals, over and above initial curiosity, lie just beneath the surface of comments on blog sites. Many contributors immediately jump from describing a condemned prisoner's end-of-life meal request to wondering aloud what they (or you) would ask for in such a situation. It brings to mind Robert Alton Harris's final remark (he was executed in California's gas chamber on April 21, 1992), paraphrasing from the movie *Bill & Ted's Bogus Journey* (1991), that "[y]ou can be a king or a street sweeper, but everyone dances with the Grim Reaper." Reminded of their mortality, the chat room writers describe end-of-life meals for themselves consisting of luxury items — often in great abundance — or comfort food, and sometimes repasts composed of both, similar to what condemned inmates have requested. Or they postulate being too anxious about their impending demise to order anything, again like many of those who faced their imminent death.

Another reason for the preoccupation with last meals is puzzlement over the character of the condemned as perhaps manifested through meal selection. "Do last meal menus somehow shed light on the inner psyche of the condemned man himself?" ask two compilers of last meals and words (Treadwell and Vernon 2001). Does "the last meal gives us a glimpse into the darkest recesses of the human mind?" inquires a blogger (Vogel n.d.). In a word, no.

Based on records combining last words and last meals of 237 inmates executed in Texas over 11 years,[5] it appears that nearly half of the prisoners requested a meal of normal size, while one-fourth asked for disproportionate amounts of food and the other fourth wanted little or nothing. Thirty-three percent expressed remorse, of whom the largest number (44 percent) specified a normal meal. The remarks of 39 percent of the inmates indicated resignation to their fate; slightly more than half (53 percent) asked for meals of normal size. Of the 13 percent insisting in their final statements on their innocence, the largest number either requested little or nothing to eat (41 percent), or a normal meal (35 percent). The three men confronting imminent death with bravado—"dying game"—specified normal, not excessive, meals. Of the three contemptuous prisoners issuing barbed statements ("Kiss my proud Irish ass"; "the prosecutor and Bill Scott are sorry sons of bitches"), two wanted normal measures of food, and one sought a meal of disproportionate size. In daily life, food choices frequently are utilized, consciously or not, to define people, places, and events and as a basis for assessing others (Jones 2007). When it comes to the last meal prior to execution, though, little can be inferred about character, guilt, or innocence from the final repast owing to the circumstances, that is, years of deprivation of certain foods and their preparations, anxiety, and the desire for solace offered by "comfort food" and the memories evoked.

Last meals and the items in them serve as symbols[35] in the discourse on crime and punishment. Jacquelyn C. Black created photographs of inmates' final repasts juxtaposed with each individual's photo, last statement, and other information. She writes (2003) that in 1984, she read a news article about Velma Barfield whose final meal before execution consisted of Cheez Doodles and a Pepsi. "That image stayed with me and years later became the impetus for educating myself about capital punishment" (Black, quoted in a review of *Last Meal*, in *Contemporary Justice Review* 8:337), which she now opposes. Those contesting retributive justice, particularly in regard to the mentally handicapped, sometimes start or end an essay with reference to a meal request. One frequently mentioned is that of Johnny Paul Penry, with an IQ less than 60, who, on hearing of his second last-minute stay of execution, asked if he could still eat his "last" meal—cheeseburgers and french fries (Hellerstein 1997; Orecklin 2000). Rickey Ray Rector has been cited by both advocates and opponents of the death penalty, albeit at cross-purposes. After shooting a police officer, he attempted to commit suicide but succeeded only in inflicting severe brain damage, thereby becoming so mentally disabled he did not know what an execution was. For his final meal he requested steak, fried chicken, cherry Kool-Aid, and pecan pie. He left the pecan pie on the side of the tray, however, telling the guards who came to take him to the execution chamber that he was saving it "for later" (Mansnerus 2001). One blogger writes about seemingly aberrant last meals and eating behavior that "[t]he obvious joke here is that you can't look at some of these requests and not know these guys are retarded" (Reynolds 2010). In contrast, an attorney representing a mentally disabled man on death row titles her op-ed piece "What Do We Gain By Taking These Childlike Lives?" (Hellerstein 1997), and an editorial in the *Dallas Morning News* (November 22, 1998) concerning Penry and Rector is called "Executing Mentally Impaired Prisoners Is Unjust and Cruel." (In June 2002, the US Supreme Court ruled that the execution of mentally disabled people is unconstitutional, violating the Eighth Amendment.)

One trope found in remarks by proponents of the death penalty is the construction of the offender as a "monster." Extravagant food requests or enormous amounts of food—monstrous portions—represent the unfettered appetites of condemned inmates, a lack of restraint also manifested in their crimes and inherent in their character. As the coup de grâce, several justify their position by noting that prisoners on death row for killing people "didn't give their victims a last meal of their choice"; one even titles his article "They Didn't Get to Choose Their Last Meals" (Greene 2001). White supremacist Lawrence Russell Brewer requested a last meal of great quantities of meat, sweets, and soft drinks but ate nothing of what was served him in ridicule of the custom. A state legislator who chairs the Senate Criminal Justice Committee demanded an immediate end to the tradition of providing a special end-of-life meal (Graczyk 2011; Oremus 2011). "He never gave his victim an opportunity for a last meal," said Senator John Whitmire. "Why in the world are you going to treat him like a celebrity two hours before you execute him? It's wrong to treat a vicious murderer in this fashion. Let him eat the same meal on the chow line as the others" (quoted in Fernandez 2011).

The custom nevertheless continues in most states, perhaps not surprisingly given food's significance as daily sustenance and its symbolic import. Ancient Egyptians included it for entombed royalty along with other necessities and comforts in the afterlife, adherents of a host of religions from Buddhism to Catholicism to Lucumí offer food and beverage to spirits and saints as a sign of respect and supplication or to seek favors, and some families host a picnic in the cemetery once a year with gifts of food for the deceased. Widely spread, the post-burial practice of providing a funerary meal at a reception, usually in the home of the deceased's survivors, focuses on the needs of the living: "Take time to stuff, O mourner. Full stomachs cannot cry" (from a poem by Jeanne Nail Adams, quoted in Yoder 1986:149).

The origins of a final repast are elusive, however. Sacrificial and scapegoating rituals in ancient Greece during calamities or in efforts to avert a future catastrophe sometimes involved selecting a criminal, poor man, or other marginal individual to be chased out of the city or even killed. The victim was treated to special food or an excellent repast in order to make this stand-in for the community appear to be a more valuable and representative member (Bremmer 1983). In Rome on the eve of entering the arena, gladiators and *bestiarii*, those who fought against wild beasts, received an elegant dinner—the *cena libera*—provided by the host of the show as symbolic compensation to those about to die, subsequently developed into a spectacle for public titillation. The Romans considered gladiatorial contests to have developed from human sacrifice to propitiate the souls of the dead; rather than kill free and noble members of society, prisoners or slaves were chosen, but they had to be made to appear higher in status—one means of which was to extend a special meal (Brettler and Poliakoff 1990). In Nuremberg in the late 1500s, the condemned "was allowed a liberal table, provided by charitable people" (not by the state) three days before execution (Calvert 1928:36). In England, some prisoners with funds, such as John Rann and Renwick Williams who were executed in the late eighteenth century, hosted their own dinner party in prison on the eve of hanging (Gatrell 1994; Johnson 1990; Smith 1996). Other condemned inmates had only bread, water, and gruel, or were even starved. Following an execution, the prison warden might schedule an official repast as closing ceremony: "We hang at eight, breakfast at nine" read one invitation (Johnson 1990:12).

By the late nineteenth century in America, the provision of a distinctive end-of-life meal for the condemned was a firmly established tradition. The custom was well enough known that on December 9, 1891, *The Roanoke Times* could print the following joke:[6]

"The Design Frustrated"

WARDEN: Now you can select anything you like for your last meal before execution.

CONVICTED MURDERER: All right. Send in a New England boiled dinner.

WARDEN: No you don't. I can't let you cheat the law by committing suicide.

Newspaper reportage of execution rituals was so pervasive that on September 13, 1891, the *Fort Worth Gazette* published the following editorial:

Some day some newspaper will forget to report the articles of food comprising the last meal eaten by a murderer under sentence of death and then the whole bottom will fall out of newspaper enterprise. It is terrible to contemplate the fearful results that might ensue were the public allowed to remain in ignorance whether a murderer, just before going to the scaffold, ate beef-steak or chicken, or whether he drank tea or coffee. There is too much attention paid to sickly details in setting forth the fact of the execution of a man too dangerous to live.

In *The Washington Times* [DC] on February 13, 1903, an anonymous author reports on the sale of relics from the infamous Newgate prison in England, then segues to the remark that "[y]ou are familiar with the nature of the breakfast often prepared in this country [the United States] by the sheriff's wife as the last meal of the condemned: coffee, rolls, chops, eggs." The writer concludes that "[t]here is a strange fascination in the accounts of executions."

THE CRUTCH OF RITUAL

Only the ritual of an execution makes it possible to endure. Without it the condemned could not give the expected measure of cooperation to the etiquette of dying. Without it, we who must preside at their deaths could not face the morning of each new execution day. Nor could you.

— Byron Eshelman, former death row chaplain at San Quentin Prison (quoted in Canan 1989:75)

At the beginning of their film *Last Supper*, Bigert and Bergström call attention to a "paradoxical ritual" in modern executions, that "human mercy and cruelty . . . share the same dinner table." Like the filmmakers, several commentators have puzzled over this, taking divergent, even contradictory, stances. Karon (2000) suggests that providing a special last meal might be "to sugarcoat what remains a grim act of violence by the state [executing the criminal] to redress a previous wrong." Focusing on the bureaucratization and routinization of the "new penology" that dehumanizes prisoners, turning them into docile automatons, LaChance (2007) contends that the state allows the condemned to choose whatever they wish for a final meal and to speak freely before dying in order to demonstrate that they possess autonomy and agency; as volitional beings who committed heinous crimes of their own free will, they deserve the punishment meted out to them. To sustain the emotional satisfaction required to uphold the death penalty, "[t]he state turns its offenders into self-made monsters" (LaChance 2007:719). In contrast to this interpretation, Gordon (2006) proposes that the ritual of the last meal constitutes "both an implicit *call* for forgiveness on the part of the citizens of the state" and "a *demonstration* of forgiveness as well, in that it shows kindness to the condemned and a recognition of their humanity and our shared humanity."

"I always thought of the last meals I prepared as a version of the Last Supper, when Christ knew that he would die the next day," said prison cook Brian Price (2004a). Some abolitionists of the death penalty draw upon the Crucifixion in pleading for "mercy, forgiveness, and respect for the dignity of life" (Lynch 2000:23), while retentionists, calling for retribution, often invoke the "eye for an eye, life for life" passage in Mosaic Law in Exodus 21:22–25. The situation is complicated by the diversity of roles, actors, and scripts in the performance of executions, beginning with the prisoners and the kitchen staff.

A number of inmates have found the offer of a special meal offensive, such as a prisoner described by Johnson (1990:106) who "was horrified by the last-meal ritual, which struck him as barbaric and cruel." On the other hand, before dying, Lawrence Buxton sent word to Texas prison cook Brian Price thanking him for his meal. Patrick Sonnier in Louisiana remarked: "Warden, tell that chef, tell him for me that he did a really great job. . . . And you tell him, Warden . . . that I am truly, truly appreciative." Warden Maggio, who earlier had said that the cook was giving "real special attention" to the meal, told Patrick: "He put himself out for you, Sonnier, he really did" (Prejean 1993:87). Brian Price, who associated the prisoner's last meal with the Lord's Supper, commented that "I took my job seriously, and it made me feel good that I was able to give the condemned at least a piece of a free world as they remembered it." He continued: "The meal requests were rarely complicated; many prisoners ordered food that they had eaten as children. I think that through their meals, they were seeking a small bit of comfort and courtesy. Food can take you back to a better time in your life, and it gave me comfort to give these dying men and women some comfort in their last hours" (Price 2004a).

Other participants in the drama of execution include the warden and the execution team, while members of the public, for whom capital punishment is an abstract symbol (Banner 2002), make inferences from the little information reported by the media. Former warden Donald Cabana maintains that the last meal is a welcome distraction in having to cope with putting someone to death. "I think you'd feel somewhat naked walking out and there was no last meal issue to talk about. Even if he doesn't want a last meal, you still have to talk to him about that.... That takes time away from thinking" (quoted in Dow 2002:189). During the final five or six hours, two officers are required to distract and comfort the prisoner as part of the task of "getting the man dead" (Johnson 1990:90). This includes a steady stream of conversation and even eating with him. "Shoot, one of 'em actually asked what to order and we didn't know what to order so we ordered McDonald's food for 'im. He ate Big Macs and I ate Big Macs, you know" (Johnson 1990:90). Given the ambivalence over the death penalty in the United States (Bonnie 1990; Dubber 1996; Lynch 2000), members of the public either develop a sympathetic identification with prisoners by recognizing their common humanity through eating and coming to terms with death (LaChance 2007:702), or they infer that "monstrous" meal portions represent an uncontrollable, monstrous character justifying death for the safety of all (see, e.g., statements on lawfreefaq.com).

In commenting on the etiquette of dying and the ritual of execution, former death row chaplain Byron Eshelman remarked that "[n]o matter how you think you feel about capital punishment, no matter how you imagine you would face the legal giving or taking of life, you would meet the reality of it by holding tightly to the crutch of ritual" (Canan 1989:75). One

scholar asks: "What purpose does all this routinization and ceremony serve?" The answer, he says, lies in the "loss of tolerance for suffering," and hence the need for a "carefully groomed image of humaneness": "[T]he modern orchestration of death lends assurance that everything is in order, everything is humane and civilized and that we aren't, after all, barbarians" (Haines 1992:126).

When executions in America were carried out in small towns and rural areas before the advent of a centralized state prison, the condemned and the local sheriff were in close contact. Not surprisingly the prisoner's last meal became transformed into a special one before dying. To extend food to another is a profoundly human act, a kindness that symbolically acknowledges a shared humanity. Whether the offer of food was intended as hospitality, a method of calming the prisoner, or a coping mechanism helping relieve the officer of stress or guilt, the fact remains that by the late nineteenth century, the tradition of a custom meal was firmly entrenched in America and often reported in newspapers. As former warden Cabana noted, this and other customs and rituals became incorporated into official procedures, which "helps the warden and the prison staff get on through the damn execution process because you've got things you have to tend to.... It is not something that any individual designed. It's kind of come together over centuries" (quoted in Dow 2002:189).

After executions were conducted in private with few witnesses, prisons disseminated scant information to the newspapers beyond the name of the condemned, the instrument of death, and the person's dying words and last food that define the event for readers. Aware of little about the ritual of execution beyond the final comments and food choice, the public nevertheless makes inferences or projects feelings and constructs opinions in opposition to or in support of the death penalty. Generally overlooked in scholarship and sometimes misinterpreted by the public, the ceremonial last meal confirms Margaret Visser's observation in *Much Depends on Dinner* (1986:12) that "[f]ood is never just something to eat"—whether for the living or, in this instance, for the dying.

ACKNOWLEDGMENTS

In developing this paper, I am indebted to discussions with Jenny McLaren, Elliott Oring, and Daniel Wojcik. Any errors of fact or interpretation, however, are mine.

NOTES

1. In his article on prison lore, Jackson mentions a "hot stick," that is, an immersion heater used by prisoners to warm food and beverages in their cells (1965). In *Death Row* (1980:125–35), Jackson and Christian list items in meals for breakfast, lunch, and dinner as part of each day's rundown of activities in a Texas prison over a three-day span, but say nothing about "last meal" or attitudes toward it. And in their book *In This Timeless Time* (2012:19–27), Jackson and Christian include photos showing a guard and porters filling trays from food trolleys and slipping the trays under cell doors as well as a porter picking up empty trays in the hall outside the cells. The same scene occurs for a brief period in their film *Death Row*, followed by the delivery of commissary items, including five cans of Dr Pepper, to one cell. There is nothing about the last meal before execution except the statement (2012:167) that everything including the food ordered is officially noted on the day of execution.

2. The source of these counts are 245 final meal requests (65 of the 310 inmates declined food) between December 7, 1982, and September 10, 2003, listed by the Texas Department of Criminal Justice at the online site web.archive.org (accessed August 8, 2010). David Shaw (2004) states that there were 314 executions since 1982. By his count, 111 death row inmates ordered fries, 85 requested hamburgers, 54 wanted steak (none was honored after 1993; see statements by Brian Price who prepared last meals—in Price 2004b and in Hannaford 2004), 56 asked for ice cream (and another 19 requested milk shakes), and 50 opted for chicken (mostly fried). In 1998, Sam Howe Verhovek, referring to the 144 men executed by Texas over the previous 15 years, notes that

> [b]urgers top the entrees. Twenty-two men chose double cheeseburgers, 15 opted for single cheeseburgers, 9 for hamburgers. Next most popular were steaks, typically T-bones, with 27 requests, and eggs (10 requests, most for scrambled). Most desired overall is a side of french fries (56 requests). Ice cream is the most popular dessert (21 requests), Coca-Cola the most popular beverage (13, just edging out 12 requests for iced tea). And 24 inmates declined any last meal at all.

At least in Texas, then, burgers and fries head the list, followed by steak and chicken.

3. These counts are based on profiles in Price (2004b), which lists the educational level of 212 inmates, for 16 of whom, however, the information is not known. In regard to 10 individuals, it is not possible for me to determine if money, vehicles, or other stolen objects were involved so I based figures on 202 people, of whom 135 benefitted materially. The examples, in order, are Richard Donald Foster, Glen Charles McGinnis, Earl Carl Heiselbetz Jr. (Price 2004b), and James David ("Cowboy") Autry (Serrill 1983). As often noted, the inmates have come from impoverished backgrounds. San Quentin warden Clifton Duffy remarked: "It seems to me the death penalty is a privilege reserved for the poor" (Dow 2002:184), echoed by John Spenkelink, electrocuted in Florida on May 25, 1979, who said: "Capital punishment: them without the capital get the punishment" (http://crime.about.com/od/history/qt/lstwrds _spnklk.htm).

4. Two recent articles lend support to this interpretation that seeking comfort through food choice is a major factor accounting for many of the items in last meal requests. In their studies of the effects of "mortality salience" (preoccupation with one's death), Friese and Hofmann (2008) confirmed the hypotheses that individuals turn to their own culture and worldview as a psychological buffer, choosing familiar and therefore comforting food and beverage over something foreign, and that in high mortality salience, there is often impaired self-control resulting in increased impulsive behavior. In "Death Row Nutrition," Wansink, Kniffin, and Shimizu (2012) analyzed the contents of 193 last meal orders of prisoners in several states, executed between 2002 and 2006. They found that the average number of calories in a last meal request was 2,756 (in four instances, it was 7,200 or more), which is greater than the 2,200 to 2,400 recommended for sedentary males for an entire day. The most frequent items asked for were meat (83.9 percent), fried food (67.9 percent), desserts (66.3 percent), and soft drinks (60 percent). In regard to starches and grains, 40.9 percent of requests were for french fries, 20.7 percent for other potato sides, and 17.1 percent for bread. Nuts appeared in only one of the orders, and yogurt, tofu, and specifically vegetarian meals were not requested at all. Their findings "are consistent with studies of how food is used to mediate feelings of stress and distress" (Wansink, Kniffin, and Shimizu 2012:837), that is, a craving for or overindulgence in fats and carbohydrates—high-caloric food consumption—when an individual is under duress and the future appears bleak.

5. I based the calculations on data in Malone (2006) concerning the last words of 355 prisoners executed in Texas from December 7, 1982, to November 16, 2005, and the final meal requests of 310 inmates from December 7, 1982, to September 10, 2003, on the archived list issued by the Texas Department of Criminal Justice (web.archive.org).

Usable records that contain both last words and final meals total 237. I coded the data into six themes evident in last words ("no last words," "innocence," "remorsefulness," "resignation," "bravado," and "defiance") and four categories of last meal requests ("no food requested," "light meal or snack," "normal meal," and "excessive"). For other efforts at thematic analysis, see Meyer (2008); and Rice, Dirks, and Exline (2009).

6. This newspaper and others cited later were accessed from http://chroniclingamerica.loc.gov/lccn/sn82016187/ and www.newspaperarchive.com.

REFERENCES CITED

Adler, Thomas. 1981. Making Pancakes on Sunday: The Male Cook in Family Tradition. *Western Folklore* 40(1): 45–54.

Anderson, Jay Allan. 1971. The Study of Contemporary Foodways in American Folklife Research. *Keystone Folklore Quarterly* 16(4):155–63.

Banner, Stuart. 2000. *The Death Penalty: An American History*. Cambridge, MA: Harvard University Press.

———. 2002. The Death Penalty's Strange Career. *Wilson Quarterly* 26(2):70–82.

Bernstein, Lee. 2010. Correctional Dining: Prison Food in the Hudson Valley. *Edible Hudson Valley*. http://edible hudsonvalley.com/editorial/summer-2010/on-the-line/.

Black, Jacquelyn C. 2003. *Last Meal*. Monroe, ME: Common Courage Press.

Bonnie, Richard J. 1990. Dilemmas in Administering the Death Penalty: Conscientious Abstention, Professional Ethics, and the Needs of the Legal System. *Law and Human Behavior* 14(1):67–90.

Bookgirl. 2002. http://www.prisontalk.com/forums/archive /index.php/t-150289.html. Accessed August 12, 2010.

Bremmer, Jan. 1983. Scapegoat Rituals in Ancient Greece. *Harvard Studies in Classical Philology* 87:299–320.

Brettler, Marc Zvi, and Michael Poliakoff. 1990. Rabbi Simeon ben Lakish at the Gladiator's Banquet: Rabbinic Observations on the Roman Arena. *Harvard Theological Review* 83(1):93–8.

Cabana, Donald A. 1996. *Death at Midnight: The Confession of an Executioner*. Boston: Northeastern University Press.

Caldwell, Andrews. 2010. *Their Last Suppers: Legends of History and Their Final Meals*. Riverside, NJ: Andrews McMeel.

Calvert, C. 1928. A Brief Account of Criminal Procedure in Germany in the Middle Ages. In *A Hangman's Diary, Being the Journal of Master Franz Schmidt, Public Executioner of Nuremberg, 1573–1617*, ed. Albrecht Keller, trans. C. Calvert and A. W. Gruner, pp. 1–71. London: Philip Allan.

Camp, Charles. 1978. America Eats: Toward a Social Definition of Foodways. PhD diss., University of Pennsylvania.

Campos, Carlos. 2003. Feeding Curiosity about the Last Meals of the Condemned. *Chicago Tribune*, December 7. http://articles.chicagotribune.com/2003-12-07/features /0312070471_1_final-meal-thomas-grasso-texas-prison -officials.

Canan, Russell F. 1989. Burning at the Wire. In *Facing the Death Penalty: Essays on a Cruel and Unusual Punishment*, ed. Michael L. Radelet, pp. 60–80. Philadelphia, PA: Temple University Press.

Cicala, John Allan. 1995. The Folk Artist as Producer: A Behavioral Study of a Sicilian Immigrant Woman's Ceremonial Cooking Style. PhD diss., Indiana University.

Collins, Nick. 2010. Last Meals: Weird Requests on Death Row. *Telegraph*, December 7. http://www.telegraph.co.uk /news/newstopics/howaboutthat/8186685/Last-meals -weird-requests-on-death-row.html.

Crowder, Carla. 2004. Mentally Ill Man Executed for 1998 Killing. *Birmingham News*, October 1. http://www.prison talk.com/forums/archive/index.php/t-81301.html.

Dow, Mark. 2002. "The Line between Us and Them": Interview with Warden Donald Cabana. In *Machinery of Death: The Reality of America's Death Penalty Regime*, ed. David R. Dow and Mark Dow, pp. 175–91. New York: Routledge.

Dubber, Markus Dirk. 1996. The Pain of Punishment. *Buffalo Law Review* 44:545–611.

Dunea, Melanie. 2007. *My Last Supper: 50 Great Chefs and Their Final Meals/Portraits, Interviews, and Recipes*. New York: Bloomsbury USA.

Executing Mentally Impaired Prisoners Is Unjust and Cruel [editorial]. 1998. *Dallas Morning News*, November 22. http://www.fdp.dk/uk/ment.htm [reprint].

Fakazis, Elizabeth. 2011. *Esquire* Mans the Kitchenette. *Gastronomica* 11(3):29–39.

Fantz, Ashley. 2007. Executed Man's Last Request Honored—Pizza for Homeless. *CNN*, May 9. http://www .cnn.com/2007/US/05/09/execution.pizza/index.html.

Fernandez, Manny. 2011. Texas Death Row Kitchen Cooks Its Last "Last Meal." *New York Times*, September 22. http://www.nytimes.com/2011/09/23/us/texas-death -row-kitchen-cooks-its-last-last-meal.html.

Fine, Gary Alan. 1980. The Kentucky Fried Rat: Legends and Modern Society. *Journal of the Folklore Institute* 17(2–3):222–43.

FoodService Director. 1999. October 15. http://www.all business.com/retail-trade/eating-drinking-places /4177194–1.html. Accessed August 12, 2010.

Freedberg, Sydney P. 1999. The 13 Other Survivors and Their Stories: Freed from Death Row. *St. Petersburg Times*, July 4:10A. http://pqasb.pqarchiver.com/sptimes /access/42911235.html?FMT=ABS&FMTS=ABS

:FT&date=Jul+4%2C+1999&author=SYDNEY+P
.+FREEDBERG&pub=St.+Petersburg+Times&edition
=&startpage=10.A&desc=The+13+other+survivors
+and+their+stories+Series%3A+FREED+FROM
+DEATH+ROW.

Friese, Malta, and Wilhelm Hofmann. 2008. What Would You Have as a Last Supper? Thoughts about Death Influence Evaluation and Consumption of Food Products. *Journal of Experimental Social Psychology* 44(5):1388–94.

Garner, Dwight. 2010. One Man's Hard Road, from Existing to Living. Review of *In the Place of Justice: A Story of Punishment and Deliverance*, by Wilbert Rideau. *New York Times*, May 5. http://www.nytimes.com/2010/05 /05/books/05book.html?scp=29&sq=last%20meal %20condemned&st=cse.

Gatrell, V. A. C. 1994. *The Hanging Tree: Execution and the English People 1770–1868*. Oxford: Oxford University Press.

Gordon, Terri J. 2006. Debt, Guilt, and Hungry Ghosts: A Foucauldian Perspective on Bigert's and Bergström's *Last Supper. Cabinet Magazine Online*. http://www.cabinet magazine.org/events/lastsuppergordon.php.

Grace, Francie. 2003. Cost Cutters Slash Prison Food Budgets. *CBS News*, May 14. http://www.cbsnews.com/stories /2003/05/14/politics/main553785.shtml.

Graczyk, Michael. 2011. Special Last Meals: Texas Prisons End Special Last Meals for Inmates Facing Execution. *Huffington Post*, September 22. http://www.huffingtonpost .com/2011/09/22/special-last-meals-texas-_n_976543 .html.

Greene, Bob. 2001. They Didn't Get to Choose Their Last Meals. *Jewish World Review*, June 12. http://www .jewishworldreview.com/bob/greene061201.asp.

Greene, David. 2010. In the Immortal Words of Gary Gilmore and NIKE, "[Just] Do It." *Entertainment Agent Blog*, June 10. entertainmentagentblog.com/2010/06/20 /in-the-ientermmortal-words-of-gary-gilmore-and-nike -just-do-it/.

Gutierrez, C. Paige. 1992. *Cajun Foodways*. Jackson: University Press of Mississippi.

Haines, Herb. 1992. Flawed Executions, the Anti-Death Penalty Movement, and the Politics of Capital Punishment. *Social Problems* 39(2):125–38.

Hannaford, Alex. 2004. Confessions of a Death Row Chef. *Observer* [UK], March 14. http://www.guardian.co.uk /lifeandstyle/2004/mar/14/foodanddrink.features12/print.

Heisley, Deborah Dale. 1990. Gender Symbolism in Food. PhD diss., Northwestern University.

Hellerstein, Dina R. 1997. What Do We Gain by Taking These Childlike Lives? *New York Times*, March 30. http:// www.deathpenaltyinfo.org/node/656.

Hickey, Jennifer G. 2001. Dining In with Capital Punishment. *Insight on the News*, May 28, 17(20):24.

Humphrey, Theodore C., and Lin T. Humphrey, eds. 1988. *"We Gather Together": Food and Festival in American Life*. Ann Arbor: UMI Research Press.

Jackson, Bruce. 1965. Prison Folklore. *Journal of American Folklore* 78(310):317–29.

Jackson, Bruce, and Diane Christian. 1979. *Death Row*. Documentary Research, Inc. 60 min., restoration copyright 2007. CD-ROM.

——. 1980. *Death Row*. Boston: Beacon Press.

——. 2012. *In This Timeless Time: Living and Dying on Death Row in America*. Chapel Hill: University of North Carolina Press, in association with the Center for Documentary Studies at Duke University.

Jeung, Stevie. 2009. "I Did Not Get My Spaghetti-O's": Death Row Consumption in the Popular Media. *UCDavis Magazine Online* 26(2). http://ucdavismagazine.ucdavis .edu/issues/win09/jeung.html.

Johnson, Robert. 1990. *Death Work: A Study of the Modern Execution Process* (2nd ed.). Belmont, CA: Wadsworth, Thomson.

Jones, Michael Owen. 2007. Food Choice, Symbolism, and Identity: Bread-and-Butter Issues for Folkloristics and Nutrition Studies (American Folklore Society Presidential Address, October 2005), *Journal of American Folklore* 120(476):129–77.

Kalčik, Susan. 1984. Ethnic Foodways in America: Symbol and the Performance of Identity. In *Ethnic and Regional Foodways in the United States: The Performance of Group Identity*, ed. Linda Keller Brown and Kay Mussell, pp. 37–65. Knoxville: University of Tennessee Press.

Karon, Tony. 2000. Why We're Fascinated by Death Row Cuisine. *Time*, August 10. http://www.time.com/time /nation/article/0,8599,52337,00.html.

Kassab, Beth. 2002. Wuornos Attracts Interest until End. *Orlando Sentinel*, October 7. http://articles.orlandosentinel .com/2002–10–07/news/0210070307_1_wuornos-serial -killers-female-serial.

Kim, Sojin, and R. Mark Livengood. 1995. Ramen Noodles & Spam: Popular Foods, Significant Tastes. *Digest: An Interdisciplinary Review of Food and Foodways* 15:2–11.

Kirshenblatt-Gimblett, Barbara. 1986. The Kosher Gourmet in the Nineteenth-Century Kitchen: Three Jewish Cookbooks in Historical Perspective. *Journal of Gastronomy* 2(4):51–89.

KRT. 2002. Florida Executes "Damsel of Death." *Sydney Morning Herald*, October 11. http://www.smh.com.au /articles/2002/10/11/1034222548910.html.

Kuntz, Tom. 1997. Word for Word/Death-Watch Logs: Banality, Nausea, Triple Execution: Guards on Inmates' Final Hours. *New York Times*, January 12. http://www .nytimes.com/1997/01/12/weekinreview/banality-nausea -triple-execution-guards-on-inmates-final-hours.html ?pagewanted=all&src=pm.

LaChance, Daniel. 2007. Last Words, Last Meals, and Last Stands: Agency and Individuality in the Modern Execution Process. *Law & Social Inquiry* 32(3):701–24.

Lancaster, John. 2011. Incredible Edibles. *New Yorker*, March 21:64–8.

The Last Meal Not Always Tasty on Death Row. 1991. *Salina Journal*, February 20:10.

Last Supper. 2005. Dir. Mats Bigert and Lars Bergström. SVT, Kultur & Samhälle, Stockholm, Sweden. DVD, 58 min.

Last Words on Death Row. 2007. *CNN*, December 31. cnn.com/2007/US/law/12/10/court.last.words/index.html.

Lloyd, Timothy Charles. 1981. The Cincinnati Chili Culinary Complex. *Western Folklore* 40(1):28–40.

Locher, Julie L., William C. Yoels, Donna Maurer, and Jillian Van Ells. 2005. Comfort Foods: An Exploratory Journey into the Social and Emotional Significance of Food. *Food & Foodways* 13(4):273–97.

Lockwood, Yvonne R., and William G. Lockwood. 1991. Pasties in Michigan's Upper Peninsula: Foodways, Interethnic Relations, and Regionalism. In *Creative Ethnicity: Symbols and Strategies of Contemporary Ethnic Life*, ed. Stephen Stern and John Allan Cicala, pp. 3–20. Logan: Utah State University Press.

Long, Lucy. 1998. Culinary Tourism: A Folkloristic Perspective on Eating and Otherness. *Southern Folklore* 55(3):181–204.

——. 2009. Introduction. In "Food and Identity in the Americas," ed. Bill Ellis. Special Issue, *Journal of American Folklore* 122(483):3–10.

Lynch, Mona. 2000. The Disposal of Inmate #85271. *Studies in Law, Politics, and Society* 20:3–34.

Magliocco, Sabina. 1993. Playing with Food: The Negotiation of Identity in the Ethnic Display Event by Italian Americans in Clinton, Indiana. In *Studies in Italian American Folklore*, ed. Luisa Del Giudice, pp. 107–26. Logan: Utah State University Press.

Malone, Dan F. 2006. Dead Men Talking: Content Analysis of Prisoners' Last Words, Innocence Claims and News Coverage from Texas' Death Row. MA thesis, University of North Texas.

Mansnerus, Laura. 2001. Damaged Brains and the Death Penalty. *New York Times*, July 21. http://www.nytimes.com/2001/07/21/arts/damaged-brains-and-the-death-penalty.html?scp=1&sq=laura%20mansnerus%20damaged%20brains&st=cse.

Masumoto, David Mas. 1987. *Country Voices.* Del Rey, CA: Inaka Countryside Publications.

McClary, Daryl C. 2007. Ex-Convicts Claude H. Ryan and Walter Seelert Kill Lewis County Deputy Sheriff Seth R. Jackson on April 7, 1937. *HistoryLink*, September 18. http://www.historylink.org/index.cfm?DisplayPage=output.cfm&file_id=8239.

McLynn, Frank. 1989. *Crime and Punishment in Eighteenth-Century England.* London: Routledge.

Meyer, Linda Ross. 2008. Rituals of Death: The Meaning of Last Words and Last Meals. http://papers.ssrn.com/sol3/papers.cfm?abstract_id=1480686.

Neustadt, Kathy. 1992. *Clambake: A History and Celebration of an American Tradition.* Amherst: University of Massachusetts Press.

Newton, Sarah E. 1992. The Jell-O Syndrome: Investigating Popular Culture/Foodways. *Western Folklore* 51(3–4):249–67.

Oklahoma Executes Third Woman This Year. 2001. *Community of Sant'Egidio*, December 5. santegidio.org/pdm/news/08_12_01_c.htm.

O'Neill, Kevin Francis. 2001. Muzzling Death Row Inmates: Applying the First Amendment to Regulations That Restrict a Condemned Prisoner's Last Words. *Arizona State Law Journal* 33:1159–218.

Orecklin, Michele. 2000. Should John Penry Die? *Time*, November 27, 156(22):76. http://www.time.com/time/magazine/article/0,9171,998589,00.html.

Oremus, Will. 2011. No More "Last Meals" on Texas Death Row. *Slatest*, September 22. http://slatest.slate.com/posts/2011/09/22/lawrence_brewer_no_more_last_meal_for_texas_inmates_on_death_row.html.

Poltilove, Josh. 2009. Death Row Last Meals Run Gamut from Lobster Tail to Tacos. *Tampa Tribune*, February 11. http://tbo.com/news/death-row-last-meals-run-gamut-from-lobster-tail-to-tacos-123223.

Prejean, Helen. 1993. *Dead Man Walking: An Eyewitness Account of the Death Penalty in the United States.* New York: Random House.

Price, Brian. 2004a. The Last Supper. *Legal Affairs*, March/April. http://www.legalaffairs.org/issues/March-April-2004/feature_price_marapr04.msp.

——. 2004b. *Meals to Die For.* San Antonio, TX: Dyna-Paige Corporation.

Pringle, Paul. 2005. Jail Food Can Be a Hard Sell. *Los Angeles Times*, January 8. http://articles.latimes.com/2005/jan/08/local/me-jailfood8.

Prison Food Service Costs Could Be Reduced. 2008. *Red Tape Blog*, June 4. http://blogpublic.lib.msu.edu/index.php/2008/06/24/prison-food-service-costs-could-be-reduc?blog=5.

Ramsland, Katherine. n.d. Gary Gilmore. *Crime Library.* http://www.crimelibrary.com/notorious_murders/mass/gilmore/begin_7.html.

Reuters, Jim Forsyth. 2011. Texas Kills Fancy Last Meal Requests on Death Row. *Los Angeles Times*, September 22. http://www.latimes.com/sns-rt-usa-executionlastmeals1e78l1zv-20110922,0,4272524.story.

Reutter, David M., Gary Hunter, and Brandon Sample. 2010. Appalling Prison and Jail Food Leaves Prisoners Hungry

for Justice. *Prison Legal News*, August 12. https://www
.prisonlegalnews.org/(S(ekstf5550c4xpv45amqxt1r2))
/displayArticle.aspx?articleid=22246&AspxAutoDetect
CookieSupport=1.

Reynolds, Jack. 2010. "Retarded Last Meals for Texas'
Death Row Inmates." *Exiled Online*, January 17. http://
exiledonline.com/retarded-last-meals-for-texas-death
-row-inmates/.

Rice, Stephen K., Danielle Dirks, and Julie J. Exline. 2009.
Of Guilt, Defiance, and Repentance: Evidence from the
Texas Death Chamber. *Justice Quarterly* 26(2):295–326.

Rich, George W., and David F. Jacobs. 1973. Saltpeter: A
Folkloric Adjustment to Acculturation Stress. *Western
Folklore* 32(3):164–79.

Riell, Howard. 2001. California Prison System Adopts
Healthy Menus. *Food Service Director*, October 15. http://
www.allbusiness.com/retail-trade/eating-drinking
-places/4179099-1.html.

Rikoon, J. Sanford. 1982. Ethnic Food Traditions: A Review
and Preview of Folklore Scholarship. *Kentucky Folklore
Record* 28(1–2):12–25.

Rose, Joseph. 2005. The Oregon State Penitentiary Surveys
Inmates on Its Meals. *Prison Talk*, March 21. http://www
.prisontalk.com/forums/showthread.php?t=113977.

Roth, LuAnne. 2011. *Last Supper* [film review]. *Journal of
American Folklore* 124(491):105–8.

Rozin, Elisabeth. 1982. The Structure of Cuisine. In *The
Psychobiology of Human Food Selection*, ed. Lewis M.
Barker, pp. 189–203. Westport, CN: AVI.

Schreiner, Bruce. 2010. DOC Officials Grilled over Bad
Aramark Food. *Real Cost of Prisons*, February 24. http://
realcostofprisons.org/blog/archives/2010/01/ky_doc
_officialn.html.

Serrill, Michael S. 1983. Thirty-One Minutes from Death.
Time, October 17. http://content.time.com/time/magazine
/article/0,9171,952204,00.html.

Shaw, David. 2004. What Would You Have for Your Last
Meal? *Los Angeles Times*, January 14. http://articles
.latimes.com/2004/jan/14/food/fo-matters14.

Siporin, Steve. 1994. From Kashrut to Cucina Ebraica: The
Recasting of Italian Jewish Foodways. *Journal of American Folklore* 107(424):268–81.

Smith, Philip. 1996. Executing Executions: Aesthetics,
Identity, and the Problematic Narratives of Capital Punishment Ritual. *Theory and Society* 25(2):235–41.

Stein, Joel. 2007. You Eat What You Are. *Time*, October
18. http://www.time.com/time/magazine/article/0,9171
,1673252,00.html.

Stossel, John. 2004. How True Is "Monster"? *ABC
News*, February 13. http://abcnews.go.com/2020/Give
MeABreak/story?id=124320&page=1.

Tan, Shannon. 2003. Joseph Trueblood Put to Death;
Relatives of Ex-Girlfriend, 2 Children Waited for Call,

Closure. *Indianapolis Star*, June 13. http://www.indystar
.com.

Texas Department of Criminal Justice. 2003. Final Meal Requests. Archived from the original on December 2, 2003.
http://web.archive.org/web/20031202214318/http://
www.tdcj.state.tx.us/stat/finalmeals.htm. Accessed August 8, 2010.

Theophano, Janet S. 1991. "I Gave Him a Cake": An Inter-
pretation of Two Italian-American Weddings. In *Creative
Ethnicity: Symbols and Strategies of Contemporary Ethnic
Life*, ed. Stephen Stern and John Allan Cicala, pp. 44–54.
Logan: Utah State University Press.

Treadwell, Ty, and Michelle Vernon. 2001. *Last Suppers:
Famous Final Meals from Death Row*. East Lansing, MI:
Loompanics Unlimited.

Turner, Patricia A. 1987. Church's Fried Chicken and the
Klan: A Rhetorical Analysis of Rumor in the Black Community. *Western Folklore* 46(4):294–306.

——. 1993. *I Heard It through the Grapevine: Rumor in
African-American Culture*. Berkeley: University of California Press.

Valdez, Tito David, Jr. n.d. It's Chow Time! If It's Prison
Food, It All Tastes the Same. http://www.inmate.com
/prison-articles/prison-chow-time.htm.

VanSickle, Abbie. 2003. Condemned Can Make Big Deal
Out of Last Meal. *Indianapolis Star*, June 13. http://www
.indystar.com.

Verhovek, Sam Howe. 1998. Word for Word/Last Meals:
For the Condemned in Texas, Cheeseburgers without
Mercy. *New York Times*, January 4. http://www.nytimes
.com/1998/01/04/weekinreview/word-for-word-last
-meals-for-the-condemned-in-texas-cheeseburgers
-without-mercy.html.

Visser, Margaret. 1986. *Much Depends on Dinner*. Toronto:
McClelland and Stewart Weidenfeld.

Vogel, Mark R. n.d. Last Meals on Death Row. http://
serialkillercalendar.com/killerextrasLASTMEALS.html.

Wansink, Brian, Matthew M. Cheney, and Nina Chan.
2003. Exploring Comfort Food Preferences across Age
and Gender. *Physiology & Behavior* 79(4–5):739–47.

Wansink, Brian, Kevin M. Kniffin, and Mitsuru Shimizu.
2012. Death Row Nutrition: Curious Conclusions of
Last Meals. *Appetite* 59(3):837–43.

Want Better Meals: Condemned Inmates. 1960. *Corpus
Christi Times*, June 18:11.

Word, Ron. 2002. Florida Executes Female Serial Killer. *St.
Petersburg Times*, October 9.

Yglesias, Linda. 1995. Grasso Orders Last Meal. *New
York Daily News*, March 13. http://articles.nydailynews
.com/1995-03-13/news/17970493_1_thomas-grasso
-oklahoma-state-penitentiary-death-penalty.

Yoder, Don. 1961. Sauerkraut in the Pennsylvania Folk-
Culture. *Pennsylvania Folklife* 12(2):56–69.

———. 1962. Pennsylvanians Called It Mush. *Pennsylvania Folklife* 13(2):27–49.

———. 1972. Folk Cookery. In *Folklore and Folklife: An Introduction*, ed. Richard M. Dorson, pp. 325–50. Chicago: University of Chicago Press.

Yoder, Lonnie. 1986. The Funeral Meal: A Significant Funerary Ritual. *Journal of Religion and Health* 25(2): 149–60.

Reading Questions

1. According to Jones's research, what is included in the final meal of most Texas inmates?

2. How might prisoners' level of education and economic status affect their choices for last meal items?

3. Based on his findings, what does Jones indicate about the relationship between a prisoner's ethnicity, his or her geographical/regional association, and his or her selection of food for the final meal?

4. What evidence does Jones present to back up the claim that "female [food] selections exhibit convenience, indulgence, and perhaps in some instances an implicit rejection of the traditional role of homemaker" (par. 21)?

5. What does Jones suggest as perhaps the most important factor affecting inmates' selection of food items for their last meal?

6. According to Jones, how do proponents of the death penalty sometimes use final-meal food-item selections to reinforce their construction of death row inmates as "monsters"?

Rhetoric Questions

7. Besides introducing the topic at hand, what purpose do paragraphs 2 to 4 of Jones's study serve? Is that purpose effectively achieved?

8. Jones presents a series of questions through which he reveals his study's purposes. Where are these questions located? Are they effectively situated in the text? Why or why not?

9. Choose any two paragraphs from one of the body sections of Jones's article. Count the number of times an outside source is cited. How would you describe Jones's strategy of development, based on your findings?

10. Jones presents an epigraph with each of his subsection titles. What purpose do these epigraphs serve for you as a reader? Do you think they are effective? Why or why not?

Response and Research Questions

11. Jones suggests that one of the reasons behind the fascination with prisoners' final meals is that the ritual compels us to consider our own final meals. What foods and beverages would you order for a final meal? Offer an explanation for your choices.

12. Jones discusses one inmate who refused to participate in the last meal ritual, calling it "barbaric and cruel" (44). Others have described the ritual as one that demonstrates "kindness to the condemned and [offers] a recognition of their humanity and our shared humanity" (42). Do you agree with either of these positions? Why or why not?

Capital Punishment in Films: The Impact of Death Penalty Portrayals on Viewers' Mood and Attitude toward Capital Punishment

BENEDIKT TILL AND PETER VITOUCH

Dr. Benedikt Till is a research associate at the Department of General Practice and Family Medicine, Center for Public Health, Medical University of Vienna and lecturer at the Medical University of Vienna. The following study was published in the *International Journal of Public Opinion Research* in 2012 with co-author Peter Vitouch, a professor of media psychology in the Department of Communication and vice-dean of the Faculty of Social Science at the University of Vienna. The article examines the impact that filmic representations of capital punishments have on viewers' moods and attitudes.

INTRODUCTION

Since several decades there has been a lively debate on the legitimacy of the death penalty between those for and those against capital punishment (see e.g., Ellsworth & Gross, 1994; Fan, Keltner, & Wyatt, 2002; Niven, 2002). The entrance of capital punishment in the forefront of debate and consciousness at nearly all levels of society is due at least in part to the plethora of movies and books on this topic (Giles, 1995). But what is the effect of such media accounts on recipients?

The Impact of Fictional and Nonfictional Death Penalty Portrayals

In a laboratory experiment, Howells, Flanagan, and Hagan (1995) demonstrated that the screening of tapes of executions leads to reduced support for the death penalty. A study by Holbert, Shah, and Kwak (2004) suggests that viewing police reality shows, crime drama, and TV news is related to the endorsement of

capital punishment. Furthermore, press coverage was found to be a driving force for opinion about capital punishment (Fan et al., 2002; Niven, 2002). An association between media use and support for the death penalty was also reported by Sotirovic (2001).

Evidence for fictional portrayals is rather heterogeneous. Slater, Rouner, and Long (2006) found increased support for the death penalty among viewers of a television drama that endorsed capital punishment. Mutz and Nir (2010) demonstrated that viewers who watched a fictional television program emphasizing flaws in the justice system, exhibit a greater rejection of the death penalty than those who viewed a more positive portrayal of the criminal justice system. Other studies, however, found no change in attitude toward the death penalty among viewers of films focusing on capital punishment (e.g., Önder & Öner-Özkan, 2003; Peterson & Thurstone, 1970). Thus, the effects of fictional entertainment narratives dealing with capital punishment on viewers' attitudes toward the death penalty are still unclear and undetermined.

Emotional Audience Responses to Dramas

According to affective disposition theory (Zillmann, 1996), viewers enjoy a film the most when the protagonist benefits from the story's outcome. If the heroes fail, we feel bad for them—this might lead to negative emotions. Evidence from several studies suggests that individuals exposed to sad film endings experience significantly higher degrees of emotional stress and a deterioration of mood (e.g., Hesse, Spies, Hänze, & Gerrards-Hesse, 1992; Tannenbaum & Gaer, 1965).

On the other hand, Festinger's (1954) social comparison theory proposes that humans tend to evaluate their values, abilities, and living conditions by comparing them with those of other people. A comparison with the undesirable situation of a person sentenced to death might improve an individual's mood. Also, people may use sad films to cope with some negative experience in their lives (see e.g., Mares & Cantor, 1992; Nabi, Finnerty, Domschke, & Hull, 2006; Tan, 2008). Till, Niederkrotenthaler, Herberth, Vitouch, and Sonneck (2010) discovered a deterioration of mood and an increase of depression in viewers of films featuring the suicide of the protagonist. Concurrently, the viewers also reacted with a rise in life satisfaction and a drop in suicidality. However, studies focusing on emotional audience reactions to films dealing with capital punishment are rare.

DETERMINANTS OF FILM EFFECTS

Audience reactions to motion pictures and television programs are partly based on the characters who populate them and on the viewers' engagement in the process of impression formation in getting to know the respective persona (Hoffner & Cantor, 1991). Identification with media characters is defined as "an imaginative process through which an audience member assumes the identity, goals, and perspective of a character" (Cohen, 2001, p. 261). Several studies provided evidence that identification has the potential to amplify media-induced reactions in terms of emotions (e.g., Slater & Rouner, 2002; Tannenbaum & Gaer, 1965; Till et al., 2010), attitude changes (e.g., Basil, 1996; Gau, James, & Kim, 2009; Greenwood, 2004), and behavior modifications (e.g., Brown & Basil, 1995; Niederkrotenthaler et al., 2009; Perry & Perry, 1976).

The impact of a motion picture can also be determined by the way certain actions are portrayed in key scenes of the movie. Print media guidelines—for example, recommended restrictions for newspaper reports on suicide—are known to influence readers' imitation behavior (Etzersdorfer & Sonneck, 1998; Niederkrotenthaler & Sonneck, 2007; Sonneck, Etzersdorfer, & Nagel-Kuess, 1994). Accordingly, removing scenes from a film has been discussed as a means to mitigate possible negative effects of movies and television programs on their viewers and has been used by television stations to moderate their broadcasts and thereby avoid public criticism (Worringham & Buxton, 1997). The effectiveness of such editing, however, has been questioned in the past, since most studies on this topic have failed to demonstrate a significant influence on film effects (e.g., Ferracuti & Lazzari, 1970; Tannenbaum, 1978; Till et al., 2010; Till & Vitouch, 2008).

The present study investigates the impact of two films featuring the portrayal of the protagonist's death via capital punishment on their viewers' mood and attitude toward the death penalty and compares the effects of these two movies to those of edited versions—thus being the first study to examine emotional, as well as cognitive, audience responses to different versions of such films. The importance of using emotional, as well as cognitive, parameters to assess the impact of a drama was recently highlighted by Till et al. (2010). The following hypotheses were formulated:

H1: The viewing of a film drama focusing on capital punishment has a negative influence on the viewers' mood.

H2: The viewing of a film drama focusing on the negative aspects of capital punishment reduces the viewers' approval of the death penalty.

H3: Excluding the protagonist's execution from a film that focuses on capital punishment reduces its impact on (a) the viewers' mood and (b) their attitudes toward the death penalty.

H4: The more a viewer identifies with the dying protagonist of a film focusing on capital punishment, the greater is (a) the deterioration of his or her mood and (b) the reduction of his or her approval of the death penalty.

METHODS

Design and Material

Group 1 viewed the movie *The Chamber* (United States, 1996), while group 2 watched *Dancer in the Dark* (Denmark/France, 2000). Both films portray the death penalty in a negative way and conclude with the explicit portrayal of (one of) the main character's execution. However, while *The Chamber* is a mainstream movie, in *Dancer in the Dark*, the plot and its depiction are rather unconventional due to the usage of different themes in the genres of the musical, the neo-realist film, and the melodrama. Furthermore, in *The Chamber* there is a certain amount of uncertainty regarding the convict's guilt, whereas in *Dancer in the Dark*, the crime—and thus the protagonist's innocence—is shown explicitly. Groups 3 and 4 saw an edited version of the respective film without the portrayal of the execution. However, it was still clear to the viewer that the protagonist was killed via death penalty. Only the execution itself was removed from the film, not the events immediately before and after the execution. The editing of the scenes was carried out in a manner one would expect from a television station to mitigate possible negative effects of its broadcasted program (see Worringham & Buxton, 1997).

In *The Chamber*, a young attorney seeks to appeal the death sentence of his grandfather, a Ku Klux Klan bomber, for the murder of a lawyer and his two small boys. Despite the attorney's efforts and the proof that his grandfather did not have the intention to kill his victims, the Ku Klux Klan bomber is executed in the gas chamber.

The film *Dancer in the Dark* involves a woman, Selma, who works day and night to save her son from the same disease she suffers from, a disease that inevitably will make her blind. When her neighbor and friend, a police officer, steals money from her to pay his debts, Selma confronts him and tries to get her money back. In the resulting turmoil, Selma shoots the police officer in self-defense. Despite her innocence, Selma gets sentenced to death. The film concludes with her execution by hanging.

Subjects

Participants were 121 individuals living in Austria ($n = 121$)—49 men (40.5%), with mean age of 34.20 years, and 72 women (59.5%), with mean age of 41.25 years.

Measures

Mood. Mood was measured by the subscales *Sorrow* and *Positive Mood* of a German short version of the *Profile of Mood States* by McNair, Lorr, and Doppleman (1971) using three items (adjectives such as "unhappy" or "sad") for sorrow and six items (adjectives such as "happy" or "merry") for positive mood on a 7-point scale ranging from 1—"not at all" to 7—"very strong" (sorrow: Cronbach's $\alpha = .89$; positive mood: Cronbach's $\alpha = .71$).

Attitude toward Capital Punishment. Attitudes toward capital punishment were measured by a questionnaire based on analogous scales developed by Önder and Öner-Özkan (2003), as well as Peterson and Thurstone (1970), using 11 items (statements such as "Life imprisonment is more effective than capital punishment") on a 5-point scale ranging from 1—"disagree" to 5—"agree." However, one item was excluded from the analysis to improve the scale's reliability (Cronbach's $\alpha = .91$).

Identification with the Protagonist. Identification was measured by a questionnaire based on an analogous scale developed by Cohen (2001) using 11 items (statements such as "I felt I knew exactly what character X was going through") on a 5-point scale ranging from 1—"disagree" to 5—"agree." However, one item was excluded from the analysis to improve the scale's reliability (Cronbach's α = .85).

In computing the parameters, scores on the negative items were reversed, so that high scores indicated a high level of the respective variable. The scores were then added together according to the instructions given in the respective manual.

Procedure

Participation in the study was voluntary and anonymous. The subjects' allocation to the experimental groups was randomized. It was ensured that the subjects had not already seen the respective film in the past. Before the film, questionnaires on mood and attitudes toward capital punishment were completed by the participants. After the movie, these parameters were measured again, as well as the subjects' identification with the respective protagonist.

Data Analysis

Nonparametric tests were applied, since normal distribution could not be assumed within the given set of data. The subjects were disproportionately low on sorrow (skew ranging between 0.47 and 2.08, and kurtosis between −1.22 and 3.61) and approval of capital punishment (skew ranging between 0.48 and 2.18, and kurtosis between −0.78 and 5.23). An overview of the medians, percentiles, means, and standard deviations of the subjects' mood and attitudes toward capital punishment is shown in Table I. Wilcoxon tests were performed to analyze the impact the films have on the subjects' mood and attitudes toward capital punishment. To examine to which extent identification influences the impact of the films, Spearman correlations were performed. An overview of the medians, percentiles, means, and standard deviations of the subjects' identification with the respective protagonist is shown in Table II. For the Wilcoxon tests, the parameters' summarized scores before and after the movie screening were used to conduct the analysis. Change scores and the summarized score for identification were used for the correlations.

RESULTS

A summary of the results of the Wilcoxon tests can be found in Table III. There was a significant deterioration of the subjects' positive mood in all four film groups (*The Chamber*: $Z = -4.06$, $n = 30$, $p < .001$; *The Chamber*, edited version: $Z = -4.27$, $n = 31$, $p < .001$; *Dancer in the Dark*: $Z = -4.61$, $n = 30$, $p < .001$; *Dancer in the Dark*, edited version: $Z = -3.57$, $n = 30$, $p < .001$). The screening of the movies also led to a significant increase of sorrow in all groups (*The Chamber*, edited version: $Z = -2.33$, $n = 31$, $p < .05$; *Dancer in the Dark*: $Z = -3.56$, $n = 30$, $p < .001$; *Dancer in the Dark*, edited version: $Z = -2.19$, $n = 30$, $p < .05$) except for the audience watching the original version of *The Chamber* ($Z = -0.70$, $n = 30$, $p = .47$). Thus, Hypothesis 1 was confirmed. Furthermore, there was a significant swing toward unfavorable assessments of capital punishment in the groups watching the edited versions of the two films (*The Chamber*: $Z = -2.95$, $n = 31$, $p < .01$; *Dancer in the Dark*: $Z = -2.78$, $n = 30$, $p < .01$), but surprisingly, not among viewers of the original versions (*The Chamber*: $Z = -1.67$, $n = 30$, $p = .09$; *Dancer in the Dark*: $Z = -0.96$, $n = 30$, $p = .33$). Therefore, Hypothesis 2 was partly confirmed. Hypotheses 3a and 3b, on the other hand, were rejected—excluding the execution from the films did not reduce the impact on the viewers' mood and their attitudes toward the death penalty.

For the correlations, the data across the four groups were collapsed and analyzed together, as only few differences were revealed between the respective films and film versions. Identification was significantly linked to the increase of sorrow (Spearman's $r = .39$, $r^2 = .15$, $n = 121$, $p < .001$) and the change of attitudes toward capital punishment (Spearman's $r = .21$, $r^2 = .04$, $n = 121$, $p < .05$), indicating that the more a viewer identified with the dying main character of the film, the more was the recipient's sadness increasing and the greater was his or her swing toward unfavorable assessments of the death penalty. Furthermore, there was a positive correlation between identification and the deterioration of positive mood close to statistical significance (Spearman's $r = .15$,

Table 1

Means (M), Standard Deviations (SD), Medians (μ), and Percentiles (P_{25}, P_{75}) for the Recipients' Mood and Attitudes toward Capital Punishment for Each Film before and after the Screening

		The Chamber (original)	Dancer in the Dark (original)	The Chamber (edited)	Dancer in the Dark (edited)
Positive mood					
Before	M (SD)	4.01 (1.24)	4.63 (1.35)	4.2 (1.26)	3.98 (1.29)
	P_{25}	3.25	3.45	3.5	2.95
	μ	4	4.66	4.33	4
	P_{75}	4.66	6	5.16	5.04
After	M (SD)	2.75 (1.41)	2.87 (1.59)	3.03 (1.37)	2.96 (1.42)
	P_{25}	1.62	1.33	1.83	1.5
	μ	2.58	2.58	3.16	3
	P_{75}	4	4.08	4	4.04
Sorrow					
Before	M (SD)	1.81 (1.38)	1.38 (0.69)	1.87 (1.3)	1.77 (1.17)
	P_{25}	1	1	1	1
	μ	1	1	1.33	1
	P_{75}	2.08	1.5	2.66	2.16
After	M (SD)	2 (1.25)	2.26 (1.37)	2.54 (1.37)	2.54 (1.68)
	P_{25}	1	1.25	1.33	1
	μ	1.5	2	2	2
	P_{75}	3	3.33	4	4
Attitudes toward capital punishment					
Before	M (SD)	2.41 (1.17)	2.12 (1.14)	2.18 (1.19)	1.98 (1.08)
	P_{25}	1.37	1.2	1.2	1.17
	μ	2.1	1.75	1.6	1.5
	P_{75}	3.32	2.92	3.3	2.85
After	M (SD)	2.28 (1.28)	2.06 (1.1)	1.96 (1.09)	1.67 (0.93)
	P_{25}	1	1	1	1
	μ	1.85	1.7	1.5	1.35
	P_{75}	3.07	2.7	2.5	2.05

Note. Values are means, standard deviations, medians, and percentiles of the parameters representing the subjects' positive mood, sorrow, and attitudes toward capital punishment based on the descriptive statistics analyzed via SPSS. The indices are based on means.

Table 2

Means (*M*), Standard Deviations (*SD*), Medians (μ), and Percentiles (P_{25}, P_{75}) for the Recipients' Identification with the Protagonist of the Respective Film

	The Chamber (original)	Dancer in the Dark (original)	The Chamber (edited)	Dancer in the Dark (edited)
M (SD)	2.59 (0.72)	3.00 (0.94)	2.83 (0.56)	3.40 (0.98)
P_{25}	2.07	2.30	2.50	2.57
μ	2.50	3.00	2.80	3.40
P_{75}	3.05	3.80	3.20	4.30

Note. Values are means, standard deviations, medians, and percentiles of the parameters representing the subjects' identification based on the descriptive statistics analyzed via SPSS. The indices are based on means.

$r^2 = .02$, $n = 121$, $p = .09$). Since identification was normally distributed, we performed regression analyses to further examine the characteristics of the associations between the viewers' identification and the film effects. The influence of identification on the change of attitudes ($B = -3.01$, Standard error = 1.46, $p < .05$, $R^2 = .09$, adapted $R^2 = .08$, $F = 11.92$) and sorrow ($B = -4.27$, Standard error = 1.18, $p < .001$, $R^2 = .19$, adapted $R^2 = .19$, $F = 29.36$) was significant—and close to statistical significance in terms of the reduction of positive mood ($B = 3.51$, Standard error = 2.49, $p = .16$, $R^2 = .02$, adapted $R^2 = .01$, $F = 3.20$). In addition, Sobel-Tests with bootstrap estimates were conducted to verify mediation (see Preacher & Hayes, 2004). However, identification was not found to be a significant mediator variable for the film-induced attitude change ($Z = 1.17$, $n = 121$, $p = .23$, 95% CI = -0.01 to 0.04), the deterioration of positive mood ($Z = 1.21$, $n = 121$, $p = .22$, 95% CI = -0.01 to 0.08), and the increase of sorrow ($Z = -0.24$, $n = 121$, $p = .80$, 95% CI = -0.09 to 0.05). Thus, hypotheses 4a and b were rejected.

Table 3

Findings from Wilcoxon-Tests Performed on the Recipients' Mood and Attitudes toward Capital Punishment for Each Film

	The Chamber (original)	Dancer in the Dark (original)	The Chamber (edited)	Dancer in the Dark (edited)
Positive mood	−4.06***	−4.61***	−4.27***	−3.57***
Sorrow	−0.70	−3.56***	−2.33*	−2.19*
Attitudes toward capital punishment	−1.67	−0.96	−2.95**	−2.78**

*p < .05. **p < .01. ***p < .001. (two-tailed)

Note. Values are Z-values from Wilcoxon-Tests representing the change of the subjects' positive mood, sorrow, and attitudes toward capital punishment.

DISCUSSION

The results of the present study show that recipients of films featuring the portrayal of the protagonist's execution are less happy and sadder after the screening than before. This effect is concordant with Zillmann's (1996) affective disposition theory proposing that an outcome victimizing the protagonist is deplored by the viewers and fits well with previous research demonstrating a deterioration of the viewers' mood after the screening of a drama (Hesse et al., 1992; Tannenbaum & Gaer, 1965; Till et al., 2010). It is interesting to note that this effect occurred in all groups showing no differences between the two motion pictures and the different film versions. The ineffectiveness of excluding scenes from a film to alter its emotional impact is consistent with findings of earlier research (see Ferracuti & Lazzari, 1970; Till et al., 2010; Till & Vitouch, 2008).

The negative portrayal of the death penalty in the two films also produced a diminished endorsement of capital punishment among the audience. This result is concordant with earlier research supporting the proposition that fictional television dramas can change peoples' opinion about the death penalty (Mutz & Nir, 2010; Slater et al., 2006). Given these results, it is plausible to assume that film dramas have the potential to affect viewers' political attitudes and influence their support not only for capital punishment, but also for other controversial public policies. However, a definite statement on this issue cannot be made based on our analyses.

It is important to point out that the viewers' attitudes toward the death penalty changed only in the groups watching the edited versions of the movies. Usually, the removal of such film scenes is meant to mitigate film effects (see Worringham & Buxton, 1997), but in this case it increased the influence on the audience's attitudes. This finding is surprising and very puzzling because of its counter-intuitive nature. A possible explanation for this result may be that recipients complement missing details in a film by using their imagination; this can lead to a more brutal or gruesome picture of an event in the viewer's imagination than actually displayed on screen, which might

aggravate the impact of a movie (see Till & Vitouch, 2008). The human mind and its imaginativeness should not be neglected or underestimated. After all, the sheer imagination of an event can change attitudes and behavior (Anderson, 1983; Gregory, Burroughs, & Ainslie, 1985; Gregory, Cialdini, & Carpenter, 1982). This is in line with earlier findings that demonstrated a counterproductive impact of removing disturbing scenes from a film. Tannenbaum (1978), for example, reported higher physiological arousal when a violent scene of a film was deleted than without editing. He also found that some viewers believe to recall the deleted film scene, even though they never actually saw this particular scene. Therefore, simply removing a possibly disturbing scene from a film cannot be deemed to be an effective tool to mitigate potentially negative film effects.

Identification with the dying protagonist was not a significant mediator variable for the film-induced audience reactions. Various persuasion theories, such as the Elaboration Likelihood Model by Petty and Cacioppo (1986a, 1986b) or the Heuristic-Systematic Model by Chaiken (1980), suggest that absorption in a narrative and response to its characters enhance persuasive effects and suppress counter arguing, which is likely to be a necessary prerequisite for behavior change (Slater & Rouner, 2002). In this study, however, there is only limited evidence for identification to produce such effects. Maybe identification is not an adequate concept to comprehend the viewers' reception process, as suggested by Zillmann (1994, 1996). Other concepts, such as involvement (Krugman, 1965), transportation (Gerrig, 1993), modes of reception (Suckfüll & Scharkow, 2009), para-social interaction (Horton & Wohl, 1956), or empathy (Zillmann, 1991), might be more adequate to explore the psychological dynamics of how film messages may influence human emotions, attitudes, and behavior.

This study also has some limitations. First, most of our hypotheses were tested in a before–after quasi experimental design with repetition of the exact measures within a 2-hr period. This approach might have attenuated the films' effects. Furthermore, the distribution of several variables was too skewed to assume normal distribution of the data. Therefore, nonparametric tests were applied that are known to have less statistical power than parametric tests (Hodges & Lehmann, 1956). The fact that the data was not normally distributed is not uncommon (Altman & Bland, 1995), but is certainly noteworthy and needs to be considered at the interpretation of the results, including their generalization to the general public. A reason for the skewed distribution of the data might be the relatively small sample size (Altman & Bland, 1995). Finally, both movies in our study featured a critical or negative portrayal of the death penalty, so our results do not refer necessarily to all films focusing on capital punishment. However, most films in today's mainstream do not glorify capital punishment (see e.g., Giles, 1995).

Our results provide no reason to believe that people will suffer emotional distress due to watching motion pictures featuring the execution of the protagonist, but these films certainly deteriorate the viewers' mood and have the potential to influence their social values and beliefs. It also challenges Tyler and Boeckmann's (1997) proposition that support for capital punishment is strongly linked to values that reflect stable and long-standing political orientations, and it supports the notion that approval of the death penalty is based on emotion rather than factual information (Ellsworth & Gross, 1994). It seems that values and priorities communicated by television dramas have a nontrivial influence on public policies (Slater et al., 2006) by shaping peoples' political views through emotions (Mutz & Nir, 2010). Our study also clearly shows that the exclusion of death scenes is not an effective tool to mitigate the impact of a brutal or gruesome film. As we were able to demonstrate, that kind of editing may even lead to adverse effects. This finding highlights the need for new schemes to protect television viewers from harmful effects.

REFERENCES

Altman, D. G., & Bland, J. M. (1995). Statistics notes: The normal distribution. *British Medical Journal, 310,* 298.

Anderson, C. A. (1983). Imagination and expectation: The effect of imagining behavioral scripts on personal intentions. *Journal of Personality and Social Psychology, 45,* 293–305.

Basil, M. D. (1996). Identification as a mediator of celebrity effects. *Journal of Broadcasting & Electronic Media, 40,* 478–495.

Brown, W. J., & Basil, M. D. (1995). Media celebrities and public health: Responses to "Magic" Johnson's HIV disclosure and its impact on AIDS risk and high-risk behaviors. *Health Communication, 7*(4), 345–370.

Chaiken, S. (1980). Heuristic versus systematic processing and the use of source versus message cues in persuasion. *Journal of Personality and Social Psychology, 39,* 752–766.

Cohen, J. (2001). Defining identification: A theoretical look at the identification of audiences with media characters. *Mass Communication & Society, 4*(3), 245–264.

Ellsworth, P., & Gross, S. (1994). Hardening of the attitudes: Americans' views of the death penalty. *Journal of Social Issues, 50*(2), 19–52.

Etzersdorfer, E., & Sonneck, G. (1998). Preventing suicide by influencing mass-media reporting. The Viennese experience 1980–1996. *Archives of Suicide Research, 4,* 67–74.

Fan, D. P., Keltner, K. A., & Wyatt, R. O. (2002). A matter of guilt or innocence: How news reports affect support for the death penalty in the United States. *International Journal of Public Opinion Research, 14*(4), 439–452.

Ferracuti, F., & Lazzari, R. (1970). Indagine sperimentale sugli effetti immediati della presentazione di scene di violenza filmata [An experimental research on the immediate effects of the presentation of scenes of violence in motion pictures]. *Bollettino di Psicologia Applicata, 100–102,* 87–153.

Festinger, L. (1954). A theory of social comparison processes. *Human Relations, 7,* 117–140.

Gau, L.-S., James, J. D., & Kim, J.-C. (2009). Effects of team identification on motives, behavior outcomes, and perceived service quality. *Asian Journal of Management and Humanity Sciences, 4*(2–3), 76–90.

Gerrig, R. J. (1993). *Experiencing narrative worlds. On the psychological activities of reading.* New Haven, CT: Yale University Press.

Giles, J. E. (1995). Pop culture portrayals of capital punishment: A review of *Dead Man Walking* and *Among the Lowest of the Dead. American Journal of Criminal Justice, 20*(1), 137–146.

Greenwood, D. N. (2004). Transporting to TV-land: The impact of idealized character identification on self and body image. *Dissertation Abstracts International: Section B. Sciences and Engineering, 65*(6), 3222.

Gregory, W. L., Burroughs, W. J., & Ainslie, F. M. (1985). Self-relevant scenarios as an indirect means of attitude change. *Personality and Social Psychology Bulletin, 11*(4), 435–444.

Gregory, W. L., Cialdini, R. B., & Carpenter, K. M. (1982). Self-relevant scenarios as mediators of likelihood estimates and compliance: Does imagining make it so? *Journal of Personality and Social Psychology, 43,* 89–99.

Hesse, F. W., Spies, K., Hänze, M., & Gerrards-Hesse, A. (1992). Experimentelle Induktion emotionaler Zustände: Alternativen zur Velten-Methode [Experimental induction of mood states: Alternatives to the Velten method]. *Zeitschrift für Experimentelle und Angewandte Psychologie, 39,* 559–580.

Hodges, J., & Lehmann, E. L. (1956). The efficiency of some nonparametric competitors of the t test. *Annals of Mathematical Statistics, 27,* 324–335.

Hoffner, C., & Cantor, J. (1991). Perceiving and responding to mass media characters. In J. Bryant & D. Zillmann (Eds.), *Responding to the screen: Reception and reaction processes* (pp. 63–101). Hillsdale, NJ: Erlbaum.

Holbert, R. L., Shah, D. V., & Kwak, N. (2004). Fear, authority, and justice: Crime-related TV viewing and endorsements of capital punishment and gun ownership. *Journalism & Mass Communication Quarterly, 81*(2), 343–363.

Horton, D., & Wohl, R. R. (1956). Mass communication and para-social interaction. Observations on intimacy at a distance. *Psychiatry, 19,* 215–224.

Howells, G. N., Flanagan, K. A., & Hagan, V. (1995). Does viewing a televised execution affect attitudes toward capital punishment? *Criminal Justice and Behavior, 22*(4), 411–424.

Krugman, H. E. (1965). The impact of television advertising: Learning without involvement. *Public Opinion Quarterly, 29,* 349–356.

Mares, M. L., & Cantor, J. (1992). Elderly viewers' responses to televised portrayals of old age. Empathy and mood management versus social comparison. *Communication Research, 19,* 459–478. doi:10.1177/009365092019004004

McNair, D. M., Lorr, M., & Doppleman, L. F. (1971). *EITS Manual for the Profile of Mood States.* San Diego, CA: Educational and Industrial Testing Service.

Mutz, D. C., & Nir, L. (2010). Not necessarily the news: Does fictional television influence real-world policy preferences? *Mass Communication and Society, 13,* 196–217.

Nabi, R. L., Finnerty, K., Domschke, T., & Hull, S. (2006). Does misery love company? Exploring the therapeutic effects of TV viewing on regretted experiences. *Journal of Communication, 56,* 689–706.

Niederkrotenthaler, T., & Sonneck, G. (2007). Assessing the impact of media guidelines for reporting on suicides in Austria: Interrupted times series analysis. *Australian and New Zealand Journal of Psychiatry, 41,* 419–428.

Niederkrotenthaler, T., Till, B., Kapusta, N. D., Voracek, M., Dervic, K., & Sonneck, G. (2009). Copycat effects after media reports on suicide: A population-based ecologic study. *Social Science & Medicine, 69*(7), 1085–1090.

Niven, D. (2002). Bolstering an illusory majority: The effects of the media's portrayal of death penalty support. *Social Science Quarterly, 83*(3), 671–689.

Önder, Ö. M., & Öner-Özkan, B. (2003). Visual perspective in causal attribution, empathy and attitude change. *Psychological Reports, 93,* 1035–1046.

Perry, D. G., & Perry, L. C. (1976). Identification with film characters, covert aggressive verbalization, and reactions to film violence. *Journal of Research in Personality, 10*(4), 399–409.

Peterson, R. C., & Thurstone, L. L. (1970). *Motion pictures and the social attitudes of children.* New York: Arno Press & The New York Times.

Petty, R. E., & Cacioppo, J. T. (1986a). *Communication and persuasion: Central and peripheral routes to attitude change.* New York: Springer.

Petty, R. E., & Cacioppo, J. T. (1986b). The elaboration likelihood model of persuasion. *Advances in Experimental Social Psychology, 19,* 123–205.

Preacher, K. J., & Hayes, A. F. (2004). SPSS and SAS procedures for estimating indirect effects in simple mediation models. *Behavior Research Methods, Instruments, and Computers, 36,* 717–731.

Slater, M. D., & Rouner, D. (2002). Entertainment-education and elaboration likelihood: Understanding the processing of narrative persuasion. *Communication Theory, 12*(2), 173–191.

Slater, M. D., Rouner, D., & Long, M. (2006). Television dramas and support for controversial public policies: Effects and mechanisms. *Journal of Communication, 56,* 235–252.

Sonneck, G., Etzersdorfer, E., & Nagel-Kuess, S. (1994). Imitative suicide on the Viennese subway. *Social Science & Medicine, 38,* 453–457.

Sotirovic, M. (2001). Effects of media use on complexity and extremity of attitudes toward the death penalty and prisoners' rehabilitation. *Media Psychology, 3,* 1–24.

Suckfüll, M., & Scharkow, M. (2009). Modes of reception for fictional films. *Communications, 34,* 361–384.

Tan, E. S. (2008). Entertainment is emotion: The functional architecture of the entertainment experience. *Media Psychology, 11,* 28–51.

Tannenbaum, P. H. (1978). Emotionale Erregung durch kommunikative Reize. Der Stand der Forschung [Emotional arousal via communicative stimuli. State of the art]. *Fernsehen und Bildung, 12*(3), 184–195.

Tannenbaum, P. H., & Gaer, E. P. (1965). Mood change as a function of stress of protagonist and degree of identification in a film viewing situation. *Journal of Personality and Social Psychology, 2,* 612–616.

Till, B., Niederkrotenthaler, T., Herberth, A., Vitouch, P., & Sonneck, G. (2010). Suicide in films: The impact of suicide portrayals on non-suicidal viewers' well-being and the effectiveness of censorship. *Suicide & Life-Threatening Behavior, 40*(4), 319–327.

Till, B., & Vitouch, P. (2008). On the impact of suicide portrayal in films: Preliminary results. In A. Herberth, T. Niederkotenthaler, & B. Till (Eds.), *Suizidalität in den Medien/Suicidality in the media: Interdisziplinäre Betrachtungen/Interdisciplinary contributions* (pp. 69–77). Münster, Germany: LIT.

Tyler, T. R., & Boeckmann, R. J. (1997). Three strikes and you are out, but why? The psychology of public support for punishing rule breakers. *Law & Society Review, 31*, 237–265.

Worringham, R., & Buxton, R. A. (1997). Censorship. In H. Newcomb (Ed.), *The encyclopedia of television* (Vol. 1, pp. 331–334). Chicago: Fitzroy Dearborn.

Zillmann, D. (1991). Empathy: Affect from bearing witness to the emotions of others. In J. Bryant & D. Zillmann (Eds.), *Responding to the screen: Reception and reaction processes* (pp. 135–167). Hillsdale, NJ: Erlbaum.

Zillmann, D. (1994). Mechanisms of emotional involvement with drama. *Poetics, 23*, 33–51.

Zillmann, D. (1996). The psychology of suspense in dramatic exposition. In P. Vorderer, H. J. Wulff, & M. Friedrichsen (Eds.), *Suspense: Conceptualizations, theoretical analyses, and empirical explorations* (pp. 199–231). Mahwah, NJ: Erlbaum.

Reading Questions

1. What do the authors present as their central research question? Where is this question located in their research report?

2. Based on their review of previous scholarship, are Till and Vitouch able to discern any areas of clear consensus among scholars? If so, what are they?

3. According to Till and Vitouch, what makes their study groundbreaking?

4. What are the researchers' four hypotheses? What are their findings in terms of accepting or rejecting each of their hypotheses?

5. Till and Vitouch indicate that one of their findings is particularly "surprising and very puzzling because of its counter-intuitive nature" (par. 23). What was the finding, and how do the researchers rationalize this result?

Rhetoric Questions

6. How does the section entitled "Emotional Audience Responses to Dramas" serve to enhance Till and Vitouch's work as social scientists? How does it foster meaning in their work?

7. Till and Vitouch discuss the results of their study in the Results section of their report, but they also provide results in the form of three different tables. Does one form of presentation provide something for the reader that the other does not? Which presentation method works best for you as a reader?

8. Analyze the structure of the study's Discussion section paragraph-by-paragraph. How is it organized, and what is the logic guiding the organization? Is this organization likely to be helpful to the intended audience? Why or why not?

9. The researchers note a number of limitations affecting their study's results. For you as a reader, what is the effect of the authors' identifying these limitations?

Response and Research Questions

10. Watch a creative film that directly concerns the death penalty. As you watch, track how your own mood and attitude shift. Evaluate Till and Vitouch's four hypotheses in light of your own experience.

11. Identify a film that has directly influenced the way you feel about a particular social issue or topic. What was the social issue or topic? In what ways were you affected? Explain why you believe the film was able to affect your beliefs or attitudes.

ACADEMIC CASE STUDY • CAPITAL PUNISHMENT   NATURAL SCIENCES

Lethal Injection for Execution: Chemical Asphyxiation?

TERESA A. ZIMMERS, JONATHAN SHELDON, DAVID A. LUBARSKY, FRANCISCO LÓPEZ-MUÑOZ, LINDA WATERMAN, RICHARD WEISMAN, AND LEONIDAS G. KONIARIS

Teresa A. Zimmers is currently an associate professor of surgery, anatomy, and cell biology at Indiana University's School of Medicine. "Lethal Injection for Execution: Chemical Asphyxiation?," a study co-written with six of her colleagues at the University of Miami Miller School of Medicine and published in the online access journal *PLoS Medicine* in 2007, offers evidence to challenge "the conventional view of lethal injection [as] leading to an invariably peaceful and painless death." According to the editor of the journal that published the study, the researchers' findings call into question the constitutionality of the current lethal injection protocol.

ABSTRACT

Background

Lethal injection for execution was conceived as a comparatively humane alternative to electrocution or cyanide gas. The current protocols are based on one improvised by a medical examiner and an anesthesiologist in Oklahoma and are practiced on an ad hoc basis at the discretion of prison personnel. Each drug used, the ultrashort-acting barbiturate thiopental, the neuromuscular blocker pancuronium bromide, and the electrolyte potassium chloride, was expected to be lethal alone, while the combination was intended to produce anesthesia then death due to respiratory and cardiac arrest. We sought to determine whether the current drug regimen results in death in the manner intended.

Methods and Findings

We analyzed data from two US states that release information on executions, North Carolina and California, as well as the published clinical, laboratory, and vet-erinary animal experience. Execution outcomes from North Carolina and California together with interspecies dosage scaling of thiopental effects suggest that in the current practice of lethal injection, thiopental might not be fatal and might be insufficient to induce surgical anesthesia for the duration of the execution. Furthermore, evidence from North Carolina, California, and Virginia indicates that potassium chloride in lethal injection does not reliably induce cardiac arrest.

Conclusions

We were able to analyze only a limited number of executions. However, our findings suggest that current lethal injection protocols may not reliably effect death through the mechanisms intended, indicating a failure of design and implementation. If thiopental and potassium chloride fail to cause anesthesia and cardiac arrest, potentially aware inmates could die through pancuronium-induced asphyxiation. Thus the conventional view of lethal injection leading to an invariably peaceful and painless death is questionable.

EDITORS' SUMMARY

Background

Lethal injection is a common form of execution in a number of countries, most prominently the United States and China. The protocols currently used in the United States contain three drugs: an ultrashort-acting barbiturate, thiopental (which acts as an anesthetic, but does not have any analgesic effect); a neuromuscular blocker, pancuronium bromide (which causes muscle paralysis); and an electrolyte, potassium chloride (which stops the heart from beating). Each of these drugs on its own was apparently intended by those who derived the protocols to be sufficient to cause death; the combination was intended to produce anesthesia then death due to respiratory and cardiac arrest. Following a number of executions in the United States, however, it has recently become apparent that the regimen as currently administered does not work as efficiently as intended. Some prisoners take many minutes to die, and others become very distressed.

Why Was This Study Done?

It is possible that one cause of these difficulties with the injections is that the staff administering the drugs are not sufficiently competent; doctors and nurses in the United States are banned by their professional organizations from participating in executions and hence most personnel have little medical knowledge or skill. Alternatively, the drug regimens used might not be effective; it is not clear whether they were derived in any rational way. The researchers here wanted to investigate the scientific basis for the protocols used.

What Did the Researchers Do and Find?

They analyzed data from some of the few states (North Carolina and California) that release information on executions. They also assessed the regimens with respect to published data from clinical, laboratory, and veterinary animal studies. The authors concluded that in the current regimen thiopental might not be fatal and might be insufficient to induce surgical anesthesia for the duration of the execution, and that potassium chloride does not reliably induce cardiac arrest. They conclude therefore that potentially aware inmates could die through asphyxiation induced by the muscle paralysis caused by pancuronium.

What Do These Findings Mean?

The authors conclude that even if lethal injection is administered without technical error, those executed may experience suffocation, and therefore that "the conventional view of lethal injection as an invariably peaceful and painless death is questionable." The Eighth Amendment of the US Constitution prohibits cruel and unusual punishment. The results of this paper suggest that current protocols used for lethal injection in the United States probably violate this amendment.

Additional Information

Please access these Web sites via the online version of this summary at http://dx.doi.org/10.1371/journal .pmed.0040156.

- *In a linked editorial the PLoS Medicine editors discuss this paper further and call for the abolition of the death penalty.*
- *The Death Penalty Information Center is a rich resource on the death penalty both in the United States and internationally.*
- *Information on challenges to lethal injection in various states, including California and North Carolina, is available from the University of California, Berkeley, School of Law.*
- *Human Rights Watch monitors executions in the United States.*
- *Amnesty International campaigns against the death penalty.*
- *A compendium of death-penalty-related links are available from a pro-death-penalty site, the Clark County Prosecuting Attorney.*

INTRODUCTION

In the United States, lethal injection can be imposed in 37 states and by the federal government and military. The origin of the lethal injection protocol can be traced to legislators in Oklahoma searching for a less expensive and potentially more humane alternative to the electric chair [1]. Both the state medical examiner and a chairman of anesthesiology appear to have been consulted in the writing of the statute. The medical examiner has since indicated that no research went into his choice of drugs—thiopental, pancuronium bromide, and potassium chloride—but rather he was guided by his own experience as a patient [2]. His expectation was that the inmate would be adequately anesthetized, and that although each individual drug would be lethal in the dosage specified, the combination would provide redundancy. The anesthesiologist's input relating to thiopental was written into law as "the punishment of death must be inflicted by continuous, intravenous administration of a lethal quantity of an ultra-short-acting barbiturate in combination with a chemical paralytic agent" [3], although in practice Oklahoma uses bolus dosing of all three drugs [4,5]. Texas, the first state to execute a prisoner by lethal injection, and subsequently other jurisdictions, copied Oklahoma's protocol without any additional medical consultation [1].

Although executioners invariably achieve death, the mechanisms of death and the adequacy of anesthesia are unclear. Used independently in sufficiently high doses, thiopental can induce death by respiratory arrest and/or circulatory depression, pancuronium bromide by muscle paralysis and respiratory arrest, and potassium chloride by cardiac arrest. When used together, death might be achieved by a combination of respiratory arrest and cardiac arrest due to one or more of the drugs used. Because thiopental has no analgesic effects (in fact, it can be antianalgesic) [6], and because pancuronium would prevent movement in response to the sensations of suffocation and potassium-induced burning, a continuous surgical plane of anesthesia is necessary to prevent extreme suffering in lethal injection.

Recently we reported that in most US executions, executioners have no anesthesia training, drugs are administered remotely with no monitoring for anesthesia, data are not recorded, and no peer review is done [7]. We suggested that such inherent procedural problems might lead to insufficient anesthesia in executions, an assertion supported by low postmortem blood thiopental levels and eyewitness accounts of problematic executions. Because of a current lack of data and reports of problems with lethal injection for executions, we sought to evaluate the three-drug protocol for its efficacy in producing a rapid death with minimal likelihood of pain and suffering.

METHODS

North Carolina lethal injection protocols were determined from Department of Corrections drug procurement records and testimony of prison personnel participating in the process. Times to death were determined from North Carolina Department of Corrections documents, including the Web site [8], official statements, and corroborating news and eyewitness reports. Start times were available for 33 executions, of which 19 could be independently confirmed. The North Carolina warden pronounces death after a flat line is displayed on the electrocardiogram (ECG) monitor for 5 min, thus time to death was calculated from start time to pronouncement of death less 5 min. Dosages were calculated from postmortem body weights taken from Reports of Investigation by the North Carolina Office of the Chief Medical Examiner. Information regarding the California protocol and execution logs and Florida and Virginia executions were obtained through available court documents [9,10,11]. Data are expressed as mean ± standard deviation. One-way ANOVA with Tukey's multiple comparison test was used for statistical analysis.

RESULTS

Data from North Carolina Executions

Three lethal injection protocols have been used in North Carolina from the first execution in 1984 to the most recent at the time of this writing in August 2006 (Figure 1A). The initial use of serial, intravenous (IV) injections of 3 g of thiopental and 40 mg of pancuronium bromide (referred to here as "Protocol A," $n = 8$, Figure 1A) was superseded by Protocol B in 1998. Protocol B consisted of serial injections of 1.5 g of thiopental, 80 mEq of potassium chloride, 40 mg of pancuronium bromide, 80 mEq of potassium chloride, and finally 1.5 g of thiopental ($n = 21$) [1,12]. After criticism from expert witnesses [13], in 2004 the injection order was changed to the current protocol of serial injections of 3 g of thiopental, 40 mg of pancuronium bromide, and 160 mEq of potassium chloride (Protocol C, $n = 11$) [14]. Each injection is performed in rapid succession with intermittent saline flushes to avoid drug precipitation. Until the last two executions in 2007, no assessment or monitoring of anesthesia was performed.

According to the North Carolina Department of Corrections, once the ECG monitor displays a flat line for 5 min, the warden declares death and a physician certifies that death has occurred [7, 12]. Execution start times and declaration times were available for 33 of the 42 lethal injections conducted in North Carolina (Figure 1B). Mean times to death were 9.88 ± 3.87 min for Protocol A, 13.47 ± 4.88 min for Protocol B, and 9.00 ± 3.71 min for Protocol C. The mean time to death for Protocol B was significantly longer than for Protocol C ($p < 0.05$, Tukey-Kramer test after one-way ANOVA). No other differences were statistically significant. These data indicate that the five-dose regimen of Protocol B slightly prolonged time to death, but more importantly, they indicate that the addition of potassium chloride did not hasten death overall.

In contrast to clinical use of these same drugs, jurisdictions invariably specify mass quantities for injection rather than dosing by body weight. We sought to determine the actual doses used in executions using postmortem body weights recorded by the Office of the Medical Examiner. North Carolina injects 3 g of thiopental; however, in Protocol B inmates were given half the thiopental at the end, once all painful stimuli were administered and death should have been achieved. Thus we considered only the first 1.5 g for Protocol B. Overall the median thiopental dose was 20.3 mg/kg (range 11.2–44 mg/kg, $n = 40$) (Figure 1C). Virtually all of the lowest doses were under Protocol B, although four very large individuals executed under Protocols A and C received less than the median dose. Eyewitness reports of inmate movement including convulsions and attempts to sit up in four executions [15] did not cluster in the lowest doses, but rather occurred at doses of 17.1, 18.9, 19.6, and 21 mg/kg, all performed under Protocol B. Calculated median doses of pancuronium bromide and potassium chloride were 0.46 mg/kg (range 0.28–0.46 mg/kg) and 1.83 mEq/kg (range 1.11–2.35 mEq/kg), respectively.

Data from California Executions

Executions in California provided a second insight into the methodologies and outcomes in lethal injections. The public version of the California protocol specifies

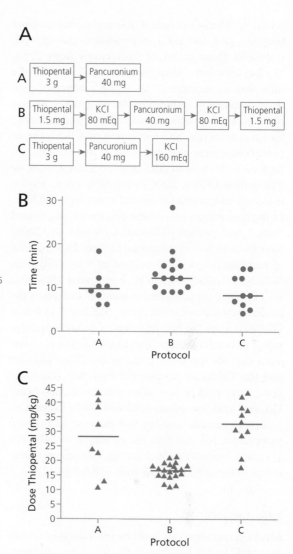

Figure 1. Lethal Injection Executions in North Carolina

(A) Schematic depicting quantity and order of drug administration in the three protocols.

(B) Time to death by protocol, calculated as the interval from execution start time to declaration of death, minus 5 min (see Methods).

(C) Actual dose of thiopental by body weight (not available for all inmates). In Protocol B, 1.5 g of thiopental was given after the pancuronium bromide and potassium chloride, once painful stimuli had been administered and death should have occurred; accordingly, only the first 1.5 g dose is plotted.

DOI:10.1371/JOURNAL.PMED.0040156.G001

injection of 5 g of thiopental, 100 mg of pancuronium bromide, and 100 mEq of potassium chloride [9]. California Department of Corrections from 226A, "Lethal Injection—Execution Record," consists of a table listing "operations," including injection of each drug, cessation of respiration, flatlining of the cardiac monitor, and pronouncement of death, with columns for time, heart rate, and respiration rate. Such execution records were available for 9 of the 11 lethal injections performed in San Quentin California State Prison from 1996 to 2006 [9,10]. One record was incomplete and contradictory and is not reported here. In the remaining 8 executions, respiration rate ceased from 1 min (inmate WB1966) to 9 min (CA2006) after the injection of thiopental (Figure 2). Cessation of respiration was noted coincident with (WB1966, SW2005, CA2006) or up to 3 min after (SA2002) injection of pancuronium bromide. Flatlining of the cardiac monitor occurred 2 min (DR2000) to 8 min (JS1999) after the last injection of potassium chloride. The records indicate that a second dose of potassium chloride was used in the execution of SA2002, and the California warden has said that additional doses were used in two other executions, one being CA2006 and the other unknown [16]. Eyewitness reports document "sudden and extreme" convulsive movements 3–4 min into the execution of MB1999 [17] and more than 30 heaving, convulsive movements of the chest and abdomen of SA2002 [18].

DISCUSSION

Most US executions are beset by procedural problems that could lead to insufficient anesthesia in executions. This hypothesis has been supported by findings of low postmortem blood thiopental levels and eyewitness accounts of problematic executions. Herein we report evidence that the design of the drug scheme itself is flawed. Thiopental does not predictably induce respiratory arrest, nor does potassium chloride always induce cardiac arrest. Furthermore, on the basis of execution data and clinical, veterinary, and laboratory animal studies, we posit that the specified quantity of thiopental may not provide surgical anesthesia for the

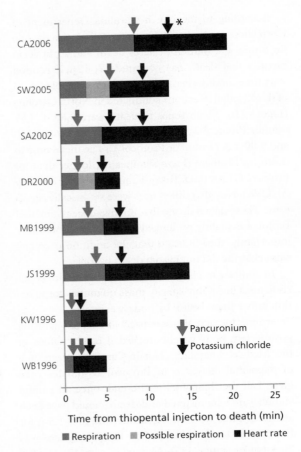

Figure 2. Lethal Injection Executions in California
Depicted are duration of respiration and heart rate after initiation of the thiopental injection at time 0. Injection of pancuronium bromide is indicated by the blue arrow, potassium chloride by the black arrow. Note that additional injections were given of potassium chloride in SA2002 and of pancuronium bromide in WB1996. SW2005 was noted to be breathing 3 min after thiopental, but not at the time of pancuronium bromide injection; the exact time respiration ceased was not recorded. DR2000 was noted to have chest movements 2 min after respiration was noted to have ceased.
*A second dose of potassium chloride was administered to CA2006, but not noted on the log. A third, unidentified inmate was also given a second dose of potassium chloride, according to the warden (see text).

DOI:10.1371/JOURNAL.PMED.0040156.G002

duration of the execution. Thus some inmates may experience the sensations of pancuronium-induced paralysis and respiratory arrest.

In the United States and Europe, techniques of animal euthanasia for clinical, laboratory, and agricultural applications are rigorously evaluated and governed by professional, institutional, and regulatory oversight. In university and laboratory settings, local oversight bodies known as Animal Care and Use Committees typically follow the American Veterinary Medical Association's guidelines on euthanasia, which consider all aspects of euthanasia methods, including drugs, tools, and expertise of personnel in order to minimize pain and distress to the animal. Under those guidelines, lethal injections of companion or laboratory animals are limited to injection by qualified personnel of certain clinically tested, Food and Drug Administration–approved anesthetics or euthanasics, while monitoring for awareness.

In stark contrast to animal euthanasia, lethal injection for judicial execution was designed and implemented with no clinical or basic research whatsoever. To our knowledge, no ethical or oversight groups have ever evaluated the protocols and outcomes in lethal injection. Furthermore, there are no published clinical or experimental data regarding the safety and efficacy of the three-drug lethal injection protocol. Until the unprecedented and controversial use of bispectral index monitoring in the last two North Carolina lethal injections [19], no monitoring for anesthesia was performed. Given this paucity of knowledge and documentation, we sought to evaluate available data in order to determine the efficacy of the three-drug protocol.

The designers of lethal injection intended that 20 each of the drugs be fatal independently and that the combination provide redundancy [2]. Moreover, in legal challenges to the death penalty, the leading expert witness testifying on behalf of the states routinely asserts that 3 g of thiopental alone is a lethal dose in almost all cases [14]. The data presented here, however, suggest that thiopental alone might not be lethal. First, extrapolating from clinical use, the lowest dosages used in some jurisdictions would not be expected to kill. Calculated dosages in North Carolina executions using 3 g of thiopental ranged from 10 to 45 mg/kg. Assuming inmates are roughly the same size across jurisdictions, the dose range would be 17–75 mg/kg in California, where 5 g of thiopental is used, and 6.6–30 mg/kg in Virginia and other jurisdictions, which use 2 g. Thus, at the lowest doses, thiopental would be given near the upper range of that recommended for clinical induction of anesthesia (3–6.6 mg/kg)—clearly not a dose designed to be fatal [20]. Second, the calculated doses used across lethal injections are only 0.1–2 times the LD_{50} (dose required to kill 50% of the tested population) of thiopental in dogs (37 mg/kg), rabbits (35 mg/kg), rats (57.8 mg/kg), and mice (91.4 mg/kg) [21, 22]. Third, intravenous delivery of thiopental alone is not recommended by the Netherlands Euthanasics Task Force, which concluded "it is not possible to administer so much of it that a lethal effect is guaranteed" [23], even in their population of profoundly ill patients.

The most compelling evidence that even 5 g of thiopental alone may not be lethal, however, is that some California inmates continued to breathe for up to 9 min after thiopental was injected. This observation directly contradicts testimony of that state's expert witness, who asserted that "this dose of thiopental sodium will cause virtually all persons to stop breathing within a minute of drug administration" and that "virtually every person given 5 grams of thiopental sodium will have stopped breathing prior to the administration of the pancuronium bromide" [24]. The witness has made identical statements regarding 3 g of thiopental [14]. Indeed, the clinical literature is replete with examples of patients experiencing respiratory failure after even low doses of thiopental [25]. Others, however, experience merely transient, nonfatal apnea. Of course, for inmates who did not stop breathing with thiopental alone, it is impossible to know whether the thiopental solution was correctly mixed, whether the entire dose was administered intravenously, or whether the apparent resistance was due to bolus dosing or individual variation. It remains possible, however, that bolus dosing of 5 g of thiopental alone might not be fatal in all persons. Indeed, nonhuman primates given as much as 60 mg/kg (the mass equivalent of 6 g for a 100 kg man) experienced prolonged sleep, but ultimately recovered [26].

If thiopental does not reliably kill the inmates, then perhaps death is effected by potassium chloride. Rapid intravenous or intracardiac administration of 1–2 mmol/kg potassium chloride under general anesthesia is considered acceptable for euthanasia of large animal species; thus the 1.11–2.35 mmol/kg doses given in North Carolina's lethal injections ought to be fatal. If potassium chloride contributes to death through cardiotoxicity, however, cardiac activity ought to cease more quickly when potassium is used than when it is not. Indeed, such is the principle behind the animal euthanasia agent, Beuthanasia-D Special, in which the cardiotoxic effects of phenytoin synergize with the central nervous system–depressive effects of pentobarbital, accelerating death over pentobarbital alone [27]. In contrast, our analysis shows that use of potassium chloride in North Carolina's Protocol C did not hasten death (defined as flatlining of the ECG) over Protocol A, which used thiopental and pancuronium alone. Moreover, in California executions, ECG flatlining was noted from 2 to 9 min after potassium chloride administration. This observation contrasts sharply with reports of accidental bolus IV administration of concentrated potassium chloride solution, in which patients experienced complete cardiopulmonary arrest almost immediately upon injection [28]. The North Carolina and California data together suggest that potassium chloride might not be the lethal agent in lethal injection.

Given that neither thiopental nor potassium chloride can be construed reliably to be the agent of death in lethal injection, death in at least some inmates might have been due to respiratory cessation from the use of pancuronium bromide. The typical use of 0.06–0.1 mg/kg pancuronium bromide under balanced anesthesia produces 100% neuromuscular blockade within 4 min, with approximately 100 min required for 25% recovery [29]. The doses used in North Carolina were some 3–11 times greater than the typical intubation dose, and thus would be expected to produce more rapid paralysis of many hours duration and complete respiratory arrest [30]. Indeed, pancuronium might have been the agent of death even in inmates who ceased breathing coincident with

or shortly after injection of pancuronium, rendering permanent the thiopental-induced apnea. In addition, because pancuronium bromide is effective even when delivered subcutaneously or intramuscularly, pancuronium is likely the sole agent of death when IV catheter misplacement or blowout impairs systemic delivery of the other two drugs. In such cases death by suffocation would occur in a paralyzed inmate fully aware of the progressive suffocation and potassium-induced sensation of burning. This was likely the experience of Florida inmate Angel Diaz, whose eyes were open and mouth was moving 24 min into his execution and who was pronounced dead after 34 min. Findings of two 30-cm burns over both antecubital fossae prompted the medical examiner to conclude that the IV lines were misplaced and the drugs were delivered subcutaneously [31].

Executions such as Diaz's, in which additional drugs were required, constitute further evidence that the lethal injection protocols are not adequate to ensure a predictable, painless death. Court documents and news reports indicate that at least Virginia [32], California [10], and Florida [31] have administered additional potassium chloride in multiple executions when the inmate failed to die as expected. If a Virginia execution takes too long and if the inmate fails to die, the protocol indicates that additional pancuronium and potassium chloride should be injected, although there is no provision for additional thiopental [32]. In cases such as Diaz's, additional drugs may have been required due to technical problems with delivery, but it remains possible that in others, the standard drug protocol failed to kill.

Given the uncertainty surrounding the mechanism of death and low postmortem blood thiopental levels in some executed inmates [7], one must ask whether adequate anesthesia is maintained to prevent awareness and suffering. Medical experts on both sides of the lethal injection debate have asserted that 3 g of thiopental properly delivered should reliably result in either death or a long, deep surgical plane of anesthesia [13,14]. In support of this contention, continuous or intermittent thiopental administration was formerly used for surgical procedures lasting

Table 1

Reported Duration of Sleep or Anesthesia after Bolus IV Injections of Thiopental in Experimental Animals

Species	Dose (mg/kg)	n	Mean Duration of Sleep[a] (min)	Mean Duration of Anesthesia[b] (min)	Reference	Calculated HED[c] (mg/kg)
Mouse	30		4.7–6.4		[43]	2.4
Rat	20		4.0–7.0		[43]	3.2
	25		22.6		[43]	4
	18	32	9.3–10.5		[44]	2.88
	22	7	30.0 ± 6.0		[44]	3.52
Rabbit	20	1	0	0	[45]	6.4
	21	10	28		[21]	6.72
	22	16	14.8–15.2		[44]	7.04
Dog	10.2	5	10.8	1.8	[46]	5.51
	10.9	5	11.4	1.4	[46]	5.89
	15	8	26	8.5	[47]	8.1
	25	22	74.4 ± 7.1		[47]	13.5
Sheep	20	4		18.3 ± 5.10	[48]	18.1
	25		30–45	15	[49]	22.6
Goat	12.7–13.9	4		12.0 ± 5.20	[48]	8.8–9.6
Swine	13.8–25.0	4		5.5 ± 2.7	[48]	12.3–22.4
Cattle	20	4		32.25 ± 14.36	[46]	28.8
Nonhuman primate	60	1	95		[43]	16.5

[a] From loss to return of righting reflex or voluntary movement.

[b] Typically corneal areflexia.

[c] Human equivalent dose was calculated as HED = animal dose (mg/kg) × (animal weight [kg]/human weight [kg])$^{0.33}$ [35,36].

doi:10.1371/journal.pmed.0040156.t001

many hours. In one study, 3.3–3.9 g given to patients over 25–50 min resulted in sleep for 4–5.5 h [33]. Depth and duration of thiopental anesthesia depends greatly upon dose and rate of administration, however, and bolus dosing results in significantly different pharmacokinetics and duration of efficacy than administration of the same quantity of drug at a lower rate [22].

In the modern practice of anesthesia, thiopental is used solely to induce a few moments of anesthesia prior to administering additional agents. Anesthesiologists are taught to administer a small test dose while assessing patient response and the need for additional doses [20]. Such stepwise administration and evaluation has been the practice from the first reports of thiopental usage in 1934, due to the known potential for barbiturate-induced respiratory arrest [34]. It was early recognized that age, body composition, health status, anxiety, premedication, and history of substance abuse clearly influence response to thiopental, with some individuals showing marked resistance to standard doses [35] and others fatal sensitivity [25]. Thus the historical and modern clinical use of thiopental results from its cautious application to prevent respiratory arrest both in the typical patient and the abnormally susceptible. In consequence, there is almost no information about duration of anesthesia following large bolus doses of thiopental in unpremedicated patients, and there are few living anesthesiologists with clinical experience relevant to lethal injection protocols.

Unlike in clinical medicine, however, bolus injection of thiopental is regularly practiced in laboratory animals and veterinary medicine. Standard texts specify from 6 to 50 mg/kg thiopental, depending on the species, for 5–10 min of anesthesia [36], including 18–22 mg/kg for 10–15 min of anesthesia in dogs, pigs, sheep, and swine [37]. Such dosages are conservative guidelines based on average responses of animals in experimental trials (Table 1), with the assumption that respiration and depth of anesthesia will be assessed in individual animals prior to onset of the procedure. (In addition, thiopental is not recommended for painful procedures in animals.) Withholding or administering additional dosages would compensate for individual variation in response.

Although species differences complicate pharmacological comparisons from animals to humans, animal studies are the basis for virtually all human drug trials. According to FDA guidelines, toxicity endpoints for drugs administered systemically to animals are typically assumed to scale well across species when doses are normalized to body surface area (i.e., mg/m^2) [38]. Calculating the human equivalent dose (HED) as recommended by the FDA [39] gives a more conservative estimate of thiopental equivalencies across species than does using simple mg/kg comparisons (Table 1). Swine in particular are regarded as an excellent model of human cardiopulmonary and cerebrovascular physiology, with comparable size, body composition, and brain perfusion rates [40]. Comparing the HED for thiopental anesthesia in swine to lethal injection dosages, we conclude that at least some inmates at the lower end of the thiopental dose range might have experienced fleeting or no surgical anesthesia, while others at the higher end of the range might have received doses predicted to induce more prolonged anesthesia (Table 1). Such a prediction is impossible to evaluate, however, because any evidence of suffering would be masked by the effects of pancuronium.

Our study is necessarily limited in scope and interpretations. Given the secrecy surrounding lethal injections, we were able to analyze only a small fraction of the 891 lethal injections in the United States to date. Indeed, the majority of executions actually take place in states such as Texas and Virginia, where the protocols and procedural problems are likely similar to the ones described, but where the states are unwilling to provide information [7]. Not only are available data limited, however, medical literature addressing the effects of these drugs at high doses and in combination is nonexistent, emphasizing the failure of lethal injection practitioners to design and evaluate rigorously a process that ensures reliable, painless death, even in animals. In consequence, the adequacy of anesthesia and mechanism of death in the current lethal injection protocol remains conjecture.

Despite such limitations, our analysis of data from 30 more forthcoming states along with reports of problematic executions and judicial findings [41] together indicate that the protocol of lethal injection for execution is deeply flawed. Technical difficulties are clearly responsible for some mishandled executions, such as Diaz's. Better training of execution personnel and altering delivery conditions may not "fix" the problem [41, 42], however, because the drug regimen itself is potentially inadequate. Our analysis indicates that as used, thiopental might be insufficient both to maintain a surgical plane of anesthesia and to predictably induce death. Consequently, elimination of pancuronium or both pancuronium and potassium, as has been suggested in California [41], could result in situations in which inmates ultimately awaken.

With the growing recognition of flaws in the lethal injection protocol, 11 states have now suspended the death penalty, with nine of those seeking resolution of issues surrounding the process [42]. In California and Florida, commissions of experts have been charged with evaluating and refining lethal injection protocols. As deliberations begin, we suggest that the secrecy surrounding protocol design and implementation should be broken. The available data or lack of data should be made public and deliberations should be open and transparent.

SUPPORTING INFORMATION

Alternative Language Abstract S1. Translation into Spanish by Francisco López-Muñoz

Found at doi:10.1371/journal.pmed.0040156 .sd001 (24 KB DOC)

ACKNOWLEDGMENTS

Author contributions. TAZ, JPS, DAL, and LGK conceived the study. TAZ and JPS obtained protocol information and execution data. TAZ, DAL, and LGK analyzed the data and published literature. DAL, LW, and RW provided clinical insights. TAZ, JPS, and FLM provided historical perspectives and references. All authors contributed to writing and editing the manuscript.

REFERENCES

[1] Denno D (2002) When legislatures delegate death: The troubling paradox behind state uses of electrocution and lethal injection and what it says about us. Ohio State Law J 63: 63–260. Available at: http://moritzlaw.osu.edu/lawjournal/issues/volume63/number1/denno.pdf. Accessed 16 March 2007.

[2] Fellner J, Tofte S (2006) So long as they die: Lethal injection in the United States. Human Rights Watch. Available at: http://hrw.org/reports/2006/us0406. Accessed 16 March 2007.

[3] Oklahoma Statute Title §22-1014(A) Available at: http://www.lsb.state.ok.us/osstatuestitle.html. Accessed 16 March 2007.

[4] United States District Court, Western District of Oklahoma (20 July 2005) Complaint and Motion to Dismiss, Anderson v. Evans. Case Number 5-825. Document Number 1, pp. 25–34.

[5] US District Court, Western District of Oklahoma (6 September 2005) Complaint and Motion to Dismiss, Anderson v. Evans. Case Number 5-825. Document Number 26, pp. 3–4.

[6] Dundee JW (1960) Alterations in response to somatic pain associated with anaesthesia. II. The effect of thiopentone and pentobarbitone. Br J Anaesth 32: 407–414.

[7] Koniaris LG, Zimmers TA, Lubarsky DA, Sheldon JP (2005) Inadequate anaesthesia in lethal injection for execution. Lancet 365: 1412–1414.

[8] North Carolina Department of Correction (2007) News regarding scheduled executions. Available at: http://www.doc.state.nc.us/dop/deathpenalty/execution_news.htm. Accessed 19 March 2007.

[9] United States District Court, Northern District of California (20 January 2006) Exhibit A to Motion for TRO, Morales v. Hickman. Case Number 6-219. San Quentin Operational Procedure No. 770. Available at: http://www.law.berkeley.edu/clinics/dpclinic/Lethal%20Injection%20Documents/California/Morales/Morales%20Dist%20Ct.Cp/Ex%20A%20to%20TRO%20motion%20(Procedure%20No.%20770).pdf. Accessed 16 March 2007.

[10] United States District Court, Northern District of California (20 January 2006) Exhibit 2 to Exhibit C in Motion for TRO, Morales v. Hickman. Case Number 6-219. Document Number 15-2. Available at: http://www.law.berkeley.edu/clinics/dpclinic/Lethal%20Injection%20Resource%20Pages/resources.ca.html. Accessed 16 March 2007.

[11] United States Supreme Court (6 March 2007) Brief for Amicus Habeas Corpus Resource Center, Hill v. McDonough. Case Number 05-8794. Available at: http://www.law.berkeley.edu/clinics/dpclinic/Lethal%20Injection%20Documents/Florida/Hill/2006.03.06%20amicus%20hcrc.pdf. Accessed 16 March 2007.

[12] United States District Court, Eastern District of North Carolina (31 October 2005) Polk Deposition, Page v. Beck. Case Number 5:04-CT-4. Document Number 98.

[13] United States District Court, Eastern District of North Carolina (3 November 2005) Second Heath Affidavit, Page v. Beck. Case Number 4-04. Document Number 102.

[14] United States District Court, Eastern District of North Carolina (27 September 2004) Affidavit of Dershwitz, Perkins v. Beck. Case Number 04-643. Document Number 7, pp. 22–31.

[15] United States District Court, Eastern District of North Carolina (7 April 2006) Order, Brown v. Beck. Case Number 5:06-CT-3018-H. Available at:

http://deathpenaltyinfo.org/Brownorder.pdf. Accessed 16 March 2007.

[16] United States District Court, Northern District of California (25 January 2006) Second Declaration of Dr. Mark Heath, Morales v. Hickman. Case Number 06-219. Document Number 22-1.

[17] United States District Court, Northern District of California (20 January 2006) Declaration of Patterson, Morales v. Hickman. Case Number 06-219. Document Number 14. Available at: http://www.law.berkeley.edu /clinics/dpclinic/Lethal%20Injection%20Documents /California/Morales/Morales%20Dist%20Ct.Cp /Ex%20B%20to%20TRO%20Motion.pdf. Accessed 16 March 2007.

[18] United States District Court, Northern District of California (20 January 2006) Declaration of Rocconi, Morales v. Hickman. Case Number 06-219. Document Number 15-4. Available at: http://www.law.berkeley.edu /clinics/dpclinic/Lethal%20Injection%20Documents /California/Morales/Morales%20Dist%20Ct.Cp /Ex%203%20to%20Heath%20Decl%20(Rocconi %20Decl%20re.%20Anderson%20execution).pdf. Accessed 16 March 2007.

[19] Steinbrook R (2006) New technology, old dilemma — Monitoring EEG activity during executions. N Engl J Med 354: 2525–2527.

[20] Abbott Laboratories (1993 November) Pentothal for injection, USP (Thiopental Sodium) Reference 06-8965-R10. A similar document is available at: http:// www.rxlist.com/cgi/generic/thiopental.htm. Accessed 16 March 2007.

[21] Werner HW, Pratt TW, Tatum AL (1937) A comparative study of several ultrashort-acting barbiturates, nembutal, and tribromethanol. J Pharmacol Exp Ther 60: 189–197.

[22] Robinson MH (1945) The effect of different injection rates upon the AD50, LD50 and anesthetic duration of pentothal in mice, and strength-duration curves of depression. J Pharmacol Exp Ther 85: 176–191.

[23] (1994) Administration and compounding of euthanasic agents. The Hague: Royal Dutch Society for the Advancement of Pharmacy.

[24] United States District Court, Northern District of California (20 January 2006) Declaration of Dershwitz, Morales v. Woodford. Case Number 06-219. Document Number 15.

[25] Harris WH (1943) Collapse under pentothal sodium. Lancet 242: 173–174.

[26] Taylor JD, Richards RK, Tabern DL (1951) Metabolism of ^{35}S thiopental (pentothal): Chemical and paper chromatographic studies of ^{35}S excretion by the rat and monkey. J Pharmacol Exp Ther 104: 93–102.

[27] (2005) Freedom of Information Summary. Original Abbreviated New Animal Drug Application. Euthanasia-III Solution. Rockville (Maryland): Food and Drug Administration. Available at: http://www.fda.gov/cvm/FOI /200-280020305.pdf. Accessed 6 March 2007.

[28] Wetherton AR, Corey TS, Buchino JJ, Burrows AM (2003) Fatal intravenous injection of potassium in hospitalized patients. Am J Forensic Med Pathol 24: 128–131.

[29] Gensia Sicor Pharmaceuticals (2003 October) Pancuronium bromide injection (prescribing information and material safety data sheet). Available at: http://www .sicor.com/products/1044.html. Accessed 16 March 2007.

[30] Mehta MP, Sokoll MD, Gergis SD (1988) Accelerated onset of non-depolarizing neuromuscular blocking drugs: Pancuronium, atracurium and vecuronium. A comparison with succinylcholine. Eur J Anaesthesiol 5: 15–21.

[31] Tisch C, Krueger C (14 December 2006) Second dose needed to kill inmate. St Petersburg Times. State/Suncoast edition. St. Petersburg. p. 1A. Available at: http:// www.sptimes.com/2006/12/14/State/Second__dose __needed__to.shtml. Accessed 16 March 2007.

[32] United States Supreme Court (6 March 2006) Brief for Amicus Curiae, Darick Demorris Walker, Hill v. McDonough. Case Number 05-8794. Available at: http://www.jenner.com/files/tbl__s69NewsDocument Order/FileUpload500/674/Brief__Amicus__Curiae __Walker.pdf. Accessed 16 March 2007.

[33] Brodie BB, Mark LC, Lief PA, Bernstein E, Papper EM (1951) Acute tolerance to thiopental. J Pharmacol Exp Ther 102: 215–218.

[34] Heard KM (1936) Pentothal: A new intravenous anesthetic. Can Med Assn J 34: 628–634.

[35] Mallison FB (1937) Pentothal sodium in intravenous anaesthesia. Lancet 230: 1070–1073.

[36] Kohn DF, Wixson SK, White WJ, Benson GJ, editors (1997) Anesthesia and analgesia in laboratory animals. New York: Academic Press. 426 p.

[37] Plumb DC (2005) Veterinary drug handbook. 5th Ed. Stockholm (Wisconsin): PharmaVet. 929 p.

[38] Mordenti J, Chappell W (1989) The use of interspecies scaling in toxicokinetics. In: Yacobi A, Kelly J, Batra V, editors. Toxicokinetics and new drug development. New York: Pergamon Press. pp. 42–96.

[39] Center for Drug Evaluation and Research (2005) Guidance for industry estimating the maximum safe starting dose in initial clinical trials for therapeutics in adult healthy volunteers. Rockville (Maryland): Food and Drug Administration. Available at: http://www .fda.gov/CDER/GUIDANCE/5541fnl.htm. Accessed 16 March 2007.

[40] Hannon JP, Bossone CA, Wade CE (1990) Normal physiological values for conscious pigs used in biomedical research. Lab Anim Sci 40: 293–298.

[41] United States District Court, Northern District of California (15 February 2006) Memorandum of Intended Decision; Request for Response from Defendants, Morales v. Tilton. Case Number C 06-219, C 06-926. Available at: http://www.deathpenaltyinfo.org/CalifLethalInjection.pdf. Accessed 16 March 2007.

[42] Koniaris LG, Sheldon JP, Zimmers TA (2007) Can lethal injection for execution really be "fixed"? Lancet 369: 352–353.

[43] Mirsky JH, Giarman NJ (1955) Studies on the potentiation of thiopental. J Pharmacol Exp Ther 114: 240–249.

[44] Richards RK, Taylor JD, Kueter KE (1953) Effect of nephrectomy on the duration of sleep following administration of thiopental and hexobarbital. J Pharmacol Exp Ther 108: 461–473.

[45] Gruber CM, Gruber JCM, Colosi N (1937) The effects of anesthetic doses of sodium thio-pentobarbital, sodium thio-ethamyl and pentothal sodium upon the respiratory system, the heart and blood pressure in experimental animals. J Pharmacol Exp Ther 60: 143–147.

[46] Ramsey H, Haag HB (1946) The synergism between the barbiturates and ethyl alcohol. J Pharmacol Exp Ther 88: 313–322.

[47] Wyngaarden JB, Woods LA, Ridley R, Seevers MH (1948) Anesthetic properties of sodium 5-allyl-5-(1-methyl-butyl)-2-thiobarbiturate (surital) and certain other thiobarbiturates in dogs. J Pharmacol Exp Ther 95: 322–327.

[48] Sharma RP, Stowe CM, Good AL (1970) Studies on the distribution and metabolism of thiopental in cattle, sheep, goats and swine. J Pharmacol Exp Ther 172: 128–137.

[49] Komar E (1991) Intravenous anaesthesia in the sheep. Proc Int Congr Vet Anesth, 4th. Utrecht (The Netherlands). pp. 209–210.

Reading Questions

1. As reported in the study, what three drugs, each supposedly administered in lethal quantities, are used as part of the execution protocol?

2. Based on your reading of the study's introduction, what is the researchers' primary concern about the effects of the lethal cocktail? On what do they base this concern?

3. The researchers suggest that the quantity of thiopental used in the execution protocol may not induce surgical anesthesia. What kinds of sensations might individuals experience during the execution process as a result?

4. What are the researchers able to suggest by comparing the human equivalent dose (HED) of thiopental anesthesia in swine to lethal injection doses?

5. According to the researchers, what does the lack of research concerning the effects of the drugs used as part of the execution protocol suggest about the protocol overall?

Rhetoric Questions

6. What elements of the study's structural components are designed to lessen any appearance of bias on the part of the researchers?

7. The study is published with an abstract and an editors' summary at the beginning. Why do you suppose both of these are offered to readers, and in what context is one likely more useful to readers than the other?

8. As part of the Discussion section, the authors include details of Angel Diaz's execution, suggesting that he was likely fully aware while experiencing suffocation and burning sensations. What is the purpose of providing this example? Is it effective? Why or why not?

9. Calculate the number of documented references in each of the study's sections—Introduction, Methods, Results, and Discussion. In what section do most of the references occur? Why do you suppose this is?

Response and Research Questions

10. According to the editors' summary, the study's results "suggest that current protocols used for lethal injection in the United States probably violate" (par. 7) the Eighth Amendment of the U.S. Constitution, which prohibits cruel and unusual punishment. Do you agree with the editors' assessment?

11. Identify three unique challenges you believe researchers face when they study controversial issues like capital punishment. How might researchers address those challenges?

ACADEMIC CASE STUDY · CAPITAL PUNISHMENT   APPLIED FIELDS

Perceptions of Law Enforcement Officers on Capital Punishment in the United States

CYNDY CARAVELIS HUGHES AND MATTHEW ROBINSON

Cyndy Caravelis Hughes is an assistant professor of criminal justice at Western Carolina University. Along with her colleague, Matthew Robinson, a professor of criminal justice at Appalachian State University, they report, in the following survey study, on perceptions of capital punishment among police officers in North Carolina. According to the authors, their study is the first "to assess death penalty opinion among criminal justice practitioners" and thus provides a new and important perspective on capital punishment opinions. This article first appeared in the June–December 2013 issue of the *International Journal of Criminal Justice Sciences*.

ABSTRACT

As scholars and legislators debate the efficacy of capital punishment, research has played a significant role in supporting arguments on both sides of the issue. Studies on the death penalty in North Carolina, United States, have ranged from examining the effects of race and sex on capital case outcomes to polling the general public on their personal support for the death penalty.

Experts have been asked about their professional opinions and murder victims' family members have added their personal experiences to the mix. There is, however, one group whose opinion has not been examined: the criminal justice practitioner. Using survey data gathered from criminal justice agencies across North Carolina, United States, the current study examines support for capital punishment among criminal justice practitioners in the state. Results show that while the law enforcement officers surveyed are overwhelmingly in favor of the continued use of capital punishment, they concurrently agree that innocent people have both been previously executed and are currently on death row today.

INTRODUCTION

At first glance, the most recent public opinion polls suggest that Americans remain in favor of capital punishment. For example, a 2011 Gallup Poll found that 61% of Americans answered yes to the question, "Are you in favor of the death penalty for a person convicted of murder?" Only 35% of Americans answered no, and 4% said they did not know or refused to answer. Yet, the percentage of people who say they favor the death penalty is down from the high of 80% in 1994, when opposition was only at 16% (Sourcebook of Criminal Justice Statistics, 2011, Table 2.51).

Further, we know from careful studies of criminologists and other social scientists that support for capital punishment is not as widespread as believed. Studies show that when Americans are given alternatives to the death penalty such as life imprisonment without the possibility of parole (LWOP), support falls to 50% or less (Robinson, 2009). As one example, a 2010 Gallup Poll asked Americans, "If you could choose between the following two approaches—the death penalty or life imprisonment with absolutely no possibility of parole—which do you think is the better penalty for murder?" It found that 49% chose the death penalty, 46% chose LWOP, and 6% said they did not know or refused to answer (Sourcebook of Criminal Justice Statistics, 2010, Table 2.49).

Research also illustrates that support for capital punishment widely varies based on certain demographic and social variables. For example, the 2011 Gallup Poll referenced above found that the death penalty is more supported by men than women (64% versus 57%, respectively); whites than nonwhites (68% versus 41%, respectively, and only 28% of blacks say they support capital punishment); older people than younger people (e.g., 65% of people 65 years and older support the death penalty, versus only 52% of 18–25 year olds); people earning lower salaries (e.g., 64% of people making less than $20,000 support the death penalty, versus 59% of those who earn $75,000 and over); Republicans than Democrats (74% versus 45%, respectively, and 65% of Independents say they support the death penalty); conservatives than liberals (72% versus 40%, respectively, and 60% of moderates say they support the death penalty); and the less educated support the death penalty the most (e.g., 65% of people with a high school diploma or lower support capital punishment, versus 47% of people with post-graduate degrees) (Sourcebook of Criminal Justice Statistics, 2011, Table 2.52).

The degree to which people support capital punishment is clearly impacted by how much they know about it or don't (Bohm, 2011). For example, a national study of expert opinion of capital punishment scholars—people who study the death penalty for a living and thus are the most informed about it—found that they overwhelmingly do not support the death penalty (Robinson, 2009). Specifically, 80% answered that they are opposed to capital punishment (only 9% expressed support for capital punishment and 11% said they were not sure). Further, not a single death penalty expert selected the death penalty when asked the question, "What is the most appropriate punishment for someone convicted of first-degree murder?" Every capital punishment expert answered either "life imprisonment without parole" (37%) or "other" (63%, and these scholars then specified various terms of imprisonment in the range of decades). The study also found that 79% of experts answered in the affirmative to the question, "Do you personally favor a temporary halt to executions (moratorium) in the United States while the practice of American capital punishment is studied?" (versus 14% who answered no and 7% who said they were not sure). And 84% of experts said they thought "states should permanently stop executing convicted murderers" due to "problems that are serious enough to make it unacceptable as a government-sanctioned punishment" (versus 14% who answered no and 2% who said they were unsure).

In spite of all we know about capital punishment opinion, there are only a handful of studies that examine the opinions of criminal justice practitioners. This is unfortunate, for as will be shown in this paper, there is ample reason to suspect that the opinion of capital punishment of criminal justice practitioners will be quite different than these experts, as well as with citizens more generally. Thus, the purpose of this paper is to report findings of our own survey of criminal justice practitioners' perceptions of capital punishment. In the paper, we report findings from our survey of law enforcement officers of all ranks working in criminal justice agencies across the state of North Carolina in the United States. Since law enforcement officers have unique experiences with regard to crime and punishment, it is important to understand their views of the death penalty.

LITERATURE REVIEW

Public opinion of capital punishment has been widely studied by criminologists, sociologists, and scholars from other academic disciplines, and is explored annually by polling firms including Gallup and Pew. From these studies and polls, we know that most Americans say they support the death penalty but that support declines when people are given alternative punishments such as life imprisonment without the possibility of parole (LWOP). We also know that certain segments of the U.S. population are more likely to support the death penalty, including men, whites, older people, the poor and less educated, and conservatives and Republicans. We also know that as people learn more about the realities of capital punishment practice, they are less likely to say they want to sentence people to death and carry out executions; such findings were noted earlier.

National polls also show that people generally do not think the death penalty is an effective deterrent to crime. For example, a 2011 Gallup Poll found that only 32% of Americans thought the death penalty deters murder, versus 64% who do not think it is a deterrent (Sourcebook of Criminal Justice Statistics, 2011, Table 2.57). Males, conservatives, and Republicans are most likely to say they think the death penalty is a deterrent (Sourcebook of Criminal Justice Statistics, 2011, Table 2.58). Also, only 52% of Americans say they think the death penalty is applied fairly, versus 41% who say it is applied unfairly (Sourcebook of Criminal Justice Statistics, 2011, Table 2.0005). Whites, males, conservatives, and Republicans are most likely to report feeling the death penalty is applied fairly; this might help account for their higher level of support.

There is evidence that public opinion of capital punishment is influenced by many other factors, including fear of crime and crime rates in the neighborhood where people live. Generally, people who are more afraid of crime and/or who live in neighborhoods with higher crime rates tend to be more supportive of capital punishment (Keil & Vito, 1991; Seltzer & McCormick, 1987). People who live in counties or regions where the death penalty has been highly politicized also are found to support the death penalty more (Jacobs & Kent, 2007). This is not surprising since the death penalty serves a political function in society, allowing legislators, prosecutors, and judges to appear tough on crime (Robinson, 2009).

Also, people who are motivated by a strong desire for retribution and who think capital punishment achieves this goal of punishment are more supportive of the death penalty (Finckenauer, 1988; Robinson, 2009). Relatedly, those with strong religious beliefs, especially white, evangelical Protestants, are most supportive of the death penalty (Grasmick & Bursik, Jr., 1993; Grasmick & Cochran, 1993; Sandys & McGarrell, 1997).

Controversially, there is some evidence that race and racial animosity correlate with support for capital punishment. That is, whites and people who feel animosity toward people of other races, especially people of color, tend to be more supportive of capital punishment (Arthur, 1998; Buckler, Davila, & Salinas, 2008; Cochran & Chamlin, 2006; Unnever & Cullen, 2007).

Meanwhile, knowledge about the realities of capital punishment is found to be inversely related to support for capital punishment (Cochran & Chamlin, 2005), so that people who learn the realities of the punishment and who have legitimate concerns about problems with the punishment—including the risk it poses to the innocent—tend to be far less supportive of the death penalty (Acker, 2009; Stinchcombe, 1994). This helps us understand the findings of death penalty experts—people who study capital punishment for a living—which show they tend *not* to support capital punishment, do *not* believe it deters murder, and believe the punishment is plagued by serious problems such as racial bias, excessive cost, and wrongful conviction for murder, among others (Radelet & Lacock, 2009; Robinson, 2009).

Some studies even find that individual personality traits correlate with support for the death penalty, which is not surprising given that personality is a measure of how people generally feel and behave (Robinson & Beaver, 2009). For example, one study found that people who rated higher on extroversion and neuroticism scales were more likely to favor the death penalty (for both men and women), while higher scores on openness to experience and agreeableness were associated with lower support of the death penalty (for men but not women) (Robbers, 2006). Another study found that people who had higher empathy scores were less likely to support capital punishment, and these people tend to be politically more liberal than conservative as well as more tolerant of different racial and ethnic groups (Unnever, Fisher, & Cullen, 2005).

In North Carolina, the state where the current study was carried out, support for capital punishment is not as strong as in other southern states. For example, a recent poll found that a large majority (68%) said they support replacing the death penalty with life imprisonment without the possibility of parole in cases where the offender must pay restitution to victims' families (LWOP+R). A sizable majority (63%) also support repealing the death penalty in order to spend more money on crime prevention, and more than half (55%) would end the death penalty if money was used to solve cold crimes and assist crime victims (Public Policy Polling, 2013).

The results of this poll are likely explained by the unique nature of capital punishment and murder in

the state. Specifically, as citizens have become aware of how rare death sentences and executions are relative to murder (suggesting the inefficacy of capital punishment), support for capital punishment has dropped. Support has dropped further in the wake of studies within the state demonstrating excessive costs, racial biases, and innocent people being released from death row (Robinson, 2011). Incredibly, as death sentences started to decline in 2001 and the state has not carried out an execution since 2006, the murder rate in the state fell from 9th highest in the country in 2001 to 18th highest in the country in 2010, and 2010 was the lowest murder rate in the state since the state started collecting data in 1973 (Robinson, 2011). So perhaps citizens do not feel the death penalty is as necessary as the state has become safer.

As of this writing, there are only two studies of which we are aware that probe the opinions of capital punishment among law enforcement officers. This is interesting because criminal justice professionals are the most likely people to have had actual experience with capital punishment, either as police officers who have arrested alleged murderers and assisted with their prosecution, prosecuted or defended them at trial, helped provide care for and custody of them within correctional facilities, and so forth. The first study, conducted by Fagan (1986), surveyed 78 law enforcement officers in the state of Washington. Fagan found that 94% of the officers surveyed supported the death penalty, while 51% of the officers disagreed with the statement, "There is no evidence that the death penalty reduces crime." In a study of 386 police chiefs, Dieter (1995) found that only 26% of chiefs felt the death penalty significantly reduces the number of homicides; when asked about ranking strategies for reducing violent crime, the chiefs cited "expanded use of the death penalty" as dead last.

In this study, we report on findings of a study of criminal justice practitioners' opinion of capital punishment using a sample of police officers in North Carolina. Given what we know about police officers, we have reason to believe that they will generally tend to be more supportive of capital punishment than the general population since males, whites,

15

and conservatives tend to be overrepresented among police officers (Worrall & Schmalleger, 2012). Further, given Skolnick's concept of the "working personality" of police officers—which suggests they are more cynical, pessimistic, distrustful, suspicious, and even prejudicial—we would expect them to be more supportive of capital punishment (Skolnick, 2000). Yet, some of these traits might lead them to be less supportive of the death penalty, especially if, through experience, they became cynical, pessimistic, distrustful, or suspicious of criminal justice practice itself and criminal sentencing in particular.

Further, since police officers, when beginning their careers, have been found to be more intelligent and empathetic, we might expect newer officers to be less supportive of the death penalty, although they also reportedly rank higher than the average person on scales of assertiveness and masculinity (Wasilewksi & Olson, 2010). Other personality traits such as authoritarianism also ought to be associated with higher support for capital punishment among police officers (Twersky-Glasner, 2005).

METHODOLOGY

The data for this study comes from a survey we created using a survey of capital punishment experts (Robinson, 2009). The new survey asked law enforcement officers questions about their opinions on both the application of capital punishment and alternatives to capital punishment. We anticipated a low response rate, due partly to the controversial nature of the survey and partly to the general reticence of sworn personnel to engage in scholarly research. In order to increase the sample size, we thus elected to send the survey to the entire population of law enforcement officers in the state of North Carolina. We contacted the North Carolina Police Chiefs Association (NCPCA) and the North Carolina Sheriffs Association (NCSA) in September 2012 and they agreed to distribute the survey to all Police Chiefs and Sheriffs in the state. The Chiefs and Sheriffs were asked to disseminate the survey to all sworn officers in their departments. The researchers followed up the initial survey distribution

with an email reminder three weeks after the original email was sent from NCPCA and NCSA and the survey was closed on November 15, 2012.

The analyses that follow are based on responses [20] provided by 215 sworn officers in 35 North Carolina counties. That only 215 officers responded is disappointing, especially since there are likely tens of thousands of officers in the state. Yet, the findings below represent the first presentation of findings on law enforcement officers' opinions of capital punishment in North Carolina or any other state.

A major limitation of this study is that it is obviously not representative of all police officers in the state of North Carolina. It is, however, the first study of its kind to attempt to discover the opinions of everyday police officers in the state in the contemporary era of capital punishment. Further, our findings raise an important question that is intriguing, even with the small sample size.

FINDINGS AND DISCUSSIONS

As shown in Table 1, the majority of the respondents are representative of the law enforcement profession as a whole in that they are white (94%) males (85%) who primarily work in urban settings (72%). Given these findings, we'd expect a high level of support for capital punishment among these officers as individuals in these groups tend to be more supportive of the death penalty. While the majority of the sample has at least some level of a college education (95%), only 42% of the sample has a Bachelor's degree or higher. This too would lead us to expect a high level of support of capital punishment among these officers.

The survey was completed by officers of all ranks (46% line officers, 33% mid-level supervisors, 21% administrators). The inclusion of officers working in an administrative capacity contributed to the fairly high number of average years in the field (15.14 years of service) as well as the average age of the respondents (39.72 years of age). It is possible that officers working in mid-level management might be less supportive of capital punishment given their many years working in the field. That is, the longer officers work

Table 1

Descriptive Variables

	Mean	S.D.
Years in policing	15.14	9.63
Age	39.72	10.19
Race/ethnicity	1.12	0.56
Gender	1.15	0.36
Rank		
Line officer		46%
Mid-level supervisor		33%
Administrator		21%
Agency location		
Rural		28%
Urban		72%
Agency type		
Municipal		73%
Sheriff's department		14%
Specialty		13%
Highest level of education		
High school diploma		5%
Some college or associate		53%
Bachelor's		30%
Master's or higher		12%

in the field, the more likely they will have experience with an actual death penalty case. This is purely speculative and reflects the literature in terms of how knowledge of the realities of the death penalty reduces support for it.

In Table 2, we present the main findings from our survey. First, it is clear that overwhelmingly, the law enforcement officers who completed the survey felt that capital punishment had a place in our society as a sentencing policy (21% agreed, 69% strongly agreed). Clearly, support among officers in

our sample is much higher than that in the general population, and especially higher than that of capital punishment experts. It is likely that this owes itself to the conservative nature of law enforcement. We also suspect that officers who answered the questions in the survey were thinking about the death penalty in theory rather than the death penalty as it is actually carried out. Experts noted how the rare nature of the death penalty relative to murder makes it ineffective in terms of achieving justice for victims' families.

When asked to select the reasons that they wanted capital punishment to remain legal, the three most frequently selected answers among our respondents were: (1) The death penalty provides closure for the victim's family; (2) With our use of DNA testing, errors in the system are minimal; and (3) There is always a chance that an offender can get out of prison, so life in prison is never guaranteed. Expert opinion is clearly different as scholars who study the death penalty for a living overwhelmingly rejected the argument that the death penalty actually serves victims' families; they also strongly believe innocent people are sentenced to death and are much more comfortable with long terms of imprisonment than they are with capital punishment.

Of the 9% of law enforcement officers that disagreed with the continued use of capital punishment, 7% cited that they strongly disagreed with the death penalty. Their three most frequently cited reasons supporting a moratorium on executions were: (1) Life in prison without parole is a viable alternative to the death penalty; (2) I do not believe that we should condone murder with murder; and (3) I believe that life in prison is a worse punishment than being executed. These were reasons also offered by capital punishment experts, who overwhelmingly rejected the death penalty in practice. In fact, not a single expert in the study by Robinson (2009) chose the death penalty as the most appropriate sentence for convicted murderers.

While 69% of the officers surveyed believe that capital punishment achieves retribution, only 28% indicated that they strongly agreed with the statement. Interestingly, 17% of the sample was unsure

Table 2

Main Findings of the Survey

Capital punishment should remain a legal punishment in the United States.

Agree	90%
Disagree	9%
Neither agree nor disagree	1%

Capital punishment, as actually practiced in the United States, achieves retribution (i.e., provides justice for murder victims, their families, and society at large).

Agree	69%
Disagree	17%
Neither agree nor disagree	15%

Capital punishment, as actually practiced in the United States, prevents future murders by killing offenders who would murder again.

Agree	66%
Disagree	24%
Neither agree nor disagree	10%

As practiced in the United States, capital punishment is disproportionately applied to people who are poor.

Agree	22%
Disagree	62%
Neither agree nor disagree	16%

As practiced in the United States, capital punishment is disproportionately applied to African Americans.

Agree	15%
Disagree	66%
Neither agree nor disagree	18%

There are wrongly convicted people on death row today.

Agree	49%
Disagree	17%
Neither agree nor disagree	34%

Innocent people have been executed for murders they did not commit in the United States.

Agree	53%
Disagree	13%
Neither agree nor disagree	34%

Support for Capital Punishment by Education

	Support DP	Against DP	Unsure
High school diploma	100%	0%	0%
Some college	90%	10%	0%
Associate degree	94%	5%	1%
Bachelor's degree	84%	16%	0%
Master's or higher	92%	4%	4%

Support for Capital Punishment by Rank

	Support DP	Against DP	Unsure
Line officers	93%	7%	0%
Mid-level supervisors	83%	15%	2%
Administrators	92%	5%	3%

as to whether capital punishment provided justice for murder victims, their families, and society at large. Even so, as indicated above, closure for the victim's family was a frequently cited reason for supporting the death penalty. Once again, these findings are quite different from those of the experts; expert opinion is that the death penalty, as actually carried out, does not achieve retribution. Here the officers might be responding to the theoretical death penalty rather than the death penalty in reality, which as noted above is so rare that it generally fails to achieve this goal.

Yet, since our question is worded, "as actually practiced in the United States," it is also possible that police officers in our sample are just unaware of how rare executions are relative to murder. Three studies of death penalty practice in North Carolina over slightly different time periods found that only between 2.4% and 2.6% of murderers are sentenced to death and far less than 1% are ever executed (Radelet & Pierce, 2010; Robinson, 2011; Unah & Boger, 2009).

When asked about the potential incapacitative effect of capital punishment, 34% of respondents either disagreed with whether capital punishment prevents future murders by killing offenders who would murder again or were unsure whether it did so. Yet, a strong majority (66%) indicated they thought the death penalty potentially saves lives. This is nearly identical to the percentage of death penalty experts who answered they believe capital punishment prevents future murders by killing offenders who would murder again. However, experts also wrote that the death penalty does not incapacitate murderers any more effectively than life imprisonment without the possibility of parole and that the research suggests most murderers would never likely murder again, making execution unnecessary.

While 62% of law enforcement officers surveyed 30 believed that the death penalty is not disproportionately applied to the poor, 22% of respondents believed that the application of capital punishment did suffer from a class bias while 16% of officers surveyed were unsure if this was the case. This is greatly different than capital punishment experts; a very large majority of them answered that the death penalty is plagued by serious social class biases. The primary

bias noted by experts was inadequate legal representation for the poor.

As to the issue of potential racial bias in the death penalty, 66% did not feel that this was the case; it is interesting that nearly one-fifth of the sample was unsure as to whether a racial bias was present in the United States' use of the death penalty. Overall, 15% of respondents agreed with the presence of a racial bias in the application of capital punishment. This, too, is greatly different than capital punishment experts; a very large majority of them answered that the death penalty is plagued by serious racial biases. The primary bias noted by experts was not a race-of-defendant bias, however, but instead a race-of-victim bias against killers of whites.

Recent studies in the state of North Carolina do in fact demonstrate that killers of whites are several times more likely to be sentenced to death than killers of other races, even after controlling for legally relevant variables (Radelet & Pierce, 2010; Robinson, 2011; Unah & Boger, 2009). Yet, these studies also show that whites are more likely to be sentenced to death (presumably because they tend to kill other whites).

As to the issue of innocence, only 17% of officers disagreed with the statement that wrongly convicted people are currently on death row, while 49% agreed and 34% were unsure as to whether that was the case. This is consistent with expert opinion, as a large majority of experts indicated that the death penalty is sometimes used against the innocent.

Over half of the sample (53%) of law enforcement officers surveyed agreed that innocent people have been executed for murders they did not commit. Of the remaining respondents, 13% disagreed and 34% neither agreed nor disagreed with that statement. This is also consistent with expert opinion.

As to the issue of how education level impacts 35 the findings, we would have anticipated that higher education is correlated with lower levels of support for capital punishment, but this is not the case. While respondents with a Bachelor's degree were the least to favor keeping capital punishment legal (16% were against the death penalty), individuals who had a Master's degree or higher had the same level of support as officers with only an Associate degree. In general, officers at all levels of education are in support of capital punishment.

Mid-level supervisors had the lowest level of support for capital punishment (83%), compared to line officers (93%) and administrators (92%). We speculated earlier that this would be the case, yet the differences are too small to draw any conclusions. And officers at all levels of rank are generally in support of capital punishment.

CONCLUSION

In our study of law enforcement opinion of capital punishment in the state of North Carolina, we found a very high level of support for the death penalty among police officers. This is not surprising given what is already known about capital punishment opinion.

As most officers in our study are white males and working in urban areas where murder rates tend to be highest, it is logical to assume that support for capital punishment will be high. Also, certain personality traits common in police officers are known to correlate with support for the death penalty, although we did not specifically assess personality traits in this study.

A logical explanation for high support of the death penalty among police officers in our sample is that officers indicated they believed capital punishment achieves important goals of punishment or benefits to society, including retribution and incapacitation, which they indicated would result in fewer murders in the future. Law enforcement officers also said they did not think the death penalty in North Carolina was disproportionately applied to the poor or African Americans; in the absence of bias, it is logical to also expect a high level of support.

What is surprising, however, is that, while a majority of officers in our sample answered that they believe innocent people are currently on death row (or they did not know) and that innocent people have been executed in the state, they still indicate they support the death penalty. Some polls of normal citizens have also found this to be true (Robinson, 2009). Yet, we are still surprised that any person could simultaneously think that innocent people are on death row and being executed and continue to support the death penalty.

One possible explanation of this finding is that those who chose to participate in the survey might possibly be among the most ardent supporters of the punishment. There are those people who would support the death penalty even knowing that innocent people are subjected to it; this is the price of justice, so to speak (Pojman & Reiman, 1998). Without a larger and more representative sample this is of course only speculation.

This study contributes to our understanding of capital punishment opinion for it is the first of its kind that assesses death penalty opinion among criminal justice practitioners. Yet, we have assessed only one branch of criminal justice—police officers—in only one state in the United States—North Carolina. Further, our sample size is unfortunately low. This is a major limitation that makes generalizing to all law enforcement officers in the state impossible.

Thus, future research in this area ought to assess opinion of criminal justice practitioners in courts, corrections, and other criminal justice agencies, as well as in other states. Further, efforts should be made to increase sample sizes so that more sophisticated analyses can be conducted. We hope that our findings generate further study into this important area of research.

REFERENCES

Acker, J. (2009). Actual innocence: Is death different? *Behavioral Sciences & the Law, 27*(3), 297.

Arthur, J. (1998). Racial attitudes and opinions about capital punishment: Preliminary findings. *International Journal of Comparative and Applied Criminal Justice, 22*(1), 131–144.

Bohm, R. (2011). *Death Quest: An Introduction to the Theory and Practice of Capital Punishment in the United States.* New York, NY: Elsevier.

Buckler, K., Davila, M., & Salinas, P. (2008). Racial differences in public support for the death penalty: Can racist sentiment and core values explain the racial divide? *American Journal of Criminal Justice, 33*(2), 151–165.

Cochran, J., & Chamlin, M. (2005). Can information change public opinion? Another test of the Marshall hypotheses. *Journal of Criminal Justice, 33*(6), 573–584.

Cochran, J., & Chamlin, M. (2006). The enduring racial divide in death penalty support. *Journal of Criminal Justice, 34*(1), 85–99.

Cochran, J., Denise, P., & Chamlin, M. (2006). Political identity and support for capital punishment: A test of attribution theory. *Journal of Crime & Justice, 29*(1), 45–80.

Death Penalty Information Center (2012). Law enforcement views on deterrence. Retrieved August 4, 2012, from http://deathpenaltyinfo.org/law-enforcement-views-deterrence

Finckenauer, J. (1988). Public support for the death penalty: Retribution as just deserts or retribution as revenge? *Justice Quarterly, 5*(1), 81–100.

Grasmick, H., & Bursik, R., Jr. (1993). Religious beliefs and public support for the death penalty for juveniles and adults. *Journal of Crime & Justice, 16*(2), 59–86.

Grasmick, H., & Cochran, J. (1993). Religion, punitive justice, and support for the death penalty. *Justice Quarterly, 10*(2), 289–314.

Jacobs, D., & Kent, S. (2007). The determinants of executions since 1951: How politics, protests, public opinion, and social divisions shape capital punishment. *Social Problems, 54*(3), 297–318.

Keil, T., & Vito, G. (1991). Fear of crime and attitudes toward capital punishment: A structural equations model. *Justice Quarterly, 8*(4), 447–464.

Pojman, L., & Reiman, J. (1998). *The Death Penalty: For and Against*. Lanham, MA: Rowman & Littlefield.

Public Policy Polling (2013). North Carolina survey results. Retrieved July 31, 2013, from http://www.publicpolicypolling.com/pdf/2011/DeathPenaltyResults.pdf

Radelet, M., & Lacock, T. (2009). Do executions lower homicide rates? The views of leading criminologists. *Journal of Criminal Law & Criminology, 99*, 489.

Radelet, M., & Pierce, G. (2010). *Race and death sentencing in North Carolina 1980–2007*. Working paper requested by author.

Robbers, M. (2006). Tough-mindedness and fair play. Personality traits as predictors of attitudes toward the death penalty—An exploratory gendered study. *Punishment & Society, 8*(2), 203–222.

Robinson, M. (2009). *Death Nation: The Experts Explain American Capital Punishment*. Upper Saddle River, NJ: Prentice Hall.

Robinson, M. (2011). The death penalty in North Carolina: A summary of the data and scientific studies. Retrieved January 24, 2013, from http://pscj.appstate.edu/ncdeathpenalty/ncdeathpenaltyfinal.pdf

Robinson, M., & Beaver, K. (2009). *Why Crime? An Interdisciplinary Approach to Explaining Criminal Behavior*. Upper Saddle River, NJ: Prentice Hall.

Sandys, M., & McGarrell, E. (1995). Attitudes toward capital punishment: Preference for the penalty or mere acceptance? *Journal of Research in Crime and Delinquency, 32*(2), 191–191.

Sandys, M., & McGarrell, E. (1997). Beyond the Bible Belt: The influence (or lack thereof) of religion on attitudes toward the death penalty. *Journal of Crime & Justice, 20*(1), 179–190.

Seltzer, R., & McCormick, J. (1987). The impact of crime victimization and fear of crime on attitudes toward death penalty defendants. *Violence and Victims, 2*(2), 99–114.

Skolnick, J. (2000). Code blue. *The American Prospect, 11*(10).

Sourcebook of Criminal Justice Statistics (2010). Table 2.49.2010. Attitudes toward the better penalty for murder. Retrieved July 31, 2012, from http://www.albany.edu/sourcebook/pdf/t2492010.pdf

Sourcebook of Criminal Justice Statistics (2011). Table 2.0005. Attitudes toward fairness of the application of the death penalty. Retrieved September 18, 2012, from http://www.albany.edu/sourcebook/pdf/t200052011.pdf

Sourcebook of Criminal Justice Statistics (2011). Table 2.51.2011. Attitudes toward the death penalty for persons convicted of murder. Retrieved July 31, 2012, from http://www.albany.edu/sourcebook/pdf/t2512011.pdf

Sourcebook of Criminal Justice Statistics (2011). Table 2.52. Attitudes toward the death penalty for people convicted of murder. Retrieved September 18, 2012, from http://www.albany.edu/sourcebook/pdf/t200052011.pdf

Sourcebook of Criminal Justice Statistics (2011). Table 2.54. Attitudes toward fairness of the application of the death penalty. Retrieved September 18, 2012, from http://www.albany.edu/sourcebook/pdf/t2542011.pdf

Sourcebook of Criminal Justice Statistics (2011). Table 2.57. Respondents reporting whether they believe the death penalty acts as a deterrent to murder. Retrieved September 18, 2012, from http://www.albany.edu/sourcebook/pdf/t2572011.pdf

Stinchcombe, A. J. (1994). The acceptability of executing the innocent. *Howard Journal of Criminal Justice, 12*(4), 304–318.

Twersky-Glasner, A. (2005). Police personality: What is it and why are they like that? *Journal of Police and Criminal Psychology, 20*(1).

Unah, I., & Boger, J. (2009). *Race, politics, and the process of capital punishment in North Carolina*. Paper presented to the annual meeting of the North Carolina Political Science Association. February. Greensboro, NC.

Unnever, J., & Cullen, F. (2007). Reassessing the racial divide in support for capital punishment: The continuing significance of race. *Journal of Research in Crime and Delinquency, 44*(1), 124–158.

Unnever, J., Fisher, B., & Cullen, F. (2005). Empathy and public support for capital punishment. *Journal of Crime & Justice, 28*(1), 1–34.

Wasilewksi, M., & Olson, A. (2010). Just a typical cop? Retrieved September 18, 2012, from http://www.officer.com/article/10232697/just-a-typical-cop?page=3

Worrall, J., & Schmalleger, F. (2012). *Policing*. Upper Saddle River, NJ: Prentice Hall.

Reading Questions

1. What does the study's introduction suggest overall about trends in attitudes toward capital punishment?

2. According to the authors, what tends to be the attitude of death penalty experts toward capital punishment? Why do they generally hold this attitude?

3. What does the study find in terms of education level and officer attitude toward capital punishment?

4. What do the researchers indicate was a particularly surprising finding of the study?

Rhetoric Questions

5. How would you describe the study's title? What impact is it likely to have on the intended audience?

6. Read the study's abstract closely, and identify its parts. What parts of the researchers' study are briefly summarized in the abstract?

7. What are the researchers' hypotheses, and where do they present them as part of their report?

8. How would you describe the central organizing strategy for the body paragraphs that make up the Findings and Discussions section? What specific pattern can you discern in the reporting of the findings?

Response and Research Questions

9. The researchers suggest that "it is important to understand [law enforcement officers'] views of the death penalty" (par. 6). For what specific reasons do you think it is important to understand police officers' views of capital punishment?

10. In the third paragraph of their introduction, the researchers provide data from the 2011 *Sourcebook of Criminal Justice Statistics* that links demographic information and attitudes toward capital punishment. Identify the demographic variables, among those reported, that best describe you. Then consider whether or not your own attitude toward capital punishment matches those provided via that data.

11. Among the main findings of the survey presented in Table 2 of the report, which is the most surprising to you? Why? Which is the least surprising? Why?

WRITING PROJECT Writing a Brief Annotated Bibliography

The readings in this chapter raise and address a host of complex questions related to crime, punishment, and justice in America, although these questions are not always stated outright. Perhaps the chapter has caused you to formulate your own questions about the topics as well.

Begin this writing project by selecting a question related to crime, punishment, or justice that is appropriate for an academic research project. You might be interested in any of the following questions, for example: Is capital punishment really a deterrent to crime? What are the implications for sentencing in light of advances in criminal brain scanning? What are the clear benefits of rehabilitation programs as opposed to jail terms for juveniles? What role does race play in sentencing for minor drug offenses?

Once you have established a workable research question, locate three to five recent and scholarly journal articles from any academic field(s) you believe will help to build an answer to your research question. Remember that Chapter 4 offers helpful instruction on conducting this kind of research.

Study the articles you select carefully, and then compose a brief annotated bibliography that includes these three parts:

- An Introduction section that establishes appropriate background and context for your research question: What led you to your research question? What makes your question important or meaningful? Why does your question need to be answered?

- A section that specifically highlights your research question.

- Full bibliographic information for each of your scholarly sources. Compose a brief summary of each article directly under each of your bibliographic entries. As part of your summaries, explain the researchers' goals (hypothesis, thesis, etc.), outline their primary research methods and findings, and briefly explain how you believe the article can help to answer your research question.

WRITING PROJECT **Composing an Evaluative Rhetorical Analysis**

Begin this assignment by locating a popular news article that explores an issue related to crime, punishment, or justice in America. Alternatively, you might choose to focus on one of the articles written for a popular audience included in the chapter offerings:

- Barbara Bradley Hagerty, "Inside a Psychopath's Brain: The Sentencing Debate"
- Sophia Kerby, "The Top 10 Most Startling Facts about People of Color and Criminal Justice in the United States: A Look at the Racial Disparities Inherent in Our Nation's Criminal-Justice System"
- Clark Merrefield, "Should Juvenile Criminals Be Sentenced Like Adults?"
- Abigail Pesta, "I Survived Prison: What Really Happens behind Bars"

After carefully reading the article, compose an evaluative rhetorical analysis in which you assess the likely effectiveness of the article in light of its intended audience.

As part of your introduction, identify the source of publication for the piece you selected (Where was it published?) and its likely intended audience (Who is likely to read the piece, given its publication source?). Then identify the specific values, beliefs, or desires you think the intended audience members of the piece likely share with one another. With these common values in mind, offer your evaluation of the likely effectiveness of the rhetorical strategies used in the article as your thesis: How effective is the writer at crafting the text, via its rhetorical elements, specifically for the intended audience?

Develop the body of your analysis by addressing the following two questions as support for your position or evaluation of the writer's rhetorical decisions:

- What does the writer successfully do that likely appeals directly to the intended audience's values, beliefs, or desires?
- What other decisions could the writer have made to appeal even more directly or successfully to the intended audience's values, beliefs, or desires?

As part of your conclusion, reflect on the piece's overall potential for connecting with, or for moving, the intended audience. Given what you've shown, what effects do you think the piece will have on its intended audience?

Food, Sustainability, and Class

The readings in this chapter offer a number of perspectives, both popular and academic, that consider both food and its sustainability, as well as their intersection with the politics of labor, economics, and class. The chapter begins with an article that explores Mexican food as a new metaphor for America, positioning it against the classic image of the melting pot. In so doing, the article broaches some of the complex economic, social, and political realities of American society. The second selection in the chapter offers a response to the notion that America once enjoyed an idyllic food past. The text asks us to consider carefully our own "food nostalgia" and the current food-reform movements in light of the realities of the country's food history. In the third selection, the author examines insects as a sustainable food option and points to various challenges and prejudices encountered by proponents of insect consumption. The final popular reading in this chapter extols the virtues of cooking for ourselves in response to the question, "Why cook?"

These readings offer a wide range of perspectives on food and its various functions and meanings. We hope they inspire you to pose your own critical questions about the role of food in our lives. Such questions might include:

- What do an individual's food choices say about him or her, if anything at all?
- What role should issues of sustainability play in our food purchase decisions?
- How does the food we eat relate to our personal identity, or how does it affect the ways we engage with other people?
- What does the food you eat mean to you?

The academic case study for this chapter provides a number of disciplinary perspectives on the topic of genetically modified (GM) foods:

- **Humanities** What are some of the ethical concerns regarding GM foods?
- **Social Sciences** Which GM and non-GM food products do consumers tolerate, prefer, and/or actually purchase?

- **Natural Sciences** What are the exposure levels of pesticides associated with GM foods among pregnant and non-pregnant women in eastern Canada?
- **Applied Fields** How do middle school students negotiate complex scientific issues in a curriculum designed to foster their knowledge of the genetically modified foods controversy?

Taco USA: How Mexican Food Became More American Than Apple Pie

GUSTAVO ARELLANO

Gustavo Arellano is an editor and writer at *OC Weekly*, an alternative newspaper in Orange County, California. He is the author of two books, *Orange County: A Personal History* (2008) and *Taco USA: How Mexican Food Conquered America* (2012), as well as the writer behind ¡Ask A Mexican!, a nationally syndicated newspaper column. In the article below, published in 2012 in *Reason* magazine online, Arellano challenges misconceptions about the appropriation of Mexican food in America. Citing concoctions such as tater tot burritos and frozen margarita machines, Arellano uses personal narrative and historical research to argue that Mexican food has, in fact, conquered North America.

MAY 14, 2012, 12:00 PM—Exit 132 off Interstate 29 in Brookings, South Dakota, offers two possibilities. A right turn will take drivers through miles of farms, flatland that stretches to the horizon, cut up into grids by country roads and picturesque barns—a scenic route to nowhere in heartland America. But take a left at the light, and you wind up coasting through a college town of 19,000 that's more than 95 percent white. The city's small Latino minority—less than 1 percent of the population—is mostly students or faculty members passing through South Dakota State University. It was here, in late 2009, that I experienced an epiphany about Mexican food in the United States.

I had been visiting the campus and found myself desperate for a taste of home. For us Southern Californians, that means burritos. Google Maps found me four Mexican restaurants in town. One, named Guadalajara, is a small South Dakota chain with outposts in Pierre and Spearfish. The food there was fine: a mishmash of tacos, burritos, and bean-and-rice pairings. But talk to the waiters in Spanish, and their faces brighten; they trot out the secret salsa they make for themselves but don't dare share with locals for fear of torching their tongues.

The most popular restaurant in town that day was Taco John's. I didn't know it then, but Taco John's is the third-largest taco chain in the United States, with nearly 500 locations. But what lured me that morning was a drive-through line snaking out from the faux-Spanish revival building (whitewashed adobe and all) and into the street. Once I inched my rental car next to the menu, I was offered an even more outrageous simulacrum* of the American Southwest: tater tots, that most midwestern of snacks, renamed "Potato Olés" and stuffed into a breakfast burrito, nacho cheese sauce slowly oozing out from the bottom of the flour tortilla.

There is nothing remotely Mexican about Potato Olés—not even the quasi-Spanish name, which has a distinctly Castilian accent. The burrito was more insulting to me and my heritage than casting Charlton

*simulacrum: the likeness or representation of a thing.

Heston as the swarthy Mexican hero in *Touch of Evil*. But it was intriguing enough to take back to my hotel room for a taste. There, as I experienced all of the concoction's gooey, filling glory while chilly rain fell outside, it struck me: Mexican food has become a better culinary metaphor for America than the melting pot.

Back home, my friends did not believe that a tater 5 tot burrito could exist. When I showed them proof online, out came jeremiads about inauthenticity, about how I was a traitor for patronizing a Mexican chain that got its start in Wyoming, about how the avaricious *gabachos* had once again usurped our holy cuisine and corrupted it to fit their crude palates.

In defending that tortilla-swaddled abomination, I unknowingly joined a long, proud lineage of food heretics and lawbreakers who have been developing, adapting, and popularizing Mexican food in El Norte since before the Civil War. Tortillas and tamales have long left behind the moorings of immigrant culture and fully infiltrated every level of the American food pyramid, from state dinners at the White House to your local 7-Eleven. Decades' worth of attempted restrictions by governments, academics, and other self-appointed custodians of purity have only made the strain stronger and more resilient. The result is a market-driven mongrel cuisine every bit as delicious and all-American as the German classics we appropriated from Frankfurt and Hamburg.

IMPERIALISM AND ENCHILADAS

Food is a natural conduit of change, evolution, and innovation. Wishing for a foodstuff to remain static, uncorrupted by outside influence — especially in these United States — is as ludicrous an idea as barring new immigrants from entering the country. Yet for more than a century, both sides of the political spectrum have fought to keep Mexican food in a ghetto. From the right has come the canard that the cuisine is unhealthy and alien, a stereotype dating to the days of the Mexican-American War, when urban legend had it that animals wouldn't eat the corpses of fallen Mexican soldiers due to the high chile content in the decaying flesh. Noah Smithwick, an observer of the aftermath of the Battle of San Jacinto in 1836, claimed "the cattle got to chewing the bones [of Mexican soldiers], which so affected the milk that residents in the vicinity had to dig trenches and bury them."

Similar knocks against Mexican food can be heard to this day in the lurid tourist tales of "Montezuma's Revenge" and in the many food-based ethnic slurs still in circulation: *beaner, greaser, pepper belly, taco bender, roach coach*, and so many more. "Aside from diet," the acclaimed borderlands scholar Américo Paredes wrote in 1978, "no other aspect of Mexican culture seems to have caught the fancy of the Anglo coiner of derogatory terms for Mexicans."

Thankfully, the buying public has never paid much attention to those prandial *pendejos*. Instead, Americans have loved and consumed Mexican food in large quantities almost from the moment it was available — from canned chili and tamales in the early 20th century to fast-food tacos in the 1960s, sit-down eateries in the 1970s, and ultra-pricey hipster mescal bars today. Some staples of the Mexican diet have been thoroughly assimilated into American food culture. No one nowadays thinks of "chili" as Mexican, even though it long passed for Mexican food in this country; meanwhile, every Major League baseball and NFL stadium sells nachos, thanks to the invention of a fast-heated chips and "cheese" combination concocted by an Italian-American who was the cousin of Johnny Cash's first wife. Only in America!

In the course of this culinary blending, a multi- 10 billion-dollar industry arose. And that's where leftist critics of Mexican food come in. For them, there's something inherently suspicious about a cuisine responsive to both the market and the *mercado*. Oh, academics and foodies may love the grub, but they harbor an atavistic view that the only "true" Mexican food is the just-off-the-grill carne asada found in the side lot of your local *abuelita* (never mind that it was the invading Spaniards who introduced beef to the New World). "Mexico's European-and-Indian soul," writes Rick Bayless, the high priest of the "authentic" Mexican food movement, in his creatively titled book, *Authentic Mexican*, "feels the intuitions of neither bare-bones Victorianism nor Anglo-Saxon productivity"—a line reminiscent of dispatches from the Raj. If it were up to these authentistas, we'd never have kimchi tacos or pastrami burritos. Salsa would not outsell ketchup in the United States. This food of the gods would be locked in Mexican households and barrios of cities, far away from Anglo hands.

That corn-fed Americans love and profit from Mexican food is viewed as an open wound in Chicano intellectual circles, a gastronomic update of America's imperial taking of the Southwest. *Yanqui* consumption and enjoyment of quesadillas and margaritas, in this view, somehow signifies a weakness in the Mexican character. "The dialectic between representation and production of Mexican cuisine offers a critical means of gauging Latino cultural power, or, more precisely, the relative lack of such power," write scholars Victor Valle and Rudy Torres in their 2000 book *Latino Metropolis*. (Another precious thought from Valle and Torres concerns Mary Sue Milliken and Susan Feniger, two midwestern girls who came to Los Angeles and learned to love Mexican food during the 1980s, parlaying that fondness into a series of television shows and books under the billing "Two Hot Tamales." The academics claim the Tamales' success arose from "neocolonial appropriations of world cuisine by reviving a gendered variant of the Hispanic fantasy discourse." Um, yeah . . .)

With due respect to my fellow lefty professors, they're full of beans. I'm not claiming equal worth for all American interpretations of Mexican food; Taco Bell has always made me retch, and Mexican food in central Kentucky tastes like . . . well, Mexican food in central Kentucky. But when culinary anthropologists like Bayless and Diana Kennedy make a big show out of protecting "authentic" Mexican food from the onslaught of commercialized glop, they are being both paternalistic and ahistorical.

That you have a nation (and increasingly a planet—you can find Mexican restaurants from Ulan Bator to Sydney to Prague) lusting after tequila, guacamole, and *tres leches* cake isn't an exercise in culinary neocolonialism but something closer to the opposite. By allowing itself to be endlessly adaptable to local tastes, Mexican food has become a primary vehicle for exporting the culture of a long-ridiculed country to the far corners of the globe. Forget Mexico's imaginary *Reconquista* of the American Southwest; the *real* conquest of North America is a peaceful and consensual affair, taking place one tortilla at a time.

I'll never forget the delight I felt a couple of years ago when I worked on a series of investigative stories on Orange County neo-Nazis. One of the photos I unearthed showed two would-be Aryans scarfing down food from Del Taco, a beloved California chain best known for its cheap and surprisingly tasty burritos. The neo-colonizers have become the colonized, and no one even fired a shot.

TAMALES AND TRUNCHEONS

As long as Mexican food has existed in this country, 15 government has tried to legislate it out of existence. This is partly because of stereotypes but mostly because government is government. The resulting underground Mexican food economy, meanwhile, has birthed some of the cuisine's most innovative trends.

In 1880s San Antonio, so-called chili queens—Mexican women who brought the Alamo City national attention by setting up impromptu stalls in city squares to sell fiery bowls of what was then known as *chile con carne*—began a decades-long game of cat and mouse with local officials. The authorities would declare a certain neighborhood legally off-limits, and the chili queens would shrug and move their tents to the outdoor plaza across the street, bringing with them their legions of loyal customers. It took until the 1940s for San Antonio bureaucrats to formally legalize the street vendors, but only if they subjected themselves to rigorous health inspections and hawked their food from white tents with screens. The public scorned these bowdlerized* women, and the chili queens disappeared within years.

The same story arc has played out nearly everywhere in the United States where there has been a Mexican with food to sell. Wandering tamale men spread across the United States during the 1890s until competitors and not-in-my-backyard types convinced

bowdlerized: stripped of offensive content.

city councils to pass laws against them. A century later, *loncheras* peddling tacos and burritos—first to construction sites, then to anywhere workers take their lunches—have encountered the same protectionism and prejudice. As the public embraces the convenience, affordability, and taste of food trucks, restaurant owners and the city officials they lobby have repeatedly attempted to squash the competition.

Any new businesses in town will always make city planners and councilmen wary and greedy, of course. But the sad, surprising reality is that most of the resistance to *loncheras* comes from brick-and-mortar businesses. Instead of refining and broadening their offerings to keep up with their new competitors, the incumbents fall back on an argument straight out of a Mafia protection racket: Since we pay more taxes and business fees than food trucks, government should squash our competition so we can continue business as usual.

It's a strategy that has long worked. In 1992 tiny Pasco, Washington, set rules limiting where taco trucks could park and requiring them to pay $45 each month per parking spot. Pasco's restaurants, by contrast, paid only $35 a year for a license. Five street vendors took Pasco all the way up to the U.S. Court of Appeals for the 9th Circuit, arguing that the double standard was unconstitutional, but they ultimately lost. Similar crackdowns have taken place in Fresno (1995), Chicago (1997), Phoenix (1999), and Dallas (1999), where Planning Commissioner James Lee Fantroy sneered during a public hearing on the subject, "The proper preparation of food is one of those things that we must carefully watch. I don't think I could bring my family to one of these [trucks] and feel comfortable."

Even in Los Angeles, the second-largest Mexi- 20
can metropolis in the world, the majority-Democrat L.A. County Board of Supervisors tried to ban food trucks as recently as four years ago. The city has destroyed carts selling unauthorized bacon dogs and even hauled off some entrepreneurs to jail, despite acknowledging that no bacon-dog customer has ever registered a complaint.

L.A. has a long history of putting the squeeze on Mexican-food peddlers. From 1900 to about 1925, the city council passed resolution after resolution

trying to ban tamale wagons from downtown Los Angeles. The *tamaleros*, knowing what they meant to their legions of customers, fought back. In 1903, when the council tried to outlaw them altogether, tamale wagons formed a mutual-aid society and presented a petition with the signatures of more than 500 customers that read in part, "We claim that the lunch wagons are catering to an appreciative public and to deprive the people of these convenient eating places would prove a great loss to the many local merchants who sell the wagon proprietors various supplies." When the city council finally kicked the vendors out as part of the effort to create the sanitized, whitewashed ethnic fantasyland now known as Olvera Street, the vendors just went underground, where they flourished for decades and eventually transformed into *loncheras*.

In 2008 the L.A. County Board of Supervisors passed a resolution making parking a truck for longer than one hour in unincorporated communities such as East L.A. a misdemeanor with a maximum penalty of a $1,000 fine and six months in jail. The plan sparked a furious backlash—not only among the *loncheros*, who created La Asociación de Loncheros L.A. Familia Unida de California (Association of Loncheros Los Angeles United Family of California) to defend themselves, but among young bloggers and hipsters who had grown up patronizing *loncheras* after clubbing or working late. Soon black T-shirts emblazoned with a white *lonchera* and the statement "Carne Asada Is Not a Crime" flowered across Southern California, and a group of foodies helped the *loncheras* sue the board of supervisors. A Los Angeles Superior Court judge eventually overturned the supes' diktat.*

But it was mostly the will of the *loncheros*—almost all immigrants who initially came to the United States with no knowledge of English, let alone an understanding of our legal system—that earned the victory. In my homeland of Orange County, Roberto Guzmán led a group of *loncheros* in 2006 to sue the city of Santa Ana to be able to park on city streets from 9 a.m. until 9 p.m., seven days a week. His Cadillac-pink truck "Alebrije's" sells food from Mexico City— buttery, crepe-like quesadillas, massive chili-soaked

---

*diktat: a mandate without consent from the populace.

sandwiches called *pambazos*, and a concoction of six tortillas covered with sautéed onions, bell peppers, jalapeños, and grilled ham, bacon, and carne asada called *alambres*.

When the city council (also majority Democrat, and all Latino, making Santa Ana the largest city in the United States with such leadership) sought to negotiate with the *loncheros* to install a lottery system giving rights to some food trucks but not all, they refused. "Please," Guzmán scoffs. "It would've been favoritism all the way. I felt as if they were going to take away the sustenance of so many families. It was going to be a huge economic loss. And it was too much a worry that, at any moment, [the city] could take away the parking spots from us." Today Santa Ana is a *lonchera* paradise—and Guzmán owns three of them, with plans for more.

MARGARITA MILLIONAIRES

The self-appointed guardians of Mexican food in this 25 country are right on one point: The popularity of Mexican food has indeed allowed many non-Mexicans to build multimillion-dollar fortunes. German immigrant William Gebhardt created Eagle Brand Chili Powder from the basement of a bar in New Braunfels, Texas, in the early 1890s, parlaying that into a canned food empire that lasts to this day. Glen Bell, founder of Taco Bell, got his idea for hard-shelled tacos from Mitla Café, a San Bernardino Mexican restaurant that stood across the street from Bell's burger stand during the early 1950s. The Frito-Lay company developed its most iconic chips, Fritos and Doritos, by purchasing the rights to those crunchy treats from Mexican immigrants. And Steve Ells, founder of Chipotle, which has mainstreamed massive burritos during the last decade, openly admits he was "inspired" by the burritos sold in San Francisco's famously Latino Mission District.

The easy response to critics of appropriation is that it's the market that decides who gets rich, not ethnic politics. Besides, obsessing over the many *gabachos* who have become Mexican-food millionaires ignores the many success stories involving Mexicans who displayed the same guile as their pasty-skinned contemporaries.

Larry Cano, for example, started out as a dishwasher at a Polynesian-themed restaurant in the Los Angeles enclave of Encino, worked his way up enough to eventually buy the place, then renamed it El Torito—the chain that pioneered sit-down Mexican dining in the United States. In Texas, the Martinez and Cuellar families created empires with their El Fenix and El Chico chains, respectively, formalizing Mexican restaurants for the rest of the country and essentially creating the genre of Tex-Mex. In Southern California during the 1990s, the Lopez family, immigrants from the southern Mexico state of Oaxaca, helped popularize regional Mexican food in this country, fighting the double challenge of introducing Oaxacan food to both Americans *and* Southern California Mexicans who looked down on the cuisine as the domain of backward Indians. Today Mexican immigrants are following the Lopez/Oaxacan lead and selling their regional specialties nationwide.

And then there's the story of Mariano Martinez, scion of the Cuellars, who in 1971 created the frozen margarita machine. At his Dallas restaurant Mariano's, which serves heroic enchilada platters, Martinez birthed an empire off the slushy tequila drink, inventing an instant mix that has powered many a house party since. Nowadays Martinez disavows the frozen margarita—he prefers his fresh, with Cointreau. But Mariano's pride in his creation and his cuisine—long dismissed by "serious" food critics as forgettable—remains.

"I've seen them all over the years," he says. "They come in and do this upscale food. . . . Some of those places aren't there anymore. My little old place I have? Forty years later, we're still pumping the same food. Same phone number. Here I am plugging away at this little Tex-Mex peasant food that no one wanted to play with, that all the ivory tower critics made fun of. And with a drink that no one can resist."

Mariano's original frozen margarita machine is 30 now in the Smithsonian. And Mexican food marches on, a combo plate of freedom giving indigestion to busybodies and authentistas everywhere.

Reading Questions

1. Describe Arellano's initial reaction to Taco John's Potato Olés.

2. According to Arellano, what "staples of the Mexican diet have been thoroughly assimilated into American food culture" (par. 9)?

3. How does Arellano respond to leftist academic critiques about the appropriation of Mexican food in America?

Rhetoric Questions

4. Arellano writes extensively about the history of local laws and ordinances that regulate Mexican food in America. Locate one of these laws or ordinances. How does the example work within his larger argument? What does the example illustrate?

5. How does Arellano use personal narrative in this essay? Are there genres in your discipline in which personal narrative would be appropriate? Why or why not?

6. Arellano's essay culminates in a description of the frozen margarita machine and its inventor. How does this example illustrate his main argument?

Response and Research Questions

7. Arellano says that a taste of home for Southern Californians like himself means burritos. What food would you consider as your "taste of home"? Explain your choice.

8. Arellano writes, "Food is a natural conduit of change, evolution, and innovation" (7). What other cultural products might be considered conduits of change? Provide and explain several examples.

9. How might researchers in other disciplines study the cultural adaptation of food? What specifically would they be looking for? How might they design their research?

10. Do you agree with Arellano's central position that "Mexican food has become a better culinary metaphor for America than the melting pot" (4)? Why or why not? If not, can you think of a better metaphor, culinary or otherwise?

Pastoral Romance

BRENT CUNNINGHAM

Brent Cunningham is a journalist and deputy editor-in-chief of the *Columbia Journalism Review*. Cunningham's writing is diverse—covering topics such as media criticism and food culture—and has appeared in publications such as the *Nation*, the *Washington Post*, and *USA Today*. His writing about food has been selected for the *Best Food Writing* anthology in 2012 and 2014. In the article below, published online in *Lapham's Quarterly* in summer 2011, Cunningham reveals insights from time spent in a small West Virginia town with his wife, Jane Black, also a food writer. Arguing against what he calls "food nostalgia," Cunningham warns his readers about the effects of romanticizing the past and ultimately calls on contemporary food writers to be more inclusive of rural and poor communities.

Betty Jo Patton spent her childhood on a 240-acre farm in Mason County, West Virginia, in the 1930s. Her family raised what it ate, from tomatoes to turkeys, pears to pigs. They picked, plucked, slaughtered, butchered, cured, canned, preserved, and rendered. They drew water from a well, cooked on a wood stove, and the bathroom was an outhouse.

Phoebe Patton Randolph, Betty Jo's thirty-two-year-old granddaughter, has a dream of returning to the farm, which has been in the family since 1863 and is an hour's drive from her home in the suburbs of Huntington, a city of nearly fifty thousand people along the Ohio River. Phoebe is an architect and a mother of one (soon to be two) boys, who is deeply involved in efforts to revitalize Huntington, a moribund Rust Belt community unsure of what can replace the defunct factories that drove its economy for a hundred years. She grew up with stories of life on the farm as she watched the empty farmhouse sag into disrepair.

Recently, over lunch in Betty Jo's cozy house in a quiet Huntington neighborhood, I listened to them talk about the farm, and I eventually asked Betty Jo what she thought of her granddaughter's notion of returning to the land. Betty Jo smiled, but was blunt: "Leave it. There's nothing romantic about it."

Leave it? But isn't Green Acres the place to be? Listening to the conversation about food reform that has unspooled in this country over the last decade, it's hard to avoid the idea that in terms of food production and consumption, we once had it right—before industrialization and then globalization sullied our Eden. Nostalgia glistens on that conversation like dew on an heirloom tomato: the belief that in a not-so-distant past, families routinely sat down to happy meals whipped up from scratch by mom or grandma. That in the 1950s, housewives had to be tricked by Madison Avenue marketers into abandoning beloved family recipes in favor of new Betty Crocker cake mixes. That the family farm was at the center of an ennobling way of life.

Evidence of the nostalgia abounds. There is an end-5 less series of books by urban food revolutionaries who flee the professional world for the simple pleasures of rural life, if only for a year or so: *Growing a Farmer: How I Learned to Live Off the Land; Coop: A Family, a Farm, and the Pursuit of One Good Egg; The Bucolic Plague: How Two Manhattanites Became Gentlemen Farmers: An Unconventional Memoir.* A new crop sprouts each year. There's Michael Pollan's admonition, in his bestselling book *Food Rules*, to not "eat anything your great-grandmother wouldn't recognize as food." And then there are countless articles about the young and educated putting off grad school to become organic farmers. A March 5 piece in the *New York Times* is typical. Under the headline "In New Food Culture, a Young Generation of Farmers Emerges," it delivers a predictable blend: twenty-somethings who quit engineering jobs to farm in Corvallis, Oregon—microbrews, Subarus, multiple piercings, indie rock, yoga. This back-to-the-landism is of a piece with the nineteenth-century, do-it-yourself fever that has swept certain neighborhoods of Brooklyn, complete with handlebar mustaches, jodhpur boots, classic cocktails, soda shops, and restaurants with wagon wheels on the walls.

The surest sign that this nostalgia has reached a critical mass, though, is that food companies have begun to board the retro bus. PepsiCo now has throwback cans for Pepsi (the red-white-and-blue one Cindy Crawford famously guzzled in the 1990s) and Mountain Dew (featuring a cartoon hillbilly from the 1960s) in which they've replaced "bad" high-fructose corn syrup with "good" cane sugar. Frito-Lay is resurrecting a Doritos chip from the 1980s (taco-flavored, a sombrero on the package). When nostalgia is co-opted by corporate America and sold back to us, as it invariably is, the backlash can't be far behind. Consider this the opening salvo.

It's unlikely that most serious food reformers think America can or should dismantle our industrial food system and return to an agrarian way of life. But the idea that "food used to be better" so pervades the rhetoric about what ails our modern food system that it is hard not to conclude that rolling back the clock would provide at least some of the answers. The trouble is, it wouldn't. And even if it would, the prospect of a return to Green Acres just isn't very appealing to a lot of people who know what life there is really like.

I came to Huntington last November with my wife, the food writer Jane Black, to research a book about the effort to build a healthier food culture there. This is where celebrity chef Jamie Oliver last year debuted his reality television show, *Jamie Oliver's Food Revolution*, after the Huntington metro area was labeled the nation's most unhealthy community by a 2008 Centers for Disease Control study. It is a place that has suffered the familiar litany of postindustrial woes: a decimated manufacturing base, a shrinking population, a drug problem. It is also precisely the kind of place where the food-reform movement must take hold if it is to deliver on its promise of large-scale and enduring change.

How would the messages and assumptions that have powered the movement in the elite enclaves where it took root over the last decade—like Brooklyn, where we live, Berkeley, Washington, DC, etc.—play in communities like Huntington? Places where most people don't consider Applebee's and Wal-Mart to be the enemy. Where the familiar and the consistent are valued over the new and the exotic, especially when it comes to what's for dinner. Where a significant portion of the population lives in poverty or perilously close to it.

Jane and I suspected that the environmental, social justice, it-just-tastes-better case for eating seasonally and sustainably that our foodie friends consider self-evident would be met with skepticism—or shrugs—by people who have more pressing concerns than the plight of tomato pickers in Florida or the fact that cows are meant to eat grass, not corn. Nostalgia, though, did not immediately register with us as part of the movement's message problem. Perhaps because we live in the same world as the people who write those My-Year-Doing-X books, foodie nostalgia only seemed an innocuous, if annoying, bit of yuppie indulgence.

But in Huntington we kept meeting people like Betty Jo. Alma Keeney, for instance, who also grew up on a farm, is baffled by her daughter-in-law Shelly's decision to launch a goat-cheese business. Shelly runs the fledgling Yellow Goat Farm with her friend, Dominique Wong, and together they tend their Nubian and Alpine dairy goats on a small plot in Proctorville, Ohio, just across the river from Huntington. The eighty-seven-year-old Alma, Shelley told us, prefers individually wrapped American slices of cheese, not "farm food," which brings back memories of hard times. Jane and I started thinking about the uncritical, even simplistic way that our agricultural past—and our kitchen-table past—are referenced in American society generally, and in the conversation about food reform specifically.

The farmer is among the most enduring figures in the American pantheon. "Those who labor in the earth are the chosen people of God," wrote Thomas Jefferson in *Notes on the State of Virginia*, his classic work on the promise of the American experiment. The agrarian ideal—a belief that the family is the soul of the nation, a pure embodiment of our democracy—is a recurring theme in the national narrative. In 1782, J. Hector St. John de Crèvecoeur, in his *Letters from an American Farmer*, celebrated the notion of independence and self-sufficiency that is central to the story: "Where is that station which can confer a more substantial system of felicity than that of an American farmer, possessing freedom of action, freedom of thoughts, ruled by a mode of government which requires but little from us?"

The exalted status of the farmer has influenced political strategy and policy decisions throughout our history: in New Deal legislation that sought to place the family farm, which struggled mightily during the Depression, on par with other industries primarily through price supports; in an amendment to the Selective Service Act of 1940, which granted deferments to young men who were "necessary to and regularly engaged in an agricultural occupation"; in the creation of the U.S. food-assistance program in 1954, which pitted the stalwart American farmer against the menace of Soviet collectivized agriculture. And it surely informs the nostalgia that shrouds today's food-reform movement. One can essentially trace a through line from Thomas Jefferson's romantic image of the farmer to a recent defense of rural America in the *Washington Post* by Tom Vilsack, the U.S. Secretary of Agriculture: "There's a value system there. Service is important for rural folks. Country is important, patriotism is important."

Today most of us are so removed from the agricultural life, and so ignorant about its realities, that this wholesome and nostalgic lens is the only one we know. Research by the FrameWorks Institute, a think tank employed by nonprofits to strategically reframe public conversation about social issues, found that for Americans, "Rural Utopia" is the dominant image of life beyond the cities and suburbs: a countryside "filled with poor but noble, tough and hard-working people living healthier and fundamentally better lives than the rest of us." This despite the fact that the reality in rural America today is one of decline: unemployment, rising divorce rates, a scramble to get out. According to the Bureau of Labor Statistics, farming is the nation's fourth-most-dangerous job.

Still, nostalgia has been a useful tool for the food-reform movement. It has provided a blueprint for how to think about and act on the daunting environmental, moral, and health problems associated with our industrial food system for people who have the resources—financial, social, and educational—that allow them to participate in the movement if they so choose, and that predispose them to be sympathetic to the cause in the first place. Whether they started raising chickens in their backyards or simply became better informed about how their food is produced, this idea that we've lost our way has helped make food *important*, and in ways that go beyond simple sustenance.

Most of these food revolutionaries won't become actual farmers, and most of those who do—including those microbrew-swilling kids in Corvallis—won't make a career of it. But the movement has, I suspect, permanently changed their attitudes toward food, and this alone is already forcing modest systemic change. Since 1994 the number of farmers' markets in the United States has risen from 1,700 to more than 6,000. And between 2000 and 2009, organic-food sales grew from $6 billion to nearly $25 billion—still

less than 4 percent of total U.S. food sales, but it's a start. Twenty years from now, most of these young "farmers" will have rejoined the professional ranks. Like their middle-class forefathers who tuned in, turned on, and dropped out in the 1960s, the appeal of financial security and a climate-controlled office will, in most cases, win out. That said, they probably won't be regulars at McDonald's, and they'll instill these values in their own kids.

Nevertheless, a "bourgeois nostalgia" pervades the food-reform movement, as Amy Trubek, an anthropologist at the University of Vermont who studies food and culture, points out. This is a perception of our food history that is the luxury of people who have little or no experience with farming, or more generally with manual labor. A perception that appeals to those who have never had to cook from scratch, let alone milk cows, kill chickens, and bake bread, just to get food on the table every day. A perception of people for whom it makes perfect sense to redefine their *leisure* time to include things like making *guanciale* or Meyer-lemon marmalade. As such, it may not resonate with great swaths of the public who don't fit this demographic profile, and it is a perception that ignores some crucial truths about our food history.

The reality of America's food past is far more complicated, and troubling, than is suggested by the romantic image at the heart of our foodie nostalgia. In *Revolution at the Table* and its sequel, *Paradox of Plenty*, the historian Harvey Levenstein provides a more sober, and ultimately more useful, accounting of that past. Levenstein shows how, starting in the late nineteenth century and continuing through the twentieth, food preparation steadily migrated outside the home. The reason is simple: if you have no choice but to plan and prepare multiple meals every day, cooking not only isn't cool, it's tedious and damned hard work.

Jane and I experienced this firsthand in West Virginia. We both are skilled and enthusiastic cooks, and as part of the reporting for the book, we wanted to see how well, and local, we could eat, and for how much money, preparing three meals a day. But we also understood that we were the kind of people for whom cooking is a hobby. Outside our door in Brooklyn, there is a cornucopia of options for the nights when we are busy or not in the mood to cook. In Huntington, though, most of those options are missing. Three months in we began to notice, with dismay, that as soon as one meal was finished, we had to start thinking about the next. Four months in, the joy of cooking was replaced by a growing irritation, a longing to amble down the block for *banh mi* or a bowl of ramen. By mid-March, Jane wrote in her journal, "Officially sick of cooking."

Between 1880 and 1930, the fruits of industrialization—canning, bottling, the growth of food manufacturers and restaurants—enabled the outsourcing of food preparation that Levenstein describes. Improved transportation—first the railroad and then the automobile—and food-preservation processes—refrigerated railcars, for instance—brought an end to seasonal and regional restrictions on what we ate. Soon, people in Kentucky had the same food choices as those in New York or California. 20

The standardization of the American diet, so bemoaned by people like me, is what many—maybe even most—people want at mealtime. It is reassuring to have what everyone else has. The desire to have the same Big Mac in Syracuse as in San Diego is a big part of why fast-food outlets became America's default dining-out option, and why suggesting that as a nation we return to a more seasonal and regional way of eating will be a tough sell.

The family farm itself was not immune to these developments. By the 1920s and '30s, the gap between city and farm diets had begun to collapse, as processed foods became high-status items in rural areas. Poor Appalachian farmers began to prefer canned hams to country hams; farm women who could afford store-bought canned vegetables and other processed food embraced this new convenience without a second thought that they were abandoning a purer, nobler way of life.

There's a reason that less than 2 percent of people in this country are engaged in farming today, and it isn't simply that they've been driven off the land by Cargill and ADM. Just like Betty Jo Patton, many of them wanted things to be easier. This revolution at the table—the one that produced the food culture that today's revolutionaries are trying to counter—was considered a tremendous leap forward. It was modern. It gave people time for things other than keeping the family fed.

There is an even more fundamental concern about our nostalgia: America's food system has always depended on the exploitation of someone, whether it was indentured servants, slaves, tenant farmers, braceros and other guest workers, or, now, immigrants. In his ode to the American farmer, Crèvecoeur made it clear that he had a little help on his farm. "My Negroes are tolerably faithful and healthy," he wrote. This is an aspect of our agricultural heritage that rarely gets mentioned in the mainstream conversation about food-system reform, and it raises thorny questions about who actually grows, harvests, processes, and prepares the food in a capitalist society. We have no history of a food system that does not depend on oppression of some sort, and it seems unlikely that we will be able to create a future system that avoids this fate. The leaders of the food revolution have, in recent years, begun to speak out on the matter of farmworker rights. But few acknowledge—at least in the public debate—that if a central goal of the movement is a more equitable food system, then the notion that we once had it right is deeply problematic.

Exploitation is as true in the kitchen as in the field. 25 Women have always borne the burden of transforming the raw to the cooked in the American home. Interestingly, it was a confluence of these two inconvenient truths about our food past—its reliance on women and exploited labor—that helped set the stage for our national embrace of fast food.

During the Gilded Age following the end of the Civil War, and continuing into the early twentieth century, America's rapidly expanding ranks of wealthy industrialists used extravagant dinner parties, featuring French haute cuisine, as a way to showcase their status. Hosts and hostesses sought to outdo one another: chefs were imported from France; eight courses were standard, as were menu cards, elaborate centerpieces, and a labor-intensive style of service known as *À la Russe*, which involved a butler carving and arranging the food on plates at a sideboard, which were then delivered to guests by servants. (The traditional style had been to fill the table with platters and bowls and let the guests serve themselves.)

The fetish for French cuisine, and all the attendant showmanship, quickly trickled down, and the nation's middle-class, which also was expanding, sought pecuniary emulation of this conspicuous consumption. Competitive dinner parties became a fixture of middle-class social life. And it wasn't just at dinner; there were also multicourse luncheons and high teas to pull together. The problem, though, was that middle-class households couldn't afford the number and quality of servants necessary for this kind of entertaining. This "servant problem," as Levenstein calls it, became something of an obsession for American housewives, who saw it as the main obstacle to fulfilling society's expectations of them.

Their plight led to various time-saving experiments, including cooperative kitchens—in which meals for multiple families were prepared for pickup in a central location—and the first home-meal delivery services. The former failed because they were regarded as a violation of the "ideal of American family life," a critique that had more than a whiff of antisocialist sentiment. The latter, it turns out, was simply an idea ahead of its time. These delivery services conformed to what was then considered the standard for a "proper meal": three courses and a menu that changed daily. As such, they were too expensive to be sustainable. The inability to solve the middle-class servant problem led, eventually, to a new conception in American society of what constituted a proper meal: simpler, cheaper, and of course, faster. We know how that story turned out.

By misrepresenting—or misunderstanding—our food history, we make a realistic conversation about what to change and how to change it more difficult than it already is. America will not revert to a nation of family farms. Convenience will always be important. Seasonal and regional limitations on what we eat can only go so far. If Americans want to cook like their grandmothers, fine, but the fact is our grandmothers, by and large, made only a handful of meals, they made them over and over again, and they used plenty of shortcuts, courtesy of the industrial age. My grandmother's cornbread, which still remains the gold standard for cornbread in my family twenty years after her death, began with a Martha White mix.

Nostalgia is part of a larger message problem that food revolutionaries face as they attempt to broaden the appeal of their cause. For example, when Wal-Mart announced earlier this year that it would, over the next five years, reduce the amount of sodium by 25 percent and added sugars by 10 percent in its house brands, and pressure other food manufacturers whose products it carries to follow suit, the overwhelming response from within the food-reform community was, "That's not good enough."

In Huntington, and in communities across the country, Wal-Mart is where a lot of people get their food. They like the way the food there tastes. If that food has less sugar and salt—incrementally less so that they will like the way it tastes—that is an important, and realistic, step toward a healthier food culture. Wal-Mart has many bad policies, but it's shortsighted to write off every initiative just because it comes from Wal-Mart. New ideas about food need to conform to people's social and economic aspirations, and those aspirations are going to be different in 2011 than they were in 1900, and they will be different, too, in Huntington, West Virginia, than in Brooklyn, New York. Achieving fundamental and lasting change in our food system will require the efforts of those yuppie farmers in Oregon who can afford to step outside the mainstream food culture and, as they say, vote with their forks. It will also require the more hardwon, incremental reforms at the big food processors and sellers, like Wal-Mart, that feed the great mass of people who either can't or won't vote with their forks.

Somewhere in the middle of these two efforts, hopefully, we can eventually arrive at a food system that makes sense for the twenty-first century. But the process of figuring out what that will look like needs to begin with a full and honest accounting of where we've been, and what's possible given where we are.

Reading Questions

1. How would the author define *food nostalgia*? How is food nostalgia used in popular food writing?

2. Explain the romantic image of farming and cooking that Cunningham writes about. How does he complicate this image?

3. What does Cunningham suggest that we do in order to move forward in an inclusive and responsible manner? What practical steps might be necessary?

4. According to Cunningham, what are some of the "crucial truths about our food history" that a "bourgeois nostalgia" (par. 17) avoids recognizing?

5. In what ways, according to Cunningham, is America's food history also a history of exploitation? Why would this be problematic for those who are nostalgic about the past?

Rhetoric Questions

6. Cunningham's article participates in a popular conversation about food. How does he review the conversation with his essay? What idea or argument is he contributing to this conversation?

7. Near the end of the article, Cunningham makes the stakes of his argument explicit: "By misrepresenting—or misunderstanding—our food history, we make a realistic conversation about what to change and how to change it more difficult than it already is" (29). Why does Cunningham make this so explicit? What are the effects of his statement? Are there moments in your own writing that would benefit from a similar statement?

Response and Research Questions

8. How does Cunningham describe the relationship between food and social class? How might people of different social classes react differently to "food nostalgia?"

9. Do you agree with the perspective that "in terms of food production and consumption, we once had it right—before industrialization and then globalization sullied our Eden" (4)? Why or why not?

10. If you were asked to contribute one policy change or one law to help your community "arrive at a food system that makes sense for the twenty-first century" (32), what would it be? Justify your choice by explaining how it takes into account your community's food past.

Grub

DANA GOODYEAR

Dana Goodyear is a poet and staff writer at the *New Yorker*, a popular American magazine. Her essays, which typically center on food and culture, have been featured in *Food & Wine*, the *Huffington Post*, and the *New Yorker*, among others. Goodyear is also the author of *Anything That Moves: Renegade Chefs, Fearless Eaters, and the Making of a New American Food Culture* (2013), a non-fiction book about shifting conceptions of food in America. In the essay below, published online in the *New Yorker* in 2011, Goodyear details the efforts of entomologists, chefs, and entrepreneurs to make insects a part of the American diet. In doing so, she makes provocative connections among academia, professional kitchens, and the business world.

Florence Dunkel, an entomologist at Montana State University, lives in a red saltbox house at the edge of the woods outside Bozeman, with her husband, Bob, whose nickname for her is Ladybug, and, until recently, with Gertrude, a fine-limbed grass-green katydid she rescued from an airplane. The walls of her kitchen are covered with pictures of her eight grandchildren, who call her Oma, or, in the case of one grandson, the Beetle Oma. In a bay window overlooking a vegetable garden, dried flowers hang next to a stained-glass dragonfly.

One freezing night at the end of February, Dunkel, who is petite, with fluffy gray curls and rosebud lips, was puttering around her kitchen, a large pair of glasses suspended from a sparkly chain around her neck and an apron tied at her waist. She pulled out her old Betty Crocker recipe binder—she has had it since 1962—and put on her glasses. She opened it to a page, yellow with use, for chocolate-chip Toll House cookies. Like many cooks, Dunkel likes to make a recipe her own. Betty Crocker called for half a cup of chopped walnuts. In the margin, in a loopy hand—the penmanship of a girl who grew up on a farm in Wisconsin in the nineteen-fifties—Dunkel had suggested a substitution: "or fresh roasted crickets."

The crickets were presenting something of a problem. Her usual supplier, in California, had run out of large ones, and instead had sent her a thousand live pinheads—babies—which she'd had to supplement with a hundred and twenty-five expensive subadults from PetSmart. Before checking her recipe, Dunkel

had picked up a pinhead. "I've never used these for food," she said, kneading it between her index finger and thumb, a chef inspecting an unfamiliar piece of meat. "I'm not even sure I'll take the head off." She'd decided to put the pinheads in the freezer to kill them—another of her nicknames, inspired by her work as an insect pathologist, is Dr. Death—and set the oven to 225 degrees for the PetSmart subadults.

"Meanwhile, we need to get the wax worms separated," she said. They were for "land shrimp cocktail," which Dunkel would serve to her Insects and Human Society class the next day, accompanied by cocktail sauce made by Bob, using horseradish from their garden. "They're going to want to wander as they get warm." She opened a plastic container secured with red tape that read "WORMS ALIVE" and dumped the worms—the larvae of the wax moth, which were plump and white and had come from a bait shop in Minnesota—onto a brown plate. They were covered in cedar shavings. My job was to separate the worms from the shavings, picking out the black ones (blackness is a sign of necrosis) and dismantling the cocoons of the ones that had started to pupate, while making sure none got away. The worms were chubby and firm, with the springiness of clementine segments. They swayed deliriously, testing the air. I got to work sorting, de-silking, herding.

"Oh! I can smell the crickets now," Dunkel said, [5] as the aroma of toasted nuts filled the kitchen. She took them out of the oven, and started to pull off the ovipositors and the legs, which can stick in the throat.

When I finished with the wax worms, she said, "The next species we're going to deal with is *Tenebrio molitor*, which is a beetle. We're going to wash them, and then we're going to fry them in butter." She handed me a container full of bran and beetle larvae—skinny, crusty, yellowish—commonly known as mealworms. I shook the mixture through a sieve; as I rinsed off the last of the bran, the worms clung to the side like sailors on a capsized ship. Dunkel dumped them in a buttery frying pan, where they hissed and squirmed before going suddenly still. They smelled of wild mushrooms, and tasted, spooned hot into my hand, like sunflower seeds.

Dunkel stayed up baking until three. The next day, at Insects and Human Society, she had her students do a honey tasting, reminding them that honey is, of course, the vomit of a bee. Then Ky-Phuong Luong, the T.A., stirred a wok full of vegetables and soy-marinated crickets, and Dunkel passed a plate of fritters with yellowish wax worms protruding from their centers. "We left out the bacon," she said, smiling sweetly. The students talked about ethnocentrism (eighty percent of the world eats insects with pleasure), sustainability, and the earth's diminishing resources. After a while, they started, tentatively, to eat. A young man in a green wool ski cap said that he would be more enthusiastic if he had some beer to wash the insects down. Standing before a plate of brownies fortified with a mash of the sautéed mealworms, he said despondently, "This is the future! You'll eat worms and like it. You gotta eat *something*."

Insects were among the original specialty foods in the American gourmet marketplace—inspired, impractical provocations that, like runway styles in retail clothing, drove the sales of more basic goods. In the early nineteen-forties, Max Ries, a German-Jewish textile manufacturer, came to Chicago and established himself as a purveyor of imported cheese to an American public that was beginning to be fascinated by exotic food. Ries was slim and dashing; he wore handmade suits and twirled his cigars. Alongside tinned tiger and elephant meat—culled from zoos and sold at department stores—he presented "French-fried ants" from Venezuela and baby bees from Japan,

conversation pieces that lent glamour to his company, Reese Finer Foods, which actually made its money selling canned water chestnuts, artichoke hearts, and baby corn. Like fashionistas, gourmets have a sense of theater. Excluded from the first Fancy Food Show, at the Sheraton-Astor, in New York, in 1955, Ries hired a limousine to shuttle buyers to a nearby hotel, where he had set up his own show, exhibiting only Reese products. (After that, the New Yorkers relented and gave him a booth, which became a mainstay.) When Reese had overstock of its Spooky Foods gift set—chocolate-covered ants, roasted butterflies, barbecue bees—it hired Bela Lugosi to appear in his Dracula costume with the product, which promptly sold out.

Insects—part delicacy, part gag—are chic again. Once a staple on *Fear Factor*, they were featured on *Top Chef Masters* this season. (The winning dish: tempura-fried crickets with sunchoke-carrot purée and blood-orange vinaigrette.) At John Rivera Sedlar's ambitious Latin restaurant Rivera, in Los Angeles, where the tasting menu includes Atlantic Cod in the Spirit of New World Discoveries, the cocktail list features the Donaji, a fourteen-dollar drink named after a Zapotec princess, which is made with artisanal Oaxacan mescal and house-made grasshopper salt. (On its own, the salt tastes like Jane's Krazy Mixed-Up Salt, crushed Bac-Os, and fish-food flakes; the bartender recommends it as a rub for grilled meat.)

Bricia Lopez supplies the bugs for Sedlar's drinks; at Guelaguetza, the Oaxacan restaurant that her parents opened in Los Angeles in 1994, she serves a scrumptious plate of *chapulines a la Mexicana*—grasshoppers sautéed with onions, jalapeños, and tomatoes, and topped with avocado and Oaxacan string cheese. Lopez, who is twenty-six and a glamorous fixture of the L.A. food scene, says that more and more Anglo hipsters are coming in to order them. "Eating grasshoppers is a thing you do here," she said. "Like, 'Oh, my God, I ate a grasshopper, *woo*.'" She went on, "There's more of a cool factor involved. It's not just 'Let's go get a burrito.' It's 'Let's get a *mole*' or 'Let's get a grasshopper.'"

The current vogue reflects not only the American 10 obsession with novelty and the upper-middle-class hunger for authenticity but also deep anxiety about the meat we already eat—which is its own kind of fashion. José Andrés, who this year won the James Beard Foundation's Outstanding Chef award, makes a very popular *chapulín* taco—sautéed shallots, deglazed in tequila; chipotle paste; and Oaxacan grasshoppers, in a hand-made tortilla—at his Washington, D.C., restaurant Oyamel. He sees bug-eating as both a gastronomic experience (he recommends the mouthfeel of a small, young, crispy *chapulín*) and a matter of survival. "We need to feed humanity in a sustainable way," he says. "Those who know how to produce protein will have an edge over everyone else. World War Three will be over control of water and food, and the insects may be an answer."

Demographers have projected that by 2050 the world's population will have increased to nine billion, and the demand for meat will grow with it, particularly in dense, industrializing countries like China and India. Last year—a year in which, according to the United Nations, nearly a billion people suffered from chronic hunger—the journal *Science* published a special issue on "food security," and included a piece on entomophagy, the unappealing name by which insect-eating properly goes. Acknowledging that the notion might be "unappetizing to many," the editors wrote: "The quest for food security may require us all to reconsider our eating habits, particularly in view of the energy consumption and environmental costs that sustain those habits."

From an ecological perspective, insects have a lot to recommend them. They are renowned for their small "foodprint"; being cold-blooded, they are about four times as efficient at converting feed to meat as are cattle, which waste energy keeping themselves warm. Ounce for ounce, many have the same amount of protein as beef—fried grasshoppers have three times as much—and are rich in micronutrients like iron and zinc. Genetically, they are so distant from humans that there is little likelihood of diseases jumping species, as swine flu did. They are natural recyclers, capable of eating old cardboard, manure, and by-products from food manufacturing. And insect husbandry is humane: bugs *like* teeming, and thrive in filthy, crowded conditions.

In December, a group of scientists at Wageningen University, in the Netherlands, published a paper concluding that insects reared for human consumption produce significantly lower quantities of greenhouse gases than do cattle and pigs. "This study therefore indicates that insects could serve as a more environmentally friendly alternative for the production of animal protein," the paper said. One of its authors was Arnold van Huis, an entomologist who is working to establish a market for insect-based products in the Netherlands, with funding from the Dutch government; the agriculture ministry recently gave him a million euros to research insect husbandry. "We have a food crisis, especially a meat crisis, and people are starting to realize that we need alternatives, and insects are just an excellent alternative," van Huis said.

On a trip to Africa, in 1995, when van Huis was on sabbatical, he traveled to a dozen countries, interviewing locals about their relationship with insects. Half the people he spoke with talked about eating them, and he finally overcame their reluctance— born of centuries of colonial opprobrium★—to share some with him. "I had termites, which were roasted, and they were excellent," he said. When he got home, he offered a bag of termites to Marcel Dicke, the head of his department—he liked them—and the two started a popular lecture series that addressed insects' potential as a food source. After van Huis and Dicke organized an insect festival that drew twenty thousand people, they were approached by several mealworm and cricket farmers who had been serving the pet-food industry but were interested in diversifying. "We know that Western peoples have some difficulties psychologically with ingesting insects, so we are looking at some ways of introducing them into food so that people will no longer recognize them," van Huis said. Insect flour was one option. "Another possibility is that you can grind insects and make them into a hot dog or a fish stick," he said. Together, van Huis and Dicke have helped get mealworms and processed snacks like Bugs Nuggets into the Dutch grocery chain Sligro.

★*opprobrium:* criticism.

The Dutch are, for reasons of geography, espe- 15 cially concerned about the effects of global warming; they are also progressive when it comes to food development. But entrepreneurs in the United States are starting to explore edible insects, too. Matthew Krisiloff, who just finished his freshman year at the University of Chicago, recently started a company called Entom Foods, which is working on de-shelling insects using pressurization technology—trade secret—in the hope of selling the meat in cutlet form. "The problem is the *ick* factor—the eyes, the wings, the legs," he said. "It's not as simple as hiding it in a bug nugget. People won't accept it beyond the novelty. When you think of a chicken you think of a chicken breast, not the eyes, wings, and beak. We're trying to do the same thing with insects, create a stepping-stone, so that when you get a bug nugget you think of the bug steak, not the whole animal." If he can overcome some of the technical challenges—like the fact that insect protein does not take the form of muscle, but is, as he put it, "goopy"—he plans to have a product out next year.

In Dicke's opinion, simply changing the language surrounding food insects could go a long way toward solving the problem that Westerners have with them. "Maybe we should stop telling people they're eating insects," he said. "If you say it's mealworms, it makes people think of ringworm. So stop saying 'worm.' If we use the Latin names, say it's a *Tenebrio* quiche, it sounds much more fancy, and it's part of the marketing." (There's a precedent for this: in the nineteenth century, English members of the Society for the Propagation of Horse Flesh as an Article of Food had French chefs prepare banquets of the meat they called *chevaline*.) The other option, Dicke said, is to cover the bugs in chocolate, because people will eat anything covered in chocolate.

The practice of ethical entomophagy started haphazardly. In 1974, Gene DeFoliart, who was the chair of entomology at the University of Wisconsin, was asked by a colleague to recommend someone who could talk about edible insects as part of a symposium on unconventional protein sources. Then, as now, entomology was more concerned with insect eradication than cultivation, and, not finding a willing

participant, DeFoliart decided to take on the project himself. He began his talk—and the paper he eventually published—with a startling statement: "C. F. Hodge (1911) calculated that a pair of houseflies beginning operations in April could produce enough flies, if all survived, to cover the earth forty-seven feet deep by August," he said. "If one can reverse for a moment the usual focus on insects as enemies of man, Hodge's layer of flies represents an impressive pile of animal protein."

DeFoliart envisioned a place for edible insects as a luxury item. The larvae of the wax moth (*Galleria mellonella*) seemed to him to be poised to become the next escargot, which in the late eighties represented a three-hundred-million-dollar-a-year business in the United States. "Given a choice, New York diners looking for adventure and willing to pay $22 for half a roasted free-range chicken accompanied by a large pile of shoestring potatoes might well prefer a smaller pile of *Galleria* at the same price," he wrote. He and a handful of colleagues, including Dunkel, began to study and promote the potential of what they called "mini-livestock," and, in *The Food Insects Newsletter*, they reported the results of nutritional analyses and assessed the efficiency of insects like crickets—the most delectable of which, entomophagists are fond of pointing out, belong to the genus *Gryllus*.

In December, a group of DeFoliart's disciples gathered at a resort in San Diego for a symposium on entomophagy at the annual conference of the Entomological Society of America. Because there is no significant funding available for entomophagy research, it has never been taken seriously by most professional entomologists. Dunkel, who in her half century in academia has many times heard colleagues discourage interested graduate students, often finds herself at odds with others in her field. It was a relief, then, to be among the like-minded. "Your soap-moth-pupae chutney—I'll never forget how that tasted!" she said, introducing a colleague from the Insectarium, in Montreal, which holds a bug banquet every other year. The entomophagists hoped to capitalize on the momentum they perceived. "We don't have to be the kooky, nerdy entomologists who eat bugs because we're crazy," an entomologist from the University of

Georgia said. "Twenty years ago, sushi was the *eww* factor; you did not see sushi in grocery stores. Now it's the cultural norm."

At the conference, Dunkel talked about her [20] frustration working in West Africa, where for decades European and American entomologists, through programs like U.S.A.I.D. and British Locust Control, have killed grasshoppers and locusts, which are complete proteins, in order to preserve the incomplete proteins in millet, wheat, barley, sorghum, and maize. Her field work in Mali focuses on the role of grasshoppers in the diets of children, who, for cultural reasons, do not eat chicken or eggs. Grasshoppers contain essential amino acids and serve as a crucial buffer against kwashiorkor, a protein deficiency that impedes physical and neurological development. In the village where Dunkel works, kwashiorkor is on the rise; in recent years, nearby fields have been planted with cotton, and pesticide use has intensified. Mothers now warn their children not to collect the grasshoppers, which they rightly fear may be contaminated.

Mainly, the entomophagists bemoaned the prejudice against insects. "In our minds, they're associated with filth," Heather Looy, a psychologist who has studied food aversions, said over dinner after the symposium. "They go dirty places, but so do fungi, and we eat those all the time. And you don't want to know about crabs and shrimp and lobster." Crabs, shrimp, and lobster are, like insects, arthropods—but instead of eating fresh lettuces and flowers, as many insects do, they scavenge debris from the ocean floor.

This injustice—lobster is a delicacy, while vegetarian crustaceans like wood lice are unfit for civilized man—is a centerpiece of the literature of entomophagy. "Why Not Eat Insects?," an 1885 manifesto by Vincent M. Holt, which is the founding document of the movement, expounds upon the vile habits of the insects of the sea. "The lobster, a creature consumed in incredible quantities at all the highest tables in the land, is such a foul feeder that, for its sure capture, the experienced fisherman will bait his lobster-pot with putrid flesh or fish which is too far gone even to attract a crab," he writes.

Holt's compelling, if Swiftian, argument addresses the food problems of his day—"What a pleasant change from the laborer's unvarying meal of bread, lard, and bacon, or bread and lard without bacon, would be a good dish of fried cockchafers or grasshoppers"—but he is innocent of the nuances of food marketing. Among the sample menus he supplies are offerings like Boiled Neck of Mutton with Wire-worm Sauce and Moths on Toast. At dinner in San Diego, it occurred to me that this naïveté had carried down. I was sitting next to Lou Sorkin, a forensic entomologist at the American Museum of Natural History who is also an expert on bedbugs, probably the most loathed insect in the United States today. He had arrived at his latest culinary discovery, he said, while experimenting with mediums for preserving maggots collected from murdered corpses. Realizing that citrus juice might denature proteins as effectively as a chemical solution, and might be more readily available in the field, he soaked large sarcophagid maggots in baths of grapefruit, lemon, lime, and pomelo juice, and voilà! Maggot ceviche. "It's a little chewy," he said. "But tasty."

Food preferences are highly local, often irrational, and defining: a Frenchman is a frog because he considers their legs food and the person who calls him one does not. In Santa María Atzompa, a community in Oaxaca where grasshoppers toasted with garlic, chile, and lime are a favorite treat, locals have traditionally found shrimp repulsive. "They would say 'some people' eat it, meaning 'the coastal people,'" Ramona Pérez, an anthropologist at San Diego State University, says. When she made scampi for a family there, she told me, they were appalled; the mother, who usually cooked with her, refused to help, and the daughters wouldn't eat. The coast is less than a hundred miles away.

Most of the world eats bugs. Australian Aborigines [25] like witchetty grubs, which, according to the authors of "Man Eating Bugs," taste like "nut-flavored scrambled eggs and mild mozzarella, wrapped in a phyllo dough pastry." *Tenebrio molitor* is factory-farmed in China; in Venezuela, children roast tarantulas. Besides, as any bug-eater will tell you, we are all already eating bugs, whether we mean to or not. According to the F.D.A., which publishes a handbook on "defect levels" acceptable in processed food, frozen or canned spinach is not considered contaminated until it has fifty aphids, thrips, or mites per hundred grams. Peanut butter is allowed to have thirty insect fragments per hundred grams, and chocolate is O.K. up to sixty. In each case, the significance of the contamination is given as "aesthetic."

In fresh vegetables, insects are inevitable. The other day, cleaning some lettuce, I was surprised by an emerald-green pentagon with antennae: a stinkbug. I got rid of it immediately. But daintiness about insects has true consequences. As Tom Turpin, an entomologist at Purdue University, said, "Attitudes in this country result in more pesticide use, because we're scared about an aphid wing in our spinach."

The antipathy that Europeans and their descendants display toward eating insects is stubborn, and mysterious. Insect consumption is in our cultural heritage. The Romans ate beetle grubs reared on flour and wine; ancient Greeks ate grasshoppers. Leviticus, by some interpretations, permits the eating of locusts, grasshoppers, and crickets. (The rest are unkosher.) The manna eaten by Moses on his way out of Egypt is widely believed to have been honeydew, the sweet excrement of scale insects.

Contemporary Westerners tend to associate insects with filth, death, and decay, and, because some insects feed on flesh, their consumption is often seen as cannibalism by proxy. Holt takes pains to stress that the insects he recommends for eating—caterpillars, grasshoppers, slugs—are pure of this taint. "My insects are all vegetable feeders, clean, palatable, wholesome, and decidedly more particular in their feeding than ourselves," he writes. "While I am confident that they will never condescend to eat *us*, I am equally confident that, on finding out how good they are, we shall some day right gladly cook and eat *them*."

In the overcoming of resistance to certain foods, Frederick J. Simoons, the author of the classic text on food taboos *Eat Not This Flesh*, says, timing is everything. He cites Emperor Meiji's consumption of beef—a Buddhist sacrilege—as the dawn of Japan's embrace of the West. Noritoshi Kanai, the eighty-eight-year-old president of Mutual Trading Company, which imports gold flakes and matsutake essence to sell to high-end sushi restaurants like Masa and Nobu, introduced sushi to the United States in the nineteen-sixties. Because sushi is raw and handled without gloves in front of the customer, everyone told him that the American public would never accept it. The convergence of three factors, he says, changed their minds: the food pyramid, which emphasized fish; the rise of the Japanese car; and *Shogun*.

Promoters of entomophagy may face a bigger obstacle. Unlike sushi, which was seen as an inedible form of an edible substance, most Westerners view insects as inappropriate for eating—the psychological equivalent of wood or paper—or dangerous, like cleaning fluid. (Insect-eaters, correspondingly, are seen as suspect, other, and possibly inhuman, an idea reinforced by countless mass-culture images, including most science fiction.) Some object to the form in which insects are presented—entire—though lobsters, mussels, oysters, clams, and even, increasingly, in this age of whole-animal cookery, pigs come to the table intact. Others locate their disgust in the fact that one has to eat the chitinous exoskeleton, but the same is true for soft-shell crab, which is rarely considered barbarous to eat.

Morphology might be at the root of the problem, however. Processing insects is labor-intensive, and they are not exactly filling. One would have to eat about a thousand grasshoppers to equal the amount of protein in a twelve-ounce steak. According to Larry Peterman, the owner of HotLix, a company that sells tequila-flavored lollipops with mealworms in them and Sour Cream & Onion Crick-ettes ("the other Green Meat"), processed crickets cost hundreds of dollars a pound. Unlike those found in the tropics, European bugs do not grow big enough to make good food, so there is no culinary tradition, and therefore no infrastructure, to support the practice. Tom Turpin told me, "If there were insects out there the size of pigs, I guarantee you we'd be eating them."

Reading Questions

1. According to the article, eating insects is not accepted in most Western cultures. What are some of the challenges facing individuals and groups in favor of using insects for human consumption?

2. How have some entrepreneurs and chefs tried to make eating insects more desirable for Westerners in particular?

3. Rhetorically, how do entomologists like Dunkle persuade others that we should include insects in our diets? What kind of arguments do they make, and for what audiences?

4. Goodyear quotes a bug supplier who indicates that the consumption of insects in some locales has a "cool factor involved" (par. 9). Why is this the case? Who are the consumers of these "chic" new insect delicacies, and why are these consumers drawn to them?

Rhetoric Questions

5. How does Goodyear use description in this piece to evoke feeling? What feelings does she evoke, and for what purposes or effects?

6. Goodyear relies heavily on crosscultural examples of insect-based diets. Locate one of these examples. How does she connect this example to her larger argument? What purpose does the example serve?

7. How are example and description typically used in your discipline? How might you use them in a paper that you're currently writing?

8. What is Goodyear's fundamental argument or position in this article? Describe her tone toward the subject matter, and explain how it impacts the way you perceive her argument.

Response and Research Question

9. In addressing the "eww" factor, a prejudice many people hold toward insects, proponents of insect consumption point to the fact that people already regularly consume fungi (which "go dirty places") and crabs (which "scavenge debris from the ocean floor"; 21). Do you see any difference between the consumption of a crab or a cricket? A grub or a mushroom? If so, how do you differentiate between the two? If not, why?

Why Cook?

MICHAEL POLLAN

Michael Pollan is one of the leading voices on food politics in America today. He is the author of numerous award-winning articles and books, including *The Omnivore's Dilemma: A Natural History of Four Meals* (2006) and *In Defense of Food: An Eater's Manifesto* (2008). In the essay below, an excerpt from *Cooked: A Natural History of Transformation* (2013), Pollan maintains that Americans are increasingly separated from the food they eat because of the industrialization and specialization of modern food production. Further, Pollan argues that we must reconnect with the act of cooking for ourselves. Then (and only then) will we reconnect with our health and happiness.

I.

At a certain point in the late middle of my life I made the unexpected but happy discovery that the answer to several of the questions that most occupied me was in fact one and the same.

Cook.

Some of these questions were personal. For example, what was the single most important thing we could do as a family to improve our health and general well-being? And what would be a good way to better connect to my teenage son? (As it turned out, this involved not only ordinary cooking but also the specialized form of it known as brewing.) Other questions were slightly more political in nature. For years I had been trying to determine (because I am often asked) what is the most important thing an ordinary person can do to help reform the American food system, to make it healthier and more sustainable? Another related question is, how can people living in a highly specialized consumer economy reduce their sense of dependence and achieve three other domestic chores that we have been only too happy to outsource — and then promptly drop from conscious awareness. But cooking somehow feels different. The work, or the process, retains an emotional or psychological power we can't quite shake, or don't want to. And in fact it was after a long bout of watching cooking programs on television that I began to wonder if this activity I had always taken for granted might be worth taking a little more seriously.

I developed a few theories to explain what I came to think of as the Cooking Paradox. The first and most obvious is that watching other people cook is not exactly a new behavior for us humans. Even when "everyone" still cooked, there were plenty of us who mainly watched: men for the most part, and children. Most of us have happy memories of watching our mothers in the kitchen, performing feats that sometimes looked very much like sorcery and typically resulted in something tasty to eat. In ancient Greece, the word for "cook," "butcher," and "priest" was the same — *mageiros* — and the word shares an etymological root with "magic." I would watch, rapt, when my mother conjured her most magical dishes, like the tightly wrapped packages of fried chicken Kiev that, when cut open with a sharp knife, liberated a pool of melted butter and an aromatic gust of herbs. But watching an everyday pan of eggs get scrambled was nearly as riveting a spectacle, as the slimy yellow goop suddenly leapt into the form of savory gold nuggets. Even the most ordinary dish follows a satisfying arc of transformation, magically becoming something more than the sum of its ordinary parts. And in almost every dish, you can find, besides the culinary ingredients, the ingredients of a story: a beginning, a middle, and an end.

Then there are the cooks themselves, the heroes 5 who drive these little dramas of transformation. Even as it vanishes from our daily lives, we're drawn to the rhythms and textures of the work cooks do, which seems so much more direct and satisfying than the more abstract and formless tasks most of us perform in our jobs these days. Cooks get to put their hands on real stuff, not just keyboards and screens but fundamental things like plants and animals and fungi.

They get to work with the primal elements, too, fire and water, earth and air, using them—mastering them!—to perform their tasty alchemies. How many of us still do the kind of work that engages us in a dialogue with the material world that concludes—assuming the chicken Kiev doesn't prematurely leak or the soufflé doesn't collapse—with such a gratifying and delicious sense of closure?

So maybe the reason we like to watch cooking on television and read about cooking in books is that there are things about cooking we really miss. We might not feel we have the time or energy (or the knowledge) to do it ourselves every day, but we're not prepared to see it disappear from our lives altogether. If cooking is, as the anthropologists tell us, a defining human activity—the act with which culture begins, according to Claude Lévi-Strauss—then maybe we shouldn't be surprised that watching its processes unfold would strike deep emotional chords.

The idea that cooking is a defining human activity is not a new one. In 1773, the Scottish writer James Boswell, noting that "no beast is a cook," called *Homo sapiens* "the cooking animal." (Though he might have reconsidered that definition had he been able to gaze upon the frozen-food cases at Walmart.) Fifty years later, in *The Physiology of Taste*, the French gastronome Jean Anthelme Brillat-Savarin claimed that cooking made us who we are; by teaching men to use fire, it had "done the most to advance the cause of civilization." More recently, Lévi-Strauss, writing in *The Raw and the Cooked* in 1964, reported that many of the world's cultures entertained a similar view, regarding cooking as the symbolic activity that "establishes the difference between animals and people."

For Lévi-Strauss, cooking was a metaphor for the human transformation of raw nature into cooked culture. But in the years since the publication of *The Raw and the Cooked*, other anthropologists have begun to take quite literally the idea that the invention of cooking might hold the evolutionary key to our humanness. A few years ago, a Harvard anthropologist and primatologist named Richard Wrangham published a fascinating book called *Catching Fire*, in which he

argued that it was the discovery of cooking by our early ancestors—and not tool making or meat eating or language—that set us apart from the apes and made us human. According to the "cooking hypothesis," the advent of cooked food altered the course of human evolution. By providing our forebears with a more energy-dense and easy-to-digest diet, it allowed our brains to grow bigger (brains being notorious energy guzzlers) and our guts to shrink. It seems that raw food takes much more time and energy to chew and digest, which is why other primates our size carry around substantially larger digestive tracts and spend many more of their waking hours chewing—as much as six hours a day.

Cooking, in effect, took part of the work of chewing and digestion and performed it for us outside of the body, using outside sources of energy. Also, since cooking detoxifies many potential sources of food, the new technology cracked open a treasure trove of calories unavailable to other animals. Freed from the necessity of spending our days gathering large quantities of raw food and then chewing (and chewing) it, humans could now devote their time, and their metabolic resources, to other purposes, like creating a culture.

Cooking gave us not just the meal but also the occasion: the practice of eating together at an appointed time and place. This was something new under the sun, for the forager of raw food would have likely fed himself on the go and alone, like all the other animals. (Or, come to think of it, like the industrial eaters we've more recently become, grazing at gas stations and eating by ourselves whenever and wherever.) But sitting down to common meals, making eye contact, sharing food, and exercising self-restraint all served to civilize us. "Around that fire," Wrangham writes, "we became tamer."

Cooking thus transformed us, and not only by making us more sociable and civil. Once cooking allowed us to expand our cognitive capacity at the expense of our digestive capacity, there was no going back: Our big brains and tiny guts now depended on a diet of cooked food. (Raw-foodists take note.) What this means is that cooking is now obligatory—it is, as it were, baked into our biology. What Winston Churchill once said of architecture — "First we shape our buildings, and then they shape us" — might also be said of cooking. First we cooked our food, and then our food cooked us.

If cooking is as central to human identity, biology, and culture as Wrangham suggests, it stands to reason that the decline of cooking in our time would have serious consequences for modern life, and so it has. Are they all bad? Not at all. The outsourcing of much of the work of cooking to corporations has relieved women of what has traditionally been their exclusive responsibility for feeding the family, making it easier for them to work outside the home and have careers. It has headed off many of the conflicts and domestic arguments that such a large shift in gender roles and family dynamics was bound to spark. It has relieved all sorts of other pressures in the household, including longer workdays and overscheduled children, and saved us time that we can now invest in other pursuits. It has also allowed us to diversify our diets substantially, making it possible even for people with no cooking skills and little money to enjoy a whole different cuisine every night of the week. All that's required is a microwave.

These are no small benefits. Yet they have come at a cost that we are just now beginning to reckon. Industrial cooking has taken a substantial toll on our health and well-being. Corporations cook very differently from how people do (which is why we usually call what they do "food processing" instead of cooking). They tend to use much more sugar, fat, and salt than people cooking for people do; they also deploy novel chemical ingredients seldom found in pantries in order to make their food last longer and look fresher than it really is. So it will come as no surprise that the decline in home cooking closely tracks the rise in obesity and all the chronic diseases linked to diet.

The rise of fast food and the decline in home cooking have also undermined the institution of the shared meal, by encouraging us to eat different things and to eat them on the run and often alone. Survey researchers tell us we're spending more time engaged in "secondary eating," as this more or less constant grazing on packaged foods is now called, and less time engaged in "primary eating" — a rather depressing term for the once-venerable institution known as the meal.

The shared meal is no small thing. It is a foundation of family life, the place where our children learn the art of conversation and acquire the habits of civilization: sharing, listening, taking turns, navigating differences, arguing without offending. What have been called the "cultural contradictions of capitalism" — its tendency to undermine the stabilizing social forms it depends on — are on vivid display today at the modern American dinner table, along with all the brightly colored packages that the food industry has managed to plant there.

These are, I know, large claims to make for the centrality of cooking (and not cooking) in our lives, and a caveat or two are in order. For most of us today, the choice is not nearly as blunt as I've framed it: that is, home cooking from scratch versus fast food prepared by corporations. Most of us occupy a place somewhere between those bright poles, a spot that is constantly shifting with the day of the week, the occasion, and our mood. Depending on the night, we might cook a meal from scratch, or we might go out or order in, or we might "sort of" cook. This last option involves availing ourselves of the various and very useful shortcuts that an industrial food economy offers: the package of spinach in the freezer, the can of wild salmon in the pantry, the box of store-bought ravioli from down the street or halfway around the world. What constitutes "cooking" takes place along a spectrum, as indeed it has for at least a century, when packaged foods first entered the kitchen and the definition of "scratch cooking" began to drift. (Thereby allowing me to regard my packaged ravioli with sage-butter sauce as a culinary achievement.) Most of us over the course of a week find ourselves all over that spectrum. What is new, however, is the great number of people now spending most nights at the far end of it, relying for the preponderance of their meals on an industry willing to do *every*thing for them save the heating and the eating. "We've had a hundred years of packaged foods," a food-marketing consultant told me, "and now we're going to have a hundred years of packaged meals."

This is a problem—for the health of our bodies, our families, our communities, and our land, but also for our sense of how our eating connects us to the world. Our growing distance from any direct, physical engagement with the processes by which the raw stuff of nature gets transformed into a cooked meal is changing our understanding of what food is. Indeed, the idea that food has *any* connection to nature or human work or imagination is hard to credit when it arrives in a neat package, fully formed. Food becomes just another commodity, an abstraction. And as soon as that happens we become easy prey for corporations selling synthetic versions of the real thing—what I call edible foodlike substances. We end up trying to nourish ourselves on images.

Now, for a man to criticize these developments will perhaps rankle some readers. To certain ears, whenever a man talks about the importance of cooking, it sounds like he wants to turn back the clock, and return women to the kitchen. But that's not at all what I have in mind. I've come to think cooking is too important to be left to any one gender or member of the family; men and children both need to be in the kitchen, too, and not just for reasons of fairness or equity but because they have so much to gain by being there. In fact, one of the biggest reasons corporations were able to insinuate themselves into this part of our lives is because home cooking had for so long been denigrated as "women's work" and therefore not important enough for men and boys to learn to do.

Though it's hard to say which came first: Was home cooking denigrated because the work was mostly done by women, or did women get stuck doing most of the cooking because our culture denigrated the work? The gender politics of cooking are nothing if not complicated, and probably always have been. Since ancient times, a few special types of cooking have enjoyed considerable prestige: Homer's

warriors barbecued their own joints of meat at no cost to their heroic status or masculinity. And ever since, it has been socially acceptable for men to cook in public and professionally—for money. (Though it is only recently that professional chefs have enjoyed the status of artists.) But for most of history most of humanity's food has been cooked by women working out of public view and without public recognition. Except for the rare ceremonial occasions over which men presided—the religious sacrifice, the July 4 barbecue, the four-star restaurant—cooking has traditionally been women's work, part and parcel of homemaking and child care, and therefore undeserving of serious—i.e., male—attention.

But there may be another reason cooking has not [20] received its proper due. In a recent book called *The Taste for Civilization*, Janet A. Flammang, a feminist scholar and political scientist who has argued eloquently for the social and political importance of "food work," suggests the problem may have something to do with food itself, which by its very nature falls on the wrong side—the feminine side—of the mind-body dualism in Western culture.

"Food is apprehended through the senses of touch, smell, and taste," she points out, "which rank lower on the hierarchy of senses than sight and hearing, which are typically thought to give rise to knowledge. In most of philosophy, religion, and literature, food is associated with body, animal, female, and appetite—things civilized men have sought to overcome with knowledge and reason."

Very much to their loss.

. . .

III.

As I grew steadily more comfortable in the kitchen, I found that, much like gardening, most cooking manages to be agreeably absorbing without being too demanding intellectually. It leaves plenty of mental space for daydreaming and reflection. One of the things I reflected on is the whole question of taking on what in our time has become, strictly speaking, optional, even unnecessary work, work for which I am not particularly gifted or qualified, and at which I may never get very good. This is, in the modern world, the unspoken question that hovers over all our cooking: Why bother?

By any purely rational calculation, even everyday home cooking (much less baking bread or fermenting kimchi) is probably not a wise use of my time. Not long ago, I read an Op-Ed piece in *The Wall Street Journal* about the restaurant industry, written by the couple that publishes the Zagat restaurant guides, which took exactly this line. Rather than coming home after work to cook, the Zagats suggested, "people would be better off staying an extra hour in the office doing what they do well, and letting bargain restaurants do what they do best."

Here in a nutshell is the classic argument for the division of labor, which, as Adam Smith and countless others have pointed out, has given us many of the blessings of civilization. It is what allows me to make a living sitting at this screen writing, while others grow my food, sew my clothes, and supply the energy that lights and heats my house. I can probably earn more in an hour of writing or even teaching than I could save in a whole week of cooking. Specialization is undeniably a powerful social and economic force. And yet it is also debilitating. It breeds helplessness, dependence, and ignorance and, eventually, it undermines any sense of responsibility.

Our society assigns us a tiny number of roles: We're producers of one thing at work, consumers of a great many other things all the rest of the time, and then, once a year or so, we take on the temporary role of citizen and cast a vote. Virtually all our needs and desires we delegate to specialists of one kind or another—our meals to the food industry, our health to the medical profession, entertainment to Hollywood and the media, mental health to the therapist or the drug company, caring for nature to the environmentalist, political action to the politician, and on and on it goes. Before long it becomes hard to imagine doing much of anything for ourselves—anything, that is, except the work we do "to make a living." For

everything else, we feel like we've lost the skills, or that there's someone who can do it better. (I recently heard about an agency that will dispatch a sympathetic someone to visit your elderly parents if you can't spare the time to do it yourself.) It seems as though we can no longer imagine anyone but a professional or an institution or a product supplying our daily needs or solving our problems. This learned helplessness is, of course, much to the advantage of the corporations eager to step forward and do all this work for us.

One problem with the division of labor in our complex economy is how it obscures the lines of connection, and therefore of responsibility, between our everyday acts and their real-world consequences. Specialization makes it easy to forget about the filth of the coal-fired power plant that is lighting this pristine computer screen, or the back-breaking labor it took to pick the strawberries for my cereal, or the misery of the hog that lived and died so I could enjoy my bacon. Specialization neatly hides our implication in all that is done on our behalf by unknown other specialists half a world away.

Perhaps what most commends cooking to me is that it offers a powerful corrective to this way of being in the world—a corrective that is still available to all of us. To butcher a pork shoulder is to be forcibly reminded that this is the shoulder of a large mammal, made up of distinct groups of muscles with a purpose quite apart from feeding me. The work itself gives me a keener interest in the story of the hog: where it came from and how it found its way to my kitchen. In my hands its flesh feels a little less like the product of industry than of nature; indeed, less like a product at all. Likewise, to grow the greens I'm serving with this pork, greens that in late spring seem to grow back almost as fast as I can cut them, is a daily reminder of nature's abundance, the everyday miracle by which photons of light are turned into delicious things to eat.

Handling these plants and animals, taking back the production and the preparation of even just some part of our food, has the salutary effect of making visible again many of the lines of connection that the supermarket and the "home-meal replacement" have succeeded in obscuring, yet of course never actually eliminated. To do so is to take back a measure of responsibility, too, to become, at the very least, a little less glib in one's pronouncements.

Especially one's pronouncements about "the environment," which suddenly begins to seem a little less "out there" and a lot closer to home. For what is the environmental crisis if not a crisis of the way we live? The Big Problem is nothing more or less than the sum total of countless little everyday choices, most of them made by us (consumer spending represents nearly three-quarters of the U.S. economy) and the rest of them made by others in the name of our needs and desires. If the environmental crisis is ultimately a crisis of character, as Wendell Berry told us way back in the 1970s, then sooner or later it will have to be addressed at that level—at home, as it were. In our yards and kitchens and minds.

As soon as you start down this path of thinking, the quotidian* space of the kitchen appears in a startling new light. It begins to matter more than we ever imagined. The unspoken reason why political reformers from Vladimir Lenin to Betty Friedan sought to get women out of the kitchen was that nothing of importance—nothing worthy of their talents and intelligence and convictions—took place there. The only worthy arenas for consequential action were the workplace and the public square. But this was before the environmental crisis had come into view, and before the industrialization of our eating created a crisis in our health. Changing the world will always require action and participation in the public realm, but in our time that will no longer be sufficient. We'll have to change the way we live, too. What that means is that the sites of our everyday engagement with nature— our kitchens, gardens, houses, cars—matter to the fate of the world in a way they never have before.

To cook or not to cook thus becomes a consequential question. Though I realize that is putting the matter a bit too bluntly. Cooking means different things at different times to different people; seldom is it an all-or-nothing proposition. Yet even to cook a few more nights a week than you already do, or to devote a Sunday to making a few meals for the week, or perhaps to try every now and again to make something you only ever expected to buy—even these modest acts will constitute a kind of a vote. A vote for what, exactly? Well, in a world where so few of us are obliged to cook at all anymore, to choose to do so is to lodge a protest against specialization—against the total rationalization of life. Against the infiltration of commercial interests into every last cranny of our lives. To cook for the pleasure of it, to devote a portion of our leisure to it, is to declare our independence from the corporations seeking to organize our every waking moment into yet another occasion for consumption. (Come to think of it, our nonwaking moments as well: Ambien, anyone?) It is to reject the debilitating notion that, at least while we're at home, production is work best done by someone else, and the only legitimate form of leisure is consumption. This dependence marketers call "freedom."

Cooking has the power to transform more than plants and animals: It transforms us, too, from mere consumers into producers. Not completely, not all the time, but I have found that even to shift the ratio between these two identities a few degrees toward the side of production yields deep and unexpected satisfactions. *Cooked* is an invitation to alter, however slightly, the ratio between production and consumption in your life. The regular exercise of these simple skills for producing some of the necessities of life increases self-reliance and freedom while reducing our dependence on distant corporations. Not just our money but our power flows toward them whenever we cannot supply any of our everyday needs and desires ourselves. And it begins to flow back toward us, and our community, as soon as we decide to take some responsibility for feeding ourselves. This has been an early lesson of the rising movement to rebuild local food economies, a movement that ultimately depends for its success on our willingness to put more thought and effort into feeding ourselves. Not every day, not

---

*quotidian: mundane; literally, a daily occurrence.

every meal—but more often than we do, whenever we can.

Cooking, I found, gives us the opportunity, so rare in modern life, to work directly in our own support, and in the support of the people we feed. If this is not "making a living," I don't know what is. In the calculus of economics, doing so may not always be the most efficient use of an amateur cook's time, but in the calculus of human emotion, it is beautiful even so. For is there any practice less selfish, any labor less alienated, any time less wasted, than preparing something delicious and nourishing for people you love?

So let's begin.

At the beginning, with fire.

35

Reading Questions

1. Why, according to Pollan, do so many people enjoy watching others cook or reading about cooking?

2. Explain the connections Pollan makes between "the 'cooking hypothesis'" (par. 8) and advances in human sociability and civility.

3. According to Pollan, what are the effects, both positive and negative, of losing our connection to cooking?

4. Pollan writes briefly about the gender politics of food. What does he mean by this? How has cooking labor traditionally been divided between the sexes?

5. How does the division of labor apply to food preparation? What, according to Pollan, does this division of labor obscure? What benefits might we gain by cooking more food at home?

Rhetoric Questions

6. Pollan argues that cooking "transformed" (11) humans and is central to our identity. What does he mean by this? What type of evidence does he provide to support this argument? Do you find his argument effective?

7. In this excerpt, Pollan admits that some of his claims may seem very large. What caveats does he offer in an effort to hedge these claims? How might you use hedging in your own writing?

8. Pollan's conclusion is a call to action for readers to cook more often. Rhetorically, how does Pollan convince readers to heed his call?

Response and Research Question

9. Consider your own experiences with cooking. What motivates you to cook when you do? What do you get from it, besides nutrition? What keeps you from cooking (more often)?

Ethical Discourse on the Use of Genetically Modified Crops: A Review of Academic Publications in the Fields of Ecology and Environmental Ethics

DANIEL GREGOROWIUS, PETRA LINDEMANN-MATTHIES, AND MARKUS HUPPENBAUER

Daniel Gregorowius, first author of "Ethical Discourse on the Use of Genetically Modified Crops: A Review of Academic Publications in the Fields of Ecology and Environmental Ethics," is an affiliated staff member at the University of Zurich's Center for Ethics–Institute for Biomedical Ethics. Along with Petra Lindemann-Matthies, professor of biology and didactics at the Karlsruhe University of Education, and Markus Huppenbauer, also of the University of Zurich's Center for Ethics, the researchers' study presented here "provides a comprehensive overview of the moral reasoning on the use of GM [genetically modified] crops expressed in academic publications from 1975 to 2008." The article was published in the *Journal of Agricultural and Environmental Ethics* in 2012.

ABSTRACT

The use of genetically modified plants in agriculture (GM crops) is controversially discussed in academic publications. Important issues are whether the release of GM crops is beneficial or harmful for the environment and therefore acceptable, and whether the modification of plants is ethically permissible per se. This study provides a comprehensive overview of the moral reasoning on the use of GM crops expressed in academic publications from 1975 to 2008. Environmental ethical aspects in the publications were investigated. Overall, 113 articles from 15 ecology, environmental ethics, and multidisciplinary science journals were systematically reviewed. Three types of moral concerns were used to structure the normative statements, moral notions, and moral issues found in the articles: concerns addressing consequences of the use of GM crops, concerns addressing the act (the technique itself), and concerns addressing the virtues of an actor. Articles addressing consequences (84%) dealt with general ecological and risk concerns or discussed specific ecological issues about the use of GM crops. Articles addressing the act (57%) dealt with the value of naturalness, the value of biotic entities, and conceptual reductionism, whereas articles addressing the actor (43%) dealt with virtues related to the handling of risks and the application of GM crops. The results of this study may help to structure the academic debate and contribute to a better understanding of moral concerns that are associated with the key aspects of the ethical theories of consequentialism, deontology, and virtue ethics.

INTRODUCTION

The use of genetically modified plants[1] in agriculture (GM crops) is controversially discussed in academic publications. An important aspect of this controversy is whether the release of GM crops in agriculture is beneficial or harmful for the environment and therefore acceptable (Hails 2000; Wolfenbarger and Phifer 2000; Clark and Lehmann 2001). Arguments against GM crops include concerns that transgenes might escape into wild populations (e.g., Pilson and Prendeville 2004; Marvier and Van Acker 2005), that the use of herbicide-resistant GM crops might lead to an increase in spraying herbicides (e.g., Firbank and Forcella 2000; Watkinson et al. 2000), and that toxins produced by GM crops might enter the food web and thus affect non-target organisms (e.g., Marvier

---

[1] A GM plant is an organism whose genetic characteristics have been modified by the insertion of an altered plant gene of the same species (intragenic modification) or a gene from other organisms (transgenic modification) using genetic engineering (Wartburg and Liew 1999).

2002; Harwood et al. 2005). Moreover, concerns have been raised over the spread of transgenic DNA by horizontal gene transfer to unrelated species (e.g., Ho et al. 1999). Arguments in favor of GM crops are, for instance, that they might be more suitable than traditional techniques to control certain pest species (e.g., Cowgill et al. 2004), that the use of herbicide-resistant GM crops might enhance agricultural biodiversity (e.g., Hails 2002), and that GM crops might require less pesticide use and reduce greenhouse gas emissions (e.g., Brookes and Barfoot 2005).

These scientific arguments are concerned with the potential consequences of the use of GM crops. In addition, it has been asked whether the modification of plants is morally permissible *per se* (Reiss and Straughan 2002). The modification of plants will be morally wrong, if it is regarded as an infringement of the integrity or dignity of plants (e.g., Balzer et al. 2000) or an interference with the natural order (e.g., Verhoog et al. 2003). Such concerns address the process of genetic modification itself. Moreover, there are concerns that are related to the character traits of an actor, such as the concerns that genetic modification is a disrespectful offense against the inherent wisdom of nature (e.g., Deane-Drummond 2002) or a sign of human hubris (e.g., Sandler 2007).

Several review articles have summed up and discussed different moral concerns in the debate on GM crops (e.g., Robinson 1999; Shelton et al. 2002; Weaver and Morris 2005). However, none so far provides a comprehensive overview of the ethical discourse in academic publications on ecological *and* environmental ethical aspects. In 2007 and 2008, we thus carried out a systematic literature review of 15 journals (seven ecology journals, five environmental ethics journals, three multidisciplinary science journals). Our aim was not to reflect the different opinions on gene technology, but to structure the academic discourse by relating the morally relevant concerns and issues expressed in the reviewed articles to established ethical theories. The structure will add a new viewpoint to ethical tools that had already been developed for the decision-making in biotechnology (e.g., Busch et al. 2002; Mepham 2008). Our article will also contribute to the current debate on the ethics of genetically modifying plants (e.g., Balzer et al. 2000).

METHODOLOGY

Preparation of the Literature Review

Before the actual literature review, we analyzed 5 moral concerns about GM crops found in various monographs, proceedings, and anthologies about gene technology, plant ethics, risk perception, and related issues (e.g., Runtenberg 1997; Balzer et al. 1998; Rolston 1999; Busch et al. 2002; Heaf and Wirz 2002; Kallhoff 2002; Reiss and Straughan 2002; Ammann et al. 2003; Stewart 2004; Deane-Drummond 2004; Sandler 2007; Stöcklin 2007). Three types of moral concerns were most prominent and thus used to structure the normative statements, moral notions, and moral issues found in the subsequent literature review: (1) concerns about the consequences of the use of GM crops in agriculture (in the following called "*moral concerns addressing consequences*"), (2) concerns about the moral permissibility of genetic modification as such ("*moral concerns addressing the act*"), and (3) concerns about human character traits and attitudes that either contribute to or are influenced by using gene technology ("*moral concerns addressing the actor*").

Relevant Ethical Theories

The three types of moral concerns can be linked to well-known theories in environmental ethics (cf. Brennan and Lo 2008)[2]: (1) moral concerns addressing consequences to *consequentialism*, (2) moral concerns addressing the act to *deontology*, and (3) moral concerns addressing the actor to *virtue ethics*.

---

[2] Besides the three mentioned normative ethical theories, other theories exist that are discussed in context of gene technology, e.g., contractualism. However, contractualism as an ethical theory of social contract could hardly be applied to the ethics of GM crops, because plants cannot be part of a social contract. Therefore, deontology, consequentialism, and virtue ethics were chosen as an underlying basis for our analysis.

CONSEQUENTIALISM

This normative theory states that the rightness or wrongness of an action has to be judged in light of the value of its consequences (von Kutschera 1999; Brink 2006). A consequentialist concept has to define the values that are worth being promoted by the outcome of an action (Brink 2006), e.g., personal pleasure, satisfaction of personal interests, or perfection of personal essential capacities. In order to find the *best* outcome, alternative actions have to be evaluated and harms and benefits of the consequences of one's action have to be weighed against each other. The one action has to be chosen that promotes the defined value in the best way, which means that harms are outweighed by benefits. Consequentialism allows trade-offs between alternative actions with the aim of maximizing the overall good for the greatest number of morally relevant entities,[3] e.g., maximizing the happiness for the greatest number of people.

DEONTOLOGY

This normative theory states that the moral evaluation of an action depends on the action's quality, i.e., certain actions are right or wrong *per se* and thus either permitted or forbidden (von Kutschera 1999; McNaughton and Rawling 2006). The rightness of an action is judged based on the action's compliance with a certain rule or principle for the sake of this rule or principle. The balancing between advantages and disadvantages of an action as in consequentialism is not a prime concern. Moral absolutists would state that, as it is the action itself that is important, a morally good act must be performed even if it has a bad consequence (Herold 2008). In addition to this approach, there is a huge diversity of theories that have been described as deontological (Gaus 2001a; Gaus 2001b). For instance, many deontologists do not agree with a moral absolutism and argue that exceptions should be made to avoid catastrophic outcomes (McNaughton and Rawling 2006). Often, deontological theories include considerations of respect for morally relevant entities for their own sake, and considerations of justice.

[3] Biotic entities can be single organisms, species, ecosystems, or the biotic community.

VIRTUE ETHICS

This normative theory is centered on the individual actor who shows certain virtues. A virtue is a character trait, state, or disposition that allows a person to act in a way that individual and collective well-being is promoted. To be named as a virtue, a character trait has to embody a commitment to an ethical value such as justice or benevolence that will provide a built-in ethical guidance for a moral agent (Annas 2006). Virtue ethics implies that acting morally right is based on the actor's moral personal attitudes and convictions. This means that the value of an action can be judged by the value of the virtues leading to this act (Rippe and Schaber 1998). The aim of a virtuous person is to develop an excellent character. Therefore, in virtue ethics an action will be judged as morally good if the actor shows a virtuous character (Annas 2006). Apart from pure forms of virtue ethics various pluralistic forms exist that allow non-virtue-based reasons that also play a role in deontology or consequentialism (Hursthouse 2003; Crisp 2003).

Although the three classical normative theories 10 form the basis of our analysis, we do not classify these concerns in the literature review as consequentialist, deontological, or virtue concerns. This would be problematic as there exist, for instance, forms of so-called non-teleological consequentialism that evaluate the outcome of an act in applying *deontological criteria* (cf. Birnbacher 2007). This means that the consequences of the act are morally judged by the number of individual rights that are respected or by the number of intrinsically right or wrong actions that result as further consequences from doing the act (Birnbacher 2007). Moreover, many deontologists include consequences in their moral reasoning. However, the normative statements, moral notions, and moral issues found in the articles can be assigned to the key issues of the normative theories, i.e., the moral concerns addressing consequences, the act itself, or the actor.

Review of the Academic Literature

We pre-selected 18 journals from the fields of ecology and environmental ethics as well as multidisciplinary science journals for review (see Table 1). The

Table 1

Overview of Journals Reviewed and Number of Relevant Articles Found (in parentheses)

Ecology journals (15)	IF	Environmental ethics journals (74)	IF	Multidisciplinary science journals (24)	IF
Trends in Ecology & Evolution (5)	14.1	Journal of Agricultural and Environmental Ethics (55)	0.7	Science (8)	30.0
Annual Review of Ecology, Evolution, and Systematics (1)	9.8	Environmental Ethics (2)		Nature (11)	26.7
Ecology Letters (0)	7.6	Environmental Values (9)		Gaia (5)	
Ecological Monographs (0)	7.1	Ethics & the Environment (3)			
Frontiers in Ecology and the Environment (2)	4.8	Ethics in Science and Environmental Politics (5)			
Molecular Ecology (1)	4.8				
Ecology (2)	4.8				
Journal of Applied Ecology (3)	4.5				
Journal of Ecology (0)	4.2				
Ecological Applications (1)	3.5				

Note. If applicable, the impact factor (IF, 2006) is shown.

period reviewed was from 1975 (first conference on the safety of recombinant DNA research in Asilomar, California; see Stewart 2004) to 2008. In the initial selection process, we asked colleagues from biology and philosophy to indicate suitable journals for the literature review. Based on this information, the ten ecology journals with the highest impact factor in 2006[4] (start of study) were selected. As for most journals in environmental ethics no impact factor was available at that time; those journals were chosen that were recommended by *all* colleagues, i.e., five renowned environmental ethics journals dealing specifically with ecological and agricultural topics. In addition, three important and well-renowned multidisciplinary science journals were selected (Table 1).

Environmental ethics journals were selected as we supposed that the ecological and environmental ethical

debate about GM crops will primarily take place in this type of journal. Nevertheless, we also wanted to investigate whether moral concerns about GM crops are raised in ecology journals. As journals in this field focus primarily on mere empirical questions, we selected a larger number of journals to have a greater chance to find relevant articles dealing with ethical concerns. As our literature review focused on the debate on GM crops in an environmental ethics context, journals from the fields of microbiology, biotechnology, or general moral philosophy were not assessed.

Online search engines of the journals or of JSTOR (Journal Storage)[5] were used to identify relevant articles for the literature review. Different types of keywords were used that referred to the genetic nature of the modification, the modification or engineering

[4] The journals were selected in 2007. At this time, the most recent impact factor was from 2006.

[5] JSTOR (Journal Storage) is an online system for archiving academic journals and provides a full-text search of digitized issues of several hundred journals. See Homepage jstor.org.

Table 2

Keywords Used in the Search for Relevant Articles

Keywords 1	Keywords 2	Keywords 3
Gene(s)	Engineering	Plant(s)
Genetic(s)	Modification(s)	Crop(s)
Genetical(ly)	Modify/ied	
Transgene(s)	(Bio)technology/ies	
Transgenic(s)		
GM(O)		

Note. Keywords in the first column were used in all different combinations with those in the second and third columns.

itself, and to plants or crops (Table 2). Keywords of one type were used in all different combinations with those of the other two types. In order not to exclude too many articles, we did not refine our search by using keywords like "value," "respect," "dignity," "integrity," "justice," or "risk." For two journals (*Environmental Ethics, Environmental Values*) no online search engines were available. Articles in these journals were selected by studying titles and abstracts.

Initially, more than 3,300 articles from 18 journals were selected and their titles and abstracts briefly examined. Articles that only briefly mentioned ecological or ethical issues or that were book reviews, editorials, and short news articles were immediately excluded. The remaining 250 original research and review articles were studied in more detail. Those articles that actually dealt with ecological or environmental concerns about GM crops from an ethical point of view were identified. Original research articles in ecology journals that did not address the moral relevance of empirical findings they discussed were excluded from the subsequent analysis. Finally, 113 articles from 15 journals remained.[6]

From the normative statements, moral notions, and issues found in the 113 articles, basic semantic

units were extracted. These basic semantic units could be, for instance, morally qualified empirical findings such as "harmful impact of GM crops on non-target insects," normative statements such as "gene technology is morally problematic because it is playing God," moral notions such as "dignity of plants," or issues that were related to principles or concepts with underlying moral implications such as the precautionary principle, global justice, or sustainable development.[7] Basic semantic units were joined to form classes of similar content. For example, the empirical finding "harmful impact of GM crops on non-target insects" was sorted under the header of "impact on species" and the notion "dignity of plants" under "individual biotic entities." The classes of similar content were finally assigned to certain clusters of moral concerns that fell under the header of one of the three moral concerns mentioned above. In order to assign semantic units to one of these concerns, it was necessary to clarify in which conceptual context they were used in the article (e.g., in context of sustainable agriculture or of the character traits of a person).

Semantic units (and thus the articles using them) that dealt with the outcome of the release of GM crops were grouped under the header of *moral concerns addressing consequences*. Articles that addressed consequences in purely empirical ecological terms (e.g., that there is a certain probability that hybrids between wild plants and GM crops can establish in the landscape) were only included in the analysis, if the moral relevance of the outcome was clearly expressed (e.g., certain consequences of the release of GM crops are beneficial or harmful for biodiversity). Articles that dealt with environmental consequences in general terms (e.g., that there are risks for the environment) were only included if their moral relevance was clarified, for instance, by relating this general concern about consequences to a concern with a normative implication (e.g., sustainability and its underlying concepts of global justice for recent and future generations). However, semantic units that questioned

---

[6] Full list of all reviewed articles is available from author 1.

[7] Only ecological concerns underlying these concepts are relevant for our analysis.

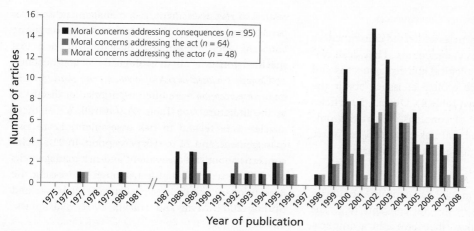

Figure 1. Number of Articles per Year in the Reviewed Period Sorted by the Three Different Types of Moral Concerns

the permissibility of genetic modification *per se* (e.g., arguing against gene technology because of its "unnaturalness") were grouped under the header of *moral concerns addressing the act itself*. Semantic units that were related to personal motivations, states, dispositions, or character traits of a moral agent and thus to a virtue or vice were grouped under the header of *moral concerns addressing the actor*.

RESULTS

Overview of Results

The great majority of articles were published in journals in the field of environmental ethics and almost half of all even in one single journal (*Journal of Agricultural and Environmental Ethics*) (see Table 1). With the exception of two articles (Cohen 1977; Dickson 1980), the reviewed literature was published between 1988 and 2008 (Fig. 1). Since then, growing attention to the use of GM crops in agriculture was apparent in the scrutinized literature. Most articles were published between 1999 and 2008.

Almost all articles from ecology journals and most of those from the other two types dealt with moral concerns addressing consequences (Table 3). However, concerns addressing the act or the actor were also prominent in the literature, especially in journals in the field of environmental ethics.

Table 3

Assignment of Articles That Express a Certain Moral Concern to Three Different Types of Journals

	Number and proportion of articles by journal type		
	Ecology journals (15)	Environmental ethics journals (74)	Multidisciplinary science journals (24)
Moral concerns addressing consequences	14/93.3%	64/86.5%	17/70.8%
Moral concerns addressing the act	5/33.3%	49/66.2%	10/41.7%
Moral concerns addressing the actor	4/26.7%	38/51.4%	6/25.0%

Note. Multiple assignments were possible. List of journals in Table 1.

Moral Concerns Addressing Consequences

More than 80% of all articles addressed consequences of the use of GM crops in agriculture. They dealt primarily with general ecological and risk concerns and also discussed specific ecological issues about the use of gene technology (Table 4). Overall, 50 articles dealt with both types of concerns, 42 articles only with general ecological and risk concerns, and three articles only with specific ecological concerns.

GENERAL ECOLOGICAL AND RISK CONCERNS

Under this header we grouped all concerns about risk assessment principles or general concepts (e.g., the concept of sustainability) that have ethical implications. Moreover, concerns about ecological risks and benefits that did not further specify the morally relevant entities affected by the presence of GM crops were grouped here. Four groups of moral concerns were present in the literature (see Table 4): concerns related to risk assessment, risk management and risk perception, concerns about (scientific) uncertainty, concerns about sustainable development, and unspecified concerns about ecological risk and benefits.

Concerns related to risk assessment, risk management, and risk perception were often mentioned or discussed in the literature (see Table 4). Overall, 62 of these articles were related to risk assessment, 12 to risk management, and 21 to risk perception. In 21 articles concerns about risk assessment and risk management were discussed in detail, most often addressing the precautionary principle (e.g., Carr 2002; Mayer and Stirling 2002; Myhr and Traavik 2002; Skorupinski 2002).

Concerns about (scientific) uncertainty were frequently present (see Table 4), but discussed in detail in only nine articles (Kasanmoentalib 1996; Carr and Levidow 2000; Carr 2002; Myhr and Traavik 2002; Myhr and Traavik 2003a; Howard and Donnelly 2004;

Table 4

Assignment of Articles to Moral Concerns Addressing Consequences of the Use of GM Crops in Agriculture

I. Moral concerns addressing consequences (95/84.1%)

1. General ecological and risk concerns (92/81.4%)	1.1. Concerns related to risk assessment, risk management, and risk perception (65/57.5%)	
	1.2. Concerns about (scientific) uncertainty (43/38.1%)	
	1.3. Concerns about sustainable development (28/24.8%)	
	1.4. Unspecified concerns about ecological risk and benefits (58/51.3%)	1.4.1. Socio-economic concerns (35/31.0%)
		1.4.2. Unspecified risk concerns (31/27.4%)
		1.4.3. Unspecified moral concerns (7/6.2%)
2. Specific ecological concerns (53/46.9%)	2.1. Concerns about the consequences for species and individual plants (29/25.7%)	
	2.2. Concerns about the consequences for ecosystems (36/31.9%)	
	2.3. Concerns about the consequences for the environment in general (10/8.8%)	

Note. Multiple assignments of articles were possible. In parentheses: number and proportion of articles.

Böschen et al. 2006; Jensen 2006; Ramjoué 2007). Articles under this header were mostly published in environmental ethics journals ($n = 27$). Those articles that merely mentioned uncertainty ($n = 34$) did this most often in the context of discussing environmental risk assessment ($n = 29$) and consequences ($n = 24$). Those articles that dealt with uncertainty in detail discussed, for instance, the ethical implications of unknown risks or unpredictable side-effects of GM crops (e.g., Kasanmoentalib 1996) or the concept of "non-knowledge" (Böschen et al. 2006).

Concerns about sustainable development were identified in about a quarter of all articles (see Table 4) and addressed in detail in ten articles. Most articles addressed the contribution of gene technology to the future development of agriculture (e.g., Duvick 1995; Wenz 1999; Pouteau 2000; Snow 2003). The sustainable development of agriculture, including societal questions, was discussed in detail in ecology journals (e.g., Hoffman and Carroll 1995), environmental ethics journals (e.g., Duvick 1995), and multidisciplinary science journals (e.g., Altmann and Ammann 1992).

Unspecified concerns about ecological risk and benefits could be sorted into socio-economic, unspecified risk, and unspecified moral concerns (see Table 4). However, socio-economic concerns were only relevant when they referred to ecological/environmental ethical issues. *Socio-economic concerns* were identified in 35 articles (see Table 4). They included, for instance, concerns about social and environmental justice (e.g., Osborn 2002), concerns about benefits or harms for future generations (e.g., Wambugu 1999), the acknowledgement of "non-scientific" concerns of the public (e.g., Devos et al. 2008), or the establishment of a societal contract with the public (e.g., Bruce 2002a).

Unspecified risk concerns addressed environmental concerns about the release of GM crops that were not further specified. They were identified in 31 articles (see Table 4) and dealt, for instance, with underlying scientific principles for ecologically based risk assessment (e.g., Regal 1994) or invoked the image of farmers as "stewards of the countryside" who are involved in environmental protection (e.g., Hails 2002). The notion "stewards of the countryside" is related to moral concerns about the actor and thus linked to virtue ethics.

Unspecified moral concerns were present in seven articles (see Table 4) that dealt with general normative aspects of consequences of gene technology. These articles discussed the consequentialist implication of the "harm principle" as such (Holtug 2001), referred to potential benefits or harms of GM crops in context of the "future benefits argument"[8] (e.g., Burkhardt 2001), or addressed ecological risks in the light of underlying research paradigms of science (e.g., Scott 2005).

SPECIFIC ECOLOGICAL CONCERNS

Articles under this header were quite common in the assessed literature and mentioned or discussed ecological consequences for individual plants as well as for species, ecosystems, or the environment in general (see Table 4). Consequences in light of the moral status of *individual plants* were of hardly any interest, even in environmental ethics journals. Only two articles (Balzer et al. 2000; Holtug 2001) went into detail about consequences for single plant organisms. Balzer et al. (2000) pointed out that the dignity of individual plants (in this article a consequentialist interpretation is favored) is violated if plants are prevented from performing the functions that members of their species can normally perform. Holtug (2001) addressed the impact of gene technology on individual organisms (in context of the consequentialist "harm principle"), but denied that plants could be violated, because they cannot suffer. Other articles discussed whether the use of GM crops is a violation of the value of *species and ecosystems* (Comstock 1989; Comstock 1990). Articles in this group also stated that certain effects such as gene flow or non-target effects might have (harmful) consequences for the *environment* in general. These articles discussed the impact on agricultural biodiversity in general (e.g., Gura 2001; Hails 2002; Kotschi 2008) or pointed out that farmland biodiversity might be increased by

---

[8] The "future benefits argument" (FBA) is a utilitarian ethical argument offered by proponents of agricultural biotechnology to justify continued research and development in gene technology.

the use of herbicide-resistant crops (e.g., Madsen and Sandøe 2001).

Articles that dealt with specific ecological concerns often discussed ecological risks for certain entities on the background of risk assessment and its underlying principles ($n = 36$), especially the precautionary principle (e.g., Mayer and Stirling 2002; Myhr and Traavik 2002; Howard and Donnelly 2004). They also discussed ecological issues in the context of general concerns about risk and benefits ($n = 36$), for instance, the question whether the use of GM crops and organic farming is incompatible or not (e.g., Bruce 2003). Moreover, unknown risks and unpredictable side-effects of GM crops on certain species or the environment in general were discussed ($n = 24$) (e.g., Kasanmoentalib 1996; Clark and Lehmann 2001; Scott 2005). Articles in this group also addressed specific consequences for the environment invoking the concept of sustainable development ($n = 16$) (e.g., Wenz 1999; Krebs et al. 1999).

Moral Concerns Addressing the Act

Articles under this header addressed concerns about the value of naturalness, the value of biotic entities, and about conceptual reductionism (Table 5). Such concerns were articulated in order to question the permissibility of gene technology *per se*. Overall, 30 articles dealt only with the value of naturalness and six only with the value of biotic entities. Moreover, one article dealt only with conceptual reductionism. However, 27 articles dealt with two different concerns and three articles with all three concerns.

The term "value"—in this context—means "intrinsic value," i.e., that objects or actions have an end in themselves and cannot be reduced to a mere instrumental value for humans (O'Neill et al. 2006). Some environmental philosophers such as Taylor (1986) distinguished between intrinsic value and inherent worth. In the literature assessed both notions were used in the same sense. The term "intrinsic value," of course, is not limited to moral concerns addressing the act.

Table 5

Assignment of Articles to Moral Concerns Addressing the Act of Genetic Modification

II. Moral concerns addressing the act (64/56.6%)		
1. Concerns about the value of naturalness (56/49.6%)	1.1. Nature as a safety mechanism (31/27.4%)	
	1.2. Nature as a guiding principle (29/25.7%)	1.2.1. Nature as a given order (18/15.9%)
		1.2.2. Nature as an autonomous identity (19/16.8%)
	1.3. Undefined concerns (9/8.0%)	
2. Concerns about the value of biotic entities (27/23.9%)	2.1. Intrinsic value of holistic biotic entities (22/19.5%)	2.1.1. Intrinsic value of species (11/9.7%)
		2.1.2. Intrinsic value of ecosystems (5/4.4%)
		2.1.3. Intrinsic value of the biotic community (14/12.4%)
	2.2. Intrinsic value of individual biotic entities (5/4.4%)	
	2.3. Undefined concerns (3/2.7%)	
3. Concerns about conceptual reductionism (11/9.7%)		

Note. Multiple assignments of articles were possible. In parentheses: number and proportion of articles.

Naturalness as a value implies that nature and its order is valuable and good *per se*. Thus, all forms of genetic modification are unnatural and therefore morally wrong. None of the articles from ecology journals or multidisciplinary science journals explicitly referred to the value of naturalness. Overall, 15 articles from the environmental ethics journals discussed concerns about the value of naturalness as such (e.g., Katz 1993; Karafyllis 2003; Verhoog et al. 2003; Siipi 2008). Articles in ecology journals only indirectly addressed concerns about naturalness. Authors argued, for instance, that gene technology just simulates a natural process (Tiedje et al. 1989). They stated that barriers that are crossed by biotechnology are comparable to those constantly crossed in nature (Tiedje et al. 1989). It was also discussed whether gene technology is unnatural in the sense that it is the ultimate manifestation of the cybernetic control of humans (Elliott and Cole 1989).

Nature as a safety mechanism was addressed in 31 articles (see Table 5). This type of concern implies that "nature knows best," because nature is the result of a long evolutionary process (cf. Reiss and Straughan 2002). Therefore, the inherent safety mechanisms of nature should be protected as otherwise there would be a violation of natural evolution (Madsen et al. 2002). The intrinsic value of nature lies in the inherent safety mechanisms of natural evolution and these mechanisms would no longer function as an insurance against disastrous consequences if humans disturb them (e.g., Madsen et al. 2002). The safety net of nature is helpful in situations where humans' assumptions about the functioning of nature might be proved wrong (e.g., Karafyllis 2003). As far as the emphasis is on the avoidance of disastrous consequences, the concept of nature as a safety mechanism can be regarded as a "moral concern addressing consequences" and grouped there. However, if nature as a safety mechanism is subsumed under the header of "moral concerns addressing the act," the intrinsic value of the safety mechanism lies in nature as such, which invokes that the violation of this intrinsic value is morally problematic *per se*.

Nature as a guiding principle was addressed in 29 articles (see Table 5). These articles dealt either with *nature as a given order* or with *nature as an autonomous identity*. The concept of *nature as a given order* defines nature as a non-human domain or as God's order that humans have to respect. The more human actions or products resemble natural actions or products, the more natural they are, and the more respect humans show for the natural order (Siipi 2008). The natural order, which has an intrinsic value, can be understood in terms of harmony and balance (Lammerts van Bueren and Struik 2005), self-realization (Katz 1993), God's creation (Comstock 1989), or "something out there" that humans must obey and should not challenge (Madsen et al. 2002). The genetic modification of crops is therefore an infringement of the given order and thus morally wrong.

The concept of *nature as an autonomous identity* states that an inherent purpose can be ascribed to nature as a whole or to single natural entities. When humans intervene in nature and create artifacts, they destroy the autonomy of nature by imposing a system of domination (Katz 1993). By inserting foreign genes into a plant's genome, borders of species are crossed and their identity is infringed. GM crops are therefore unnatural and, in consequence, morally wrong. Human beings are called to respect the autonomy of nature. The concept of nature as an autonomous identity can be linked to the virtue of appreciation (cf. Katz 1993).

Articles under this header regarded gene technology as a violation of the intrinsic value of biotic entities, i.e., a disrespect to organisms and life in general. The term "intrinsic value" was either mentioned directly or indirectly by using terms like "integrity" or "dignity." Integrity is defined as the intrinsic value of a biotic entity that accomplishes its natural aim (Lammerts van Bueren and Struik 2005), which includes both individual and holistic entities, whereas dignity is assigned only to individual organisms (Balzer et al.

[9] The term "biotic entities" refers to individual organisms as well as to species, ecosystems, or the biotic community.

2000).[10] No one article in the ecology journals or the multidisciplinary science journals dealt with concerns about the value of biotic entities. In six articles published in the *Journal of Agricultural and Environmental Ethics* and in two articles published in the journal *Environmental Values* concerns about the value of biotic entities were discussed in detail. Among these articles, three dealt with the concepts "integrity" and "dignity" (Balzer et al. 2000; Melin 2004; Lammerts van Bueren and Struik 2005), three with the concept of "integrity" (Verhoog et al. 2003; Dobson 1995; Westra 1998), and one with the concept of "dignity" (Heeger 2000). Another article discussed the intrinsic value of animals and also mentioned that of plants (Verhoog 1992).

The *intrinsic value of holistic biotic entities* was addressed in 22 articles (see Table 5). In these articles, an intrinsic value is ascribed to species, (agricultural) ecosystems, or the whole biotic community. The *intrinsic value of species* lies in the "wholeness" of species, their ability to fulfill species-specific characteristics, and their being in balance with the environment (Lammerts van Bueren and Struik 2005). Every human action that hinders species to fulfill their species-specific characteristics would be morally wrong. Overall, 11 articles addressed such concerns about the intrinsic value of species (see Table 5).

Only five articles addressed the *intrinsic value of ecosystems* (see Table 5), which lies in the harmony and balance of their biotic and abiotic elements (Verhoog et al. 2003; Deckers 2005; Lammerts van Bueren and Struik 2005). Humans should follow the "ecological knowledge of nature" in cultivating the land (Verhoog et al. 2003). As "ecological integrity" results from natural, evolutionary processes, human-induced interferences such as gene technology must be banned (Westra 1998).

The *intrinsic value of the biotic community* was expressed in 14 articles (see Table 5). This value lies in the ability of life for self-regulation in order to ac-

complish a certain inherent purpose (Lammerts van Bueren and Struik 2005). In this context, integrity is understood as the state of "wholeness" or "completeness" of life allowing it to perform all the functions that are characteristic for the biotic community. Verhoog (1992) discussed this concept in terms of something (recognizable by phenomena such as homeostasis, stability, balance, and equilibrium) that can be disturbed by human actions. Dobson (1995) understood the intrinsic value of the biotic community in a similar way, stating that genetic engineering could be problematic because it is a technology that expresses a worldview of human mastery over the non-human world.[11] Overall, eight articles dealing with the value of the biotic community addressed the "land ethics" and cited the well-known notion about the "integrity, stability, and beauty of the biotic community" (Comstock 1989; Verhoog 1992; Dobson 1995; Saner 2000). This integrity can be irreversibly disturbed by human actions such as gene technology (Verhoog 1992).

The *intrinsic value of individual biotic entities* was addressed in five articles (see Table 5). Three articles dealt with both the *concept of integrity* and the *concept of dignity*. One article referred only to the *concept of integrity* and stated that integrity can only be guaranteed if the specific phenotype of an individual plant is in balance with its environment (e.g., Lammerts van Bueren and Struik 2005). Another article pointed to the *concept of dignity*: Balzer et al. (2000) critically discussed a deontological interpretation of dignity and also an interpretation based on the concept of the "telos" (aim of an organism) that corresponds with the genetic make-up of an organism. This interpretation defines a plant's well-being as the potential of the individual (characterized by its genetic make-up) to develop to maturity. According to these meanings of dignity, changing the genome through genetic modification would collide with the integrity or dignity of an organism. This is in line with a deontological interpretation of dignity or integrity

[10] Balzer et al. (2000) discussed different meanings and understanding of dignity, including deontological meanings. However, they favored a consequentialist meaning.

[11] Concerns about the human mastery over the non-human world are also topics within virtue concerns.

and was thus grouped under the header of "moral concerns addressing the act." However, Balzer et al. (2000) favored a consequentialist interpretation of the "dignity of plants."

CONCERNS ABOUT CONCEPTUAL REDUCTIONISM

Articles under this header addressed the reductionist perspective in handling gene technology. Two different types of reductionism can be distinguished (Woese 2004): a *methodological reductionism* that is the mode of scientific analysis, and a *conceptual reductionism* that is part of a worldview stating that the whole is no more than the sum of its parts. Concerns about conceptual reductionism represent a fundamental critique of the materialistic worldview and of the treatment of biotic entities only as a means to an end and not as ends in themselves. For opponents of gene technology, such a conceptual reductionism is inherent in the genetic modification of plants. In consequence, they condemn gene technology *per se*.

Concerns about conceptual reductionism were rarely expressed in the literature (see Table 5). Articles that dealt with the concern often addressed naturalness or the intrinsic value of organisms. For instance, one article stated that in a "process of reduction" the distinctions between the living and the non-living and between the "nature" of plants, animals, and humans disappears at the molecular level (Verhoog 1992). As the idea of "crossing species barriers" seems to be irrelevant at the molecular level, humanity is getting further and further away from nature as given to humans (Verhoog 1992). This "reduction of life to the digital code of DNA" is critically related to the fictional character of Frankenstein (Scott 2000) and thus to concerns about the value of naturalness. Moreover, the critique of reductionism was addressed in context of the perception of risks and scientific uncertainties about risks (e.g., Verhoog et al. 2003; Deckers 2005). Linked to this conceptual reductionism were concerns about the moral status of biotic entities (Verhoog et al. 2003; Deckers 2005).

Moral Concerns Addressing the Actor

Articles under this header referred to virtues related to the handling of risks or to the application of GM crops (Table 6). Overall, 26 articles dealt only with virtues related to the handling of risks, 19 only with virtues related to the application of GM crops, and three with both types. As concerns addressing the actor are linked to a person's character traits and

Table 6

Assignment of Articles to Moral Concerns Addressing the Actor

III. Moral concerns addressing the actor (48/42.5%)		
1. Virtues related to the handling of risks (29/25.7%)	1.1. Virtues related to trust in actors to handle risks (22/19.5%)	1.1.1. Trustworthiness
	1.2. Virtues related to responsible behavior and awareness of consequences (12/10.6%)	1.2.1. Responsibility
2. Virtues related to the application of GM crops (22/19.5%)	2.1. Virtues related to temperance in application of GM crops (16/6.4%)	2.1.1. Humility (11/9.7%)
		2.1.2. Wisdom (6/5.3%)
	2.2. Virtues related to integration into nature (8/3.2%)	2.2.1. Care (5/4.4%)
		2.2.2. Justice (4/3.5%)
	2.3. Virtues related to respect for non-human life (7/2.8%)	2.3.1. Appreciation

Note. Multiple assignments of articles were possible. In parentheses: number and proportion of articles.

want to define what constitute a "good life" of humans, they are part of virtue ethics.

Most articles did not discuss virtues as such (*n* = 34), but dealt indirectly with concerns about the actor by speaking of trust, precaution, or responsibility in handling risks (e.g., Altmann and Ammann 1992; Segal 2001). Nevertheless, in 14 articles concerns about the actor were addressed in detail: five articles discussed different types of virtue concerns (Bruce 2002b; Deane-Drummond 2002; Pascalev 2003; Sandler 2004; Kirkham 2006) and nine articles dealt with certain virtues such as trustworthiness, precaution, respect, or humility (Scott 2000; Mayer and Stirling 2002; Myhr and Traavik 2002; Bruce 2002a; Bruce 2003; Vogel 2003; Scott 2003; Munnichs 2004; Paula and Birrer 2006).

VIRTUES RELATED TO THE HANDLING OF RISKS
Virtues related to the handling of risks are trustworthiness and responsibility (see Table 6). The virtue of *trustworthiness* referred to trust (or distrust) of the public toward scientific researchers, regulatory procedures, as well as political and economic institutions (e.g., Scott 2003; Munnichs 2004). The virtue of *responsibility* referred to a general awareness of humans of the outcomes of their work and research (Altmann and Ammann 1992), care for the environment (Myhr and Traavik 2002), and care for the future (Deblonde and du Jardin 2005). Virtues related to the handling of risks are only indirectly dealing with environmental concerns as they focus on how scientists should behave and what the public (as consumers) can expect from sciences, politics, and the market. Thus, they are linked to socio-economic questions.

VIRTUES RELATED TO THE APPLICATION OF GM CROPS
Virtues referring to the application of GM crops were humility, wisdom, care, justice, and appreciation (see Table 6). The virtues *humility* and *wisdom* call for *temperance in the application of GM crops*. Humility acknowledges that humans can never entirely know the outcomes of their actions (Vogel 2003). This virtue is morally required for a proper understanding of humans' relationship with the natural environment (Sandler 2004) and implies a certain handling

of scientific procedures and knowledge (Mayer and Stirling 2002). Seen this way, the precautionary principle embodies humility regarding scientific procedures and knowledge (Mayer and Stirling 2002). The virtue of wisdom acknowledges that humans have to interact cautiously with their environment to avoid a domination of nature. Wisdom is closely related to the virtues of prudence, temperance, precaution, and practical wisdom (Deane-Drummond 2002).[12]

The virtues of *care* and *justice* apply to motivations and attitudes concerning humans' *integration into nature*. Care is related, for instance, to questions regarding the technological development (Atkinson 2002) or the sustainable approach in agriculture (Osborn 2002; Verhoog et al. 2003). The virtue of justice is understood as a disposition that takes into account the importance of non-human species as part of the overall ecological community (e.g., Deane-Drummond 2002). Justice is said to embody questions dealing with the precautionary principle (Deane-Drummond 2002; Osborn 2002).

The virtue of *appreciation* is *related to the respect for non-human life*, e.g., the respect for the abilities and vulnerabilities of non-human life (Wenz 1999), the respect for the existence of individual life-projects and goals (Westra 1998), or the reverence for the autonomy of nature as a whole (Katz 1993; Dobson 1995). As appreciation is dealing with the relationship of humans with nature, it is linked to deontological questions concerning the value of nature and its biotic entities (cf. Westra 1998).

DISCUSSION

Overview of the Academic Debate on GM Crops

We have identified three types of moral concerns in the academic debate on GM crops: (1) *moral concerns about the consequences* of the modification or of the outcomes of GM crops in the environment

---

[12] We agree with Celia Deane-Drummond (2002), who states that the virtue of wisdom includes the virtues of prudence, temperance, precaution, and practical wisdom. Therefore, as long as these virtues were mentioned, they were considered as the virtue of wisdom.

(associated with *consequentialist ethics*), (2) *moral concerns addressing the act* of modifying the genome of plants *per se* (associated with *deontological ethics*), and (3) *moral concerns addressing the actor's character traits and attitudes* affected by applying gene technology (associated with *virtue ethics*).

The ethical literature on gene technology often conceives the discussion as a disagreement between two moral concerns: consequentialist and deontological concerns (e.g., Runtenberg 1997; Reiss and Straughan 2002). However, our study shows that virtue concerns were also present in the debate, especially since 2001. This might reflect the growing interest in virtue concerns in environmental ethics in general (cf. Deane-Drummond 2004; Sandler and Cafaro 2004; Sandler 2007). Nevertheless, our results have to be taken with care: they might not be representative for the entire academic debate on moral concerns about the release of GM crops in agriculture as we deliberately selected certain types of journals.

Moral Concerns about the Use of GM Crops in the Academic Debate

Moral concerns addressing consequences invoked rarely 50 the impact on individual plants (but see Balzer et al. 2000). Holtug (2001) stated that in context of the "harm principle," which in his opinion has to be the moral basis for the regulation of GM food, holistic entities such as biotic communities and plants as non-sentient entities are often excluded as they cannot suffer. However, in recent years it is discussed how to ascribe a morally relevant value to certain characteristics of plants in a consequentialist sense. One example is the "value of flourishing"[13] by Kallhoff (2002). This concept implies that it is in the "interest" of a plant to develop and grow according to its species-specific characteristics, complete its life cycle, and flourish in a stress-free environment. In a similar way, Attfield (2003) ascribed an intrinsic value to individual plants, including GM crops, as they can grow, photosynthesize and respire, reproduce and self-repair.

[13] In German: "*Wert des pflanzlichen Gedeihens*."

The lack of articles dealing with the intrinsic value of individual organisms in a consequentialist way might be due to our focus on plants. Plants have no interests as they lack the ability to feel and express pain, which is crucial for sentientist* consequentialism** to assign the intrinsic value to a biotic entity. Reiss and Straughan (2002) pointed out that questions about the moral status of organisms are more important in the debate on transgenic animals. Regarding transgenic plants, socio-economic questions are said to be more prominent (cf. Reiss and Straughan 2002; Gonzalez 2007). This was also reflected by our finding that articles referring to general environmental consequences of GM crops often dealt with questions concerning socio-economic aspects (e.g., Goga and Clementi 2002; Bruce 2002; Bruce 2003). Even articles in natural sciences journals (*Science* and *Nature*) dealt with socio-economic concerns such as concerns about food security and living conditions of farmers in developing countries (e.g., Serageldin 1999; Wambugu 1999).

General ecological concerns were often directed to risk assessment and risk management. This can be explained by the controversial debate on the underlying principles of risk assessment, following the adoption of the Cartagena Protocol in 2000 (cf. Nisbet and Huge 2007). Since then, the ethical implications of the precautionary principle and of the concept of substantial equivalence[14] were broadly discussed (e.g., Pouteau 2000). This is also reflected in the increasing number of articles addressing risk assessment (especially the precautionary principle) after the turn of the century in our literature review (e.g., Mayer and Stirling 2002; Skorupinski 2002; Myhr and Traavik 2003a; Myhr and Traavik 2003b). One element of this discourse [involves] concerns about (scientific)

sentientist: someone who believes that other creatures have sentience, or distinct thoughts.
**consequentialism:* the theory that an action should be judged based on its consequences.
[14] Sustainable equivalence is a concept that states that GM food should be considered the same as conventional food if it shows the same characteristics and composition as the conventional food.

uncertainty that are frequently addressed in the literature (e.g., Kasanmoentalib 1996; Carr and Levidow 2000; Myhr and Traavik 2002; Böschen et al. 2006). Uncertainty is closely related to questions about the acceptability of certain risks, the trade-off between benefits and harms, and scientific research or risk assessment as such. In this context, questions arise with which scientists are unfamiliar, for example, how to define acceptable ecological risks, how to address different risk perceptions in a liberal society (e.g., Jensen 2006), or how to deal with different approaches in risk assessment in Europe and in the United States (e.g., Ramjoué 2007).

General ecological concern not only addressed risk assessment, but also the future of agriculture and the possible contribution of gene technology to a sustainable development. In articles discussing sustainable agriculture most often the safety of GM crops, the value of naturalness (used especially in context of organic farming), or socio-economic questions like the market concentration in global seed industry are addressed. However, the contribution of gene technology to a sustainable agriculture is a controversially discussed concern in the literature, i.e., whether gene technology is a sustainable approach or not. This controversy might be based on different understandings and definitions of sustainable agriculture. This is especially true if only organic farming is considered as a sustainable form of agriculture (cf. Verhoog 1997).

Moral concerns addressing the act, in particular those about naturalness, were common in the reviewed literature. Using naturalness in a normative sense either for or against gene technology is seen as a "naturalistic fallacy" (e.g., criticized by Comstock 1989 and Myskja 2006). A naturalistic fallacy is committed whenever a statement or argument attempts to prove that something *is* in a certain way natural and therefore *ought to be* that way. It has also been criticized that concerns about naturalness are quite meaningless, as there are many different meanings and types of naturalness (Cooley and Goreham 2004; Siipi 2008).

Concerns about the value of biotic entities were less prominent in the reviewed literature than concerns about the value of naturalness. Most often, an intrinsic value was assigned to holistic biotic entities such as species, ecosystems, or the biotic community, whereas only few articles assigned an intrinsic value to individual plants. Even among environmental ethicists no consensus exists whether an intrinsic value can be assigned to individual plants (e.g., Melin 2004).

Moral concerns addressing the actor were linked in several articles to moral concerns addressing the act (pointing to deontological ethics) (e.g., Katz 1993; Westra 1998; Kirkham 2006). For instance, notions such as "vexing nature" or "playing God," which are used in context of act-orientated concerns, also have virtue-based implications invoking questions about the purpose of technology and the place of humanity within the natural environment (Kirkham 2006). Among actor-based concerns, *virtues that are related to the handling of risks* were important. Most often, the virtues of trustworthiness (of science as well as of politics and the market) and responsibility were mentioned. These virtues imply that actors are concerned about their actions and act in ways that promote or maintain environmental goods or values. When focusing on risks and benefits, i.e., on the outcome of gene technology, virtues like responsibility can be linked to concerns about consequences.

In the last decade, virtues such as humility, wisdom, care, justice, and appreciation have received increasing attention in environmental ethics. These virtues, which we grouped under the header of "*virtues related to the application of GM crops,*" are justified by the worth of living organisms and humans' relationship with nature (cf. Sandler 2007). Because living organisms are valuable, humans have to behave prudently and respectfully toward them. Seen in this way, virtues related to the application of GM crops deal with the respect for living organisms and can overlap with act-orientated concerns. For example, the virtue of humility and the closely related virtue of caution can be linked to the concept of ecological integrity (Westra 1998). Moreover, virtues related to the application of GM crops can be linked to concerns addressing consequences. For instance, the precautionary principle with its aim to minimize ecological risks is based on consequentialist concerns. However, precaution is also related to attitudes of an actor, especially to the virtues of wisdom and care (cf. Deane-Drummond 2002; Mayer and Stirling 2002). To have such a virtue-based interpretation of the precautionary principle in mind is helpful to avoid misunderstandings in the public debate.

Virtue concerns can be linked to other types of moral concerns, i.e., concerns addressing the act and concerns addressing consequences. Moral concerns addressing the actor can thus help to overcome the often presupposed dichotomy of consequentialist and deontological concerns in the debate on the use of GM crops. Pluralistic forms of virtue ethics theories exist that integrate non-virtue-based reasons that play a role in deontology or consequentialism (Crisp 2003). For instance, it was stated by Hursthouse (2003) that virtue ethics appear to stand "shoulder to shoulder" with deontology. With the focus on the individual person's character traits, virtue ethics add a new viewpoint to the overall ethical debate, as the actor is not the prime focus in consequentialism or deontology.

In the reviewed literature, environmental concerns were closely linked to socio-economic concerns in several articles, for example, to questions about ecological and social justice or to the trustworthiness of science, politics, and the market (e.g., Wambugu 1999; Scott 2000; Scott 2003; Goga and Clementi 2002; Bruce 2002a; Bruce 2003). This shows that the debate about the ecological and environmental ethical aspects of GM crops is also a debate about the role of science, the role of politics and the market, and the role of laypersons in public as consumers. It is therefore doubtful whether the environmental debate on GM crops can be held separately from the debate on socio-economic aspects or whether they are mutually dependent.

Comparison of the Academic and Laypersons' Debate on the Use of GM Crops

Moral concerns of laypersons play an important role in the public debate on GM crops. Although moral concerns and arguments similar to those expressed by academics are put forward by laypersons in the public debate, laypersons' concerns do not only reflect scientific arguments associated with gene technology (cf. Harlander 1991), but also more fundamental personal beliefs (Hoban et al. 1992). Moreover, the risk perception between laypersons and scientific experts (in the field of biological sciences) differs in certain points: experts significantly and systematically perceive biotechnology as less risky than laypersons do (Savadori et al. 2004; Sjöberg 2008) and consider its applications in food production as more useful (Savadori et al. 2004). However, despite these dissimilarities *moral concerns addressing consequences* are prominent in the public debate on GM crops or GM food, too (e.g., Frewer et al. 1997a; Saba et al. 1998; Gaskell 2000; Gaskell et al. 2000; Magnusson and Koivisto Hursti 2002; Amin et al. 2007; Chen and Li 2007; Henson et al. 2008).

Moral concerns addressing the act are often invoked in the moral reasoning of laypersons (Hansen et al. 2003; Frewer et al. 2004; Siegrist 2008; Tanner et al. 2008). This is especially true for concerns about naturalness: about 65% of the participants in the 2002 Eurobarometer survey agreed that GM food threatens the natural order of things (Peters and Sawicka 2007). Concerns about the loss of naturalness have been recognized as important constituents of unease among the public (e.g., Reif and Melich 1996; Frewer et al. 1997b; Melich 2000). Naturalness concerns are often addressed by the public to express a desire for a world untouched by humans (Dürnberger 2008). However, laypersons are less concerned about the infringement of the intrinsic value in modifying plants than in the modification of animals (cf. Frewer et al. 1997a; Kinsey and Senauer 1997; Ganiere et al. 2006). In the academic debate, the moral status of plants appears to be less important.

In contrast to concerns addressing consequences of the act itself, *moral concerns addressing the actor* were rarely found in recent studies on the laypersons' perception of gene technology. However, several surveys have shown that trustworthiness is crucial for laypersons (Brown and Ping 2003; Frewer 2003; Gaskell et al. 2003; Hansen et al. 2003; Frewer et al. 2004; Savadori et al. 2004; Chen and Li 2007; Siegrist 2008).

Therefore, virtues essential for handling risks are important for initiating and establishing a dialogue between academic experts and laypersons.

Similar to academic experts, laypersons base their moral reasoning about GM crops on concerns about perceived risks, unnaturalness, and personal ethical beliefs. However, conflicts within the public about GM crops are not likely to be solved by more knowledge about potential ecological risks. These conflicts are deeply rooted in personal ideas about life and nature, i.e., deontological and virtue concerns, which are important for the moral reasoning of laypersons, as recent psychological research showed (Tanner et al. 2008). Social and psychological scientists could help to identify factors that motivate and lead people to certain attitudes toward gene technology. Knowing the motivations of others makes it easier to take their position seriously, accepting that they do not act in bad faith but simply against a different normative backdrop. In this regard, ethicists are important for the dialogue between academic experts and laypersons in the public: they can discuss how moral concerns are used by laypersons and how a sound and well-grounded moral reasoning has to be established. Moreover, natural scientists can contribute to the debate with their expertise on ecological concerns. Knowledge of risks and benefits is fundamental for moral reasoning, especially for consequentialist ethics.

CONCLUSIONS

The literature review showed that there is no single dichotomy between moral concerns addressing consequences and the act, i.e., consequentialist and deontological concerns. Moral concerns addressing the actor, i.e., virtue concerns, were also present and linked with the other two concerns (cf. Crisp 2003; Hursthouse 2003). Environmental virtue ethics with its focus on the individual actor could help to bridge the split between deontological and consequentialist concerns. Psychological research on act choices (Tanner et al. 2008) indicates that deontological and consequentialist concerns are not mutually exclusive in the reasoning of laypersons: different types of moral concerns are often intertwined in laypersons' decision-making on act choices.

The perception of gene technology by academic experts, especially by natural scientists, differs from that of laypersons. The moral reasoning of academic experts is well founded on ecological concerns; their arguments are carefully considered and critically discussed. However, among laypersons, ecological concerns are more often associated with personal lifestyles and individual preferences (Korthals 2001; Meijboom et al. 2003). Ethics as the discipline that analyzes and justifies moral reasoning could help to take into account moral concerns of the general public in the debate on the use of GM crops by establishing an "empirically informed ethics" (cf. Musschenga 2005). Empirically informed ethics combines doing empirical research with philosophical analysis and reflection (Musschenga 2005). It could improve the context sensitivity in the debate on GM crops, for example, by addressing the personal lifestyles of laypersons. As consumers, laypersons are not only concerned with risk and safety of GM crops, but also follow personal preferences in their decisions (Korthals 2001). Ethicists could bridge the gap between the moral perception of (natural) scientists and laypersons with the help of an empirically informed ethics.

In moral philosophy, models are used that help to structure and analyze a moral debate. Moreover, practical tools for decision-making processes that integrate different moral concerns are provided. Such models and tools were developed, for instance, by Fraser (2001), Busch et al. (2002), Forsberg (2007), and Mepham (2008). The aim of such tools is to support a systematic public deliberation about the ethical aspects of agricultural biotechnologies (Beekman and Brom 2007). However, they rarely include virtue concerns and, if so, only address the virtue of justice. The present results exemplify the relevance of different virtues in the ecological discourse on the release of GM crops that should be integrated in the respective models and tools. They can help to overcome the focus in the debate on deontology and consequentialism. An example of how to integrate virtue concerns is the tool for ethical decision-making by Bleisch and Huppenbauer (2011).

Our study is the first to provide a comprehensive overview of the moral reasoning expressed in academic publications on the use of GM crops. It shows which types of moral concerns are expressed in the debate, how they are mutually linked, and could thus contribute to a better understanding of the academic debate on the release of GM crops. It would be helpful to investigate the public debate in the same way. To know the various types of moral concerns and their different usage in the academic as well as in the public debate would be a crucial starting point to develop a fruitful dialogue between sciences and the general public.

ACKNOWLEDGMENTS

We would like to thank the University Research Priority Programme Ethics (Universitärer Forschungsschwerpunkt Ethik) of the Ethics-Center, University of Zurich, for financial support, and Bernhard Schmid, Roger Busch, Marc Hall, and Oliver Jütersonke for providing valuable comments on the original manuscript. We would also like to thank the reviewers for helpful comments on a previous version of this manuscript.

REFERENCES

Altmann, M., & Ammann, K. (1992). Gentechnologie im gesellschaftlichen Spannungsfeld: Züchtung transgener Kulturpflanzen. *GAIA, 1*(4), 204–213.

Amin, L., Jahi, J., Nor, A. R., Osman, M., & Mahadi, N. M. (2007). Public acceptance of modern biotechnology. *Asia Pacific Journal of Molecular Biology and Biotechnology, 15*(2), 39–51.

Ammann, K., Jacot, Y., & Braun, R. (Eds.). (2003). *Methods for risk assessment of transgenic plants, IV. Biodiversity and biotechnology.* Basel: Birkhäuser Verlag.

Annas, J. (2006). Virtue ethics. In D. Copp (Ed.), *The Oxford handbook of ethical theory* (pp. 515–536). New York: Oxford University Press.

Atkinson, D. (2002). Agriculture—reconciling ancient tensions. *Ethics in Science and Environmental Politics, 2*(2002), 52–58.

Attfield, R. (2003). *Environmental ethics.* Cambridge: Polity Press.

Balzer, P., Rippe, K. P., & Schaber, P. (1998). *Menschenwürde vs. Würde der Kreatur.* München: Alber.

Balzer, P., Rippe, K. P., & Schaber, P. (2000). Two concepts of dignity for humans and non-human organisms in the context of genetic engineering. *Journal of Agricultural and Environmental Ethics, 13*(1), 7–27.

Beekman, V., & Brom, F. W. A. (2007). Ethical tools to support systematic public deliberations about the ethical aspects of agricultural biotechnologies. *Journal of Agricultural and Environmental Ethics, 20*(1), 3–12.

Birnbacher, D. (2007). *Analytische Einführung in die Ethik.* Berlin and New York: Walter de Gruyter.

Bleisch, B., & Huppenbauer, M. (2011). *Ethische Entscheidungsfindung. Ein Handbuch für die Praxis.* Zürich: Versus Verlag.

Böschen, S., Kastenhofer, K., Marschall, L., Rust, I., Soentgen, J., & Wehling, P. (2006). Scientific cultures of non-knowledge in the controversy over genetically modified organisms (GMO). *GAIA, 15*(4), 294–301.

Brennan, A., & Lo, Y.-S. (2008). Environmental ethics. In *Stanford Encyclopedia of Philosophy,* first published Mon Jun 3, 2002; substantive revision Thu Jan 3, 2008, plato.stanford.edu/entries/ethics-environmental/.

Brink, D. O. (2006). Some forms and limits of consequentialism. In D. Copp (Ed.), *The Oxford handbook of ethical theory* (pp. 380–423). New York: Oxford University Press.

Brookes, G., & Barfoot, P. (2005). GM crops: The global economic and environmental impact—the first nine years 1996–2004. *AgBioForum, 8*(2&3), 187–196.

Brown, J. L., & Ping, Y. (2003). Consumer perception of risk associated with eating genetically engineered soybeans is less in the presence of a perceived consumer benefit. *Journal of the American Dietetic Association, 103*(2), 208–214.

Bruce, D. (2002a). A social contract for biotechnology: Shared visions for risky technologies? *Journal of Agricultural and Environmental Ethics, 15*(3), 279–289.

Bruce, D. (2002b). GM ethical decision making in practice. *Ethics in Science and Environmental Politics, 2*(2002), 75–78.

Bruce, D. (2003). Contamination, crop trials, and compatibility. *Journal of Agricultural and Environmental Ethics, 16*(6), 595–604.

Burkhardt, J. (2001). Agricultural biotechnology and the future benefits argument. *Journal of Agricultural and Environmental Ethics, 14*(2), 135–145.

Busch, R. J., Knoepffler, N., Haniel, A., & Wenzel, G. (2002). *Grüne Gentechnik. Ein Bewertungsmodell.* München: Utz Verlag.

Carr, S. (2002). Ethical and value-based aspects of the European commission's precautionary principle. *Journal of Agricultural and Environmental Ethics, 15*(1), 31–38.

Carr, S., & Levidow, L. (2000). Exploring the links between science, risk, uncertainty, and ethics in regulatory controversies about genetically modified crops. *Journal of Agricultural and Environmental Ethics, 12*(1), 29–39.

Chen, M.-F., & Li, H.-L. (2007). The consumer's attitude toward genetically modified foods in Taiwan. *Food Quality and Preference, 18*(4), 662–674.

Clark, E. A., & Lehmann, H. (2001). Assessment of GM crops in commercial agriculture. *Journal of Agricultural and Environmental Ethics, 14*(1), 3–28.

Cohen, S. N. (1977). Recombinant DNA: Fact and fiction. *Science, 195*(4279), 654–657.

Comstock, G. (1989). Genetically engineered herbicide resistance, Part One. *Journal of Agricultural and Environmental Ethics, 2*(4), 263–306.

Comstock, G. (1990). Genetically engineered herbicide resistance, Part Two. *Journal of Agricultural and Environmental Ethics, 3*(2), 114–146.

Cooley, D. R., & Goreham, G. A. (2004). Are transgenic organisms unnatural? *Ethics and the Environment, 9*(1), 46–55.

Cowgill, S. E., Danks, C., & Atkinson, H. J. (2004). Multitrophic interactions involving genetically modified potatoes, nontarget aphids, natural enemies and hyperparasitoids. *Molecular Ecology, 13*(3), 639–647.

Crisp, R. (2003). Modern moral philosophy and the virtues. In R. Crisp (Ed.), *How should one live? Essays on the Virtues* (pp. 1–18). Oxford: Oxford University Press.

Deane-Drummond, C. E. (2002). Wisdom with justice. *Ethics in Science and Environmental Politics, 2*(2002), 65–74.

Deane-Drummond, C. E. (2004). *The ethics of nature.* Malden: Blackwell Publications.

Deblonde, M., & du Jardin, P. (2005). Deepening a precautionary European policy. *Journal of Agricultural and Environmental Ethics, 18*(4), 319–343.

Deckers, J. (2005). Are scientists right and non-scientists wrong? Reflections on discussions of GM. *Journal of Agricultural and Environmental Ethics, 18*(5), 451–478.

Devos, Y., Maeseele, P., Reheul, D., van Speybroeck, L., & de Waele, D. (2008). Ethics in the societal debate on genetically modified organisms: A (re)quest for sense and sensibility. *Journal of Agricultural and Environmental Ethics, 21*(1), 29–61.

Dickson, D. (1980). Patenting living organisms—how to beat the bug-rustlers. *Nature, 283*(5743), 128–129.

Dobson, A. (1995). Biocentrism and genetic engineering. *Environmental Values, 3*(4), 227–239.

Dürnberger, C. (2008). Der Mythos der Ursprünglichkeit: Landwirtschaftliche Idylle und ihre Rolle in der öffentlichen Wahrnehmung. *Forum TTN, 2008*(19), 45–52.

Duvick, D. N. (1995). Biotechnology is compatible with sustainable agriculture. *Journal of Agricultural and Environmental Ethics, 8*(2), 112–125.

Elliott, E. T., & Cole, C. V. (1989). A perspective on agroecosystem science. *Ecology, 6*(70), 1597–1602.

Firbank, L. G., & Forcella, F. (2000). Genetically modified crops and farmland biodiversity. *Science, 289*(5484), 1481–1482.

Forsberg, E.-M. (2007). Value pluralism and coherentist justification of ethical advice. *Journal of Agricultural and Environmental Ethics, 20*(1), 81–97.

Fraser, V. (2001). What's the moral of the GM food story? *Journal of Agricultural and Environmental Ethics, 14*(2), 147–159.

Frewer, L. J. (2003). Societal issues and public attitudes towards genetically modified foods. *Trends in Food Science and Technology, 14*(5–8), 319–332.

Frewer, L. J., Hedderley, D., Howard, C., & Shepherd, R. (1997a). "Objection" mapping in determining group and individual concerns regarding genetic engineering. *Agriculture and Human Values, 14*(1), 67–79.

Frewer, L. J., Howard, C., & Shepherd, R. (1997b). Public concerns in the United Kingdom about general and specific applications of genetic engineering: Risk, benefit, and ethics. *Science, Technology and Human Values, 22*(1), 98–124.

Frewer, L. J., Lassen, J., Kettlitz, B., Scholderer, J., Beekman, V., & Berdal, K. G. (2004). Societal aspects of genetically modified foods. *Food and Chemical Toxicology, 42*(7), 1181–1193.

Ganiere, P., Chern, W., & Hahn, D. (2006). A continuum of consumer attitudes toward genetically modified foods in the United States. *Journal of Agricultural and Resource Economics, 31*(1), 129–149.

Gaskell, G. (2000). Agricultural biotechnology and public attitudes in the European Union. *AgBioForum, 3*(2–3), 87–96.

Gaskell, G., Allum, N., Bauer, M., Durant, J., Allansdottir, A., Bonfadelli, H., et al. (2000). Biotechnology and the European public. *Nature Biotechnology, 18*(9), 935–938.

Gaskell, G., Allum, N., & Stares, S. (2003). Europeans and biotechnology in 2002—Eurobarometer 58.0 (2nd Edn. March 21st 2003). A report to the EC Directorate General for Research from the project "Life Sciences in European Society" QLG7-CT-1999-00286.

Gaus, G. F. (2001a). What is deontology? Part one: Orthodox views. *Journal of Value Inquiry, 35*(1), 27–42.

Gaus, G. F. (2001b). What is deontology? Part two: Reasons to act. *Journal of Value Inquiry, 35*(2), 179–193.

Goga, B. T. C., & Clementi, F. (2002). Safety assurance of foods: Risk management depends on good science but it is not a scientific activity. *Journal of Agricultural and Environmental Ethics, 15*(3), 305–313.

Gonzalez, C. G. (2007). Genetically modified organisms and justice: The international environmental justice implications of biotechnology. *Georgetown International Environmental Law Review, 19*(4), 583–610.

Gura, T. (2001). The battlefields of Britain. *Nature, 412*(6849), 760–763.

Hails, R. S. (2000). Genetically modified plants—the debate continues. *Trends in Ecology & Evolution, 15*(1), 14–18.

Hails, R. S. (2002). Assessing the risks associated with new agricultural practices. *Nature, 418*(6898), 685–688.

Hansen, J., Holma, L., Frewer, L. J., Robinson, P., & Sandøe, P. (2003). Beyond the knowledge deficit: Recent research into lay and expert attitudes to food risks. *Appetite, 41*(2), 111–121.

Harlander, S. K. (1991). Social, moral, and ethical issues in food biotechnology. *Food Technology, 45*(5), 152–159.

Harwood, J. D., Wallin, W. G., & Obrycki, J. J. (2005). Uptake of Bt endotoxins by nontarget herbivores and higher order arthropod predators: Molecular evidence from a transgenic corn agroecosystem. *Molecular Ecology, 14*, 2815–2823.

Heaf, D., & Wirz, J. (Eds.) (2002). Genetic engineering and the intrinsic value and integrity of animals and plants. Proceedings of a Workshop at the Royal Botanic Garden, Edinburgh. Hafan: Ifgene.

Heeger, R. (2000). Genetic engineering and the dignity of creatures. *Journal of Agricultural and Environmental Ethics, 13*(1), 43–51.

Henson, S., Annou, M., Cranfield, J., & Ryks, J. (2008). Understanding consumer attitudes toward food technologies in Canada. *Risk Analysis, 28*(6), 1601–1617.

Herold, N. (2008). Pflicht ist Pflicht! Oder nicht? Eine Einführung in die Deontologische Ethik. In J. S. Ach, K. Bayertz, & L. Siep (Eds.), *Grundkurs Ethik. Band 1: Grundlagen* (pp. 71–90). Paderborn: Mentis Verlag.

Ho, M.-W., Ryan, A., & Cummins, J. (1999). Cauliflower mosaic viral promoter—a recipe for disaster? *Microbial Ecology in Health and Disease, 11*(4), 194–197.

Hoban, T. J., Woodrum, E., & Czaja, R. (1992). Public opposition to genetic engineering. *Rural Sociology, 57*(4), 476–493.

Hoffman, C. A., & Carroll, C. R. (1995). Can we sustain the biological basis of agriculture? *Annual Review of Ecology, Evolution and Systematics, 26*(1995), 69–92.

Holtug, N. (2001). The harm principle and genetically modified food. *Journal of Agricultural and Environmental Ethics, 14*(2), 169–178.

Howard, J. A., & Donnelly, K. C. (2004). A quantitative safety assessment model for transgenic protein products produced in agricultural crops. *Journal of Agricultural and Environmental Ethics, 17*(6), 545–558.

Hursthouse, R. (2003). Normative virtue ethics. In R. Crisp (Ed.), *How should one live? Essays on the virtues* (pp. 19–36). Oxford: Oxford University Press.

Jensen, K. K. (2006). Conflict over risks in food production: A challenge for democracy. *Journal of Agricultural and Environmental Ethics, 19*(3), 269–283.

Kallhoff, A. (2002). *Prinzipien der Pflanzenethik. Die Bewertung pflanzlichen Lebens in Biologie und Philosophie.* New York and Frankfurt: Campus Verlag.

Karafyllis, N. C. (2003). Renewable resources and the idea of nature—what has biotechnology got to do with it? *Journal of Agricultural and Environmental Ethics, 16*(1), 3–28.

Kasanmoentalib, S. (1996). Science and values in risk assessment: The case of deliberate release of genetically engineered organisms. *Journal of Agricultural and Environmental Ethics, 9*(1), 42–60.

Katz, E. (1993). Artefacts and functions: A note on the value of nature. *Environmental Value, 2*(3), 223–232.

Kinsey, J., & Senauer, B. (1997). Food marketing in an electronic age: Implications for agriculture. *Choices, 12*(2nd Quarter), 32–35.

Kirkham, G. (2006). "Playing god" and "vexing nature": A cultural perspective. *Environmental Values, 15*(2), 173–195.

Korthals, M. (2001). Taking consumers seriously: Two concepts of consumer sovereignty. *Journal of Agricultural and Environmental Ethics, 14*(2), 201–215.

Kotschi, J. (2008). Transgenic crops and their impact on biodiversity. *GAIA, 17*(1), 36–41.

Krebs, J. R., Bradbury, R. B., Wilson, J. D., & Siriwardena, G. M. (1999). The second silent spring? *Nature, 400*(6753), 611–612.

Lammerts van Bueren, E., & Struik, P. (2005). Integrity and rights of plants: Ethical notions in organic plant breeding and propagation. *Journal of Agricultural and Environmental Ethics, 18*(5), 479–493.

Madsen, K. H., Holm, P. B., Lassen, J., & Sandøe, P. (2002). Ranking genetically modified plants according to familiarity. *Journal of Agricultural and Environmental Ethics, 15*(3), 267–278.

Madsen, K. H., & Sandøe, P. (2001). Herbicide resistant sugar beet—What is the problem? *Journal of Agricultural and Environmental Ethics, 14*(2), 161–168.

Magnusson, M. K., & Koivisto Hursti, U.-K. (2002). Consumer attitudes towards genetically modified foods. *Appetite, 39*(1), 9–24.

Marvier, M. (2002). Improving risk assessment for nontarget safety of transgenic crops. *Ecological Applications, 12*(4), 1119–1124.

Marvier, M., & Van Acker, R. C. (2005). Can crop transgenes be kept on a leash? *Frontiers in Ecology and Environment, 3*(2), 99–106.

Mayer, S., & Stirling, A. (2002). Finding a precautionary approach to technological developments—lessons for the evaluation of GM crops. *Journal of Agricultural and Environmental Ethics, 15*(1), 57–71.

McNaughton, D., & Rawling, P. (2006). Chapter 15. Deontology. In D. Copp (Ed.), *The Oxford handbook of ethical theory* (pp. 425–458). New York: Oxford University Press.

Meijboom, F. L. B., Verweij, M. F., & Brom, F. W. A. (2003). You eat what you are: Moral dimensions of diets tailored to one's genes. *Journal of Agricultural and Environmental Ethics, 16*(6), 557–568.

Melich, A. (2000). Modern biotechnology, quality of life, and consumers' access to justice—Eurobarometer 52.1 (Nov–Dec 1999). Conducted by INRA (Europe), Brussels. ICPSR02893-v4. Cologne, Germany: GESIS/Ann Arbor, MI. Inter-University Consortium for Political and Social Research [distributors].

Melin, A. (2004). Genetic engineering and the moral status of non-human species. *Journal of Agricultural and Environmental Ethics, 17*(6), 479–495.

Mepham, B. (2008). *Bioethics. An introduction for the biosciences* (2nd ed.). Oxford, New York: Oxford University Press.

Munnichs, G. (2004). Whom to trust? Public concerns, late modern risks, and expert trustworthiness. *Journal of Agricultural and Environmental Ethics, 17*(2), 113–130.

Musschenga, A. (2005). Empirical ethics, context-sensitivity, and contextualism. *Journal of Medicine and Philosophy, 30*(5), 467–490.

Myhr, A. I., & Traavik, T. (2002). The precautionary principle: Scientific uncertainty and omitted research in the context of GMO use and release. *Journal of Agricultural and Environmental Ethics, 15*(1), 73–86.

Myhr, A. I., & Traavik, T. (2003a). Genetically modified (GM) crops: Precautionary science and conflicts of interests. *Journal of Agricultural and Environmental Ethics, 16*(3), 227–247.

Myhr, A. I., & Traavik, T. (2003b). Sustainable development and Norwegian genetic engineering regulations: Applications, impacts, and challenges. *Journal of Agricultural and Environmental Ethics, 16*(4), 317–335.

Myskja, B. K. (2006). The moral difference between intragenic and transgenic modification of plants. *Journal of Agricultural and Environmental Ethics, 19*(3), 225–238.

Nisbet, M. C., & Huge, M. (2007). Where do science debates come from? Understanding attention cycles and framing. In D. Brossard, J. Shanahan, & T. C. Nesbitt (Eds.), *The media, the public and agricultural biotechnology* (pp. 193–230). London: CABI Publishing.

O'Neill, J., Holland, A., & Light, A. (2006). *Environmental values (Routledge Introductions to Environment)*. New York: Routledge Group.

Osborn, D. (2002). Stretching the frontiers of precaution. *Ethics in Science and Environmental Politics, 2*(2002), 37–41.

Pascalev, A. (2003). You are what you eat: Genetically modified foods, integrity, and society. *Journal of Agricultural and Environmental Ethics, 16*(6), 583–594.

Paula, L., & Birrer, F. (2006). Including public perspectives in industrial biotechnology and the biobased economy. *Journal of Agricultural and Environmental Ethics, 19*(3), 253–267.

Peters, H. P., & Sawicka, M. (2007). German reactions to genetic engineering in food production. In D. Brossard, J. Shanahan, & T. C. Nesbitt (Eds.), *The public, the media and agricultural biotechnology* (pp. 57–96). Wallingford (UK): CABI Publishing.

Pilson, D., & Prendeville, H. R. (2004). Ecological effects of transgenic crops and the escape of transgenes into wild populations. *Annual Review of Ecology, Evolution, and Systematics, 35*(1), 149–174.

Pouteau, S. (2000). Beyond substantial equivalence: Ethical equivalence. *Journal of Agricultural and Environmental Ethics, 13*(3–4), 271–291.

Ramjoué, C. (2007). The transatlantic rift in genetically modified food policy. *Journal of Agricultural and Environmental Ethics, 20*(5), 419–436.

Regal, P. J. (1994). Scientific principles for ecologically based risk assessment of transgenic organisms. *Molecular Ecology, 3*(1), 5–13.

Reif, K., & Melich, A. (1996). Biotechnology and genetic engineering: What Europeans think about biotechnology—Eurobarometer 39.1 (First ICPSR Edition, April 1996). Conducted by INRA (Europe), Brussels. ICPSR ed. Ann Arbor, MI. Interuniversity Consortium for Political and Social Research [producer], Köln. Zentralarchiv für Empirische Sozialforschung/ Ann Arbor, MI. Inter-University Consortium for Political and Social Research [distributors].

Reiss, M. J., & Straughan, R. (2002). *Improving nature.* Cambridge: Cambridge University Press.

Rippe, K. P., & Schaber, P. (1998). Einleitung. In K. P. Rippe & P. Schaber (Eds.), *Tugendethik* (pp. 7–18). Stuttgart: Philipp Reclam jun.

Robinson, J. (1999). Ethics and transgenic crops: A review. *Electronic Journal of Biotechnology, 2*(2), 71–81.

Rolston, H., III. (1999). *Genes, genesis and god. Values and their origins in natural and human history.* Cambridge: Cambridge University Press.

Runtenberg, C. (1997). Argumentationen im Kontext angewandter Ethik: das Beispiel Gentechnologie. In N. Herold & S. Mischer (Eds.), *Philosophie: Studium, Text and Argument* (pp. 179–193). Münster: LIT-Verlag.

Saba, A., Moles, A., & Frewer, L. J. (1998). Public concerns about general and specific applications of genetic engineering: A comparative study between the UK and Italy. *Nutrition and Food Science, 98*(1), 19–29.

Sandler, R. (2004). An aretaic objection to agricultural biotechnology. *Journal of Agricultural and Environmental Ethics, 17*(3), 301–317.

Sandler, R. (2007). *Character and environment. A virtue-oriented approach to environmental ethics.* New York: Columbia University Press.

Sandler, R., & Cafaro, P. (2004). *Environmental virtue ethics.* Lanham: Rowman and Littlefield.

Saner, M. A. (2000). Biotechnology, the limits of Norton's convergence hypothesis, and implications for an inclusive concept of health. *Ethics and the Environment, 5*(2), 229–241.

Savadori, L., Savio, S., Nicotra, E., Rumiati, R., Finucane, M., & Slovic, P. (2004). Expert and public perception of risk from biotechnology. *Risk Analysis, 24*(5), 1289–1299.

Scott, I. M. (2000). Green symbolism in the genetic modification debate. *Journal of Agricultural and Environmental Ethics, 13*(3–4), 293–311.

Scott, D. (2003). Science and the consequences of mistrust: Lessons from recent GM controversies. *Journal of Agricultural and Environmental Ethics, 16*(6), 569–582.

Scott, D. (2005). The magic bullet criticism of agricultural biotechnology. *Journal of Agricultural and Environmental Ethics, 18*(3), 259–267.

Segal, H. P. (2001). Victor and victim. *Nature, 412*(6850), 861.

Serageldin, I. (1999). Biotechnology and food security in the 21st century. *Science, 285*(5426), 387–389.

Shelton, A. M., Zhao, J.-Z., & Roush, R. T. (2002). Economic, ecological, food safety, and social consequences of the deployment of Bt transgenic plants. *Annual Review of Entomology, 47*(2002), 845–881.

Siegrist, M. (2008). Factors influencing public acceptance of innovative food technologies and products. *Trends in Food Science and Technology, 19*(11), 603–608.

Siipi, H. (2008). Dimensions of naturalness. *Ethics and the Environment, 13*(1), 71–103.

Sjöberg, L. (2008). Genetically modified food in the eyes of the public and experts. *Risk Management, 10*(3), 168–193.

Skorupinski, B. (2002). Putting precaution to debate — about the precautionary principle and participatory technology assessment. *Journal of Agricultural and Environmental Ethics, 15*(1), 87–102.

Snow, A. (2003). Genetic engineering: Unnatural selection. *Nature, 424*(6949), 619.

Stewart, C. N. (2004). *Genetically modified planet. Environmental impacts of genetically engineered plants.* New York: Oxford University Press.

Stöcklin, J. (2007). Die Pflanze. Moderne Konzepte der Biologie. Eidgenössische Ethikkommission für die Biotechnologie im Ausserhumanbereich EKAH (Eds.). Beiträge zur Ethik und Biotechnologie, Band 2.

Tanner, C., Medin, D. L., & Iliev, R. (2008). Influence of deontological versus consequentialist orientations on act choices and framing effects: When principles are more important than consequences. *European Journal of Social Psychology, 38*(5), 757–769.

Taylor, P. (1986). *Respect for nature: A theory of environmental ethics.* Princeton: Princeton University Press.

Tiedje, J. M., Colwell, R. K., Grossman, Y. L., Hodson, R. E., Lenski, R. E., Mack, R. N., et al. (1989). The planned introduction of genetically engineered organisms: Ecological considerations and recommendations. *Ecology, 70*(2), 298–315.

Verhoog, H. (1992). The concept of intrinsic value and transgenic animals. *Journal of Agricultural and Environmental Ethics, 5*(2), 147–160.

Verhoog, H. (1997). Organic agriculture versus genetic engineering. *NJAS Wageningen Journal of Life Sciences, 54*(4), 387–400.

Verhoog, H., Matze, M., van Bueren, E. L., & Baars, T. (2003). The role of the concept of the natural (naturalness) in organic farming. *Journal of Agricultural and Environmental Ethics, 16*(1), 29–49.

Vogel, S. (2003). The nature of artifacts. *Environmental Ethics, 25*(2), 149–168.

von Kutschera, F. (1999). *Grundlagen der Ethik.* Berlin and New York: Walter de Gruyter.

Von Wartburg, W. P., & Liew, J. (1999). *Gene technology and social acceptance.* Lanham, Md: University Press of America.

Wambugu, F. (1999). Why Africa needs agricultural biotech. *Nature, 400*(6739), 15–16.

Watkinson, A. R., Freckleton, R. P., Sutherland, W. J., & Robinson, R. A. (2000). Predictions of biodiversity response to genetically modified herbicide-tolerant crops. *Science, 289*(5484), 1554–1557.

Weaver, S. A., & Morris, M. C. (2005). Risks associated with genetic modification: An annotated bibliography of peer-reviewed natural science publications. *Journal of Agricultural and Environmental Ethics, 18*(2), 157–189.

Wenz, P. S. (1999). Pragmatism in practice: The efficiency of sustainable agriculture. *Environmental Ethics, 21*(4), 391–410.

Westra, L. (1998). Biotechnology and transgenics in agriculture and aquaculture: The perspective from ecosystem integrity. *Environmental Values, 7*(1), 79–96.

Woese, C. R. (2004). A new biology for a new century. *Microbiology and Molecular Biology Reviews, 68*(2), 173–186.

Wolfenbarger, L. L., & Phifer, P. R. (2000). The ecological risks and benefits of genetically engineered plants. *Science, 290*(5499), 2088–2093.

Reading Questions

1. The researchers identify three general types of moral concerns across the 113 articles that were ultimately analyzed as part of their final review of the scholarship. What are those three types of moral concerns?

2. The researchers analyzed the articles' content by a process of extracting and classifying "basic semantic units" (par. 15). In your own words, explain what this means.

3. According to Table 3 in the study, what percentage of environmental ethics journals expressed concern about the consequences of the use of genetically modified crops?

4. The researchers found the concept *nature as a safety mechanism* addressed in how many of the articles?

5. What are the three more specific "moral concerns addressing the act" (5) that are identified as part of this study?

Rhetoric Questions

6. In the report's Introduction, where do the authors switch from providing background and context for their study to presenting their specific aims? What makes the location of this switch appropriate?

7. In light of its central topic, the researchers' perspective, and the genre of presentation, could you make a case that this report should be classified as social science research? If so, on what basis would you make such an argument? If not, why not?

8. Look closely at the study's Results section. Explain the section's organizational logic. Account for the role of headings and subheadings.

Response and Research Questions

9. Do you find it surprising that moral concerns addressing the actor were identified least in the laypersons' debate on the use of genetically modified crops? Why or why not?

10. What are your personal concerns about the use of genetically modified crops? Do any of the specific moral concerns identified by the researchers as part of their literature review project intersect with your own concerns about genetically modified crops? If so, which ones?

Willingness to Pay for Foods with Varying Production Traits and Levels of Genetically Modified Content

JOHN C. BERNARD, KATIE GIFFORD, KRISTIN SANTORA, AND DARIA J. BERNARD

John C. Bernard is a professor of applied economics and statistics in the College of Agriculture and Natural Resources at the University of Delaware. He has published a number of research articles on the likelihood and willingness of consumers to purchase various types of novel or genetically modified products. In "Willingness to Pay for Foods with Varying Production Traits and Levels of Genetically Modified Content," published in 2009 in the *Journal of Food Distribution Research*, Bernard and his team of researchers report on a study that "examined consumer willingness to pay for first- and second-generation genetically modified (GM) and organic foods and for non-GM foods, dependent on [customers'] tolerance for GM content."

This study examined consumer willingness to pay for first- and second-generation genetically modified (GM) and organic foods and for non-GM foods, dependent on tolerance for GM content. Data from a survey of students were examined using a heteroskedastic two-limit Tobit model. Results showed consumers were willing to pay significantly more for organic and second-generation foods over first-generation GM foods, which suggests a niche market for second-generation GM foods may be possible. For non-GM foods, consumers were indifferent between a 100 and 99 percent threshold, but did not view 95 percent non-GM foods as more valuable than foods with unknown GM.

Consumers today face food choices resulting from a variety of production techniques. At the forefront of these changes has been the development and rapid expansion of genetically modified (GM) foods. The first generation of these products has been those that feature production benefits for the farmer such as pest or disease resistance. Second-generation GM foods, where the benefit will focus on the consumer by having improved nutrition, taste, or flavor, or lower fat or calories, are currently being developed and should soon be on the market. At the other end of the spectrum, the market for organic foods has experienced tremendous growth. Organic methods entail numerous production traits, including the requirement that they not contain GM ingredients.

How these foods are perceived and labeled could have a significant influence on consumer acceptance and willingness to pay (WTP). In the United States, the creation of the USDA National Organic Program in 2002 and accompanying "Certified Organic" labels has aided an already growing niche market. In contrast, GM food labeling is voluntary unless the product has substantially different qualities from its non-modified counterpart (U.S. Food and Drug Administration 2001). Under these regulations, first-generation GM foods do not require labels; as a result, labeling of GM foods is almost nonexistent. More visible are foods labeled non-GM. However, this claim typically appears as an additional point of information on products with the Certified Organic logo. More importantly, second-generation GM foods by definition will require a label.

Unlike the United States, many nations have established mandatory labeling policies for GM foods. A key element of these policies is the establishment of threshold levels for GM ingredients allowed within non-GM foods. In a recent survey, Gruère and Rao (2007) found the European Union to be among the more extreme: a food labeled as non-GM can not contain more than 0.9 percent GM ingredients. Countries with less strict threshold levels include Brazil and Australia at 1 percent and Japan, Taiwan, and Thailand at 5 percent. China was noted as having a zero-tolerance level.

The establishment of a tolerance level for GM ingredients allowed in non-GM foods may be forthcoming in the United States as second-generation GM foods are approved and begin to appear on the market. Given the size and complexity of the food system, a zero-tolerance policy may be infeasible without major changes in production operations to enable strict segregation. The magnitude of the threshold limit on GM content could have a significant effect not only on producers but also on consumer acceptance and WTP for the affected food products. Currently, little is known about how alternative threshold limits affect consumer purchasing decisions.

The goals of this study were thus twofold. First was to determine consumer WTP for foods produced with different production traits: first-generation GM, second-generation GM, and organic. The second was to examine consumer WTP for non-GM foods with a given tolerance level for GM ingredients that may have inadvertently entered the production process. The tolerance levels selected were zero, 1, and 5 percent (equivalently 100, 99, and 95 percent non-GM) to coincide with existing standards elsewhere. As a secondary objective, the two goals were investigated with respect to two products: milk, which represented a fresh food product, and cereal, which represented a processed food product.

LITERATURE

While extensive research has been conducted on consumer acceptance of and WTP for non-GM foods, few studies have looked at the effects of various thresholds on consumer WTP. Matsumoto (2006) used the contingent-valuation method to elicit Japanese consumers' WTP for GM segregation programs. Since April 2001, Japanese consumers have had access to GM labels on food products if the product contains GM ingredients accounting for more than 5 percent of the product's total weight. The GM food used in this study was a potato snack product made with GM potatoes. The author noted that the sale of

GM potato seeds in the United States had ceased in March 2001. Using threshold levels of zero, 1, and 2 percent, results showed that Japanese consumers were not willing to pay significantly more as the threshold level decreased. In addition, government certification did not affect consumer WTP.

Noussair, Robin, and Ruffieux (2004) used experimental auctions to elicit French consumers' WTP for similar food products that differed only in their content of GM ingredients. Specifically, four biscuit products were used that were considered to be close substitutes. One product was identified as non-GM and organic. One product—soy—was identified as containing GM ingredients. The two remaining products differed in the content of GM ingredients: less than 0.1 percent and no more than 1 percent. The authors found that bids for the thresholds were significantly different. Subjects also had significantly higher WTP for the 1 percent threshold compared to a product identified as "contains genetically modified organisms." In addition, the 0.1 percent threshold was not considered to be GM-free by subjects.

Rousu et al. (2004) was the only study that examined the impact of various tolerance levels for GM content on U.S. consumers' WTP. Experimental auctions for three GM food products (32-ounce bottle of canola oil, 16-ounce bag of corn tortilla chips, and 5-pound bag of russet potatoes) were used to test whether U.S. consumers prefer foods with zero, 1, or 5 percent tolerance levels for GM material. Results suggested that subjects reduced their valuation by an average of about 10 percent relative to the GM-free baseline, regardless of the threshold level. In addition, results suggested that bids were not significantly different when comparing the two threshold levels. If the United States were to establish a tolerance level, the authors recommended it be set at 5 percent. This would be less costly to meet and would not significantly lower demand compared to a 1 percent tolerance level. From these three studies, it appears that WTP for GM content levels vary across countries and reflect government policies with regard to the allowed limit.

An area where there has been a growing volume of research is the acceptance of and WTP for second-generation GM products. A review of several studies, which considered GM products nutritionally enhanced, revealed that differences exist not only across countries but also within a given country. First, Burton and Pearse (2002) reported that 30 percent of Australian respondents were not willing to purchase a beer having any GM component regardless of the price or health benefits. However, a group of consumers who were concerned about cholesterol were willing to pay an AU$0.83 premium for a bottle of beer made with yeast genetically modified to leave increased antioxidants, which would reduce cholesterol.

O'Connor et al. (2006) reported Irish consumer acceptance of a hypothetical GM yogurt product that included a GM ingredient proven to help protect against cancer as part of a healthy diet. Using cluster analysis, 21.2 percent of respondents demonstrated clear support for GM foods offering specific consumer benefits. Another 20.5 percent were receptive to second-generation products but had a number of reservations about accepting such products.

Bugbee, Loureiro, and Hine (2004) reported U.S. consumer acceptance of different types of a GM tomato plant. Respondents had the highest WTP premium (mean of 10.49 cents per pound) for GM enhanced flavor. The second-highest WTP premium (mean of 8.72 cents per pound) was for GM nutritionally enhanced. However, 32.87 percent of respondents were not willing to pay a premium for GM nutritionally enhanced. Interestingly, the third-highest WTP premium (mean of 3.05) was for GM pesticide reduction.

Onyango and Nayga Jr. (2004) reported U.S. consumer willingness to consume a breakfast cereal made from GM grains nutritionally enhanced with calcium, omega fatty acids, or antioxidants. The majority of respondents were at least somewhat willing to consume the three versions of the breakfast cereal (82, 77, and 74 percent, respectively) provided the product was derived from plant-to-plant GM technology. Animal-to-plant GM technology was less acceptable in each case.

Onyango and Govindasamy (2005) reported U.S. consumer WTP for GM product attributes in bananas, cereal, and beef. Consumers were not willing to pay significantly more for added antioxidants in bananas. However, they were willing to pay 18.8 percent more for this attribute in cereals and 7.16 percent more in the case of beef. In addition, consumers were willing to pay 4.55 percent more for added compounds for energy in beef.

DATA AND METHODS

Data were collected through a survey of University of Delaware (UD) and Wesley College (WC) students in fall 2005.[1] As students represent up-and-coming consumers, they play a substantial role in determining the success of current and second-generation GM foods. How their opinions would compare to those of general adult consumers was uncertain. One argument suggests that students, having been exposed to GM foods for much of their lives, have a more positive outlook toward them and consider them significantly less risky than adults do (Zhao and Widdows 2001; Chern et al. 2002). Others have suggested students' attitudes toward and WTP for GM foods match those of adults. Fritz et al. (2003) compared youths (under 18), college students, and adults and found that while youths and adults had significantly different views, college students and adults did not. Similarly, Chern et al. (2002) showed that students and adults in the United States and Norway had similar willingness to consume GM foods, with or without the presence of an environmental benefit of pesticide reduction. Lusk et al. (2005) noted that student valuations tended to be on par with those from general population samples. In either situation, student WTP for these products and technologies would be of importance to marketers. The survey was distributed in classes and residence halls. No monetary incentive or class credit was provided. Classes were selected from different course levels and from different fields encompassing natural

[1]Prior to the administration of the survey it was pretested among students in two classes and with two faculty members. Feedback from these participants was used to refine several components of the survey and clarify some of the questions. Afterward, another small group of students gave final suggestions, which were also incorporated.

and social sciences and the humanities to capture a wide spectrum of students. Instructors allowed class time for completion of the survey, and all students in attendance completed the survey, a total of 198 responses. The distribution of the survey to students living in residence halls was added to try to improve the size and randomness of the sample. Six hundred surveys and return envelopes were sent to students' dorm rooms, with 138 returned, a response rate of 23 percent.

In total, 336 responses were received, with 151 from WC and 175 from UD. Only 10 surveys were not usable due to missing information. The UD portion had a higher percentage of white and female students, while the WC students were more racially diverse (87.4 percent white, 0.04 percent black or African American, and 68.9 percent female for the UD sample compared to 69.7 percent white, 20.6 percent black or African American, and 44.6 percent female for the WC sample). The demographic profile of the sample compared favorably with regard to race to both the U.S. Census 2000 and the state of Delaware (U.S. Census Bureau 2006).

The survey was constrained to three pages. The top of the first page was reserved for brief definitions of GM and organic foods, as shown in Table 1. The remainder of the survey was divided into three sections. The first dealt with questions regarding respondents' knowledge and rating of GM and organic foods, opinions regarding labeling, and confidence in the ability of agencies to ensure the safety of the food supply. The second section contained the two WTP questions, and the last section included demographic information.

The primary part of the survey was the two questions asking respondents about their WTP for various attributes compared to a version of the product with an unknown GM content. Given current products available and the labeling requirements, having the base product be one with an unknown GM content reflected the typical version of the foods found on store shelves. The product attributes were 100 percent non-GM, 99 percent non-GM, 95 percent non-GM, GM to improve production, GM to improve

Table 1

Definitions Presented on the Surveys

Genetically modified (GM) foods are foods in which the genetic material has been altered or inserted from other species, using biotechnology, to create desired characteristics or remove undesired characteristics.

Organic foods are foods that were produced without synthetic pesticides, chemical or sewage-sludge-based fertilizers, or the use of hormones or antibiotics, contain no GM ingredients, and are not irradiated.

nutrition, and organic. The first three were designed to test differences in WTP due to varying tolerance levels for GM ingredients within non-GM foods, while the latter three were designed to examine how different production techniques and the reasons for using them influenced WTP.

The two questions differed only in the product involved, the first being for the fresh product, milk, and the second for the processed product, cereal. The products were chosen because of their likely inclusion in the average diet, and as products that would be familiar to students. Additionally, milk was one of few products where GM-free (non-rBST) and organic versions were readily available in local supermarkets. Students' familiarity with these choices should have improved interest and aided them in forming their answers. As neither product was available in a GM version to improve nutrition, these were posed as hypothetical options.

Several possible methods were available to determine consumer WTP (for a good discussion see Lusk and Hudson 2004). Gathering WTP estimates from survey questions could be difficult due to their hypothetical nature. Since no actual purchase is made, respondents' indicated WTP tends to be inflated (Lee and Hatcher 2001; Voelckner 2006). A typical alternative—using experimental auctions, where participants make actual purchases—was not feasible since some of the products do not exist. A second concern was that many students would be unfamiliar with current market prices, which may serve as a reference point for WTP responses, an issue that could also cause problems with an auction experiment.

In consideration of these issues, a rating system for WTP was implemented. For each attribute combination, respondents were asked to rate their WTP compared with the unknown-GM-content version on a scale of 1 (pay much less) to 9 (pay much more), with 5 labeled as indicating indifference. This design had the benefit of not requiring students to directly come up with a price or to have knowledge of current prices.

Table 2 summarizes the responses to the WTP questions. Most means were significantly greater than 5, suggesting a higher WTP for those versions relative to the base product with unknown GM content. The entries that were not significantly different from 5 were the 95 percent non-GM for both milk and cereal and the 99 percent non-GM for cereal, which indicates that respondents were indifferent between purchasing those versions and versions with an unknown quantity of GM ingredients. These findings provide an early suggestion that consumers may not value a 95 percent non-GM tolerance level and that the value of a 99 percent non-GM tolerance level may depend on product type.

The only entries with means significantly less than 5 were the milk and cereal products that had been genetically modified to improve production. These were viewed less favorably than were versions with unknown GM contents. Genetic modification to improve nutrition appears to have sizeable consumer interest, with average WTP not significantly different from that for organic. This finding suggests there may be a niche market for second-generation GM foods similar to that for organic.

Comparisons between the milk and cereal means yielded two interesting observations. First, WTP for each threshold was higher for milk than for cereal. It may be that for a fresh product such as milk there was greater interest in avoiding a GM component. The other finding was that for the two GM versions and organic there was no difference between milk and cereal, suggesting differences between product types may not be pronounced for these production traits.

A more detailed analysis of WTP was conducted [25] using heteroskedastic 2-limit Tobit models in SAS. These models were necessary because the data were

Table 2

Descriptive Statistics for WTP Measures

Product	Variable	Definition	Mean	SD
Milk	100	WTP for milk 100% non-GM	5.3354*	1.6555
	99	WTP for milk 99% non-GM	5.2267*	1.3790
	95	WTP for milk 95% non-GM	5.0609	1.2719
	Production	WTP for milk GM to improve production	4.8100*	1.4699
	Nutrition	WTP for milk GM to improve nutrition	5.3354*	1.5976
	Organic	WTP for organic milk	5.3670*	1.7972
Cereal	100	WTP for cereal 100% non-GM	5.2043*	1.4749
	99	WTP for cereal 99% non-GM	5.0621	1.2663
	95	WTP for cereal 95% non-GM	5.0093	1.1983
	Production	WTP for cereal GM to improve production	4.7143*	1.3917
	Nutrition	WTP for cereal GM to improve nutrition	5.3591*	1.5447
	Organic	WTP for organic cereal	5.3700*	1.6181

*Indicates value is significantly different from 5 at the 5% level.

censored on both sides, as the survey responses for WTP were limited to whole-number values from 1 to 9. A possible issue, however, was that the data may be considered ordinal. In other words, respondents may not have used a uniform ratings scale. The alternative for censored data that accounts for this possibility would be an ordered probit model, which depends on the parallel-slopes assumption (Long 1997). For this data set the assumption was rejected, making ordered probit inappropriate. Previous studies have shown that Tobit and probit models yield comparable results (see, for example, Harrison, Gillespie, and Fields 2005).[2] Another issue with the models was the need to account for possible subject heterogeneity, which has been identified in similar models (Bernard, Zhang, and Gifford 2006). To alleviate these concerns the models were tested and, where appropriate, corrected for heteroskedasticity using demographics.

To analyze the data, four models were developed, two for each food product. The first set of models examined the effect of the different threshold levels on WTP. The second set of models examined the effect of production method on WTP. In each case the dependent variable was WTP relative to a version with unknown GM content. Dummy variables were created for each attribute variable, included as independent variables. For both milk and cereal, the equations below describe the basic models:

$$(1) \quad WTP_{ij} = \beta_0 + \beta_1 99 + \beta_2 95 + \beta_3 KnowGM + \beta_4 OpinionGM + \beta_5 Religion + \beta_6 Black + \beta_7 Female + \varepsilon_i$$

$$(2) \quad WTP_{ij} = \beta_0 + \beta_1 Nutrition + \beta_2 Organic + \beta_3 KnowGM + \beta_4 OpinionGM + \beta_5 Religion + \beta_6 Black + \beta_7 Female + \varepsilon_i$$

For both equations, i and j represent respondent number and product version, respectively, and the variables are as defined in Tables 2 and 3.

While the attitude and demographic variables in the two models could be useful, potentially more interesting would be interactions between them and the product-attribute variables. This would be especially true for Model 2, where a variable such as OpinionGM could be expected to increase consumer interest in a product genetically modified to improve nutrition but to lower interest in an organic version. Interaction terms were thus added to both sets of models. To keep the models from becoming overly complex, likelihood-ratio tests were conducted to determine which interaction terms were significant. Sets of interaction terms that were jointly insignificant were removed.

Hypotheses were similar for both sets of models. For the main variables of interest in the first set, it was believed that WTP would decrease as the tolerance level for GM content increased, with the lowest WTP coming with the 95 percent non-GM level. For the second set, it was hypothesized that WTP for GM versions to improve production would be lower, while WTP for both GM versions to improve nutrition and organic would be higher. Of the two, it was further anticipated that organic would have the higher WTP over the base.

For the remaining independent variables, the effect of knowledge of GM foods was uncertain. It has been argued that knowledge could either reduce or increase concerns over GM foods.[3] For example, Rimal, Moon, and Balasubramanian (2006) found that consumers who had read or heard a great deal about GM technology were more likely to buy organic. Interestingly, though, Schilling et al. (2003) found that most consumers in fact know very little about GM foods. With regard to the effect of opinion, respondents who had favorable opinions of GM foods were expected to have higher WTP for products that were genetically modified for either production or nutrition and to have lower WTP for organic and non-GM foods, as they would see less necessity for

[2] Ordered probit models were run for comparison despite the violation of the assumption. Results differed from the Tobit in only one case, where female was significant in the probit version of the cereal GM-content model.

[3] A more detailed discussion of the effect of individuals' knowledge on acceptance of GM foods can be found in Costa-Font, Gil, and Traill (2008)

Table 3

Variable Definitions and Descriptive Statistics

Variable	Definition	Mean	SD
KnowGM	Knowledge of GM food from 1 = no knowledge to 5 = very knowledgeable	2.1389	1.1976
OpinionGM	Opinion of GM foods from 1 = very negative to 5 = very positive	2.9838	0.8392
Religion	Frequency religious or moral beliefs influence food choices from 1 = never to 4 = always	1.4246	0.7102
Black	1 = black or African American; 0 = other race	0.1288	0.3355
Hispanic	1 = Hispanic; 0 = other race	0.0368	0.1886
Female	1 = female; 0 = male	0.5583	0.4974

these categories. Those indicating that religious or moral beliefs influenced food choice were expected to yield the opposite pattern.

Gender was considered the key demographic, with the expectation that females would have lower WTP for all GM versions, since past literature has shown that women tend to perceive more risk from GM food and have lower WTP (see, for example, Baker and Burnham 2001). Racial differences were included without expectations to sign. However, Hossain et al. (2003) found that white consumers were more willing to consume GM breakfast cereals. In contrast, Rimal, Moon, and Balasubramanian (2006) found no significant difference based on race. Due to the small number of Hispanic respondents, black or African American was the only race separated for consideration in the final model. Other demographic variables, such as age and income, were not considered appropriate given the homogeneous nature of college students (Kraus 1995).

RESULTS

Beginning with results from the first section of the survey, it was found that 52 percent of the students were unsure if they had eaten GM products. Less than

half, 44 percent, were sure they had, and about 5 percent believed they had never eaten GM food. Hallman et al. (2003) found that 26 percent of respondents reported having consumed food containing GM ingredients while 58 percent said they had not and 15 percent were unsure. This study's higher percentage of respondents may simply reflect the passage of time, resulting in increased awareness. A large majority of the students had eaten organic food (73 percent), with a small proportion remaining uncertain (14 percent).

The vast majority of students responded that they supported labeling of GM food products. This was unsurprising, since consumers consistently report a desire to see labeling when directly asked (see, for example, Hallman and Aquino 2005). Students were asked to rate their desire for labeling for five food-product categories: snack foods, grains, fruits and vegetables, meat and poultry, and dairy products. Snack foods received the highest rating, with 90 percent of respondents in support, while the lowest-ranked category was grains, at 81 percent support. Results for the remaining categories fell within this narrow range. Students had high confidence in government to ensure the safety of the food supply. Farmers were ranked second in this regard. Food companies and grocery stores were lower, but still in the upper half of the scale. Lastly, students were asked to rank the importance of five different attributes of organic: no synthetic pesticides, no chemical fertilizers, no hormones/antibiotics, non-GM, and not irradiated. Lack of pesticides and fertilizers were considered the most important. Non-GM was considered the least important of the requirements, which may be because of the low awareness of GM in the food supply, as previously discussed.

Results for the GM-content models appear in Table 4. In examining these, recall that the base WTP, stated in the intercepts, reflected the WTP for a product that was 100 percent non-GM relative to a version with an unknown GM content. Also note that the final model was the basic model. The likelihood-ratio tests conducted showed the interaction terms to be insignificant, meaning that there was no difference in the influence of attitudes and demographics toward different tolerance levels.

For both milk and cereal there was no statistically 35 significant change from the 100 percent non-GM version to the 99 percent non-GM version. However,

for both there was a significant decrease in WTP for products at the 95 percent non-GM level. The adjustments in predicted WTP correspond to a 4.2 percent decrease for cereal and a 5.3 percent decrease for milk. These percentages were slightly lower than those reported by Rousu et al. (2004), but similar enough to suggest the findings may be somewhat robust.

In terms of the remaining explanatory variables, consumers' knowledge and opinion of GM foods both played key roles in WTP. The opinion coefficients were as expected, with WTP for the non-GM versions decreasing as an individual's opinion of the technology increased. While knowledge tends to be a point of contention, findings here showed that more knowledgeable respondents had significantly higher WTP for versions with limited GM content. This provided evidence that better-informed subjects were not necessarily more accepting of the technology.

Significant demographic variables differed between the milk and cereal models. For milk, females expressed a higher WTP than did males to avoid GM content. This could relate to Creamer et al.'s (2002)

Table 4
Estimated Heteroskedastic Two-Limit Tobit Models for GM Content

Variable	Milk model		Cereal model	
	Estimate	p-value	Estimate	p-value
Intercept	5.6739	<0.0001	5.5788	<0.0001
99	−0.1172	0.3084	−0.1604	0.1125
95	−0.3027	0.0085	−0.2353	0.0200
KnowGM	0.1110	0.0057	0.1336	0.0002
OpinionGM	−0.2873	<0.0001	−0.3035	<0.0001
Religion	0.0914	0.1890	0.1934	0.0017
Black	0.0198	0.9120	−0.4813	0.0064
Female	0.3368	0.0005	0.1178	0.1699
Observations	326		326	
Log likelihood	−1623		−1518	

observation that milk was seen, especially by women, as a product of special concern due to its perceived importance in the diet. With the cereal model, respondents with religious or moral issues had significantly higher WTP, while African Americans expressed lower WTP. The former finding was as expected, while the latter suggested differences along racial lines that should be given further attention.

Table 5 contains results from the production traits models. The base WTP was for a product that was genetically modified for improved production relative to a version with unknown GM content. For this set of models, likelihood-ratio tests showed that the interaction terms with the organic production trait belonged in the model. Compared to GM for production, organic and GM for nutrition versions had significantly higher WTP for both products. Evaluating the equations at the means, the predicted adjustments were a 24.5 percent increase for cereal and a 17.3 percent increase for milk with GM nutritional benefits, and 23.1 percent and 18.7 percent increases for organic cereal and milk, respectively. While it had been expected that the WTP for organic would be higher than for GM with nutritional benefits, these numbers were not significantly different in either model. This result should be viewed favorably by those looking to market second-generation GM products and those promoting organic products.

Table 5

Estimated Heteroskedastic Two-Limit Tobit Models for Production Traits

Variable	Milk model		Cereal model	
	Estimate	p-value	Estimate	p-value
Intercept	3.3352	<0.0001	2.9145	<0.0001
Nutrition	0.5754	<0.0001	0.7129	<0.0001
Organic	3.0202	<0.0001	3.1807	<0.0001
KnowGM	−0.0671	0.2345	−0.0532	0.2858
OpinionGM	0.5465	<0.0001	0.6927	<0.0001
Religion	−0.1701	0.0824	−0.2109	0.0145
Black	0.0561	0.8191	0.1134	0.6265
Female	0.3313	0.0146	0.1856	0.1254
Organic*KnowGM	0.2816	0.0040	0.2454	0.0045
Organic*OpinionGM	−1.1393	<0.0001	−1.2074	<0.0001
Organic*Religion	0.3483	0.0415	0.5111	0.0006
Organic*Black	−0.8402	0.0482	−1.2168	0.0026
Organic*Female	0.0248	0.9161	−0.0078	0.9702
Observations	326		326	
Log likelihood	−1719		−1633	

The interaction terms demonstrated that attitudes and demographics were significant in determining which types of consumers might be more interested in GM for improved nutrition or for organic. Consumers with greater knowledge of GM did express significantly higher WTP for organic. This corresponded well with the results from Table 4 that more knowledge of GM foods leads people to desire substitutes. Those who took religious and moral beliefs into account when making food purchases similarly had greater interest in organic versions for both products. In contrast, the higher a consumer's opinion of GM foods was, the lower their WTP for organic. Racial differences also existed, with black consumers having lower WTP for organic. This appeared again to follow that group's lower interest in non-GM products in the first two models. The lack of significant differences between males and females suggests that other factors would be better at segmenting consumers in the marketplace.

Results for all models have been adjusted for het- 40 eroskedasticity. Variances in WTP were found to differ by both school attended and race. For the former, the responses from WC students had a higher variance than did those from UD. This was found despite the lack of significant differences in the mean responses between the schools. Responses from black or African American students also were found to have a larger variance. As with the racial differences in means, there was no clear explanation for this and thus further study is warranted.

DISCUSSION AND CONCLUSIONS

This research examined both consumers' WTP for different thresholds for GM content in non-GM foods and consumers' WTP for foods produced either organically or genetically modified for varying reasons. The implication from the models for the former was that if the United States does implement a threshold level of GM content in non-GM foods, 1 percent would be a reasonable limit. This was an encouraging result, as a zero-percent tolerance would be difficult to achieve, given the proliferation of GM foods in the United States and the expenses to achieve a 100 percent non-GM standard. However, 5 percent GM content was enough to significantly decrease WTP to a level no different from that for current products where the quantity of GM content is unknown. Thus our recommendation is that foods beyond 1 percent GM content be referred to as "GM," and that it would not be worth the expense and effort of implementing a 95 percent non-GM standard. This result varies from Rousu et al. (2004), who failed to find a difference between a 1 and 5 percent tolerance level and therefore proposed 5 percent as adequate. Their small sample though, as they noted, meant care was needed in making a general conclusion. The larger sample here of future consumers suggests a more stringent level would be required.

Evidence additionally shows that acceptable tolerance levels and their respective WTP may vary by degree of processing. Indications of WTP for milk, the fresh product, were higher than for the processed product, cereal, at all tolerance levels. For milk, based on the descriptive statistics, WTP premiums existed for both the 100 and 99 percent non-GM levels while cereal only had a significant premium for the former. In the models, the WTP for 99 percent non-GM cereal was marginally not significantly less than the WTP for the 100 percent version. It seems, then, that non-GM is a more important attribute for fresh products, although the tolerance for GM within non-GM processed products may be smaller. Interest in a 5 percent tolerance level for non-GM processed foods seemed nearly nonexistent.

For the comparison of production traits, consumers' WTP was significantly more for either organic foods or those genetically modified to have nutrition benefits over foods genetically modified to improve production. Of greater interest, the WTP between organic and GM for nutrition benefits foods were not significantly different from one another based on either the statistics or the model estimates. These results suggested a large potential consumer interest in niche markets for both product categories. The findings for GM for improved nutrition foods, in particular, suggested that such foods could command a premium, as is seen with organic products. This should be considered by any company concerned about needing to label second-generation GM foods. Fears regarding negative consumer reaction toward GM labeling of second-generation products may be unfounded and unnecessarily slowing the appearance of such products. From these results it would seem that producers may be overcautious about GM labeling and that a potentially profitable market exists for such products.

While the differences in WTP for organic and GM to improve nutrition were not significantly different overall, the types of consumers interested in each respective product market were. Those with greater knowledge of GM foods or with religious or moral concerns about their foods were much more interested in organic versions. In contrast, blacks and those with higher opinions of genetic modification favored foods genetically modified to improve nutrition. A final finding is that, unlike in the tolerance-level results, there were no noticeable differences between fresh and processed products.

Some limitations and corresponding possible extensions should be noted. An expanded subject pool from the general population and other states would help judge the extent of these results. The additional investigation of other food products would also be useful. Finally, given the varieties of methods to gauge WTP, other formats could be used as comparisons. Regardless, the results should be carefully considered by marketers and policy analysts.

REFERENCES

Baker, G. A., and T. A. Burnham. 2001. "Consumer Response to Genetically Modified Foods: Market Segment Analysis and Implications for Producers and Policy Makers." *Journal of Agricultural and Resource Economics* 26:387–403.

Bernard, J. C., C. Zhang, and K. Gifford. 2006. "An Experimental Investigation of Consumer Willingness to Pay for Non-GM Foods When an Organic Option Is Present." *Agricultural and Resource Economics Review* 35:374–385.

Bugbee, M., M. Loureiro, and S. Hine. 2004. "A Risk Perception Analysis of Genetically Modified Foods Based on Stated Preferences." Dept. of Agricultural and Resource Economics, Fort Collins, CO. Colorado State Cooperative Extension. ABMR 04-01.

Burton, M., and D. Pearse. 2002. "Consumer Attitudes towards Genetic Modification, Functional Foods and Microorganisms: A Choice Modeling Experiment for Beer." *AgBioForum* 5:51–58.

Chern, W. S., K. Rickertsen, N. Tsuboi, and T. Fu. 2002. "Consumer Acceptance and Willingness to Pay for Genetically Modified Vegetable Oil and Salmon: A Multiple-Country Assessment." *AgBioForum* 5:105–112.

Costa-Font, M., J. M. Gil, and B. Traill. 2008. "Consumer Acceptance, Valuation of and Attitudes towards Genetically Modified Foods: Review and Implications for Food Policy." *Food Policy* 33:99–111.

Creamer, L. K., L. E Pearce, J. P. Hill, and M. J. Boland. 2002. "Milk and Dairy Products in the 21st Century." *Journal of Agricultural and Food Chemistry* 50:7187–7193.

Fritz, S., D. Husmann, G. Wingenback, T. Rutherford, V. Egger, and P. Wadhwa. 2003. "Awareness and Acceptance of Biotechnology Issues among Youth, Undergraduates, and Adults." *AgBioForum* 6:178–184.

Gruère, G. P., and S. R. Rao. 2007. "A Review of International Labeling Policies of Genetically Modified Food to Evaluate India's Proposed Rule." *AgBioForum* 10:51–64.

Hallman, W. K., and H. L. Aquino. 2005. "Consumers' Desire for GM Labels: Is the Devil in the Details?" *Choices* 20:217–22.

Hallman, W. K., W. C. Hebden, H. L. Aquino, C. L. Cuite, and J. T. Lang. 2003. *Public Perceptions of Genetically Modified Foods: A National Study of American Knowledge and Opinion* (Publication number RR-1003-004). New Brunswick, NJ: Food Policy Institute, Cook College, Rutgers—The State University of New Jersey.

Harrison, R. W., J. Gillespie, and D. Fields. 2005. "Analysis of Cardinal and Ordinal Assumptions in Conjoint Analysis." *Agricultural and Resource Economics Review* 34:238–252.

Hossain, F., B. Onyango, A. Adelaja, B. Schilling, and W. Hallman. 2003. "Nutritional Benefits and Consumer Willingness to Buy Genetically Modified Foods." *Journal of Food Distribution Research* 34:24–29.

Kraus, S. J. 1995. "Attitudes and the Prediction of Behavior: A Meta-Analysis of the Empirical Literature." *Personality and Social Psychology Bulletin* 21:58–75.

Lee, K. H., and C. B. Hatcher. 2001. "Willingness to Pay for Information: An Analyst's Guide." *Journal of Consumer Affairs* 35:120–140.

Long, J. S. 1997. *Regression Models for Categorical and Limited Dependent Variables*. California: Sage Publications.

Lusk, J. L., and D. Hudson. 2004. "Willingness-to-Pay Estimates and Their Relevance to Agribusiness Decision Making." *Review of Agricultural Economics* 26:152–169.

Lusk, J. L., M. Jamal, L. Kurlander, M. Roucan, and L. Taulman. 2005. "A Meta-Analysis of Genetically

Modified Food Valuation Studies." *Journal of Agricultural and Resource Economics* 30:28–44.

Matsumoto, S. 2006. "Consumers' Valuation of GMO Segregation Programs in Japan." *Journal of Agricultural and Applied Economics* 38:201–211.

Noussair, C., S. Robin, and B. Ruffieux. 2004. "Do Consumers Really Refuse to Buy Genetically Modified Food?" *Economic Journal* 114:102–120.

O'Connor, E., C. Cowan, G. Williams, J. O'Connell, and M. P. Boland. 2006. "Irish Consumer Acceptance of a Hypothetical Second-Generation GM Yogurt Product." *Food Quality and Preference* 17:400–411.

Onyango, B., and R. Govindasamy. 2005. "Consumer Willingness to Pay for GM Food Benefits: Pay-Off or Empty Promise? Implications for the Food Industry." *Choices* 20:223–226

Onyango, B., and R. M. Nayga Jr. 2004. "Consumer Acceptance of Nutritionally Enhanced Genetically Modified Food: Relevance of Gene Transfer Technology." *Journal of Agricultural and Resource Economics* 29:567–583.

Rimal, A., W. Moon, and S. K. Balasubramanian. 2006. "Perceived Risks of Agro-Biotechnology and Organic Food Purchases in the United States." *Journal of Food Distribution Research* 37:70–79.

Rousu, M., W. E. Huffman, J. F. Shogren, and A. Tegene. 2004. "Are United States Consumers Tolerant of Genetically Modified Foods?" *Review of Agricultural Economics* 26:19–31.

Schilling, B. J., W. Hallman, F. Hossain, and A. O. Adelaja. 2003. "Consumer Perceptions of Food Biotechnology: Evidence from a Survey of U.S. Consumers." *Journal of Food Distribution Research* 34:30–35.

U.S. Census Bureau. 2006. *United States Census 2000*. Available at http://www.census.gov/main/www/cen2000.html.

U.S. Food and Drug Administration. 2001. *Voluntary Labeling Indicating Whether Foods Have or Have Not Been Developed Using Bioengineering*. Available at http://www.cfsan.fda.gov/?dms/biolabgu.html.

Voelckner, F. 2006. "An Empirical Comparison of Methods for Measuring Consumers' Willingness to Pay." *Marketing Letters* 17:137–149.

Zhao, J., and R. Widdows. 2001. "Consumers' Attitudes to Biotechnology and Food Products: A Survey of Younger, Educated Consumers." *Consumer Interest Annual*.

Reading Questions

1. Explain how the researchers differentiate between first-generation genetically-modified (GM) foods, second-generation GM foods, and organic foods.

2. According to the researchers, why does labeling of first-generation GM foods rarely occur in the United States?

3. What rationalizations do the researchers provide for their selection of college students as the target population for their data collection?

4. Based on what specific findings do the researchers propose that "foods beyond 1 percent GM content be referred to as 'GM,' and that it would not be worth the expense and effort of implementing a 95 percent non-GM standard" (par. 41)?

5. According to the researchers, why is it the case that "producers may be overcautious about GM labeling" (43) for certain kinds of genetically modified foods?

Rhetoric Questions

6. The authors of this study have multiple audiences. One of these is clearly other researchers who might endeavor to explore this topic further. What other group is an intended audience for this research? How do you know?

7. The study presents results of the research in a number of areas of the report. Besides the Results section, where else can you locate the reporting of findings? What is the effect on you, as a reader, of the researchers' decisions to report their findings in this manner? As part of your response, explore the location of tables in the report.

8. What two goals of social sciences reporting could the report's final paragraph be said to achieve?

Response and Research Questions

9. Would you be willing to pay more for a gallon of milk (a fresh product) produced organically than a gallon of milk that is GM to improve nutrition (enriched with calcium and vitamin D)? Why or why not? Would you be willing to pay more for a box of cereal (a processed product) produced organically than a box of cereal that is GM to improve nutrition (enriched with vitamins and minerals)? Why or why not?

10. When you are shopping, for what products do you consider GM status as part of your decision to purchase? For what products does GM status not matter at all? Why do you think this is the case?

ACADEMIC CASE STUDY • GENETICALLY MODIFIED FOOD   NATURAL SCIENCES

Maternal and Fetal Exposure to Pesticides Associated to Genetically Modified Foods in Eastern Townships of Quebec, Canada

AZIZ ARIS AND SAMUEL LEBLANC

Aziz Aris is an investigator for the Mother and Child Axis at the Clinical Research Center and associate professor of obstetrics and gynecology at the University of Sherbrooke Hospital in Quebec, Canada. With Samuel Leblanc, co-author of the study below, the researchers report on their investigation into the presence of pesticides associated with genetically modified foods in women (pregnant and nonpregnant) in eastern Canada. As the authors indicate, one of the goals of their research is to help "develop procedures to avoid environmentally induced disease in susceptible populations such as pregnant women and their fetuses." This article first appeared in the journal *Source: Reproductive Toxicology* in 2011.

ABSTRACT

Pesticides associated to genetically modified foods (PAGMF) are engineered to tolerate herbicides such as glyphosate (GLYP) and gluphosinate (GLUF) or insecticides such as the bacterial toxin bacillus thuringiensis (Bt). The aim of this study was to evaluate the correlation between maternal and fetal exposure, and to determine exposure levels of GLYP and its metabolite aminomethyl phosphoric acid (AMPA), GLUF and its metabolite 3-methylphosphinicopropionic acid (3-MPPA), and Cry1Ab protein (a Bt toxin) in Eastern Townships of Quebec, Canada. Blood of thirty pregnant women (PW) and thirty-nine nonpregnant women (NPW) was studied. Serum GLYP and GLUF were detected in NPW and not detected in PW. Serum 3-MPPA and CryAb1 toxin were detected in PW, their fetuses, and NPW. This is the first study to reveal the presence of circulating PAGMF in women with and without pregnancy, paving the way for a new field in reproductive toxicology including nutrition and utero-placental toxicities.

1. INTRODUCTION

An optimal exchange across the maternal-fetal unit (MFU) is necessary for a successful pregnancy. The placenta plays a major role in the embryo's nutrition and growth, in the regulation of the endocrine functions, and in drug biotransformation [1–3]. Exchange involves not only physiological constituents, but also substances that represent a pathological risk for the fetus such as xenobiotics that include drugs, food additives, pesticides, and environmental pollutants [4]. The understanding of what xenobiotics do to the MFU and what the MFU does to the xenobiotics should provide the basis for the use of the placenta as a tool to investigate and predict some aspects of developmental toxicity [4]. Moreover, pathological conditions in the placenta are important causes of intrauterine or perinatal death, congenital anomalies, intrauterine growth retardation, maternal death, and a great deal of morbidity for both mother and child [5].

Genetically modified plants (GMP) were first approved for commercialization in Canada in 1996 then became distributed worldwide. Global areas of these GMP increased from 1.7 million hectares in 1996 to 134 million hectares in 2009, an 80-fold increase [6]. This growth rate makes GMP the fastest-adopted crop technology [6]. GMP are plants in which genetic material has been altered in a way that does not occur naturally. Genetic engineering allows gene transfer (transgenesis) from an organism into another in order to confer them new traits. Combining GMP with pesticides-associated GM foods (PAGMF) allows the protection of desirable crops and the elimination of unwanted plants by reducing the competition for nutrients or by providing insect resistance. There is a debate on the direct threat of genes used in the preparation of these new foods on human health, as they are not detectable in the body, but the real danger may come from PAGMF [6–10]. Among the innumerable PAGMF, two categories are largely used in our agriculture since their introduction in 1996: (1) residues derived from herbicide-tolerant GM crops such as glyphosate (GLYP) and its metabolite aminomethyl phosphoric acid (AMPA) [11], and glyphosinate ammonium (GLUF) and its metabolite 3-methylphosphinicopropionic acid (MPPA) [12]; and (2) residues derived from insect-resistant GM crops such as Cry1Ab protein [13,14].

Among herbicide-tolerant GM crops, the first to be grown commercially were soybeans which were modified to tolerate glyphosate [11]. Glyphosate [N-(Phosphonomethyl) glycine] is a nonselective, post-emergence herbicide used for the control of a wide range of weeds [15]. It can be used on non-crop land as well as in a great variety of crops. GLYP is the active ingredient in the commercial herbicide Roundup®. Glyphosate is an acid, but usually used in a salt form, most commonly the isopropylamine salt. The target of glyphosate is 5-enolpyruvoylshikimate 3-phosphate synthase (EPSPS), an enzyme in the shikimate pathway that is required for the synthesis of many aromatic plant metabolites, including some amino acids. The gene that confers tolerance of the herbicide is from the soil bacterium *Agrobacterium tumefaciens* and makes an EPSPS that is not affected by glyphosate. Few studies have examined the kinetics of absorption, distribution, metabolism, and elimination (ADME) of glyphosate in humans [15,16]. Curwin et al. [17] reported detection of urinary GLYP concentrations among children, mothers, and fathers living in farm and nonfarm households in Iowa. The ranges of detection were 0.062–5.0 ng/ml and 0.10–11 ng/ml for nonfarm and farm mothers, respectively. There was no significant difference between farm and nonfarm mothers and no positive association between the mothers' urinary glyphosate levels and glyphosate dust concentrations. These findings suggest that other sources of exposure such as diet may be involved.

Gluphosinate (or glufosinate) [ammonium dl-homoalanin-4-(methyl) phosphinate] is a broad-spectrum, contact herbicide. Its major metabolite is 3-methylphosphinicopropionic acid (MPPA), with which it has similar biological and toxicological effects [18]. GLUF is used to control a wide range of weeds after the crop emerges or for total vegetation control on land not used for cultivation. Gluphosinate herbicides are also used to desiccate (dry out) crops before harvest. It is a phosphorus-containing amino acid. It inhibits the activity of an enzyme, glutamine synthetase, which is necessary for the production of the amino acid glutamine and for ammonia detoxification [12]. The application of GLUF leads to reduced glutamine and increased ammonia levels in the plant's tissues. This causes photosynthesis to stop and the plant dies within a few days. GLUF also inhibits the same enzyme in animals [19]. The gene used to make plants resistant to gluphosinate comes from the bacterium *Streptomyces hygroscopicus* and encodes an enzyme called phosphinothricine acetyl transferase (PAT). This enzyme detoxifies GLUF. Crop varieties carrying this trait include varieties of oilseed rape, maize, soybeans, sugar beet, fodder beet, cotton, and rice. As for GLYP, its kinetics of absorption, distribution, metabolism, and elimination (ADME) is not well studied in humans, except for a few poisoned-case studies [16,20,21]. Hirose et al. reported the case of a 65-year-old male who ingested BASTA, which contains 20% (w/v) of GLUF ammonium, about 300 ml, more than the estimated human toxic dose [20]. The authors studied the serial change of serum GLUF concentration every 3–6 h and assessed the urinary excretion of GLUF every 24 h. The absorbed amount of GLUF was estimated from the cumulative urinary excretion. The changes in serum GLUF concentration exhibited $T_{1/2\alpha}$ of 1.84 and $T_{1/2\alpha}$ of 9.59 h. The apparent distribution volume at b-phase and the total body clearance were 1.44 1/kg and 86.6 ml/min, respectively. Renal clearance was estimated to be 77.9 ml/min.

The Cry1Ab toxin is an insecticidal protein produced by the naturally occurring soil bacterium *Bacillus thuringiensis* [22,23]. The gene (truncated *cry1Ab* gene) encoding this insecticidal protein was genetically transformed into maize genome to produce a transgenic insect-resistant plant (Bt-maize; MON810) and, thereby, provide specific protection against Lepidoptera infestation [13,14]. For more than 10 years, GM crops have been commercialized and approved as an animal feed in several countries worldwide. The Cry toxins (protoxins) produced by GM crops are solubilized and activated to Cry toxins by gut proteases of susceptible insect larvae. Activated toxin binds to specific receptors localized in the midgut epithelial cells [24,25], invading the cell membrane and forming cation-selective ion channels that lead to the disruption of the epithelial barrier and larval death by osmotic cell lysis [26–28].

Since the basis of better health is prevention, one would hope that we can develop procedures to avoid environmentally induced disease in susceptible populations such as pregnant women and their fetuses. The fetus is considered to be highly susceptible to the adverse effects of xenobiotics. This is because environmental agents could disrupt the biological events that are required to ensure normal growth and development [29,30]. PAGMF are among the xenobiotics that have recently emerged and extensively entered the human food chain [9], paving the way for a new field of multidisciplinary research, combining human reproduction, toxicology, and nutrition, but not as yet explored. Generated data will help regulatory agencies responsible for the protection of human health to make better decisions. Thus, the aim of this study was to investigate whether pregnant women are exposed to PAGMF and whether these toxicants cross the placenta to reach the fetus.

2. MATERIALS AND METHODS

2.1. Chemicals and reagents

For the analytical support (Section 2.3), GLYP, AMPA, GLUF, APPA, and N-methyl-N-(tert-butyl-dimethylsilyl) trifluoroacetamide (MTBSTFA) + 1% tertburyldimethylchlorosilane (TBDMCS) were purchased from Sigma (St. Louis, MO, USA). 3-MPPA was purchased from Wako Chemicals USA (Richmond, VA, USA), and Sep-Pak Plus PS-2 cartridges, from Waters Corporation (Milford, MA, USA). All other chemicals and reagents were of analytical grade (Sigma, MO, USA). The serum samples for validation were collected from volunteers.

2.2. Study subjects and blood sampling

At the Centre Hospitalier Universitaire de Sherbrooke (CHUS), we formed two groups of subjects: (1) a group of healthy pregnant women ($n = 30$), recruited at delivery; and (2) a group of healthy fertile nonpregnant women ($n = 39$), recruited during their tubal ligation of sterilization. As shown in Table 1 of clinical characteristics of subjects, eligible groups were matched for age and body mass index (BMI). Participants were not known for cigarette or illicit drug use or for medical condition (i.e., diabetes, hypertension, or metabolic disease). Pregnant women had vaginal delivery and did not have any adverse perinatal outcomes. All neonates were of appropriate size for gestational age (3423 ± 375 g).

Blood sampling was done before delivery for pregnant women or at tubal ligation for nonpregnant

Table 1

Characteristics of subjects

	Pregnant women (n = 30)	Nonpregnant women (n = 39)	P value[a]
Age (year, mean ± SD)	32.4 ± 4.2	33.9 ± 4.0	NS
BMI (kg/m², mean ± SD)	24.9 ± 3.1	24.8 ± 3.4	NS
Gestational age (week, mean ± SD)	38.3 ± 2.5	N/A	N/A
Birth weight (g, mean ± SD)	3364 ± 335	N/A	N/A

BMI, body mass index; N/A, not applicable; data are expressed as mean ± SD; NS, not significant.

[a]P values were determined by Mann-Whitney test.

women and was most commonly obtained from the median cubital vein, on the anterior forearm. Umbilical cord blood sampling was done after birth using the syringe method. Since labor time can take several hours, the time between taking the last meal and blood sampling is often a matter of hours. Blood samples were collected in BD Vacutainer 10 ml glass serum tubes (Franklin Lakes, NJ, USA). To obtain serum, whole blood was centrifuged at 2000 rpm for 15 min within 1 h of collection. For maternal samples, about 10 ml of blood was collected, resulting in 5–6.5 ml of serum. For cord blood samples, about 10 ml of blood was also collected by syringe, giving 3–4.5 ml of serum. Serum was stored at −20°C until assayed for PAGMF levels.

Subjects were pregnant and nonpregnant women living in Sherbrooke, an urban area of Eastern Townships of Quebec, Canada. No subject had worked or lived with a spouse working in contact with pesticides. The diet taken is typical of a middle-class population of Western industrialized countries. A food market-basket, representative for the general Sherbrooke population, contains various meats, margarine, canola oil, rice, corn, grain, peanuts, potatoes, fruits and vegetables, eggs, poultry, meat, and fish. Beverages include milk, juice, tea, coffee, bottled water, soft drinks, and beer. Most of these foods come mainly from the province of Quebec, then the rest of Canada and the United States of America. Our study did not quantify the exact levels of PAGMF in a market-basket study.

However, given the widespread use of GM foods in the local daily diet (soybeans, corn, potatoes,...), it is conceivable that the majority of the population is exposed through their daily diet [31,32].

The study was approved by the CHUS Ethics Human Research Committee on Clinical Research. All participants gave written consent.

2.3. Herbicide and metabolite determination

Levels of GLYP, AMPA, GLUF, and 3-MPPA were measured using gas chromatography-mass spectrometry (GC–MS).

2.3.1. CALIBRATION CURVE

According to a method described by Motojyuku et al. [16], GLYP, AMPA, GLUF, and 3-MPPA (1 mg/ml) were prepared in 10% methanol, which is used for all standard dilutions. These solutions were further diluted to concentrations of 100 and 10 µg/ml and stored for a maximum of 3 months at 4°C. A 1 µg/ml solution from previous components was made prior to herbicide extraction. These solutions were used as calibrators. A stock solution of DL-2-amino-3-phosphonopropionic acid (APPA) (1 mg/ml) was prepared and used as an internal standard (IS). The IS stock solution was further diluted to a concentration of 100 µg/ml. Blank serum samples (0.2 ml) were spiked with 5 µl of IS (100 µg/ml), 5 µl of each calibrator solution (100 µg/ml), or 10, 5 µl of 10 µg/ml solution, or 10, 5 µl of 1 µg/ml solution, resulting in calibration samples containing 0.5 μg of IS (2.5 μg/ml), with 0.5 μg (2.5 μg/ml), 0.1 μg (0.5 μg/ml), 0.05 μg (0.25 μg/ml), 0.01 μg (0.05 μg/ml), or 0.005 μg (0.025 μg/ml) of each compound (i.e., GLYP, AMPA, GLUF, and 3-MPPA). Concerning extraction development, spiked serum with 5 μg/ml of each compound was used as a control sample.

2.3.2. EXTRACTION PROCEDURE

The calibration curves and serum samples were extracted by employing a solid phase extraction (SPE) technique, modified from manufacturers' recommendations and from Motojyuku et al. [16]. Spiked serum (0.2 ml), prepared as described above, and acetonitrile (0.2 ml) were added to centrifuge tubes. The tubes were then vortexed (15 s) and centrifuged (5 min, 1600 × g). The samples were purified by SPE using 100 mg Sep-Pak Plus PS-2 cartridges, which were conditioned by washing with 4 ml of acetonitrile followed by 4 ml of distilled water. The samples were loaded onto the SPE cartridges, dried (3 min, 5 psi), and eluted with 2 ml of acetonitrile. The solvent was evaporated to dryness under nitrogen. The samples were reconstituted in 50 μl each of MTBSTFA with 1% TBDMCS and acetonitrile. The mixture was vortexed for 30 s every 10 min, 6 times. Samples of solution containing the derivatives were used directly for GC–MS (Agilent Technologies 6890N GC and 5973 Invert MS).

2.3.3. GC–MS ANALYSIS

Chromatographic conditions for these analyses were as follows: a 30 m × 0.25 mm Zebron ZB-5MS fused-silica capillary column with a film thickness of 0.25 μm from Phenomenex (Torrance, CA, USA) was used. Helium was used as a carrier gas at 1.1 ml/min. A 2 μl extract was injected in a split mode at an injection temperature of 250°C. The oven temperature was programmed to increase from an initial temperature of 100°C (held for 3 min) to 300°C (held for 5 min) at 5°C/min. The temperatures of the quadrupode, ion source, and mass-selective detector interface were respectively 150, 230, and 280°C. The MS was operated in the selected-ion monitoring (SIM) mode. The following ions were monitored (with

quantitative ions in parentheses): GLYP (454), 352; AMPA (396), 367; GLUF (466); 3-MPPA (323); IS (568), 466.

The limit of detection (LOD) is defined as a signal of three times the noise. For 0.2 ml serum samples, LOD was 15, 10, 10, and 5 ng/ml for GLYP, GLUF, AMPA, and 3-MPPA, respectively.

2.4. Cry1Ab protein determination

Cry1Ab protein levels were determined in blood using a commercially available double antibody sandwich (DAS) enzyme-linked immunosorbent assay (Agdia, Elkhart, IN, USA), following manufacturer's instructions. A standard curve was prepared by successive dilutions (0.1–10 ng/ml) of purified Cry1Ab protein (Fitzgerald Industries International, North Acton, MA, USA) in PBST buffer. The mean absorbance (650 nm) was calculated and used to determine samples concentration. Positive and negative controls were prepared with the kit Cry1Ab positive control solution, diluted 1/2 in serum.

2.5. Statistical analysis

PAGMF exposure was expressed as number, range and mean ± SD for each group. Characteristics of cases and controls and PAGMF exposure were compared using the Mann–Whitney U-test for continuous data and by Fisher's exact test for categorical data. Wilcoxon matched pairs test compared two dependent groups. Other statistical analyses were performed using Spearman correlations. Analyses were realized with the software SPSS version 17.0. A value of $P < 0.05$ was considered as significant for every statistical analysis.

3. RESULTS

As shown in Table 1, pregnant women and nonpregnant women were similar in terms of age and body mass index. Pregnant women had normal deliveries and birth-weight infants (Table 1).

GLYP and GLUF were non-detectable (nd) in maternal and fetal serum, but detected in nonpregnant women (Table 2, Fig. 1). GLYP was [2/39 (5%),

Table 2

Concentrations of GLYP, AMPA, GLUF, 3-MPPA, and Cry1Ab protein in material and fetal cord serum

	Maternal (*n* = 30)	Fetal cord (*n* = 30)	*P* value[a]
GLYP			
Number of detection	nd	nd	nc
Range of detection (ng/ml)			
Mean ± SD			
AMPA			
Number of detection	nd	nd	nc
Range of detection (ng/ml)			
Mean ± SD (ng/ml)			
GLUF			
Number of detection	nd	nd	nc
Range of detection (ng/ml)			
Mean ± SD (ng/ml)			
3-MPPA			
Number of detection	30/30 (100%)	30/30 (100%)	*P* < 0.001
Range of detection (ng/ml)	21.9-417	8.76-193	
Mean ± SD (ng/ml)	120 ± 87.0	57.2 ± 45.6	
Cry1Ab			
Number of detection	28/30 (93%)	24/30 (80%)	*P* = 0.002
Range of detection (ng/ml)	nd-1.50	nd-0.14	
Mean ± SD (ng/ml)	0.19 ± 0.30	0.04 ± 0.04	

GLYP, glyphosate; AMPA, aminomethyl phosphoric acid; GLUF, gluphosinate ammonium; 3-MPPA, 3-methylphosphinicopropionic acid; Cry1Ab, protein from bacillus thuringiensis; nd, not detectable; nc, not calculable because not detectable. Data are expressed as number (*n*, %) of detection, range, and mean ± SD (ng/ml).

[a]*P* values were determined by Wilcoxon matched pairs test.

range (nd-93.6 ng/ml), and mean ± SD (73.6 ± 28.2 ng/ml)] and GLUF was [7/39 (18%), range (nd-53.6 ng/ml), and mean ± SD (28.7 ± 15.7 ng/ml). AMPA was not detected in maternal, fetal, and nonpregnant women samples. The metabolite 3-MPPA was detected in maternal serum [30/30 (100%), range (21.9-417 ng/ml), and mean ± SD (120 ± 87.0 ng/ml), in fetal cord serum [30/30 (100%), range (8.76-193 ng/ml), and mean ± SD (57.2 ± 45.6 ng/ml) and

in nonpregnant women serum [26/39 (67%), range (nd-337 ng/ml), and mean ± SD (84.1 ± 70.3 ng/ml)]. A significant difference in 3-MPPA levels was evident between maternal and fetal serum (*P* < 0.001, Table 2, Fig. 1), but not between maternal and nonpregnant women serum (*P* = 0.075, Table 3, Fig. 1).

Serum insecticide Cry1Ab toxin was detected in: (1) pregnant women [28/30 (93%), range (nd-1.5 ng/ml), and mean ± SD (0.19 ± 0.30 ng/ml)]; (2)

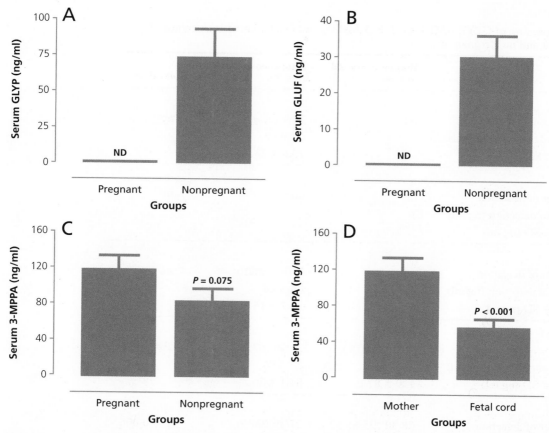

Figure 1. Circulating concentrations of glyphosate (GLYP: A), gluphosinate (GLUF: B), and 3-methylphosphinicopropionic acid (3-MPPA: C and D) in pregnant and nonpregnant women (A–C) and in maternal and fetal cord blood (D). Blood sampling was performed from 30 pregnant women and 39 nonpregnant women. Chemicals were assessed using GC-MS. *P* values were determined by Mann-Whitney test in the comparison of pregnant women to nonpregnant women (A–C). *P* values were determined by Wilcoxon matched pairs test in the comparison of maternal to fetal samples (D). A *P* value of 0.05 was considered as significant.

nonpregnant women [27/39 (69%), range (nd-2.28 ng/ml), and mean ± SD (0.13 ± 0.37 ng/ml)]; and (3) fetal cord [24/30 (80%), range (nd-0.14 ng/ml), and mean ± SD (0.04 ± 0.04 ng/ml)]. A significant difference in Cry1Ab levels was evident between pregnant and nonpregnant women's serum (*P* = 0.006, Table 3, Fig. 2) and between maternal and fetal serum (*P* = 0.002, Table 2, Fig. 2).

We also investigated a possible correlation between the different contaminants in the same woman. In pregnant women, GLYP, its metabolite AMPA, and GLUF were undetectable in maternal blood and therefore impossible to establish a correlation between them. In nonpregnant women, GLYP was detected in 5% of the subjects, its metabolite AMPA was not detected, and GLUF was detected in 18%; thus, no significant correlation emerged from these contaminants in the same subjects. Moreover, there was no correlation between 3-MPPA and Cry1AB in the same women, both pregnant and not pregnant.

Table 3

Concentrations of GLYP, AMPA, GLUF, 3-MPPA, and Cry1Ab protein in serum of pregnant and nonpregnant women

	Pregnant women (n = 30)	Nonpregnant women (n = 39)	P value[a]
GLYP			
Number of detection	nd	2/39 (5%)	nc
Range of detection (ng/ml)		nd-93.6	
Mean ± SD		73.6 ± 28.2	
AMPA			
Number of detection	nd	nd	nc
Range of detection (ng/ml)			
Mean ± SD (ng/ml)			
GLUF			
Number of detection	nd	7/39 (18%)	nc
Range of detection (ng/ml)		nd-53.6	
Mean ± SD (ng/ml)		28.7 ± 15.7	
3-MPPA			
Number of detection	30/30 (100%)	26/39 (67%)	P = 0.075
Range of detection (ng/ml)	21.9-417	nd-337	
Mean ± SD (ng/ml)	120 ± 87.0	84.1 ± 70.3	
Cry1Ab			
Number of detection	28/30 (93%)	27/39 (69%)	P = 0.006
Range of detection (ng/ml)	nd-1.50	nd-2.28	
Mean ± SD (ng/ml)	0.19 ± 0.30	0.13 ± 0.37	

GLYP, glyphosate; AMPA, aminomethyl phosphoric acid; GLUF, gluphosinate ammonium; 3-MPPA, 3-methylphosphinicopropionic acid; Cry1Ab, protein from bacillus thuringiensis; nd, not detectable; nc, not calculable because not detectable. Data are expressed as number (n, %) of detection, range, and mean ± SD (ng/ml).

[a]P values were determined by Mann-Whitney test.

4. DISCUSSION

Our results show that GLYP was not detected in maternal and fetal blood, but present in the blood of some nonpregnant women (5%), whereas its metabolite AMPA was not detected in all analyzed samples. This may be explained by the absence of exposure, the efficiency of elimination, or the limitation of the method of detection. Previous studies report that glyphosate and AMPA share similar toxicological profiles. Glyphosate toxicity has been shown to be involved in the induction of developmental retardation of fetal skeleton [33] and significant adverse effects on the reproductive system of male Wistar rats at puberty and during adulthood [34]. Also, glyphosate was harmful to human placental cells [35,36] and embryonic cells [36]. It is interesting to note that all

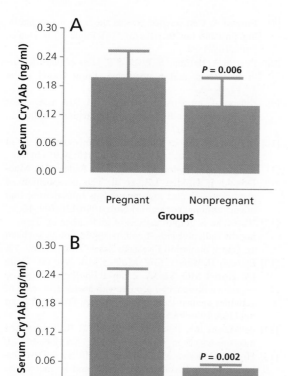

Figure 2. Circulating concentrations of Cry1Ab toxin in pregnant and nonpregnant women (A), and maternal and fetal cord (B). Blood sampling was performed from 30 pregnant women and 39 nonpregnant women. Levels of Cry1Ab toxin were assessed using an ELISA method. P values were determined by Mann-Whitney test in the comparison of pregnant women to nonpregnant women (A). P values were determined by Wilcoxon matched pairs test in the comparison of maternal to fetal samples (B). A P value of 0.05 was considered as significant.

of these animal and *in vitro* studies used very high concentrations of GLYP compared to the human levels found in our studies. In this regard, our results represent actual concentrations detected in humans and therefore they constitute a referential basis for future investigations in this field.

GLUF was detected in 18% of nonpregnant women's blood and not detected in maternal and fetal

blood. As for GLYP, the non-detection of GLUF may be explained by the absence of exposure, the efficiency of elimination, or the limitation of the method of detection. Regarding the non-detection of certain chemicals in pregnant women compared with nonpregnant women, it is assumed that the hemodilution caused by pregnancy may explain, at least in part, such non-detection. On the other hand, 3-MPPA (the metabolite of GLUF) was detected in 100% of maternal and umbilical cord blood samples, and in 67% of the nonpregnant women's blood samples. This highlights that fetal this metabolite is more detectable than its precursor and seems to easily cross the placenta to reach the fetus. Garcia et al. [37] investigated the potential teratogenic effects of GLUF in humans and found increased risk of congenital malformations with exposure to GLUF. GLUF has also been shown in mouse embryos to cause growth retardation, increased death, or hypoplasia [18]. As for GLYP, it is interesting to note that the GLUF concentrations used in these tests are very high (10 ug/ml) compared to the levels we found in this study (53.6 ng/ml). Hence, our data, which provide the actual and precise concentrations of these toxicants, will help in the design of more relevant studies in the future.

On the other hand, Cry1Ab toxin was detected in 93% and 80% of maternal and fetal blood samples, respectively, and in 69% of tested blood samples from nonpregnant women. There are no other studies for comparison with our results. However, trace amounts of the Cry1Ab toxin were detected in the gastrointestinal contents of livestock fed on GM corn [38–40], raising concerns about this toxin in insect-resistant GM crops: (1) that these toxins may not be effectively eliminated in humans and (2) there may be a high risk of exposure through consumption of contaminated meat.

5. CONCLUSIONS

To our knowledge, this is the first study to highlight the presence of pesticides-associated genetically modified foods in maternal, fetal, and nonpregnant women's blood. 3-MPPA and Cry1Ab toxin are clearly detectable and appear to cross the placenta to the fetus. Given the potential toxicity of these environmental pollutants and the fragility of the fetus, more studies are needed, particularly those using the placental transfer approach [41]. Thus, our present results will provide baseline data for future studies exploring a new area of research relating to nutrition, toxicology, and reproduction in women. Today, obstetric-gynecological disorders that are associated with environmental chemicals are not known. This may involve perinatal complications (i.e., abortion, prematurity, intrauterine growth restriction, and preeclampsia) and reproductive disorders (i.e., infertility, endometriosis and gynecological cancer). Thus, knowing the actual PAGMF concentrations in humans constitutes a cornerstone in the advancement of research in this area.

CONFLICT OF INTEREST STATEMENT

The authors declare that they have no competing interests.

ACKNOWLEDGMENTS

This study was supported by funding provided by the Fonds de Recherche en Santé du Québec (FRSQ). The authors wish to thank Drs. Youssef AinMelk, Marie-Thérèse Berthier, Krystel Paris, François Leclerc, and Denis Cyr for their material and technical assistance.

REFERENCES

[1] Sastry BV. Techniques to study human placental transport. Adv Drug Deliv Rev 1999;38:17–39.

[2] Haggarty P, Allstaff S, Hoad G, Ashton J, Abramovich DR. Placental nutrient transfer capacity and fetal growth. Placenta 2002;23:86–92.

[3] Gude NM, Roberts CT, Kalionis B, King RG. Growth and function of the normal human placenta. Thromb Res 2004;114:397–407.

[4] Myllynen P, Pasanen M, Pelkonen O. Human placenta: a human organ for developmental toxicology research and biomonitoring. Placenta 2005;26:361–71.

[5] Guillette EA, Meza MM, Aquilar MG, Soto AD, Garcia IE. An anthropological approach to the evaluation of preschool children exposed to pesticides in Mexico. Environ Health Perspect 1998;106:347–53.

[6] Clive J. Global status of commercialized biotech/GM crops. In: ISAAA 2009. 2009.

[7] Pusztai A. Can science give us the tools for recognizing possible health risks of GM food? Nutr Health 2002;16:73–84.

[8] Pusztai A, Bardocz S, Ewen SW. Uses of plant lectins in bioscience and biomedicine. Front Biosci 2008; 13:1130–40.

[9] Magana-Gomez JA, de la Barca AM. Risk assessment of genetically modified crops for nutrition and health. Nutr Rev 2009;67:1–16.

[10] Borchers A, Teuber SS, Keen CL, Gershwin ME. Food safety. Clin Rev Allergy Immunol 2010;39:95–141.

[11] Padgette SR, Taylor NB, Nida DL, Bailey MR, MacDonald J, Holden LR, et al. The composition of glyphosate-tolerant soybean seeds is equivalent to that of conventional soybeans. J Nutr 1996;126:702–16.

[12] Watanabe S. Rapid analysis of glufosinate by improving the bulletin method and its application to soybean and corn. Shokuhin Eiseigaku Zasshi 2002;43:169–72.

[13] Estruch JJ, Warren GW, Mullins MA, Nye GJ, Craig JA, Koziel MG. Vip3A, a novel *Bacillus thuringiensis* vegetative insecticidal protein with a wide spectrum of activities against lepidopteran insects. Proc Natl Acad Sci USA 1996;93:5389–94.

[14] de Maagd RA, Bosch D, Stiekema W. Toxin-mediated insect resistance in plants. Trends Plant Sci 1999;4:9–13.

[15] Hori Y, Fujisawa M, Shimada K, Hirose Y. Determination of the herbicide glyphosate and its metabolite in biological specimens by gas chromatography–mass spectrometry. A case of poisoning by roundup herbicide. J Anal Toxicol 2003;27:162–6.

[16] Motojyuku M, Saito T, Akieda K, Otsuka H, Yamamoto I, Inokuchi S. Determination of glyphosate, glyphosate metabolites, and glufosinate in human serum by gas chromatography-mass spectrometry. J Chromatogr B: Anal Technol Biomed Life Sci 2008;875:509–14.

[17] Curwin BD, Hein MJ, Sanderson WT, Striley C, Heederik D, Kromhout H, et al. Urinary pesticide concentrations among children, mothers and fathers living in farm and non-farm households in Iowa. Ann Occup Hyg 2007;51:53–65.

[18] Watanabe T, Iwase T. Developmental and dysmorphogenic effects of glufosinate ammonium on mouse embryos in culture. Teratog Carcinog Mutagen 1996; 16:287–99.

[19] Hoerlein G. Glufosinate (phosphinothricin), a natural amino acid with unexpected herbicidal properties. Rev Environ Contam Toxicol 1994;138:73–145.

[20] Hirose Y, Kobayashi M, Koyama K, Kohda Y, Tanaka T, Honda H, et al. A toxicokinetic analysis in a patient with acute glufosinate poisoning. Hum Exp Toxicol 1999;18:305–8.

[21] Hori Y, Fujisawa M, Shimada K, Hirose Y. Determination of glufosinate ammonium and its metabolite, 3-methylphosphinicopropionic acid, in human serum

by gas chromatography–mass spectrometry following mixed-mode solid-phase extraction and t-BDMS derivatization. J Anal Toxicol 2001;25:680–4.

[22] Hofte H, Whiteley HR. Insecticidal crystal proteins of *Bacillus thuringiensis*. Microbiol Rev 1989;53:242–55.

[23] Schnepf E, Crickmore N, Van Rie J, Lereclus D, Baum J, Feitelson J, et al. *Bacillus thuringiensis* and its pesticidal crystal proteins. Microbiol Mol Biol Rev 1998;62:775–806.

[24] Van Rie J, Jansens S, Hofte H, Degheele D, Van Mellaert H. Receptors on the brush border membrane of the insect midgut as determinants of the specificity of *Bacillus thuringiensis* delta-endotoxins. Appl Environ Microbiol 1990;56:1378–85.

[25] Aranda E, Sanchez J, Peferoen M, Guereca L, Bravo A. Interactions of *Bacillus thuringiensis* crystal proteins with the midgut epithelial cells of Spodoptera frugiperda (Lepidoptera: Noctuidae). J Invertebr Pathol 1996;68:203–12.

[26] Slatin SL, Abrams CK, English L. Delta-endotoxins form cation-selective channels in planar lipid bilayers. Biochem Biophys Res Commun 1990;169:765–72.

[27] Knowles BH, Blatt MR, Tester M, Horsnell JM, Carroll J, Menestrina G, et al. A cytolytic delta-endotoxin from *Bacillus thuringiensis* var. israelensis forms cation-selective channels in planar lipid bilayers. FEBS Lett 1989;244:259–62.

[28] Du J, Knowles BH, Li J, Ellar DJ. Biochemical characterization of *Bacillus thuringiensis* cytolytic toxins in association with a phospholipid bilayer. Biochem J 1999;338(Pt 1):185–93.

[29] Dietert RR, Piepenbrink MS. The managed immune system: protecting the womb to delay the tomb. Hum Exp Toxicol 2008;27:129–34.

[30] Dietert RR. Developmental immunotoxicity (DIT), postnatal immune dysfunction and childhood leukemia. Blood Cells Mol Dis 2009;42:108–12.

[31] Chapotin SM, Wolt JD. Genetically modified crops for the bioeconomy: meeting public and regulatory expectations. Transgenic Res 2007;16:675–88.

[32] Rommens CM. Barriers and paths to market for genetically engineered crops. Plant Biotechnol J 2010; 8:101–11.

[33] Dallegrave E, Mantese FD, Coelho RS, Pereira JD, Dalsenter PR, Langeloh A. The teratogenic potential of the herbicide glyphosate-roundup in Wistar rats. Toxicol Lett 2003;142:45–52.

[34] Dallegrave E, Mantese FD, Oliveira RT, Andrade AJ, Dalsenter PR, Langeloh A. Pre- and postnatal toxicity of the commercial glyphosate formulation in Wistar rats. Arch Toxicol 2007;81:665–73.

[35] Richard S, Moslemi S, Sipahutar H, Benachour N, Seralini GE. Differential effects of glyphosate and roundup on human placental cells and aromatase. Environ Health Perspect 2005;113:716–20.

[36] Benachour N, Seralini GE. Glyphosate formulations induce apoptosis and necrosis in human umbilical, embryonic, and placental cells. Chem Res Toxicol 2009;22:97–105.

[37] Garcia AM, Benavides FG, Fletcher T, Orts E. Paternal exposure to pesticides and congenital malformations. Scand J Work Environ Health 1998;24:473–80.

[38] Chowdhury EH, Shimada N, Murata H, Mikami O, Sultana P, Miyazaki S, et al. Detection of Cry1Ab protein in gastrointestinal contents but not visceral organs of genetically modified Bt11-fed calves. Vet Hum Toxicol 2003;45:72–5.

[39] Chowdhury EH, Kuribara H, Hino A, Sultana P, Mikami O, Shimada N, et al. Detection of corn intrinsic and recombinant DNA fragments and Cry1Ab protein in the gastrointestinal contents of pigs fed genetically modified corn Bt11. J Anim Sci 2003;81:2546–51.

[40] Lutz B, Wiedemann S, Einspanier R, Mayer J, Albrecht C. Degradation of Cry1Ab protein from genetically modified maize in the bovine gastrointestinal tract. J Agric Food Chem 2005;53:1453–6.

[41] Myren M, Mose T, Mathiesen L, Knudsen LE. The human placenta—an alternative for studying foetal exposure. Toxicol in Vitro 2007;21:1332–40.

Reading Questions

1. The researchers establish early in the introduction that their focus is not concerned with the effects of genetically modified (GM) foods on humans; instead, their focus is on the effects of pesticides associated with GM foods (PAGMF): "There is a debate on the direct threat of genes used in the preparation of these new foods on human health, as they are not detectable in the body, but the real danger may come from PAGMF" (par. 3). What are the two categories of pesticides the researchers focus on?

2. According to the researchers, what are the potential benefits of their findings for the general public as well as for other academic researchers?

3. Describe the two study groups created by the researchers. What characteristics of each group did the researchers consider as they created these two groups?

4. In the Discussion section, the researchers report that they detected 3-MPPA (a metabolite of gluphosinate, or GLUF, an herbicide) "in 100% of maternal and umbilical cord blood samples" (25). However, they also take caution to note the concentration levels of the detected herbicide. Why is the detected concentration important?

5. In light of their findings regarding the insecticide Cry1Ab toxin, what are two concerns that the researchers express?

Rhetoric Questions

6. The researchers frequently take caution not to overstate the implications of their findings. What strategies do the researchers use to hedge these implications?

7. The study's Introduction reviews previous research conducted on the pesticides under investigation. On average, how many previous studies are referenced in each paragraph of the introduction? What, if anything, might this number suggest about previous research in this area?

8. This research report includes a number of tables and figures. What are the main differences between the ways these visual elements are labeled? Do you find the tables or the figures easier to navigate and understand? Why?

9. What features of the study (structure, language, and reference) contribute to the appearance of objectivity or otherwise serve to enhance the researchers' credibility (ethos)? Explain your choices.

Response and Research Question

10. The researchers suggest that their work could "pav[e] the way for a new field of multi-disciplinary research, combining human reproduction, toxicology, and nutrition" (7). In your estimation, what could each of these fields likely contribute to the continued study of the potential toxicity of pesticides associated with GM foods?

Genetically Modified Food in Perspective: An Inquiry-Based Curriculum to Help Middle School Students Make Sense of Tradeoffs

SHERRY SEETHALER AND MARCIA LINN

Sherry Seethaler holds a PhD in math and science education. She is a science writer and educator at the University of California–San Diego and the author of *Lies, Damned Lies, and Science: How to Sort through the Noise around Global Warming, the Latest Health Claims, and Other Scientific Controversies* (2009), along with other books aimed at translating the work of science for a general readership. Marcia Linn is a professor of development and cognition at the University of California–Berkeley Graduate School of Education. She specializes in math, science, and technology education and has published a number of books and articles on the topics. In the following article, Seethaler and Linn report on a study they conducted to understand how middle school students learn about a controversial scientific issue, genetically modified foods. The article was published in the November 2004 issue of the *International Journal of Science Education.*

To understand how students learn about science controversy, this study examines students' reasoning about tradeoffs in the context of a technology-enhanced curriculum about genetically modified food. The curriculum was designed and refined based on the Scaffolded Knowledge Integration Framework to help students sort and integrate their initial ideas and those presented in the curriculum. Pre-test and post-test scores from 190 students show that students made significant (p < 0.0001) gains in their understanding of the genetically modified food controversy. Analyses of students' final papers, in which they took and defended a position on what type of agricultural practice should be used in their geographical region, showed that students were able to provide evidence both for and against their positions, but were less explicit about how they weighed these tradeoffs. These results provide important insights into students' thinking and have implications for curricular design.

INTRODUCTION

Making sound political and personal decisions about cloning, gene therapy, stem cell research, genetic engineering of food, and a vast array of other issues entails understanding and weighing complex tradeoffs involving economics, human health and safety, the environment, and ethics. Since science will continue to play an ever-increasing role in our lives, science educators face the challenging task of preparing students who will be autonomous learners of science even after they have completed their formal science education. This study examines how eighth-grade students learn about a complex scientific controversy, the genetically modified food[1] (GMF) controversy, including how these students synthesize evidence to evaluate tradeoffs.

Motivation for the curriculum

Classroom studies have shown that students are rarely called upon to engage in reflective thinking about mathematics and science (Driver et al. 2000; Stigler and Hiebert 1999). Furthermore, only about 1% of space in science textbooks is devoted to any discussion of science controversy, and science textbooks dominate instruction (Champagne 1998; Knain 2001; Schmidt et al. 1996). Most children and adults, including science teachers, hold the perspective that scientific knowledge is unchanging and uncontroversial, other than the accumulation of new knowledge (Driver et al. 1996). This would make people less likely to seek out competing viewpoints of scientists when making science-based decisions. On the other hand, over the past half-century, there has been a shift among philosophers and sociologists of science, away from seeing science as a purely empirical process, to seeing it as a social process of knowledge construction in which imagination and argument play an important role (Driver et al. 2000; Latour and Woolgar 1986). Science standards have called for changes in the way science is taught; in particular, drawing attention to the centrality of debate in science, the importance of the interactions between science and society, and the need for students to understand and apply the concept of a tradeoff in making decisions (American Association for the Advancement of Science 1993; National Committee on Science Education Standards and Assessment 1996).

Context for the curriculum

The GMF controversy generates a great deal of media attention, and has direct relevance to the daily lives of students because we are all eating GMF.[2] The topic also fits well with key content standards including: sexual reproduction in plants, the role of genes in inheritance, the interdependence of organisms in ecosystems (National Committee on Science Education Standards and Assessment 1996), the idea that technologies have side effects, and agriculture and the impact humans have on the environment (American Association for the Advancement of Science 1993). It was also possible to frame the final assignment (paper) in terms of a "decision" about whether to grow GMF or use another form of agriculture. This asked students to integrate what they had learned in a coherent way in order to choose and defend a position, in keeping with the goal of helping students develop a rich, connected set of ideas about the controversy.

The GMF controversy involves a complex set of tradeoffs, because it is difficult to predict the long-term impact of GMF, and because different genetically modified crops have different risks and benefits. Not including the ethical questions, there are three main themes of tradeoffs in the controversy:

- *Human health.* Genetic engineering of food has been touted as a way of growing enough food for an increasing world population, and improving the nutrient intake of populations at risk for deficiencies—as in the case of golden rice, which contains a precursor to vitamin A (Ye et al. 2000). Genetic engineering also has the power to remove allergens in food, and while research shows that this is feasible (Tada et al. 1996) critics contend that genetic engineering, by allowing us to introduce genes from completely unrelated species, could result in the introduction of novel allergens into the human food chain (Holdredge and Talbott 2001).

- *The environment.* Proponents of genetic engineering believe that crops engineered to express their own pesticides could reduce the use of chemicals on crops (Thayer 1999). Others are concerned that these crops may increase insecticide resistance in insect pests, lead to herbicide resistance in weeds, and may harm beneficial insects such as monarch butterflies (Losey et al. 1999; Wolfenbarger and Phifer 2000).

- *Economics.* Disease-resistant crops could benefit farmers; for example, a genetically modified disease-resistant papaya variety is credited with saving the livelihood of Hawaiian papaya farmers whose crops were being destroyed by a virus (Yoon 1999). On the other hand, opponents point to increasing difficulties exporting GMF to certain countries, and to the risks of corporate control of agriculture.

Further complicating the issue is what to use as the basis to compare the risks and benefits of genetically modified crops. All farming impacts the environment, so it is not fair to compare the impact of these crops with "virgin land," or even with idealized forms of organic farming. In reality, even organic farmers use chemicals on their crops to control insects, weeds, and plant diseases.[3] Furthermore, most food is grown using intensive (also called conventional) farming in large monocultures with use of synthetic pesticides and fertilizers. Moving away from use of these pesticides usually comes with a price; organic farmers often get lower yields, thus requiring more land to grow the same amount of food (Munn et al. 1998). While this is far from an exhaustive list of the issues in this debate, it makes it clear that the GMF controversy offers a meaningful and substantive context for science learning.

How do students learn about complex scientific issues?

We need to better understand how to scaffold students as they compare and combine "pieces" of knowledge about an issue to form an integrated understanding. We have gained some understanding of how students learn to make connections between ideas in areas such as Newtonian mechanics, heat and temperature, and plate tectonics, but our knowledge remains tentative (diSessa 1988; Gobert 2000; Linn and Hsi 2000). Even less is known about how students integrate sets of ideas, like those in the GMF controversy, which cut across different scientific domains and connect to social issues.

In this curriculum, students must sift through and synthesize what they have learned about GMF and agriculture to take a position on what agricultural method they think should be used in their geographical region. This requires students to make use of evidence to defend their position. There is research that has yielded insight into some of the difficulties people of all ages have in constructing arguments about everyday issues (Driver et al. 1996; Kuhn 1991; Means and Voss 1996; Ranney and Schank 1998; Voss and Means 1991). For example, they are often unable to use evidence appropriately or to generate counterarguments. However, in these studies subjects were not usually given the opportunity to learn about the domain in question. Bell (1998, 2000) has shown that in the context of a curriculum about light, when students were given specific prompts and the debate was framed in terms of two alternative theories, students were able to make appropriate use of evidence to evaluate a theory. Thus, in a rich context, with appropriate scaffolding, students may be better at using evidence appropriately.

The findings reported here provide insight into how students grapple with complex, multidisciplinary scientific issues. Specifically, this study addresses the question: How successful are students in the eighth grade at learning to weigh the tradeoffs involved in using one method of agriculture or another, and supporting their position with appropriate evidence?

Overview of the curriculum

The curriculum described in this paper was designed to help students come to an integrated understanding of the GMF controversy. In other words, the curriculum should help students develop a rich, well-connected network of ideas about the controversy. The Scaffolded Knowledge Integration (SKI) Framework was used to guide the design of the GMF curriculum. SKI is a result of nearly 20 years of classroom research (Linn 1995; Linn and Hsi 2000). The overarching goal of SKI is to promote knowledge integration. SKI consists of four meta-principles that guide the development of new curricula: (1) to make science accessible; (2) to make thinking visible; (3) to help students learn from others; and (4) to promote autonomous lifelong science learning.

A team of educational researchers, teachers, and scientists designed the curriculum. The curriculum was built in the Web-based Inquiry Science Environment (WISE) (http://wise.berkeley.edu/), which was created to support students based on the principles and philosophy of the SKI Framework (Linn and Slotta 2000). (The GMF curriculum is available online at http://wise.berkeley.edu). The WISE environment provides students with an inquiry map to keep track of what step they are on in the overall flow of the project, hints on demand, links to Web pages, tools like the online discussion tool, and prompts to take notes.

At the beginning of the curriculum, students were asked whether or not they would eat GMF or plant it in their garden, to encourage them to think about what they had already heard regarding this food, and record their initial beliefs about it. In the next activity, students learned the history of corn, which introduced them to the importance of crosses in crop development. Next they learned what it means to genetically engineer a plant, and they investigated the differences between crosses and genetic engineering. Students participated in an in-class activity where they tasted genetically engineered food (pilot run only) and/or examined ingredient labels from common food products, and discussed how many foods were likely to contain genetically engineered ingredients. Students also read and discussed a short article on an anti-GMF incident in their local area. In the next part of the project, a variant of the jigsaw approach was used to allow students to explore the evidence for or against GMF, and for or against organic food (Aronson 1978; Brown and Palincsar 1989). (See Table 1 for a summary of the evidence students explored in the jigsaw.) The curriculum designers sought to present as balanced a view of GMF and agriculture as possible. We presented GMF in the context of other methods of agriculture to help students understand that all agricultural practices have both risks and benefits.

After they researched one of four positions (for or against GMF, for or against organic), pairs or groups of students prepared posters and short oral presentations to teach their classmates about the evidence they explored. As students listened to the presentations,

they took notes on a form designed to scaffold their note taking and promote reflection. After each presentation, there was opportunity for discussion and debate. Once students heard all of the evidence for and against each position, they chose what type of agriculture they thought should be used in their geographical region—GMF, organic agriculture, or conventional (intensive) farming methods—and they each wrote a paper defending their position. Students were scaffolded in writing their paper by the use of pages designed to help them organize arguments and evidence for the position they had chosen (handouts can be downloaded from http://wise.berkeley.edu). The curriculum took about 10 class periods each of 45 minutes. For a more detailed description of how the curriculum was designed in accordance with the SKI principles, see Seethaler (2003).

The curriculum was refined following a pilot run with one class, as described in Seethaler (2002). The changes were modest with the basic structure of the project remaining the same between runs. To increase the generalizability of our findings on students' reasoning about tradeoffs, results from both runs were pooled in the detailed analysis of students' reasoning.

Table 1
The four pieces of the jigsaw

Position	Evidence
For GMF	GMF saves Hawaiian papaya crop
	GMF can reduce allergens in food
	GMF can improve nutrient content of food: golden rice example
Against GMF	GMF insecticide-producing corn may harm monarch butterflies
	GMF could introduce novel allergens into food
	GMF could lead to herbicide-resistant superweeds
For organic	Organic farmers use crop rotation to enrich soil
	Organic farmers do not use synthetic chemicals
	Organic farms must undergo a rigorous certification procedure
Against organic	Organic farmers must still combat weeds and insects (practical issues)
	Organic farmers do use chemicals on their crops
	Organic farmers often get lower yields

METHODS

Participants

The pilot run of the curriculum took place in an eighth-grade classroom (17 students) in a school in an urban, middle-class neighborhood with an ethnically diverse student body. After the redesign of the curriculum (about two months later), it was run again by a different teacher in her six eighth-grade classrooms (173 students) in a moderately diverse, suburban, middle-class neighborhood. Both teachers have a strong scientific background: the teacher of the pilot class has a PhD in environmental science, and the teacher at the second school has a Bachelor's degree in biology. However, since the initial runs of the curriculum reported here, many other teachers with a variety of science backgrounds have reported success using this curriculum in their classrooms.

Sources of data

Data sources include students' written work, pre-tests 15 and post-tests consisting of short-answer questions designed to promote reflective thinking, online notes that the students took as they were working through the project, offline notes taken during the poster presentations, and the position paper. Since students worked in pairs in the online portion of the project, notes were generated by pairs of students. All other written work was individual. Additional data includes classroom observations (pilot run), and audiotapes of interviews with individual students (pilot), with the teacher (pilot), and of whole class discussions (second run).

Scoring

Pre-tests and post-tests. The pre-tests and post-tests were used to assess changes in students' understanding of GMF and agriculture before and after the curriculum. They consisted of eight short-answer questions designed to encourage students to reflect on the risks and benefits of agricultural practices. For example, the questions "Why might an organic farmer think that organic food is safer for the environment than genetically engineered food?" and "Why

might a farmer planting genetically engineered seeds choose to grow genetically modified food?" ask students to consider the benefits and risks of two different agricultural methods.

The marking scheme assigned points for each unique, correct (normative) response that a student generated. For most questions, there were a number of possible normative answers that a student could give. This meant that the total number of points that could be assigned was quite high, but not even an expert would be expected to get a perfect score since one respondent is unlikely to give every possible example or argument. The scoring scheme was set up this way to minimize the ceiling effect and to make sure that all possible normative responses were valued. Partial points were allotted if a response was consistent with a scientifically accepted response but was only partially elaborated. If a response contained one normative idea and one non-normative idea, students would receive points for the normative idea, as long as the non-normative idea given did not contradict it. A second coder graded a subset of the tests, with a greater than 85% inter-rater reliability. The following is an example of the coding scheme for one of the questions.

Why might an organic farmer think that organic food is safer for the environment than genetically engineered food? (10 points possible)

- Some genetically modified food that produces its own insecticides (1) is harmful to beneficial insects (1).

- Organic farmers do not use synthetic chemicals (1). Some synthetic pesticides have been shown to harm wildlife (1). For example, DDT got into the food chain (1) and caused some birds to lay soft-shelled eggs/die off (1).

- Organic food does not lead to superweeds (Other examples of benefits of organic food are allowed.) (1). Superweeds may occur when genetically modified food crosses with weeds (1).

- Most genetically modified food contains antibiotic resistance genes (1). Some people think that the presence of these genes in the environment could lead to the antibiotic resistance of disease-causing bacteria (1).

- (It is more natural (0). Organic farmers do not use pesticides (0).)

Position papers. Position papers were analyzed to better understand how students were using evidence in their arguments and making sense of tradeoffs in the controversy. In their papers, students were to decide what form of agriculture they thought should be used in California: organic farming, intensive farming of non-GMF, or farming of GMF. They were instructed to give evidence to support their positions, and explain what evidence someone with an opposing viewpoint might use.

Seven aspects of students' position papers were considered: (1) the number of pieces of evidence used; (2) the themes (topics) of evidence used; (3) scientific normativity; (4) the degree of elaboration of evidence students presented *in favor* of their position; (5) the degree of elaboration of evidence students presented *against* their position; (6) the degree of elaboration of the evidence used by the students to *address the evidence against* their position; and (7) the quality of students' conclusions.

To study the first two of these aspects of students' position papers, each piece of evidence students used in their position papers was tabulated, and classified as either one of the 12 corresponding to those in the jigsaw (see Table 1) or as "other." The other category is an umbrella category that contains evidence that came up in the class discussion, or was derived from the curriculum (by students following additional web links), or came from students' experiences and discussions outside the classroom. Evidence in the "other" category was listed and then grouped into global categories based on the themes that arose from the analysis of students' responses.

To assess the remaining five aspects of students' position papers, each position paper was scored according to a 10-point knowledge integration (KI) scale. The presence or absence of non-normative conceptions was scored on a binary (0, 1) scale. If there were any non-normative ideas present in the paper, the normativity score was zero. Three-point KI scales were used to score: the evidence students presented in favor of their position, evidence against their position (i.e., possible challenges), and evidence to counter the challenges to their position. Usually, there was

more than one of each of these three types of evidence presented, and students were assigned a score based on the best (most normative, most elaborated) piece of each type of evidence presented. Students could receive a score of 0, 1, or 2 (highest). Evidence was classified as present but not elaborated (KI = 1) or as present and elaborated (KI = 2). If it was absent entirely, or confusing, it was assigned a score of 0.

This scoring scheme for the position papers was inspired by the work of Toulmin (1958). Toulmin was the first and most influential individual to make a distinction between the idealized notion of arguments employed in logic and mathematics, and the everyday practice of arguments in a wide range of contexts. Toulmin's scheme for analyzing arguments identifies four major components of an argument: data, claim, warrant, and backing. Data are used to support a claim. A warrant is the justification stating why that data can be used to support the claim. The warrant thus functions as a bridge between the data and the claim. The warrant may be implicit in an argument, to be made explicit if there are challenges to the validity of using a particular piece of data to support the claim. Often drawing a sharp distinction between the data and the warrant is impossible, but, in general, the data is factual information, and the warrant contains more general rule-like statements (van Eemeren et al. 1996). If the authority of the warrant is not accepted right away, a backing may be required. The backing is not general like the warrant; rather, it is more like data in that it consists of specific facts, incidences, or examples. For example, in a legal argument it would consist of a citation of a specific piece of legislation (Toulmin 1958). While the components are common to arguments in different domains, what counts as data, warrant, backing, and claims is field-dependent.

In our scoring scheme, evidence considered elaborated contained an explicit warrant or backing, or both, as well as data and claim; whereas "unelaborated" evidence consisted of data and claim only. An example of this coding scheme applied to students' "Con Evidence" (evidence against their chosen position) is shown in the following (bold type indicates

data, <u>claims</u> are underlined, *warrants* are in italics, and ***backings*** are in bold italics). More examples are provided later (see Results).

Con KI = 0
Absent or non-scientific.
3MF (Paper is pro GMF): "…You are not letting the plant be natural, you could start a wipe out, and you could mess up the food."

Con KI = 1
Gives one or more normative pieces of evidence, but does not really elaborate on any of them.
1DT (Paper is pro GMF): GM foods "<u>could cause allergic reactions to people</u> [claim] because **the gene put in it could be from something that they are allergic to [data].**"

Con KI = 2
Elaborates on at least one of the pieces of evidence given.
4KB (Paper is pro GMF): "<u>GM foods are important</u> [claim] because they **keep the papaya crop in Hawaii healthy [data]**. *It is important to keep the papaya crop health [sic] and free of diseases because it is one large part of Hawaii's economy, and food source [warrant].* ***If we had GM the potato crops in Ireland there would not have been such devastation [sic]. What happened was around the 1940's [sic] the potato crops in Ireland all died from a disease and lots of people died of starvation…*** [backing]" (pro, KI = 2).

Finally, a four-point scale was used to assess the conclusion students gave to their essays. A maximum conclusion score meant that the student gave an explicit rationale that was completely normative from a scientific standpoint, of why the evidence in favor of their position outweighed the evidence against. Since the conclusion should not involve the presentation of any new evidence, but rather the weighing of evidence already presented, Toulmin's scheme was not applied to the conclusion. A score of zero was assigned when the conclusion was absent. One point was assigned if the student simply stated that there was more or better evidence for than against their position. A conclusion that merited a score of two points contained an indication that the student realized there were tradeoffs and offered some rationale as to why the evidence for their position outweighed the evidence against, but may have had some minor misconceptions. To merit a score of three the student would have to weigh only

Table 2
KI scoring scheme

Element of argument	Possible scores
Evidence in favor of chosen position	0, 1, 2
Evidence against chosen position	0, 1, 2
Normativity (presence/absence of non-normative ideas)	0/1
Counter-evidence to evidence against their position	0, 1, 2
Conclusions to overall argument	0, 1, 2, 3
Total possible Knowledge Integration points	10

evidence that would be considered valid from a scientific or public policy standpoint.

In summary, students could receive a total of five points for the evidence in favor of, and against, their positions, and normativity. There were another five points possible for the evidence countering the challenges to their position, and the conclusion. Thus, this scheme treats students' papers as an extended argument, where the scoring of the evidence is based on Toulmin's scheme. The structure of the KI scheme is presented in Table 2. A second coder scored a subset of students' position papers. Initially, the second coder agreed with the primary coder greater than 70% of the time. Following discussion, particularly regarding what ideas about agriculture should be considered non-normative, the second coder agreed with the primary coder greater than 90% of the time.

RESULTS

Changes in students' conceptions and attitudes over the course of the curriculum

Students came to the curriculum with a variety of ideas about GMF and agriculture. Some of their non-normative pre-test conceptions are presented in Table 3.

Table 3
Examples of students' non-normative pre-test conceptions

To genetically engineer a plant means:

"It is to grow something un-naturaly [*sic*]. To be grown with chemicals"

"...a plant is artificially grown in a sense....Plants are crossbred that don't usually do"

"...I guess to make plants grow faster, become alive like in the movies!"

"...To grow a plant with other parts of plants. It isn't grown outside with water and sun but they are grown with chemicals to make it grow faster"

"Maybe it means that you inject it with hormones or make its growing process different [*sic*]"

"See what kind of water or inviorment [*sic*] it can live in"

"...When people take plants to make food from them, like corn chips for example [...] These chips don't look like corn kernels"

An organic farmer might think that organic food is safer for the environment (than GMF) because:

"Because organic food has no chemicals and stuff like that"

"Because organic food is grown safely and without any chemicals or breeding..."

"It's all natural"

"Nature has always grown the food that way and humans have never tampered with them"

The overall pre-test to post-test gains for each school are presented in Table 4. As shown by a paired *t*-test, students had significant pre-test to post-test gains at each school. There were no significant gender differences in pre-test to post-test gains at either school (not shown).

The following pre-test and post-test responses show how one student, Sam, developed a more elaborated understanding of GMF over the course of the curriculum. The statements are Sam's responses to "Why might some people be afraid to eat food which comes from a plant that has been genetically engineered?"

> Some people are afraid to eat food from G.E. plants because they think there might be a bad chemical in them. (Sam, pre-test)

> Some people are afraid to eat GM foods because they think that there will be some effect on their body from genes that have been put into the plant. They could also have an allergic reaction because of a new gene in the plant. (Sam, post-test)

Sam's post-test response cited a more specific risk than his pre-test response, and it indicates that Sam understood that genetic engineering involves the transfer of new genes to the plant. Overall, students' pre-test and post-test responses tended to be brief, possibly because they are not accustomed to being required to provide extensive detail in test situations. However, in general, their responses moved to being more normative and less vague from the pre-test to post-test, indicating that they had come to a

Table 4
Pre-test to post-test gains for each run of the eighth-grade GMF curriculum

School	Number of students	Pre-test	Post-test	*t*-value	*p*-value
1. Pilot	17 (one class)	5.3, SD=4.0	10.5, SD=4.6	6.527	<0.0001
2. Second run	173 (six classes)	7.6, SD=3.3	11.2, SD=3.5	12.794	<0.0001

better understanding of GMF and agriculture over the course of the curriculum.

Students' attitudes about agricultural methods. Overall, students' attitudes toward GMF tended toward positive both before the curriculum (as indicated by the notes they took initially) and after (as indicated by the position they chose for the final paper). Initially, 80% of students said that they would eat GMF and 70% said they would grow it. At the end of the curriculum, 62% of students wrote papers in favor of GMF. In their final papers, students gave a much more extensive rationale for their stance than they did in these initial notes. For a more detailed discussion of students' attitudes, see Seethaler (2003).

How do students construct arguments in the context of this debate, and how successful are students in the eighth grade at learning to support their position with appropriate evidence and weighing the tradeoffs involved in using one method of agriculture or another?

Numbers and themes of evidence used. In their final papers, students in the pilot run used an average of 2.5 (standard deviation [SD], 1.3) pieces of evidence of the 12 they explored in the jigsaw (14 papers), and students in the second run used 3.7 (SD, 1.7) of these pieces of evidence (147 papers). These averages include only normative uses of the evidence. Very few students used "jigsaw" evidence inappropriately, or cited it incorrectly. There were only 26 instances of incorrect evidence use/misquoting of evidence, compared with more than 500 correct uses, suggesting that students understood the ideas presented in the curriculum. The most commonly cited incorrect evidence was that organic farmers do not use chemicals on their crops (12 students).

A little more than one-half of the evidence students used in their papers was presented as evidence in favor of their position, while just under one-half was described as possible counter-evidence to their position. This shows that, in a content-rich context, where students are given appropriate scaffolds, they can provide counter-evidence to their position. Furthermore, this observation, and the fact that nearly one-third of students wrote their paper in favor of a position other than the one they explored in the jigsaw, shows that students learned from their peers. The breakdown of the evidence used by students depending on their position on agriculture is presented in Table 5.

Some evidence was important for students independent of what position on agriculture they chose. For example, over one-half of the students used evidence about yield in their papers. Students who wrote papers in favor of genetic engineering or intensive farming could cite "increasing yields" in favor of their position, and this was especially common among students choosing intensive agriculture. However, well over one-half of the students writing papers about organic farming also addressed the yield issue (as evidence against their position). On the other hand, some evidence was not used very frequently, regardless of what position students chose. For example, only one in 20 students made use of the fact that organic agriculture is carefully regulated. Even students who wrote position papers in favor of organic farming did not usually make use of this evidence.

Another trend that can be observed is that while students made use of evidence both in favor of and against their positions, they usually did not draw from evidence presented about *another* agricultural method. For example, students writing position papers in favor of GMF drew on evidence presented in favor of this method and evidence presented against this method. However, with the exception of yield, they did not draw from evidence presented in favor of, or against, organic agriculture. This same trend is also observed for students writing papers in favor of intensive farming, but is slightly less prevalent among students defending organic methods of farming. Evidence about other agricultural methods was relevant to their position. For example, the fact that insects and weeds are difficult to control is a perfectly valid reason to give for choosing to grow GMF, but less than one-quarter of pro-GMF students used this to support their position. Like the observation that only a relatively small number of students wrote papers in favor of intensive farming, this observation also seems to indicate that students find it challenging to take evidence presented in one context and restate it in another. The evidence on yield is an exception,

Table 5

Percentage of students using each piece of evidence by position chosen for final paper

Evidence		Pro organic	Pro intensive	Pro GMF	Overall % of students using this evidence
Pro GMF	Papayas	*21*	*8*	**59**	45
	Reduce allergens	*13*	*17*	**40**	31
	Vitamin A rice	*26*	*0*	**57**	45
Against GMF	Risks to other insects	**18**	**8**	*43*	34
	Introduce allergens	**34**	**25**	*46*	41
	Superweeds	**21**	**0**	*35*	29
Pro organic	Crop rotation	**32**	*17*	*5*	13
	Synthetic chemicals	**55**	*92*	*12*	29
	Regulations	**13**	*0*	*3*	5
Against organic	Weeds and insects	*29*	**67**	**21**	26
	Chemicals are used	*42*	**42**	**10**	21
	Yields	*63*	**92**	**46**	54

Italics, evidence against position; **bold**, evidence in favor of position.

suggesting that students can do this under certain circumstances. Yield came up frequently in class discussions, possibly increasing connections across contexts.

In addition to the pieces of evidence from the jigsaw, students also cited evidence that had come up in class discussions, that they had learned from following other links to the web in the project, or that they had learned outside the classroom. On average, students used 1.8 (SD, 1.3) pieces of "other" evidence. This number includes only evidence that was normative and was not just a matter of opinion, or ethics. This evidence fell roughly into four broad categories: quality of food and cost to consumer, safety of the food, environmental risks and benefits of the method, and benefits and disadvantages to the farmer. The overwhelmingly most popular arguments used by students were about using genetic engineering to improve quality of the food, such as the taste of the food (37 students) or the size or shape of the food (44 students). Students also gave, on average, 1.3 (SD, 0.96) pieces of ethical/opinion-based evidence. ("Evidence" that was actually non-normative, not just a matter of opinion, was not counted.) Most cited in the ethical/opinion-based category is "organic food is natural" or more natural than other food (used by 33 students), and genetic engineering is morally wrong or is playing God (used by 23 students). Students used these both in favor of their position, and as counter-arguments someone might give.

Normativity. About one-third of students had non-normative ideas in their final papers. It was rare for there to be more than one or two non-normative ideas in a student's paper. Note that the non-normative ideas were not included in statistics presented earlier of total evidence used by students. (Thus, in reality, students actually gave more evidence than we counted.) Non-normative ideas included: the belief that organic farmers do not use chemicals on their crops, that GMF may give you cancer, that you can (physically) remove genes from food, that no pesticides are used on genetically modified crops, and so on. There were a wide range of these sorts of ideas, and some students' ideas were the opposite of others (GMF may give you cancer/has made us healthier). Recall that students rarely used evidence from the jigsaw incorrectly. Thus, the non-normative ideas appearing in students' papers are not usually ideas that were a major focus of the curriculum. Some may have been ideas that students brought with them to the curriculum (like GMF giving you cancer); others may be due to students extrapolating from something that they learned in the curriculum (if you can remove toxins from food, this must mean you excise the genes). An unpaired *t*-test on the total KI scores not including the normativity score, grouped by the normativity score, indicated that otherwise the quality of students' papers was similar whether or not they included non-normative ideas ($t = 1.7$, $p = 0.08$). This is not surprising since non-normative ideas tended to be listed as additional evidence for or against a student's position rather than being a central idea in their argument. Thus, over the course of the curriculum, students gained a more integrated understanding of the controversy, but will need more experience with it to continue to refine their network of ideas.

Level of integration of evidence used by students. The KI analysis based on Toulmin's scheme reveals how students were using evidence and comparing trade-offs in the controversy. In the following excerpts, bold type indicates **data**, claims are underlined, *warrants* are in italics, and ***backings*** are in bold italics. (Note: evidence considered in favor of a student's position may be evidence against a competing position.)

The following is an example of normative, but less integrated evidence:

> We should grow GMF. "**GM foods can keep away disease, viruses, and even harmful bugs that destroy crops**" (pro, KI = 1).

All students achieved at least one on the KI scale for evidence in favor of their position, and most (90%) achieved at least one for the evidence against their

position. Many students (nearly one-half) also elaborated, showing that they had a detailed understanding of what the consequences/benefits of using a particular technology could be.

> 4AG (Paper is pro organic): We should not use genetically modified food. "... **Superweeds occur when a food that has been given immunity to a certain type of herbicide, crosses with nearby weeds. The weeds then produce offspring that contain the same immunity to herbicides.** This produces a problem for the farmers. *They are forced to use a more powerful herbicide to kill weeds. That poses a threat to the environment and it can create a serious economic problem...*" (pro, KI = 2).

> 2DD (Paper is pro organic): "... Another argument that would make [...] intensively grown food worse than organically grown food is that **the pesticides they use have endangered two types of birds one of them was the Brown Pelican.** The pesticide that caused this was called DDT although it is no longer legal in the United States the bird's population is still just starting to recover. *Pesticides cause a sort of chain reaction. **For example worms eat the infected dirt then a fish eats the worms and then a bigger fish eats the smaller fish and then a human eats the fish. Now all of the pesticide combined is in the human...***" (pro, KI = 2).

Fewer students were able to give good counter-evidence to the evidence against their positions. The following quotations show how some students did effectively address counter-evidence to their positions.

> 2CH: "Another argument against genetically modified food is that if you put pesticides into it, it would kill beneficial bugs as well as harmful ones. **My response is that other external pesticides do that too.** So that isn't really a good argument" (counter to evidence against position, KI = 1).

> 3CN (Paper is pro intensive): "... The assumption that natural chemicals are safer than synthetic ones is the premise on which the argument against intensive farming is based. In most cases, however, it is the opposite. **For example, one chemical organic farmers use is copper sulfate, which kills honeybees.** *Many arguments have been made that synthetic chemicals kill all bugs, whereas organic chemicals kill only the bad insects. Clearly this isn't the case...*" (KI = 2).

Both of these quotations also reveal that students were evaluating agricultural methods in relation to one another. For example, the first student recognized that dangers to beneficial insects are not specific to insecticide-producing plants. In fact, as the student pointed out, traditional insect sprays have these risks as well.

Students' papers also yield some insights into how students weighed specific risks and benefits of each agricultural method to conclude their argument. For example:

> 7WB: "I think that the arguments for my position outweighs the opposing arguments because not only do I prove that genetically modified foods cost a significant amount of money, they also require a lot of experiment time and research. All arguments that I proposed against GM foods gave examples of situations that would be hard to resolve if they happened. They were all slim chances that something could go wrong, such as the superweeds, or allergic reactions, but cannot afford to take these chances when human lives are involved" (conclusion, KI = 2).

> 1CW: "I am for the genetic manipulation of these crops to serve our purposes. I believe this because of what it has done for the people of Europe with the European Corn Borer, in Asia for its role with Gold Rice and for helping the agricultural economy with lower prices for foods everywhere. I know of the problems with the Tomato with the Peanut allergens, and the Monarch Butterflies being destroyed, but I still believe that Genetic Engineering is a good way to help ailing people around the world by improving their diet" (conclusion, KI = 2).

Both of these students gave some rational comment as to how they weighed the risks and benefits of GMF in their conclusions. For example, the first student decided on his position as a way of minimizing risk. These conclusions contain some misconceptions about GMF; for example, GMF has helped with the European corn borer in the United States and other countries, but not in Europe (where GMF is not commercially grown). None of the students provided a conclusion that achieved a KI score of 3.

Table 6 presents the number of students achieving a given KI score for each element of their position paper.

Overall, students had a KI score of 4.6 (SD, 1.3). Their KI score was 3.3 (SD, 0.9) out of 5 for their pro and con evidence, and 1.4 (SD, 0.8) out of 5 for their conclusions and the rebuttals. In other words, students were able to identify and explain specific benefits and risks of a particular method of agriculture. However, in general, they tended to list these benefits and risks without explicitly concluding *why* they thought the benefits outweighed the risks. It seems that students either tended not to see the importance of giving an elaborated conclusion and rebuttals once they had detailed the evidence for and against their positions, or that they find giving an integrated conclusion rather challenging.

DISCUSSION

This study provides important insight into students' thinking about multi-domain, multi-faceted, problematic science. In addition, the in-depth analysis of students' reasoning in the context of the curriculum can be used to re-inform the pedagogical principles used in the initial design.

Students' use of evidence

Over the course of the GMF curriculum, as shown by the analysis of students' work, students developed a more sophisticated understanding of GMF and agricultural methods. Furthermore, students were able to make appropriate use of evidence to argue for their positions on agriculture. On average, students used between three and four pieces of evidence gleaned from the curriculum in their papers, plus another three from various other sources. Importantly, they did not ignore evidence counter to their position. In fact, this accounted for almost one-half of the evidence students presented in their papers. This is an especially significant finding because others have found that students tend to fixate on one or two claims and have particular difficulty coming up with counter-evidence to their position (Driver et al. 1996; Kuhn 1991, 1992, 1993; Voss and Means 1991). People often ignore evidence that is not consistent with their own position (Chinn and Brewer 1993).

There are at least three possible reasons for the differences in our results regarding students' use of evidence. First, here the students wrote their position papers in the context of a curriculum where they were

Table 6

Distribution of knowledge integration scores

Element of argument	Percentage of students achieving each KI score and average scores for each element
Evidence in favor of chosen position	KI = 0, 0% KI = 1, 57% KI = 2, 43% Mean = 1.4, SD = 0.5
Evidence against chosen position	KI = 0, 10% KI = 1, 60% KI = 2, 30% Mean = 1.2, SD = 0.6
Normativity	KI = 0, 36% KI = 1, 64% Mean = 0.6, SD = 0.5
Counter-evidence to evidence against their position	KI = 0, 78% KI = 1, 20% KI = 2, 2% Mean = 0.2, SD = 0.5
Conclusions to overall argument	KI = 0, 15% KI = 1, 58% KI = 2, 27% KI = 3, 0% Mean = 1.1, SD = 0.6

learning about agricultural methods, and were specifically challenged by the teacher and other students, who exposed them to new arguments and evidence. In other words, students were not being asked to come up with evidence "out of the blue," as in many studies that examine students' ability to use evidence (Kuhn 1991; Voss and Means 1991). Rather, they were synthesizing their ideas at the culmination of a set of activities designed to challenge them to come to a more integrated understanding about GMF and agriculture. In these activities, students were scaffolded as they learned new ideas and compared and sifted through them.

Second, the expectations for the position paper were made completely explicit to students, and students were provided with a number of scaffolds. Instructions for the paper showed students how to structure their papers and gave them some sentence starter prompts. To help them plan their papers, they were also given idea-organizing pages, and were encouraged to list all the arguments and evidence about agriculture they had heard. Students were free to choose the agricultural method that seemed most ideal to them, and the evidence they thought best supported their position. However, they were reminded on a number of occasions that a scientific paper cannot be written solely "from the heart," but that opinions must be supported by evidence.

Third, in many of the studies that found students had difficulty using evidence appropriately, students were asked to generate evidence "on the spot," often orally (Kuhn 1991; Voss and Means 1991). Here, the students had time to reflect as they were writing their position papers. The generation of evidence to support a position requires time and reflection, and it seems unrealistic to think that students could generate good evidence in a short period of time about something they may never previously have given much thought.

The fact that students' papers contained evidence both for and against their position on agriculture shows that students recognized that there are trade-offs in the controversy, and could give examples of them. However, in general, students tended not to be explicit about how they were weighing the tradeoffs in the controversy (as indicated by the low conclusion KI scores). From the data we have collected thus far, it is not possible to say whether this is because students find it particularly challenging to weigh tradeoffs or because they believe that just laying out the evidence for and against their position is sufficient for making their point. Students may need further instruction about what is a good conclusion to an argument.

Design principles

Three principles might be derived from these observations. First, a subprinciple could be added to the SKI principle "help students learn from others." In order to help students learn to support their arguments with evidence, give students exposure to building arguments in a content-rich domain where they are exposed to multiple forms of evidence and have the opportunity to discuss the evidence with a community of peers and teachers. Ideally, over the course of multiple curricula like that described here, these communities would develop criteria for the evaluation of evidence in multiple domains.

Second, a subprinciple under the SKI principle "make science accessible" could be added: make goals for students explicit. Students need to understand the expectations placed on them in particular contexts. For example, an English teacher might want students to write "from the heart" on a creative writing assignment, but may have different expectations

when students are writing a critique. This difference is not obvious to someone inexperienced in different forms of writing. Furthermore, many students are completely unaccustomed to "writing" in science class. In fact, Seethaler recently found that the undergraduate science students in her class at a major university (juniors and seniors) had minimal experience writing in their science classes, and they were not certain how to structure their papers (2001, unpublished data).

Third, to elaborate the principle "make thinking visible," it is important to note that students need to be given time to engage in the act of reflecting. Scaffolds can both prompt such reflection and sustain reasoning.

While these principles are derived from a study examining a single subject matter domain, and a single grade level, we believe that they will transfer to other contexts as well. The biggest challenge is in translating these principles into effective classroom practice. The teachers of the classes studied here both had strong domain knowledge, and were very self-motivated to bring science controversy into the classroom. Many teachers have since used this curriculum and reported success. Some had minimal subject matter preparation, but all chose to bring the genetically modified food controversy into their classrooms because they believed it was something their students should learn about. These are most likely to be the teachers who work to create a classroom culture where students engage in reflective thinking. Curricula like the one described here can give students the opportunity to learn to construct arguments and use evidence, but the generalizability of these results is likely to depend on classroom culture.

Students' use of warrants

It is difficult to compare our students' use of warrants with other researchers' findings, because studies in the literature tend to differ along multiple lines. Jiménez-Aleixandre et al. (2000) studied a ninth-grade classroom where students were engaged in small group discussions trying to explain the reason for the differences observed between wild and domesticated chicks' coloration. Students had time to reflect, but they were not given specific scaffolds in the discussion, other than the problem scenario, and the instruction to give reasons for their answer. In their study, warrants were used for about one-third of claims, but two students really dominated the group discussion, so it is not possible to generalize. Chinn and Anderson (1998) studied fourth-grade students' argumentative discourse about issues raised in stories the students had read. In general, they found that students' arguments were logical, but that warrants were not generally made explicit. Students may have different norms for the construction of arguments in conversation versus in written work; however, there are not enough data on this to make a definitive statement. In a study by Bell (2000), where students were scaffolded to provide warrants, specifically an explanation of *why* a particular piece of evidence could be used to support or challenge one of two theories about how light travels, students included warrants in over 70% of argument explanations. Bell's students were providing written explanations in the form of notes. We did not specifically prompt our students to use warrants in their position papers, and just under one-half of our students made use of warrants in their papers. In Toulmin's (1958) work on argumentation, he posited that warrants may only be made explicit if there are challenges to the validity of using particular data to support a claim; thus, getting students to use warrants even more consistently may require specific explicit challenges to their positions.

The role of context in students' reasoning

Despite our students' ability to use evidence appropriately and provide warrants spontaneously in nearly one-half of the papers, there are three lines of observations that show limits in their flexible use of evidence across contexts, suggesting that the students would benefit from more support to understand how evidence could be used in different ways to support or challenge various positions. First, students here used evidence for and against their positions, but tended not to use relevant evidence presented in the context of another position. For example, students writing a paper in favor of GMF used evidence from the curriculum that was presented in the context of arguments

for and against GMF, but rarely used evidence that came up in discussions of organic food. Second, the fact that very few students wrote papers on intensive farming may reflect the lack of visibility to students of the evidence for this position, rather than students' dislike of this method of farming. (Recall that the jigsaw categories were for and against organic and for and against GMF, so the evidence in favor of intensive farming would have to be drawn from evidence against the other methods.) Finally, an observation that students in the pilot run had trouble deciding what to put on their posters, in particular a pair of students who had no difficulty explaining the papaya evidence (see Table 1), but still did not understand why it could be used by supporters of GMF, also illustrates this (Seethaler 2002). This difficulty on the part of students in using evidence flexibly is consistent with the literature on transfer (for a review, see Bransford and Schwartz 1999). Studies suggest that transfer is an active rather than passive process (Gick and Holyoak 1980). This implies that asking students to think more about *why* a particular piece of evidence can be used to support or challenge a position might help them use evidence more flexibly across contexts. An anecdotal observation that students seemed to have less trouble deciding what evidence to present in their poster presentations in the second run of the project, after we had added prompts for them to think about why pieces of evidence were good support for a particular position, could be explained by viewing transfer as an active process (Seethaler 2002). The recommendation that students discuss evidence with their peers and the teacher, and work together as a community to develop criteria for the evaluation of evidence in various contexts, is also consistent with the goal of helping students to use evidence more flexibly, since it is known that presenting concepts in multiple contexts can increase transfer. This would argue for the inclusion of projects like the WISE GMF controversy project at various points in students' educational trajectories.

In summary, our results show that students made gains in their understanding of GMF over the course of the curriculum. Eighth-grade students constructed arguments with evidence to support their positions.

These students also presented evidence counter to their positions, which shows that they understood both the risks and benefits of agriculture and thus that there were tradeoffs involved with their chosen method of agriculture. However, students were generally not explicit about how they weighed the tradeoffs they had identified, and this is an area that needs future work. Indeed, there is little research into how students make sense of tradeoffs, despite the fact that being able to identify and assess risks and benefits of technologies is so important in our daily lives. Having students construct arguments about scientific issues is important because it means that students are using what they know, rather than just recalling it piecemeal. The inclusion of science controversy into the middle school curriculum can help students start to become autonomous science learners by assisting them to think critically about important issues that will affect their lives.

ACKNOWLEDGMENTS

This work was supported by the National Science Foundation under grant numbers 9873180 and 9805420. The data and opinions expressed here are those of the authors and do not necessarily reflect those of the National Science Foundation. Special thanks to Professor Andrea diSessa, Stephanie Sisk-Hilton, Michelle Williams, and Timothy Zimmerman for their feedback on drafts of this manuscript.

NOTES

This work was completed while Seethaler was at U.C. Berkeley.

1. In reality, nearly all of the food we eat is "genetically modified" by cross-breeding. However, in this paper, as is general practice in the media, the term *genetically modified* is used more restrictively to describe food derived from plants altered using biotechnological techniques to directly manipulate genes or gene expression.

2. A number of food crops in the United States are now genetically modified, including well over one-half of the nation's soybean crop and about one-third of the corn (Kaeppler 2000). Other modified foods include potatoes, canola, papaya, and squash (*Wall Street Journal*, Tuesday, 12 October 1999). This genetically modified food, especially soybeans and corn, is found in a wide array of processed foods; for example, soy and corn oils, soy flour, and corn starch are added to cakes, crackers, candies, and so on.

3. For a list of chemicals approved for use on organic crops, see http://www.ams.usda.gov/nop/NationalList/FinalRule .html.

REFERENCES

American Association for the Advancement of Science (1993). *Benchmarks for Science Literacy* (New York: Oxford University Press).

Aronson, E. (1978). *The Jigsaw Classroom* (Beverly Hills, CA: Sage Publications).

Bell, P. (1998). Designing for students' conceptual change in science using argumentation and classroom debate. Unpublished doctoral dissertation, University of California at Berkeley, Berkeley, CA.

Bell, P. (2000). Scientific arguments as learning artifacts: Designing for learning from the web with KIE. *International Journal of Science Education*, 22(8), 797–817.

Bransford, J.D., and Schwartz, D.L. (1999). Rethinking transfer. A simple proposal with multiple implications. In A. Iran-Nejad and P.D. Peason (eds.), *Review of Research in Education* (vol. 24) (Washington, DC: AERA), 61–100.

Brown, A.L., and Palinscar, A.S. (1989). Guided, cooperative learning and individual knowledge acquisition. In L.B. Resnick (ed.), *Knowing, Learning, and Instruction: Essays in Honor of Robert Glaser* (Hillsdale, NJ: Lawrence Erlbaum Associates), 393–451.

Champagne, A. (1998). Kill all the mosquitoes or cure malaria. Symposium conducted at the meeting of the American Association for the Advancement of Science (AAAS), Philadelphia, PA.

Chinn, C.A., and Anderson, R.C. (1998). The structure of discussions that promote reasoning. *Teachers College Record*, 100(2), 315–368.

Chinn, C., and Brewer, W. (1993). The role of anomalous data in knowledge acquisition: A theoretical framework and implications for science instruction. *Review of Educational Research*, 63(1), 1–49.

diSessa, A. (1988). Knowledge in pieces. In G. Forman and P. Pufall (eds.), *Constructivism in the Computer Age* (Hillsdale, NJ: Lawrence Erlbaum Associates), 49–70.

Driver, R., Leach, J., Millar, R., and Scott, P. (1996). *Young People's Images of Science* (Buckingham: Open University Press).

Driver, R., Newton, P., and Osborne, J. (2000). Establishing the norms of scientific argumentation in classrooms. *Science Education*, 84, 287–312.

Gick, M., and Holyoak, K. (1980). Analogical problem solving. *Cognitive Psychology*, 12(3), 306–355.

Gobert, J. (2000). A typology of causal models for plate tectonics: Inferential power and barriers to understanding. *International Journal of Science Education*, 22(9), 937–977.

Holdredge, C., and Talbott, S. (2001). Sowing technology: The ecological argument against genetic engineering down on the farm. *Sierra: The Magazine of the Sierra Club*, 24–72.

Jiménez-Aleixandre, M., Pilar, R., Anxela, B., and Duschl, R.A. (2000). Doing the lesson or doing science: Argument in high school genetics. *Science Education*, 84(6), 757–792.

Kaeppler, H. (2000). Food safety assessment of genetically modified crops. *Agronomics Journal*, 92, 793–797.

Knain, E. (2001). Ideologies in school science textbooks. *International Journal of Science Education*, 23(3), 319–329.

Kuhn, D. (1991). *The Skills of Argument* (Cambridge: Cambridge University Press).

Kuhn, D. (1992). Thinking as argument. *Harvard Educational Review*, 62(2), 155–178.

Kuhn, D. (1993). Science as argument: Implications for teaching and learning scientific thinking. *Science Education*, 77(3), 319–337.

Latour, B., and Woolgar, S. (1986). *Laboratory Life: The Construction of Scientific Facts* (Princeton, NJ: Princeton University Press).

Linn, M. (1995). Designing computer learning environments for engineering and computer science: The Scaffolded Knowledge Integration Framework. *Journal of Science Education and Technology*, 4(2), 103–126.

Linn, M.C., and Hsi, S. (2000). *Computers, Teachers, Peers: Science Learning Partners* (Mahwah, NJ: Lawrence Erlbaum Associates).

Linn, M., and Slotta, J. (2000). WISE Science. *Educational Leadership*, 58(2), 29–32.

Losey, J., Raylor, R., and Carter, M. (1999). Transgenic pollen harms monarch larvae. *Nature*, 399, 214.

Means, M., and Voss, J. (1996). Who reasons well? Two studies of informal reasoning among children of different grade, ability and knowledge levels. *Cognition and Instruction*, 14(2), 139–178.

Munn, D.A., Coffing, G., and Sautter, G. (1998). Response of corn, soybean and wheat crops to fertilizer and herbicides in Ohio compared with low-input production practices. *American Journal of Alternative Agriculture*, 13(4), 181–189.

National Committee on Science Education Standards and Assessment (1996). *National Science Education Standards: 1996* (Washington, DC: National Academy Press).

Ranney, M., and Schank, P. (1998). Toward an integration of the social and the scientific: Observing, modeling, and promoting the explanatory coherence of reasoning. In S.J. Read and L.C. Miller (eds.), *Connectionist Models of Social Reasoning and Social Behavior* (Mahwah, NJ: Lawrence Erlbaum Associates), 245–274.

Schmidt, W., McKnight, C., and Raizen, S. (1996). Splintered vision: An investigation of U.S. mathematics and science education. U.S. National Research Center for the Third International Mathematics and Science Study, Michigan State University.

Seethaler, S. (2002). Can middle school students learn to construct arguments that balance tradeoffs in the genetically modified food controversy? Paper presented at the annual meeting of the American Educational Research Association, New Orleans, LA.

Seethaler, S. (2003). Controversy in the classroom: How eighth-grade and undergraduate students reason about tradeoffs of genetically modified food. Unpublished doctoral dissertation, University of California at Berkeley, CA.

Stigler, J.W., and Hiebert, J. (1999). *The Teaching Gap: Best Ideas from the World's Teachers for Improving Education in the Classroom* (New York: The Free Press).

Tada, Y., Nakase, M., Adachi, T., Nakamura, R., Shimoda, H., Takahashi, M., Fujimura, T., and Matsuda, T. (1996). Reduction of 14–16 kDa allergenic proteins in transgenic rice plants by antisense gene. *FEBS Letters*, 391, 341–345.

Thayer, A. (1999). Transforming agriculture: Transgenic crops and the application of discovery technologies are altering the agrochemical and agricultural business. *Chemical and Engineering News*, 19 April, pp. 21–35.

Toulmin, S. (1958). *The Uses of Argument* (Cambridge: Cambridge University Press).

van Eemeren, F.H., Grootendorst, R., Henkemans, F.S., Blair, J.A., Johnson, R.H., Krabbe, E.C.W., Plantin, C., Walton, D.N., Willard, C.A., et al. (1996). *Fundamentals of Argumentation Theory: A Handbook of Historical Backgrounds and Contemporary Developments* (Hillsdale, NJ: Lawrence Erlbaum Associates).

Voss, J., and Means, M. (1991). Learning to reason via instruction in argumentation. *Learning and Instruction*, 1, 337–350.

Wolfenbarger, L., and Phifer, P. (2000). The ecological risks and benefits of genetically engineered plants. *Science*, 290, 2088–2093.

Ye, X., Al-Babali, S., Klöti, A., Zhang, J., Lucca, P., Beyer, P., and Potrykus, I. (2000). Engineering the provitamin-A (β-carotene) biosynthetic pathway into (carotenoid-free) rice endosperm. *Science*, 287(5451), 303–305.

Yoon, C. (1999). Stalked by deadly virus, papaya lives to breed again. *The New York Times*, 20 July.

Reading Questions

1. What do the researchers mean by their use of the term *tradeoff* when it comes to making decisions about scientific controversies?

2. In the Scoring section of their report, the researchers provide details about what two forms of data used to assess students' learning?

3. According to the researchers, what incorrect piece of evidence did students cite most often in their papers?

4. What three reasons do the researchers provide as possible supporting explanations for why, in their papers, students did not ignore evidence counter to their position?

5. In response to the problem of transfer, what do the researchers suggest instructors should have students do?

Rhetoric Questions

6. Where do the researchers present their central research question? What makes this placement appropriate in the overall design of their research report?

7. What role does the discussion of Sam's responses on the pre-test and post-test play in the reporting of the results? How does it figure into the discussion of "Changes in students' conceptions and attitudes over the course of the curriculum" covered in the Results section of the report?

8. Carefully read the section labeled "Design Principles," and make a note of every instance of hedging that appears in the authors' reporting. Looking specifically at those instances, offer an explanation for why the writers hedge when they do.

Response and Research Questions

9. The researchers report that "there has been a shift among philosophers and sociologists of science, away from seeing science as a purely empirical process, to seeing it as a social process of knowledge construction in which imagination and argument play an important role" (par. 3). In your opinion, what roles do imagination and argument play in the construction of scientific knowledge?

10. The researchers suggest that "many students are completely unaccustomed to 'writing' in science class" (47). What kinds of writing have you done in science classes? What kinds of writing do you feel you should do in those classes?

11. The researchers conclude that exploration of scientific controversies "can help students start to become autonomous science learners by assisting them to think critically about important issues that will affect their lives" (52). Make a list of scientific controversies with which you are familiar. Choose one, and briefly explain the sides of the controversy.

Writing a Persuasive Narrative

Many of the writers whose work for popular audiences is presented in this chapter offer compelling stories about their own and others' experiences as support for their larger claims about food, sustainability, and/or class, among other concerns. Gustavo Arellano, in "Taco USA: How Mexican Food Became More American Than Apple Pie," for instance, explains how he came to experience an "epiphany about Mexican food in the United States." Michael Pollan, in the introduction to his book *Cooked*, recounts his own "magical" experiences watching others prepare food to support his contention about the importance of returning to the practice of cooking for ourselves. In both cases, these personal narratives serve powerful persuasive purposes.

For this project, we invite you to craft a personal narrative that explores your own experience(s) with food in order to make a larger point or to support a claim about food, its sustainability, and/or its connections to larger concerns for American culture or society.

Consider first what you want to suggest to your readers, as you'll want to craft your text with that persuasive intent in mind: What is the overall point you want to emphasize in your narrative? For example, you might choose to make a case that we should eat organically as much as possible, or you might argue that we need to do more to support community gardens. You'll also need to decide if you want to state your position or argument outright or, instead, merely imply the position you're taking. Make the decision that best suits your needs.

Since your evidence for this argument is your personal experience(s), you'll want to consider carefully the structure of your narrative: Will you focus on a single event or experience? Will you focus on your engagement with food more broadly over a span of years? Regardless of the final organizational scheme you employ, remember that your experiences are meant to serve as evidence to support a claim.

WRITING PROJECT **Translating a Scholarly Work for a Popular Audience**

For this project, we ask you to "translate" one of the academic, or scholarly, works included in the chapter for a popular audience. In order to do this, you'll first need to choose the work you'd like to be the focus of your translation:

- Daniel Gregorowius, Petra Lindemann-Matthies, and Markus Huppenbauer's "Ethical Discourse on the Use of Genetically Modified Crops: A Review of Academic Publications in the Fields of Ecology and Environmental Ethics" (*Humanities*)

- John C. Bernard, Katie Gifford, Kristin Santora, and Daria J. Bernard's "Willingness to Pay for Foods with Varying Production Traits and Levels of Genetically Modified Content" (*Social Sciences*)

- Aziz Aris and Samuel Leblanc's "Maternal and Fetal Exposure to Pesticides Associated to Genetically Modified Foods in Eastern Townships of Quebec, Canada" *(Natural Sciences)*
- Sherry Seethaler and Marcia Linn's "Genetically Modified Food in Perspective: An Inquiry-Based Curriculum to Help Middle School Students Make Sense of Tradeoffs" *(Applied Fields)*

Once you've selected your target text for translation, you'll need to decide on the form your translation will take. For example, you might choose to translate Bernard et al.'s social science report for a popular audience by composing a news article about it. Or you might choose to translate the substance of Aris and Leblanc's natural science report into the form of a press release.

Regardless of the public, or popular, genre you choose (news article, press release, etc.), you'll likely want to study examples of that form of writing to become more aware of the conventional rhetorical features associated with the genre. As you review each example, take care to note the structural, language, and reference features of the public genre:

- What kind of title does the example have?
- Can you discern a patterned presentation of information throughout the example?
- In what ways does the example attempt to connect to its intended audience?
- Typically, how long are the paragraphs? How long is the typical sentence?
- How would you assess the level of diction used in the piece? Is jargon employed?
- Are visuals typically used? If so, what kind?
- How does the writer of the example reference outside research?
- Are quotations used? If so, how often? Are they documented? If so, how?

Your final product should look and read as much as possible like a professional example of the genre you're producing.

Global Climate Change and Natural Catastrophes

This chapter of readings offers an array of perspectives, from both the civic and the academic points of view, on issues related to global climate change and natural disasters. The popular article that opens the chapter suggests future devastating effects of climate change and warns readers of the consequences of delaying preparations. Written after the December 2004 earthquake and resulting tsunami that ravaged parts of coastal Indonesia, the second article argues that the rising tolls of destruction resulting from increased natural disasters may be driven by socioeconomic factors like population growth and human migration patterns. The third article relies on economic principles to probe ethical questions concerning what should be done about climate change, and the final popular selection explores the intersections of politics, deregulation, and the effects of natural disasters.

More than providing specific answers about the causes of climate change, or about a region's level of preparedness for a potential natural disaster, we hope the readings in this chapter will compel you, in light of your own experiences, to begin asking questions and considering potential answers to the complex dilemmas presented by global climate change:

- Is there a link between global climate change and the severity of some natural disasters?

- What is my local government doing to prepare for potential disasters?

- What makes a regulation effective? Should the government be interested in deregulation?

- What should/can I do about global warming?

- How do local, regional, and national politics factor into discussions of global climate change?

In the academic case study for this chapter, we take a closer look at what has been described as one of the deadliest and costliest disasters in American history—the 2005 hurricane Katrina and its impacts. Collectively, these readings provide a glimpse into the myriad ways scholars have approached understanding the disaster and its effects:

- **Humanities** What were the hurricane's effects, both regionally and nationally, on the production of music?

- **Social Sciences** What issues related to environmental justice emerged in the disaster area created by Hurricane Katrina?

- **Natural Sciences** What were the levels of toxic trace elements at sites in and around New Orleans, before and after the hurricane struck?

- **Applied Fields** How could nurses identify individuals who might be suffering from post-traumatic stress disorder as a result of their experience of the hurricane's destruction?

Are You Ready for More?

SHARON BEGLEY

Sharon Begley is a senior U.S. health and science correspondent for Reuters. She has covered science and medicine for *Newsweek* and is the author of three books about the human brain, including *The Mind and the Brain* (2002) and *Train Your Mind, Change Your Brain* (2007). Her article "Are You Ready for More?" was published online in May 2011 in the U.S. News section of the *Daily Beast*, a popular news reporting and opinion website. In her article, Begley explores the ubiquitous nature of severe weather events and their effects during 2010 as a sign of events to come. She provides numerous examples of anticipated changes that communities will have to grapple with as a result of the forces of climate change. Her article further suggests that few communities are planning for such changes and fewer still are actually preparing for them.

Joplin, Mo., was prepared. The tornado warning system gave residents 24 minutes' notice that a twister was bearing down on them. Doctors and nurses at St. John's Regional Medical Center, who had practiced tornado drills for years, moved fast, getting patients away from windows, closing blinds, and activating emergency generators. And yet more than 130 people died in Joplin, including four people at St. John's, where the tornado sucked up the roof and left the building in ruins, like much of the shattered city.

Even those who deny the existence of global climate change are having trouble dismissing the evidence of the last year. In the U.S. alone, nearly 1,000 tornadoes have ripped across the heartland, killing more than 500 people and inflicting $9 billion in damage. The Midwest suffered the wettest April in 116 years, forcing the Mississippi to flood thousands of square miles, even as drought-plagued Texas suffered the driest month in a century. Worldwide, the litany of weather's extremes has reached biblical proportions. The 2010 heat wave in Russia killed an estimated 15,000 people. Floods in Australia and Pakistan killed 2,000 and left large swaths of each country under water. A months-long drought in China has devastated millions of acres of farmland. And the temperature keeps rising: 2010 was the hottest year on earth since weather records began.

From these and other extreme-weather events, one lesson is sinking in with terrifying certainty. The stable climate of the last 12,000 years is gone. Which

means you haven't seen anything yet. And we are not prepared.

Picture California a few decades from now, a place so hot and arid the state's trademark orange and lemon trees have been replaced with olive trees that can handle the new climate. Alternating floods and droughts have made it impossible for the reservoirs to capture enough drinking water. The picturesque Highway 1, sections of which are already periodically being washed out by storm surges and mudslides, will have to be rerouted inland, possibly through a mountain. These aren't scenes from another deadly-weather thriller like *The Day after Tomorrow.* They're all changes that California officials believe they need to brace for within the next decade or two. And they aren't alone. Across the U.S., it's just beginning to dawn on civic leaders that they'll need to help their communities brave coming dangers brought by climate change, from disappearing islands in Chesapeake Bay to dust bowls in the Plains and horrific hurricanes in the Gulf of Mexico. Yet only 14 states are even planning, let alone implementing, climate-change adaptation plans, says Terri Cruce, a climate consultant in California. The other 36 apparently are hoping for a miracle.

The game of catch-up will have to happen quickly 5 because so much time was lost to inaction. "The Bush administration was a disaster, but the Obama administration has accomplished next to nothing either, in part because a significant part of the Democratic Party is inclined to balk on this issue as well," says economist Jeffrey Sachs, head of the Earth Institute at Columbia University. "We [are] past the tipping point." The idea of adapting to climate change was once a taboo subject. Scientists and activists feared that focusing on coping would diminish efforts to reduce carbon emissions. On the opposite side of the divide, climate-change deniers argued that since global warming is a "hoax," there was no need to figure out how to adapt. "Climate-change adaptation was a nonstarter," says Vicki Arroyo, executive director of the Georgetown Climate Center. "If you wanted to talk about that, you would have had to talk about climate change itself, which the Bush administration didn't want to do." In fact, President Bush killed what author Mark Hertsgaard in his 2011 book, *Hot*, calls "a key adaptation tool," the National Climate Assessment, an analysis of the vulnerabilities in regions of the U.S. and ideas for coping with them. The legacy of that: state efforts are spotty and local action is practically nonexistent. "There are no true adaptation experts in the federal government, let alone states or cities," says Arroyo. "They've just been commandeered from other departments."

The rookies will struggle to comprehend the complex impacts of climate change. The burning of fossil fuels has raised atmospheric levels of heat-trapping carbon dioxide by 40 percent above what they were before the Industrial Revolution. The added heat in the atmosphere retains more moisture, ratchets up the energy in the system, and incites more violent and extreme weather. Scientists disagree about whether climate change will bring more intense or frequent tornadoes, but there is wide consensus that the 2 degrees Fahrenheit of global warming of the last century is behind the rise in sea levels, more intense hurricanes, more heat waves, and more droughts and deluges. Even if the world went carbon-neutral tomorrow, we'd be in for more: because of the CO_2 that has already been emitted, we're on track for another 5 degrees of warming. Batten down the hatches. "You can no longer say that the climate of the future is going to be like the climate of today, let alone yesterday," says Judi Greenwald, vice president of innovative solutions at the Pew Center on Global Climate Change. "In all of the plausible climate scenarios, we are going to have to change the way we do things in ways we can't even predict."

Changing temperatures will have a profound effect on the plants and animals among us. Crops that flourished in the old climate regime will have to adapt to the new one, as some pests are already doing. Tropical diseases such as malaria, dengue fever, and yellow fever are reaching temperate regions, and ragweed and poison ivy thrive in the hothouse world. Yet most of us are naive about what climate-change adaptation will entail. At the benign extreme, "adapting" sounds as easy as home gardeners adjusting to their new climate zones—those colorful bands on the back of the package of zinnia seeds. It sounds as pleasant as cities planting more trees, as Chicago, New York, Boston, and scores of others are doing (with species native to the warmer climes: Chicago is subbing heat-loving sweet gum and swamp oak for the traditional white oak). And it sounds as architecturally interesting as changing roofs: New York, which is looking at an average temperature increase of up to 3 degrees Fahrenheit by 2020, is planning to paint 3 million square feet of roofs white, to reflect sunlight and thus reduce urban heat-island effects.

But those steps don't even hint at how disruptive and expensive climate-change adaptation will be. "Ten years ago, when we thought climate change would be slow and linear, you could get away with thinking that 'adaptation' meant putting in permeable pavement" so that storm water would be absorbed rather than cause floods, says Bill McKibben, author of the 2010 book *Eaarth*. "Now it's clear that's not going to be at all sufficient, as we see already with disruptions in our ability to grow food, an increase in storms, and the accelerated melting of Greenland that could raise sea levels six feet. Adaptation is going to have to be a lot more than changing which trees cities plant."

As tomorrow's climate wreaks havoc on agriculture—this spring's deluges have already kept farmers from getting tractors into fields to plant corn—

McKibben foresees tens of thousands more Americans having to work on farms, since human hands can do what machines cannot, like planting seeds in flooded fields. Until now, maximizing yield has been the agricultural imperative, but in the future, stability and resilience will be more important. In much of the Northeast, farmers will be unable to grow popular varieties of apples, blueberries, and cranberries, for instance; in Vermont, maple sugaring will likely go the way of ox-drawn plows.

States and cities will have to make huge investments in infrastructure to handle the encroaching sea and raging rivers. Keene, N.H., for instance, has been a pioneer in climate-change adaptation, says Missy Stults, climate director of ICLEI-Local Governments for Sustainability USA. The city recently enlarged culverts along its highways so storm runoff would be less likely to wash out roads. In the San Francisco Bay area, planners are considering increasing the height of the seawall on the city's waterfront and the levees at the San Francisco and Oakland airports. In Ventura, Calif., construction crews moved Surfer's Point 65 feet inland, the state's first experiment in "managed retreat." Because warmer air provides less lift, airport runways the world over will have to be lengthened in order for planes to take off.

In Norfolk, Va., where the combination of global sea-level rise and local-land subsidence has brought water levels 13.5 inches higher since 1930, the city has fought a battle to stay ahead of the tide by elevating one often-flooded roadway by 18 inches. But the neighborhood may have to be abandoned—and residents may not be much happier in neighboring parts of Maryland. An expected sea-level rise there of twice the global average means that 371 miles of highway are at risk of looking more like canals, while 2,500 historic and archeological sites could become real-life versions of Atlantis. Thousands of septic systems— 5,200 in a single county near Chesapeake Bay—are in flood zones, says Zoe Johnson, who directs the climate-change adaptation program at the Department of Natural Resources.

Already, 13 islands in the bay are submerged, 400,000 acres on the eastern shore are on the way

to joining them, and 580 acres of shoreline are lost every year as intense storms erode beaches and wetlands. Homeowners can no longer automatically get a permit to "harden" their beaches by erecting bulkheads and seawalls; they must instead plant vegetation, which may not do the trick. "It's inevitable that some of our low-lying communities will need to be relocated or abandoned," says Johnson.

Maryland is not the only place that will have to decide which communities it can afford to protect and which will have to be sacrificed. Environmental scientist Thomas Wilbanks of Oak Ridge National Laboratory, who chaired a 2011 panel of the National Research Council on adapting to climate change, says: "We'll identify places with iconic value and protect them whatever the cost, even if that means Miami and New Orleans become islands" as surrounding communities are sacrificed. Given that Manhattan is already an island, architects asked to imagine its future have gone a step further: designing Venice-like canals for the southern tip.

In Alaska, six indigenous villages on the coast, including Newtok and Shishmaref, are likely to get swamped as seas rise and storm surges intensify, says Gary Kofinas of the University of Alaska–Fairbanks. They also sit on permafrost, which isn't "perma" anymore. As the ground melts beneath the villages, the state is figuring out how and where to relocate them. Around the world, nearly 1 billion people live in low-lying river deltas, from Guangzhou to New Orleans, that will be reclaimed by the sea, forcing tens of millions of people to migrate. It threatens to be a trail of human misery that will make the exodus after Hurricane Katrina look like a weekend getaway.

The U.S. could take some advice from other coun- 15 tries like the Netherlands, which has more than a little experience keeping the ocean at bay. The Dutch seem to understand just how radically different life will be. As part of a 200-year plan, the country has launched a €1.5 billion project to broaden river channels so they aren't overwhelmed as a result of the higher flows, says Pier Vellinga, professor of climate change at Wageningen University. Rotterdam raised by 2 feet a storm gate at the port that holds back the (rising) North Sea and elevated the ground the new 1,700-acre port sits on by a foot and a half to keep it from being submerged, all at a cost of some €50 million. The country is also adding millions of cubic yards of sand to dunes that hold back the North Sea. All told, it will soon be spending some €4 billion a year to cope with what's coming down the pike. Britain, too, is taking adaptation seriously, planning to raise the height of the floodgates protecting central London from the Thames by 12 inches.

So what lies behind America's resistance to action? Economist Sachs points to the lobbying power of industries that resist acknowledgment of climate change's impact. "The country is two decades behind in taking action because both parties are in thrall to Big Oil and Big Coal," says Sachs. "The airwaves are filled with corporate-financed climate misinformation." But the vanguard of action isn't waiting any longer. This week, representatives from an estimated 100 cities are meeting in Bonn, Germany, for the 2nd World Congress on Cities and Adaptation to Climate Change. The theme is "Resilient Cities." As Joplin, Mo., learned in the most tragic way possible, against some impacts of climate change, man's puny efforts are futile. But time is getting short, and the stakes are high. Says Daniel Sarewitz, a professor of science and society at Arizona State University: "Not to adapt is to consign millions of people to death and disruption."

Reading Questions

1. Begley's article begins by describing the efforts of residents of Joplin, Missouri, to prepare for an impending tornado. What do those efforts consist of?

2. Begley notes that only fourteen states are preparing climate-change adaptation plans. What does she suggest are the reasons so few states are engaged in preparing for the consequences of climate change?

3. Begley identifies a number of potentially devastating consequences of climate change for some American cities and states. What, according to Begley, are some of the possible consequences for San Francisco, Norfolk, and Alaska?

Rhetoric Questions

4. Begley's article makes use of a fairly dramatic photograph. What is its impact on you as a reader? Consider the placement of the photo in the article. What is the benefit of placing it at the beginning of the piece?

5. Begley cites a number of experts in the area of climate change. Look closely at the people she cites. Do her choices present a good balance of opinions on the issue? Why or why not?

Response and Research Questions

6. Begley's article is centrally concerned with learning to adapt to climate change. What does she mean by "adapting" or "adaptation"? Is there a difference between short-term and long-term adaptation plans?

7. At the end of her article, Begley returns briefly to the scene described in her opening: "As Joplin, Mo., learned in the most tragic way possible, against some impacts of climate change, man's puny efforts are futile. But time is getting short, and the stakes are high." What message do these lines convey to you?

8. Begley identifies the Netherlands as an example of a country that has done the kind of adaptation planning the United States needs to undertake. Based on the Dutch example, what does the United States (or your community, as part of the United States) need to do?

Rising Tide

DANIEL SAREWITZ AND ROGER A. PIELKE JR.

Daniel Sarewitz is a professor of science and society and co-director of the Consortium for Science, Policy & Outcomes at Arizona State University. He has published a number of works that explore the connections among science policy, research, and social outcomes, including *Frontiers of Illusion: Science, Technology, and the Politics of Progress* (1999), *Prediction: Science, Decision-Making, and the Future of Nature* (2000), and *Living with the Genie: Essays on Technology and the Quest for Human Mastery* (2003). Roger A. Pielke Jr. is a professor of environmental studies and a former director of the Center for Science and Technology Policy Research at the University of Colorado. He has co-authored or written a number of books, including *The Honest Broker: Making Sense of Science in Policy and Politics* (2007) and *The Climate Fix: What Scientists and Politicians Won't Tell You about Global Warming* (2010). In their article, "Rising Tide," published

in the *New Republic* magazine in January 2005, Sarewitz and Pielke claim that due to the "increase in vulnerability because of growing populations, expanding economies, rapid urbanization, and migrations to coasts and other exposed regions," we should prioritize our energies and focus our response to global climate change on reducing our vulnerability to natural disasters.

The increasing threat of natural disasters has long been cited as one of many reasons why society should reduce greenhouse gas emissions, and the horrendous toll of the December 26 Indonesian earthquake and resulting tsunami has only made those calls louder. A December 30 article in *Salon* portrays the effects of the recent tsunami as "visions of just the kind of tumultuous weather that scientists have long viewed as a symptom of global warming." A day later, Sir David King, Britain's chief science adviser, told the BBC, "What is happening in the Indian Ocean underlines the importance of the Earth's system to our ability to live safely. And what we are talking about in terms of climate change is something that is really driven by our own use of fossil fuels."

Such arguments have a rich pedigree. Only nine days before the tsunami, Klaus Toepfer, executive director of the U.N. Environment Programme, said, "Climate scientists anticipate an increase [in] intensity of extreme weather events." Environmental groups use the threat of increasing disasters to advocate decisive action to reduce the emission of greenhouse gases and implement the Kyoto Protocol on climate change. The advocacy group Scientists and Engineers for Change supported John Kerry in the 2004 election by posting billboards in storm-ravaged Florida with the message, GLOBAL WARMING = WORSE HURRICANES. GEORGE BUSH JUST DOESN'T GET IT.

Global climate change is real, and developing alternative energy sources and reducing global carbon-dioxide emission is essential. But the claim that action to slow climate change is justified by the rising toll of natural disasters—and, by extension, that reducing emissions can help stanch these rising losses—is both scientifically and morally insupportable. To minimize damage from tsunamis and the like, we need to focus not on reducing emissions but on reducing our vulnerability to disasters.

★ ★ ★

The first thing to understand about disasters is that they have indeed been rapidly increasing worldwide over the past century, in both number and severity, and that the causes of this increase are well understood—and have nothing to do with global warming. Data from the Center for Research on the Epidemiology of Disasters in Brussels, Belgium, as well as the Red Cross and the reinsurance industry, show that the number of disasters affecting at least 100 people or resulting in a call for international assistance has increased from an average of about 100 per year in the late '60s to between 500 and 800 per year by the early twenty-first century. The reason is not an increase in the frequency or severity of storms, earthquakes, or similar events, but an increase in vulnerability because of growing populations, expanding economies, rapid urbanization, and migrations to coasts and other exposed regions.

These changes are reflected in the costs of major 5 disasters, which, according to the German insurance company Munich Re, rose more than tenfold in the second half of the twentieth century, from an average of about $4 billion per year in the 1950s to more than $40 billion in the 1990s, in inflation-adjusted dollars. The great Miami hurricane of 1926, for example, caused about $76 million in damage; when Hurricane Andrew, of similar force, struck South Florida in 1992, it caused more than $30 billion in damage, again adjusted for inflation. Research suggests that if the same 1926 storm were to hit Miami today, it would cost more than $80 billion.

The economic losses from disasters are increasingly concentrated in the affluent world. But, as a percentage of GNP, the economic effects of natural disasters on poor countries can be hundreds of times greater. Damages from Hurricane Mitch, for example, which devastated Central America in 1998, were estimated at between $5 and $7 billion—or almost the annual combined total economic activity of the two hardest-hit nations, Honduras and Nicaragua. Their economies still have not recovered. By comparison, the magnitude 6.7 earthquake that struck California in 1994, one of the costliest disasters in U.S. history, caused an estimated $20 to $40 billion in losses, but this amounted to only 2 to 4 percent of California's economic activity.

Disasters disproportionately harm poor people in poor countries because those countries typically have densely populated coastal regions, shoddily constructed buildings, sparse infrastructure, and grossly inadequate public health capabilities. Poor land use leads to widespread environmental degradation, such as deforestation and wetlands destruction, which in turn exacerbates flooding and landslides. Emergency preparation and response capabilities are often inadequate, and hazard insurance is usually unavailable, further slowing recovery. Thus, while the world's poorest 35 countries make up only about 10 percent of the world's population, they suffered more than half of the disaster-related deaths between 1992 and 2001.

Disparities in disaster vulnerability between rich and poor will continue to grow. About 97 percent of population growth is occurring in the developing world. This growth, in turn, drives urbanization and coastal migration. The result is that, in the next two decades, the population of urban areas in the developing world will likely increase by two billion people. And this population is being added to cities that are mostly located on coastal or flood plains—or in earthquake zones—and are unable to provide the quality of housing, services, infrastructure, and environmental protection that can help reduce vulnerability.

Faced with the inescapable momentum of these socioeconomic trends as we clean up from the South Asian disaster, the crucial question is this: What can be done to better prepare the world—especially the developing world—for future disasters? It is absurd to suggest that reducing greenhouse gas emission is an important part of the answer.

The chief reason is that the role of demographics in making a country vulnerable to disaster overwhelms

that of a warming atmosphere. Indeed, the most recent assessment of the scientifically authoritative Intergovernmental Panel on Climate Change (IPCC) found no evidence to support the idea that human-caused climate change has discernibly influenced the rapidly increasing disaster toll of recent decades. While IPCC data and predictions indicate that human-caused climate change may have an effect on future disasters, our analysis of hurricanes and tropical cyclones, using IPCC data and assumptions, shows that for every $1 of additional disaster damage scientists expect will be caused by the effects of global warming by 2050, an additional $22 to $60 of damages will result from the growth of economies and populations. Other studies of hurricanes, flooding, and heat waves lead to a similar conclusion: Socioeconomic trends, not climate change, will continue to drive increasing disaster losses.

The example of rising sea levels provides further illustration. Scientists expect that, by 2050, average global sea levels will rise by two to twelve inches. But no research suggests that the Kyoto Protocol, or even more ambitious emissions-reduction proposals, would significantly reduce this increase. Meanwhile, coastal populations will continue to grow by hundreds of millions, mostly in developing countries. Bangladesh alone, which suffered about 140,000 deaths from a cyclone in 1991, may add up to 100 million people to its population by 2050. The world will indeed be more vulnerable to tsunamis in the future, but, once again, the causes are primarily socioeconomic change, not climate change.

Yet assertions that global warming is directly linked to rising disaster losses persist. Such assertions may have short-term political benefits in the global warming debate, but they detract from serious efforts to prepare for disasters. Global climate change has been a potent focusing lens for environmental groups, governments, the scientific research establishment, and international bodies, especially the United Nations. The U.N. Framework Convention on Climate Change—and its Kyoto Protocol mandating emissions reductions—occupies thousands of advocates, diplomats, scientists, lawyers, and journalists. The climate change policy agenda has also sucked into its maw a wide range of other issues, such as energy policy, water policy, public health and infectious diseases, deforestation, and, of course, disasters. Climate change thus captures a huge proportion of the public attention, political energy, and financial and intellectual resources available for addressing global environmental challenges — including disaster preparedness. Uncontrolled urban growth exacerbates hazards and urban growth.

The U.N. Framework Convention, for example, refused to fund disaster preparedness efforts at its last conference in December unless states could demonstrate exactly how the disasters they feared were linked to climate change. Consider, too, the amount spent on scientific research. According to a recent RAND study, U.S. funding of disaster loss-reduction research in 2003 amounted to about $127 million — only 7 percent of the amount invested in climate change research for that year. Efforts in Congress to create a coordinated research program focused on reducing disaster losses have never gained momentum. By contrast, the U.S. government has sponsored a coordinated, multi-agency framework for climate change research for more than 15 years, with total investments, by our calculations, of more than $30 billion, adjusted for inflation.

This is not to say that many thousands of people and hundreds of organizations worldwide are not productively confronting disaster vulnerability, but their efforts do not begin to address the magnitude of the problem. Thousands of participants from most of the world's nations, along with scientists and political advocates, have come together every year since 1995 to work toward concerted international action on climate change. But, when the U.N. World Conference on Disaster Reduction convenes later this week, it will be the first such meeting in more than a decade.

While the prospects for global climate change are constantly in the public eye, the South Asian earthquake and tsunami poignantly demonstrate that the crisis of growing disaster vulnerability only becomes news after disaster strikes. Yet we know that effective action is possible to reduce disaster losses even in the face of poverty and dense population. During the 2004 hurricane season, Haiti and the Dominican Republic, both on the island of Hispaniola, provided a powerful lesson in this regard. As Julia Taft of the U.N. Development Program explained: "In the Dominican Republic, which has invested in hurricane shelters and emergency evacuation networks, the death toll was fewer than ten, as compared to an estimated two thousand in Haiti. . . . Haitians were a hundred times more likely to die in an equivalent storm than Dominicans."

Most tools needed to reduce disaster vulnerability already exist, such as risk assessment techniques, better building codes and code enforcement, land-use standards, and emergency-preparedness plans. The question is why disaster vulnerability is so low on the list of global development priorities. Says Brian Tucker, president of GeoHazards International, "The most serious flaw in our current efforts is the lack of a globally accepted standard of acceptable disaster vulnerability, and an action plan to put every country on course to achieve this standard. Then we would have a means to measure progress and to make it clear which countries are doing well and which are not. We need a natural disaster equivalent to the Kyoto Protocol."

Those who justify the need for greenhouse gas reductions by exploiting the mounting human and economic toll of natural disasters worldwide are either ill-informed or dishonest. This is not, as Britain's Sir David King suggested, "something we can manage" by decreasing our use of fossil fuels. Prescribing emissions reductions to forestall the future effects of disasters is like telling someone who is sedentary, obese, and alcoholic that the best way to improve his health is to wear a seat belt.

In principle, fruitful action on both climate change and disaster should proceed simultaneously. In practice, this will not happen until the issues of climate change and disaster vulnerability are clearly separated in the eyes of the media, the public, environmental activists, scientists, and policymakers. As long as people think that GLOBAL WARMING = WORSE HURRICANES, global warming will also equal less preparation. And disasters will claim ever more money and lives.

Reading Questions

1. What is Sarewitz and Pielke's position on the reality of global climate change?

2. One of the authors' points is that taking steps to address global climate change will not alter the magnitude of future natural disasters. What reasons do they provide to support this statement?

3. What question do the authors think we should really be trying to answer in terms of future disasters?

Rhetoric Questions

4. How would you describe the strategy that Sarewitz and Pielke use to structure the opening paragraph of their article? What does the opening seek to establish for the reader, and how does it accomplish that?

5. What evidence do Sarewitz and Pielke provide as support for the following statement: "The world will indeed be more vulnerable to tsunamis in the future, but, once again, the causes are primarily socioeconomic change, not climate change" (par. 11)? In your opinion, is their evidence for this statement sufficient? Why or why not?

Response and Research Questions

6. Sarewitz and Pielke conclude by arguing that disaster preparedness hinges on separating the issues of climate change and disaster vulnerability "in the eyes of the media, the public, environmental activists, scientists, and policymakers" (18). Review Sharon Begley's article, "Are You Ready for More?" (see p. 546), and consider whether or not her arguments conflate the issues of climate change and disaster vulnerability in ways that Sarewitz and Pielke would find problematic.

7. Consider the community in which you live. Assess its efforts to reduce greenhouse gases, and compare those efforts to the community's disaster preparedness. Are the two efforts somehow linked? Should they be separated? Why? Where should the priority be?

8. Explain Sarewitz and Pielke's reasoning behind this statement: "Prescribing emissions reductions to forestall the future effects of disasters is like telling someone who is sedentary, obese, and alcoholic that the best way to improve his health is to wear a seat belt" (17).

The Ethics of Climate Change

JOHN BROOME

John Broome is Emeritus White's Professor of Moral Philosophy and an Emeritus Fellow of Corpus Christi College at the University of Oxford. He has researched and published extensively on the issues of climate change. In 1992, he published a book-length treatment of the matter: *Counting the Cost of Global Warming*. The following article was first published in the June 2008 edition of *Scientific American* and later republished in Tim Folger and Elizabeth Kolbert's *The Best American Science and Nature Writing, 2008*. In the article, Broome explains why what we should do about climate change is an ethical question, and he proposes strategies for thinking about how to answer that question.

What should we do about climate change? The question is an ethical one. Science, including the science of economics, can help discover the causes and effects of climate change. It can also help work out what we can do about climate change. But what we should do is an ethical question.

Not all "should" questions are ethical. "How should you hold a golf club?" is not, for instance. The climate question is ethical, however, because any thoughtful answer must weigh conflicting interests among different people. If the world is to do something about climate change, some people—chiefly the better-off among the current generation—will have to reduce their emissions of greenhouse gases to save future generations from the possibility of a bleak existence in a hotter world. When interests conflict, "should" questions are always ethical.

Climate change raises a number of ethical questions. How should we—all of us living today—evaluate the well-being of future generations, given that they are likely to have more material goods than we do? Many people, some living, others yet to be born, will die from the effects of climate change. Is each death equally bad? How bad are those deaths collectively? Many people will die before they bear children, so climate change will prevent the existence of children who would otherwise have been born. Is their non-existence a bad thing? By emitting greenhouse gases, are the rich perpetrating an injustice on the world's poor? How should we respond to the small but real chance that climate change could lead to worldwide catastrophe?

Many ethical questions can be settled by common sense. Sophisticated philosophy is rarely needed. All of us are to some extent equipped to face up to the ethical questions raised by climate change. For example, almost everyone recognizes (with some exceptions) the elementary moral principle that you should not do something for your own benefit if it harms another person. True, sometimes you cannot avoid harming someone, and sometimes you may do it accidentally without realizing it. But whenever you cause harm, you should normally compensate the victim.

Climate change will cause harm. Heat waves, [5] storms, and floods will kill many people and harm many others. Tropical diseases, which will increase their range as the climate warms, will exact their toll in human lives. Changing patterns of rainfall will lead to local shortages of food and safe drinking water. Large-scale human migrations in response to rising sea levels and other climate-induced stresses will impoverish many people. As yet, few experts have predicted specific numbers, but some statistics suggest the scale of the harm that climate change will cause. The European heat wave of 2003 is estimated to have killed 35,000 people. In 1998 floods in China adversely affected 240 million. The World Health Organization estimates that as long ago as 2000 the annual death toll from climate change had already reached more than 150,000.

In going about our daily lives, each of us causes greenhouse gases to be emitted. Driving a car, using electric power, buying anything whose manufacture or transport consumes energy—all those activities generate greenhouse gases that contribute to climate change. In that way, what we each do for our own benefit harms others. Perhaps at the moment we cannot help it, and in the past we did not realize we were doing it. But the elementary moral principle I mentioned tells us we should try to stop doing it and compensate the people we harm.

This same principle also tells us that what we should do about climate change is not just a matter of weighing benefits against costs—although it is partly that. Suppose you calculate that the benefit to you and your friends of partying until dawn exceeds the harm done to your neighbor by keeping her awake all night. It does not follow that you should hold your party. Similarly, think of an industrial project that brings benefits in the near future but emits greenhouse gases that will harm people decades hence. Again suppose the benefits exceed the costs. It does not follow that the project should go ahead; indeed it may be morally wrong. Those who benefit from it should not impose its costs on others who do not.

ETHICS OF COSTS AND BENEFITS

But even if weighing costs against benefits does not entirely answer the question of what should be done about climate change, it is an essential part of the answer. The costs of mitigating climate change are the sacrifices the present generation will have to make to reduce greenhouse gases. We will have to travel less and better insulate our homes. We will have to eat less meat. We will have to live less lavishly. The benefits are the better lives that future people will lead: they will not suffer so much from the spread of deserts, from the loss of their homes to the rising sea, or from floods, famines, and the general impoverishment of nature.

Weighing benefits to some people against costs to others is an ethical matter. But many of the costs and benefits of mitigating climate change present themselves in economic terms, and economics has useful methods of weighing benefits against costs in complex cases. So here economics can work in the service of ethics.

The ethical basis of cost-benefit economics was recognized recently in a major report, the *Stern Review on the Economics of Climate Change*, by Nicholas Stern and his colleagues at the U.K. Treasury. The Stern Review concentrates mainly on comparing costs and benefits, and it concludes that the benefit that would be gained by reducing emissions of greenhouse gases would be far greater than the cost of reducing them. Stern's work has provoked a strong reaction from economists for two reasons. First, some economists think economic conclusions should not be based on ethical premises. Second, the review favors strong and immediate action to control emissions, whereas other economic studies, such as one by William Nordhaus of Yale University, have concluded that the need to act is not so urgent.

Those two issues are connected. Stern's conclusion differs from Nordhaus's principally because, on ethical grounds, Stern uses a lower "discount rate." Economists generally value future goods less than present ones: they discount future goods. Furthermore, the more distant the future in which goods become available, the more the goods are discounted. The discount rate measures how fast the value of goods diminishes with time [see box opposite]. Nordhaus discounts at roughly 6 percent a year; Stern discounts at 1.4 percent. The effect is that Stern gives a present value of $247 billion for having, say, a trillion dollars' worth of goods a century from now. Nordhaus values having those same goods in 2108 at just $2.5 billion today. Thus, Stern attaches nearly 100 times as much value as Nordhaus does to having any given level of costs and benefits 100 years from now.

The difference between the two economists' discount rates is enough to explain the difference between their conclusions. Most of the costs of controlling climate change must be borne in the near future, when the present generation must sacrifice some of its consumption. The benefits will mostly come a century or two from now. Because Stern judges the present value of those benefits to be higher than Nordhaus does, Stern can justify spending more today on mitigating climate change than Nordhaus can.

How Much Do We Care about the Future?

Economists usually value goods received in the future less highly than goods received today. But how much less? If the discount rate is 6 percent a year, goods worth $1 trillion received one year from today are worth only about $940 billion today. (Because economists discount continuously, the actual present value is $941.8 billion.) Economists Nicholas Stern and William Nordhaus have recently reached dramatically divergent conclusions, embodied in the discount rates they apply, about how much to spend today on goods available only to future generations.

HOW DISCOUNTING EVALUATES FUTURE GOODS
The graph shows how the value economists assign today to receiving goods worth $1 trillion in the future depends both on the discount rate and on how far into the future the trillion dollars' worth of goods will be received.

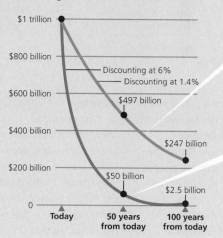

Nicholas Stern's 1.4 percent discount rate places a relatively high value on the well-being of future generations. A trillion dollars' worth of goods received in 100 years is valued at $247 billion today. In fact, Stern argues, the world needs to begin investing 1 percent of its total production, or about $500 billion today, on efforts to reduce greenhouse gases.

William Nordhaus's 6 percent discount rate places far less value than Stern's rate does on the well-being of future generations. A trillion dollars' worth of goods in 100 years is valued at only $2.5 billion today, hardly enough to justify the costs of greatly reducing greenhouse gases.

THE RICHER FUTURE

Why discount future goods at all? The goods in question are the material goods and services that people consume—bicycles, food, banking services, and so on. In most of the scenarios predicted for climate change, the world economy will continue to grow. Hence, future people will on average possess more goods than present people do. The more goods you already have, the less valuable are further goods, and so it is sound economic logic to discount them. To have one bathroom in your house is a huge improvement to your life; a second bathroom is nice but not so life-changing. Goods have "diminishing marginal value," as economists put it.

But there may be a second, purely ethical reason for discounting goods that come to relatively rich people. According to an ethical theory known as prioritarianism, a benefit—by which I mean an increase in an individual's well-being—that comes to a rich person should be assigned less social value than the same benefit would have if it had come to a poor person. Prioritarianism gives priority to the less well off. According to an alternative ethical theory known as utilitarianism, however, a benefit has the same value no matter who receives it. Society should simply aim to maximize the total of people's well-being, no matter how that total is distributed across the population [see box on p. 558].

What should the discount rate be? What determines how fast the value of having goods in the future diminishes as the future time in question becomes more remote? That depends, first, on some nonethical factors. Among them is the economy's rate of growth, which measures how much better off, on average, people will be in the future than they are today. Consequently, it determines how much less benefit future

15

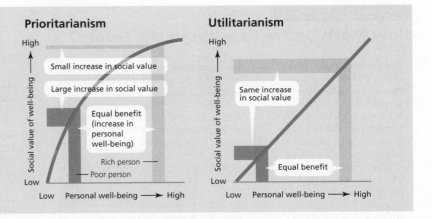

Theories of value disagree about the social value of distributing equal benefits to rich and poor. Prioritarianism assigns greater social value to a given increase in well-being if it reaches a poor person. Utilitarianism assigns the same social value no matter how benefits are distributed.

people will derive from additional material goods than people would derive now from those same goods. A fast growth rate makes for a high discount rate.

The discount rate also depends on an ethical factor. How should benefits to those future, richer people be valued in comparison to our own? If prioritarianism is right, the value attached to future people's benefits should be less than the value of our benefits, because future people will be better off than we are. If utilitarianism is right, future people's benefits should be valued equally with ours. Prioritarianism therefore makes for a relatively high discount rate; utilitarianism makes for a lower one.

The debate between prioritarians and utilitarians takes a curious, even poignant turn in this context. Most debates about inequality take place among the relatively rich, when they consider what sacrifices they should make for the relatively poor. But when we think about future people, we are considering what sacrifices we, the relatively poor, should make for the later relatively rich. Usually prioritarianism demands more of the developed countries than utilitarianism does. In this case, it demands less.

TEMPORAL DISTANCE

Another ethical consideration also affects the discount rate. Some philosophers think we should care more about people who live close to us in time than about those who live in the more distant future, just because of their temporal distance from us. If those philosophers are right, future well-being should be discounted just because it comes in the future. This position is called pure discounting. It implies we should give less importance to the death of a 10-year-old 100 years in the future than to the death of a 10-year-old now. An opposing view is that we should be temporally impartial, insisting that the mere date on which a harm occurs makes no difference to its value. Pure discounting makes for a relatively high discount rate; temporal impartiality makes for a lower one.

To determine the right discount rate, therefore, the economist must answer at least two ethical questions. Which should we accept: prioritarianism or utilitarianism? And should we adopt pure discounting or be temporally impartial?

These questions are not matters of elementary [20] morality; they raise difficult issues in moral philosophy. Moral philosophers approach such questions by combining tight analytical argument with sensitivity to ethical intuitions. Arguments in moral philosophy are rarely conclusive, partly because we each have mutually inconsistent intuitions. All I can do as a philosopher is judge the truth as well as I can and present my best arguments in support of my judgments. Space prevents me from setting forth my arguments here, but I have concluded that prioritarianism is mistaken and that we should be temporally impartial.

Measuring Catastrophe?

Climate change raises much harder and more important ethical issues than the appropriate value of the discount rate. One is the chance of utter catastrophe. The Intergovernmental Panel on Climate Change reports several studies of how global temperatures will increase in the long run if atmospheric greenhouse gases reach the warming equivalent of about 550 parts per million of carbon dioxide (a level expected within a few decades). Most of the studies estimate the probability is 5 percent or more that the increase will be above 8 degrees Celsius (14.4 degrees Fahrenheit). The disruption caused by such temperatures would pose some risk—no one can say how much—of a devastating collapse of the human population, perhaps even to extinction. Any such event would be so bad that even multiplied by its small chance of occurrence, its badness could dominate all calculations

of the harm that climate change will cause. Working out how bad such an event would be is an urgent but very difficult ethical problem.

For example, a population collapse will cause the premature deaths of billions of people. So one must try to estimate how bad, ethically speaking, it is for a person to die early. That may sound like a hard-hearted question, but the value of human life is already recognized as a necessary element in public policy. For example, the World Health Organization has developed a measure of the "burden of disease"—the harm done to people by disease, including the harm suffered by those who are killed by disease. The WHO is already applying the measure to estimate the harm done by climate change.

Catastrophe raises an even harder ethical question. If humanity becomes extinct or the human population collapses, vast numbers

of people who would otherwise have existed will not in fact exist. The absence of so much potential humanity seems an overwhelmingly bad thing. But that is puzzling. If nonexistence is a harm, it is a harm suffered by nobody, since there is nobody who does not exist. How can there be a harm that harms nobody?

Some philosophers insist there can be no such harm. They think that extinction or population collapse will do no harm apart from causing early deaths. Other philosophers disagree; they think the loss of future humanity would indeed be exceedingly bad. If they are right, they will still have to judge in quantitative terms just how bad it would be.

The issue remains one of the hardest and most debated problems in practical philosophy. But until a satisfactory answer is found, it will be impossible to properly judge the badness of climate change.

For more detail, see Chapter 10 of my book *Weighing Goods* (1991) and Section 4.3 of my book *Weighing Lives* (2004).

MARKET DISCOUNT RATES?

Stern reaches those same ethical conclusions. Since both tend toward low discounting, they—together with Stern's economic modeling—lead him to his 1.4 percent rate. His practical conclusion follows: the world urgently needs to take strong measures to control climate change.

Economists who oppose Stern do not deny that his practical conclusion follows from his ethical stance. They object to his ethical stance. Yet most of them decline to take any ethical position of their own, even though they favor an interest rate higher than Stern's. As I have explained, the correct discount rate depends on ethical considerations. So how can

economists justify a discount rate without taking an ethical position?

They do so by taking their higher discount rate from the money market, where people exchange future money for present money, and vice versa. They adopt the money-market interest rate as their interest rate. How can that be justified?

First, some values are determined by people's tastes, which markets do reveal. The relative value of apples and oranges is determined by the tastes revealed in the fruit market. But the value that should be attached to the well-being of future generations is not determined by tastes. It is a matter of ethical judgment.

So does the money market reveal people's ethical judgments about the value of future well-being? I doubt it. The evidence shows that, when people borrow and lend, they often give less weight to their own future well-being than to their present well-being. Most of us are probably not so foolish as to judge that our own well-being is somehow less valuable in old age than in youth. Instead our behavior simply reflects our impatience to enjoy a present benefit, overwhelming whatever judgment we might make about the value of our own future. Inevitably, impatience will also overwhelm whatever high-minded arguments we might make in favor of the well-being of future generations.

But for the sake of argument, suppose people's market behavior genuinely reflected their judgments of value. How could economists then justify proclaiming an ethically neutral stance and taking the discount rate from the market? They do so, purportedly, on democratic grounds—leaving ethical judgments to the public rather than making them for themselves. The economists who criticize Stern claim the democratic high ground and accuse him of arrogantly trying to impose his own ethical beliefs on others.

They misunderstand democracy. Democracy requires debate and deliberation as well as voting. Economists—even Stern—cannot impose their beliefs on anyone. They can only make recommendations and argue for them. Determining the correct discount rate requires sophisticated theory, and we members of the public cannot do it without advice from experts. The role of economists in the democratic process is to work out that theory. They should offer their best recommendations, supported by their best arguments. They should be willing to engage in debate with one another about the ethical bases of their conclusions. Then we members of the public must reach our own decisions with the experts' help. Without their help, our choices will be uninformed and almost worthless.

Once we have made our decisions through the democratic process, society can act. That is not the job of economists. Their recommendations are inputs to the process, not the output of it. The true arrogance is imagining that you are the final arbiter of the democratic process.

Ethical considerations cannot be avoided in determining the discount rate. Climate change raises many other ethical issues, too; one crucial one, the problem of catastrophic outcomes, is mentioned in the box on page 559. It will require serious work in ethics to decide what sacrifices we should make to moderate climate change. Like the science of climate change, the ethics of climate change is hard. So far it leaves much to be resolved. We face ethical as well as scientific problems, and we must work to solve them.

Reading Questions

1. According to Broome, what makes the question of what we *should* do about climate change a matter for ethics?

2. Broome argues that at least one way to approach the question of what we should do about climate change is to weigh benefits and costs. However, he also suggests that just because the benefits of an action outweigh the costs, this does not mean we should necessarily take that action. Explain his reasoning for this.

3. What is the "discount rate"? How does it explain the difference between Stern's and Nordhaus's conclusions and recommendations for action regarding climate change?

4. Define the concepts of "prioritarianism," "utilitarianism," and "temporal distance," in your own words.

Rhetoric Questions

5. Why do you think Broome, an economist and philosopher, spends so much time in his article defining concepts?

6. Describe the structural organization of Broome's article. How is it organized?

7. Read the concluding paragraphs of Broome's argument closely. Then evaluate the conclusion's likely effectiveness on his intended audience. In your opinion, what are its strengths? What are its weaknesses?

Response and Research Questions

8. Broome distinguishes between the kinds of insights that science and ethics can provide to the issues surrounding climate change. What kinds of insights do you think each area of knowledge provides?

9. Broome suggests that prioritarianism is mistaken and that we should be temporally impartial. Do you agree with his conclusions? Why or why not? One way to begin considering your position is to provide an answer to a question that ran with the original article: "Which is worse, the death of a child in 2108 or the death of a child today?"

10. What moral principle do you think guides Broome's conclusion, and what moral principle(s) do you feel should guide any response to climate change?

Disasters and Deregulation

TED STEINBERG

Ted Steinberg is the Adeline Barry Davee Distinguished Professor of History and Professor of Law at Case Western University in Cleveland, Ohio. He is an expert in environmental, social, and legal history and has published extensively in these areas. His recent book-length projects include *Acts of God: The Unnatural History of Natural Disaster* (2000), *Down to Earth: Nature's Role in American History* (2002), and *American Green: The Obsessive Quest for the Perfect Lawn* (2006). In "Disasters and Deregulation," published in 2006 in the *Chronicle of Higher Education*, Steinberg explores the history of deregulation since the 1980s and its relationship to the problems of governmental response to natural hazards.

From a statistical perspective, our nation's recent hurricane problem comes down to a case of bad luck. Even though 32 major hurricanes developed in the North Atlantic from 1998 to 2003, only three reached the mainland in the United States. Then came two very active seasons that brought a record number of hurricanes. "We went from being very, very lucky to being very unlucky in 2004 and 2005," Phil Klotzbach, of Colorado State University's Tropical Meteorology Project, told the *Times-Picayune*. "Hopefully, we get back to being lucky again."

A little luck is always a good thing, especially with another hurricane season now under way. But we can help load the dice in our favor by understanding what has gone wrong with the federal government's approach to natural hazards.

To date the Katrina disaster has been presented in the news media as primarily a textbook example of failed Republican politics. If only President Bush had left the Federal Emergency Management Agency alone and not incorporated it into the Department of Homeland Security. If only he had appointed a FEMA director with experience in disaster preparedness. If only he had not slashed funds to strengthen the levees, then things would have gone better down South.

There is little doubt that the Bush administration badly mishandled the disaster. Nor can there be any question that concern with terrorism drained away resources and distracted political leaders from the threat of natural disasters. But ultimately our nation's problem with such calamities goes back much further than the rise of Republicans to power in the 2000 election or the attacks of September 11, 2001. The dilemma stems from the deregulatory ethos that has dominated U.S. politics since 1980. That disregard for limits — be they on coastal development or storm-susceptible housing — is something that both Republicans and Democrats have conspired to bring about.

The ethos is part of a more general trend since 5 the late 1970s toward a neoliberal agenda. As described by the geographer David Harvey in his recent *A Brief History of Neoliberalism* (Oxford University Press, 2005), neoliberalism involves "an institutional framework characterized by strong private property rights, free markets, and free trade." It is a philosophy centered on nearly absolute economic freedom that flourished during the Reagan administration and, as the economist Joseph E. Stiglitz has pointed out in *The Roaring Nineties* (W. W. Norton, 2003), carried over into the Clinton era.

Consider, for example, the National Flood Insurance Program, established in 1968 and based on the idea that the federal government would help people in flood-prone locales insure their property. In return, local municipalities would enact regulations limiting land use in vulnerable areas and thereby reduce exposure to flood risk. Unfortunately, a 1983 General Accounting Office report revealed that FEMA — first charged with administering the program under Jimmy Carter — had failed to monitor state and local regulations.

A bipartisan assault on the program soon followed. What was once a requirement that local authorities adopt flood-plain rules became "the preferred approach" under the Reagan administration. The Clinton administration then abandoned land-use regulation

entirely, drafting a new policy that sought to "encourage positive attitudes toward flood-plain management."

Meanwhile FEMA allowed the maps defining flood zones to go out of date, a move that understated the risk of inundation and thus helped encourage coastal development in vulnerable areas. Back in the 1970s, mapping those areas subject to a 1 percent risk of annual flooding occurred every three to five years. But the deregulatory climate that began the following decade led to a lackadaisical attitude at FEMA's cartography department.

By the time Hurricane Katrina struck, some of the flood-insurance maps were a full generation old. A map depicting part of Hancock County, Miss., for example, allowed homeowners to build some 10 feet below the elevation that an accurate estimate of a 100-year flood would have permitted — a disaster waiting to happen if ever there was one.

Sadly, the same deregulatory agenda also applied 10 to vulnerable barrier islands. In 1982 the Coastal Barrier Resources Act set aside 186 units of dynamic barrier land and denied those areas federal support for bridges, water and sewer systems, and national flood insurance. The problem is that the law applied only to those barrier islands not yet developed. It also did not prevent people from using their own money to build on private land.

A 1992 report by the General Accounting Office found that two out of 10 federal agencies provided assistance to undeveloped barrier islands covered by the legislation. Indeed, the barrier-resources act has done virtually nothing to contain development on those high-risk land masses. It has no teeth because Democrats and Republicans both support strong property rights; neither group has had the backbone to rein in real-estate developers.

Nothing better demonstrates the lack of respect for rules than policy trends in governing the construction of mobile homes, a form of housing extremely prone to destruction from hurricane-force winds. Such manufactured homes — popular housing in the South — have been regulated by the Department of Housing and Urban Development since the 1970s. But the agency has fallen down on the job.

In the 1980s, engineers at Texas Tech University exposed flaws in the wind-design standards in the manufactured-housing code. That did not, however, stop dealers from selling as "hurricane resistive" mobile homes that could not withstand winds of more than 80 mph—just barely a Category 1 hurricane. HUD spent years ignoring the troubling evidence. It took Hurricane Andrew, which destroyed 97 percent of the mobile homes along the hurricane's path in Dade County, Fla., or roughly 10,000 structures, to force the department, over objections from industry, to upgrade wind-safety standards. (The tougher wind code applies only to mobile homes built after 1994.)

Recent developments in mobile-home regulation are even more troubling. In 2000 President Bill Clinton signed the Manufactured Housing Improvement Act. The legislation further deregulated an industry that had never been stringently supervised. The law established a "consensus committee" of 21 voting members to interpret and revise mobile-home construction and safety standards—11 members of the committee, a majority, were even allowed to have a "significant financial interest" in the very industry they are supposed to be regulating.

Unsurprisingly, only two weeks after Katrina 15 ripped through the South, David Roberson, president and chief executive of Alabama-based Cavalier Homes Inc. and a representative of the Manufactured Housing Institute, a trade group, went to Congress to argue for suspending wind-safety standards. The idea was to facilitate the installation of mobile homes in areas affected by the storm—places that remain vulnerable to hurricanes.

Last spring FEMA issued a flood-insurance guideline requiring those New Orleans homeowners whose houses were more than 50 percent damaged by Hurricane Katrina to elevate rebuilt structures three feet off the ground. The three-foot figure seems arbitrary—though FEMA claims it is not—based less on hard science than faith in unrestrained real-estate development. Computer models reveal that even a Category 3 storm could inundate the city to a depth of more than 10 feet above sea level, and that's assuming the levees hold. The lenient rule fits with the larger

generation-long pattern that has come to define U.S. natural-hazards policy.

Although the gravity of the recent Katrina disaster inspired some members of Congress to put forth a tougher and more meaningful set of flood-insurance regulations, they found little support. Michael G. Oxley, an Ohio Republican, and Barney Frank, a Massachusetts Democrat, sponsored legislation in the House of Representatives that would have beefed up the federal program by including those areas subject annually to a fifth of a percent chance of flooding. Such a move would have expanded the areas deemed at risk to nearly the entire nation—floods, after all, have been recorded in all 50 states—and would have allowed the program to build up the necessary reserves for a future calamity on a par with what happened last August.

Developers have opposed such legislation because it would presumably increase construction costs. David L. Pressly Jr., of the National Association of Home Builders, told the *New York Times* that the flood-insurance program "may need a tune-up, but I don't think it needs radical change." Congress appears to agree. Instead of substantive reform, both chambers are considering bills that tinker with the flood-insurance program. The House version calls for increasing premiums on vacation homes and businesses and instructs the comptroller general to study the program, the latter move a favorite ploy by those seeking to stave off any truly meaningful environmental reform, as the history of studying global-warming policy attests. The Senate version is somewhat stronger, but it would do little to correct the federal government's role in underwriting life on the edge of obliteration.

If we find mobile homes reduced to rubble and water 10 feet deep in the streets this summer, people ought not simply blame President Bush or his political appointees. The real problem is the bipartisan disregard for rules and limits that has made our nation's approach to natural disaster so much like playing Russian roulette. With $7 trillion in insured property along the stretch from Texas to Maine, now is the time for more, not less, regulation of coastal development.

Reading Questions

1. Steinberg suggests that the response to the disaster created by Hurricane Katrina in New Orleans, Louisiana, needs to be understood within a larger trend that characterizes both Republican and Democratic agendas since 1980. What is that trend?

2. According to Steinberg, how is the neoliberal agenda consistent with the policies of deregulation?

3. Steinberg uses the example of the deregulation of the mobile home construction industry to support his argument. Based on his recounting of the history of the related regulation, what seems to be a core motivation for deregulating that industry?

Rhetoric Questions

4. Steinberg's article was published in the *Chronicle of Higher Education*. What does this tell you about his likely intended audience?

5. Steinberg offers a number of extended examples to underscore his claims. What claim does he support by reporting on the history of the National Flood Insurance Program?

6. The conclusion of Steinberg's argument makes a call to action. What specific action is he asking for? Do you think that his call will effectively move his audience to action?

Response and Research Questions

7. Do you agree with Steinberg when he states in the final paragraph that "now is the time for more, not less, regulation of coastal development" (19)? Why or why not?

8. Why do you think neoliberalism, as defined by David Harvey, has been embraced by both Republican and Democratic federal administrations?

9. Consider another federal regulation or policy related to natural hazards. Research the history of the regulation or policy to determine if it can be characterized as deregulatory in nature.

"My FEMA People": Hip-Hop as Disaster Recovery in the Katrina Diaspora

ZENIA KISH

Zenia Kish is an instructor in American studies at New York University. In her article, published in 2009 in the academic journal *American Quarterly*, Kish examines musical responses to "the violence, racism, displacement, and vulnerability that came to represent the experiences of the Katrina diaspora" as evidenced in a number of hip-hop songs. She complicates her examination of these representations by placing her explorations in the larger context of the historical "migrant" or "refugee" image of the African American.

Within two weeks of Hurricane Katrina touching down on the coast just east of New Orleans on August 29, 2005, Mos Def had penned, recorded, and performed a searing critique of the rescue effort in his song "Katrina Klap." Later renamed "Dollar Day," the song laments the "water water everywhere and babies dead in the street," and damns President George W. Bush's "policy for handlin the niggaz and trash." Ending with a call to action, Def urges sympathizers to not only "talk about it," but "be about it."[1] A year later, on August 31, 2006, the rapper pulled a flatbed truck in front of Radio City Music Hall in New York City where the MTV Video Music Awards were being recorded, and launched an impromptu performance of "Katrina Klap." Drawing a large crowd, he was promptly arrested by New York City police for disorderly conduct. Discharged the following day, Def's publicist issued a statement that declared: "Mos Def chose to use his voice to speak for those who are losing their own during this critical period of reconstruction."[2]

The immediate effects of Katrina were stark: more than 800,000 Gulf residents displaced, approximately 1,500 dead, and tens of thousands left behind in the flooding city without food, water, or a means of escape.[3] Appalled by the suffering, many hip-hop artists, from New Orleans and nationwide, recorded tracks decrying the tragedy and branding those seen to be responsible. From underground New Orleans bounce artists like the 504 Boyz, Mia X, and

5th Ward Weebie to some of mainstream hip-hop's most recognized names, including Lil Wayne, Jay-Z, and Public Enemy, a veritable subgenre of Katrina hip-hop was born on waves of backlash against the unnecessary suffering and institutional failure that transformed the natural disaster of Katrina into a national one. Folding individual stories of suffering into larger structural critiques of the human catastrophe, these musical responses both engaged the violence, racism, displacement, and vulnerability that came to represent the experiences of the Katrina diaspora, and became a cultural force of identification and activism that intervened in constructions of the event as a national emergency.

Although politicians, the media, and witnesses repeatedly asserted that Katrina was without precedent in U.S. history, the experience of massive upheaval and displacement in the face of natural disaster was not new for the African American community. The Great Mississippi Flood of 1927 and the Vanport Flood of 1948 in Oregon both provoked massive waves of African American relocation. In each case, black and often poor communities bore a disproportionate share of the environmental and economic risks of natural disaster as underwritten by discriminatory housing, job distribution, and rescue efforts.[4] These floods, along with epochal forces such as Abolition, Reconstruction, and the Dust Bowl, have made migration one of the enduring thematics of black cultural production: musical forms from minstrelsy to the blues to hip-hop work through the dislocation and urgency of cultural survival provoked by a history of forced migration. Often unable to return, the African American migrant is repeatedly figured as a stranger in search of a new home. To the surrounding community, this stranger was a *refugee* whose foreignness marks the limits of majoritarian identity and hospitality.[5]

The United States' ambivalence toward refugees greeted Katrina's predominantly poor and black evacuees in the wake of the storm. Literally called refugees by most politicians and the mass media in the first week after the hurricane, the displaced population was also figuratively construed as outside the norms of middle-class white citizenship—and indeed, a threat to it. Across the mediascape, evacuees were depicted as anonymous black masses, poor and often dangerous, and their apparent vulnerability became framed as a long-term drain on American resources and government spending.[6] The designation of refugee helped construct the exceptional—and exceptionally *un*-American—nature of the emergency: images of the disaster defied the belief that a humanitarian catastrophe of this magnitude couldn't happen *here*, in the United States.

The black public sphere responded immediately. 5 Black activists protested the xenophobic racism and disenfranchisement suggested by the use of the term *refugee*, and post-Katrina hip-hop became vital in disrupting such discourse by asserting a politics of voice against a regime of representation in which black and poor suffering bodies were everywhere seen, but very rarely heard from. As a political strategy, giving voice to "those who are losing their own" is an attempt to lay claim to what Peter Nyers calls the "onto-political status of a speaking being," by which outsiders or aliens, defined by legal or other forms of social exclusion, may interrupt the dominant political—which is to say *speaking*—order, "not just to be heard, but to be recognized as a speaking being as such."[7]

I will explore how the aesthetic strategies and logics of intelligibility given form in Katrina protest hip-hop narrate experiences of exile and persecution, expendability and community, vulnerability and renewal in the wake of an American tragedy. Attempting to speak for the voiceless is always a fraught project, and hip-hop artists combined musical modes of resistance with strains of self-critique that recognized the contradictory location of rap within the commercial music industry, which itself capitalizes off of a culture of consumption that valorizes spectacle, violence, and racialized exploitation. In Katrina hip-hop we can thus hear a plurality of speaking positions, grappling with identification, empowerment, and objectification in response to a collective trauma that was both local and constitutive of what Mos Def identifies as "the storm called . . . America."

In particular, I am interested in the ways in which these themes are refracted through the figure of the refugee. I will examine how both national and local New Orleans artists identify with and rebel against the forces of marginalization that produced different senses of being a refugee, and also how they exploit marginality and the hustle as strategies to return home, however different or new that home may be. Providing listeners with an affective mapping of the social, economic, and discursive contradictions that produced the Katrina diaspora as refugees, post-Katrina hip-hop is a critical site for interrogating the ongoing tragedy of African American bodies that don't matter.

MUSIC AND DISPLACEMENT

Surveying twentieth-century black American migration narratives in fiction and song, Farah Jasmine Griffin observes that far from tending toward integrated or static representations of displacement, these narratives are "as diverse as the people and the times that create them."[8] Interpreting new urbanisms, articulating the development of modern black power, and, in some cases, expressing a desire to return to the South, migration narratives voice the complex emotional and social experiences of divided communities and structural homelessness that follow in the wake of displacement. Survival, however, often became the starting point for cultural rebirth among African American communities as scattered evacuees regrouped in new areas, forged new musical collaborations, and invented expressions for their experiences and hopes.

Flooding 26,000 square miles up to a depth of 30 feet and displacing an estimated 700,000 people, up to 300,000 of whom were African Americans, the Great Mississippi Flood of 1927 sparked a phenomenal outpouring of blues music that transcribed this historical moment.[9] This creative proliferation of music contributed to the elaboration of what Clyde Woods terms the "blues epistemology." For Woods, the blues grew out of specific social and historical conditions grounded in the plantation economy to become not just an aesthetic movement but also a complex *epistemology*, a mode of knowing and interpreting the world, motivated to achieve an "autonomy of thought and action in the midst of constant surveillance and violence."[10] Where the early blues served to "sp[ea]k the desires which were released in the dramatic shift in social relations that occurred in a historical moment of crisis and dislocation," as Hazel Carby observes, I would argue that the post-Katrina moment is the first time that mainstream American hip-hop has taken up the thematic of *contemporary* black migration as a mass phenomenon in any significant way.[11] The resulting musical structure of feeling marks a significant contribution to the history of black American creative output in response to disaster.

Inheriting much from the blues tradition, hip-hop continues to develop the productive tension in the blues between a narrative drive for coherence and development, and the reflexivity of structured repetition and recursion. On the one hand, William Jelani Cobb identifies hip-hop as the "folklore of the twenty-first century" wherein MCs' narratives extend the blues tradition of story-telling such that hip-hop is now "so central to the development of the post-civil-rights generation of black people that it's nearly impossible to separate the music from our politics, economic realities, gains, and collective shortcomings."[12] Supplementing hip-hop's narrative functions, Robert Walser stresses the importance of the music's creation of "horizons of expectation that enable dialogue and participation" and the joy it takes

in repetition, thus destabilizing and challenging the flow of the very narrative that it tells. This is especially so in the case of diasporic* narratives, which are invested in the teleological progression from origin to resettlement.[13] "The homeland," writes Jasbir Puar of diasporic cultural productions, "is not represented only as a demographic, a geographical place, nor primarily through history, memory, or even trauma, but is cohered through sensation, vibrations, echoes, speed, feedback loops, recursive folds, and feelings."[14]

The tension thus produced between musical and lyrical forms, and between progression and repetition, opens up access points to the political interventions animating Katrina hip-hop. These tensions, however, also expose the seams of unequal power relations that can be reconstituted through restrictive models of gender, agency, sexuality, racial identity, exploitation, and representation mobilized in the music. Space and time are also reconfigured through narrative and musical forms, and it is often claims for repetition and return in Katrina protest hip-hop, rather than demands for a clean break from the past, that are its most revolutionary features. At the same time, investing in repetition as return — to New Orleans as well as to African American histories of migration — hip-hop narrates the progressive adaptations and innovations of black American communities.

WHERE NEW ORLEANS AT? BOUNCE AND KATRINA

Musicologist David Evans observed of the blues music produced after the 1927 flood in Mississippi that most of the songs were written from the position of having personally experienced the storm, even when the songwriter had not. It is striking that so much hip-hop about Katrina likewise directly addresses audiences from a first-person speaking voice, regardless of the artist's origins in or lack of connection to New Orleans, lending the music candor and emotional urgency. This is particularly the case in bounce, a form

diasporic: relating to the diaspora, or the migration and dispersion of a group.

of hip-hop born in New Orleans. From New Orleans resident Mia X's colorful rap "My FEMA People" to Chopper's "Crescent City Crisis" to 5th Ward Weebie's disaster anthem, "Fuck Katrina (The Katrina Song)," much of the hip-hop after the flood narrated, from an often collective first-person perspective, the frustrations, humiliations, and pleasures grounded in specifically local knowledge of the multiple socioeconomic disasters that intersected with Katrina. Deeply rooted in, and for the most part bounded by, the geography and social relations of New Orleans, bounce was transformed by a new activist engagement that arose as the music remapped its conventional identifications with its audience, the spaces of the city, and its own musical forms.

Born in the late 1980s and oriented toward dancing, bounce has consistently used two basic, up-tempo beats—Triggaman and Brown Beat—as well as highly repetitive hooks, a heavy reliance on call-and-response with the audience, and simple lyrics. Music journalist Nik Cohn notes that "In days gone by, 95 percent were sex and violence songs" meant to get people dancing in the clubs or courtyards of housing developments where bounce has always been a fixture of block parties.[15] The music has always been explicitly articulated in relation to the city's geographical features and social world, with constant references to natural landmarks, famous shops, housing projects, and neighborhood rivalries. Many rappers, for example, assume aliases that cite (and site) where they grew up, including 5th Ward Weebie and 10th Ward Buck. Songs often fix on specific spatial referents, such as Juvenile's 2003 song "Nolia Clap,"[16] which is named after a housing project nicknamed the Magnolia, and is filled with shout-outs to different areas of the city ("Where that Iberville at? The Eighth Ward at?").

The music emerges from the charged social networks formed in New Orleans's high density public housing, which was one of the poorest and most ghettoized cities in the country when Katrina hit, and rappers often addressed their music to audiences they knew intimately.[17] In addition to lyrical self-referentiality, bounce also reproduces localism musically through sampling patterns, rhythms, and sounds drawn largely from autochthonous* music history. After Katrina, signification of the local inhabited these familiar musical forms in entirely new ways, pushing them to express new configurations of space, distance, and community by engaging with the meaning of home now that most bounce artists were far away from it. It was, according to some observers, a radical politicization of a previously ludic** form of music-making.[18]

In her song "My FEMA People," veteran Seventh Ward resident Mia X raps,

> Ride through my city
> Beirut. Iraq. Ride through my city
> I ride and cry all through the city
> Looking for the culture all through the city
> We were left for dead for vultures all through the city
> It's so much bigger than the weather[19]

Rather than attempting to speak for those apparently losing their voices, as Mos Def claimed to do, Mia X situates herself in conversation with those she hears all around her. Her relationship to the site of devastation allows her to move through the city and recognize how it has changed, but it also moves her to link New Orleans to a global matrix not of natural disasters, but of foreign war zones.

New Orleans is presented in the song as a city under siege on multiple fronts. The reference to Beirut connotes a long drawn-out civil war, analogizing the violence and self-destructive crime that made New Orleans one of the most dangerous cities in the United States prior to Katrina. But the Lebanese Civil War was also fought against external occupying forces, and X's reference implicates foreign forces in the local proliferation of violence.[20] X is commenting on the violent rhetoric that saturated public discourse in the chaos immediately following the storm. In response to the appearance of anarchy in the streets, martial law was imposed in the disaster zone and Louisiana governor Kathleen Blanco issued her infamous "shoot-to-kill" order to soldiers to halt looting.

---

autochthonous: indigenous.
**ludic:* playful or spontaneous.

"These troops are . . . under my orders to restore order in the streets," Blanco told the media. "They have M16s, and they are locked and loaded. These troops know how to shoot and kill and they are more than willing to do so if necessary and I expect they will."[21]

Mia X's reference to Iraq suggests parallels between local and international occupation by U.S. imperial interests, but also cites economic exploitation by the oil industry—whether the extractive industries of the Persian Gulf, or the refineries off the Louisiana shore in the Mexican Gulf—which generates enormous wealth in areas that consistently rank among the poorest in their respective regions. Implicit in Mia X's "ride through my city" is an open predicate that implies the singer is moving through her city, looking for the life that used to be there, but it could also be read to take Beirut and Iraq as its subjects, as though these foreign disasters are themselves moving through her city, hunting down local lives and cultural forms as its targets.

New Orleans artist 5th Ward Weebie also expresses the ire of forced homelessness on his track "Fuck Katrina (The Katrina Song)," which became something of an anthem for the Katrina diaspora after he first improvised it onstage at a club night for evacuees in Houston, October 2005. Working up the audience, he played the prerecorded FEMA phone message that frustrated many evacuees trying to contact the Federal Emergency Management Agency for assistance or the infamous second support check that everyone was promised and no one seemed to receive. After playing the message, he burst into a chorus of "Fuck Katrina!" calling back and forth with the audience as it erupted in dance to the novel combination of political invective and a familiar bounce beat. Weebie disses George Bush and the Red Cross for abandoning storm victims, and personifies Hurricanes Katrina and Rita as "hoes" who "fuck over my people." At the end of the song, Weebie inverts the practice of shouting out to specific locations in the city as a metonymic address to one's friends or acquaintances. Instead, Weebie invokes the city's wards, districts, and housing projects like Calliope and Iberville to name not the people who lived there, but rather their absence

and the suffering they continue to experience now that they have left:

> Ninth Ward shattered
> Eighth Ward suffered
> Seventh Ward gone but my man said fuck it
> Sixth Ward empty
> Fifth Ward through
> Calliope and Iberville ain't a thing we can do[22]

Many bounce songs written post-Katrina channeled the anger, fear, and sadness of evacuating New Orleans as it drowned. These songs were often born at music nights in relocation centers such as Houston and Atlanta, and served as much to reclaim community bonds and suggest strategies for getting home as to lodge criticism. Cursing Katrina, George Bush, and FEMA, the dancehall music addresses audiences directly and invites the release and spontaneity of dance and being together. Strength, they suggest, will arise collectively. In the post-Katrina context, bounce takes on new meanings as both strategy and metaphor for survival, a rebounding on the dance floor as well as into new ways of life, a pleasure-filled resilience in the face of adverse conditions. Two months after Katrina touched down, New Orleans producers Master P and the 504 Boyz released a compilation CD dedicated to disaster victims titled "Hurricane Katrina: We Gon' Bounce Back." The theme of bouncing runs throughout the collection, and proposes the music itself as an inseparable aspect of New Orleans's renewal. As Halleluyah raps on the title track, "Now let me tell you we gon' bounce back, bounce back / I'm straight New Orleans like a bounce track, bounce track."[23]

MAINSTREAM HIP-HOP REPRESENTS

While New Orleans rappers spoke from direct experience, refusing alienating labels such as "refugees" by expressing the traumas of Katrina as something artists and audiences underwent together and could only recover from collectively, many mainstream hip-hop artists took up Katrina as a political cause with broader import. Some mainstream artists like Lil Wayne and Juvenile grew up in New Orleans, continue to have strong ties to the city, and in several cases, lost property, friends, or family members to the

20

storm. Others such as Kanye West, Papoose, Chuck D, and Mos Def had no direct links to the region, but felt moved by their identification with the victims of entrenched racism and hierarchies of power. Appearing on an NBC telethon for Katrina survivors in the first days of September, West went off-script, saying, "I hate the way they portray us in the media. You see a black family, it says, 'They're looting.' You see a white family, it says, 'They're looking for food.'"[24] From this perspective, then, it wasn't only residents of the disaster zone who were being victimized, but the African American community more generally. Blame for the systemic disenfranchisement was frequently attributed to George Bush and the government for devaluing the lives of the poor and African Americans to the extent that they were abandoned and, following Foucault's* formulation of the racist calculus of biopower, "let die" while others were made to live.[25]

The mainstream hip-hop discourse shared some features with New Orleans–based artists, but often diverged in its political agenda and scope of critique. Continuous with some New Orleans rappers, many professional artists anchor their critiques in the geography of human disaster by mapping the local in relation to global sites of poverty, such as Haiti, or zones of U.S. military intervention, such as Iraq and Afghanistan. Numerous rappers also comment on the spatial refraction of the disaster via technologies of representation and surveillance, which distorted images of the disaster and distanced the media (and by extension, media audiences) from the unfolding events, discouraging personal involvement. Jay-Z, for example, raps, "Helicopter swooped down just to get a scoop / Through his telescopic lens but he didn't scoop you"[26] and Juvenile concurs, "Fuck Fox News! I don't listen to y'all ass / Couldn't get a nigga off the roof with a star pass."[27]

One of the catchiest songs to hit the street following Katrina was "George Bush Doesn't Care about Black People"[28] by The Legendary K.O., also known as K-Otix, a rap group out of Houston. One of the largest destinations for those fleeing the disaster zone,

*Michel Foucault: a mid-twentieth-century social theorist.

Houston extended assistance and shelter to many thousands in need through a broad network of grassroots and national non-profit organizations, but also manifested xenophobic fears of hurricane transplants. Media reports sensationalized violent crime committed by evacuees, and high-profile comments by locals such as Barbara Bush betrayed a deep ambivalence regarding the influx of apparent outsiders.[29]

K-Otix released "George Bush Doesn't Care about Black People" online on September 6, just one week after the storm, and it very quickly gained publicity through radio play and Internet-circulated videos; the first day the song was available online, it received 10,000 downloads.[30] The song in part ventriloquizes a first-hand account of living through the storm, thus constructing intimacy with diaspora audiences in Houston, and in part lashes out at those deemed responsible for the rescue failure, especially George Bush. K-Otix member Micah Nickerson comments that the song was born of a desire to put the lived experiences of the storm in the context of the structural problems that multiplied human suffering: "I had really wanted to write about this in the first-person, as someone stuck in New Orleans and left by this administration to basically fend for myself, but was having trouble putting the emotions I felt into words. When I heard Kanye during the benefit, the rest as they say was history."

The group raps over the music of Kanye West's popular 2005 song "Gold Digger," in which West slams a woman he perceives as a materialistic manipulator who uses her wiles and sex appeal to seduce him, and then drains his bank account. In the chorus of the West song, Jamie Foxx sings, "She take my money, well I'm in need / Yeah she's a trifflin' friend indeed / Oh she's a gold digger way over time / That digs on me."[31] West's song is itself an inversion of Ray Charles's song "I Got a Woman" in which Charles extols the beauty and generosity of a lover who gives him money and "saves her lovin just for me"[32] (Charles's vocals can be heard in the background of the K-Otix version). In the K-Otix song, West's music and Foxx's vocal line are kept, but George Bush is interpolated as the gold digger, and West's infamous denunciation of Bush on the

NBC telethon, "George Bush doesn't care about black people," is paraphrased and made into the chorus:

> (Foxx: She take my money…)
> I ain't sayin he a gold digger
> (…when I'm in need)
> But he ain't messin with no broke niggaz
> (I gotta leave)
> George Bush don't like black people[33]

The song shifts voices and perspective, at times speaking from the perspective of a New Orleans resident stuck on his roof, at others turning to directly address George Bush, who took nearly a week to visit the Gulf Coast because he was on vacation: "Five damn days, five long days / And at the end of the fifth you walkin' in like, 'Hey!'"[34] The narration then reverts to third-person references to Bush, and decries the president's apparent indifference to the region's most exposed, and apparently disposable, populations:

> I guess Bush said niggaz been used to dyin
> He said, "I know it looks bad, just have to wait"
> Forgettin folks who too broke to evacuate
> Niggaz starvin and they dyin of thirst
> I bet he had to go and check on them refineries first
> Makin a killin off the price of gas
> He woulda been up in Connecticut twice as fast[35]

The seemingly simple musical structure of the song, which sounds at first listen like an endlessly repeating series of Foxx's background vocal line set over a spare syncopated beat, is belied by complexities of voice, address, and shifting referents. Where Ray Charles celebrates a woman who saves her loving for him morning and night and gives him money when he's in need, West's female gold digger and K-Otix's feminized Bush ("She take my money") both benefit from not "messin with no broke niggaz."[36] The lack of musical embellishment and repetitive rhythm collaborate with the constantly revolving historical referents of the song in ways that call on the cultural competence of audiences. "George Bush Doesn't Care about Black People," in other words, encourages an active listening that hears not only the changing gender and power relations implied in the evolving narratives of exploitation, but also, significantly, the deliberate repetition of elements that are retained across these versions of the song.

Whereas Bush and the state are portrayed as heartless gold (and grave) diggers by K-Otix, many other rappers testify to the devaluation of black life using language that draws attention to the ways in which the color line in the United States is often experienced through structural economic inequities. Mos Def's "Katrina Klap (Dollar Day)" is dedicated to "the streets, the streets everywhere / The streets affected by the storm called…America" and situates the poverty of the U.S. South within the global context in which almost half the world subsists on a dollar a day.[37] Dismissing "Mr. President" who is "'bout that cash," Mos Def notes that in the United States, "if you poor you black."[38] He connects the racially selective rescue efforts of the state with George Bush's larger biopolitical designs, such that the administration's response to Katrina serves as a synecdoche* for the pervasive systems of racial oppression structuring American life. While asserting that Bush is "out treatin' niggaz worse than they treat the trash," he reasons through the mathematics of racialized state violence:

> No opinion my man it's mathematical fact
> Listen, a million poor since 2004
> And they got illions and killions to waste on the War
> And make you question what the taxes is for
> Or the cost to reinforce the broke levee wall
> Tell the boss he shouldn't be the boss anymore[39]

Critiquing "dollar day" in New Orleans as symptomatic of the nation's hierarchies of distribution, Def's song also recognizes the individuals who suffered in the storm and pays tribute to local musical production by deriving his clap from the 2003 hit "Nolia Clap" by New Orleans rapper Juvenile. While he implores God to "save these streets / One dollar per every human being," he also admonishes those around him to do more to help: "Quit bein cheap nigga, freedom ain't free!…Let's make them dollars stack / And rebuild these streets." Although part of his declared agenda is "to use his voice to speak for those who are losing their own," Def is also adamant that talk isn't enough and ends his song by exhorting

---

*synecdoche: a figure of speech wherein a part of something represents the whole thing.

his listeners, "Don't talk about it, be about it." Mos Def himself continued to be active in fundraising and drawing public attention to the inequitable conditions of resettlement and reconstruction after the storm.

While many rappers from Mos Def to K-Otix to Jay-Z narrate cycles of poverty and racism that set the stage for the human disaster long before Katrina hit shore, others work to undo the fiction that the black residents of the disaster zone were all economic deadweights. As wealthy residents of New Orleans, many local rappers situate themselves within the matrix of loss by enumerating their personal property losses: Lil Wayne, for example, laments losing two Jags in his song "Georgia Bush,"[40] and rapper Juvenile and producer Master P were both known to have lost houses in the storm surge. Brooklynite Papoose takes his cue from New Orleans rappers when he opens his elegiac song "Mother Nature" boasting of his wealth, and asks why the property and citizenship of black residents are so easily devalued by the state and mass media:

> A lotta property was lost, crushed by the trees
> Evacuated the city they was forced to leave
> They was forced outta their homes; they would never leave
> So why the media keep callin' 'em refugees?[41]

He refutes the stereotype that urban black residents of New Orleans, and the Ninth Ward in particular, were unproductive or second-class members of society, inclined to homelessness like refugees: many in the most devastated neighborhoods were in fact homeowners. The Ninth Ward, renowned for being a working-class neighborhood in a low-lying section of the city that was virtually razed by the floods, had a homeownership rate of more than 50 percent, one of the highest rates in the city. Many thus did not want to flee, and a large proportion of the evacuated had strong reasons to return. However, media sensationalism, combined with racist xenophobia in different evacuation receiver sites, produced a moral panic that gave local and national news media a good scoop.

Fear of the storm's poor spilling over into the rest of the country became highly territorialized and at times assumed the language of sovereign protection against foreign invaders. For example, one white resident of Greensburg, 80 miles northwest of New Orleans, articulated his fears several weeks after the storm at a meeting regarding the temporary resettlement of evacuees in the town:

> The only thing we see about these people in the news is what happened in the Superdome. They're rapists and thugs and murderers. I'm telling you, half of them have criminal records. I've worked all my life to have what I have. I can't lose it, and I can't stand guard 24 hours a day.[42]

Similarly, the black mayor of Baton Rouge lent authority to the racially charged prejudices already circulating when he declared to the press, "I want to make sure that some of these thugs and looters that are out shooting officers in New Orleans don't come here and do the same. I am not going to allow a New Orleans situation, shooting at people and looting, to happen here in Baton Rouge."[43] In the many cases like these where surrounding populations—but also farther afield in centers like Houston and Atlanta—feared the invasion of Katrina "refugees," the storm survivors were cast as a threat to property and white privilege. They embodied a dangerous "remainder or excess" which, for Prem Kumar Rajaram, is recognizable in the figure of the refugee as "that which is expelled or which cannot fit, and is *out of place*, following the territorialization of life and of existence."[44] It is within these various public discourses that Katrina hip-hop had to situate itself—both as a response to what was being said in the public sphere, and as a means to reinforce a sense of community, or at least shared suffering, by those being labeled and treated as refugees.

Chuck D assiduously observes that the devaluation of the racialized other is not merely a domestic issue, but is also reflected in the discursive and physical exporting of America's problems to "faraway places" where they can appear to belong to someone else. In his protest lyric "Hell No (We Ain't Alright)," written and recorded with Flavor Flav days after Katrina hit, Chuck D lashes out at the widespread objectification of victims, intoning that this is no longer "the same old keep it real," in spite of what audiences are hearing:

> Disgraces, all I been seein is hurtin black faces
> Moved out to harm in faraway places

(FLAVOR FLAV: Emergency) statements, corpses,
    alligators, and snakes
. . . (This ain't no TV show) ain't no video (this is
    really real!)
Y'all hearin the same old keep it real[45]

While the mass media frequently resorted to representing the disaster zone as a place literally *other*,
rendered vivid in frequent comparisons between the
U.S. Gulf Coast and the 2004 Tsunami in Asia, third
world refugee camps, and war zones, Katrina hip-hop
often cut through such uncritical analogies to make
not metaphorical but causal connections between the
tragedy unfolding on home soil and foreign conflict
zones. Juvenile, in his song "Get Your Hustle On,"
points to government abandonment when he de-
claims, "We starving! We livin like Haiti without no
government,"[46] while Mos Def bemoans the "illions
and killions"[47] spent on the Iraq war instead of re-
inforcing levees and rescuing people, and Papoose is
shocked that George Bush "took a whole army wit
him when he came to war / But when he traveled to
New Orleans he came with his dog."[48] Chuck D also
observes that the making of an American third world
is connected as much to dehumanizing regimes of
mass media representation as to the Bush administration's complicity with the global military industrial
complex (to the neglect of, what rapper Chopper
identifies as, "the battlefield"[49] at home). Chuck D:

Now I see we be the new faces of refugees
We ain't even overseas, but stuck here on our knees
Forget the plasma TV, ain't no electricity
New world's upside down and out of order
Shelter? Food? Wassup (FLAVOR FLAV: where's the
    water?)
No answers from disaster, them masses hurtin
So who the f— we call—Halliburton?
Son of a Bush, how you wanna just trust that cat
To fix shit, when all the help is stuck in Iraq?
Makin war plans, takin more stands than
    Afghanistan
2,000 soldiers there dyin in the sand . . .
But that's over there, right? (What's over here?)
Is a noise so loud
That some can't hear
But on TV I know that I can see
Bunches of people
Looking just like me
And they ain't all right[50]

With the "New world upside down and out of order,"
it is clear to Chuck D that the apparently exceptional
nature of the disaster is in reality a corollary of the
military, economic, and cultural colonization sub-
tending the project of the American modern.

While much post-Katrina hip-hop is deeply critical of the reifying gaze of the mass media, the failure
of politicians, and the discriminatory actions of local
and state police who Lil Wayne notes are "killas in my
home,"[51] there also emerged in the Katrina hip-hop
epistemology a strain of heightened self-knowledge
and self-criticism by rappers who recognized their
own position in the structures of power and consumerism that contributed to the injustices they critiqued.
Artists like Kanye West, Jay-Z, and Mos Def grapple
in their music and public statements with being denigrated, as black men and as commercial musicians,
by the same racist state, commercial media industry,
and social structures that they buy into and profit
from. When Kanye West went off script on the NBC
Katrina fundraiser, he not only railed against the bun-
gling rescue effort, media misrepresentations, and
President Bush, but he also admitted his own culpability, telling TV audiences that

> even for me to complain about it, I would be a
> hypocrite because I've tried to turn away from the TV
> because it's too hard to watch. I've even been shopping
> before giving a donation, so now I'm calling my busi-
> ness manager to see what is the biggest amount I can
> give, and just to imagine if I was down there, and those
> are my people down there.

Jay-Z concurs in his song "Minority Report,"

> Sure I ponied up a mill, but I didn't give my time
> So in reality I didn't give a dime,
> I just put my monies in the hands of the same people
>   that left my people stranded
> Nothin' but a bandit
> Left them folks abandoned
> Damn, that money that we gave was just a band-aid[52]

These references point up the self-consciousness
some rappers feel about benefiting from the very
structures of capitalist accumulation, exploitation,
and consumerism that help perpetuate the polarization of privilege that divided those who could escape
the storm from those who couldn't. The dynamic of

us and *them* — the citizens successfully integrated into the American capitalist dream and those relegated to its peripheries — is therefore problematized in relation to the color line. On the one hand, rappers like Kanye and others with no personal links to New Orleans embrace all the victims of the storm as "my people," while on the other, they are forced to admit that economic privilege in fact carves up the very racial community they wish to produce.

In response to the structures of exploitation and dehumanization acting on Katrina evacuees, many rappers call out to survivors to hustle their way back to agency, autonomy, and the restoration of selfhood. The hustler is seen to be economically productive and to construct new social networks. In "Georgia Bush," New Orleans native Lil Wayne suggests that people in receiving cities show their goodwill by providing the displaced with means that will help them recover because Bush "ain't gonna drop no dollas." "See us in ya city, man," he raps, "give us a pound / Cuz if a nigga still movin then he holdin it down."[53] 5th Ward Weebie and the 504 Boyz call for those who are in distant evacuation centers to hustle their way home, and Jay-Z promotes hustling as the only means by which Katrina evacuees can hold their own in the racialized economy of scarcity:

> For life is a chain, cause and effected
> Niggas off the chain because they affected
> It's a dirty game so whatever is effective
> From weed to selling kane, gotta put that in effect
> Wouldn't you loot, if you didn't have the loot?
> Baby needed food and you stuck on the roof[54]

Pointing out, along with K-Otix and others, the structural inequalities that already criminalize the black, especially male, body even before he acts, Jay-Z concludes that if the white person's "finding food" in a flooded store is automatically the black person's "looting," then agency and indeed survival can only be obtained by black minoritized bodies outside the law.

The call to hustle carries problematic connotations of both economic and sexual exploitation since the hustling recommended by these rappers reproduces their wealth through the exploitation of women's bodies and of the already impoverished drug-users

in inner-city neighborhoods. These economic enterprises tend to maintain themselves through cultures of violence; New Orleans was especially devastated by the drug wars of the 1990s and consistently high rates of murder, violent crime, and incarceration afflicted the music industry as much as the wider community.[55] Others, however, counter that it is too simplistic to read figures such as pimps and hustlers in these reductive terms. Mark Anthony Neal, for example, suggests that rappers use these tropes to position themselves above the relations of exploitation: "It's the ultimate hustle, a hustle predicated on the hustle, or as writer Beth Coleman described it, an example of the pimp's ability to 'exploit exploitation.'"[56]

Juvenile's Katrina song "Get Your Hustle On" supports this interpretation, urging evacuees to hustle the government — which is itself depicted as the ultimate exploitation operation under Bush the golddigger — for FEMA checks that they can turn around for profit by drug-dealing:

> Fuck [*New Orleans Mayor Ray*] Nagin!
> Ah-listen to me, I got the remedy
> Save your money up and find out who got 'em for 10
>   a ki'
> Bubble, if you don't hustle don't use your energy
> Cause you gon' be a cellmate or wind up as a memory
> …Everybody need a check from FEMA
> So he can go and sco' him some co-ca-llina[57]

The (presumably male) listeners addressed by Juvenile are expected not only to regain economic leverage where the state-built levees failed them, but also to rebuild their sense of community. This community is founded not only on a rejection of the state that does not care for them ("your mayor ain't your friend, he's the enemy / Just to get your vote, a saint is what he pretend to be"), but also in the shared practice of preparing and selling street drugs. In the video for the song, Juvenile stands with his friends in a circle in the debris of the Lower Ninth Ward, collectively demonstrating with their hands how they prepare crack in Pyrex pipes: "We take the Pyrex and then we rock with it, roll with it / Take the Pyrex and then we rock with it, roll with it!"[58]

Arguably, these mainstream rappers are immersed 35 in a musical economy that itself explicitly capitalizes off of sampling the works of other artists and turning their profit to some extent through their own creative recombinatory skills in circulating pre-existing cultural capital ("rock with it, roll with it!"). Hip-hop artists are deeply implicated in circuits of capital, branding, marketing, and consumption-fueled lifestyles, and their glamorized accumulation of private wealth and power is often perceived to be connected to (and profit from) the drug trade and cultures of violence—if not directly, then at least through their representations of drugs and violence. These discourses are reproduced through a typically gendered and homophobic logic that defines agency against the dependence and even abjection imputed to women and practitioners of nonnormative sexuality. This situates the music and its artists ambivalently in regard to many of their post-Katrina critiques of the violence of the biopolitical state, the production of categories of subhumanity, and the capitalist system of exploitation.

However, acknowledging, as some self-conscious rappers do, that these contradictions are constitutive of their ability to position themselves so as to voice political interventions in the public sphere, I would argue that it is important to recognize that the hustler—whether seen as liberated entrepreneur or as predator who capitalizes on further exploiting the exploited—functions in some significant ways as an answer to the figure of the refugee. The hustler is not cast outside the dominant political/speaking order by the sovereign right of exclusion like the refugee, but is instead conceived in Katrina hip-hop as a self-defining free agent who takes responsibility for himself and his immediate community. The aggressive gendering and heteronormativity of the hustler derives in large part from a defensive masculinity incubated in hip-hop culture, but also, in this context, serves to compensate for the dominant discursive splicing of Katrina survivors into criminally violent and looting young men on the one hand, and helpless racialized women, children, and elderly on the other. Rejecting these two denigrated models of deviance, the hustler positions himself outside the reach of law enforcement and dependence on government aid, and instead fashions an autonomous social and economic sphere in which his wealth and social standing are strengthened through predominantly masculine networks within his community and in the cities he visits.

The hustle is also a means of ensuring self-reproduction into the future: Juvenile raps that unless you're hustling, you will wind up in jail or just "a memory," and Jay-Z justifies hustling to meet the basic needs of feeding and sheltering one's children. Unlike the refugee, who, as Jay-Z reminds us, "seeks refuge," the hustler does not ask for or presumably desire inclusion in any preexisting community; spurning inclusion in the dominant political order, the hustler instead springs from necessity to empowerment, and, unlike the refugee, exposes no public vulnerability. Enriching himself and his immediate circle through recurrent circuits of exploitation, in some ways similar to the commercial hip-hop artist, the hustler also adapts to the challenges of his permuting environment and innovates new strategies of survival. Many post-Katrina rappers suggest that this figure has the power to resist the chronic homelessness characterizing the dominant African American migration narrative by promising self-determination, and perhaps the only means to return home for those most disenfranchised by America's recurrent un-natural disasters.

CONCLUSION

As soon as Katrina degenerated into a human disaster, the discourse of Katrina "refugees" erupted into a charged controversy with some, such as Lou Dobbs, validating the label by claiming that it best reflected reality, while many others vocally disavowed the term as disenfranchising and demeaning.[59] Although many major news outlets and even President Bush came to denounce the use of the term, the aftereffects of the widely circulated portrait of the Katrina refugee remained. Everywhere depicted—when not "looting"—as long-suffering, unfortunate multitudes in need of rescue, Katrina survivors continued to be seen but not heard, used as an emblem of otherness for consumption by a presumptively white, middle-class public, but excluded from the rights and protections of full citizenship.[60] As blues and jazz artists have historically responded to the displacement of African Americans, hip-hop artists from New Orleans and the national stage intervened against regimes of representation that they saw to be inherently racist.

Voicing alternative interpretations of what was really going on was a vital practice of resistance for post-Katrina hip-hop, as both an epistemological project and as political activism. As an epistemological project, the music worked through various forms of racism, penetrating political and mass media responses to the disaster, and proposed new frameworks for understanding what was happening. These frameworks included historicizing the economic and racial marginalization of Katrina victims as entrenched modes of biopolitical governance not only in the South, but as a national problem. They also included spatial mappings of the connections between events in the Gulf and U.S. interventions overseas, and attempted to make sense of the complex, and at times contradictory, vectors of distance that seamlessly collapsed New Orleans into the third world or Iraq, but at the same time rendered photographers and George Bush flying over the devastation too far away to assist those stranded on roofs. These epistemological frameworks destabilized the exceptionalist claims made throughout public discourse that Katrina was an unprecedented natural disaster, and forced a greater accounting of the inequities that have supported such human tragedies, including U.S. imperialism, throughout history.

As political expression, post-Katrina hip-hop voiced concern for those whose representation as refugees in their own land silenced them and devalued their lives. Many rappers negotiated the constitutive contradictions of, as Lil Wayne points out, being "born right here in the USA / But due to tragedy, looked on by the whole world as a refugee,"[61] and recognized that the story of Katrina is now a story of diaspora as much as it is about rebuilding New Orleans and the Gulf Coast. While Katrina didn't incite a large-scale return of the protest ethic that marked the early days of hip-hop, the hip-hop artists who did interrupt the silences of the storm registered self-conscious

dissent against the historic cycles that produce black American diasporas as vulnerable and homeless.[62] Corresponding with Jacques Rancière's assertion that "Politics exists because those who have no right to be counted as speaking beings make themselves of some account," Katrina hip-hop calls for return but also, in the same act, disrupts the repetition of African American disaster migration.[63] It locates new points of departure for politics: through professional artists who donate their money, music and voices; through the music's aesthetic innovations; through local underground rappers who convene community in the diaspora and enact rites of return; and through the listeners who engage with those who do not deserve to be silenced yet again.

NOTES

I would like to thank Clyde Woods, Michael Ralph, and Tavia Nyong'o for their help and input on this article, as well as the editors at *American Quarterly* for their feedback. I would also like to express gratitude to Darwin Bond-Graham for his suggestions at the earliest stages of this project.

1. Mos Def, "Dollar Day," *True Magic*, Geffen, 2006.

2. Jayson Rodriguez, "Mos Def Arrested after Impromptu Performance outside VMAs," *MTV News*, September 1, 2006, http://www.mtv.com/news/articles/1539981/20060901/mos_def.jhtml (accessed June 30, 2007).

3. John L. Beven II et al., "Annual Summary: Atlantic Hurricane Season of 2005," *Monthly Weather Review* 136.6 (March 2008): 1110–73; "Katrina's Diaspora," *New York Times*, October 2, 2005, http//www.nytimes.com/imagepages/2005/10/02/national/nationalspecial/20051002diaspora_graphic.html (accessed April 28, 2007); "Katrina Index Monthly Summary of Findings: March 2, 2006," Brookings Institution, http://www.brookings.edu/metro/pubs/200603_Katrina Indexes.pdf (accessed April 26, 2008). Another 750 were still missing and presumed dead more than a year later. Michelle Krupa, "Presumed Missing," *Times-Picayune*, March 5, 2006.

4. Jason David Rivera and DeMond Shondell Miller, "Continually Neglected: Situating Natural Disasters in the African American Experience," *Journal of Black Studies* 37.4 (March 2007): 502–22.

5. See Cornel West, *Keeping Faith: Philosophy and Race in America* (New York: Routledge, 1993), xiii. On the development

of the migration narrative in black music, see Farah Jasmine Griffin, *"Who Set You Flowin'?": The African-American Migration Narrative* (New York: Oxford University Press, 1995).

6. The term *refugee* was ubiquitous in the mass media in the week following the storm and was generally deployed to reinforce the exceptionality of the event in American history. Media watchdog Global Language Monitor released findings one week after the storm that the term *refugee* appeared in world media five times more frequently than the more neutral term *evacuee*. "Media Abounds with Apocalyptic-Type References in Coverage of Katrina," *Global Language Monitor*, September 7, 2005, http://www.languagemonitor.com/Katrina.html (accessed October 17, 2005).

7. Peter Nyers, "Abject Cosmopolitanism: The Politics of Protection in the Anti-Deportation Movement," *Third World Quarterly* 24.6 (December 2003): 1078–93.

8. Griffin, *"Who Set You Flowin'?"* 4.

9. "Delta Geography," Delta Cultural Center of the Department of Arkansas Culture, http://www.deltaculturalcenter.com/geography/ (accessed October 8, 2008).

10. Clyde Woods, *Development Arrested: The Blues and Plantation Power in the Mississippi Delta* (New York: Verso, 1998), 29.

11. Hazel Carby, "Policing the Black Woman's Body in an Urban Context," *Critical Inquiry* 18.4 (Summer 1992): 738–56. I do not mean to suggest, however, that the themes of historical migration and diaspora are absent in hip-hop. Indeed, much American hip-hop production (as well as earlier blues, jazz, dub, and arguably electronic music and rock) is very much interested in themes of displacement, exile, and longing for distant homelands, usually in the South, the Caribbean, and Africa; just listen to Afrika Bambaataa or the Fugees or Talib Kweli, for example. Such music, however, generally relates diasporization to imagined and experienced *historical* displacements rather than contemporary migration.

12. William Jelani Cobb, *To the Break of Dawn: A Freestyle on the Hip-Hop Aesthetic* (New York: New York University Press, 2007), 4.

13. Robert Walser, "Rhythm, Rhyme, and Rhetoric in the Music of Public Enemy," *Ethnomusicology* 39.2 (Spring–Summer 1995): 193–217.

14. Jasbir Puar, *Terrorist Assemblages: Homonationalism in Queer Times* (Durham, NC: Duke University Press, 2007), 171.

15. Quoted in Bonisteel, Sara. "F— Katrina: New Orleans Hip-Hop Remembers the Hurricane." Fox News, August 28, 2006. Retrieved June 27, 2007, from http://www.foxnews.com/story/0,2933,210845,00.html.

16. Juvenile/Skip/Wacko, "Nolia Clap," *The Beginning of the End*, Rap-A-Lot Records, ASYO 42046-CD, 2005.

17. 100 percent of public housing residents were black. See David Dante Troutt, "Many Thousands Gone, Again," in *After the Storm: Black Intellectuals Explore the Meaning of Hurricane Katrina*, ed. David Dante Troutt (New York: New Press, 2006), 3–28. A Brookings Institution study shows that in the 1990s, New Orleans was second among the nation's large metropolitan areas for locating such housing in predominantly black neighborhoods; Lance Freeman, "Siting Affordable Housing: Location and Neighborhood Trends of Low Income Housing Tax Credit Developments in the 1990s," Brookings Institution (April 2004), http://www.brookings.edu/metro/katrina.htm (accessed April 13, 2007). For more on the relations between the history of bounce and the geography of New Orleans, see Matt Miller, "Bounce: Rap Music and Cultural Survival in New Orleans," *HypheNation* 1.1 (April 2006): 15–31.

18. Bonisteel, 2006.

19. Mia X cited in Bonisteel, 2006.

20. In 2004, New Orleans logged a murder rate of 56 per 100,000 people, four and a half times the average for cities of similar size in the United States. The New Orleans police force has long been known for racism, internal corruption, and abuses of power. Nicole Gelinas, "New Orleans Still Drowning in Crime," *Dallas Morning News*, May 13, 2007, http://www.dallasnews.com/sharedcontent/dws/dn/opinion/points/stories/DN-gelinas_13edi.ART.State.Edition1.4310bb0.html (accessed November 15, 2008).

21. Commenting on Blanco's order and media reports of wanton criminality among the stranded, right-wing pundit Robert Tracinski wrote, "There were many decent, innocent people trapped in New Orleans when the deluge hit. But they were trapped alongside large numbers of people from two groups: criminals—and wards of the welfare state, people selected, over decades, for their lack of initiative and self-induced helplessness." "Hurricane Katrina Exposed the Man-Made Disaster of the Welfare State," *Pittsburgh Tribune Review*, September 11, 2005.

22. 5th Ward Weebie, "Fuck Katrina (The Katrina Song)," "Bounce Back," 2005. Retrieved June 10, 2007 from http://www.myspace.com/fifthwardweebie.

23. Master-P and Halleluyah, "Bounce Back," *Hurricane Katrina: We Gon' Bounce Back*, Guttar, 2005.

24. Lisa De Moraes, "Kanye West's Torrent of Criticism, Live on NBC," *Washington Post*, September 3, 2005, http://www.washingtonpost.com/wp-dyn/content/article/2005/09/03/AR2005090300165.html (accessed June 30, 2007).

25. In his later lectures, Foucault discusses how, to manage the question of who will live and who will die, govern-

mentality increasingly regulates populations along the axis of race, with racism functioning as "the basic mechanism of power, as it is exercised in modern States." This mechanism consists in "making live and *letting die.*" Michel Foucault, *Society Must Be Defended: Lectures at the Collège de France, 1975–76,* ed. Mauro Bertani and Alessandro Fontana (New York: Picador, 2003): 254, 247. Peter Nyers brings this discussion to bear on the question of refugees: national sovereignty consists, in part, in the power to decide membership—the right to permit or refuse entry and citizenship. Nyers, "Abject Cosmopolitanism," 1071.

26. Jay-Z, "Minority Report, " *Kingdom Come,* Roc-A-Fella/Island Def Jam, DEJ B000804502, 2006.

27. Juvenile, "Get Ya Hustle On," *Reality Check,* Atlantic, 2006.

28. The Legendary K.O., "George Bush Doesn't Care about Black People," 2005, digital download at http://www.rappersiknow.com/2005/09/06/day-24-myone-hands-up-featuring-kay-produced-by-symbolyc-one-bw-the-legendary-ko-george-bush-doesnt-care-about-black-people-produced-by-kanye-west/.

29. Visiting the Houston Astrodome, where many evacuees were being sheltered, Barbara Bush commented to the media, "What I'm hearing, which is sort of scary, is they all want to stay in Texas. Everyone is so overwhelmed by the hospitality. And so many of the people in the arena here, you know, were underprivileged anyway, so this is working very well for them." "Barbara Bush Calls Evacuees Better Off," *New York Times,* September 7, 2005, 22.

30. Press release, www.k-otix.com, September 11, 2005 (accessed October 11, 2008).

31. Kanye West, "Gold Digger," *Late Registration,* Roc-A-Fella/Island Def Jam, 2005.

32. Ray Charles, "I Got a Woman," *Hallelujah I Love Her So,* Atlantic 8006, 1962.

33. The Legendary K.O., "George Bush Doesn't Care about Black People," 2005.

34. Ironically, when Bush did finally make it to the Gulf, he went straight to Biloxi, Mississippi, which is 71 percent white and has a Republican mayor and governor and two Republican senators. It took him another couple of days to get to New Orleans and other hard-hit areas that were majority black and Democrat before the storm. Jacob Weisberg, "An Imperfect Storm: How Race Shaped Bush's Response to Katrina," *Slate,* September 7, 2005, http://www.slate.com/?id=2125812 (accessed May 17, 2007).

35. The Legendary K.O., "George Bush Doesn't Care about Black People," 2005.

36. Feminization is repeatedly deployed in post-Katrina hip-hop as a form of intense denigration. Bush is often figured as a woman, as in Lil Wayne's "Georgia Bush." Another trope is the personification of Hurricane Katrina (and sometimes category 3 Hurricane Rita, which devastated parts of the Louisiana coastline on September 24, 2005) as a bitch or ho. For example, 5th Ward Weebie raps in "The Katrina Song," "I say fuck Katrina that ho is a creeper for hangin' with Rita."

37. "A Dollar a Day," BBC World Radio Service, December 7, 2007, http://www.bbc.co.uk/worldservice/documentaries/2007/12/071227_dollar_a_day_1.shtml (accessed November 15, 2008).

38. Mos Def, 2006.

39. Ibid.

40. Lil Wayne and DJ Drama, "Georgia Bush," *Dedication 2,* 101 Distribution 2120, 2006.

41. Papoose, "Mother Nature," *The Best of Papoose: The Mixtape,* 2006.

42. Jeremy Alford, "In One Parish, Divide over Housing Newcomers," *New York Times,* September 28, 2005, http://www.nytimes.com/2005/09/28/national/nationalspecial/28race.html?ex=1182571200&en=fdb4073ff3592a7c&ei=5070 (accessed June 18, 2007).

43. Quoted in John Valery White, "The Persistence of Race Politics and the Restraint of Recovery in Katrina's Wake," in *After the Storm,* ed. Troutt, 41–62.

44. Prem Kumar Rajaram, "Making Place: The 'Pacific Solution' and Australian Emplacement in the Pacific and on Refugee Bodies," *Singapore Journal of Tropical Geography* 24.3 (November 2003): 290–306.

45. Public Enemy, "Hell No (We Ain't Alright)," *Rebirth of a Nation,* Guerilla Funk 31021, 2005.

46. Juvenile, 2006.

47. Mos Def, 2006.

48. Papoose, 2006.

49. New Orleans rapper Chopper narrates the self-reproducing cycle of racialized poverty that trapped him growing up: "I came from the slums where we were on welfare because we had to be," he said in an interview with MTV. "It's hard for a black man to get a job. I'm 19, but I've never had a job in my life. I applied for them when I was 16, but no one wants to hire you. So you gotta do what you can 'cause bills won't wait. It's hard for black people there. Louisiana is ranked the #2 worst-educated state. Mississippi is #1. You come on the battlefield and see how it really is." Corey Moss, "Juvenile, 3 Doors Down among Those Affected by Disaster," MTV.com, September 7, 2005, http://

www.mtv.com/news/articles/1509095/20050907/juvenile
.jhtml (accessed October 12, 2008).

50. Public Enemy, 2005.

51. Lil Wayne and DJ Drama, 2006.

52. Jay-Z, 2006.

53. Lil Wayne and DJ Drama, 2006.

54. Jay-Z, 2006.

55. Louisiana has the highest incarceration rate in the country, with 816 sentenced prisoners for every 100,000 residents. Although Louisiana's population is made up of 32 percent African Americans, 72 percent of inmates are black, and most of them end up in the main penitentiary of Angola, a former slave plantation. Henry Giroux, "Reading Hurricane Katrina: Race, Class, and the Biopolitics of Disposability," *College Literature* 33.3 (Summer 2006): 171–96.

56. I would like to thank Darwin Bond-Graham for pointing out this argument. Mark Anthony Neal, *New Black Man: Rethinking Black Masculinity* (New York: Routledge, 2005), 135.

57. Juvenile, 2006.

58. Ibid.

59. Lou Dobbs, "Seeking Refuge from Political Correctness," September 8, 2005, http://www.cnn.com/2005/US /09/08/political.correctness/index.html (accessed October 8, 2005).

60. Hazel Rose Markus remarks that "the talk of refugees and the third world allows people to imagine that poverty and non-whiteness are non-American things." "Race and Representation" (lecture delivered October 24, 2005, for "Confronting Katrina: Race, Class, and Disaster in American Society," Stanford Special Course), http://ccsre .stanford.edu/EV_events.htm#katrina (accessed March 29, 2007). It is important to note that the racism laid bare in the "refugee" controversy was not only directed against African Americans, but simultaneously revealed how refugees generally have been so degraded in popular opinion as to automatically summon the image of an abject, racialized, and expendable population.

61. Lil Wayne, "Tie My Hands," *Tha Carter III*, Cash Money B0013ABI48, 2008.

62. Several commentators, including rap reviewer Steve "Flash" Juon and Steven Waddy of the National Hip Hop Political Convention, suggest that many mainstream rappers were scared away from writing about Katrina for fear of censorship or political backlash. Steve "Flash" Juon, "Papoose: The Best of Papoose," RapReviews.com, April 10, 2007, http://www.rapreviews.com/archive/2007_04_bestofpapoose .html (accessed November 18, 2008); Bonisteel, 2006.

63. Jacques Rancière, *Disagreement: Politics and Philosophy* (Minneapolis: University of Minnesota Press, 1999), 27.

Reading Questions

1. Kish proposes that there are a number of instances in the history of the African American experience when African Americans have experienced forced migration. What are these historical instances?

2. Kish suggests that the traditions of hip-hop music have many of their roots in blues music. What blues traditions, according to Kish, are echoed now in hip-hop music?

3. Kish explores lyrics from songs from Mia X and Weebie to suggest that bounce itself was transformed by the experience of Katrina. According to Kish, in what ways was bounce changed?

4. Kish also examines the musical response of national hip-hop music to the devastation and destruction caused by Katrina. How, according to Kish, do the responses of regional artists differ from those of national hip-hop artists, like Jay-Z and the Legendary K.O.?

5. In what ways does Kish see representations of the "hustler" and the "hustle" in hip-hop as a response to the figure of the "refugee"?

Rhetoric Questions

6. How would you describe the title of Kish's study? What might it suggest about the relationship between the writer and her readers?

7. Kish announces exactly what she intends to explore throughout her article. What do you see as her central thesis? Where is it located?

8. Kish's article is developed in four distinct sections. Identify and describe each of these stages. In addition, briefly explain how each section functions to help the researcher support her central aims.

Response and Research Questions

9. Locate and examine closely one of the Katrina protest hip-hop songs Kish explores as a part of her study. What elements of the song's lyrics and music, in your opinion, make it a protest song?

10. Notice the pattern Kish establishes for presenting a number of lyrics from a song and then offering an analysis of those lines. Choose one of the lyric segments that Kish cites, and perform your own analysis of the lines.

ACADEMIC CASE STUDY • HURRICANE KATRINA   SOCIAL SCIENCES

Environmental Justice, Local Knowledge, and After-Disaster Planning in New Orleans

BARBARA L. ALLEN

Barbara L. Allen is a professor and a director of the Graduate Program in Science and Technology Studies at the Virginia Polytechnic Institute and State University's Northern Virginia Center. Her study, published in 2007 in the journal *Technology in Society*, examines a number of social and political issues "in light of failures in after-disaster planning during the rebuilding of the city [New Orleans] in the year following" the Hurricane Katrina disaster.

ABSTRACT

This article addresses issues of environmental justice and historic preservation in the aftermath of Hurricane Katrina in New Orleans. Specifically, four main areas are examined in light of failures in after-disaster planning during the rebuilding of the city in the year following the storm. The first area of critique is the problem of public trust in government environmental officials in Louisiana. The second area is the lack of planning for debris disposal, and the possibility that this may create future public health and environmental injustice sites. Third, the article addresses problems faced by residents, particularly the poor and working class, who are trying to clean up and rebuild after the storm. And last, the article highlights issues unique to rebuilding in New Orleans's 20 historic districts, in particular the tensions between local knowledge and the federal response to the disaster.

1. INTRODUCTION

The aftermath of Hurricane Katrina provides an important lens into the various dimensions of environmental justice (EJ)[1] in New Orleans. In particular, the hurricane served to highlight disparities in health and well being that already existed in the region, and to bring into public view the vulnerabilities of the poor, working class, and minority communities. Disputes over local vs. cosmopolitan knowledge, and questions about whose science and whose knowledge "counts" in the reclamation of the city, continue to play out in the politics of rebuilding this historic place.

2. LOCAL EMPOWERMENT AND ENVIRONMENTAL JUSTICE CONCERNS

For analytic purposes, a disaster can be thought of in three distinct event timeframes: before, during, and after. This article examines post-disaster issues and planning preparedness disconnects that became apparent after Hurricane Katrina. Four broad areas, all directly related to local empowerment and environmental justice concerns, are:

1. environmental knowledge and public trust
2. debris disposal problems
3. equal access to rebuilding tools and repatriation
4. building science and historic preservation

2.1. Environmental knowledge and public trust— a bad history

After Hurricane Katrina, there were endless reports of flooding that submerged Superfund sites and up-

ended oil-storage tanks. Wall breaches on drainage canals released an enormous rush of water into the city, scraping about a foot of sediment from the bottoms of the canals and re-depositing it in other parts of the city. This effectively released several decades of previously "dormant" hazardous material into the urban landscape.

The content of the sediment represented some of 5 the worst years of Louisiana's industrial waste disposal practices and pesticide use, before the days of much regulation and enforcement.[2] The material dried and formed a cracked, grayish "moonscape" in yards and streets throughout the city. Wilma Subra, an environmental scientist who has worked with many community groups in Louisiana, was asked to sample numerous sites around the metro area. She found elevated levels of heavy metals, with particularly high levels of arsenic in 92% of her samples. In the Lower Ninth Ward, for example, after the flood arsenic was 74 times higher than the US Environmental Protection Agency (EPA) standard.[3] While this might seem very high, the State of Louisiana has much lower standards for arsenic: the same sample is only 2.5 times more than the state allowable limit, giving the appearance of being less toxic. That the state would set its toxicity limits for arsenic so much higher than the federal standards is suspicious to many environmental health practitioners and informed citizen

---

[1] The U.S. environmental justice (EJ) movement of the past several decades, a synergistic hybrid of traditional environmentalism and social justice concerns, has focused primarily on two issues: (1) the siting and expansion of hazardous facilities in poor and minority communities, and (2) the push for remediation, damages, and/or relocation for poor and minority communities impacted by previous or on-going pollution. Louisiana has been at the forefront of this movement, providing important case studies, such as fighting a variety of injustices from hazardous waste generated by large concentrations of chemical plants to affordable housing built on polluted Superfund sites [1,2].

[2] My information on the cause and composition of the floodwaters was taken from two interviews: Wilma Subra, a self-employed environmental scientist, whom I interviewed on January 25, 2006, at her office in New Iberia, Louisiana; and Ivor van Heerden, coastal geologist, LSU Hurricane Center, interviewed on February 6, 2006, in Washington, D.C.

[3] The environmental data that Subra and other scientists collected in the aftermath of Hurricanes Katrina and Rita is available at <http://www.leanweb.org/katrina/katrinadata.html> (accessed 22 February 2006). Interestingly, the EPA website provides easy access to federal heavy metal standards, but the Louisiana Department of Environmental Quality (LDEQ) website appears to have a manual that can be downloaded, but it is over 700 pages long and uses codes that are hard to interpret—in short, one would have to be an environmental lawyer to decipher it.

groups. Subra also found many toxic chemicals present that are associated with now-defunct polluting industries, such as old creosote facilities, in the material re-deposited by Hurricane Katrina.

According to Subra, the biggest problem with the sediment, besides its toxicity, was that it was very available and easily dispersed via skin contact and airborne pathways, and thus dangerous to human health. The EPA and the US Federal Emergency Management Agency (FEMA) were reluctant to comment or act, according to Subra, as state officials were anxious to open up neighborhoods for citizens to return. Government agencies were simply hoping it would rain and the material would simply go away. It did rain and the sludge was still there—lots of it—and it was still highly toxic.

Six months after the hurricane I contacted public health officials and researchers, many of whom were reluctant to talk. One who did talk asked that I did not use her name, but she made some interesting observations. According to my informant, health officials were in a difficult position. Half a year after the devastation, only 25% of the city's residents had returned; a year after the storm, that number rose to about 40%. Negative publicity regarding public health issues would deter such repatriation, particularly families with children who had not returned in any large numbers to the city. The informant also told me to pursue the state public health websites, where the most prominent worries were still smoking and obesity, not Hurricane Katrina. While the information on various public health websites did eventually reflect concerns about mold, mildew, and other contamination, it was never presented as the health threat that independent environmental scientists, such as Wilma Subra, thought it was.

Further complicating citizens' confidence in their state public health officials has been those officials' complicity with polluting industries in the past. There are numerous examples of state regulators and public health officials protecting industry and refusing to address serious public concerns. One such example was the state's neglect in addressing elevated lead levels in children who live near oilfield waste sites [3].

More recently, the taxpayer-funded state cancer data collection agency, the Louisiana Tumor Registry, was taken to court by concerned citizens and medical researchers who tried to obtain zip-code-specific information for rare cancers (such as pediatric cancers) occurring in residents living near petrochemical facilities. The state has fought for a decade to block access to public location-specific cancer data, raising many questions among the citizens as to whose interests this agency serves [4]. To date, the state still refuses to release cancer data by zip code, citing both patient privacy rights and cost of data production as its primary reasons.

For citizens, the source of scientific information is very important to its believability [5]. In Louisiana, citizens' trust in their state public health system to distribute accurate information has been eroded by questionable activity or, in some cases, inactivity. Trust in the source of information is paramount to ensuring full participation in any public health and remediation efforts. Unfortunately, this has been compromised by many years of industry-complicit behavior.

2.2. Debris disposal problems

Another potential EJ issue related to Hurricane Katrina's aftermath is where the debris being removed from New Orleans is being dumped. For months after the storm, debris was piled on the curbs and in the street and removed by contractors. Some people hired workers to scrape the sediment from their property so the toxic sludge could be removed. The heaps of discarded material included household waste, building products, cars, electronics, appliances, furniture, toys, and clothing.

Although some efforts were made to separate the waste into hazard categories to target environmentally sound removal, these efforts were thwarted by the lack of leadership and a lack of information sharing that plagued the cleanup. Large out-of-state contractors, hired by FEMA for waste removal, simply pushed the separated piles of debris together and carted them off to dumpsites. Thus local efforts at environmentally sound cleanup were not adequately coordinated with the large corporate firms hired to remove debris. Adding to the problem was the fact that state maps of the allowable hurricane debris disposal areas showed sites that were closed long ago for failing to meet federal standards. These sorts of knowledge disconnects degraded the cleanup process and may even create Superfund sites of the future.

Unfortunately, this would not be the first time a hurricane's refuse created a toxic zone. The Agricultural Street landfill in New Orleans was one of the main sites for waste from Hurricane Betsy 40 years earlier. It had been closed for years prior to Hurricane Betsy due to complaints from local citizens, but the mountains of waste generated by the hurricane led to the emergency re-opening of the landfill. Fifteen years later the US Department of Housing and Urban Development built affordable homes on the then-reclaimed landfill and sold them to mostly African-American families. In 1990, it was designated a Superfund site, with heavy metal concentrations many time the EPA allowable levels for public safety. Government officials declared that "there was no apparent public hazard" to the citizens living on the site [6]. It became a legendary EJ battle and the residents, citing health problems, are still fighting for relocation.

About five months after Hurricane Katrina, I received an e-mail from a high school student living in a rural parish west of New Orleans along the Mississippi River (an area EJ advocates have renamed Cancer Alley). After Hurricane Katrina, an old landfill near her house was opened to receive waste and began emitting noxious odors. She took samples of the "black ooze" from the site and contacted the Louisiana Department of Environmental Quality, only to be told that the landfill was accepting only construction waste, and the smell she described was probably decaying gypsum board. I suspect her story will be repeated many times across south Louisiana as these marginal waste sites receive the debris from homes and businesses ruined by the hurricane. The full environmental impact of Hurricane Katrina's waste and its hastily designated removal sites will not be known for many years.

2.3. Equal access to rebuilding tools and repatriation

As people were first allowed to come back to examine the damage to their homes, in some cases to remove debris and search for what was salvageable, neither local, state, or federal officials recommended any type of protection. Finally, at the insistence of environmental groups, the EPA told residents not to come into contact with the sediment, and FEMA handed out a list of recommended protective gear (masks, gloves, Tyvek suits, etc.) to returning residents stopped at police checkpoints before they entered their devastated neighborhoods. Unfortunately, there was no place within 100 miles to buy any of these items, even if the residents could have afforded them; finally nonprofits began distributing protective gear, free of charge, to residents as they returned.

While wealthier homeowners hired people to clean and gut their homes, working-class and poor residents did the work themselves. Furthermore, many of the immigrant workers brought in by large government contractors to remove the debris wore little or no protection (some, by their own choice or due to a lack of education, had masks dangling around their necks) as they cleaned. Unprotected cleaning and demolition was extremely risky in much of the city (especially in the areas most heavily flooded and having the most sludge). There was no electricity, no emergency phone system, no medical clinics, and no running water, further adding to the dangerous nature of the work.

But cleanup information and assistance were not the only tools needed. Fortunately, much of the housing stock in New Orleans was built appropriately for a floodplain. Many houses in the Lower Ninth Ward, for example, were constructed of mold- and rot-resistant cypress, raised 2–4 ft off the ground on piers, and built to flood and drain.[4] This neighborhood ranges in elevation from a low point of 4 ft below sea level to a high point of 8 ft above sea level closer to the river. The reason the area was so heavily flooded was because of a breech in the canal walls, not necessarily because of elevation.

[4] From an interview with Elizabeth English on *To the Point*, National Public Radio, 13 January 2006.

Unfortunately "many of the houses that are good candidates for recovery have been labeled 52% or 56% damaged by FEMA."[5] In order to get a building permit and thus money from FEMA and an insurance company to rebuild, a house must have sustained less than 50% damage. According to one construction engineer who has worked with ACORN,[6] FEMA's experts have not only overstated damage, but in some cases, they have allowed further damage to occur by inaction. For example, FEMA would declare 100% roof damage when in actuality the damage was minimal to moderate. This declaration meant that FEMA would not provide blue plastic protective material for the roof, thus allowing rain to further damage the property.

Further adding to homeowners' frustration was the fact that in order to challenge FEMA's damage determination, a homeowner had to be present in New Orleans and present evidence contradicting FEMA's damage determination. This was difficult, as many of the residents were living in other locations well removed from New Orleans and had no way to file a grievance. Assembling a counter claim to substantiate a differing technological assessment of their property was complicated and deterred many poor owners who simply gave up.

A related issue that brought citizens and the insurance industry together in a struggle between local and non-local knowledge was the assessment of damage by private insurance company claims adjustors, not FEMA. Citizens again were caught in the middle, forced to dispute what their insurance company would pay toward rebuilding their homes via the Louisiana Hurricane mediation program. But the homeowners were outgunned in mediation, as they were often on their own to prepare and present the technical evidence disputing the assessment. The insurance companies had likely seen thousands of cases

and they were ready with a winning strategy prepared by experts.

In adjacent, majority-white Jefferson Parish, many neighborhoods had street after street of houses with small FEMA trailers in every yard, enabling the owner to rebuild while living on site. There was no such evidence of this scale of activity in Orleans Parish. A year after the flood waters subsided, some neighborhoods still had no electricity or water that they could connect to a FEMA trailer even if they had one. Compounding the problem was New Orleans's own zoning regulations, which forbid parking trailers on the street or blocking sidewalks. Where will these residents live while repairing their homes?

A big question is: what happens when the residents of a community are dispersed and have difficulty forming a cohesive voice? This was and is one of the largest problems Hurricane Katrina presents. Communities were asked to assemble a list of those willing to come back and rebuild in order to receive assistance. This task was much easier for wealthier residents who had Internet access and other high-tech means of communication. The poor were at a definite disadvantage in this planning phase of rebuilding, and that disadvantage may mean that their neighborhoods do not get needed funding. The longer people stay away and build their lives elsewhere, the less likely they are to return.

2.4. Knowledge of building science and historic preservation

The conflict of local and non-local knowledge has been also a problem in the salvage, triage, and rebuilding of New Orleans's older structures. One example was the policy and process by which blue plastic protective material was nailed to roofs after the storm to prevent further weather damage. The US government's operation blue roof program, which put tarps on roofs in New Orleans after Hurricane Katrina, would not tarp older roofs of slate and tile, leaving some of the most historic structures open to the elements and further ruin. They claimed that the plastic could not be nailed to the hard surface, so these structures were neglected. Student groups from Tulane University and

[5] From a phone interview I conducted with Elizabeth English on 17 February 2006.

[6] ACORN is the acronym for the Association of Community Organizations for Reform Now, an umbrella group that supports community development in poor communities.

the local Preservation Resource Center (PRC) tried to put tarps on as many hard-surface roofs as they could, but many sustained additional damage from rain and the elements due to either a delayed response or no response from the FEMA program.

Important knowledge has been generated over many decades by local preservation and neighborhood groups in New Orleans. This knowledge about building materials and practices would have a profound impact on the cost, ability, and even possibility of owners rebuilding and returning to their homes. In the nineteenth and early twentieth centuries, houses were built in a climate- and locale-appropriate fashion. The houses, designed by local craftsmen, were built of materials more forgiving to water damage. For example, many interior walls were built of plaster over lath—both somewhat impermeable and mildew resistant—and cypress floorboards that were rot resistant, unlike most new materials. Some of the older houses were even framed with bargeboard taken from dismantled river barges and noted for their durability and climate appropriateness. Vinyl tiles, drywall, and vinyl siding did not fare well and had to be removed after homes were flooded. Ironically, the houses with fewer upgrades were in better shape for re-habitation if they were not in dilapidated condition to begin with.[7] In some flooded areas, new materials often had to be removed, taking the house somewhat back to its original condition, at least on the lower levels.

After Hurricane Katrina and owing to the slow federal response, many community groups from all over the United States rushed in to help New Orleans rebuild, bringing with them their own local knowledge. While some worked with local groups that shared their long-time knowledge, others worked in a more isolated fashion. Unfortunately, FEMA and some outside volunteers instructed residents to rip everything out of the houses. People were removing cypress flooring, plaster, and other materials that would have both saved them rebuilding costs and strengthened the ability of their homes to withstand future flooding.

The demolition of the Naval Brigade Hall in the warehouse/arts district is a sad example of outsiders bringing their local practices to New Orleans. The building dated to 1903 and was one of the city's important jazz landmarks. An incubator of early ragtime music, it served as a school that was attended by many noted jazz musicians, and a place where blacks and whites played together during the long era of segregation. A few weeks after the hurricane, city inspectors placed a sign on the building saying it was unsafe for habitation. Within hours a group of firefighters from Chicago arrived and using a high-pressure water-spraying device they had brought with them called "the strong arm," they knocked the building down, reducing it to a pile of bricks. One resident of the neighborhood complained to the firefighters that the building was not on fire and was a historic structure, to which one firefighter replied "we have to do it for safety reasons" [7]. The building had sustained wind damage and the third floor had collapsed, but the first floor was intact and its unusually thick walls were still plumb. This important monument to the early history of jazz probably could have been saved.

Business interests also played a part in rebuilding after Hurricane Katrina. For example, within a week after the hurricane, Michael Carliner, an economist and author of a study on the impact of Hurricane Katrina on housing stock in New Orleans for the National Association of Home Builders, reported that "every wood structure that stood in more than 6 ft of floodwater will have to be demolished" [8]. Professional outside viewpoints, driven by specific interests, can be counter to the reality of the local residents. Local preservationists knew that older housing stock, originally constructed in a climate-appropriate manner, was among the easiest to save. These older neighborhoods embodied communality, fostered social interaction and cultural practices, and were the cornerstone of city life—a catalyst for bringing New Orleans back to some semblance of its former days.

---

[7] A number of nineteenth-century structures in Orleans, particularly those in historic African-American and Creole neighborhoods, were in a state of neglect before the storm. One concern of the historic preservation community is that these areas will be demolished, thus losing an important chapter in the diverse history of the city. Some feel that extra care and consideration should be afforded these structures to ensure that they too are rebuilt.

Outside knowledge, which drove regulations and technical knowledge, impacted the ability of citizens to rebuild.

The influence of insurance companies on the city is exemplified by their pressure to adopt stricter, traditional building codes. Some insurance assessments required houses to be raised in order to be eligible for payout; others required that the structure be brought up to new city and state building codes, often making it more expensive. Unfortunately, the bill to create a statewide building code for homeowners established a 19-member council to impose and revise the standard code. No preservationists were asked to sit on the council—a concern to many in New Orleans, a city comprised of 20 historic districts [9]. Although building codes are devised for public safety, historic structures often need special consideration rather than a blanket application of uniform standards.

Some local architects claimed that insurance companies have a "penchant for demolition" in order to save paperwork—even though the buildings in the historic parts of the town were some of the most rehabitable. Too many drive-by assessors looked, saw an "old dilapidated wood building," and labeled it unsalvageable [10]. Local architects understood the typical local construction better than outside adjustors who wanted to avoid paperwork and developers hungry for a blank slate provided by building demolition. These examples point to a disjunction between local and cosmopolitan knowledge, a disconnect that may have consequences for the citizens of New Orleans.

In Brian Wynne's analysis of the contamination of sheep herds in the United Kingdom after Chernobyl [11], he pointed out that experts did not take into account local knowledge when intervening, thus causing even greater economic disaster to the local agricultural community. Similarly, examples in New Orleans, such as neglecting to tarp hard-roof surfaces, not talking to local preservationists about appropriate building materials, and over-zealous demolition of "hazardous" structures, have caused even more damage to the oldest, most historic buildings in the city. Thus, FEMA and other outside guidelines for post-disaster response were damaging to many older neighborhoods, which are economically important

for tourism. The failure of the post-Katrina triage program was both technical and social by not taking into account local knowledge and conditions. If they had listened to, and collaborated with, local citizens and experts, it would have resulted in better practices and better policy recommendations for working toward the reconstruction of the historic building fabric.

3. CONCLUSION

The aftermath of Hurricane Katrina offers an expanded lesson in the importance of local knowledge and environmental justice for after-disaster planners. Social factors such as race, class, culture, and education level are important considerations when devising equitable aftermath strategies. Disconnects between on-the-ground and tacit knowledge and knowledge generated by experts from afar can hinder efforts to rebuild communities. Maybe it would be possible to garner ideas from previous EJ controversies that would positively inform after-disaster planning in the future.

My own research on the EJ movement in Louisiana has shown that the strongest and most effective citizens' groups have the following: (1) alliances with well-organized national and multi-national environmental and social justice groups, (2) have enrolled the support of activist and independent scientists and professional experts to work on their behalf, and (3) are cross-class and multi-ethnic in composition [1]. Alliances with national groups, such as ACORN, are happening, and the prominence of the storm's aftermath in the media has ensured wider visibility of the struggles of poor and displaced citizens. In the case of New Orleans, the participation of the National Trust for Historic Preservation and other outside preservation groups has been a lifeline for those who are trying to save older structures in the post-Katrina demolition frenzy. Slowly, more scientists and independent experts are participating in the historic preservation and environmental debates on behalf of citizens who are not necessarily well represented in the voices of the corporate and government experts. It is also important that outside experts be heard so that state economic interests do not override community health and well being. More could be done to engage citizens with scientists who are asking questions in concert with communities and trying to find answers to those issues that citizens find most urgent. And lastly, an effort toward creating heterogeneous citizen groups would enable the marshalling of the social and political capital of the disparate groups. Their collective voices would be far stronger in their fight for justice, equality, and appropriateness in rebuilding their communities.

ACKNOWLEDGMENTS

I would like to thank Carl Mitcham, Robert Frodeman, and all the participants of the Cities and Rivers II conference in New Orleans, March 21–25, 2006. The ideas and discussions at this event enabled me to think in a more interdisciplinary manner about the disaster and its impact as well as about my own assumptions regarding environmental justice and citizen participation in science.

In addition, I would like to thank the American Academy in Rome for giving me the time to think and write about this important topic. Conversations with my colleagues at the academy were invaluable in helping me to think in new ways about historic preservation and rebuilding.

REFERENCES

[1] Allen B. Uneasy alchemy: citizens and experts in Louisiana's chemical corridor disputes. Cambridge, MA: MIT Press; 2003.

[2] Roberts JT, Toffolon-Weiss M. Chronicles from the environmental justice frontline. New York: Cambridge University Press; 2001.

[3] Allen B. Shifting boundary work: issues and tensions in environmental health science in the case of Grand Bois, Louisiana. Sci Cult 2004;13(4):429–448.

[4] Allen BL. The problem with epidemiology data in assessing environmental health impacts of toxic sites. In: Aral MM, Brebbia CA, Maslia ML, Sinks T, editors. Environmental exposure and health. Boston: MIT Press; 2005. p. 467–475.

[5] Irwin A, Dale A, Smith D. Science in hell's kitchen: the local understanding of hazard issues. In: Irwin A, Wynne B, editors. Misunderstanding science. The public reconstruction of science and technology. New York: Cambridge University Press; 1996. p. 47–64.

[6] Toffolon-Weiss MM, Roberts TJ. Who wins, who loses? Understanding outcomes of environmental injustice struggles. In: Pellow P, Brulle R, editors. Power, justice, and the environment. Cambridge, MA: MIT Press; 2005. p. 77–90.

[7] Russell G. Historic jazz building sent to early grave. Times-Picayune, 5 October 2005.

[8] Kessler J. Preservationists fear bulldozing of neighborhoods. Atlanta Journal-Constitution, 12 September 2005.

[9] Anderson E. Debate on state-wide building code revs up. Times-Picayune, 19 November 2005.

[10] Barron E, quoted in Dean A. Architects weigh in on rebuilding. Architectural Record 2005;193:9, cited from: http://archrecord.construction.com, accessed 6/2/06.

[11] Wynne B. Misunderstood misunderstandings: social identities and public uptake of science. In: Irwin A Wynne B, editor. Misunderstanding science? The public reconstruction of science and technology. New York: Cambridge University Press; 1996. p. 19–46.

Reading Questions

1. In the Introduction section of her article, Allen suggests that the aftermath of Hurricane Katrina is an important site for examining issues related to environmental justice. What does she mean by environmental justice?

2. What evidence does Allen provide to suggest that "[i]n Louisiana, citizens' trust in their state public health system to distribute accurate information has been eroded" (par. 9)?

3. Allen notes a clear disparity in the rebuilding experiences in predominantly black communities (like Orleans Parish) and predominantly white ones (like Jefferson Parish). What evidence or examples does she provide to support her assessment?

4. In what ways does Allen suggest that FEMA did more damage than good in terms of the preservation of New Orleans history?

Rhetoric Questions

5. Consider the amount and forms of evidence Allen uses in her study. Do you think these are both sufficient? Why or why not?

6. Beyond simply ending her report, what do you think Allen's conclusion is meant to achieve for her audience? Do you think it is successful? Why or why not?

Response and Research Questions

7. Allen recounts receiving an e-mail from a high school student about a smell coming from a landfill near her house. What do you think Allen is trying to suggest by telling this story?

8. Identify a physical site in your local or regional area that could be used to examine issues of environmental justice. What are the specific environmental issues related to the site?

ACADEMIC CASE STUDY • HURRICANE KATRINA   NATURAL SCIENCES

Distribution of Toxic Trace Elements

TINGZHI SU, SHI SHU, HONGLAN SHI, JIANMIN WANG, CRAIG ADAMS, AND EMITT C. WITT

The first author of this article, Tingzhi Su, was a doctoral student in environmental engineering at the University of Missouri–Rolla at the time of its publication in *Environmental Pollution* in 2008. She completed the degree in 2010 and is currently a senior associate at ENVIRON, an international consulting agency on environmental and health issues. In the article, Su and her fellow researchers report the results of a comparative study of toxic trace elements in the soil and sediments in the regions of New Orleans after the devastating landfall of Hurricane Katrina in August 2005.

ABSTRACT

This study provided a comprehensive assessment of seven toxic trace elements (As, Pb, V, Cr, Cd, Cu, and Hg) in the soil/sediment of Katrina-affected greater New Orleans region 1 month after the recession of flood water. Results indicated significant contamination of As and V and non-significant contamination of Cd, Cr, Cu, Hg, and Pb at most sampling sites. Compared to the reported EPA Region 6 soil background inorganic levels, except As, the concentrations of the other six elements had greatly increased throughout the studied area; St. Bernard Parish and Plaquemines Parish showed greater contamination than other regions. Comparison between pre- and post-Katrina data in similar areas, and data for surface, shallow, and deep samples, indicated that the trace element distribution in post-Katrina New Orleans was not obviously attributed to the flooding. This study suggests that more detailed study of As and V contamination at identified locations is needed.

1. INTRODUCTION

Hurricane Katrina was one of the worst natural disasters in U.S. history (CDC, 2006a). The storm caused by Katrina damaged coastal Mississippi, Louisiana,

Alabama, and as far east as the Florida panhandle (CDC, 2006b). The consequences induced by Katrina were catastrophic in southeastern Louisiana, especially in the greater New Orleans region, including Orleans Parish, St. Bernard Parish, Plaquemines Parish, and Jefferson Parish. After Katrina made its landfall in south Plaquemines Parish, the entire Mississippi Delta was almost devastated, including much of the fleet that supported the state's fishing industry (Adams et al., 2007). Approximately 80% of the New Orleans city was flooded after the storm-induced levee breaches in Lake Pontchartrain, with water reaching 20 feet (6 m) in some locations (CDC, 2006b; Pardue et al., 2005). The torrent removed homes from their foundations, scattered fuel oil tanks and their contents, damaged oil refineries, and created large piles of moving debris (Adams et al., 2007).

Southeastern Louisiana held 21 oil refineries and accounted to a total of 47% of U.S. distillates. During Katrina, most of the refineries were severely affected or damaged and more than 7 million gallons of oil were estimated to spill from industrial plants, storage depots, hundreds of rigs and other damaged facilities, and scattered at sites throughout southeastern Louisiana (McCaskill, 2006). Lake Pontchartrain, which greatly contributed to the catastrophic flooding in New Orleans, was also a historic environmental sink. It received the agricultural runoff from north shore, poorly treated or untreated sewage from many communities throughout the Pontchartrain Basin, and the storm water runoff from New Orleans metropolitan area during rain events (Anonymous, 1995; Williams, 2002). The contaminated water and associated sediment from Lake Pontchartrain mixed with a great variety of other contaminants, and was spread all over the flood-affected areas. The concern was that these contaminants may have significantly degraded the environmental quality in New Orleans. Pardue et al. (2005) reported that Pb, As, and in some cases, Cr concentrations in the flood water exceeded the drinking water standards. Extensive mud deposits left in some areas of New Orleans had the potential to carry contaminants from Lake Pontchartrain to the affected neighborhoods. Because metal

contamination in Louisiana has been a serious health problem since the early 1970s (Brown et al., 2000), it was necessary to assess the amounts of major toxic trace elements of concern in the soil/sediment across the entire area affected by Hurricane Katrina and associated flood in southeastern Louisiana, to determine the extent of toxic trace elements contamination in these areas.

Several researchers have studied the post-Katrina toxic element concentrations in soil/sediment and water samples from New Orleans (Cobb et al., 2006; Dubey et al., 2007; Mielke et al., 2006; Presley et al., 2006; Wang et al., 2004), and concluded that Pb and As contamination could be a great concern. However, samples in these studies were mainly collected from very limited areas along major thoroughfares. These included areas between the 17th Street Canal and the Industrial Canal in Orleans Parish, around the Superdome, and along St. Charles Avenue on the Mississippi River front. Although a broader area, in both Orleans Parish and St. Bernard Parish, was also investigated (Schwab et al., 2007), the study only focused on As and Pb contamination in the soil/sediment.

Very little information is available concerning the 5 presence of a group of high-priority toxic trace elements in the flood-affected areas in Jefferson Parish, the refinery region in St. Bernard Parish, the northeastern region of Orleans Parish along the lakefront area, and the Mississippi Delta in Plaquemines Parish through where the eye of Hurricane Katrina passed, except some preliminary leaching data published by us recently for a subset of 46 samples (Adams et al., 2007). To further provide a more comprehensive assessment of Hurricane Katrina's impact on toxic trace element contamination, this research analyzed the extended 157 soil/sediment samples collected from the Katrina- and flood-impacted greater New Orleans region, including Jefferson Parish, Orleans Parish, St. Bernard Parish, and Plaquemines Parish (64 sampling sites), using an approach that is consistent with the current regulations, i.e., the determination of total concentration of seven high-priority toxic trace elements, As, Pb, Cd, Cu, Cr, V, and Hg.

2. MATERIALS AND METHODS

2.1. Sample collection

During the period October 6–18, 2005, a total of 238 soil/sediment samples were collected from 64 sampling sites (Figs. 1 and 2). The sampling area covered the most seriously damaged places, and was divided into four regions. Region 1 was in Jefferson Parish, close to the lakefront and along Esplanade Avenue, including neighborhoods at the 17th Street Levee breach, and southward to the river front along Woodvine Avenue. Region 2 was in Orleans Parish, including the 17th Street Canal breach and the Industrial Levee breach-affected area along Lake Pontchartrain, the London Avenue Canal breach-affected neighborhoods (east), the northeast region of Orleans Parish along the lakefront area, and the neighborhoods between Highways 90 and 3139 at the Mississippi River front. Region 3 was in St. Bernard Parish, from the Industrial Canal to the refineries in eastern New Orleans along the Mississippi River. Region 4 was along Highway 23 on the Mississippi Delta in Plaquemines Parish, including

Empire (near the location where the eye of Hurricane Katrina passed through) and Venice, LA.

A coring procedure and a surface sediment collection procedure were used for sample collection. The coring procedure was our primary sampling method. It allowed assessment of how contaminants may have penetrated into the ground and/or determination of the baseline concentrations of contaminants not caused by the flooding. In this procedure, a 2-cm diameter hand-held soil corer was used to take a 0–10 cm "shallow" core. Totally 213 "shallow" core samples were collected; at 20 such locations, a 10–20 cm "deep" core was also collected in addition to the shallow core. Five surface sediment samples were taken from the top 1 cm of sediment on the ground, from the top of and beneath automobiles, from sidewalks, and from the inside and outside of structures.

All soil/sediment samples were kept in 60-mL amber glass vials with Teflon-lined caps. The samples were labeled and immediately double-bagged into plastic bags, and placed in a cooler. Samples were kept in a

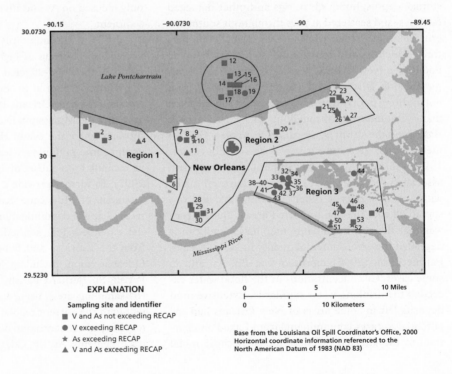

Figure 1. Sampling sites in New Orleans, Louisiana—sampling regions 1 (Jefferson Parish), 2 (Orleans Parish), 3 (St. Bernard Parish). (For interpretation of the references to color in this figure legend, the reader is referred to the web version of this article.)

EXPLANATION

Sampling site and identifier
■ V and As not exceeding RECAP
● V exceeding RECAP
★ As exceeding RECAP
▲ V and As exceeding RECAP

Base from the Louisiana Oil Spill Coordinator's Office, 2000
Horizontal coordinate information referenced to the
North American Datum of 1983 (NAD 83)

refrigerator until analysis in the Environmental Research Center at the Missouri University of Science & Technology. Before analysis, 35 of the samples became unlabeled or broken, or the amount of samples was too little for analysis. As a result, the total number of samples analyzed was 203. Our preliminary study analyzed 46 samples for their element leaching characteristics (Adams et al., 2007). In this continuous study, all the remaining 157 samples, including at least one surface and/or shallow sample from each sampling site, were analyzed for their total element concentrations. The total elements' concentrations were compared against the regulated values and background values.

2.2. Chemicals and reagents

Trace metal grade nitric acid and hydrochloric acid were purchased from Fisher Scientific. The metal standard solutions were purchased from PerkinElmer (Waltham, Massachusetts, USA). Deionized (DI) water was generated from a Millipore water purification system at conductivity of 18 MΩ/cm.

2.3. Microwave-assisted acid digestion

All 157 samples were digested with a Multiwave 3000 microwave digestion system (PerkinElmer, Waltham, Massachusetts, USA), following EPA Method 3051A (US EPA, 2007a). This digestion method is designed to extract the most environmentally significant elements from a sample, rather than to achieve the total dissolution of sequestered elements in a sample. In the method, 0.35–0.50 g of each sample was digested with a mixture of 9 mL of trace metal grade HNO_3 and 3 mL of trace metal grade HCl. After digestion, samples were diluted to 50 mL with DI water. Further dilutions were made before analysis. The quality control requirements of this digestion method were processed on a routine basis. For precision control, a duplicate sample was processed with each batch of 20 samples. Relative percentage difference of duplicated sample (RPD) for each element was ranged from 2.7 to 14.7% for V, 0.7 to 12.3% for Cr, 0.8 to 12.6% for Cu, 1.3 to 16.8% for Cd, 0.6 to 6.9% for Pb, 6.6 to 16.1% for As, 0 to 19.2% for Hg, and 1.9 to 17.6% for

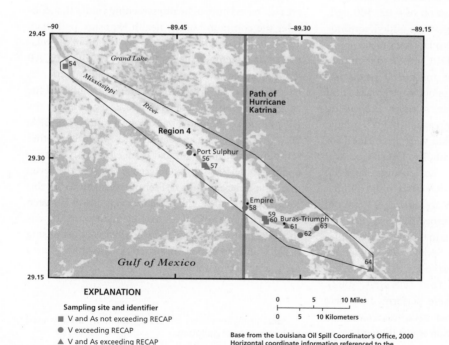

Figure 2. Sampling sites on Mississippi Delta in Plaquemines Parish—sampling region 4. (For interpretation of the references to color in this figure legend, the reader is referred to the web version of this article.)

EXPLANATION

Sampling site and identifier
■ V and As not exceeding RECAP
● V exceeding RECAP
▲ V and As exceeding RECAP

0   5   10 Miles
0   5   10 Kilometers

Base from the Louisiana Oil Spill Coordinator's Office, 2000
Horizontal coordinate information referenced to the
North American Datum of 1983 (NAD 83)

Fe. For accuracy confirmation, a spiked sample was processed with each batch of 20 samples. The spiked recovery for each element was ranged from 82.3 to 120.2% for V, 93.1 to 103.4% for Cr, 80.6 to 102.6% for Cu, 66.7 to 93.2% for Cd, 77.7 to 125.8% for Pb, 84.2 to 111.7% for As, and 92.8 to 119.2% for Hg. Fe was not planned for the analysis initially and spike recovery was not performed.

2.4. Chemical analysis

As, Pb, Cd, Cu, Cr, and V were analyzed by following EPA Method 200.8 (US EPA, 1994). An Elan DRCe (Dynamic Reaction Cell) ICP-MS (inductively coupled plasma-mass spectrometry) instrument equipped with a cyclonic spray chamber, Meinhard nebulizer, and nickel cones (PerkinElmer SCIEX, Concord, Ontario, Canada) was used for analysis. The RF (Radio Frequency) power was 1500 W. Argon flow rates for the plasma and auxiliary gas were 15 and 1.0 L/min, respectively. Nebulizer gas follow rate was 1.02 L/min. Samples were delivered at 1.0 mL/min by a peristaltic pump. The initial instrument calibration was carried out at a concentration of 0.02–500 µg/L linear range. Internal standards were added continuously online as a mixture for quantitation purposes. As (AsO) was detected with DRC mode to eliminate the chloride interference due to the HCl addition during acid digestion and possible interference from any chloride in the soil/sediment samples. For quality assurance, at least one or more reagents blanks, sample duplications, and sample spikes were performed for each batch of 20 or fewer samples. Quality control (QC) and spiking recovery were ensured between 90% and 110%. The method detection limits (MDL) for As, Pb, Cd, Cu, Cr, and V were 0.12, 0.07, 0.06, 0.36, 0.59, and 0.14 mg/kg, respectively.

The total Hg concentrations in the digested samples were analyzed using a Tekran Series 2600 Ultra-trace Mercury Analysis System (Tekran Inc., Toronto, Canada), following EPA Method 1631 (US EPA, 2002). The same quality controls were performed as were used for detection of the other toxic trace elements. The MDL for mercury detection was 0.02 mg/kg.

Fe was detected using the flame atomic absorption spectrometry method. The digested solutions were directly aspirated into the air–acetylene oxidizing flame of a PerkinElmer Model 3110 flame atomic absorption spectrometer (PerkinElmer SCIEX, Concord, Ontario, Canada) after appropriate dilution with DI water. A Fe single-element hollow cathode lamp was used. The absorbance was detected at the wavelength 248.3 nm. The Fe concentration was obtained with an external calibration method at the linear range of calibration curve (0.1–20 mg/L). The MDL for Fe was 15 mg/kg.

3. RESULTS AND DISCUSSION

3.1. Regulations

Two regulations served as the basis for this assessment: EPA Region 6 Human Health Medium-Specific Screening Levels (HHMSSL) for residential soils (US EPA, 2008), and Louisiana Department of Environmental Quality Risk Evaluation/Corrective Action Program remediation levels (LDEQ 2003). HHMSSL are risk-based human health screening values that consider the common human health exposure pathways, and they were used for an initial evaluation of the relative environmental concern for a site. LDEQ RECAP levels were used to determine if corrective action is necessary for the protection of human health and the environment. In addition to these regulations, the EPA Region 6 inorganic background values (US EPA, 2007b) were used as a reference to evaluate whether sampling areas have elevated trace elements contamination. Table 1 shows the reference levels of the seven toxic trace elements for residential soils studied in this research. To analyze the possible relationship between the distributions of these toxic elements and the anthropogenic* activities in the studied area, the housing density and dominant industries in the studied area are referred to in Table 2.

*anthropogenic: effects caused by humans, usually used with reference to pollution.

Table 1

Regulation limits of toxic trace elements (mg/kg), US EPA Region 6 soil inorganic background value (mg/kg) and percentage of sampling sites with increased toxic trace elements concentration in the sampling regions

Toxic trace elements	As[n]	As[c]	As[t]	Pb	V	Cr[t]	Cu	Cd	Hg
HHMSSL2007 (US EPA, 2008) (mg/kg)	22	0.39		400	390	210	2900	39	23
RECAP (LDEQ) (mg/kg)			12	400	55		310	3.9	2.3
US EPA Region 6 soil background (US EPA, 2007b) (mg/kg)			1.1–16.7	10–18	66	38	20	0.1–1	0.1

As[n] — non-cancer endpoint; As[c] — cancer endpoint; As[t] — total arsenic; Cr[t] — total chromium.

3.2. Arsenic

Arsenic contamination in New Orleans has been rec- [15] ognized since the early 1970s, when As was found to have contaminated the streams, rivers, and lakes where hunting and fishing were popular (Brown et al., 2000). Additionally, in 1995, high concentrations of methyl As were found in the bodies of *Micropterus*

salmoides and *Procambarus clarkii* (red crawfishes) obtained from several commercial lakes and streams in New Orleans (Brown et al., 2000).

In this research, all 157 soil/sediment samples exceeded the 0.39 mg/kg EPA Region 6 HHMSSL cancer endpoint level. Approximately 15% of samples (from 28% of sampling sites) exceeded the 12 mg/kg

Table 2

Pre-Katrina housing density (United States Census Bureau, 2000) and main industries (City-data.com) in the four sampling regions, and elevation of the seven toxic trace elements concentration in post-Katrina samples in each region

Sampling region	Housing density (/km²)	Main industries	Sites exceeding Region 6 background level (%)							
			As	Pb	V	Cr	Cu	Cd	Hg	Pb
Jefferson	237	Printing: food, chemical, machinery, plastic & rubber, fabricated metal, manufacturing	0	100	17	17	50	17	83	0
Orleans	460	Food, transportation manufacturing	16	92	4	16	56	24	92	16
St. Bernard	22	Petroleum & coal products manufacturing	9	95	50	41	86	18	59	9
Plaquemines	5	Oil & gas; fishing; petrochemical industry	9	100	55	55	73	18	27	9

LDEQ RECAP remediation levels, and 4% of samples (from 9% of sampling sites) exceeded the 22 mg/kg EPA Region 6 HHMSSL non-cancer endpoint level.

The maximum As concentration of 49.07 mg/kg was found in Site 57 along Highway 23 on the Mississippi Delta in Plaquemines Parish, which is 125 times greater than the EPA HHMSSL for cancer endpoint level. Sampling sites with As concentrations above the median level (6.14 mg/kg) were generally located in St. Bernard Parish and on the Mississippi Delta of Plaquemines Parish. The percentages of sampling sites with at least one sample above the median level in these two regions were 95% and 82%, respectively. The sampling sites with As concentrations greater than LDEQ RECAP remediation level of 12 mg/kg are shown in Figs. 1 and 2 in star (only As exceeding LDEQ RECAP) and triangle (both As and V exceeding LDEQ RECAP). Approximately 17% of the sampling sites in Jefferson Parish had at least one sample with As concentration exceeding the LDEQ RECAP remediation level. The values were 24% in Orleans Parish, 36% in St. Bernard Parish, and 27% along Highway 23 in Plaquemines Parish.

Arsenic has been widely used in pesticides in agriculture, pigments, medicine, treated lumber, and semiconductor materials. Our sampling sites were located on the reclaimed land from wetlands close to Lake Pontchartrain in Jefferson Parish and Orleans Parish (Connor et al., 2002), lands with more than 50% owner-occupied housing in Orleans Parish and close to the Industrial Canal area in St. Bernard Parish (ULI, 2005), or the refinery sites in eastern St. Bernard Parish and Plaquemines Parish. Therefore, the As contamination in the soil/sediment in the sampling sites would be caused by industrial contamination, the Lake Pontchartrain sediment, and household contamination from paints and treated lumber.

The As contamination results from this study are consistent with those reported previously (Schwab et al., 2007; Presley et al., 2006; Cobb et al., 2006) for the overlapped areas in Regions 2 and 3. In this research, the highest As concentration of 33.75 mg/kg within the New Orleans area was found on Site 9, close to the 17th Street Canal breach, which is also consistent with data by Schwab et al. (2007).

3.3. Vanadium

Vanadium is toxic to humans and other animals (Perez-Benito, 2006). No studies were found regarding the V contamination in soil/sediment in New Orleans or on the Louisiana Delta previously. This study showed that 26% of the 157 soil/sediment samples (from 48% of sampled sites) had V concentrations greater than the LDEQ RECAP remediation levels (55 mg/kg). The maximum concentration was 92.06 mg/kg, and the median V concentration was 36.89 mg/kg.

Sampling sites with at least one sample exceeding the LDEQ RECAP level were shown in circle (only V exceeding LDEQ RECAP) and triangle (both V and As exceeding LDEQ RECAP) in Figs. 1 and 2. Spatially, at least one sample that exceeded the LDEQ RECAP Remediation levels for V was observed in 17 and 24% of sampling sites in Jefferson Parish and New Orleans Parish, respectively, and in 73% of sampling sites in both St. Bernard Parish and the Plaquemines Parish had V concentrations greater than the median level. Since V has been widely used in refineries and fisheries (Lazaridis et al., 2003), the high V concentrations found in the soil/sediment in these regions might come from these sources. The highest V concentration was found on Site 62, between Buras and Triumph in Plaquemines Parish. Even though all V concentrations in the samples were within the EPA Region 6 HHMSSL level of 390 mg/kg, the contamination was still significant because a large number of samples and sampling sites had already exceeded the LDEQ RECAP vanadium remediation level.

3.4. Lead

Urban accumulation of lead is a global problem, and there is a significant correlation between median Pb levels in the blood of children and the median Pb concentration in soils (Mielke et al., 1999). According to previous studies on post-Katrina soil/sediment samples, there was significant Pb contamination in some downtown areas of New Orleans after Katrina (Presley et al., 2006; Plumlee et al., 2006). It was reported that, based on a small set of preliminary sample analyses, approximately 30% of leachates using simulated acid rain contained elevated concentrations of Pb (Adams et al., 2007).

In general, Pb concentrations in all soil/sediment samples studied in this research were within the LDEQ RECAP and EPA HHMSSL limits of 400 mg/kg, except for two samples: one with a concentration of 495 mg/kg from Site 9 (located on the Robert E. Lee Boulevard, close to Canal Boulevardin Orleans Parish), and the other with a concentration of 551 mg/kg from Site 31 (located at the intersection of Toledano Street and South Dervigny Street in Orleans Parish, near a playground). Pb distribution was not very different throughout the studied area; 50–72% of the sampling sites in the four sampling regions had at least one sample with Pb concentrations of greater than the median Pb level (35.10 mg/kg), with Orleans Parish and St. Bernard Parish showing relatively higher soil/sediment lead concentrations. This is probably attributed to the broad application of lead in housing, transportation tools, and industrial practices.

The 400 mg/kg Pb concentration was also regulated by EPA as Corrective Action Strategy (CAS) High Priority Bright Line Screening (HPBLS) level (US EPA, 2000). Similar Pb contaminations in locations near Site 9 were also reported by Schwab et al. (2007) and Cobb et al. (2006). Site 9 was located on the land reclaimed from Lake Pontchartrain (Connor et al., 2002), which has been used as a recreational and commercial seafood boating hub for the city. There was also a landfill site in the corner of interstate 10E and 17th Street Canal. These sources and the filling materials during land reclamation could contribute to the Pb contamination on this site. Based on EPA reports (OMB Watch, 2004, 2005), there was no potential toxic chemical site near sampling Site 31. Therefore, the Pb contamination on Site 31 may be derived by historic Pb-based petroleum contamination related to its location between Highway 90 and the Pontchartrain Expressway.

3.5. Chromium, cadmium, copper, and mercury

With two exceptions, there was no significant contamination of Cr, Cd, Cu, or Hg based on the findings that none of the above four elements in the 157 samples exceeded the limits set by the two regulations. One sample from the Plaquemines Parish (Site 57)

had a Cd concentration of 4.3 mg/kg. Another sample from Jefferson Parish (Site 4) had a Cu concentration of 960 mg/kg. The concentrations of Cd or Cu in two samples exceeded LDEQ RECAP remediation levels.

The median concentrations of Cr, Cd, Cu, and Hg in the 157 samples were 21.19, 0.33, 19.58, and 0.12 mg/kg, respectively. Compared with the median concentrations, St. Bernard Parish had higher Cr, Cd, and Cu (more than 91% of the sampling sites had at least one sample with Cr, Cd, or Cu higher than the median). Plaquemines Parish had higher Cr and Cu (91% of the sampling sites had at least one sample with Cr greater than the median; for Cu, the ratio was 82%). Orleans Parish had higher Hg concentrations (84% of its sampling sites had at least one sample with Hg higher than the median). The high Cr, Cd, and Cu concentrations in St. Bernard Parish and Plaquemines Parish were attributed to the industrial practices in these two regions. The higher Hg concentration in Orleans Parish could be caused by the waste disposal (such as landfill), and gasoline from concentrated traffic in this region.

3.6. Correlations of Fe with As, V, and Pb

Correlation analysis showed that iron was significantly correlated ($\alpha = 0.05$) to both As and V in the soil/sediment samples, with corresponding correlation coefficients (r) of 0.54 for Fe vs As, and 0.85 for Fe vs V, respectively (Fig. 3). However, there was no significant correlation ($\alpha = 0.05$) between Fe and Pb ($r < 0.1$).

It should be noted that Fe oxides or hydroxides are strong sorbents of anions such as As or V (Ford et al., 1997). Therefore, As and V can accumulate on the Fe oxide particles in the environment. Our preliminary data using sequential extraction confirmed that As and V are most related to iron oxides fraction. Studies are currently being conducted to determine the details of element binding to different fractions of soil/sediment samples, including those that are exchangeable, bound to carbonate, bound to iron and manganese oxides, bound to organic matter, and the biologically unavailable part that stayed in residue. Camm et al. (2004) also reported that in As-contaminated sites, As was mostly in the form of Fe–As oxides such as scorodite (hydrated $FeAsO_4$) in

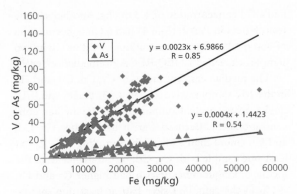

Figure 3. Relationship between V, As, and the iron concentration in soil/sediment samples based on the microwave-assisted acid-digested samples.

soil samples. These studies support the linear correlation found between As and Fe in this study.

3.7. Trace element concentrations in surface, shallow, and deep samples

Five surface samples were collected at 0–1 cm from on top of cars or inside houses. Shallow samples were collected at 0–10 cm on each of our sampling stops. A total of 20 deep samples were collected randomly at 10–20 cm in addition to the shallow core. Comparison between the surface, shallow, and deep samples will indicate how contaminants penetrated into the ground, and/or determine the baseline concentrations of contaminants that were not caused by the flooding. If the element concentration in the deeper sample is the same or greater than that in the surface sample, the element on this sampling spot (the spot where the core was applied) would be hypothesized to have been there before Katrina. On the other hand, if the element concentration is lower in the deeper sample than that in the corresponding surface sample, it might suggest that this sampling point had increased element contamination due to more recent (possibly Katrina-related) deposition.

Comparison of surface (0–1 cm) vs shallow (0–10 cm) samples showed that there was no significant difference ($\alpha = 0.05$) in concentrations for As, Cr, Cu, Cd, Pb, and Hg (although the mean value was always higher for the surface samples than shallow

samples except for Hg). However, V was significantly ($\alpha = 0.05$) greater in the surface samples (0–1 cm) as compared to the shallow (0–10 cm) samples by 43%. Since two out of the five surface samples were collected near parked cars, the higher V in surface samples may have been caused by oil contamination during flooding because V is abundant in gasoline. Comparison of shallow (0–10 cm) vs deep (10–20 cm) samples showed that there was no significant difference for any of the seven elements ($\alpha = 0.05$) between these two types of samples. The Hg concentrations in the deep sample and the surface sample were correlated with each other ($r = 0.81$, $\alpha = 0.05$). This correlation may or may not be due to the increased mobility of this element.

Based on the above observation, the element concentrations in the three types of samples were not very different, indicating that the impact of Katrina on toxic element distribution was not significant.

3.8. Effect of Katrina on toxic element re-distribution in New Orleans

EPA (US EPA, 2007b) reported the typical pre-Katrina background inorganic concentrations in soils for Region 6 (updated in 1997), including Louisiana (shown in Table 1). In our study, percentages of samples with element concentrations exceeding the highest background level were 6% for As, 79% for Pb, 15% for V, 17% for Cr, 49% for Cu, 10% for Cd, and 54% for Hg. This suggested that the trace element concentrations in soil/sediment samples of post-Katrina New Orleans had increased, especially for Pb, Cu, and Hg. The elevation of these toxic element concentrations in our sampling regions is shown in Table 2. Element concentrations in soil/sediment samples in St. Bernard Parish and the Plaquemines Parish generally increased more significantly. Since the EPA Region 6 soil background value was updated 8 years before Hurricane Katrina, the observed elevation of trace element concentrations in the soil/sediment in the studied area may be attributed more by the contamination from the fast-increasing social and industrial development than by Hurricane Katrina.

Table 3

Pre-Katrina and post-Katrina toxic trace element concentrations in soil/sediment in the area between the 17th Street Canal and Industrial Canal of Orleans Parish

Trace element		Pre-Katrina concentration (Wang et al., 2004)[a] (mg/kg)	Post-Katrina concentration[b] (mg/kg)
Pb	Low	3.2	7.55
	High	5195	551.48
	Average	579.7	120.33
Cd	Low	0.3	0.14
	High	6.7	2.05
	Average	2.52	0.55
Cu	Low	2.3	2.77
	High	116	223.42
	Average	34.96	29.83
Cr	Low	0.4	**0.59**
	High	13.9	**46.39**
	Average	2.085	**20.18**
V	Low	0.7	**5.7**
	High	12.2	**82.47**
	Average	5.17	**33.67**

[a]Average concentration was recalculated by combining all their data (Wang et al., 2004) in this area.

[b]Values in bold are substantially higher than the according pre-Katrina values.

Wang et al. (2004) studied the Pb, Cd, Cu, Cr, and V concentrations in soil/sediment in pre-Katrina New Orleans in areas similar to part of our Region 2, which were located between the 17th Street Canal and the Industrial Canal in Orleans Parish. The comparison between the pre-Katrina data and our post-Katrina data in this area is shown in Table 3. The Pb, Cd, and Cu concentrations in post-Katrina samples from Region 2 were lower than those of the pre-Katrina samples. However, Cr and V concentrations increased significantly. The results are consistent with Schwab et al.'s (2007) report for post-Katrina soil/sediment Pb concentrations in the same area. The pre-Katrina As and Hg data are not available in any of our studied regions.

Since there was no soil cleanup action between the time of Wang's pre-Katrina study (Wang et al., 2004) and our post-Katrina study in this region, the decreased Pb, Cd, and Cu in soil/sediment samples could be a result of the dilution by floods. Because Cr and V are widely used in industrial practices (Lazaridis et al., 2003; Marsh and McInerney, 2003), they could be carried to the city by flood water from Industrial Canal and/or Lake Pontchartrain. Another possible contamination source may be from gasoline, because V is abundant in crude oils and Cr is often used as additives in gasoline (Du et al., 1997; Lazaridis et al., 2003). As a result, Hurricane Katrina's impact on the distribution of toxic trace elements in the studied area seems to be typically similar to that of severe storm water.

4. CONCLUSIONS

Results generated in this research suggest that As and V contamination could be a serious issue throughout the Katrina-affected greater New Orleans region due to the large number of sampling sites having at least one sample that exceeded the LDEQ RECAP standards for remediation. No significant Pb, Cd, Cu, Hg, and Cr contamination was found in studied areas, except for few specific sampling locations. Pb contamination at two sites exceeded 400 mg/kg, which suggested the need for immediate attention: one was Site 9 (along the Robert E. Lee Boulevard close to the lakefront), and the other was Site 31 (on Toledano Street close to the river front).

Concentrations of As, V, Cu, and Cr were relatively greater in both St. Bernard Parish and Plaquemines Parish than in other sampling regions. Pb concentrations in both St. Bernard Parish and Orleans Parish were higher. Cd concentrations were relatively higher in St. Bernard Parish. Hg concentrations were greater in Orleans Parish. Data also suggested that toxic element concentrations in the soil/sediment of the Katrina-affected greater New Orleans region had increased significantly since 1997, especially for Pb, Cu, and Hg. Comparison of the toxic trace elements' concentrations in surface, shallow, and deep samples showed no significant difference, indicating Katrina's impact on toxic trace elements re-distribution is not significant. Compared to pre-Katrina studies, Pb, Cd, and Cu concentrations decreased while Cr and V concentrations increased in soil/sediment in Orleans Parish. Both As and V had significant correlations with the total Fe in soil/sediment.

ACKNOWLEDGMENTS

This research was sponsored by a grant from the U.S. Geological Survey (USGS) Mid-Continent Geographic Science Center, through the Geographic Analysis and Monitoring Program. Analyses and additional support were provided by the Environmental Research Center (ERC) at the Missouri University of Science and Technology (formerly University of Missouri–Rolla). Special thanks to the OCSNER Medical Group of New Orleans, Calvin O'Neal and the USGS National Wetland Science Center, Lafayette, Louisiana, for facilitating our sampling effort. Authors also wish to thank Mr. Harmanjit Mallhi for his assistance for mercury analysis. Conclusions and statements made in this paper are those of the authors, and in no way reflect the endorsement of the aforementioned funding agencies. Any use of trade, product, or firm names is for descriptive purposes only and does not imply endorsement by the U.S. Government.

APPENDIX A. SUPPLEMENTARY DATA

Supplementary data associated with this article can be found, in the online version, at http://sciencedirect .com/science/article/pii/S0269749108002595.

REFERENCES

Adams, C., Witt, E.C., Wang, J., Shaver, D.K., Summers, D., Filali-Meknassi, Y., Shi, H., Luna, R., Anderson, N., 2007. Chemical quality of depositional sediments and associated soils in New Orleans and the Louisiana peninsula following Hurricane Katrina. Environmental Science & Technology 41, 3437–3443.

Anonymous, 1995. Lake Pontchartrain Restoration Working. Louisiana Environmentalist Magazine Online Special Features Available from: http://www.leeric.lsu.edu /le/special/pontchartrain.htm.

Brown III, L.R., Brown, Q.C., Miller, R. H., 2000. Effects of arsenic on *Poecilia reticulata*: ecotoxicity and biomagnification in the aquatic food chain in Southeast New Orleans. Abstracts, 220th ACS National Meeting, Washington, DC, August 20–24, 2000.

Camm, G.S., Glass, H.J., Bryce, D.W., Butcher, A.R., 2004. Characterization of a mining-related arsenic-contaminated site, Cornwall, UK. Journal of Geochemical Exploration 82, 1–15.

CDC, 2006a. Public health response to Hurricanes Katrina and Rita—Louisiana, 2005. Morbidity and Mortality Weekly Report 55, 29–30.

CDC, 2006b. Public health response to Hurricanes Katrina and Rita—United States, 2005. Morbidity and Mortality Weekly Report 55, 229–231.

City-data com. Louisiana Business Data. Available from: http://www.city-data.com.

Cobb, G.P., Abel, M.T., Rainwater, T.R., Austin, G.P., Cox, S.B., Kendall, R.J., Marsland, E. J., Anderson, T.A., Leftwich, B.D., Zak, J.C., Presley, S.M., 2006. Metal distributions in New Orleans following hurricanes Katrina and Rita: a continuation study. Environmental Science & Technology 40, 4571–4577.

Connor Jr., P., Maygarden, D., Caridas, V., Penland, S., Kindinger, J., 2002. Bathymetry of south shore Lake Pontchartrain. In: Environment Atlas of the Lake Pontchartrain Basin, U.S. Geological Survey Open-File Report 02–206.

Du, B., Wei, Q., Wang, S., Yu, W., 1997. Application of microemulsions in determination of chromium naphthenate in gasoline by flame atomic absorption spectroscopy. Talanta 44, 1803–1806.

Dubey, B., Solo-Gabriele, H.M., Townsend, T.G., 2007. Quantities of arsenic-treated wood in demolition debris generated by Hurricane Katrina. Environmental Science & Technology 41, 1533–1536.

Ford, R.G., Bertsch, P.M., Farley, K.J., 1997. Changes in transition and heavy metal partitioning during hydrous iron oxide aging. Environmental Science & Technology 31, 2028–2033.

Lazaridis, N.K., Jekel, M., Zouboulis, A.I., 2003. Removal of Cr(VI), Mo(VI), and V(V) ions from single metal aqueous solutions by sorption or nanofiltration. Separation Science and Technology 38, 2201–2219.

LDEQ, 2003. LDEQ RECAP Table 1 Screening Standards for Soil and Groundwater. Available from: http://www.deq.louisiana.gov/portal/Portals/0/technology/recap/2003/RECAP%202003%20Text%20Table%201.pdf.

Marsh, T.L., McInerney, M.J., 2003. Microbial transformations of hexavalent chromium. Recent Research Developments in Microbiology 7, 499–529.

McCaskill, J.R., 2006. Natural disasters and oil: the effect of Hurricane Katrina on oil production in the Gulf of Mexico. Submitted to GP200A. Available from: http://srb.stanford.edu/nur/GP200A%20Papers/jolene_mccaskill.pdf.

Mielke, H.W., Gonzales, C.R., Smith, M.K., Mielke Jr., P.W., 1999. The urban environment and children's health: soils as an integrator of lead, zinc, and cadmium in New Orleans, Louisiana, USA. Environmental Research 81, 117–129.

Mielke, H.W., Powell, E.T., Gonzales, C.R., Mielke Jr., P.W., Ottesen, R.T., Langedal, M., 2006. New Orleans soil lead (Pb) cleanup using Mississippi River alluvium: need, feasibility and cost. Environmental Science & Technology 40, 2784–2789.

OMB Watch, 2004. Potential small-source toxic chemical sites in New Orleans. Available from: http://www.ombwatch.org/info/NewOrleans/smalltoxic.html.

OMB Watch, 2005. Toxic chemical sites in New Orleans. Available from: http://www.ombwatch.org/article/articleview/3088.

Pardue, J.H., Moe, W.M., Mcinnis, D., Thibodeaux, L.J., 2005. Chemical and microbiological parameters in New Orleans floodwater following Hurricane Katrina. Environmental Science & Technology 39, 8591–8599.

Perez-Benito, J.F., 2006. Effects of chromium(VI) and vanadium(V) on the lifespan of fish. Journal of Trace Elements in Medicine and Biology 20, 161–170.

Plumlee, G.S., Meeker, G., Demas, C.R., Foreman, W.T., Lovelace, J.K., Hageman, P.L., Morman, S.A., Lamothe, P.J., Sutley, S., Breit, G.N., Brownfield, I., Furlong, E.T., Goldstein, H., Adams, M., Rosenbauer, R.J., Nilsen, E., 2006. Sources, mineralogy, chemistry, environmental reactivity, and metal bioaccessibility of flood sediments deposited in the New Orleans area by hurricanes Katrina and Rita. In: Proceedings, 232nd ACS National Meeting, San Francisco, CA.

Presley, S.M., Rainwater, T.R., Austin, G.P., Platt, S.G., 2006. Assessment of pathogens and toxicants in New Orleans, LA, following Hurricane Katrina. Environmental Science & Technology 40, 468–474.

Schwab, K.J., Gibson, K.E., Williams, D.L., Kulbicki, K.M., Lo, C.P., Mihalic, J.N., Breysse, P.N., Curriero, F.C., Geyh, A.S., 2007. Microbial and chemical assessment of regions within New Orleans, LA, impacted by Hurricane Katrina. Environmental Science & Technology 41, 2401–2406.

ULI, 2005. A strategy for rebuilding New Orleans, LA. Drafted report for review, subject to technical editing. Available from: http://law.wustl.edu/landuselaw/Articles/ULI_Draft_New_Orleans%20Report.pdf.

US Census Bureau, 2000. Census data used: year 2000. Available from: http://quickfacts.census.gov/qfd/states/22/2255000.html.

US EPA, 1994. Determination of trace elements in waters and wastes by inductively coupled plasma—mass spectrometry, v5.4. EPA Method 200.8.

US EPA, 2000. CAS high priority bright line screening table. Available from: http://www.epa.gov/earth1r6/6pd/rcra_c/pd-o/capp-dhpblt.pdf, p. 24.

US EPA, 2002. Mercury in water by oxidation, purge and trap, and cold vapor atomic fluorescence spectrometry. EPA Method 1631 Rev. E. EPA-821-R-02-019.

US EPA, 2007a. Microwave-assisted acid digestion of sediments, sludges, soils, and oils. EPA Method 3051A.

US EPA, 2007b. EPA region 6 human health medium—specific screening levels. Available from: http://www.epa.gov/region6/6pd/rcra_c/pd-n/r6screenbackground.pdf.

US EPA, 2008. Region 6 human health medium—specific screening levels 2008. Available from: http://www.epa.gov/Region6/6pd/rcra_c/pd-n/screenvalues.pdf.

Wang, G., Mielke, H.W., Quach, V., Gonzales, C., Zhang, Q., 2004. Determination of polycyclic aromatic hydrocarbons and trace metals in New Orleans soils and sediments. Soil & Sediment Contamination 13, 313–327.

Williams, S.J., 2002. Lake Pontchartrain Basin: Bottom Sediments and Regional Scientific and Educational Resources. U.S. Geological Survey Open-file Report No. 98-805.

Reading Questions

1. In the Introduction section of their report, Su et al. provide an overview of research that has taken place on the issue of toxic element contamination in New Orleans. What do the authors suggest their article contributes to the professional discussion of this topic that is new?

2. In your own words, describe the data collection methods followed by the researchers in this study. Then briefly describe the procedures the researchers used to analyze that data.

3. The Results and Discussion section of this professional report includes a number of tables. Look carefully at Table 3. How do Su et al. rationalize the reduced levels of Pb, Cd, and Cu in post-Katrina Region 2?

4. Look at the Conclusions section of the study again, and make a list of findings that the researchers indicate are "significant."

Rhetoric Questions

5. The report produced by Su et al. is clearly intended for an audience of the researchers' peers. However, how do you think the findings of this research might be useful for another audience—say, a residential zoning board, or city planners? Identify other potential audiences for this research report or its findings.

6. Look at the study's abstract. Compare the construction of the abstract to the description of what is conventional content for an abstract on pages 174–75 of this text. Do you see anything extra in this professional example? Does anything appear to be left out?

7. Identify what you believe to be the study's hypothesis. Assess the appropriateness of the researchers' placement of their hypothesis in their report.

Response and Research Questions

8. If possible, access the study's supplementary data at the weblink provided under "Appendix A. Supplementary Data." What kind of data is there, and what do you think is the purpose behind providing this additional data?

9. Identify an organization that could benefit from an awareness of this study's results. Describe the organization and the ways it could potentially benefit.

Posttraumatic Stress Disorder after Hurricane Katrina

JACQUELINE RHOADS, FAYE MITCHELL, AND SUSAN RICK

Dr. Jacqueline Rhoads is a registered nurse and professor at the Louisiana State University Health Science Center School of Nursing. The following article was written and published with her colleagues, Faye Mitchell and Susan Rick, who are also professors and clinical nurse specialists, in the *Journal for Nurse Practitioners* (January 2006). In addition to peer-reviewed research reports, the journal publishes articles designed to support the continuing education of nurse practitioners. In this instance, the authors provide nurses with insight into the signs and symptoms of post-traumatic stress disorder (PTSD) in the aftermath of Hurricane Katrina in an effort "to prevent serious sequelae that can disrupt and even end a person's life."

ABSTRACT

All who viewed the horror caused by Hurricane Katrina could see the reactions of terror, paralysis, loss, and grief. For those who lived through the event itself, these same symptoms are often continued as the survivor relives the horror over and over again. Posttraumatic stress disorder (PTSD) is a psychological and physical reaction to a stressful event that any of us might face, whether we live through it or just witness it repeatedly on television. But emotional distress differs from posttraumatic stress disorder. Why do some persons suffer more extensively? How do you tell when someone has PTSD? How can you help? The lessons learned in the aftermath of this terrible natural disaster may be applied to many other situations for patients or providers alike.

For a week the country watched Hurricane Katrina, packing 160 mph winds, move slowly toward New Orleans with an expected landfall as a Category 4 or 5 sometime Monday morning, August 29. About 1.3 million persons live in New Orleans and its suburbs, and many began evacuating before Sunday morning; others waited to see whether the storm would turn as storms had done in the past seasons.[1] By Sunday evening, nearly 1 million persons had fled the city and its surrounding parishes. Between 20,000 and 25,000 others remained in the city and sought shelter in the Louisiana Superdome, lining up for what they thought would be an uncomfortable but bearable 2 to 4 days.[1] Approximately 20,000 stranded tourists were told to remain in the city's hotels, on third-floor levels or higher, and away from windows.[1] Any hopes of evacuation out of the city were clearly impossible.

Two days after the hurricane a reporter from Fox News correctly estimated the death toll in the thousands and the damage higher than $200 billion, topping Hurricane Andrew as the most expensive natural disaster in US history.[1] More than a million persons had been displaced—a huge humanitarian crisis unseen in the United States since the Great Depression.[1] No large American city had ever been evacuated since Richmond and Atlanta in the Civil War.[1]

STORM'S EFFECTS ON THE PEOPLE OF NEW ORLEANS

The people who directly experienced the hurricane's effects can be seriously affected by the storm's psychological effects. Many of these people have now been displaced from their homes and are being cared for in new communities. Although these people will suffer the most, some other persons who only witnessed the effects of the hurricane repeatedly on television may also be at risk of posttraumatic stress disorder (PTSD). They all may encounter behavioral and emotional readjustment problems that are normal responses to the hurricane's aftermath. Their exposure to the stress of the storm can change their focus and create confusion about what they need to do.[2] How serious these effects will be depend on such things as each person's overall ability to cope with stress, how serious the traumatic event was, and what kind of help and support he or she gets from family, friends, and professionals following the trauma.[2]

Most survivors will think the feelings they have are indications they are having a nervous breakdown or that there is something wrong with them because other persons who experienced the same trauma do not appear to be experiencing the same feelings. Some may turn to drugs or alcohol to make them feel or rest better. Others may turn away from friends and family who do not seem to be as affected or understand what they are feeling.[2]

The Katrina survivors from New Orleans faced not only the danger of death and physical injury but also the loss of their homes, possessions, and communities. Many were separated from their families and were moved to shelters far away from the life that was familiar.

Even before the hurricane, New Orleans was recorded in the *Louisiana Health Care Report Card* as a city with many poor, impoverished persons. Many environmental, social, and economic factors contribute to the ranking of New Orleans and the State of Louisiana at the top of the charts of poor health outcomes.[3] The median family income for New Orleans residents is $22,276.[3] Approximately 34% of family households are at or below the poverty level.[3] In the entire state, one in three children lives in poverty.[3] In New Orleans, that number changes to about one in two.[3] Ninety-seven percent of Louisiana parishes are designated as either totally or partially medically underserved.[3]

Hurricane Katrina only added to the stress of the poor, for they were the ones most affected. They were the ones stranded on the overpasses, roofs, and in the Superdome and Convention Center without food or water. They were the ones who became overwhelmed with fear and a sense of hopelessness.

Unfortunately, these also are the persons who most likely will mentally and physically reexperience the trauma. These feelings make them more susceptible to PTSD.[2]

POSTTRAUMATIC STRESS DISORDER

PTSD is different from most mental health diagnoses in that it is tied to a particular traumatic life experience that typically involves the potential for death or serious injury.[4] Several types of experiences and the

Table 1

Percentage of persons experiencing disasters who are diagnosed with PTSD[2,4]

Event	Percentage
Bombing	34
Mass shooting	33
Plane crash	29
Violent assault	19
Motor vehicle accident	14
Assault, burn, industrial accident	13
Natural disaster	4–5

percentage of survivors who develop PTSD are listed in Table 1. These experiences result in intense fear, helplessness, or horror. It is reasonable to expect that many of those most affected by Hurricane Katrina will have one or more of the common stress reactions for several days and possibly weeks (Box 1).[2,5] Patients may experience temporary psychological reactions, cognitive reactions, physical complaints, or changes in psychosocial behavior that cause them to avoid large crowds or social activities at which they may be asked about the event.[4] Work is often impaired or the person calls in sick to avoid any chances for recall.[4]

Most who were affected by Hurricane Katrina will most likely experience only mild, normal stress reactions. The literature[2,4-6] documents that in many instances disaster experiences can promote personal growth and strengthen relationships. However, one of every three persons who experienced this disaster will have symptoms that are more than the normal stress reactions—what is called PTSD.[4]

WHO IS AT RISK

By just watching the television the first few days after Hurricane Katrina, it is evident that the experiences of New Orleans residents place them at a higher than normal risk of severe stress symptoms and lasting PTSD. Other persons who watched the event

Box 1. Common symptoms of reactions to traumatic stress

Emotional Reactions

Shock

Terror

Irritability

Blame

Anger

Guilt

Grief or sadness

Emotional numbing

Helplessness

Loss of pleasure derived from familiar activities

Difficulty feeling happy

Difficulty experiencing loving feelings

Cognitive Reactions

Impaired concentration

Impaired decision-making ability

Memory impairment

Disbelief

Confusion

Nightmares

Decreased self-esteem

Decreased self-efficacy

Self-blame

Intrusive thoughts or memories

Worry

Dissociation (e.g., tunnel vision, dreamlike or "spacey" feeling)

Physical Reactions

Fatigue, exhaustion

Insomnia

Cardiovascular strain

Startle response

Hyperarousal

Increased physical pain

Reduced immune response

Headaches

Gastrointestinal upset

Decreased appetite

Decreased libido

Vulnerability to illness

Psychosocial Reactions

Increased relational conflict

Social withdrawal

Reduced relational intimacy

Alienation

Impaired work or school performance

Decreased satisfaction

Distrust

Externalization of blame

Externalization of vulnerability

Feeling abandoned/rejected

Overprotectiveness

Note. Modified from the *Disaster Mental Health Response Handbook*[2] and Young et al.[5]

repeatedly on television also feel a sense of hopelessness, shock, and despair. This is especially true if they have had a history of exposure to other traumas (such as severe accidents, abuse, assault, combat, rescue work); chronic medical illness or psychological disorders; chronic poverty, homelessness, unemployment, or discrimination; recent or subsequent major life stressors or emotional strain (such as single parenting), which many did.[6] It will bring back memories of other times or other traumas that will intensify current problems, including magnitude, duration, and type of traumatic exposure. Variables such as age when exposed to the trauma and a lower level of education are also associated with increased risk of developing PTSD.[7]

Additional factors related to vulnerability for developing PTSD include severity of initial reaction; peritraumatic dissociation (i.e., feeling numb and having a sense of unreality during and shortly after a trauma); early conduct problems; childhood adversity; family history of psychiatric disorder; poor social support after a trauma; and personality traits such as hypersensitivity, pessimism, and negative reactions to stressors.[7] Women are more likely to develop PTSD than men, independent of exposure type and level of stressor, and a history of depression in women increases the vulnerability for developing PTSD.[7]

Although exposure to a traumatic event may result in an increased vulnerability to subsequent traumas, several studies have also reported that exposure to trauma can have an inoculation effect and strengthen a person's protective factors.[4] This occurs when a person has experience in successfully mastering traumatic events.[7]

School-aged children show greater psychological impairment after disasters than do adults.[7] A longitudinal study of young children and adolescents exposed to Hurricane Andrew found that younger children are at greater risk of PTSD than older adults. Studies of the effects after Hurricane Hugo showed that age interacted with most stressors (e.g., life threat, injury, loss).[7-9] Middle-aged persons experienced the highest levels of disaster-related symptoms of depression, anxiety, and posttraumatic stress. A study of firefighters by Ursano et al.[10] showed that psychosocial resources, such as hardiness, perceived control, and social support, afford critical protection for disaster victims.[10]

Several factors can aggravate stress reactions and increase the risk of developing negative outcomes.[4] These factors include lack of support before and after the disaster, poor coping strategies before the event, bad experiences at the scene of the disaster, lack of information about the disaster, and impersonal attention to the victims[4] (Table 2).

PHASES OF PTSD

Published studies[4,7-10,12] have identified the following phases of PTSD:

- Phase 1: Impact
- Phase 2: Immediate postdisaster: recoil and rescue

- Phase 3: Recovery
- Phase 4: Problematic stress responses

Each phase has significant signs and symptoms that assist the health care provider in diagnosing the disorder.[4,7-10,12]

Phase 1: Impact

Most persons respond appropriately during the impact of a disaster and react to protect their own lives and the lives of others. This is a natural and basic reaction.[11] They may cry, panic, or run away, and these behaviors need to be addressed in the postdisaster period.[4] After the fact, persons may judge their actions during the disaster as inappropriate or foolish or not having fulfilled their own or others' expectations.[4] They may be disorganized and in shock and may not be able to respond appropriately to protect themselves. Such fragmented behavior may be short-lived or last indefinitely.[4]

The person may experience several events that may compound the traumatic event. For example, threat to life and encounters with death; feelings of helplessness and powerlessness; loss (e.g., loved ones, home, possessions), dislocation (i.e., separation from loved ones, home, familiar settings, neighborhood, community); feeling responsible (e.g., feeling as though more could have been done); inescapable horror (e.g., being trapped or tortured); and human malevolence. (It is particularly difficult to cope with a disaster if it is seen as the result of deliberate human actions.[4])

Phase 2: Immediate Postdisaster: Recoil and Rescue

During this phase, witnesses recoil from the impact, and the initial rescue activities commence.[4] Initial mental effects may appear (e.g., persons show confusion, are stunned, or show levels of high anxiety).[4] Emotional reactions will depend on how the person responds to those events. The emotional reactions may include numbness, denial or shock, flashbacks and nightmares, grief reactions to loss, anger, despair, sadness, or hopelessness.[4] In this phase relief and survival may lead to feelings of joy, which may be difficult to accept in the face of the destruction the disaster has wrought. These feelings of joy may

Table 2

Factors that affect risk of PTSD[2]

Factors That Increase Chance of PTSD	Factors That Decrease Chance of PTSD
Specific	Social support
Lack of emotional and social support	Higher income and education
Presence of other stressors such as fatigue, cold, hunger, fear, uncertainty, loss, dislocation, and other psychologically stressful experiences	Successful mastery of past disasters and traumatic events
Difficulties at the scene	Limited exposure to any stressor that may precipitate PTSD
Lack of information about the nature and reasons for the event	Provision of information about expectations and availability of recovery services
Lack of or interference with self-determination and self-management	Care, concern, and understanding on the part of the recovery services personnel
Treatment [given] in an authoritarian or impersonal manner	Provision of regular and appropriate information about the emergency and reasons for action
Lack of follow-up support in the weeks after the exposure	
General	
Female sex	
Age of 40 to 60 years	
Little previous experience or training relevant to coping with disaster	
Ethnic minority	
Low socioeconomic status	
Children present in the home	
For women, the presence of a spouse, especially if he is significantly distressed	
Psychiatric history	
Severe exposure to the disaster, especially injury, life threat, and extreme loss	
Living in a highly disrupted or traumatized community	
Secondary stress and resource loss	

make the person feel guilty or shameful that he or she survived or were able to escape without problems (survivor's guilt).[4]

Phase 3: Recovery

The recovery phase is the prolonged period of adjustment or return to normalcy that everyone must go through.[4] It begins when rescue is completed and persons face the task of getting their lives and activities back to normal. Much of what happens during this phase depends on the extent of devastation that has occurred, as well as injuries and lives lost.[4]

During this phase, the person receives the aid that usually comes after disaster. The disillusionment phase sets in when the disaster is no longer on the front pages of newspapers and attention is gone.[4] Then the person becomes withdrawn, and the realities of loss, bureaucratic constraints, and the changes caused by the disaster become evident, and, in many cases, overwhelming.[4]

During acute danger the person's priority is basic safety and survival. Once this is secured, other needs emerge that are physical, social, and psychological. These needs are typically left frustrated and unfulfilled for a prolonged period. This frustration may result in feelings of retribution or violence that place the person or others in the community in greater jeopardy for PTSD.[4]

Emotional needs are very important, especially for those who have been severely affected, and may only start to appear during this phase. Persons may also be hesitant to express their needs, feeling they should be grateful for the aid given or because they have suffered less than others have. Note that sometimes these emotional reactions may present as physical health symptoms, such as sleep disturbance, indigestion, and fatigue, or they may present as social distress, such as relationship or work difficulties.[4]

However, some persons during this phase also show resilience, relief, and elation at surviving disaster; a sense of excitement and a feeling of greater self-worth; changes in the way they view the future; and feelings of "learning about one's strengths" and growing from the experience.[4]

Phase 4: Problematic Stress Responses

In the fourth phase responses that are less common are seen and indicate that the person will likely need assistance from a medical or mental health care provider.[4] These responses include the following:

- Severe dissociation (feeling as if the world is unreal, not feeling connected to own body, losing sense of identity or taking on a new identity, amnesia)[4]
- Severe intrusive reexperiencing (flashbacks, terrifying screen memories or nightmares, repetitive automatic reenactment)[4]

- Extreme avoidance (agoraphobic-like social or vocational withdrawal, compulsive avoidance)[4]
- Severe hyperarousal (panic episodes, terrifying nightmares, difficulty controlling violent impulses, inability to concentrate)[4]
- Debilitating anxiety (ruminative worry, severe phobias, unshakable obsessions, paralyzing nervousness, fear of losing control or going crazy)[4]
- Severe depression (lack of pleasure in life, feelings of worthlessness, self-blame, dependency, early awakenings)[4]
- Problematic substance use (abuse or dependency, self-medication)[4]
- Psychotic symptoms (delusions, hallucinations, bizarre thoughts or images)[4]

Some persons will be more affected by a traumatic event for a longer period than others, depending on the nature of the event and the physical and mental condition of the person who experienced it. It is during this phase that PTSD is often diagnosed, with severity depending on how vulnerable the person is, how well he or she copes with stress, and the degree of exposure to the disaster.[4]

PATHOLOGY OF PTSD

PTSD is marked by clear biological changes and psychological symptoms and is complicated because it frequently occurs in conjunction with related disorders such as depression, substance abuse, problems of memory and cognition, and other problems of physical and mental health.[4] The disorder is also associated with an impaired ability to function in social or family life, leading to occupational instability, marital problems and divorces, family discord, and difficulties in parenting. Common traumatic stress reactions are listed in Box 1.[2,5]

Stable neurobiological alterations in both the central and autonomic nervous systems, such as altered brain wave activity, decreased volume of the hippocampus, and abnormal activation of the amygdala, are seen in those with PTSD.[4] Both the hippocampus and the amygdala are involved in the processing and integration of memory. The amygdala is involved in coordinating the body's fear response.[4] Psychophysiological alterations associated with PTSD include hyperarousal of the sympathetic nervous system, increased sensitivity of the startle reflex, and sleep abnormalities.[4]

Persons with PTSD tend to have abnormal levels of key hormones involved in the response to stress.[4] Increased thyroid function seems to be present with PTSD. Some studies have shown that cortisol levels in those with PTSD are lower than normal, and epinephrine and norepinephrine levels are higher than normal.[4] Persons with PTSD also continue to produce higher than normal levels of natural opiates after the trauma has passed.[4] An important finding is that the neurohormonal changes seen in PTSD are distinct from, and actually opposite to, those seen in major depression.[4]

PTSD is associated with the increased likelihood of co-occurring psychiatric disorders. In a large-scale study,[4] 88% of men and 79% of women with PTSD met criteria for another psychiatric disorder. The co-occurring disorders most prevalent for men with PTSD were alcohol abuse or dependence (51.9%), major depressive episodes (47.9%), conduct disorders (43.3%), and drug abuse and dependence (34.5%). The disorders most frequently comorbid with PTSD among women were major depressive disorders (48.5%), simple phobias (29%), social phobias (28.4%), and alcohol abuse or dependence (27.9%).[4] PTSD also significantly affects psychosocial functioning, independent of comorbid conditions, and includes problems in family and other interpersonal relationships, with employment, and involvement with the criminal justice system.[4]

Headaches, gastrointestinal complaints, immune system problems, dizziness, chest pain, and discomfort in other parts of the body are common in persons with PTSD. Often, medical doctors treat the symptoms without being aware that they stem from PTSD.[13]

DIAGNOSING PTSD

Unlike the common and milder response to trauma that anyone might experience, the criteria in the *Diagnostic and Statistical Manual of Mental Disorders (DM-IV-TR)*[11] for PTSD are long and complex (Box 2). The symptoms are divided into six criteria groups, and persons must display symptoms within each criterion. Diagnostic assessment of PTSD involves careful assessment of symptoms and relation to criterion; persons first describe experiencing a trauma (criterion A1) and then report whether their reactions are of fear, helplessness, or horror (criterion A2).[11] If either part of criterion A is not met, the diagnosis of PTSD cannot be made; therefore, asking persons about criteria B (five reexperiencing symptoms), C (seven avoidance symptoms), D (five arousal symptoms), E, and F is not indicated. But if criterion A is identified, the other criteria should be examined.[11]

Criterion A: The Experience

With criterion A, a person has been exposed to a catastrophic event involving actual or threatened death or injury, or a threat to the physical integrity of him/herself or others. During this traumatic exposure, the survivors will experience intense fear, helplessness, or horror.

Criterion B: The Traumatic Event Is Persistently Reexperienced

Criterion B includes symptoms that are easily identified symptoms of PTSD: the traumatic event remains, sometimes for decades or a lifetime, a dominating factor in the person's psychological status, with the ability to cause panic, terror, dread, grief, or despair whenever the person is reexposed to trauma-related stimuli. These emotions manifest in daytime fantasies, traumatic nightmares, and flashbacks. Flashbacks evoke mental images, emotional responses, and psychological reactions associated with the trauma. Some severely traumatized individuals may dissociate during a stressor or have a blunted response due to defensive avoidance and numbing. Often, the intense emotional response to the stressor may not occur

Box 2. PTSD symptoms

1. Exposure to an event that threatened life of self or others
2. Event was reexperienced through nightmares, flashbacks, or recurring memories
3. Individual avoids anything that might trigger memory of the trauma
   - Drugs, ETOH
   - Decreased memory
   - Flat affect
4. Individual has symptoms of hyperactive states:
   - Insomnia
   - Anger—outbursts
   - Difficulty concentrating

until considerable time has elapsed after the incident has terminated.

Criterion C: Persistent Avoidance of Stimuli Associated with the Trauma and Numbing of General Responsiveness

This criterion consists of symptoms that reflect behavioral, cognitive, or emotional responses PTSD patients use in an attempt to reduce the chances that they will be exposed to anything that resembles the trauma-related stimuli. They will attempt to minimize the intensity of their psychological response by avoiding any situation in which they perceive a risk of confronting trauma-related stimuli. This may involve individuals cutting off the conscious experience of trauma-based memories and feelings. Individuals may also have diminished interest in once significant activities and may have a sense of a foreshortened future. Finally, because individuals with PTSD cannot tolerate strong emotions, especially those associated with the traumatic experience, they separate the cognitive from the emotional aspects of psychological experience and perceive only the former. Such "psychic numbing" is an emotional anesthesia that makes it extremely difficult for people with PTSD to participate in meaningful interpersonal relationships.

Criterion D: Persistent Symptoms of Increased Arousal (not present before the trauma)

Symptoms included in Criterion D most closely resemble those seen in panic and generalized anxiety disorders. While symptoms such as insomnia and irritability are generic anxiety symptoms, hyper-vigilance and startle are more characteristic of PTSD. The hyper-vigilance in PTSD may sometimes become so intense it may appear like paranoia. This hyper-vigilance response can actually be the most significant PTSD symptom. These individuals also have difficulty concentrating.

Criterion E

The duration of the disturbance (symptoms in criteria B, C, and D) is more than 1 month.

Criterion F: Functional Ability

Criterion F, or functional ability, specifies that the survivor must experience significant social, occupational, or other distress as a result of these symptoms. This means that the symptoms must endure for more than 1 month. They must cause clinically significant distress or impairment in social, occupational, or other important areas of functioning.

A diagnosis of acute PTSD will involve the presence of symptoms for less than 3 months. If symptoms persist for 3 months or more a chronic PTSD diagnosis is noted. Delayed onset of PTSD occurs when the symptoms occur at least 6 months after the stressor.

TREATMENT

The most common therapeutic protocol for patients with PTSD was published in the comprehensive book on PTSD treatment by Foa, Keane, and Friedman.[15] The protocol includes cognitive-behavioral therapy (CBT) and medication. Excellent results have been obtained with some CBT combinations of exposure therapy and cognitive restructuring, especially with female victims of childhood or adult sexual trauma.[14] Sertraline (Zoloft) and paroxetine (Paxil) are selective serotonin reuptake inhibitors (SSRIs) that are the first medications to receive approval by the Food and Drug Administration as indicated treatments for PTSD. Success was reported with eye movement desensitization and reprocessing (EMDR), although rigorous scientific data are lacking, and it is unclear whether this approach is as effective as CBT.[15]

Perhaps the best therapeutic option for mildly to moderately affected patients with PTSD is group therapy. In such a setting, the patient with PTSD can discuss traumatic memories, symptoms, and functional deficits with others who have had similar experiences. This approach was most successful with war veterans, rape or incest victims, and survivors of natural disaster.[14] It is important that therapeutic goals be realistic because, in some cases, PTSD is a chronic and severely debilitating psychiatric disorder that is refractory to current available treatments. The hope remains, however, that growing knowledge about PTSD will enable the design of interventions that are more effective for all patients with this disorder.[14]

Currently, there is controversy about which interventions work best during the immediate aftermath of a trauma. Research on critical incident stress debriefing (CISD), an intervention used widely, has brought disappointing results with respect to its efficacy to attenuate posttraumatic distress or to forestall the later development of PTSD. Promising results have been shown with brief CBT.[15]

Families are extremely important systems, and it is most important that postdisaster treatment and intervention efforts be aimed at the family unit. Outreach efforts for intensive services should focus on areas where at-risk persons and families are most likely to live. Treatments and interventions known to be effective for them should be implemented. It is important to provide support also to the families, especially wives and mothers, of persons with PTSD.[15]

CONCLUSION

Traumas happen to many competent, healthy, strong, good persons. No one can completely protect himself or herself from traumatic experiences. Up to 8% of persons will have PTSD at some time in their lives, and most likely everyone would develop PTSD if they were exposed to trauma that was severe enough.

Because trauma is common, it is important that practitioners consider PTSD in their differential when seeing patients. Prompt recognition of PTSD, the pathology, signs, and symptoms, is important and enables quick action to prevent serious sequelae that can disrupt and even end a person's life.

REFERENCES

[1] Smith S. Fox News Live Broadcast. New York, NY: Fox Broadcasting Company, Twentieth Century Fox Film Corporation; September 2005.

[2] Disaster Mental Health Response Handbook. NSW Health. State Health Publication No: (CMH) 00145. July 2000. Available at: http://www.nswiop.nsw.edu.au.

[3] Louisiana Health Care Report Card. Louisiana Department of Health and Hospitals, Office of Public Health. Baton Rouge, LA: 2003. Available at: http://www.oph.dhh.state.la.us/recordsstatistics/statistics/page359d.html?page=557.

[4] Friedman MJ. National Posttraumatic Stress Disorder: An Overview. A National Center for PTSD Fact Sheet. National Center for PTSD. December 2005. Available at: http://www.ncptsd.va.gov/.

[5] Young BH, Ford JD, Ruzek JI, Friedman MJ, Gusman FD. Disaster Mental Health Services: A Guidebook for Clinicians and Administrators. St Louis, MO: National Center for PTSD, Department of Veteran Affairs Employee Education System; 1998.

[6] Koopman C, Classen CC, Cardena E, Spiegel D. When disaster strikes. J Trauma Stress. 1995;8:29–46.

[7] Norris FH, Friedman MJ, Watson PJ. 60,000 Disaster victims speak: Part II, summary and implications of the disaster mental health research. Psychiatry. 2002;65:240–260.

[8] Bryant RA, Harvey AG. Acute stress disorder: A critical review of diagnostic issues. Clinical Psychol Rev. 1997;17:757–773.

[9] Kessler RC, Sonnega A, Bromet EJ, Hughes M, Nelson CB. Posttraumatic stress disorder in the National Comorbidity Survey. Arch General Psychiatr. 1995;52:1048–1060.

[10] Ursano RJ, Grieger TA, McCarroll JE. Prevention of posttraumatic stress: consultation, training, and early treatment. In: Van der Kolk BA, McFarlane AC, Weisaeth L, editors. Traumatic Stress: The Effects of Overwhelming Experience on Mind, Body, and Society. New York, NY: Guilford Press; 1996. p. 441–462.

[11] DSM-IV-TR 2000: Diagnostic and Statistical Manual of Mental Disorders. 4th Edition. Washington, DC: The American Psychiatric Association Publishing Inc.; 2000. p. 463–468.

[12] Brady KT. Posttraumatic stress disorder and comorbidity: recognizing the many faces of PTSD. J Clin Psychiatry. 1997;58(suppl 9):12–15.

[13] Blank AS Jr. Clinical detection, diagnosis, and differential diagnosis of post-traumatic stress disorder. Psychiatr Clin North Am. 1994:17:351–383.

[14] Friedman MJ. Current and future drug treatment for posttraumatic stress disorder patients. Psychiatr Ann. 1998;28:461–468.

[15] Foa E, Keane T, Friedman MJ. Treatments for PTSD: Practice Guidelines from the International Society for Traumatic Stress Studies. New York, NY: The Guilford Press; 2000.

Reading Questions

1. According to the authors, why are the poor more susceptible to experiencing PTSD?

2. How do the authors estimate the number of individuals who, after enduring the horrors of Hurricane Katrina, could potentially experience symptoms of PTSD, or symptoms beyond the "normal stress reactions" (par. 11)?

3. During what phase of PTSD are individuals often diagnosed?

4. According to the article, what co-occuring disorder is most prevalent in men with PTSD? In women with PTSD?

5. How do the authors differentiate between a diagnosis of acute PTSD and chronic PTSD?

Rhetoric Questions

6. What elements of the article make it read like a traditional academic research report? By contrast, what elements make it read more like a news report?

7. Describe the authors' diction in light of their intended audience.

8. What is the article's central informative purpose? How do you know this? Does the article make an argument? If so, what is it?

Response and Research Questions

9. Study Table 2 (p. 605) of the article carefully. Imagine for a moment that you have just witnessed a traumatic event that could potentially cause you to develop PTSD. Based on the information in the table and your analysis of yourself, identify the factors that would increase or decrease your likelihood of developing PTSD.

10. The authors of this article provide information they believe is important for a specific audience. Imagine for a moment, however, that you need to create a presentation explaining PTSD to a group of law enforcement officers. What information from the article would you include in your presentation? What would you omit? Why?

11. Identify a section in the article that you feel could be presented in the form of a table or box. Create that table or box. Once you're done, write a brief assessment of its usefulness for a potential audience when contrasted with the text version of that section of the article.

WRITING PROJECT **Composing a Research Proposal**

For this assignment, construct a proposal for research that will help others under-stand some aspect of a recent natural disaster or catastrophe. Imagine that your audience is an organization that could potentially fund your research proposal.

As you plan your proposal, use the following questions to help you generate ideas and organize your writing:

- What natural disaster or catastrophe would you like to study? With what specific aspect of the disaster will you engage?

- Why is this a significant topic or phenomenon for your potential readers?

- What have others from your discipline already written about this topic or a similar one?

- What are your research questions? What types of questions might someone from your discipline ask about your topic?

- What type of data will you need to collect to help you engage your research questions?

- How will you collect your data? What research methods will enable you to collect the data that you need?

Use the pieces in this chapter to help guide your writing. Think in particular about the types of research questions that writers from various academic disciplines have posed. Consider also the ways that they designed their studies to engage these questions: What research methods did they use? What type of data did they collect?

As you write, remember that research proposals are persuasive documents. As such, your proposal should be crafted to make your reader want to fund your research. Include the following sections in your proposal, in response to the ques-tions posed above:

- **Introduction**   Use the Introduction to establish the significance of the topic at hand. Provide background and context about the topic. Consider carefully the needs and desires of your target audience.

- **Methods**   Use the Methods section to explain to your audience exactly how you will conduct your research: What are your research questions? How will you go about finding answers to those questions?

- **Conclusion**   Use the Conclusion to reiterate the reasons why you believe it is important to conduct this research. You would probably be well served to underscore the potential positive impacts that the research could have for your target audience.

- **Bibliography**   Use your bibliography of sources to demonstrate that you are educated on the topic, that you are aware of the other major scholarly conver-sations surrounding your topic. The documentation system you follow (MLA, APA, etc.) should be appropriate for your research area.

Writing a Comparative Rhetorical Analysis: Popular and Academic Sources

In this assignment, we invite you to explore rhetorical strategies that writers in this chapter use to address scholarly and popular audiences. Select two pieces from this chapter, and write an essay in which you compare how each writer tailors his or her writing for a specific audience. Choose one piece written for a scholarly audience and one piece written for a popular audience.

Before you begin writing, you might reread each piece carefully with attention to the following questions:

- Who is the intended audience?
- What are the audience's views on the topic before reading the text? What prior knowledge do they bring to their reading experience?
- What belief systems or values inform the audience's views on the topic?
- What is the author's purpose for writing (i.e., to persuade, to inform)?
- What medium was the piece originally published in?
- What type of evidence does the author rely on? Is this the most persuasive type of evidence for the audience?
- What rhetorical strategies does the author use (i.e., word choice, writing voice, tone, evidence) to write most effectively for the intended audience?
- How might the author have written this piece differently for a new audience?

As you read and engage these questions, mark passages in the text that you might use as supporting evidence for your claims. At the same time, jot down your thoughts in the margins or make a comparison chart with a column for each text as you work toward analysis.

Introduce the two articles, and assert a thesis near the beginning of your analysis. Compare and contrast the two articles' rhetoric in the body of your analysis: what structural, reference, and/or language conventions do they employ? In your conclusion, assess the appropriateness of the articles' construction in light of their intended audiences.

Introduction to Documentation Styles

You've likely had some experience with citing sources in academic writing, both as a reader and as a writer. Many students come to writing classes in college with experience only in MLA format, the citation style of the Modern Language Association. The student research paper at the end of Chapter 4 is written in MLA style, which is the most commonly required citation style in English classes. Although MLA is the citation style with which English and writing teachers are usually most familiar, it is not the only one used in academic writing—not by a long shot.

Some students don't realize that other citation styles exist, and they're often surprised when they encounter different styles in other classes. Our goal in this appendix is to help you understand (1) why and when academic writers cite sources and (2) how different citation styles represent the values and conventions of different academic disciplines. This appendix also provides brief guides to MLA, APA (American Psychological Association), and CSE (Council of Science Editors) styles—three styles that are commonly used in the first three chapters in Part Two of this book. These citation styles are discussed in some detail in Chapter 4 as well. Near the end of this appendix, you'll find a table with other citation styles commonly used in different disciplines, including some of the applied fields discussed in Chapter 9.

Why Cite?

There are several reasons why academic writers cite sources that they draw upon. The first is an ethical reason: academic research and writing privilege the discovery of new knowledge, and it is important to give credit to scholars who discover new ideas and establish important claims in their fields of study. Additionally, academic writers cite sources to provide a "breadcrumb trail" to show how they developed their current research projects. Source citations show what prior work writers are building on and how their research contributes to that body of knowledge. If some of the sources are well respected, that ethos helps to support the writers' research as well. It demonstrates that the writers have done their homework; they know what has already been discovered, and they are contributing to an ongoing conversation.

These two values of academic writing—the necessity of crediting the person or persons who discover new knowledge, and the importance of understanding prior work that has led to a specific research project—shape the choices that academic writers make when citing sources. Anytime you quote, summarize, or paraphrase the work of someone else in academic writing, you must give credit to that person's work. *How* academic writers cite those sources, though, differs according to their academic discipline and writing situation.

Disciplinary Documentation Styles

Citation styles reflect the values of specific disciplines, just like other conventions of academic writing that we've discussed in this book. When you compare the similarities and differences in citation styles, you might notice that some conventions of particular citation styles that seemed random before suddenly have meaning. For example, if we compare the ways that authors and publication dates are listed in MLA, APA, and CSE styles, we'll notice some distinctions that reflect the values of those disciplines:

Author's full name

Year of publication listed near the end

MLA

Carter, Michael. "Ways of Knowing, Doing, and Writing in the Disciplines." *College Composition and Communication* 58.3 (2007): 385-418. Print.

Only author's last name included in full

Year included toward the beginning, in a place of importance

APA

Carter, M. (2007). Ways of knowing, doing, and writing in the disciplines. *College Composition and Communication, 58*(3), 385-418.

Only last name given in full, and first and middle initials are not separated from last name by any punctuation

Year also has a place of prominence and isn't distinguished from the name at all, emphasizing that timeliness is as important as the name of the author

CSE

Carter M. 2007. Ways of knowing, doing, and writing in the disciplines. Coll Compos Commun. 58(3):385-418.

MLA lists the author's full name at the beginning of the citation, emphasizing the importance of the author. Date of publication is one of the last items in the citation, reflecting that a publication's currency is often not as important in the humanities as it is in other disciplines. By contrast, APA and CSE list the date of publication near the beginning of the citation in a place of prominence.

Interestingly, CSE does not use any unique punctuation to distinguish the author from the date other than separating them by a period, reflecting that they are of almost equal importance.

Citation styles reflect the values of the respective disciplines. In a very real sense, citation styles are rhetorically constructed: they are developed, revised, updated, and used in ways that reflect the purpose and audience for citing sources in different disciplines. Some rules in documentation styles don't seem to have a clear reason, though, and this is why it's important to know how to verify the rules of a certain system. Our goal is to help you understand, on a rhetorical level, the way three common citation styles work. Memorizing these styles is not always the most productive endeavor, as the styles change over time. Really understanding how they work will be much more useful to you long-term.

Modern Language Association (MLA) Style

WHAT IS UNIQUE ABOUT MLA STYLE?

MLA style is generally followed by researchers in the disciplines of the humanities such as foreign languages and English. One of the unique aspects of MLA style, when compared with other styles, is that the page numbers of quoted, summarized, or paraphrased information are included in in-text citations. While other styles sometimes also include page numbers (especially for exact quotations), the use of page numbers in MLA allows readers to go back to find the original language of the referenced passage. In the disciplines that follow MLA style, the way in which something is phrased is often quite important, and readers might want to review the original source to assess how you are using evidence to support your argument.

We offer some basic guidelines here for using MLA style, but you can learn more about the style guides published by the Modern Language Association, including the *MLA Handbook for Writers of Research Papers* and the *MLA Style Manual and Guide to Scholarly Publishing*, at http://www.mla.org.

IN-TEXT CITATIONS IN MLA STYLE

When sources are cited in the text, MLA style calls for a parenthetical reference at the end of a sentence or at the end of the information being cited (if in the middle of a sentence). The author's name and the page number of the reference appear in parentheses with no other punctuation, and then the end-of-sentence punctuation appears after the parenthetical reference.

> The popularity of crystals and crystallization in chemical research can be traced to the Zantac patent case (Davey 1463).

1. Paraphrase from article

2. Last name of author

3. Page number where paraphrased material can be found

WORKS CITED CITATIONS IN MLA STYLE

The citations list at the end of an academic paper in MLA style is called a Works Cited page. Citations are listed on the Works Cited page in alphabetical order by the authors' last names.

> Davey, Roger J. "Pizzas, Polymorphs, and Pills." *Chemical Communications* 13 (2003): 1463-67. Print.

1. Author's name is listed first, with the last name preceding the first name and any middle initials. The first name is spelled out.

2. Article titles and book chapters are given in quotation marks. All words in the title are capitalized except for articles and prepositions (unless they are the first words). Include a period after the title, inside the last quotation mark.

3. Book, journal, magazine, and newspaper titles appear in italics. No punctuation follows the title.

4. For a journal, the volume number follows the title of the journal. If the journal starts new pagination at the beginning of each issue, include a period and the issue number (13.1).

5. The year of publication appears in parentheses, followed by a colon.

6. Inclusive page numbers are provided in the MLA citation of a journal article, followed by a period.

7. Medium of publication (Print, Web, DVD, etc.) comes last, followed by a period.

CITING DIFFERENT TYPES OF SOURCES IN MLA STYLE

Comparison of Different Kinds of Sources in MLA Style

Type of Source	Example of Works Cited Entry	Notes
Book	Davies, Alice, and Kathryn Tollervey. *The Style of Coworking: Contemporary Shared Workspaces.* Munich: Prestel Verlag, 2013. Print.	When more than one author is listed, only the first author's name is reversed in MLA style.
Book chapter	Hochman, Will, and Mike Palmquist. "From Desktop to Laptop: Making Transitions to Wireless Learning in Writing Classrooms." *Going Wireless: A Critical Exploration of Wireless and Mobile Technologies for Composition Teachers and Researchers.* Ed. Amy C. Kimme Hea. Cresskill: Hampton, 2009. 109-31. Print.	Be sure to list both the book chapter and the title of the book when citing a chapter from an edited collection.
Scholarly journal article	Bemer, Amanda Mertz, Ryan M. Moeller, and Cheryl E. Ball. "Designing Collaborative Learning Spaces: Where Material Culture Meets Mobile Writing Processes." *Programmatic Perspectives* 1.2 (2009): 139-66. Print.	If the source is taken electronically from a database, the database is also listed.
Magazine or newspaper article	Goel, Vindu. "Office Space Is Hard to Find for Newcomers." *New York Times* 2 Apr. 2015: F2. Print.	Periodical articles can differ in print and online, so be sure to cite where you found your version of the article.
Website	Arieff, Allison. "Collaborative Workspaces: Not All They're Cracked Up to Be." *CityLab.* Atlantic Monthly Group, 18 Jan. 2012. Web. 2 Apr. 2015.	
Website with no individual author listed	Sage One. "Eight Ideas for Designing a More Collaborative Workspace." *Microsoft for Work.* Microsoft Corporation, 10 Jul. 2014. Web. 2 Apr. 2015.	When no author is listed, you can begin the citation with the title of the article or site. If an organization or some other entity is sponsoring the article (as in this case), that can be listed as the author.

SAMPLE MLA WORKS CITED PAGE

Works Cited

Arieff, Allison. "Collaborative Workspaces: Not All They're Cracked Up to Be." *CityLab*. Atlantic Monthly Group, 18 Jan. 2012. Web. 2 Apr. 2015.

Bemer, Amanda Mertz, Ryan M. Moeller, and Cheryl E. Ball. "Designing Collaborative Learning Spaces: Where Material Culture Meets Mobile Writing Processes." *Programmatic Perspectives* 1.2 (2009): 139-66. Print.

Davies, Alice, and Kathryn Tollervey. *The Style of Coworking: Contemporary Shared Workspaces*. Munich: Prestel Verlag, 2013. Print.

Goel, Vindu. "Office Space Is Hard to Find for Newcomers." *New York Times* 2 Apr. 2015: F2. Print.

Hochman, Will, and Mike Palmquist. "From Desktop to Laptop: Making Transitions to Wireless Learning in Writing Classrooms." *Going Wireless: A Critical Exploration of Wireless and Mobile Technologies for Composition Teachers and Researchers*. Ed. Amy C. Kimme Hea. Cresskill: Hampton, 2009. 109-31. Print.

Sage One. "Eight Ideas for Designing a More Collaborative Workspace." *Microsoft for Work*. Microsoft Corporation, 10 Jul. 2014. Web. 2 Apr. 2015.

American Psychological Association (APA) Style

WHAT IS UNIQUE ABOUT APA STYLE?

Researchers in many areas of the social sciences and related fields generally follow APA documentation procedures. Although you'll encounter page numbers in the in-text citations for direct quotations in APA documents, you're less likely to find direct quotations overall. Generally, researchers in the social sciences are less interested in the specific language or words used to report research findings than they are in the results or conclusions. Therefore, social science researchers are more likely to paraphrase information from sources than to quote information.

Additionally, in-text documentation in the APA system requires that you include the date of publication for research. This is a striking distinction from the MLA system. Social science research that was conducted fifty years ago may not be as useful as research conducted two years ago, so it's important to cite the date of the source in the text of your argument. Imagine how different the results would be for a study of the effects of violence in video games on youth twenty years ago versus a study conducted last year. Findings from twenty years ago probably have very little bearing on the world of today and would not reflect the same video game content as today's games. Including the date of research publication as part of the in-text citation allows readers to quickly evaluate the currency, and therefore the appropriateness, of the research you reference. Learn more about the *Publication Manual of the American Psychological Association* and the APA itself at http://www.apa.org.

IN-TEXT CITATIONS IN APA STYLE

When sources are cited in the text, APA style calls for a parenthetical reference at the end of a sentence or at the end of the information being cited (if in the middle of a sentence). The author's name and the year of publication are included in parentheses, separated by a comma, and then the end-of-sentence punctuation appears after the parenthetical reference. Page numbers are only included for direct quotations.

> The popularity of crystals and crystallization in chemical research can be traced to the Zantac patent case (Davey, 2003).

1. Paraphrase from article
2. Last name of author
3. Year of publication

Often, the author's name is mentioned in the sentence, and then the year is listed in parentheses right after the author's name.

According to Davey (2003), the popularity of crystals and crystallization in chemical research can be traced to the Zantac patent case.

1. Name of author mentioned in the sentence
2. Year of publication listed in parentheses directly following author's name
3. Paraphrase from article

REFERENCE PAGE CITATIONS IN APA STYLE

The citations list at the end of an academic paper in APA style is called a References page. Citations are listed on the References page in alphabetical order by the authors' last names.

Davey, R. J. (2003). Pizzas, polymorphs, and pills. *Chemical Communications, 13*, 1463-1467.

1. The author's name is listed first, with the last name preceding first and middle initials. Only the last name is spelled out.
2. The year directly follows the name, listed in parentheses and followed by a period.
3. Article titles and book chapters are listed with no punctuation other than a period at the end. Only the first word in the title and any proper nouns are capitalized. If there is a colon in the title, the first word after the colon should also be capitalized.
4. Journal titles appear in italics, and all words are capitalized except articles and prepositions (unless they are the first words). A comma follows a journal title.
5. The volume number follows the title, also in italics. If there is an issue number, it is listed in parentheses following the volume number, but not in italics. This is followed by a comma.
6. Inclusive page numbers appear at the end, followed by a period.

CITING DIFFERENT TYPES OF SOURCES IN APA STYLE

Comparison of Different Kinds of Sources in APA Style

Type of Source	Example of Reference Page Entry	Notes
Book	Davies, A., & Tollervey, K. (2013). *The style of coworking: Contemporary shared workspaces.* Munich: Prestel Verlag.	In APA, multiple authors are linked with an ampersand (&).
Book chapter	Hochman, W., & Palmquist, M. (2009). From desktop to laptop: Making transitions to wireless learning in writing classrooms. In A. C. Kimme Hea (Ed.), *Going wireless: A critical exploration of wireless and mobile technologies for composition teachers and researchers* (pp. 109-131). Cresskill, NJ: Hampton Press.	Be sure to list both the book chapter and the title of the book when citing a chapter from an edited collection.
Scholarly journal article	Bemer, A. M., Moeller, R. M., & Ball, C. E. (2009). Designing collaborative learning spaces: Where material culture meets mobile writing processes. *Programmatic Perspectives, 1*(2), 139-166.	In APA, the journal number is italicized with the journal title, but the issue number (in parentheses) is not.
Magazine or newspaper article	Goel, V. (2015, April 2). Office space is hard to find for newcomers. *The New York Times*, p. F2.	Periodical articles can differ in print and online, so be sure to cite where you found your version of the article.
Website	Arieff, A. (2012, January 18). Collaborative workspaces: Not all they're cracked up to be. *CityLab*. Retrieved from http://www.citylab.com/	
Website with no individual author listed	Sage One. (2014, July 10). Eight ideas for designing a more collaborative workspace [Web log post]. Retrieved from http://blogs.microsoft.com/	When no author is listed for a web-based source, you can begin the citation with the title of the article or site. If an organization or some other entity is sponsoring the article (as in this case), that can be listed as author.

SAMPLE APA REFERENCE PAGE

RUNNING HEAD   7

References

Arieff, A. (2012, January 18). Collaborative workspaces: Not all they're cracked up to be. *CityLab*. Retrieved from http://www.citylab.com/

Bemer, A. M., Moeller, R. M., & Ball, C. E. (2009). Designing collaborative learning spaces: Where material culture meets mobile writing processes. *Programmatic Perspectives, 1*(2), 139-166.

Davies, A., & Tollervey, K. (2013). *The style of coworking: Contemporary shared workspaces*. Munich: Prestel Verlag.

Goel, V. (2015, April 2). Office space is hard to find for newcomers. *The New York Times*, p. F2.

Hochman, W., & Palmquist, M. (2009). From desktop to laptop: Making transitions to wireless learning in writing classrooms. In A. C. Kimme Hea (Ed.), *Going wireless: A critical exploration of wireless and mobile technologies for composition teachers and researchers* (pp. 109-131). Cresskill, NJ: Hampton Press.

Sage One. (2014, July 10). Eight ideas for designing a more collaborative workspace [Web log post]. Retrieved from http://blogs.microsoft.com/

Council of Science Editors (CSE) Style

WHAT IS UNIQUE ABOUT CSE STYLE?

As the name suggests, the CSE documentation system is most prevalent among disciplines of the natural sciences, although many of the applied fields of the sciences, like engineering and medicine, rely on their own documentation systems. As with the other systems described here, CSE requires writers to document all materials derived from sources. Unlike MLA or APA, however, CSE allows multiple methods for in-text citations, corresponding to alternative forms of the reference page at the end of research reports. The three styles—**Citation-Sequence**, **Citation-Name**, and **Name-Year**—are used by different publications. In this book, we introduce you to the Name-Year system.

For more detailed information on CSE documentation, you can consult the latest edition of *Scientific Style and Format: The CSE Manual for Authors, Editors, and Publishers,* and you can learn more about the Council of Science Editors at its website: http://www.councilscienceeditors.org.

IN-TEXT CITATIONS IN CSE STYLE

When sources are cited in the text, CSE style calls for a parenthetical reference directly following the relevant information. The author's name and the year of publication are included in parentheses with no other punctuation.

> The popularity of crystals and crystallization in chemical research can be traced to the Zantac patent case (Davey 2003).

1. Paraphrase from article
2. Last name of author
3. Year of publication

REFERENCE PAGE CITATIONS IN CSE STYLE

The citations list at the end of an academic paper in CSE style is called a References page. Citations are listed on the References page in alphabetical order by the authors' last names.

> Davey RJ. 2003. Pizzas, polymorphs, and pills. Chem Comm.
> 13:1463-1467.

1. The author's name is listed first, with the full last name preceding the first and middle initials. No punctuation separates elements of the name.
2. The year directly follows the name, followed by a period.
3. Article titles and book chapters are listed with no punctuation other than a period at the end. Only the first word in the title and any proper nouns

are capitalized. If there is a colon in the title, the first word after the colon should not be capitalized.

4. Journal titles are often abbreviated, and all words are capitalized. A period follows the journal title.

5. The volume number follows the title. If there is an issue number, it is listed in parentheses following the volume number, but not in italics. This is followed by a colon. No space appears after the colon.

6. Inclusive page numbers appear at the end, followed by a period.

CITING DIFFERENT TYPES OF SOURCES IN CSE STYLE

Comparison of Different Kinds of Sources in CSE Style

Type of Source	Example of Reference Page Entry	Notes
Book	Davies A, Tollervey K. 2013. The style of coworking: contemporary shared workspaces. Munich: Prestel Verlag. 159 p.	Listing the number of pages is optional in CSE, but useful.
Book chapter	Hochman W, Palmquist M. 2009. From desktop to laptop: making transitions to wireless learning in writing classrooms. In: Kimme Hea AH, editor. Going wireless: a critical exploration of wireless and mobile technologies for composition teachers and researchers. Cresskill (NJ): Hampton Press. p. 109-131.	
Scholarly journal article	Bemer AM, Moeller RM, Ball CE. 2009. Designing collaborative learning spaces: where material culture meets mobile writing processes. Prog Persp. 1(2):139-166.	Some journal titles in CSE are abbreviated.
Magazine or newspaper article	Goel V. 2015 Apr 2. Office space is hard to find for newcomers. New York Times (National Ed.). Sect. F:2 (col. 1).	
Website	Arieff A. 2012 Jan 18. Collaborative workspaces: not all they're cracked up to be [Internet]. CityLab; [accessed 2015 Apr 2]. Available from http://www.citylab.com/design/2012/01 /collaborative-workspaces-not-all-theyre -cracked-be/946/	CSE calls for the exact URL and an access date for web-based sources.
Website with no individual author listed	Sage One. 2014. Eight ideas for designing a more collaborative workspace [blog]. Microsoft at Work; [accessed 2015 Apr 2]. Available from http://blogs.microsoft.com/work/2014/07/10 /eight-ideas-for-designing-a-more-collaborative -workspace/	

SAMPLE CSE REFERENCE PAGE

Running head 7

References

Arieff A. 2012 Jan 18. Collaborative workspaces: not all
they're cracked up to be [Internet]. CityLab; [accessed
2015 Apr 2]. Available from http://www.citylab.com
/design/2012/01/collaborative-workspaces-not-all-theyre
-cracked-be/946/

Bemer AM, Moeller RM, Ball CE. 2009. Designing collaborative
learning spaces: where material culture meets mobile
writing processes. Prog Persp. 1(2):139-166.

Davies A, Tollervey K. 2013. The style of coworking:
contemporary shared workspaces. Munich: Prestel
Verlag. 159 p.

Goel V. 2015 Apr 2. Office space is hard to find for newcomers.
New York Times (National Ed.). Sect. F:2 (col. 1).

Hochman W, Palmquist M. 2009. From desktop to laptop:
making transitions to wireless learning in writing
classrooms. In: Kimme Hea AH, editor. Going wireless:
a critical exploration of wireless and mobile technologies
for composition teachers and researchers. Cresskill (NJ):
Hampton Press. p. 109-131.

Sage One. 2014. Eight ideas for designing a more collaborative
workspace [blog]. Microsoft at Work; [accessed 2015
Apr 2]. Available from http://blogs.microsoft.com
/work/2014/07/10/eight-ideas-for-designing-a-more
-collaborative-workspace/

Other Common Documentation Styles

Many disciplines have their own documentation styles, and some are used more commonly than others. The following chart lists a few of the most popular.

Name of Citation Style	Disciplines	Website
American Chemical Society (ACS)	Chemistry and Physical Sciences	http://pubs.acs.org/series/styleguide
American Institute of Physics (AIP)	Physics	http://publishing.aip.org/authors
American Mathematical Society (AMS)	Mathematics	http://www.ams.org/publications/authors
American Medical Association (AMA)	Medicine	http://www.amamanualofstyle.com/
American Political Science Association (APSA)	Political Science	http://www.apsanet.org/Portals/54/files/APSAStyleManual2006.pdf
American Sociological Association (ASA)	Sociology	http://www.asanet.org/documents/teaching/pdfs/Quick_Tips_for_ASA_Style.pdf
Associated Press Stylebook (AP Style)	Journalism	https://www.apstylebook.com/
Bluebook style	Law, Legal Studies	https://www.legalbluebook.com/
Chicago Manual of Style (CMoS)	History and other humanities disciplines	http://www.chicagomanualofstyle.org/
Institute of Electrical and Electronics Engineers (IEEE)	Engineering	http://www.ieee.org/documents/ieeecitationref.pdf

Name of Citation Style	Disciplines	Website
Linguistic Society of America (LSA)	Linguistics	http://www.linguisticsociety.org/files/style-sheet.pdf
Modern Humanities Research Association (MHRA)	Humanities	http://www.mhra.org.uk/Publications/Books/StyleGuide/StyleGuideV3.pdf

TRACKING RESEARCH

There are many useful, free digital tools online that can help you track your research and sources. Three of the best are personalized research-tracking tools and social applications that enable you to find additional resources through other users of the application:

- **Diigo (https://www.diigo.com/)** Diigo is a social bookmarking application that solves two dilemmas faced by many writers. First, you can access all of the bookmarks that you save in a browser on multiple devices. Additionally, you can tag your sources and share them with others. That means you can search using tags (not very different from searching with key words in a database) and find other sources that users of Diigo have tagged with the same words and phrases that you have chosen.

- **Zotero (https://www.zotero.org/)** Zotero is a robust research tool that helps you organize, cite, and share sources with others. You can install Zotero into your web browser and quickly save and annotate sources that you're looking at online. Zotero can help you generate citations, annotated bibliographies, and reference lists from the sources that you have saved.

- **Mendeley (http://www.mendeley.com/)** Similar to Zotero, Mendeley is a free reference manager and academic social network that allows you to read and annotate PDFs on any device.

Your school may also have licenses for proprietary tools such as RefWorks and EndNote, which are also very useful research-tracking applications. Most of these applications can help you generate citations and reference lists as well. However, you need to understand how a documentation style works in order to check what is generated from any citation builder. For example, if you save the title of a journal article as "Increased pizza consumption leads to temporary euphoria but higher long-term cholesterol levels," a citation builder will not automatically change the capitalization if you need to generate a citation in MLA format. You have to be smarter than the application you use.

ACKNOWLEDGMENTS

Text Credits

Barbara L. Allen. "Environmental Justice, Local Knowledge, and After-Disaster Planning in New Orleans." Reprinted from *Technology in Society*, Vol. 29, Issue 2. Copyright © 2007. Reproduced with permission from Elsevier.

Gustavo Arellano. "Taco USA: How Mexican Food Became More American Than Apple Pie." From *Reason Magazine*, June 2012. © 2012 Gustavo Arellano. Reproduced with permission of the author.

Aziz Aris and Samuel Leblanc. "Maternal and Fetal Exposure to Pesticides Associated to Genetically Modified Foods in Eastern Townships of Quebec, Canada." From *Reproductive Toxicology*, Vol. 31, Issue 4, May 2011, pp. 528–33. Copyright © 2011. Reproduced with permission from Elsevier.

Sharon Begley. "Are You Ready for More?" From *Newsweek*, May 29, 2011. Reproduced with permission of the author.

John C. Bernard, Katie Gifford, Kristin Santora, Daria J. Bernard. "Willingness to Pay for Foods with Varying Production Traits and Levels of Genetically Modified Content." From *Journal of Food Distribution Research*, Vol. 40, Issue 2, pp. 1–11. Reproduced by permission of JFDR and the author.

John Broome. "The Ethics of Climate Change." From *Scientific American*, June 1, 2008. © 2008 Scientific American, Inc. All rights reserved. Reproduced with permission.

Mike Brotherton. Excerpt from "Hubble Space Telescope Spies Galaxy/Black Hole Evolution in Action." From press release posted on mikebrotherton.com, June 2, 2008. Reproduced with permission of the author.

Mike Brotherton, Wil Van Breugel, S. A. Stanford, R. J. Smith, B. J. Boyle, Lance Miller, T. Shanks, S. M. Croom, and Alexei V. Filippenko. Excerpt from "A Spectacular Poststarburst Quasar." From *The Astrophysical Journal*, August 1, 1999. Copyright © 1999 The American Astronomical Society. Reproduced with permission of the authors.

Wanda Cassidy, Karen Brown, and Margaret Jackson. "'Under the Radar': Educators and Cyberbullying in Schools." From *School Psychology International*, October 2012, Vol. 33, No. 5, pp. 520–32. Copyright © 2012 Psychology International. Reproduced with permission of SAGE.

Andrew J. Cherlin. Excerpt from "Chapter 1: How American Family Life Is Different." From *The Marriage-Go-Round: The State of Marriage and the Family in America Today*, by Andrew J. Cherlin. Copyright © 2009 Andrew J. Cherlin. Reprinted by permission of Alfred A. Knopf, an imprint of the Knopf Doubleday Publishing Group, a division of Penguin Random House LLC. All rights reserved.

Brent Cunningham. "Pastoral Romance." From *Lapham's Quarterly*, August 15, 2011. Reproduced with permission of the author.

EBSCO Health. "Sample Discharge Orders." From www.ebscohost.com. Reproduced with permission from EBSCO Information Services.

Dana Goodyear. "Grub." From *Anything That Moves: Renegade Chefs, Fearless Eaters, and the Making of a New American Food Culture*, by Dana Goodyear. Copyright © 2013 by Dana Goodyear. Reproduced by permission of Riverhead, an imprint of Penguin Publishing Group, a division of Penguin Random House LLC.

Daniel Gregorowius, Petra Lindemann-Matthies, and Markus Huppenbauer. "Ethical Discourse on the Use of Genetically Modified Crops: A Review of Academic Publications in the Fields of Ecology and Environmental Ethics." From *Journal of Agricultural & Environmental Ethics*, Vol. 25, Issue 3, January 1, 2001, pp. 265–93. © 2011 Springer. Reproduced with kind permission from Springer Science and Business Media.

Arthur L. Greil, Kathleen Slauson-Blevins, and Julia McQuillan. "The Experience of Infertility: A Review of Recent Literature." From *Sociology of Health & Illness*, Vol. 32, Issue 1. Copyright © 2010 by Blackwell Publishing Ltd. Reproduced with permission of Blackwell Publishing Ltd. in the format Book via Copyright Clearance Center.

Barbara Bradley Hagerty. "Inside a Psychopath's Brain: The Sentencing Debate." From an NPR news report originally published on NPR.org on June 30, 2010. © 2010 National Public Radio, Inc. Reproduced with permission of NPR. Any unauthorized duplication is strictly prohibited.

Cyndy Caravelis Hughes and Matthew Robinson. "Perceptions of Law Enforcement Officers on Capital Punishment in the United States." From *International Journal of Criminal Justice Sciences*, Vol. 8, Issue 2, June–December 2013. Reproduced with permission.

Dale Jacobs. "More Than Words: Comics as a Means of Teaching Multiple Literacies." From *English Journal*, Vol. 96, No. 3, January 2007. Copyright © 2007 National Council of Teachers of English. Reproduced with permission.

Michael Owen Jones. "Dining on Death Row: Last Meals and the Crutch of Ritual." From *Journal of American Folklore*, Winter 2014. Copyright © 2014 by the Board of Trustees of the University of Illinois. Reproduced with permission of the University of Illinois Press.

Charles Kerns and Kenneth Ko. "Exploring Happiness at Work." From *Leadership & Organizational Management Journal*. Copyright © 2009. Reproduced with permission of the authors.

Carolyn W. Keys. "Revitalizing Instruction in Scientific Genres: Connection Knowledge Production with Writing to Learn in Science." From *Science Education*, Vol. 83. Copyright © 1999 John Wiley & Sons. Reproduced with permission.

Zenia Kish. "'My FEMA People': Hip-Hop as Disaster Recovery in the Katrina Diaspora." *American Quarterly*, Vol. 61, Issue 3, 2009, 671–92. © 2009 The American Studies Association. Reproduced with permission of Johns Hopkins University Press.

Donatella Marazziti and Domenico Canale. "Hormonal Changes When Falling in Love." From *Psychoneuroendocrinology*, August 2004, Vol. 29, Issue 7, pp. 931–36. Copyright © 2004 Elsevier. Used with permission of Elsevier.

Clark Merrefield. "Should Juvenile Criminals Be Sentenced Like Adults?" From *The Daily Beast*, November 26, 2012. © 2012 The Daily Beast Company LLC. All rights reserved. Reproduced with permission and protected by the copyright laws of the United States. The printing, copying, redistribution, or retransmission of this content without express written permission is prohibited.

Margaret Shandor Miles, Diane Holditch-Davis, Suzanne Thoyre, and Linda Beeber. "Rural African-American Mothers Parenting Prematurely Born Infants: An Ecological Systems Perspective." From *Newborn and Infant Nursing Reviews*, Vol. 5, Issue 3, September 2005, pp. 142–48. Copyright © 2005 Elsevier. Reproduced with permission from Elsevier.

Warren E. Milteer Jr. "The Strategies of Forbidden Love: Family across Racial Boundaries in Nineteenth-Century North Carolina." From *Journal of Social History*, Vol. 47, Issue 3, Spring 2014, by George Mason University. Reproduced with permission of George Mason University in the format "reuse in a book" via Copyright Clearance Center.

Myra Moses. "Lesson Plan" and "IEP." Reproduced with permission of the author.

Kalervo Oberg. Excerpt from "Cultural Shock: Adjustments to New Cultural Environments." From *Practical Anthropology*, 1960, Vol. 7. Copyright © 1960 American Association of Missiology. Reproduced with permission.

Abigail Pesta. "I Survived Prison: What Really Happens behind Bars." From *Marie Claire*, March 19, 2009. © 2009 Hearst Communications. Reproduced with permission.

Cara O. Peters, Jane B. Thomas, and Richard Morris. "Looking for Love on Craigslist: An Examination of Gender Differences in Self-Marketing Online." From *Journal of Marketing Development and Competitiveness*, Vol. 7, Issue 3, 2013. © 2013 North American Business Press. Reproduced with permission.

Michael Pollan. "Why Cook?" From *Cooked: A Natural History of Transformation*, by Michael Pollan. Copyright © 2013 Michael Pollan. Reproduced by permission of Penguin Press, an imprint of Penguin Publishing Group, a division of Penguin Random House LLC.

Brian Powell, Catherine Bolzendahl, Claudia Geist, and Lala Carr Steelman. "Changing Counts, Counting Change: Toward a More Inclusive Definition of Family." From *Counted Out: Same-Sex Relations and Americans' Definitions of Family*. Reproduced with permission of Russell Sage Foundation in the format "republish in a book" via Copyright Clearance Center.

Kevin Rathunde and Mihaly Csikszentmihalyi. "Middle School Students' Motivation and Quality of Experience: A Comparison of Montessori and Traditional School Environments." From *American Journal of Education*, 2005, Vol. 111, Issue 3. Copyright © 2005 University of Chicago Press. Reproduced with permission.

Jacqueline Rhoads, Faye Mitchell, and Susan Rick. "Posttraumatic Stress Disorder after Hurricane Katrina." From *The Journal for Nurse Practitioners*, Vol. 2, Issue 1, pp. 18–26. Copyright © 2006 Elsevier Limited. Reproduced with permission.

Gary Ritchison. "Hunting Behavior, Territory Quality, and Individual Quality of American Kestrels (*Falco sparverius*)." From Eastern Kentucky University Web page. Reproduced with permission of author.

Daniel Sarewitz and Roger A. Pielke Jr. "Rising Tide." From the *New Republic*, January 17, 2005. Reproduced with permission of the authors.

Susan Saulny. "In Strangers' Glances at Family, Tensions Linger." From the *New York Times*, October 13, 2011. © 2011 The New York Times. All rights reserved. Reproduced with permission and protected by the copyright laws of the United States. The printing, copying, redistribution, or retransmission of this content without express permission is prohibited.

Sherry Seethaler and Marcia Linn. "Genetically Modified Food in Perspective: An Inquiry-Based Curriculum to Help Middle School Students Make Sense of Tradeoffs." From *International Journal of Science Education*,

Vol. 26. Copyright © 2004. Reproduced by permission of Taylor & Francis Ltd, http://www.tandfonline.com.

Jack Solomon. "Masters of Desire: The Culture of American Advertising." From *The Signs of Our Time: Semiotics—the Hidden Messages of Environments, Objects, and Cultural Images*, by Jack Fisher Solomon. Copyright © 1988 by Jack Solomon. Reproduced with permission of Tarcher, an imprint of Penguin Publishing Group, a division of Penguin Random House LLC.

Ted Steinberg. "Disasters and Deregulation." From *The Chronicle of Higher Education*, July 21, 2006. Copyright © 2006 The Chronicle of Higher Education. Reprinted with permission.

Tingzhi Su, Shi Shu, Honglan Shi, Jianmin Wang, Craig Adams, and Emitt C. Witt. "Distribution of Toxic Trace Elements." From *Environmental Pollution*,

Vol. 156, Issue 3, December 2008, pp. 944–50. Copyright © 2008. Reproduced with permission from Elsevier.

Benedikt Till and Peter Vitouch. "Capital Punishment in Films: The Impact of Death Penalty Portrayals on Viewers' Mood and Attitude toward Capital Punishment." From *International Journal of Public Opinion Research*. © 2012 Oxford University Press. *International Journal of Public Opinion Research* by World Association for Public Opinion Research. Reproduced with permission of Oxford University Press in the format "reuse in a book/e-book" via Copyright Clearance Center.

Susan K. Whitbourne. "The Myth of the Helicopter Parent." From *Psychology Today, Fulfillment at Any Age* blog, posted February 23, 2013. Reproduced with permission of the author.

Index

LaunchPad Solo Additional video material may be found online in LaunchPad Solo when the ⊙ icon appears.

A

abstracts, 174–75
Academic Case Studies
  Capital Punishment
    applied fields: "Perceptions of Law
      Enforcement Officers on Capital
      Punishment in the United States"
      (Hughes and Robinson), 438–49
    humanities: "Dining on Death Row:
      Last Meals and the Crutch of Ritual"
      (Jones), 396–416
    natural sciences: "Lethal Injection for
      Execution: Chemical Asphyxiation?"
      (Zimmers et al.), 426–38
    social sciences: "Capital Punishment in
      Films: The Impact of Death Penalty
      Portrayals on Viewers' Mood and
      Attitude toward Capital Punishment"
      (Till and Vitouch), 416–26
  Genetically Modified Food
    applied fields: "Genetically Modified
      Food in Perspective: An Inquiry-Based
      Curriculum to Help Middle School
      Students Make Sense of Tradeoffs"
      (Seethaler and Linn), 525–42
    humanities: "Ethical Discourse on the
      Use of Genetically Modified Crops: A
      Review of Academic Publications in the
      Fields of Ecology and Environmental
      Ethics" (Gregorowius et al.), 478–500
    natural sciences: "Maternal and Fetal
      Exposure to Pesticides Associated to
      Genetically Modified Foods in Eastern
      Townships of Quebec, Canada" (Aris
      and Leblanc), 513–24
    social sciences: "Willingness to Pay for
      Foods with Varying Production Traits
      and Levels of Genetically Modified
      Content" (Bernard et al.), 501–13
  Hurricane Katrina
    applied fields: "Posttraumatic Stress
      Disorder after Hurricane Katrina"
      (Rhoads et al.), 601–10
    humanities: "'My FEMA People': Hip-
      Hop as Disaster Recovery in the Katrina
      Diaspora" (Kish), 565–80

Academic Case Studies *(continued)*
  Hurricane Katrina *(continued)*
    natural sciences: "Distribution of Toxic
      Trace Elements" (Su et al.), 588–600
    social sciences: "Environmental Justice,
      Local Knowledge, and After-Disaster
      Planning in New Orleans" (Allen),
      580–88
  Perspectives on Love
    applied fields: "Looking for Love on
      Craigslist: An Examination of Gender
      Differences in Self-Marketing Online"
      (Peters et al.), 363–80
    humanities: "The Strategies of Forbidden
      Love: Family across Racial Boundaries
      in Nineteenth-Century North Carolina"
      (Milteer), 336–48
    natural sciences: "Hormonal Changes
      When Falling in Love" (Marazziti and
      Canale), 356–62
    social sciences: "Women and Men in
      Love: Who Really Feels It and Says
      It First?" (Harrison and Shortall),
      348–56
academic disciplines
  conventions of writing in, 90
  defined, 7–8
  genres in, 90
  number of, 8–9
  research in, 89–90
academic journals, 69
academic literacy, 14
academic presses, books published by, 69
academic research, 59–85
  avoiding plagiarism in, 75–76
  choosing primary and secondary sources in,
    60–62
  conducting, 59
  developing a supported argument on a
    controversial issue in, 79–84
  developing research question in, 59–60
  documentation systems in, 76–77
  evaluating sources in, 69–71
  generating search terms in, 65

  paraphrasing in, 72–73
  quoting in, 74
  searching for journal articles by discipline in,
    67–68
  searching for sources in, 62–68
  summarizing in, 71–72
  using journal databases in, 66–67
  writing an annotated bibliography in,
    77–79
academic writers
  reasons for citing sources, 613–14
  reasons for writing, 10–13
academic writing
  analyzing genres and conventions in,
    91–92
  using structure, language, and reference
    (SLR) to analyze, 94–96
  values of, 613–14
acknowledgments, 175
active voice, 136–37, 176–77
Adams, Craig. *See* Su, Tingzhi; Shu, Shi; Shi,
    Honglan; Wang, Jianmin; Adams, Craig;
    and Witt, Emitt C.; "Distribution of Toxic
    Trace Elements"
advertisement
  rhetorical analysis of, 48–52
  student analysis of, 52–57
Allen, Barbara L., "Environmental Justice, Local
    Knowledge, and After-Disaster Planning
    in New Orleans," 580–88
American Chemical Society (ACS), 626
American Institute of Physics (AIP), 626
American Mathematical Society (AMS), 626
American Medical Association (AMA), 626
American Political Science Association (APSA),
    626
American Psychological Association (APA), 77,
    97, 613, 614–15
  citing different types of sources in, 621
  in-text citations in, 619–20
  reference page citations in, 620
  sample reference page in, 621
  uniqueness of, 619
American Sociological Association (ASA), 626

annotated bibliography, 77
  writing an, 77–79
appeals, rhetorical, 38
appendixes, 175–76
applied fields, 261–303
  business as, 282–94
  defined, 261
  education as, 272–94
  genres in selected, 264–304
  law as, 294–304
  nursing as, 264–72
  research in, 262
  rhetoric and, 263–64
  scholars in, 9
Arellano, Gustavo, "Taco USA: How Mexican
    Food Became More American Than Apple
    Pie," 452–57
"Are You Ready for More?" (Begley), 546–50
arguments, 37–58
  analysis of, 48
  assumptions in, 45–46
  audience expectations in, 45
  claims in, 37, 39–40
  counterarguments and, 47–48
  defined, 37
  developing reasons in, 41–42
  developing supported, on a controversial
    issue, 79–84
  expert testimony in, 44
  personal experience in, 43
  proofs and appeals in, 38–39
  statistical data and research findings in,
    44–45
  supporting reasons with evidence in, 43–45
  thesis versus hypothesis in, 40–41
Aris, Aziz, and Leblanc, Samuel, "Maternal
    and Fetal Exposure to Pesticides
    Associated to Genetically Modified Foods
    in Eastern Townships of Quebec, Canada,"
    513–24
artistic proofs, 38
artistic texts, 149
Associated Press Stylebook (AP Style), 626
assumptions, 45–46

audience, 24
  analyzing expectations of, 45
  for a lab report, 263–64
  primary, 21
  secondary, 21
authors, 24

B

Bahls, Patrick (mathematics), 29, 219, 225
  on genres ⊙
  on research contexts ⊙
  on research questions ⊙
Baumgartner, Jody (political science), 28, 60
  on using evidence ⊙
  on writing process ⊙
Beeber, Linda. See Miles, Margaret Shandor;
    Holditch-Davis, Diane; Thoyre, Suzanne;
    and Beeber, Linda; "Rural African-American
    Mothers Parenting Prematurely Born
    Infants: An Ecological Systems Perspective"
Begley, Sharon, "Are You Ready for More?"
    546–50
Bernard, Daria J. See Bernard, John C.; Gifford,
    Katie; Santora, Kristin; and Bernard, Daria
    J.; "Willingness to Pay for Foods with
    Varying Production Traits and Levels of
    Genetically Modified Content"
Bernard, John C.; Gifford, Katie; Santora,
    Kristin; and Bernard, Daria J.; "Willingness
    to Pay for Foods with Varying Production
    Traits and Levels of Genetically Modified
    Content," 501–13
bias, addressing, 164
Bluebook style, 626
Bolzendahl, Catherine. See Powell, Brian;
    Bolzendahl, Catherine; Geist, Claudia;
    and Steelman, Lala Carr; "Changing
    Counts, Counting Change: Toward a More
    Inclusive Definition of Family"
Boyle, B. J., "A Spectacular Poststarburst
    Quasar," 98–99
Broome, John, "The Ethics of Climate Change,"
    555–56

Brotherton, Mike (astronomy), 47, 93, 96, 97, 100
"A Spectacular Poststarburst Quasar," 98–99
on developing arguments ◎
"Hubble Space Telescope Spies Galaxy/Black
Hole Evolution in Action," 94–95
on qualifiers ◎
Bruegel, Wil Van, "A Spectacular Poststarburst
Quasar," 98–99
Bush, George H. W., "Letter to Saddam
Hussein," 31–32
business, 282–94
business plan in, 285–94
memorandum in, 282–84
business plan, 285–94

C

Canale, Domenico. See Marazziti, Donatella, and
Canale, Domenico, "Hormonal Changes
When Falling in Love"
"Capital Punishment in Films: The Impact of
Death Penalty Portrayals on Viewers' Mood
and Attitude toward Capital Punishment"
(Till and Vitouch), 416–26
"Changing Counts, Counting Change: Toward
a More Inclusive Definition of Family"
(Powell et al.), 318–31
Cherlin, Andrew, "How American Family Life Is
Different," 310–15
Chicago Manual of Style, 139–40, 626
Chopin, Kate, "The Story of an Hour," 124–25,
126–28
citations, reasons for making, 613–14
claims, 37, 39–40
in arguments, 37
close reading
in the humanities, 113–23
strategies for, 123–28
collaboration, cooperation and, in natural
sciences, 226
college(s)
choosing, 5
comparing writing in, with writing in other
contexts, 12–13
differences between universities and, 4–5
purpose of, 5–6
writing about, 7
community colleges, 4
comparative experiments, 219
"Comparing the Efficiency of Various Batteries
Being Used over Time" (Lemon),
230–39
complex thesis statement, 41
content/form-response grid, 123
control groups, 219
controversial issue, developing supported
arguments on a, 79–84
conventions, 10
language
active and passive voice, 136–37, 176–77
description and rhetorical language, 136
hedging, 137, 177
reference
in the humanities, 138–39
in-text documentation, 178
paraphrase, 179
summary, 179
structural, 130
abstracts as, 174–75
in the humanities, 135
IMRAD (Introduction, Methods, Results,
and Discussion) format and, 166–74
titles as, 174
of writing
in humanities, 129
in the natural sciences, 221–26
in the social sciences, 165–74
cooperation, collaboration and, in natural
science, 226
Council of Science Editors (CSE), 77, 613,
614–15
citing different types of sources in, 624
in-text citations in, 623
reference page citations in, 623–24
sample reference page, 625
uniqueness of, 623
Council of Writing Program Administrators
(CWPA), 13

counterarguments, 47
   anticipating, 47–48
   dealing with, 48
Crime, Punishment, and Justice, 381–450
   "Capital Punishment in Films: The Impact of Death Penalty Portrayals on Viewers' Mood and Attitude toward Capital Punishment" (Till and Vitouch), 416–26
   "Dining on Death Row: Last Meals and the Crutch of Ritual" (Jones), 396–416
   "Inside a Psychopath's Brain: The Sentencing Debate" (Hagerty), 382–85
   "I Survived Prison: What Really Happens behind Bars" (Pesta), 392–96
   "Lethal Injection for Execution: Chemical Asphyxiation?" (Zimmers et al.), 426–38
   "Perceptions of Law Enforcement Officers on Capital Punishment in the United States" (Hughes and Robinson), 438–49
   "Should Juvenile Criminals Be Sentenced Like Adults?" (Merrefield), 388–92
   "The Top 10 Most Startling Facts about People of Color and Criminal Justice in the United States: A Look at the Racial Disparities Inherent in Our Nation's Criminal-Justice System" (Kerby), 385–88
Croom, S. M., "A Spectacular Poststarburst Quasar," 98–99
Csikszentmihalyi, Mihaly, "Happiness in Everyday Life: The Uses of Experience Sampling," 181–82
"Cultural Shock: Adjustments to New Cultural Environments" (Oberg), 155–58
Cunningham, Brent, "Pastoral Romance," 457–63

D

databases, using journal, 66–67
deconstruction, 113
description
   movement to speculation in natural sciences, 214–18
   in the natural sciences, 213–14

descriptive language, 136
descriptive writing, 214
details, replicability and, 224
Dieckmann, Janna (nursing), 265
Diigo, 627
"Dining on Death Row: Last Meals and the Crutch of Ritual" (Jones), 396–416
"Disasters and Deregulation" (Steinberg), 561–64
discharge instructions in nursing, 268–72
disciplinarity, 9
disciplinary discourse, 90
discipline, searching for journal articles by, 67–68
disciplines, reflection of, in choice of documentation style, 614–15
discourse communities, 90
"Distribution of Toxic Trace Elements" (Su et al.), 588–600
doctoral-granting universities, 4
documentation, recency and, 225
documentation styles, 76
   American Chemical Society (ACS), 626
   American Institute of Physics (AIP), 626
   American Mathematical Society (AMS), 626
   American Medical Association (AMA), 626
   American Political Science Association (APSA), 626
   American Psychological Association (APA), 77, 97, 613, 614–15
      citing different types of sources in, 621
      in-text citations in, 619–20
      reference page citations in, 620
      sample reference page in, 621
      uniqueness of, 619
   American Sociological Association (ASA), 626
   Associated Press Stylebook (AP Style), 626
   Bluebook style, 626
   Chicago Manual of Style, 139–40, 626
   Council of Science Editors (CSE), 77, 613, 614–15
      citing different types of sources in, 624

documentation styles *(continued)*
  Council of Science Editors (CSE) *(continued)*
    in-text citations in, 623
    reference page citations in, 623–24
    sample reference page, 625
    uniqueness of, 623
  Institute of Electrical and Electronics
    Engineers (IEEE), 626
  Linguistic Society of America (LSA), 627
  Modern Humanities Research Association
    (MHRA), 627
  Modern Language Association (MLA), 76,
    97, 139, 613, 614
    citing different types of sources in, 617
    in-text citations in, 615–16
    sample works cited page, 618
    uniqueness of, 615
    works cited citations in, 616
  reflection of disciplines using, 614–15
drafting, 28

E

editing, 29
education, 272–94
  individualized education program (IEP) in,
    276–94
  lesson plans in, 273–76
"Effects of Sleep Deprivation: A Literature
  Review" (O'Brien), 187–95
"Electricity Monitor Company, The" (Mills),
  286–93
e-mail correspondence, 302–4
"Environmental Justice, Local Knowledge, and
  After-Disaster Planning in New Orleans"
  (Allen), 580–88
"Ethical Discourse on the Use of Genetically
  Modified Crops: A Review of Academic
  Publications in the Fields of Ecology and
  Environmental Ethics" (Gregorowius
  et al.), 478–500
"Ethics of Climate Change, The" (Broome),
  555–61
ethos, appeals to, 38

"Evaluation of the Attribution Theory"
  (Kapadia), 199–207
evidence, 43
  supporting reasons with, 43–45
experiments
  comparative, 219
  freewriting about, 220–21
expert testimony, 44

F

Feminist Theory, 113
Filippenko, Alexei V., "A Spectacular
  Poststarburst Quasar," 98–99
five-paragraph essay, 134
Food, Sustainability, and Class, 451–544
  "Ethical Discourse on the Use of Genetically
    Modified Crops: A Review of Academic
    Publications in the Fields of Ecology and
    Environmental Ethics" (Gregorowius
    et al.), 478–500
  "Genetically Modified Food in Perspective:
    An Inquiry-Based Curriculum to Help
    Middle School Students Make Sense
    of Tradeoffs" (Seethaler and Linn),
    525–42
  "Grub" (Goodyear), 464–70
  "Maternal and Fetal Exposure to Pesticides
    Associated to Genetically Modified Foods
    in Eastern Townships of Quebec, Canada"
    (Aris and Leblanc), 513–24
  "Pastoral Romance" (Cunningham),
    457–63
  "Taco USA: How Mexican Food Became
    More American Than Apple Pie"
    (Arellano), 452–57
  "Why Cook?" (Pollan), 471–77
  "Willingness to Pay for Foods with Varying
    Production Traits and Levels of Genetically
    Modified Content" (Bernard et al.),
    501–13
for-profit institutions, 5
freewriting, 27–28
  about experiments, 220–21

G

Garrigan, Shelley (Spanish language and literature), 129

Gay, Kaitie (student), interview of Malecha, Marvin, 16–19

Geiger, Paige (molecular and integrative physiology), 212, 227

Geist, Claudia. *See* Powell, Brian; Bolzendahl, Catherine; Geist, Claudia; and Steelman, Lala Carr; "Changing Counts, Counting Change: Toward a More Inclusive Definition of Family"

"Genetically Modified Food in Perspective: An Inquiry-Based Curriculum to Help Middle School Students Make Sense of Tradeoffs" (Seethaler and Linn), 525–42

genres
 defined, 23, 90
 in the humanities, 141
 in the natural sciences, 227
 in the social sciences, 180
 understanding, 23–24

Gifford, Katie. *See* Bernard, John C.; Gifford, Katie; Santora, Kristin; and Bernard, Daria J.; "Willingness to Pay for Foods with Varying Production Traits and Levels of Genetically Modified Content"

Global Climate Change and Natural Catastrophes
 "Are You Ready for More?" (Begley), 546–50
 "Disasters and Deregulation" (Steinberg), 561–64
 "Distribution of Toxic Trace Elements" (Su et al.), 588–600
 "Environmental Justice, Local Knowledge, and After-Disaster Planning in New Orleans" (Allen), 580–88
 "The Ethics of Climate Change" (Broome), 555–61
 "'My FEMA People': Hip-Hop as Disaster Recovery in the Katrina Diaspora" (Kish), 565–80
 "Posttraumatic Stress Disorder after Hurricane Katrina" (Rhoads et al.), 601–10
 "Rising Tide" (Sarewitz and Pielke), 550–55

Goodyear, Dana, "Grub," 464–70

Google Scholar, 64

Gregorowius, Daniel; Lindemann-Matthies, Petra; and Huppenbauer, Markus; "Ethical Discourse on the Use of Genetically Modified Crops: A Review of Academic Publications in the Fields of Ecology and Environmental Ethics," 478–500

"Grub" (Goodyear), 464–70

H

Hagerty, Barbara Bradley, "Inside a Psychopath's Brain: The Sentencing Debate," 382–85

"Happiness in Everyday Life: The Uses of Experience Sampling" (Csikszentmihalyi and Hunter), 181–82

Harrison, Marissa A., and Shortall, Jennifer C., "Women and Men in Love: Who Really Feels It and Says It First?" 348–56

hedging, 137, 177

higher education
 defined, 3
 differences between colleges and universities in, 4–5

Holditch-Davis, Diane. *See* Miles, Margaret Shandor; Holditch-Davis, Diane; Thoyre, Suzanne; and Beeber, Linda; "Rural African-American Mothers Parenting Prematurely Born Infants: An Ecological Systems Perspective"

Holtzhauser, Timothy (student), analysis of advertisement, 52–57

"Hormonal Changes When Falling in Love" (Marazziti and Canale), 356–62

"How American Family Life Is Different" (Cherlin), 310–15

"Hubble Space Telescope Spies Galaxy/Black Hole Evolution in Action" (Brotherton), 94–95

Hughes, Cyndy Caravelis, and Robinson, Matthew, "Perceptions of Law Enforcement Officers on Capital Punishment in the United States," 438–49
humanities, 108–51
  artistic texts in, 149
  close reading in the, 113–23
  conventions of writing in, 129
  developing effective thesis statements in, 132–34
  developing research questions and thesis statements in, 130–33
  documentation in, 139–41
  five-paragraph essays and other thesis-driven templates in, 134–35
  genres of writing in, 141
  language conventions in, 136–37
    active and passive voice in, 136–38
    description and rhetorical language, 136
    hedging in, 137
  observation and interpretation in, 110–11
  reference conventions in, 138–39
  research in, 111–12
  responding to the interpretations of others in, 128–29
  role of theory in the, 113
  scholars in, 8
  strategies for close reading and observation in, 123–28
  structural conventions in, 130, 135
    paragraphs and transitions, 135
    title, 135
  texts and meaning in, 109–10
  textual interpretation in, 141–49
human subjects, institutional review board process and, 165
Hunter, Jeremy, "Happiness in Everyday Life: The Uses of Experience Sampling," 181–82
"Hunting Behavior, Territory Quality, and Individual Quality of American Kestrels (*Falco sparverius*)" (Ritchison), 242–48
Huppenbauer, Markus. *See* Gregorowius, Daniel; Lindemann-Matthies, Petra; and Huppenbauer, Markus; "Ethical Discourse on the Use of Genetically Modified Crops: A Review of Academic Publications in the Fields of Ecology and Environmental Ethics"
hypothesis
  defined, 40
  replicability and, 224
  research questions and, 158–60
  versus thesis, 40–41

I

idea mapping, 28
IMRAD (Introduction, Methods, Results, and Discussion) format, 92, 97
  in conveying objectivity, 222–23
  structural conventions and, 166–74
inartistic proofs, 38
individualized education program (IEP), 276–94
"Inside a Psychopath's Brain: The Sentencing Debate" (Hagerty), 382–85
Institute of Electrical and Electronics Engineers (IEEE), 626
institutional review board process, human subjects and, 165
"In Strangers' Glances at Family, Tensions Linger" (Saulny), 332–36
interdisciplinary fields, 211
interpretations
  observation and, 110–11
  responding to, 128–29
  textual, 141–49
in-text documentation, 178
IRAC (introduction, rule, application, and conclusion), 295
"I Survived Prison: What Really Happens behind Bars" (Pesta), 392–96

J

Jackson, Karen Keaton (writing studies), 12, 21, 75, 90, 111, 130, 134
  on citation practices ⊙

on comparing high school and college writing ▶

on drafting and the writing process ▶

on purpose and audience ▶

on research and writing ▶

on rhetorical context and critical awareness ▶

on scholarly and popular sources ▶

Jacobs, Dale, "More Than Words: Comics as a Means of Teaching Multiple Literacies," 114–22

jargon in conveying objectivity, 223

Jones, Michael Owen, "Dining on Death Row: Last Meals and the Crutch of Ritual," 396–416

journal articles, searching for, by discipline, 67–68

journal databases, using, 66–67

K

Kapadia, Matt (student), "Evaluation of the Attribution Theory," 199–207

Kerby, Sophia, "The Top 10 Most Startling Facts about People of Color and Criminal Justice in the United States: A Look at the Racial Disparities Inherent in Our Nation's Criminal-Justice System," 385–88

Kish, Zenia, " 'My FEMA People': Hip-Hop as Disaster Recovery in the Katrina Diaspora," 565–80

Koniaris, Leonidas G. *See* Zimmers, Teresa A.; Sheldon, Jonathan; Lubarsky, David A.; López-Muñoz, Francisco; Waterman, Linda; Weisman, Richard; and Koniaris, Leonidas G.; "Lethal Injection for Execution: Chemical Asphyxiation?"

L

lab reports, 248–59

audience for, 263–64

Lambrecht, Gena (student), 11

on academic writing ▶

language conventions

active and passive voice, 136–37, 176–77

description and rhetorical language, 136

hedging, 137, 177

LaRue, Michelle, 218, 219, 222

law, 294–304

e-mail correspondence in, 302–4

legal briefs, 295–302

Leblanc, Samuel. *See* Aris, Aziz, and Leblanc, Samuel, "Maternal and Fetal Exposure to Pesticides Associated to Genetically Modified Foods in Eastern Townships of Quebec, Canada"

legal briefs, 295–302

Lemon, Kedric (student)

"Comparing the Efficiency of Various Batteries Being Used over Time," 230–39

"Which Type of Battery Is the Most Effective When Energy Is Drawn Rapidly?, 250–59

lesson plans, 273–76

"Lethal Injection for Execution: Chemical Asphyxiation?" (Zimmers et al.), 426–38

"Letter to Saddam Hussein" (Bush), 31–32

liberal arts colleges/universities, 4

"Life May Be Possible on Other Planets" (Nastasi), 102–5

Lindemann-Matthies, Petra. *See* Gregorowius, Daniel; Lindemann-Matthies, Petra; and Huppenbauer, Markus; "Ethical Discourse on the Use of Genetically Modified Crops: A Review of Academic Publications in the Fields of Ecology and Environmental Ethics"

Linguistic Society of America (LSA), 627

Linn, Marcia. *See* Seethaler, Sherry, and Linn, Marcia, "Genetically Modified Food in Perspective: An Inquiry-Based Curriculum to Help Middle School Students Make Sense of Tradeoffs"

listing, 28

literacy, 10

academic, 14

social and/or cultural, 15

literacy *(continued)*
  technological, 14
  workplace, 14
literacy narrative
  composing, 14–15
  defined, 14
literature review, 180–207
  writing, 182–86
logos, appeals to, 38
"Looking for Love on Craigslist: An Examination
    of Gender Differences in Self-Marketing
    Online" (Peters et al.), 363–80
Lopez, Sofia (student), "The Multiple Audiences
    of George H. W. Bush's Letter to Saddam
    Hussein," 33–34
López-Muñoz, Francisco. *See* Zimmers, Teresa
    A.; Sheldon, Jonathan; Lubarsky, David
    A.; López-Muñoz, Francisco; Waterman,
    Linda; Weisman, Richard; and Koniaris,
    Leonidas G.; "Lethal Injection for
    Execution: Chemical Asphyxiation?"
Love, Marriage, and Family, 309–79
  "Changing Counts, Counting Change:
    Toward a More Inclusive Definition of
    Family" (Powell et al.), 318–31
  "Hormonal Changes When Falling in Love"
    (Marazziti and Canale), 356–62
  "How American Family Life Is Different"
    (Cherlin), 310–15
  "Looking for Love on Craigslist: An
    Examination of Gender Differences in
    Self-Marketing Online" (Peters et al.),
    363–80
  "The Myth of the Helicopter Parent"
    (Whitbourne), 316–18
  "In Strangers' Glances at Family, Tensions
    Linger" (Saulny), 332–36
  "The Strategies of Forbidden Love: Family
    across Racial Boundaries in Nineteenth-
    Century North Carolina" (Milteer),
    336–48
  "Women and Men in Love: Who Really
    Feels It and Says It First?" (Harrison and
    Shortall), 348–56

Lubarsky, David A. *See* Zimmers, Teresa A.;
    Sheldon, Jonathan; Lubarsky, David A.;
    López-Muñoz, Francisco; Waterman,
    Linda; Weisman, Richard; and Koniaris,
    Leonidas G.; "Lethal Injection for
    Execution: Chemical Asphyxiation?"

M

magazines, 70
main points, 71
Malecha, Marvin, student interview of, 16–19
Marazziti, Donatella, and Canale, Domenico,
    "Hormonal Changes When Falling in
    Love," 356–62
Marxism, 113
master's granting institutions, 4
"Masters of Desire: The Culture of American
    Advertising" (Solomon), 49–52
"Maternal and Fetal Exposure to Pesticides
    Associated to Genetically Modified Foods
    in Eastern Townships of Quebec, Canada"
    (Aris and Leblanc), 513–24
Matsuda, Aya (linguistics), 166, 180
McCracken, Moriah (writing studies), 23, 44,
    61, 92, 128
  on citation practices ⊙
  on genres ⊙
  on important writing skills ⊙
  on reading scholarly texts ⊙
  on research methods ⊙
McCurdy, John (history), 109
memorandum, 282–84
Mendeley, 627
Merrefield, Clark, "Should Juvenile Criminals
    Be Sentenced Like Adults?" 388–92
Miles, Margaret Shandor; Holditch-Davis,
    Diane; Thoyre, Suzanne; and Beeber,
    Linda; "Rural African-American Mothers
    Parenting Prematurely Born Infants:
    An Ecological Systems Perspective,"
    266–68
Miller, Lance, "A Spectacular Poststarburst
    Quasar," 98–99

Mills, Daniel Chase, "The Electricity Monitor Company," 286–93

Milteer, Warren E., Jr., "The Strategies of Forbidden Love: Family across Racial Boundaries in Nineteenth-Century North Carolina," 336–48

Mitchell, Faye. *See* Rhoads, Jacqueline; Mitchell, Faye; and Rick, Susan; "Posttraumatic Stress Disorder after Hurricane Katrina"

mixed-methodology studies, 163–64

MLA Handbook for Writers of Research Papers, 615

MLA Style Manual and Guide to Scholarly Publishing, 615

Modern Humanities Research Association (MHRA), 627

Modern Language Association (MLA), 76, 97, 139, 613, 614
    citing different types of sources in, 617
    in-text citations in, 615–16
    sample works cited page, 618
    uniqueness of, 615
    works cited citations in, 616

"More Than Words: Comics as a Means of Teaching Multiple Literacies" (Jacobs), 114–22

Morris, Jonathan (political science), 28, 60, 69, 164
    on avoiding bias ◎
    on scholarly literature ◎
    on using evidence ◎
    on the writing process ◎

Morris, Richard. *See* Peters, Cara O.; Thomas, Jane B.; and Morris, Richard; "Looking for Love on Craigslist: An Examination of Gender Differences in Self-Marketing Online"

"Multiple Audiences of George H. W. Bush's Letter to Saddam Hussein, The" (Lopez), 33–34

"'My FEMA People': Hip-Hop as Disaster Recovery in the Katrina Diaspora" (Kish), 565–80

"Myth of the Helicopter Parent, The" (Whitbourne), 316–18

N

Nastasi, Jonathan (student), "Life May Be Possible on Other Planets," 102–5

natural sciences, 209–60
    collaboration and cooperation in, 226
    conventions of writing in, 221–22
    designing a research study in, 218–21
    detail in, 224
    documentation in, 225
    genres of writing in, 227–28
    hypotheses in, 224
    lab reports in, 248–59
    moving from description to speculation in, 214–18
    objectivity in, 222–24
    observation and description in, 213–14
    observation logbook in, 227–39
    precision in, 224
    recency in, 225
    reference selection in, 225
    replicability in, 224
    research in, 212–13
    research proposal in, 240–48
    scholars in, 9

neutrality, 164

New Criticism, 113

New Historicism, 113

newspapers, 69

non-academic audience, using rhetorical context to analyze writing for, 94–96

numbers, in conveying objectivity, 223

nursing, 264–72
    discharge instructions, 268–72
    scholarly research report in, 265–68

O

Oberg, Kalervo, "Cultural Shock: Adjustments to New Cultural Environments," 155–58

objectivity, 164
    rhetorical features conveying, 222–23

O'Brien, William (student), "Effects of Sleep Deprivation: A Literature Review," 187–95

observation, 89
  interpretation and, 110–11
  in the natural sciences, 213–14
  strategies for, 123–28
  systematic, 213, 214
observation logbook, 227–40

P

paragraphs, 135
paraphrasing, 72–73, 179
passive voice, 136–37, 176–77
"Pastoral Romance" (Cunningham), 457–63
pathos, appeals to, 38
peer review, 28
"Perceptions of Law Enforcement Officers
    on Capital Punishment in the United
    States" (Hughes and Robinson),
    438–49
personal experience, 43
Pesta, Abigail, "I Survived Prison: What Really
    Happens behind Bars," 392–96
Peters, Cara O.; Thomas, Jane B.; and Morris,
    Richard; "Looking for Love on Craigslist:
    An Examination of Gender Differences in
    Self-Marketing Online," 363–80
Pielke, Roger A., Jr. *See* Sarewitz, Daniel, and
    Pielke, Roger A., Jr., "Rising Tide"
plagiarism, avoiding, 75–76
Pollan, Michael, "Why Cook?" 471–77
popular sources, 69
  examples of, 69
Postcolonialism, 113
"Posttraumatic Stress Disorder after Hurricane
    Katrina" (Rhoads et al.), 601–10
Powell, Brian; Bolzendahl, Catherine; Geist,
    Claudia; and Steelman, Lala Carr;
    "Changing Counts, Counting Change:
    Toward a More Inclusive Definition of
    Family," 318–31
precision, replicability and, 224
prewriting, 27–29
primary audience, 21
primary evidence, collecting, 61

primary research, 89
primary sources, 60–62
  using, 62
Proctor, Sian (geology), 210
proofreading, 29
proofs
  artistic, 38
  inartistic, 38
*Publication Manual of the American Psychological
    Association*, 178, 619
purpose, 24

Q

qualifying claims, 47
qualitative methods, 162–63
quantitative methods, 160–62
Queer Theory, 113
quoting, 74

R

Rathunde, Kevin (social sciences), 153, 161
Ray, Sarah (student), "Till Death Do Us Part:
    An Analysis of Kate Chopin's 'The Story
    of an Hour,'" 143–49
reader response, 113
reading, rhetorically, 24
reasons
  developing, 41–42
  supporting with evidence, 43–45
rebuttals, 47
recency in natural sciences, 225–26
  documentation in, 225
  reference selection in, 225
reference conventions
  in the humanities, 138–39
  in-text documentation, 178
  paraphrase, 179
  summary, 179
references, 175
reference selection, recency and, 225
replicability in natural sciences, 224
  detail in, 224

hypotheses in, 224
 precision in, 224
reports
 lab, 248–59
 scholarly research, 265–68
research, 28. *See also* academic research
 in the humanities, 111–12
 in the natural sciences, 212–13
 in the social sciences, 154
 tracking, 627
researchers
 presentation of names of, 226
 treatment of other, 226
research-intensive universities, 4
research proposal, 240–48
research questions, 59, 130
 developing, 59–60, 130–32
 hypotheses and, 158–60
 writing a, 60
revising, 29
rhetoric, 12
 applied fields and, 263–64
rhetorical analysis, 25
 of an advertisement, 48–58
 of a text, 34–35
 writing a, 30–31
 writing a comparative, 101
rhetorical appeals, 38
rhetorical context, 71
 adapting to different, 92–93
 analyzing, 27
 in analyzing writing for a non-academic
  audience, 94–96
 defined, 21
 identifying, 22
 translating scholarly writing for different,
  102–6
 understanding, 21–22
rhetorical language, 136
rhetorical writing processes, 27–30
 drafting in, 28
 editing/proofreading in, 29
 freewriting in, 27–28
 idea mapping in, 28

listing in, 28
 peer review in, 28
 prewriting/invention in, 27–29
 research in, 28
 revising in, 29
Rhoads, Jacqueline; Mitchell, Faye; and Rick,
  Susan; "Posttraumatic Stress Disorder after
  Hurricane Katrina," 601–10
Richter, Michelle, 45, 263
 on comparing quantitative and qualitative
  research ⊙
 on the role of audience ⊙
Rick, Susan. *See* Rhoads, Jacqueline; Mitchell,
  Faye; and Rick, Susan; "Posttraumatic
  Stress Disorder after Hurricane Katrina"
"Rising Tide" (Sarewitz and Pielke), 550–55
Ritchison, Gary, "Hunting Behavior, Territory
  Quality, and Individual Quality of
  American Kestrels (*Falco sparverius*),"
  242–48
Robinson, Matthew. *See* Hughes, Cyndy
  Caravelis, and Robinson, Matthew,
  "Perceptions of Law Enforcement Officers
  on Capital Punishment in the United
  States"
"Rural African-American Mothers Parenting
  Prematurely Born Infants: An Ecological
  Systems Perspective" (Miles et al.),
  266–68

S

Santora, Kristin. *See* Bernard, John C.; Gifford,
  Katie; Santora, Kristin; and Bernard, Daria
  J.; "Willingness to Pay for Foods with
  Varying Production Traits and Levels of
  Genetically Modified Content"
Sarewitz, Daniel, and Pielke, Roger A., Jr.,
  "Rising Tide," 550–55
Saulny, Susan, "In Strangers' Glances at Family,
  Tensions Linger," 332–36
scholarly research report, 265–68
scholarly sources, 69
 examples of, 69

scholarly writing, translating for different
    rhetorical contexts, 102–6
scholars, interviewing with a, 15–16
schools with a specific focus, 4–5
scientific writing process, 210–11
search terms, 63
    generating, 65–66
    identifying, 63–67
secondary audience, 21
secondary research, 89
secondary sources, 60–62
    using, 62
Seethaler, Sherry, and Linn, Marcia, "Genetically
    Modified Food in Perspective: An Inquiry-
    Based Curriculum to Help Middle School
    Students Make Sense of Tradeoffs,"
    525–42
Shanks, T., "A Spectacular Poststarburst
    Quasar," 98–99
Sheldon, Jonathan. *See* Zimmers, Teresa A.;
    Sheldon, Jonathan; Lubarsky, David A.;
    López-Muñoz, Francisco; Waterman,
    Linda; Weisman, Richard; and Koniaris,
    Leonidas G.; "Lethal Injection for
    Execution: Chemical Asphyxiation?"
Shi, Honglan. *See* Su, Tingzhi; Shu, Shi; Shi,
    Honglan; Wang, Jianmin; Adams, Craig;
    and Witt, Emitt C.; "Distribution of Toxic
    Trace Elements"
Shortall, Jennifer C. *See* Harrison, Marissa A.,
    and Shortall, Jennifer C., "Women and
    Men in Love: Who Really Feels It and Says
    It First?"
"Should Juvenile Criminals Be Sentenced Like
    Adults?" (Merrefield), 388–92
Shu, Shi. *See* Su, Tingzhi; Shu, Shi; Shi,
    Honglan; Wang, Jianmin; Adams, Craig;
    and Witt, Emitt C.; "Distribution of Toxic
    Trace Elements"
simple thesis statement, 41
Sims, Ashlyn (student), argument on condom
    distribution, 80–84
Smith, R. J., "A Spectacular Poststarburst
    Quasar," 98–99

social and/or cultural literacy, 15
social sciences, 152–208
    conventions of writing in, 165–74
        abstracts in, 174–75
        acknowledgments in, 175
        appendixes in, 175–76
        references in, 175
        structural conventions and IMRAD format
            in, 166–74
        titles in, 174
    genres of writing in, 180
    IRB process and use of human subjects in, 165
    language conventions in, 176–78
        active and passive voice in, 176–77
        hedging in, 177
    literature review in, 180–207
    methods in
        addressing bias in, 164
        mixed, 163–64
        qualitative, 162–63
        quantitative, 160–62
    reference conventions in, 178–79
        in-text documentation, 178
        summary and paraphrase, 179
    research in, 154
    research questions and hypotheses in, 158–60
    role of theory in, 154–58
    scholars in, 9
Solomon, Jack, "Masters of Desire: The Culture
    of American Advertising," 49–52
sources
    distinguishing between scholarly and popular,
        69
    evaluating, 70–71
    examples of popular, 69
    examples of scholarly, 69
    searching for, 62–68
    summarizing, paraphrasing, and quoting from,
        71–75
    synthesizing, 184
"Spectacular Poststarburst Quasar, A"
    (Brotherton et al.), 98–99
speculation, movement from description to, in
    natural sciences, 214–18

speculative writing, 214

Stanford, S. A., "A Spectacular Poststarburst Quasar," 98–99

statistical data and research findings, 44–45

Steelman, Lala Carr. *See* Powell, Brian; Bolzendahl, Catherine; Geist, Claudia; and Steelman, Lala Carr; "Changing Counts, Counting Change: Toward a More Inclusive Definition of Family"

Steinberg, Ted, "Disasters and Deregulation," 561–64

"Story of an Hour, The" (Chopin), 124–25, 126–28

Stout, Sam (student), 11
  on academic writing ◉

"Strategies of Forbidden Love: Family across Racial Boundaries in Nineteenth-Century North Carolina, The" (Milteer), 336–48

structural conventions, 130
  abstracts as, 174–75
  in the humanities, 135
  IMRAD (Introduction, Methods, Results, and Discussion) format and, 166–74
  titles as, 174

structure, language, and reference (SLR), in analyzing academic writing, 94–96

Su, Tingzhi; Shu, Shi; Shi, Honglan; Wang, Jianmin; Adams, Craig; and Witt, Emitt C.; "Distribution of Toxic Trace Elements," 588–600

summarizing, 71–72, 179

systematic observations, 213, 214

T

"Taco USA: How Mexican Food Became More American Than Apple Pie" (Arellano), 452–57

technological literacy, 14

texts, 109
  artistic, 149
  rhetorical analysis of, 34–35

textual interpretation, 141–49

theory
  in the humanities, 113
  in the social sciences, 154–58

theory response essay, 196–98

thesis-driven templates, 134–35

thesis statements, 39, 40, 130
  complex, 41
  constructing, 42–43
  developing, 130–34
  simple, 41

thesis versus hypothesis, 40–41

Thomas, Jane B. *See* Peters, Cara O.; Thomas, Jane B.; and Morris, Richard; "Looking for Love on Craigslist: An Examination of Gender Differences in Self-Marketing Online"

Thoyre, Suzanne. *See* Miles, Margaret Shandor; Holditch-Davis, Diane; Thoyre, Suzanne; and Beeber, Linda; "Rural African-American Mothers Parenting Prematurely Born Infants: An Ecological Systems Perspective"

Till, Benedikt, and Vitouch, Peter, "Capital Punishment in Films: The Impact of Death Penalty Portrayals on Viewers' Mood and Attitude toward Capital Punishment," 416–26

"Till Death Do Us Part: An Analysis of Kate Chopin's 'The Story of an Hour'" (Ray), 143–49

titles, 135, 174
  in conveying objectivity, 222

"Top 10 Most Startling Facts about People of Color and Criminal Justice in the United States: A Look at the Racial Disparities Inherent in Our Nation's Criminal-Justice System, The" (Kerby), 385–88

topic, 24

transitions, 135

U

universities, differences between colleges and, 4–5

V

visuals, reading rhetorically, 25
Vitouch, Peter. *See* Till, Benedikt, and Vitouch,
    Peter, "Capital Punishment in Films:
    The Impact of Death Penalty Portrayals
    on Viewers' Mood and Attitude toward
    Capital Punishment"
voice, active and passive, 136–38, 176–77

W

Wang, Jianmin. *See* Su, Tingzhi; Shu, Shi; Shi,
    Honglan; Wang, Jianmin; Adams, Craig;
    and Witt, Emitt C.; "Distribution of Toxic
    Trace Elements"
Waterman, Linda. *See* Zimmers, Teresa A.;
    Sheldon, Jonathan; Lubarsky, David A.;
    López-Muñoz, Francisco; Waterman,
    Linda; Weisman, Richard; and Koniaris,
    Leonidas G.; "Lethal Injection for
    Execution: Chemical Asphyxiation?"
Weisman, Richard. *See* Zimmers, Teresa A.;
    Sheldon, Jonathan; Lubarsky, David A.;
    López-Muñoz, Francisco; Waterman,
    Linda; Weisman, Richard; and Koniaris,
    Leonidas G.; "Lethal Injection for
    Execution: Chemical Asphyxiation?"
"Which Type of Battery Is the Most Effective
    When Energy Is Drawn Rapidly?"
    (Lemon), 250–59
Whitbourne, Susan Krauss, "The Myth of the
    Helicopter Parent," 316–18
"Why Cook?" (Pollan), 471–77
"Willingness to Pay for Foods with Varying
    Production Traits and Levels of
    Genetically Modified Content" (Bernard
    et al.), 501–13
Witt, Emitt C. *See* Su, Tingzhi; Shu, Shi; Shi,
    Honglan; Wang, Jianmin; Adams, Craig;
    and Witt, Emitt C.; "Distribution of Toxic
    Trace Elements"
"Women and Men in Love: Who Really Feels It
    and Says It First?" (Harrison and Shortall),
    348–56
Woods, Alexandria (student), 11
    on academic writing ◎
workplace literacy, 14
writing
    conventions of, 10, 90
        in humanities, 129
        in the social sciences, 165–74
        of writing
            in humanities, 129
            in the natural sciences, 221–26
            in the social sciences, 165–74
    descriptive, 214
    reasons for academic, 10–13
    a rhetorical analysis, 30–31
    rhetorically, 25–26
    speculative, 214

Z

Zimmers, Teresa A.; Sheldon, Jonathan;
    Lubarsky, David A.; López-Muñoz,
    Francisco; Waterman, Linda; Weisman,
    Richard; and Koniaris, Leonidas G.;
    "Lethal Injection for Execution: Chemical
    Asphyxiation?" 426–38
Zotero, 627